Lecture Notes in Computer Science

Lecture Notes in Computer Science

Vol. 1: GI-Gesellschaft für Informatik e.V. 3. Jahrestagung, Hamburg, 8.–10. Oktober 1973. Herausgegeben im Auftrag der Gesellschaft für Informatik von W. Brauer. XI, 508 Seiten. 1973.

Vol. 2: GI-Gesellschaft für Informatik e.V. 1. Fachtagung über Automatentheorie und Formale Sprachen, Bonn, 9.–12. Juli 1973. Herausgegeben im Auftrag der Gesellschaft für Informatik von K.-H. Böhling und K. Indermark. VII, 322 Seiten. 1973.

Vol. 3: 5th Conference on Optimization Techniques, Part I. (Series: I.F.I.P. TC7 Optimization Conferences.) Edited by R. Conti and A. Ruberti. XIII, 565 pages. 1973.

Vol. 4: 5th Conference on Optimization Techniques, Part II. (Series: I.F.I.P. TC7 Optimization Conferences.) Edited by R. Conti and A. Ruberti. XIII, 389 pages. 1973.

Vol. 5: International Symposium on Theoretical Programming. Edited by A. Ershov and V. A. Nepomniaschy. VI, 407 pages. 1974.

Vol. 6: B. T. Smith, J. M. Boyle, J. J. Dongarra, B. S. Garbow, Y. Ikebe, V. C. Klema, and C. B. Moler, Matrix Eigensystem Routines – EISPACK Guide. XI, 551 pages. 2nd Edition 1974. 1976.

Vol. 7: 3. Fachtagung über Programmiersprachen, Kiel, 5.–7. März 1974. Herausgegeben von B. Schlender und W. Frielinghaus. VI, 225 Seiten. 1974.

Vol. 8: GI-NTG Fachtagung über Struktur und Betrieb von Rechensystemen, Braunschweig, 20.–22. März 1974. Herausgegeben im Auftrag der GI und der NTG von H.-O. Leilich. VI, 340 Seiten. 1974.

Vol. 9: GI-BIFOA Internationale Fachtagung: Informationszentren in Wirtschaft und Verwaltung. Köln, 17./18. Sept. 1973. Herausgegeben im Auftrag der GI und dem BIFOA von P. Schmitz. VI, 259 Seiten. 1974.

Vol. 10: Computing Methods in Applied Sciences and Engineering, Part 1. International Symposium, Versailles, December 17–21, 1973. Edited by R. Glowinski and J. L. Lions. X, 497 pages. 1974.

Vol. 11: Computing Methods in Applied Sciences and Engineering, Part 2. International Symposium, Versailles, December 17–21, 1973. Edited by R. Glowinski and J. L. Lions. X, 434 pages. 1974.

Vol. 12: GFK-GI-GMR Fachtagung Prozessrechner 1974. Karlsruhe, 10.–11. Juni 1974. Herausgegeben von G. Krüger und R. Friehmelt. XI, 620 Seiten. 1974.

Vol. 13: Rechnerstrukturen und Betriebsprogrammierung, Erlangen, 1970. (GI-Gesellschaft für Informatik e.V.) Herausgegeben von W. Händler und P. P. Spies. VII, 333 Seiten. 1974.

Vol. 14: Automata, Languages and Programming – 2nd Colloquium, University of Saarbrücken, July 29–August 2, 1974. Edited by J. Loeckx. VIII, 611 pages. 1974.

Vol. 15: L Systems. Edited by A. Salomaa and G. Rozenberg. VI, 338 pages. 1974.

Vol. 16: Operating Systems, International Symposium, Rocquencourt 1974. Edited by E. Gelenbe and C. Kaiser. VIII, 310 pages. 1974.

Vol. 17: Rechner-Gestützter Unterricht RGU '74, Fachtagung, Hamburg, 12.–14. August 1974, ACU-Arbeitskreis Computer-Unterstützter Unterricht. Herausgegeben im Auftrag der GI von K. Brunnstein, K. Haefner und W. Händler. X, 417 Seiten. 1974.

Vol. 18: K. Jensen and N. E. Wirth, PASCAL – User Manual and Report. VII, 170 pages. Corrected Reprint of the 2nd Edition 1976.

Vol. 19: Programming Symposium. Proceedings 1974. V, 425 pages. 1974.

Vol. 20: J. Engelfriet, Simple Program Schemes and Formal Languages. VII, 254 pages. 1974.

Vol. 21: Compiler Construction, An Advanced Course. Edited by F. L. Bauer and J. Eickel. XIV. 621 pages. 1974.

Vol. 22: Formal Aspects of Cognitive Processes. Proceedings 1972. Edited by T. Storer and D. Winter. V, 214 pages. 1975.

Vol. 23: Programming Methodology. 4th Informatik Symposium, IBM Germany Wildbad, September 25–27, 1974. Edited by C. E. Hackl. VI, 501 pages. 1975.

Vol. 24: Parallel Processing. Proceedings 1974. Edited by T. Feng. VI, 433 pages. 1975.

Vol. 25: Category Theory Applied to Computation and Control. Proceedings 1974. Edited by E. G. Manes. X, 245 pages. 1975.

Vol. 26: GI-4. Jahrestagung, Berlin, 9.–12. Oktober 1974. Herausgegeben im Auftrag der GI von D. Siefkes. IX, 748 Seiten. 1975.

Vol. 27: Optimization Techniques. IFIP Technical Conference. Novosibirsk, July 1–7, 1974. (Series: I.F.I.P. TC7 Optimization Conferences.) Edited by G. I. Marchuk. VIII, 507 pages. 1975.

Vol. 28: Mathematical Foundations of Computer Science. 3rd Symposium at Jadwisin near Warsaw, June 17–22, 1974. Edited by A. Blikle. VII, 484 pages. 1975.

Vol. 29: Interval Mathematics. Procedings 1975. Edited by K. Nickel. VI, 331 pages. 1975.

Vol. 30: Software Engineering. An Advanced Course. Edited by F. L. Bauer. (Formerly published 1973 as Lecture Notes in Economics and Mathematical Systems, Vol. 81) XII, 545 pages. 1975.

Vol. 31: S. H. Fuller, Analysis of Drum and Disk Storage Units. IX, 283 pages. 1975.

Vol. 32: Mathematical Foundations of Computer Science 1975. Proceedings 1975. Edited by J. Bečvář. X, 476 pages. 1975.

Vol. 33: Automata Theory and Formal Languages, Kaiserslautern, May 20–23, 1975. Edited by H. Brakhage on behalf of GI. VIII, 292 Seiten. 1975.

Vol. 34: GI – 5. Jahrestagung, Dortmund 8.–10. Oktober 1975. Herausgegeben im Auftrag der GI von J. Mühlbacher. X, 755 Seiten. 1975.

Vol. 35: W. Everling, Exercises in Computer Systems Analysis. (Formerly published 1972 as Lecture Notes in Economics and Mathematical Systems, Vol. 65) VIII, 184 pages. 1975.

Vol. 36: S. A. Greibach, Theory of Program Structures: Schemes, Semantics, Verification. XV, 364 pages. 1975.

Vol. 37: C. Böhm, λ-Calculus and Computer Science Theory. Proceedings 1975. XII, 370 pages. 1975.

Vol. 38: P. Branquart, J.-P. Cardinael, J. Lewi, J.-P. Delescaille, M. Vanbegin. An Optimized Translation Process and Its Application to ALGOL 68. IX, 334 pages. 1976.

Vol. 39: Data Base Systems. Proceedings 1975. Edited by H. Hasselmeier and W. Spruth. VI, 386 pages. 1976.

Vol. 40: Optimization Techniques. Modeling and Optimization in the Service of Man. Part 1. Proceedings 1975. Edited by J. Cea. XIV, 854 pages. 1976.

Vol. 41: Optimization Techniques. Modeling and Optimization in the Service of Man. Part 2. Proceedings 1975. Edited by J. Cea. XIII, 852 pages. 1976.

Vol. 42: James E. Donahue, Complementary Definitions of Programming Language Semantics. VII, 172 pages. 1976.

Vol. 43: E. Specker und V. Strassen, Komplexität von Entscheidungsproblemen. Ein Seminar. V, 217 Seiten. 1976.

Vol. 44: ECI Conference 1976. Proceedings 1976. Edited by K. Samelson. VIII, 322 pages. 1976.

Vol. 45: Mathematical Foundations of Computer Science 1976. Proceedings 1976. Edited by A. Mazurkiewicz. XI, 601 pages. 1976.

Vol. 46: Language Hierarchies and Interfaces. Edited by F. L. Bauer and K. Samelson. X, 428 pages. 1976.

Vol. 47: Methods of Algorithmic Language Implementation. Edited by A. Ershov and C. H. A. Koster. VIII, 351 pages. 1977.

Vol. 48: Theoretical Computer Science, Darmstadt, March 1977. Edited by H. Tzschach, H. Waldschmidt and H. K.-G. Walter on behalf of GI. VIII, 418 pages. 1977.

Lecture Notes in Computer Science

Edited by G. Goos and J. Hartmanis

73

Graph-Grammars and Their Application to Computer Science and Biology

International Workshop
Bad Honnef, October 30 – November 3, 1978

Edited by
Volker Claus, Hartmut Ehrig and Grzegorz Rozenberg

Springer-Verlag
Berlin Heidelberg New York 1979

Editors
Volker Claus
Universität Dortmund
Lehrstuhl Informatik II
Postfach 500500
D-4600 Dortmund 50

Hartmut Ehrig
Technische Universität Berlin
Fachbereich Informatik
Otto-Suhr-Allee 18/20
D-1000 Berlin 10

Grzegorz Rozenberg
Rijksuniversiteit te Leiden
Subfaculteit der Wiskunde
Wassenaarseweg 80
Postbus 9512
2300 RA Leiden

AMS Subject Classifications (1970): 68-00, 68A30
CR Subject Classifications (1974): 4.0, 5.0

ISBN 3-540-09525-X Springer-Verlag Berlin Heidelberg New York
ISBN 0-387-09525-X Springer-Verlag New York Heidelberg Berlin

Printed in Germany

Printing and binding: Beltz Offsetdruck, Hemsbach/Bergstr.
2145/3140-543210

Preface

One of the older and by now well-established areas of theoretical computer science is formal language theory. Roughly speaking it deals with finite specifications of (possibly infinite) sets of strings. The sets of strings (called string languages) turn out to be useful for describing quite a variety of phenomena in a number of disciplines of science such as for example linguistics, computer science, engineering, psychology and biology. However in many applications of formal language theory applying string languages was considered to be the first step only, leading to a more general theory where sets of multidimensional objects, as well as various tranformations of them could be (finitely) described and studied. Then for example various problems in data bases, semantics of programming languages, two-dimensional programming languages, data flow analysis or incremental compilers call for finite grammatical definitions of sets of graphs, whereas various problems in picture processing and biological pattern generation require finite grammatical (or machine) descriptions of sets of maps. Extending the theory of formal (string) languages to a theory of formal multidimensional languages is a very natural step from the mathematical point of view.

Consequently there is a need, justified by both practical and theoretical considerations, to built up a theory of languages able to accomodate structures more general than strings - for example graphs and maps. Indeed various efforts were made in this direction within the last 10 years. However it is clear that the theory available (which we loosely refer to as "graph grammar theory" for historical reasons) so far does not match the theory of formal string languages. One obvious reason for this is that from the mathematical point of view the sets of structures like graphs and maps are intrinsically more difficult to deal with than the sets of strings. However another reason may be that in spite of the genuine interest in the topic there is a lack of concentrated effort in building up the desired theory. The "graph grammar community" appears to be quite scattered, not communicating well with each other and not communicating its findings very well to the outside world.

It was our perception of this lack of communication that gave us the idea to organize a meeting of researchers from very diversified areas of science who are either active workers in the theory of graph grammars or have a genuine interest in this area. This meeting took place in Bad Honnef, West Germany, in the fall of 1978 and the present collection is a direct consequence of this meeting. Not all of the papers presented at the meeting appear in this volume: some of them were already committed somewhere else, others did not make it through the selection process. Also some papers from this volume were not presented at the above mentioned meeting, but in our opinion their inclusion gives a better view of the current state of art in graph grammar theory. Of special character are the two first papers of this volume together presenting a rather complete survey of graph grammar theory. They certainly form a good starting point for perusing this volume.

In our opinion the meeting was successful in the sense that it certainly broadened our understanding of what the whole area is about, as well as making most of the participants even more decided than before to devote their scientific efforts to the further development of this well motivated and mathematically very challenging area.

This meeting would not have been possible without the generous help we have received from

Minister für Wissenschaft und Forschung des Landes Nordrhein-Westfalen

Deutsche Forschungsgemeinschaft

Hewlett-Packard, Frankfurt

Mathematischer Beratungs- und Programmierdienst, Dortmund.

We are very grateful for that. We are also very indebted to A.Poigné for helping us so much in the organization of the meeting and editing this volume. Of course we are most grateful to all the participants of the meeting for turning it into a week of very useful scientific and very pleasant personal contacts.

V.Claus,
H.Ehrig,
G.Rozenberg.

Table of contents

INTRODUCTION TO THE ALGEBRAIC THEORY OF GRAPH GRAMMARS (A SURVEY)

Hartmut Ehrig

Technical University Berlin, FB 20

August 1978

ABSTRACT

The aim of this survey is to motivate and introduce the basic constructions and results which have been developed in the algebraic theory of graph grammars up to now. The complete material is illustrated by several examples, especially by applications to a "very small data base system", where consistent states are represented as graphs, operation rules and operations as productions and derivations in a graph grammar respectively. Further applications to recursively defined functions, record handling, compiler techniques and development and evolution in Biology are sketched in the introduction. This survey is divided into the following sections:

1. INTRODUCTION

The algebraic theory of graph grammars is an attempt to describe sequential and parallel graph grammars using graph morphisms and gluing constructions for graphs as basic concepts for the construction of derivations. These gluing constructions arc very useful because on one hand they are generalizing the concatenation of strings and on the other hand they are special cases of pushout resp. colimit constructions in categorical algebra so that universal diagram techniques can be used in most of the constructions and proofs. Unfortunately categorical concepts are not known to most researchers in Computer Science and Biology (and there are still many mathematicians not familiar with these constructions!) Actually this had been a disadvantage in making the algebraic approach widely known and we hope that this introductory paper may help to remove this (artificial) burden. Hence we avoid categorical terminology as far as possible in the following sections but the concepts of category theory which are implicitely used are summerized in an appendium.
The aim of this survey is to motivate and introduce the basic constructions and results which have been developed in the algebraic theory of graph grammars. Except of two typical cases we don't give full proofs since they can be found in the literature. Let us point out that this paper is neither a survey on different approaches to graph grammars, for which we refer to /OV.Na 78/, nor a survey on applications. But we will briefly sketch the main fields of applications in 1.1 before summerizing the contents of this survey in 1.2 and giving some technical remarks in 1.3.

1.1 MAIN AREAS OF APPLICATIONS

The development of the algebraic theory of graph grammars was mainly influenced by problems in those areas of applications where "dynamic graph models" can be used (dynamic in the sense of any manipulation of the graph structure).
The main areas of those applications are the following:

- Semantics of recursively defined functions
- Record handling
- Data base systems
- Compiler techniques
- Development and evolution in Biology

In the first three of these areas Church-Rosser properties for graph derivations play an important role. The use of Church-Rosser properties in various areas of Theoretical Computer Science (with correctness of operational semantics being a most "transparent" case) is well-known. Here the data structures to be manipulated are strings or trees. Graph grammar theory allows to extend these applications to arbitrary linked data structures. We will briefly discuss and illustrate the first three of the application areas while the last two are only sketched.

1. Semantics of Recursively Defined Functions

Recursion in programming has often been explicated in terms of macro-expansions of trees. However, efficiency considerations have led to the use of collapsed trees.

Taking for example the recursive definition

f(u,v)=ite(u=0,0,f(u-1,f(u,v)))

we can represent the right hand side by the collapsed tree in Fig. 1.1 instead of a tree which avoids to represent same variables and constants by different nodes.

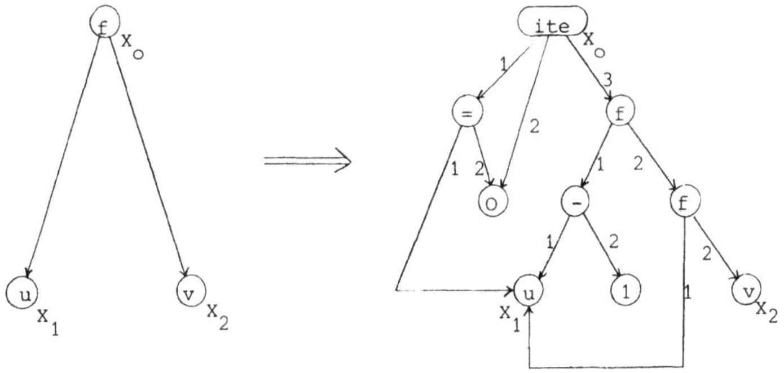

Figure 1.1: Graph Grammar Production for a Recursive Definition

Hence we can express the recursive definition by the graph grammar production in Fig. 1.1 (where the meaning of the gluing items x_o, x_1, x_2 will be given in Sections 2 and 3)

Now expressions, like $f^{\#}(4,f(3,u))+u$, can be represented as "expression graphs" and a macroexpansion of f as an application of the production defined above. Using the Church-Rosser properties for graph derivations we are able to show that all those macroexpansions are satisfying the Church-Rosser property which means that they can be applied in arbitrary order leading to the same result in all cases. Also all or nothing evaluation of a function can be represented as a direct derivation of expression graphs and evaluations and macroexpansions together define a Church-Rosser system. Hence we obtain in /AP.EhRo 76/ a mathematical proof of the following result:

With all or nothing evaluation of given functions, recursively defined functions, represented as expression graphs instead of trees, are single-valued.

An extension of these results including partial evaluation is studied in /AP.Pa 78/.

2. Record Handling

/AP.Eh Ro 77/ discusses a mathematical foundation for reasoning about the correctness and computational complexity of record handling algorithms using algebraic graph theory. A class of pattern matching and replacement rules for graphs is specified, such that applications of rules in the class can readily be programmed as rapid transformations of record structures. When transformations of record structures are formalized as applications of rules to appropriate graphs we can use

Church-Rosser properties to prove that families of transformations are well behaved. In particular, it is shown that any Church-Rosser family of transformations satisfying mild conditions can be combined with housekeeping operations involving indirect pointers and garbage collection without losing the Church-Rosser property. Moreover parallel derivations are used to express the net effect of two transformations as a single transformation. These results and the general theorems that support them can be used to analyze the behavior of a large structure that can be updated asynchronously by several parallel processes or users.

A typical example of a Church-Rosser property involving indirect pointers is given in Fig. 1.2 where in all steps indirection productions are applied (if the target of an arc is colored I the indirection production allows to change the target of this arc to its successor). Let us point out that in Fig. 1.2 starting with the arc colored C we need three while starting with z we only need two applications of the indirection production to end up with the same resulting graph.

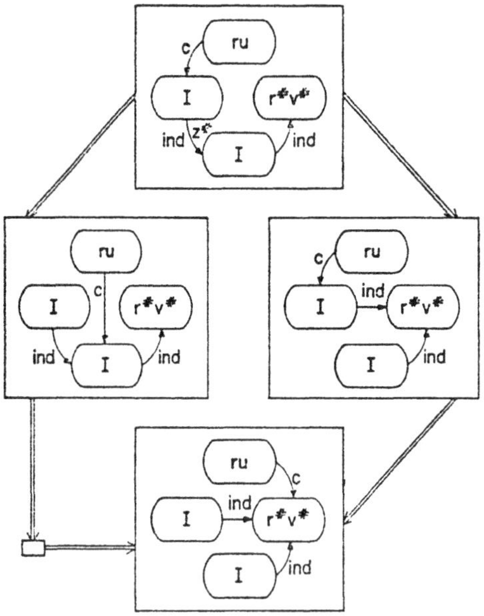

Figure 1.2: Church-Rosser Property of Indirection

3. Data Base Systems

A convenient way to represent a semantic network, the semantic structure of a data base system, is that of using (colored) graphs. In /AP.Eh Kr 76a/,/AP.Kr 78/ and /AP.Eh Kr 78/ it is suggested that manipulations in semantic networks can be expressed using graph productions and derivations. A simple example of a library is given and it is shown how to formalize operations like registering, ordering, lending and returning a book using graph grammar productions and derivations. A typical example for returning a book with catalogue number K 12345 by reader L 0815 is given in Fig. 1.3 (the upper row is the production representing the operation "returning" and the lower row is the direct derivation representing the change of (a small part of) the state of the library system).

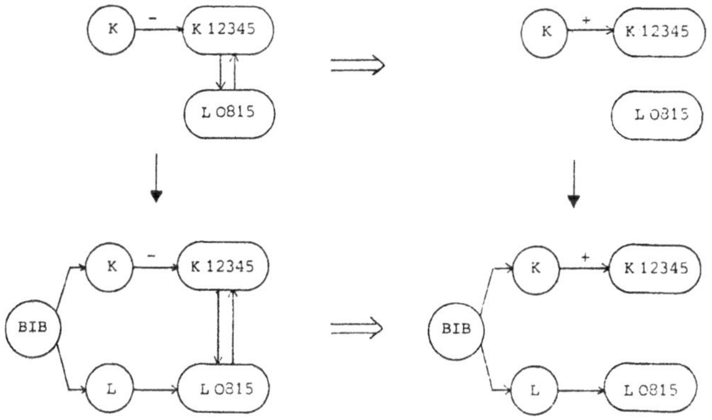

Figure 1.3: Production and Direct Derivation for Returning a Book

More details of this library system will be given in Sections 2 up to 5 where this example is used to illustrate most of the constructions and results in the Algebraic Theory of Graph Grammars. Expecially the operations and consistent states of the library are defined in 3.2 and 3.4.2 as examples of productions and the language of a graph grammar respectively. Using the notion of "independence" for graph derivations (see 4.1) it is shown in Example 4.2 which of the library operations are independent such that they can be applied in arbitrary order or in parallel. Moreover it is discussed in Example 4.8 how the productions ordering and registering (which are not independent if they are applied to the same book) can be combined to a "concurrent production" which has exactly the same effect like sequential application of ordering and registering. The corresponding results (4.4, 4.5, 4.7 and 4.11) in the theory of graph grammars seem to be a basic tool for synchronization problems in data base systems (see /AP.Kr 78/ or /AP.Eh Kr 78/). An extension of some of these results to generalized data base systems is studied in /AP.NePa 77/

and /AP.St 78/.

Since the structure of a semantic network can be defined by a graph grammar the correctness of these structures can be checked using parsing techniques. Two examples of approaches to realize conceptional schemes for data base systems using graph grammars are given in /AP.Go Fu 74/ and /AP.Sc 76/.

4. Compiler Techniques

In several cases compiler techniques can be considered as manipulations of (colored) graphs. We will give two examples: 1. Implementing an incremental compiler, we must consider various lists and a lot of references between them in order to allow insertion, deletion, or substitution of increments. Since the structure is not always a tree it is shown in /AP.Sc 75/ how to establish a syntax-directed concept for implementing incremental compilers using the graph grammar approach for partial graphs in /AP.Sc Eh 76/. 2. For code optimization in a compiler we need program data flow analysis. One of the standard approaches is to construct the control flow graph.

To construct this graph it is standard to group instructions into basic blocks, take these blocks as the nodes, and so on. In /AP.Fa Ke Zu 76/, however, it is shown that most of these graphs can be generated by a graph grammar. A slightly extended version of the algorithm in /AP.Fa Ke Zu 76/ can test in linear time whether a given graph can be generated and construct a parse in the case where the answer is YES.

5. Development and Evolution in Biology

The use of L-systems to model the development of filamental organisms is widely known. The string representation in the mathematical models, however, restrict the application to very simple organisms. In /GL.Lu Li 74/ A. Lindenmayer and K.Culik II have given a mathematical model to extend L-systems to graphs. This allows to model the development of slightly more general (and perhaps also of some higher dimensional) organisms. The main idea is to predict the development of such an organism by calculation of derivation sequences in parallel graph grammars (which are also called graph L-systems). Algebraic approaches to parallel graph grammars are given in /GL.Eh Kr 76/, /GL.Eh Rb 76/, /GL.Ld 78/ and /GL.Eh Ld 78/. In the last two papers the construction of locally star gluing formulas (generalizing locally catenative formulas) is given for graph sequences of (special) parallel graph grammars. This allows to predict the development of organisms by a recursive procedure without calculating the complete derivation sequence.

Finally let us mention that an approach of N. Rashewsky to describe the spezialization and evolution process of organisms was formulated in terms of (sequential) graph grammars in /AP.Eh Ti 75/.

1.2 CONTENTS OF THIS SURVEY AND HISTORICAL REMARKS

Motivated by several other graph grammar approaches (which are reviewed in /OV.Na 78/) the algebraic approach was introduced by H. Ehrig, M. Pfender and H.J. Schneider in

/GG.Eh Pf Sc 73a,b/. Extended versions were given in /GG.Ro 75b/, /AP.Eh Kr 76b/, /GG.Sc Eh 76/ and /GG. Eh Kr Ma Ro Wi 78/ to cover all the applications sketched in 1.1.1 up to 1.1.4. But for this survey we only consider a simplified version of gluing constructions and derivations underlying this approach which is given in Section 2 and 3.

The embedding theorem given in /GG.Eh Pf Sc 73b/ (and improved in /GG.Eh Kr 76/, /GG.Eh 77/, /GG. Kr 77a/ and /GG.Eh Kr Ma Ro Wi 78/ was the first basic result in the Algebraic Theory of Graph Grammars:

Given a derivation sequence $G_o \Longrightarrow \ldots \Longrightarrow G_n$ of graphs and an embedding $h_o : G_o \longrightarrow \bar{G}_o$ then it is possible to obtain an extended sequence $\bar{G}_o \Longrightarrow \ldots \Longrightarrow \bar{G}_n$ using the same productions provided that a suitable JOIN-condition is satisfied. This condition, the embedding theorem (including also the inverse CLIP-construction in 5.3), and some other properties of derivation sequences are discussed in Section 5.

A second basic contribution to the algebraic theory of graph grammars was given by B.K. Rosen in /GG.Ro 75a/, where he started to study Church-Rosser properties of derivations in graph grammars. The results obtained in this and subsequent papers /GG.Eh Kr 75b/, /AP.Eh Ro 76/, /AP.Eh Kr 76a/, /GG.Kr 77b/ and /AP.Eh Ro 78b/ are summarized in the Church-Rosser-, Parallelism-, and Concurrency Theorems in Section 4 (see 4.4, 4.5, 4.7 and 4.11) and in Theorem 5.6 on canonical derivation sequences.

A third basic contribution to the algebraic theory was given by H. Ehrig, H.-J. Kreowski and G. Rozenberg in /GL.Eh Kr 76/ and /GL.Eh Rb 76/ where approaches to parallel graph grammars were given generalizing L-systems from strings to graphs. These algebraic approaches were basically motivated by the original paper /GL.Cu Li 74/ of Culik II and Lindenmayer and by the algebraic approach in the sequential case mentioned above. While some technical results for the algebraic approaches to parallel graph grammars are given in /GL.Eh Kr 76/, /GL.Eh Rb 76/, and /GL.Eh 75/ the first basic result is given in /GL.Ld 78/ resp. /GL.Eh Ld 78/: The construction of a locally catenative formula for dependent PDOL-systems is generalized to the graph case (see 7.4 and 7.6). All this is discussed in Sections 6 and 7. The basic parallel gluing construction, however, is given already in 2.9.

Let us point out that readers which are only interested in parallel graph grammars may skip Sections 3,4 and 5. On the other hand Sections 6 and 7 may be skipped by those which are only interested in the sequential case.

In Section 8 several results concerning graph languages generated by algebraic graph grammars (sequential and parallel case) are summarized with a pumping lemma for type2-graph grammars (proved in /GG.Kr 78/)being of central importance.

As mentioned above there is an appendium in Section 9 on the basic notions of Category Theory which are implicitly used in the other sections. Moreover, the proofs of two results in Section 2 and 4 are given in 9.6 and 9.7 which are typical for the proof techniques used in the Algebraic Theory of Graph Grammars.

References using the first bibliography on graph grammars (prepared by Manfred Nagl) are given in Section 10.

For readers more familiar with the material let us point out that in this survey we only consider productions $p=(B_1 \longleftarrow K \longrightarrow B_2)$ where $K \longrightarrow B_1$ and $K \longrightarrow B_2$ are injective and (colorpreserving) graph morphisms. This is convenient for the presentation but not adequate for some of the applications mentioned in 1.1. On the other hand we are quite sure that most of the constructions and results can be generalized to "structures" (in the sense of /GG.Ra 75/ and /GG.Eh Kr Ma Ro Wi 78/) instead of graphs so that we can cover all these applications (and some more) using only one unified approach.

1.3 TECHNICAL REMARKS

As mentioned above already the reader is not supposed to be familiar with algebraic or categorical notation. All what we need will be carefully motivated and introduced. We only assume basic knowledge of sets and mappings and formal language theory in the string case.
Finally let us remark that (in order to avoid brackets) we sometimes use notations like fx for a map f applied to the argument x, fA for the set $\{fx/x \in A\}$ but not to be confused with gf for the composition of maps applied in the order first f and then g. The notation for graphs and graph morphisms will be introduced in 2.3 and 2.5.

1.4 ACKNOWLEDGEMENTS

Many thanks to Barry K. Rosen, Hans-Jörg Kreowski and Grzegorz Rozenberg for carefully reading of the first draft of this survey, stimulating remarks, discussions and suggestions which led to a considerably improved exposition. Sections 6 and 7 of this survey can be considered as a first part of the paper /GL.Eh Ld 78/ by Axel Liedtke and myself. In fact this is an improved and simplified version of his master thesis /GL.Ld 78/. The bibliography on graph grammars used in this survey was prepared by Manfred Nagl. Last but not least I am thankful to Helga Barnewitz for excellent typing of the paper.

2. GLUING CONSTRUCTIONS FOR GRAPHS

The first major problems to be tackled in building the algebraic theory of graph grammars is to generalize catenation of strings to catenation of graphs, referred to as gluing of graphs. Let us consider a Chomsky production of the form p=(u,v) with nonempty v. Then for each context x,y we obtain a direct derivation $xuy \Rightarrow xvy$ in such a way that u is replaced by v. More precisely we replace u by v and connect the first symbol v_1 of $v=v_1 \ldots v_s$ with the last symbol x_n of $x=x_1 \ldots x_n$ and the last v_s of v with the first y_1 of $y=y_1 \ldots y_t$. Regarding x,v and y as graphs

$$o \xrightarrow{x_1} o \;\ldots\; o \xrightarrow{x_r} \underset{1}{o} \xrightarrow{v_1} o \;\ldots\; o \xrightarrow{v_s} \underset{2}{o} \xrightarrow{y_1} o \;\ldots\; o \xrightarrow{y_t} o$$

we have two "gluing items" 1 and 2 connecting v with the context x and y. (Note that also the case $v=\varepsilon$ (empty word) can be included where the corresponding graph consists of a single node.)

In the general graph case u,v and (x,y) become arbitrary graphs B_1, B_2 and D respectively.

Since the gluing items 1 and 2 in our example are part of v (resp. u) and of the context x and y we will consider in the graph case an "interface" graph K, which is "part" of B_2 (resp. B_1) and D, where B_2 (resp. B_1) and D are disjoint elsewhere. In other words K is exactly the intersection of B_2 (resp. B_1) and D. In this special case we can define the "gluing of B_2 (resp. B_1) and D along K" as the union of B_2 (resp. B_1) and D. Hence the string xuy coresponds to the gluing of B_1 and D along K and xvy to the gluing of B_2 and D along K. This means that a direct derivation in the graph case will consist of two gluing constructions.

For the special case mentioned above where K is exactly the intersection of B and D the gluing of B and D along K is very simple: it is the union of B and D. But this definition of gluing depends essentially on the representations of B, D and K. In general we will have the situation that B, D and K are arbitrary disjoint graphs and that the connection between them is given by graph morphisms $b:K \longrightarrow B$ and $d:K \longrightarrow D$. In this case the gluing G of B and D along K can be defined by the following iterative procedure for G:

```
procedure gluing, parameter (G), input parameters (B, D, K, b, d)
begin G:=B+D        < disjoint union >
for all nodes and arcs k in K do
    G:= identification (G, bk, dk)
end
```

where identification (G, bk, dk) is a procedure which identifies the items bk and dk in the graph G. (Note, that for a more explicit version of the gluing procedure we also have to define graph morphisms $c:D \longrightarrow G$ and $g:B \longrightarrow G$).

Let us consider the following example:

2.1 EXAMPLE

In Fig. 2.1 the graph K consists of the three nodes numbered 1,2,3, graph B is the right one in the upper row and D the left in the lower row. The graph morphisms b:K⟶ B and d:K⟶ D are defined by the images 1,2,3 in B resp. D where k corresponds to bk resp. dk for k=1,2,3. Such a notation will be used in most of our examples.

The procedure gluing yields in step 0 the disjoint union of B and D where we have two copies for each of the nodes k=1,2,3. The procedure identification glues together node k in B with node k in D for k=1,2,3 leading to the graph G in Fig. 2.1. Actually in Fig. 2.1 K can be considered as the common subgraph of B and D and hence G as the union of B and D. However the gluing procedure is not limited to that special case. If nodes 2 and 3 in K would have the same color they could be mapped by graph morphism d:K⟶ D to the same node, say 2 in D. Hence the gluing would be the graph G in Fig. 2.1 where nodes 2 and 3 are identified.

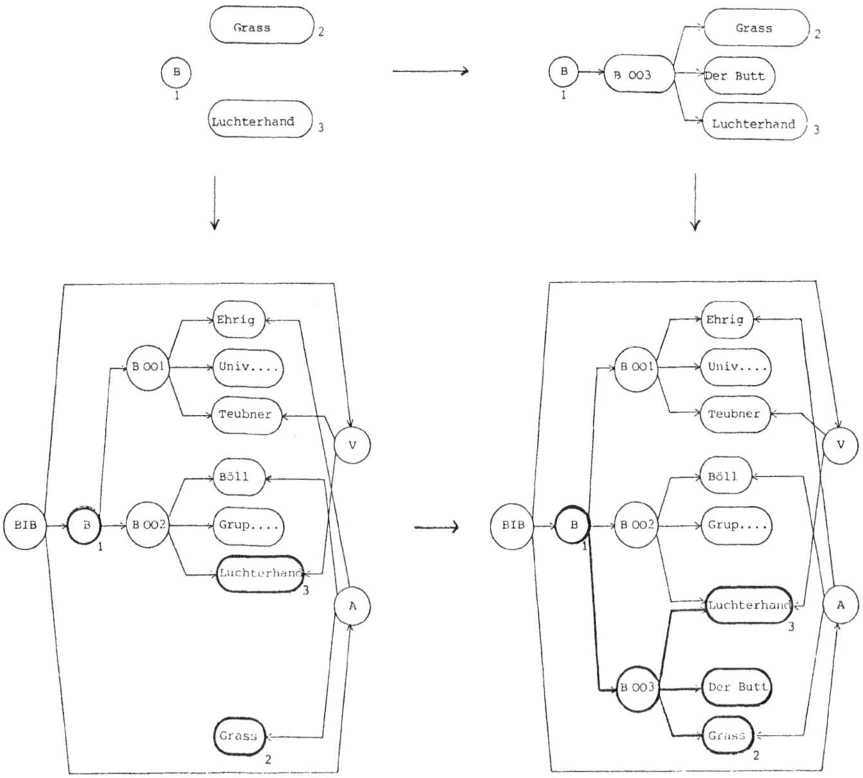

Figure 2.1: Gluing Construction

From the mathematical point of view the gluing procedure is nothing else but a stepwise construction of quotient graphs where in each step we have only a single identification. This version of the gluing procedure is suitable for implementation because such an identification can be done moving one pointer only (resp. using one indirect pointer), provided that the arcs in the graph are implemented as pointers. However, this stepwise construction is unpleasent for theoretical investigations, especially in proofs. Actually we can also do the same construction in one step: Consider the relation $bk \sim dk$ for all k in K defined on B+D and let $\approx$ the reflexive, symmetric and transitive closure of $\sim$, i.e. $\approx$ is the equivalence relation generated by $\sim$ which becomes a "graph congruence" on B+D. Then the gluing is given by the quotient graph

$$G = B + D/_{\approx}$$

A mathematical precise definition of this construction is given in the Appendium in 9.3.

Although this construction is easier to handle than the stepwise construction this quotient construction is still unpleasent in most of the proofs for derivation sequences of graphs because we have to consider 2n different gluing constructions for a derivation of length n. This motivates one to look for an abstract characterization of this gluing construction. As pointed out in the introduction it is the main idea of the algebraic approach to give such an abstract algebraic characterization: The pushout construction (abbreviated PO) in the category of graphs. This algebraic characterization is a universal property of the gluing construction which will be given in 2.6. The important point is that we don't consider the gluing G only, but also the connection with B and D given by graph morphisms $g:B \longrightarrow G$ and $c:D \longrightarrow G$. Together with the given graph morphisms $b:K \longrightarrow B$ and $d:K \longrightarrow D$ we obtain the following commutative diagram which is called pushout of b and d:

$$\begin{array}{ccc} K & \xrightarrow{\quad b \quad} & B \\ {\scriptstyle d}\downarrow & (PO) & \downarrow{\scriptstyle g} \\ D & \xrightarrow{\qquad} & G \end{array}$$

Note that in Example 2.1 we have constructed such a PO where the graph morphisms g and c are the obvious inclusions from B into G resp. D into G.

Using PO-diagrams instead of quotient graphs for the gluing construction we can apply results for composition and decomposition of PO-diagrams, known from Category Theory, in the Algebraic Theory of Graph Grammars. Otherwise we would have all the difficulties arising from quotient set and case constructions concerning well-definedness of functions on these sets. Especially this makes sense in Section 4 and 5 when we consider properties of derivation sequences where several gluing constructions are envolved. To be fair, however, we must admit that for some constructions we cannot use the universal properties of PO-diagrams and have to go back to the explicit set theoretical constructions. Summerizing we have:

2.2 DIFFERENT LEVELS OF DESCRIPTION

For the gluing construction and other basic notions in the Algebraic Theory of Graph Grammars we have three different levels of description:

1. Algorithmic description
2. Set-theoretical description
3. Algebraic-categorical description

The algorithmic description usually is the most intuitive one, at least for people in Computer Science. Moreover it is useful for the implementation of the construction. For mathematical precise definitions of the constructions we have to use the set-theoretical or, as far as possible, the algebraic-categorical description. Finally for most of the proofs in the Algebraic Theory of Graph Grammars we use the algebraic-categorical level.

In this introduction we only use the basic concept of PO-diagrams to give a short and precise formulation of our definitions, constructions and results. The basic categorical constructions used in the theory are given in the Appendium together with two typical proofs. Especially the equivalence of the set-theoretical and algebraic-categorical description is proved in 9.3 resp. 9.6. Our algorithmic description is not precise enough to allow an equivalence proof. The main reason to present it is to give an intuitive meaning of the constructions and some hints for implementation.

Before we study the gluing construction for graphs in more detail let us give the basic notions of graph theory which are used in the following sections.

2.3 DEFINITION

1) Let $C=(C_A,C_N)$ be a pair of sets, called pair of color alphabets for arcs and nodes respectively, which will be fixed in the following.
2) A (colored) graph $G=(G_A, G_N, s, t, m_A, m_N)$ consists of sets G_A, G_N, called set of arcs and nodes respectively, and mappings $s:G_A \longrightarrow G_N$, $t:G_A \longrightarrow G_N$, called source resp. target map, $m_A:G_A \longrightarrow C_A$, $m_N:G_N \longrightarrow C_N$, called arc resp. node coloring map, these data can be summarized in the diagram

$$G: C_A \xleftarrow{m_A} G_A \overset{s}{\underset{t}{\rightrightarrows}} G_N \xrightarrow{m_N} C_N$$

3) A graph G is called discrete if G_A is empty.

4) Graph G' is called subgraph of G if $G'_A \subseteq G_A$, $G'_N \subseteq G_N$ and all the mappings s',t', m'_A und m'_N are restrictions of the corresponding ones from G.

Remarks:

1. Our definition of graphs allows parallel arcs including those with same color. As pointed out in /GT.Ro 77/ this seems to be the adequate notion for graphs in Computer Science.

2. If we don't want to distinguish between arcs and nodes we use the notation item and $x \in G$ means $x \in G_A$ or $x \in G_N$.

3. For a node $n \in G_N$ all the arcs in $s^{-1}(n) \cup t^{-1}(n)$ will sometimes be referred as the adjacent arcs of node n.

2.4 EXAMPLE

An explicit description of the graph B in Fig. 2.1 (the right graph in the upper row) is given by:

$B=(B_A, B_N, s, t, m_A, m_N)$ with

$B_A = \{a_1,\dots,a_4\}$, $B_N = \{n_1,\dots,n_5\}$

$s\ a_1=v_1$, $s\ a_i=v_4$ for i=2,3,4

$t\ a_1=v_4$, $t\ a_2=v_2$, $t\ a_3=v_3$, $t\ a_4=v_5$

$m_N\ v_1$=B, $m_N\ v_2$=Grass, $m_N\ v_3$=Luchterhand, $m_N\ v_4$=BOO3, $m_N\ v_5$=Der Butt

$m_A\ a_i = \varepsilon$ (empty word) for i=1,...,4

The graph K in Fig. 2.1 is discrete.

2.5 DEFINITION

Given two graphs G and G' a graph morphism $f:G \longrightarrow G'$, f or $G \longrightarrow G'$ for short, is a pair of maps $f=(f_A:G_A \longrightarrow G'_A,\ f_N:G_N \longrightarrow G'_N)$ such that $f_N\ s=s' f_A$, $f_N\ t=t' f_A$, $m'_A f_A = m_A$, and $m'_N f_N = m_N$, i.e. the following diagram commutes for source and target mappings separately:

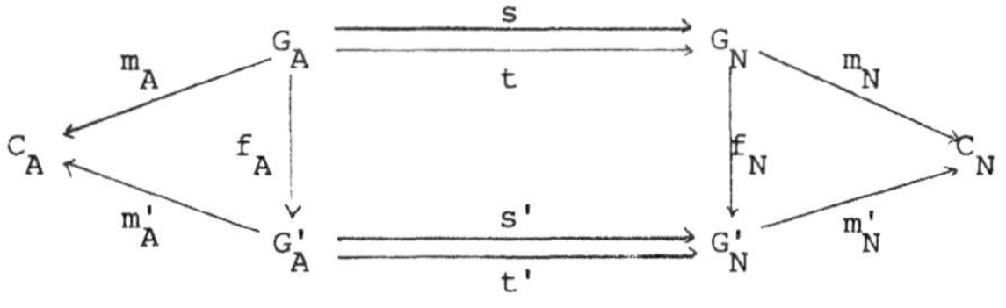

A graph morphism $f=(f_A,f_N)$ is called injective resp. surjective if both f_A and f_N are injective resp. surjective mappings. If $f:G \longrightarrow G'$ is injective and surjective it is called an isomorphism, and there is also an inverse isomorphism $f':G' \longrightarrow G$. The composition $f'f:G \longrightarrow G''$ of two graph morphisms $f=(f_A,f_N):G \longrightarrow G'$ and

$f':(f'_A, f'_N):G' \longrightarrow G''$ is defined by $f'f=(f'_A f_A, f'_N f_N)$.
The disjoint union of graph morphisms $f:G \longrightarrow G'$ and $g:H \longrightarrow H'$ is the graph morphism $f+g:G+H \longrightarrow G'+H'$ defined by $(f+g)=(f_A+g_A, f_N+g_N)$ where also the disjoint union of graphs G+H is defined as disjoint union in both components.

Remark:

In the graphical notation of a graph, like B of Example 2.4 in Fig. 2.1, we don't give the set of arcs and nodes explicitly. Hence also a graph B' with a_i and n_j replaced by a'_i resp. n'_j for $i=1,\dots,4$ and $j=1,\dots,5$ in 2.4 would have the same graphical notation as B in Fig. 2.1. Actually B and B' are isomorphic under the isomorphism $f:B \longrightarrow B'$ with $f_A\, a_i=a'_i$ and $f_N\, n_j=n'_j$. Hence the graph B in Fig. 2.1 represents an isomorphism class of graphs and it makes no sense to distinguish one special representative in this class. In the literature such an isomorphism class of graphs is sometimescalled abstract graph in opposite to concrete graphs as given in 2.3.

Consequently the graphical notation of a graph morphism is based on abstract graphs and we will sometimes use additional indices 1,2,3,... to indicate that node with index i in K is mapped by b_N to that with the same index in B. In several cases it is not necessary to give the mappings b_A and b_N explicitly because there is only one choice for b_A and b_N such that $b=(b_A, b_N)$ becomes a graph morphism. In Fig. 2.1 we have the following four injective graph morphisms satisfying gb=cd:

$b:K \longrightarrow B$, $d:K \longrightarrow D$, $c:D \longrightarrow G$ and $g:B \longrightarrow G$.

Now we are able to give the algebraic definition of the gluing construction which is the basic concept in the Algebraic Theory of Sequential Graph Grammars. A corresponding gluing construction for parallel graph grammars will be given in 2.8.

2.6 DEFINITION (ALGEBRAIC GLUING CONSTRUCTION AND PUSHOUT)

Given graph morphism $K \longrightarrow B$ and $K \longrightarrow D$ a graph G together with two graph morphisms $B \longrightarrow G$ and $D \longrightarrow G$ is called gluing of B and D along K or pushout of $K \longrightarrow B$ and $K \longrightarrow D$ if we have

1. (Commutativity): $K \longrightarrow B \longrightarrow G = K \longrightarrow D \longrightarrow G$, and
2. (Universal Property): For all graphs G' and graph morphisms $B \longrightarrow G'$ and $D \longrightarrow G'$ satisfying $K \longrightarrow B \longrightarrow G' = K \longrightarrow D \longrightarrow G'$ there is a unique graph morphism $G \longrightarrow G'$ such that

$B \longrightarrow G \longrightarrow G' = B \longrightarrow G'$ and $D \longrightarrow G \longrightarrow G' = D \longrightarrow G'$

The situation can be illustrated by the following diagram

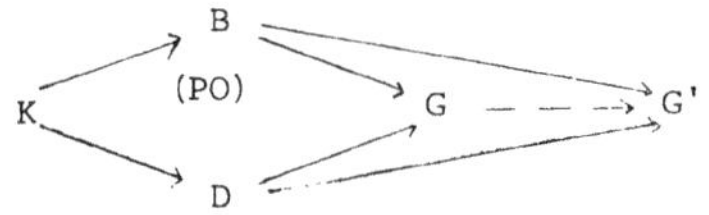

Also the diagram (PO) above is referred to as pushout if it satisfies the commutativity and universal property in 1. and 2.

Interpretation:

The commutativity means that the items of B and D coming from the "interface" graph K are identified in G. On the other hand we want to make sure that no other items of B and D are glued together and that G does not contain other items which are not coming from B or D. These both requirements are expressed by the universal property of G where G is compared with any other G' satisfying a similar commutativity as G. This will be illustrated by the following Example 2.7.

Remark:

The gluing graph G is uniquely determined up to isomorphism by the commutativity and universal property above. Moreover the gluing procedure and the set-theoretical gluing construction sketched in the introduction of this section are satisfying these properties. An explicit gluing construction for injective $K \longrightarrow B$ will be given in 2.8. The equivalence of the algebraic and different set-theoretical gluing constructions is proved in 9.3 and 9.6.

2.7 EXAMPLE

We will show that the diagram in Fig. 2.1 is a PO-diagram. Without loss of generality we can assume that K, B and D are subgraphs of G. Given any graph G' with graph morphisms $B \longrightarrow G'$ and $D \longrightarrow G'$ satisfying $K \longrightarrow B \longrightarrow G' = K \longrightarrow D \longrightarrow G'$ we know that $B \longrightarrow G'$ and $D \longrightarrow G'$ coincide on the intersection K of B and D. Hence the unique graph morphism $G \longrightarrow G'$ can be defined on subgraph B by $B \longrightarrow G'$ and on subgraph D of G by $D \longrightarrow G'$.

For the case of injective morphisms $K \longrightarrow B$ we have the following set-theoretical description of the gluing construction which avoids quotient sets but includes several case constructions:

2.8 LEMMA (GLUING CONSTRUCTION)

Given graph morphisms $b:K \longrightarrow B$ and $d:K \longrightarrow D$ the following gluing construction is a pushout in the sense of 2.6 provided that b is injective.

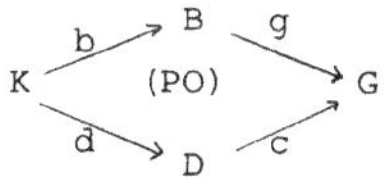

1) $G=D+(B-bK)$ for the sets of arcs and nodes respectively where s_G, t_G for all $a \in G_A$ and m_G are defined by:

   $s_G\ a = \underline{\text{if}}\ a \in D_A\ \underline{\text{then}}\ s_D\ a$

   $\qquad \underline{\text{else}}\ \underline{\text{if}}\ s_B\ a \in (B-bK)_N\ \underline{\text{then}}\ s_B\ a$

   $\qquad\qquad \underline{\text{else}}\ dk \quad \text{where } s_B\ a = bk \text{ for } k \in K_N$

   $t_G\ a$ is defined similar replacing "s" by "t" simultaneously

   $m_G\ x = \underline{\text{if}}\ x \in D\ \underline{\text{then}}\ m_D\ x\ \underline{\text{else}}\ m_B\ x$ for each item $x \in G$.

2) $c:D \longrightarrow G$ is the inclusion from D into G.

3) $g: B \longrightarrow G$ is defined for all items $x \in B$ by

$gx =$ <u>if</u> $x \in B - bK$ <u>then</u> x <u>else</u> dk where $x = bk$ for $k \in K$.

Note that s_G, t_G and g are well-defined because b is injective. The proof of this lemma is given in 9.6 (see also /GG.Ro 75b/ and /OV.De Eh 76/. The reader is referred to Example 2.1 to make sure that the set-theoretical description above has the same effect as the gluing procedure.

Finally we will consider the gluing concept for parallel graph grammars which will be used in Section 6 and 7. In the sequential case we only need the gluing of two graphs but in the parallel case - because of parallel replacement - we need the gluing of $n \geq 2$ graphs $B_1, \ldots, B_n$ in one step. Since we will allow that each B_i will be glued together with each other B_j we need $n(n-1)/2$ interface graphs K_{ij} with $1 \leq i < j \leq n$ instead of one in the sequential case. Hence we obtain the following construction generlizing 2.6.

<u>2.9 DEFINITION (STAR GLUING AND PUSHOUT-STAR)</u>

A graph star of degree $n \geq 1$ is a diagram

$$S = (B_i \longleftarrow K_{ij} \longrightarrow B_j)_{1 \leq i < j \leq n}$$

consisting of graphs B_i, B_j, K_{ij} and graph morphisms $k_{ij}: K_{ij} \longrightarrow B_i$ resp. $k_{ji}: K_{ij} \longrightarrow B_j$.
In the case $n=1$ we only have the single graph B_1 and for $n=2$ we have a pair of graph morphisms $K_{12} \longrightarrow B_1$ and $K_{12} \longrightarrow B_2$ as given in 2.6.
Due to 2.2 let us give a procedure for the star gluing before we give the algebraic description, while the set-theoretical one is sketched in the remark below:

<u>procedure</u> star gluing <u>parameter</u> (G) <u>input parameters</u> $((B_i \xleftarrow{k_{ij}} K_{ij} \xrightarrow{k_{ji}} B_j)_{1 \leq i < j \leq n})$

<u>begin</u> $G := B_1 + \ldots + B_n$ <disjoint union>

<u>for</u> all $1 \leq i < j \leq n$ and x in K_{ij} <u>do</u>

  $G :=$ identification $(G, k_{ij}\,x, k_{ji}\,x)$

<u>end</u>

Obviously the star gluing procedure generalizes the gluing procedure to case $n > 2$. The same is true for the pushout-star defined as follows:
Given a star $S = (B_i \longleftarrow K_{ij} \longrightarrow B_j)_{1 \leq i < j \leq n}$ a graph G together with graph morphisms $B_i \longrightarrow G$ for $i = 1, \ldots, n$ is called <u>star gluing of S</u> or <u>pushout-star of S</u>, POS for short, if we have:

<u>1. (Commutativity):</u> $K_{ij} \longrightarrow B_i \longrightarrow G = K_{ij} \longrightarrow B_j \longrightarrow G$ for all $i<j$, and
<u>2. (Universal Property):</u> For all graphs G' and graph morphisms $B_i \longrightarrow G'$ satisfying $K_{ij} \longrightarrow B_i \longrightarrow G' = K_{ij} \longrightarrow B_j \longrightarrow G'$ for all $i<j$ there is a unique graph morphism $G \longrightarrow G'$ such that $B_i \longrightarrow G \longrightarrow G' = B_i \longrightarrow G'$ for all $i = 1, \ldots, n$ in the following diagram:

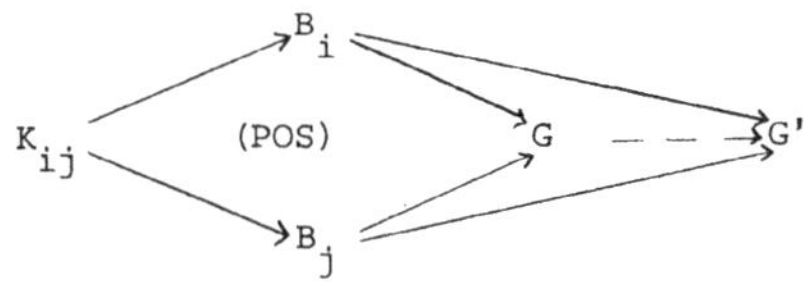

Also the diagram (POS) above is referred to as pushout-star which has in the case n=3 the following shape:

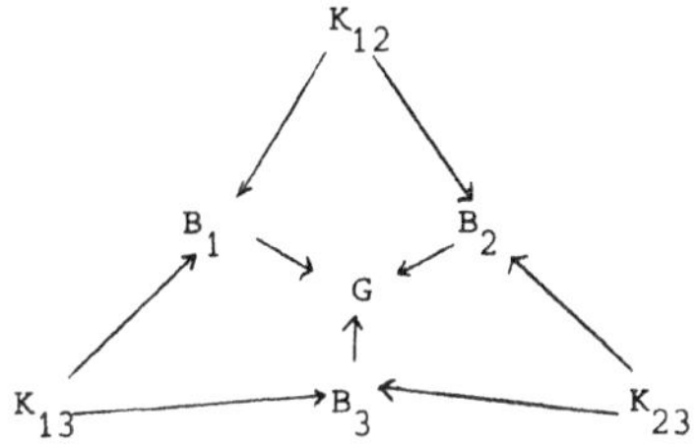

Remark: As in the case of gluing of graphs the graph G=STARGLUING(S) is uniquely determined up to isomorphism and (see 9.3) there is also an explicit set-theoretical description for the star gluing which can be performed for arcs and nodes independently. In each component we obtain the quotient set

$$G=B_1+\ldots+B_n/\approx$$

where $\approx$ is the equivalence relation generated by the relation $\sim$ defined by $k_{ij}\ z \sim k_{ji}\ z$ for all z in k_{ij} and all $1 \leq i < j \leq n$.

2.10 EXAMPLE

In Fig. 2.2 the graph G together with the three graph morphisms in the center is the pushout star of the graph star given by the remaining graph morphisms. All the graph morphisms are injective in this example.

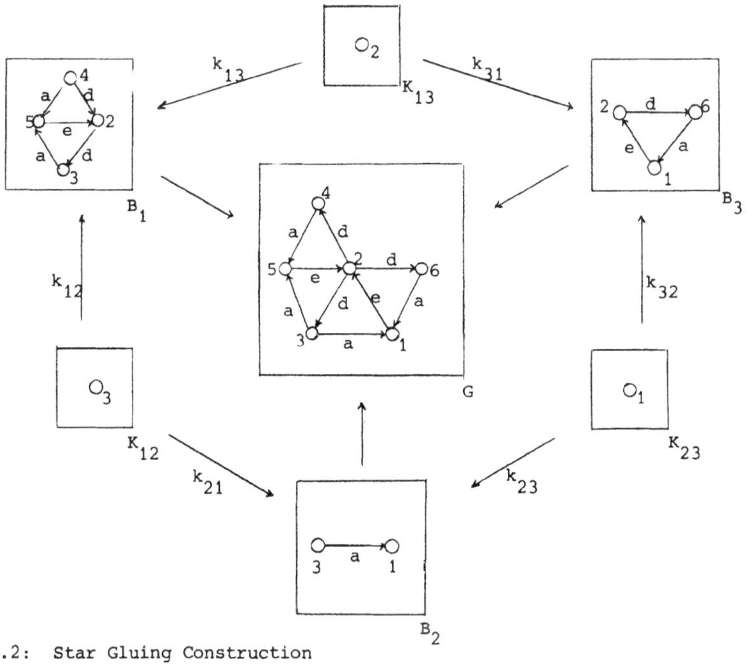

Figure 2.2: Star Gluing Construction

3. SEQUENTIAL GRAPH GRAMMARS

Using the motivation and the gluing construction for graphs from Section 2 we are now able to define graph productions, derivations and grammars for the sequential case of graph grammars. This generalizes Chomsky grammars to the case of graphs. As mentioned in 1.2 the algebraic approach treated in this section was introduced in /GG.Eh Pf Sc 73a,b/ and extended in various other papers. For a survey on other approaches to graph grammars we refer to /OV.Na 78/. The generalization of L-systems to graphs will be treated in Section 6.

3.1 DEFINITION (PRODUCTIONS, DIRECT DERIVATIONS)

1) A *graph production* p is a pair of graph morphisms

   $p=(B_1 \longleftarrow K \longrightarrow B_2)$

   where the graphs B_1, B_2 and K are called *left side*, *right side* and *interface* of p respectively.

   The production p is called *fast*, if $K \longrightarrow B_1$ and $K \longrightarrow B_2$ are injective.

2) Given a production $p=(B_1 \longleftarrow K \longrightarrow B_2)$ and a graph D, called *context*, together with a graph morphism $K \longrightarrow D$ a *direct derivation* consists of the following two pushouts $(PO)_1$ and $(PO)_2$

$$\begin{array}{ccccc} B_1 & \longleftarrow & K & \longrightarrow & B_2 \\ \downarrow & (PO)_1 & \downarrow & (PO)_2 & \downarrow \\ G & \longleftarrow & D & \longrightarrow & H \end{array}$$

   We write then $G \Longrightarrow_p H$ and we also say that $B_1 \longrightarrow G$ (resp. $B_2 \longrightarrow H$) is the *occurence* of p in G (resp. H). $G \Longrightarrow H$ is also called a direct derivation *via* p *based on* $B_1 \longrightarrow G$.

3) A *derivation* $G \Longrightarrow_* H$ means G=H or a sequence of direct derivations

   $G=G_1 \Longrightarrow_{p_1} G_2 \Longrightarrow_{p_2} \cdots \Longrightarrow_{p_{n-1}} G_n=H.$

Interpretation:

The interface graph K of a production p consists of the gluing items which are mapped by $K \longrightarrow B_i$ to B_i for i=1,2. With respect to the generative power it sufficies to consider only discrete interface graphs K but concerning independence of derivations (see 4.1) it is useful to include as many arcs in K as possible. In the direct derivation $G \Longrightarrow_p H$ given by the pushouts $(PO)_1$ and $(PO)_2$ the production p and the context graph D are defining G (resp. H) as gluing of B_1 (resp. B_2) and D along K. In other words we obtain H from G by deleting B_1 and adding B_2 (in both cases without gluing items). Actually the gluing items are included in the context graph D which is the intermediate result deleting only B_1 from G. Generating a direct derivation in general a production p, and graph G and the occurence $B_1 \longrightarrow G$ will be given but not the context graph D. In this case D must be constructed in a first step, called "gluing analysis" (see 3.7), in such a way that G becomes the gluing of B_1 and D along K in $(PO)_1$. In the second step H is constructed as gluing of B_2 and D along K by pushout $(PO)_2$. The interpretation of "fast" productions will be given in Remark 1 of 3.8.

3.2 EXAMPLES

In Fig. 3.1 seven productions, corresponding to the operations of a small library system considered in /AP.Eh Kr 78/ are given. In each case the interface graph K is discrete consisting of all the indices given in the left (or in the right) hand side of the production. The graph morphisms $K \longrightarrow B_1$ and $K \longrightarrow B_2$ are the corresponding inclusions. All the node colors, except B and K, are parameters which have to be "recolored" by actual parameters before applying the production. The production KATALOGISIEREN for example is recolored with the actual parameters "B001", "K54321", "KAMIDI", "Univ...", and "Teubner" and applied to the graph G left in the lower row of Fig. 3.2. The occurence of the production is given in bold face. The context graph D in this example is G without the node colored B001 and all its adjacent arcs. The graph H in the direct derivation $G \Longrightarrow H$ is given by the right one in the lower row of Fig. 3.2.
Another direct derivation, now using the production BESTELLEN, is given in Fig. 2.1. Since K and B_1 are equal in this example, also D and G become equal. Hence the direct derivation $G \Longrightarrow H$ is completely determined by pushout $(PO)_2$ which is given in Fig. 2.1.
An example of a direct derivation with non injective occurences $B_1 \longrightarrow G$ and $B_2 \longrightarrow H$ is given in Fig. 4.4 and will be studied in Example 4.12.

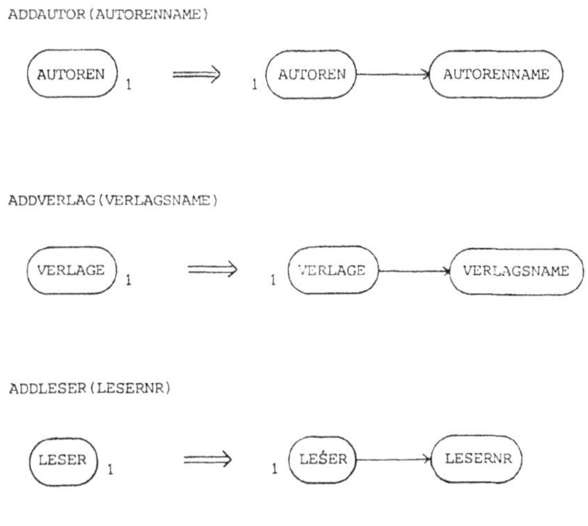

Figure 3.1: List of Productions with Discrete K

BESTELLEN(BEST-NR,AUTORENNAME,TITEL,VERLAGSNAME)

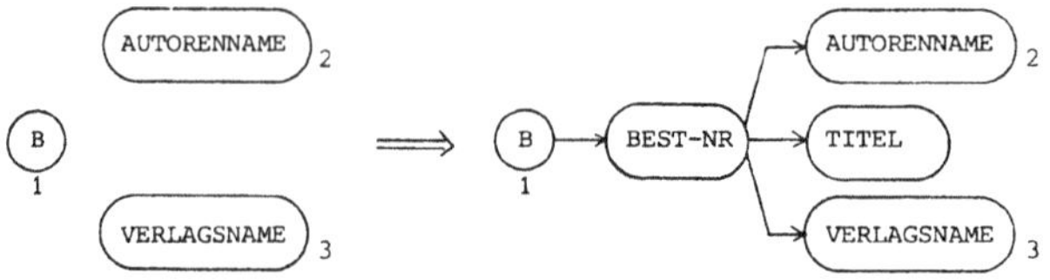

KATALOGISIEREN(BEST-NR,KAT-NR)

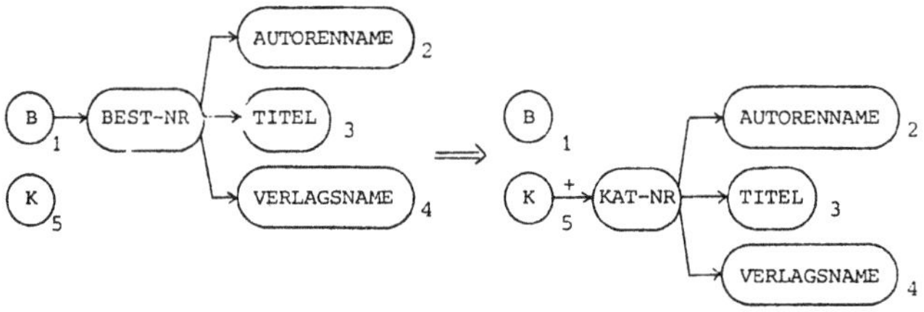

AUSLEIHEN(KAT-NR,LESERNR)

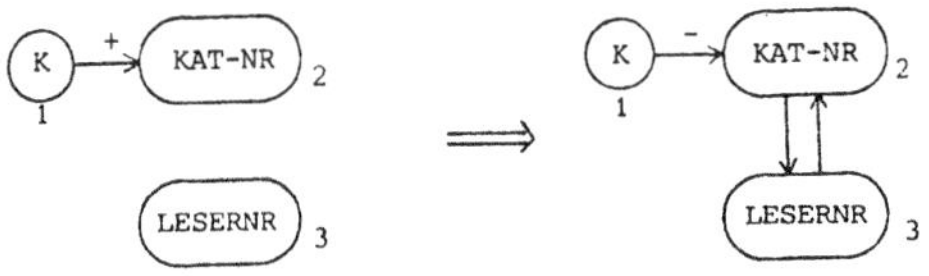

LÖSCHEN(KAT-NR)

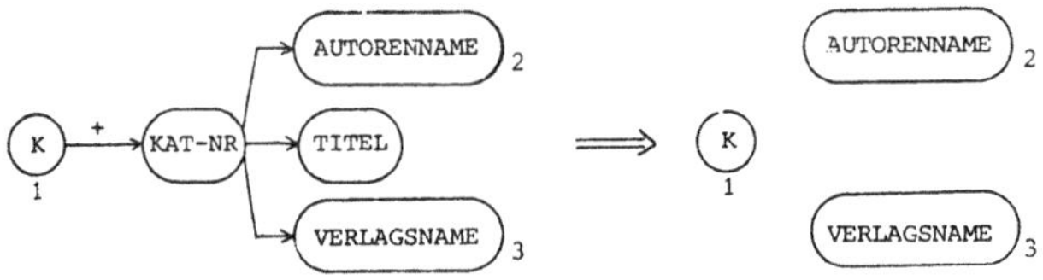

Figure 3.1: List of Productions with Discrete K (cont'd)

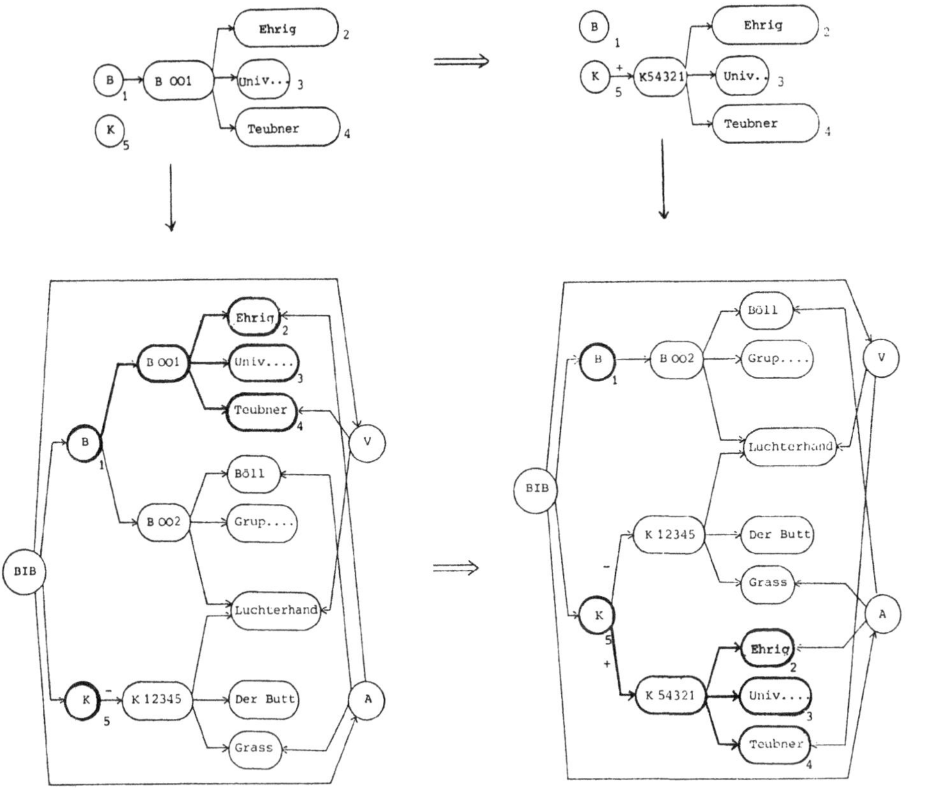

Figure 3.2: Direct Derivation G$\Longrightarrow$H

3.3 DEFINITION (GRAPH GRAMMARS AND LANGUAGES)

1) A (sequential) graph grammar

$$GG=(C,T,PROD,START)$$

consists of a pair of color alphabets $C=(C_A, C_N)$ (see 2.3), a pair of terminal color alphabets $T=(T_A, T_N)$ included in C, a finite set of productions PROD and a start graph START where all graphs are finite. Moreover we assume that the start graph START and all the left hand sides of the productions are not terminal colored. (For some applications, however, we will take T=C and drop this last assumption.)

2) The graph language L(GG) of a graph grammar GG is defined to be the set of all terminal colored graphs derivable from the start graph. More precisely

$$L(GG)=\{H \in GRAPHS_T \ / \ START \Longrightarrow_* H\}$$

Remark:

Since the pushout construction is only unique up to isomorphism (see 2.6) we have for each direct derivation $G \Longrightarrow H$ also $G \Longrightarrow H'$ and hence for each $H \in L(GG)$ also $H' \in L(GG)$ for all graphs H' isomorphic to H. Thus we can consider L(GG) as a language of abstract graphs (see 2.5). See 8.2 for more about graph languages.

3.4 EXAMPLES

1. Using the procedure in the introduction of Section 2 we can show that each Chomsky grammar can be considered as a graph grammar consisting of totally ordered graphs. Hence also each Chomsky Language can be considered as a graph language.

2. The list of productions in Fig. 3.1 together with the startgraph in Fig. 3.3 constitutes a graph grammar GG. More precisely we would have to consider the (infinite) set of productions which arise from those in Fig. 3.1 by recoloring the parameters by actual parameters (see 3.2). Moreover we take T=C and drop the assumption concerning not terminal colored graphs in 3.3.1). In spite of these slight modifications we will speak of a graph grammar GG. The corresponding graph language L(GG) is the set of all consistent states of the library specified in /AP.Eh Kr 78/ which are satisfying the following five conditions:

1) There is a node colored "BIB(LIOTHEK)" which is source of five arcs with targets colored "A(UTOREN)", "V(ERLAGE)", "B(ESTELLUNGEN)", "K(ATALOG)", and "L(ESER)" respectively.
2) The nodes colored "A", "V", "B", "K" and "L" respectively are sources of a finite number of arcs. For the arcs with source colored "A" or "V" the target is colored by a string over the Latin alphabet, called A- or V-name, which are supposed to be disjoint. For arcs with source colored "B", "K", or "L" the target is colored with the same letter followed by 3, 5 and 4 digits called B-, K-, and L-numbers respectively. Each arc with source "K" is colored "+" or "-" corresponding to the status "present" or "lent out" of a book.
3) Each K- and B-number is source of exactly three arcs where the targets are colored with an A-, V- and T-name. A T-name (title of a book) is a string over the Latin alphabet including a blank and the node colored with a T-name is target of no other arc.
4) For each arc colored "-"pointing to a K-number there is exactly one node colored with an L-number and two arcs between the corresponding nodes in opposite direction.
5) There are no other nodes and arcs except those specified in 1)-4).

The interpretation of a consistent state should be clear by definition and the example in Fig. 3.4. A derivation sequence deriving Fig. 3.4 from Fig. 3.3 will be given in Example 5.7.

3. An example of an "arc-context-free" graph grammar, where the left hand sides of the productions are single arcs together with source and target node, is given in /GG.Kr 77a/ resp. /GG.Kr 78/.

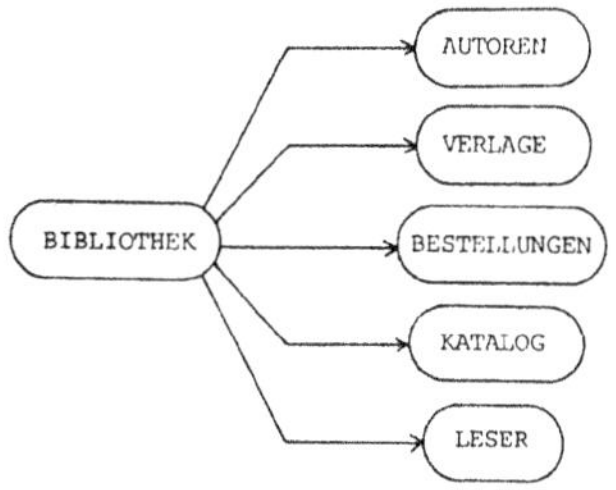

Figure 3.3: Startgraph of a Bibliography Graph Grammar

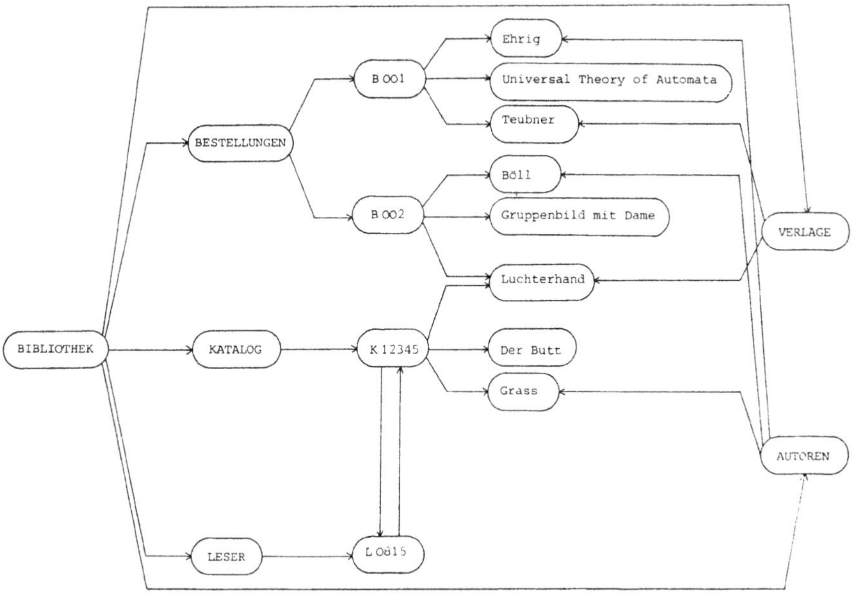

Figure 3.4: Consistent State of a Bibliography

Now we turn to the problem of constructing a direct derivation $G \underset{p}{\Longrightarrow} H$ in the case that a fast production $p=(B_1 \xleftarrow{b_1} K \xrightarrow{b_2} B_2)$, a graph G and the occurence $g:B_1 \longrightarrow G$ of p in G are given. However, it is not always possible to get a well-defined derived graph H. If, for example, there is a context arc a in G, which itself is not in $g\,B_1$ but with source $s_G a$ in gB_1, then we must know how to connect arc a with $h\,B_2$ in the derived graph H. However, we don't have such an information unless $s_G a$ is a gluing item gb_1k for some $k\in K$. In this case there is a corresponding gluing item hb_2k in H which can be used as source $s_H a$ of the context arc a. These items $s_G a$ (and similarly defined $t_G a$) will be called "dangling" because they are left dangling in G after removing gB_1. For technical reasons we also call the corresponding nodes x in B_1 with $gx=s_G a$ (resp. $gx=t_G a$) dangling nodes. If the occurence $g:B_1 \longrightarrow G$ is not injective there may be another difficulty to obtain a direct derivation. We have to assume that all items identified by g, called identification items, are gluing items $b_1\,k$ for some $k\in K$. Otherwise we also can construct the context graph D and $d:K \longrightarrow D$, but the gluing G' of B_1 and D along K will not be the graph G exactly. Actually if we have $gb_1k=gx$ in G for some $x\in B_1 - b_1k$ then the images of b_1k and x in G' are different (see Example 3.6.3). Dangling and identification items together will be called boundary. Hence we have to require that boundary items are gluing items. Actually this condition, called gluing condition, is necessary and sufficient to obtain a direct derivation:

3.5 DEFINITION (GLUING CONDITION)

Given a fast production $p=(B_1 \xleftarrow{b_1} K \xrightarrow{b_2} B_2)$ and a graph morphism $g:B_1 \longrightarrow G$ let us define the following subgraphs of B_1:

GLUING = $b_1\,K$

DANGLING = $\{x\in(B_1)_N \ / \ \exists\ a\in(G-g\,B_1)\ \ gx=s_G a \text{ or } gx=t_G a\}$

IDENTIFICATION = $\{x\in B_1 \ / \ \exists\ y\in B_1 \ \ x\neq y \text{ and } gx=gy\}$

BOUNDARY = DANGLING $\cup$ IDENTIFICATION

Now the GLUING CONDITION for p with respect to g states that boundary items are gluing items, i.e. BOUNDARY $\subseteq$ GLUING.

3.6 EXAMPLES

1. The GLUING CONDITION is satisfied trivially for all those productions satisfying a) and b) below with respect to arbitrary $g:B_1 \longrightarrow G$:

a) There are no different nodes (resp. no parallel arcs) in B_1 having the same color. (This implies IDENTIFICATION = $\emptyset$ (empty graph).)

b) All nodes in B_1 are gluing items. (This implies DANGLING $\subseteq$ GLUING)

Hence the GLUING CONDITION is always satisfied for all the productions in Fig. 3.1 except KATALOGISIEREN and LÖSCHEN.

2. The GLUING CONDITION is also satisfied for KATALOGISIEREN (using actual parameter B001 resp. B002 for BEST-NR and suitable ones for the other parameters) with respect to the inclusion of B_1 into the graph G of Fig. 3.4. But it would not be satisfied if there would be an additional arc in G connecting the node colored B001 with any other node in G. In this case BEST-NR in B_1 would be a dangling but no gluing node.

The production LÖSCHEN cannot be applied to Fig. 3.4.

3. The GLUING CONDITION is not satisfied in the following situation of Fig. 3.5 because IDENTIFICATION = $\{2,3\}$ is not contained in GLUING = $\{1,2\}$

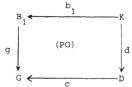

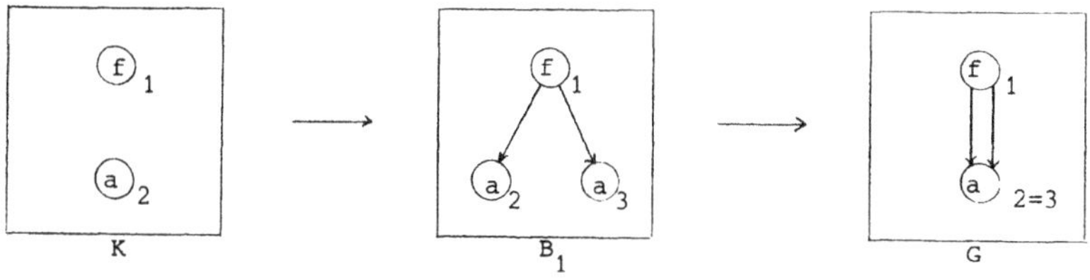

Figure 3.5: Graph Morphisms not Satisfying the Gluing Condition

Using the GLUING CONDITION we are now able to construct the context graph D in pushout $(PO)_1$ of 3.1 provided that $b_1:K \longrightarrow B_1$ and $g:B_1 \longrightarrow G$ are given. Intuitively the context (including the gluing items) of B_1 in G is given by CONTEXT = $(G-gB_1) + gb_1K$. However, this construction on the sets of arcs and nodes does not become a graph iff not DANGLING $\subseteq$ GLUING, the first part of the GLUING CONDITION, is satisfied. The second part, IDENTIFICATION $\subseteq$ GLUING, makes sure that the gluing of B_1 and CONTEXT along K becomes G.

3.7 LEMMA (CONTEXT GRAPH AND GLUING ANALYSIS)

Given graph morphisms $b_1:K \longrightarrow B_1$ and $g:B_1 \longrightarrow G$ with b_1 injective there exists a unique (up to isomorphism) graph D with graph morphisms $d:K \longrightarrow D$ and $c:D \longrightarrow G$ such that the diagram

$$\begin{array}{ccc} B_1 & \xleftarrow{\;b_1\;} & K \\ {\scriptstyle g}\downarrow & (PO) & \downarrow{\scriptstyle d} \\ G & \xleftarrow[\;c\;]{} & D \end{array}$$

becomes a pushout iff the GLUING CONDITION is satisfied. In this case D is called <u>CONTEXT of B_1 in G</u> and D together with d and c, given by the construction below, is called <u>gluing analysis</u> or <u>pushout-complement</u> of b_1 and g.

1) $D=(G-g\,B_1)+g\,b_1\,K$ is a subgraph of G
2) $c:D \longrightarrow G$ is the inclusion of D into G
3) $d:K \longrightarrow D$ is defined for all items $k \in K$ by $dk=g\,b_1\,k$

<u>Remark:</u>

If b_1 is not injective the lemma remains true without uniqueness. This means we will have different (nonisomorphic) context graphs in general (see /GG.Eh Pf Sc 73b/, /GG.Ro 75b/, /AP.Eh Kr 76b/, /OV.De 76/ for constructions and proofs).
Examples are given in 3.2 and implicitly in 3.6.1:
For the productions ADDAUTOR, ADDVERLAG, ADDLESER and BESTELLEN in Fig. 3.1 the

context graph D will always be equal to the graph G. If KATALOGISIEREN, AUSLEIHEN and LÖSCHEN in Fig. 3.1 can be applied to a graph G the context graph D will be the subgraph of G where the images of the nongluing nodes in B_1 colored BEST-NR, KAT-NR or TITEL and all the arcs coming from B_1 are deleted.

3.8 COROLLARY (CONSTRUCTION OF DIRECT DERIVATIONS)

Given a fast production $p=(B_1 \longleftarrow K \longrightarrow B_2)$, a graph G and an occurence $g:B_1 \longrightarrow G$ of p in G there is a unique (up to isomorphism) direct derivation $G \underset{p}{\Longrightarrow} H$ based on g iff the GLUING CONDITION is satisfied. In this case we have a two step construction:

Step 1: Gluing analysis in diagram $(PO)_1$ using Lemma 3.7

Step 2: Gluing construction in diagram $(PO)_2$ using Lemma 2.8

$$\begin{array}{ccccc} B_1 & \longleftarrow & K & \longrightarrow & B_2 \\ g \downarrow & (PO)_1 & \downarrow & (PO)_2 & \downarrow h \\ G & \longleftarrow & D & \longrightarrow & H \end{array}$$

Remarks:

1. Under very mild conditions on the representation of (finite) graphs (see Thm.3.4 in /GG.Eh Kr Ma Ro Wi 78/) there is also a "fast algorithm" for the construction of direct derivations $G \underset{p}{\Longrightarrow} H$ with fast p which is independent on the size of G. Actually this algorithm avoids copying and constructs H from G making only local changes in G.

2. It is clear that the construction above can be iterated to obtain a derivation sequence $G_1 \Longrightarrow G_2 \Longrightarrow \ldots \Longrightarrow G_n$. But using the same concepts and constructions we also get a parsing sequence $G_n \Longrightarrow G_{n-1} \Longrightarrow \ldots \Longrightarrow G_1$: The symmetry of our definition of productions and direct derivations in 3.1 allows to obtain a reduction step $H \underset{p}{\Longrightarrow} G$ by applying the "inverse production" $\bar{p}=(B_2 \longleftarrow K \longrightarrow B_1)$ of $p=(B_1 \longleftarrow K \longrightarrow B_2)$ to H. This yields a direct derivation $H \underset{\bar{p}}{\Longrightarrow} G$ which again can be constructed by two steps as in Corollary 3.8.

3. The proof of 3.8 follows immediately from 3.1, 3.7 and 2.8 (see also /GG.Ro 75b/ /OV.De Eh 76/)

3.9 SOME REMARKS ON MEMBERSHIP AND PARSING PROBLEM

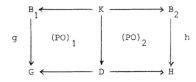

The membership problem for graph grammars is defined as followed: Given an arbitrary graph grammar GG and an arbitrary graph G does G belong to the language L(GG)? Using the same techniques as in the string case for Chomsky grammars one can show that the membership problem is not decidable for arbitrary graph grammars (corresponding to Type 0 Chomsky grammars) but it is decidable for "context-sensitive" graph grammars. By "context-sensitive" we mean that for each production $p=(B_1 \longleftarrow K \longrightarrow B_2)$ the number of arcs and nodes of B_1 is less or equal to that of B_2. Much more difficult than in the string case is the problem of efficient syntax analysis for graph grammars which is studied in /GG.Fr 77/ and /GG.De Gh 78/. For the class of precedence graph grammars (which are based on the precedence context-free grammars) the syntax analysis problem is solved. In /GG.Fr 77/ it requires linear time only and is implemented in SIMULA 67.

4. CHURCH-ROSSER PROPERTIES, PARALLELISM AND CONCURRENCY THEOREMS

In this section we consider Church-Rosser properties of graph derivations and parallel productions and derivations. Moreover we will study the problem how to reduce a derivation sequence to a single derivation step using the concept of concurrent productions and derivations. Let us consider the strong Church-Rosser property: Given a graph G and two direct derivations $G \Longrightarrow H$ via p and $G \Longrightarrow H'$ via p' with $H \neq H'$, is it possible to find a graph X such that there are direct derivations $H \Longrightarrow X$ via p' and $H' \Longrightarrow X$ via p. Of course this will not be true in general but by Church-Rosser-Property I it is true if the given derivations $G \Longrightarrow H$ via p and $G \Longrightarrow H'$ via p' are "parallel independent". Parallel independence does not only include the fact that the occurences of B_1 from p and B_1' from p' are disjoint in G, but also that they have a nonempty intersection which has to consist of common gluing items. Similar we are able to define sequential independence of $G \Longrightarrow H \Longrightarrow X$ via (p,p'). Dualizing the first result we can show in Church-Rosser-Property II that in the case of sequential independence there is also a graph H' and derivations $G \Longrightarrow H'$ via p' and $H' \Longrightarrow X$ via p. Moreover we have a parallel production p+p', defined as the disjoint union in each component, so that for each sequential independent sequence $G \Longrightarrow H \Longrightarrow X$ via (p,p') there is a direct derivation $G \Longrightarrow X$ via p+p' (Synthesis). Conversely each parallel derivation $G \Longrightarrow X$ via p+p' can be decomposed into an independent sequence $G \Longrightarrow H \Longrightarrow X$ via (p,p') (Analysis). These constructions "Synthesis" and "Analysis" are uniquely defined and they are inverses of each other (Parallelism Theorem). Finally we are also able to drop the assumption that the sequence $G \Longrightarrow H \Longrightarrow X$ via (p,p') is independent. In this case p and p' are "R-related" and we are able to construct a "concurrent production" $p *_R p'$ such that there is a bijective correspondence between "R-related" sequences $G \Longrightarrow H \Longrightarrow X$ via (p,p') and direct "concurrent" derivations $G \Longrightarrow X$ via the concurrent production $p *_R p'$ (Concurrency Theorem). This allows to reduce arbitrary finite derivation sequences to one direct derivation using an interated concurrent production. Moreover the Parallelism Theorem turns out to be a special case of the Concurrency Theorem.

We start with the notions of parallel and sequential independence in two different formulations. The first one is more intuitive,the second one is algebraic and will be used to prove Church-Rosser-Property I in 9.7.

4.1 DEFINITION (INDEPENDENCE)

Given two fast productions $p=(B_1 \xleftarrow{b_1} K \xrightarrow{b_2} B_2)$ and $p'=(B_1' \xleftarrow{b_1'} K' \xrightarrow{b_2'} B_2')$ two direct derivations $G \Longrightarrow H$ via p based on g and $G \Longrightarrow H'$ via p' based on g' are called parallel independent if the intersection of B_1 and B_1' (which are the occurences of p and p' in G) consist of common gluing items. That means precisely

1) $g\,B_1 \cap g'\,B_1' \subseteq g\,b_1\,K \cap g'\,b_1'\,K'$

Dually the derivation sequence $G \Longrightarrow H \Longrightarrow X$ via (p,p') based on g and g' is called sequential independent if

2) $h\, B_2 \cap g'\, B_1' \subseteq h\, b_2\, K \cap g'\, b_1'\, K'$

Remark:

The inclusion in 1) resp. 2) can also be replaced by equality because the other inclusion is trivially satisfied.

4.2 EXAMPLE

The derivations in Fig. 4.1 via the productions KATALOGISIEREN resp. ABBESTELLEN in Fig. 3.1 are not parallel independent because the node colored "B1" is in the intersection of the occurences but not a gluing item.
However, the derivations in Fig. 4.2 via the same productions but with different actual parameters are parallel independent. Moreover both derivation sequences in Fig. 4.2 are sequential independent which is a consequence of Church-Rosser-Property I (see 4.4). The existence of the parallel derivation in Fig. 4.2 is an application of the Parallelism Theorem 4.6 given below.

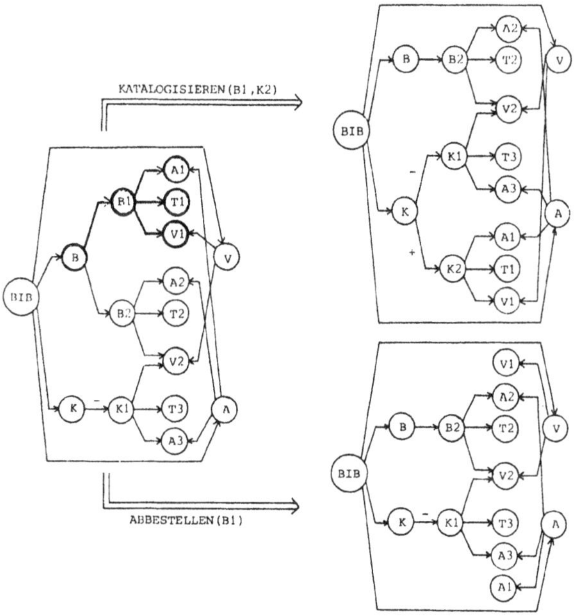

Figure 4.1: Derivations which are not Parallel Independent

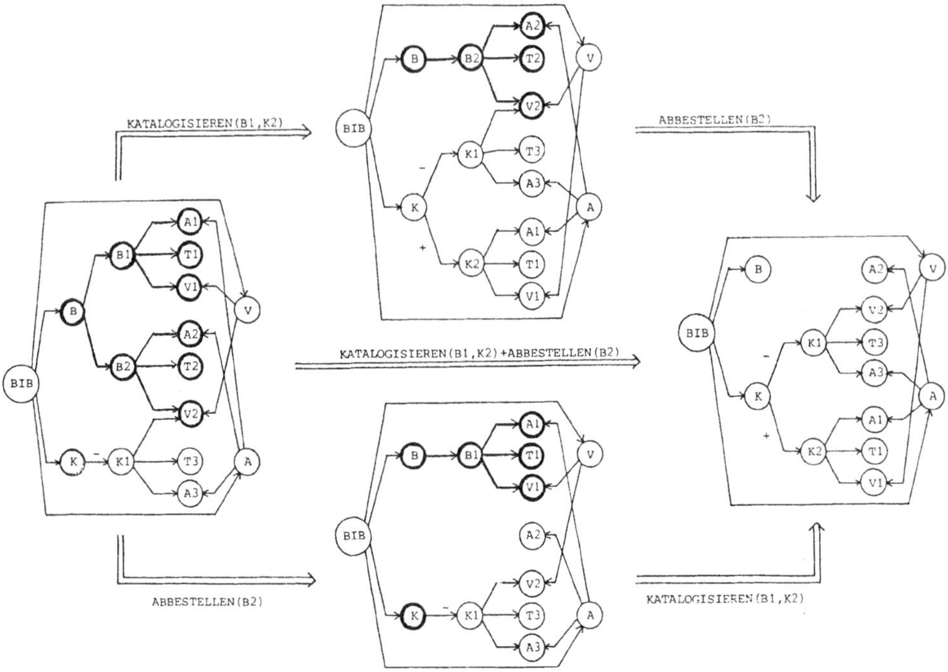

Figure 4.2: Independent and Parallel Derivations

Interpretation of Parallel Independence:

Parallel independence of $G \Longrightarrow H$ via p and $G \Longrightarrow H'$ via p' means that the occurence B_1 of p (resp. B_1' of p') in G will not be destroyed by the other derivation $G \Longrightarrow H'$ via p' (resp. $G \Longrightarrow H$ via p) because gluing items are preserved in the derivation process. Hence we can also apply p to H' (resp. p' to H). In other words B_1 is included in the context graph D' of $G \Longrightarrow H'$ (resp. B_1' is included in context D of $G \Longrightarrow H$). This second formulation will be given more precisely in the following characterization:

4.3 LEMMA (ALGEBRAIC FORMULATION OF INDEPENDENCE)

The derivations $G \Longrightarrow H$ via p and $G \Longrightarrow H'$ via p' based on g resp. g' are parallel independent iff there are graph morphisms $B_1 \longrightarrow D'$ and $B_1' \longrightarrow D$ such that

$$B_1 \xrightarrow{g} G = B_1 \longrightarrow D' \xrightarrow{c_1'} G \quad \text{and} \quad B_1' \xrightarrow{g'} G = B_1' \longrightarrow D \xrightarrow{c_1} G$$

where c_1 and c_1' are the corresponding context graph injections.

Now we are able to state Church-Rosser-Property I (first announced in /GG.Ro 75a/) which is proved in 9.7 using Lemma 4.3. For the proof of 4.3 see /AP.Eh Ro 76/ and /OV.Dè Eh 76/.

4.4 THEOREM (CHURCH-ROSSER-PROPERTY I)

Let p and p' be fast productions and $G \Longrightarrow H$ and $G \Longrightarrow H'$ be parallel independent direct derivations via p resp. p'. Then there is a graph X and direct derivations $H \Longrightarrow X$ via p' and $H' \Longrightarrow X$ via p such that both sequences in the following picture become sequentially independent.

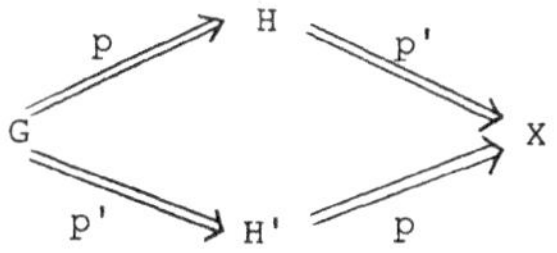

The proof of this theorem is typical for the use of algebraic pushout techniques. For this reason it is given explicitly in the appendium in 9.7 (see also /GG.Eh Kr 75b/, /AP.Eh Ro 76/, /AP.Eh Kr 76a/)

Now we want to obtain a similar result starting with a sequential independent sequence $G \Longrightarrow H \Longrightarrow X$ via (p,p'). Due to Remark 2 in 3.8 each direct derivation $G \Longrightarrow H$ via p can also be considered as a direct derivation $H \Longrightarrow G$ via the inverse production $\bar{p}$ of p. However, sequential independence of $G \Longrightarrow H \Longrightarrow X$ via (p,p') is equivalent to parallel independence of $H \Longrightarrow G$ via $\bar{p}$ and $H \Longrightarrow X$ via p'. This follows immediately from Def. 4.1. Using this idea we obtain the following corollary of Theorem 4.4 (see /GG.Eh Kr 75/, /AP.Eh Kr 76a/)

4.5 COROLLARY (CHURCH-ROSSER-PROPERTY II)

Given a sequentially independent sequence $G \underset{p}{\Longrightarrow} H \underset{p'}{\Longrightarrow} X$ via fast productions p and p' there exists another sequentially independent sequence $G \underset{p'}{\Longrightarrow} H' \Longrightarrow X$ between the same graphs G and X. Moreover $G \underset{p}{\Longrightarrow} H$ and $G \underset{p'}{\Longrightarrow} H$ become parallel independent.

As we have seen in Example 4.2 another consequence of parallel independence of $G \Longrightarrow H$ via p and $G \Longrightarrow H'$ via p' is the fact that we can apply the parallel production p+p' to G leading to a parallel derivation $G \Longrightarrow X$ via p+p'.

4.6 DEFINITION (PARALLEL PRODUCTIONS AND DERIVATIONS)

Let $p=(B_1 \xleftarrow{b_1} K \xrightarrow{b_2} B_2)$ and $p'=(B_1' \xleftarrow{b_1'} K' \xrightarrow{b_2'} B_2')$ be fast productions. Then the parallel production p+p' is defined by

$$p+p' = (B_1+B_1' \xleftarrow{b_1+b_1'} K+K' \xrightarrow{b_2+b_2'} B_2+B_2')$$

where + denotes the disjoint union of graphs resp. graph morphisms (see 2.5 and note that p+p' becomes also a fast production). A derivation $G \Longrightarrow X$ via p+p' will be called parallel derivation (not to be confused with derivations in parallel graph grammars which will be defined in Section 6).

Parallel derivations and independent sequences are related in the following way (see /GG.Kr 76/, /GG.Kr 77b/, /AP.Eh Kr 76a/):

4.7 PARALLELISM THEOREM

1. ANALYSIS: Given a parallel derivation

$$G \Longrightarrow X \text{ via } p+p'$$

there is a canonical analysis into two sequentially independent sequences

$$G \Longrightarrow H \Longrightarrow X \text{ via } (p,p') \text{ and } G \Longrightarrow H' \Longrightarrow X \text{ via } (p',p)$$

2. SYNTHESIS: Given a sequentially independent sequence

$$G \Longrightarrow H \Longrightarrow X \text{ via } (p,p')$$

there is a canonical synthesis to one parallel derivation

$$G \Longrightarrow X \text{ via } p+p'$$

3. The operations ANALYSIS and SYNTHESIS are inverse of each other in the following sense: Given p,p' and p+p' there is a bijective correspondende between sequentially independent sequences $G \Longrightarrow H \Longrightarrow X$ via (p,p') and parallel derivations $G \Longrightarrow X$ via p+p'.

Now we want to drop the assumption that the sequence $G \Longrightarrow H \Longrightarrow X$ via (p,p') is sequentially independent. That means we allow that the occurences B_2 of p and B_1' of p' have an intersection which consists not only of gluing items. Before we give the technical details let us consider an example:

4.8 EXAMPLE

Consider the productions p=BESTELLEN and p'=KATALOGISIEREN for the same order number Bn (actual parameter of BEST-NR). Then for any graph G not containing (a node colored) Bn any derivation sequence $G \Longrightarrow H \Longrightarrow X$ via (p,p') will not be sequentially independent because Bn (and it's adjacent arcs) will be in the intersection of the occurences B_2 of p and B_1' of p' which are not gluing items. Actually we have a fixed intersection R of B_2 and B_1' for all possible graphs H which in this special case is equal to B_2. Hence we will say that the productions BESTELLEN and KATALOGISIEREN (using the same actual parameters) are "R-related" (see 4.9). Although we cannot apply the parallel production p+p' to G there is a possibility to handle both productions in common with the same effect like sequential application: The production NEUKATALOGISIEREN in Fig. 4.3. Actually this production turns out to be the"R-concurrent production"of BESTELLEN and KATALOGISIEREN using the relation R above. The general definition of R-concurrent productions(with interpretation) will be given in 4.10. Roughly spoken the R-concurrent production $p *_R p' = (B_1^* \longleftarrow K^* \longrightarrow B_2^*)$ is constructed as follows: B_1 is the gluing of B_1 and a subgraph B_{10}' of B_1' where B_{10}' does not contain the R-related items of B_1' except of the gluing items coming from K. In our example B_{10}' consists of the nodes colored B, K, AUTORENNAME and VERLAGSNAME such that the gluing with B_1 yields the graph B_1 which is the left one in Fig.4.3. Dually B_2 is the gluing of B_2' and B_{20} where B_{20} does not contain the R-related items of B_2 except of the gluing items coming from K'. In our example B_{20} consists of the nodes colored B, AUTORENNAME, TITEL and VERLAGSNAME such that the gluing with B_2 yields the graph B_2 which is the right one in Fig. 4.3.

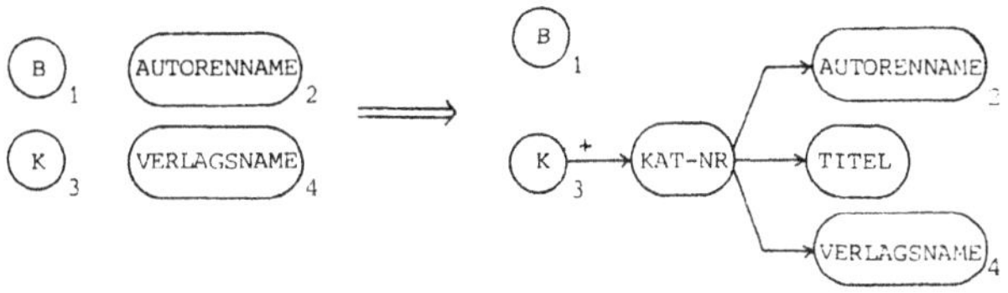

Figure 4.3: Concurrent Production

For the construction of the corresponding gluing items we refer to 4.9 and 4.10.

The following Definitions 4.9 and 4.10 include technical details like pullbacks (see 9.5) which are only used for the precise formulation of the Concurrency Theorem in 4.11. This theorem states that R-related sequences and direct derivations via the R-concurrent productions have essentially the same effect.

4.9 DEFINITION (R-RELATED PRODUCTIONS AND DERIVATIONS)

1) A <u>relation</u> R for a <u>pair of fast productions</u> (p,p') is a pair of graph morphisms $B_2 \leftarrow R \rightarrow B_1'$ such that in the following diagrams there are (unique) PO-complements (see 3.7) $L_1 \rightarrow B_{10}' \rightarrow B_1'$ and $L_2 \rightarrow B_{20} \rightarrow B_2$ of $L_1 \rightarrow R \rightarrow B_1'$ and $L_2 \rightarrow R \rightarrow B_2$ respectively.
   Note, that p and p' are given in the bottom row and L_1 and L_2 are constructed as the intersection of K and R resp. K' and R. More precisely L_1 and L_2 are the pullbacks (see 9.5) in the following diagrams.

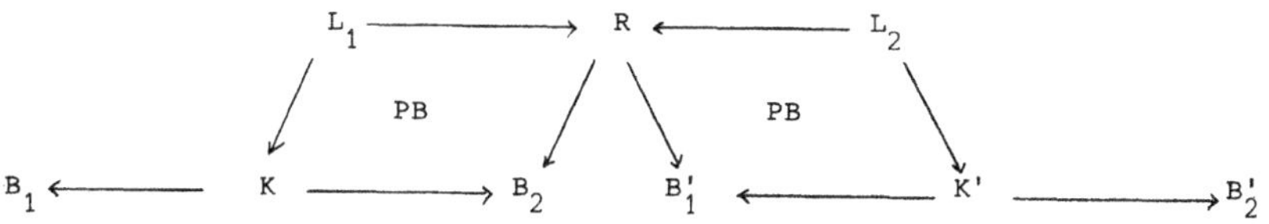

   The PO-complements are pairs of morphisms such that the following squares become PO

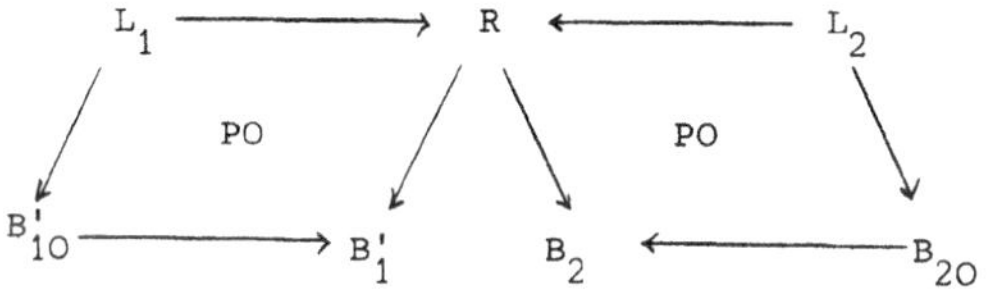

2) Given a relation R for (p,p') a derivation sequence $G \Longrightarrow H \Longrightarrow X$ via (p,p') is called R-related if in the following diagram (1) commutes and if there are (unique) morphisms $B_{20} \longrightarrow D'$ and $B'_{10} \longrightarrow D$ making (2) and (3) commutative where D and D' are the context graphs of $G \Longrightarrow H$ and $H \Longrightarrow X$ respectively.

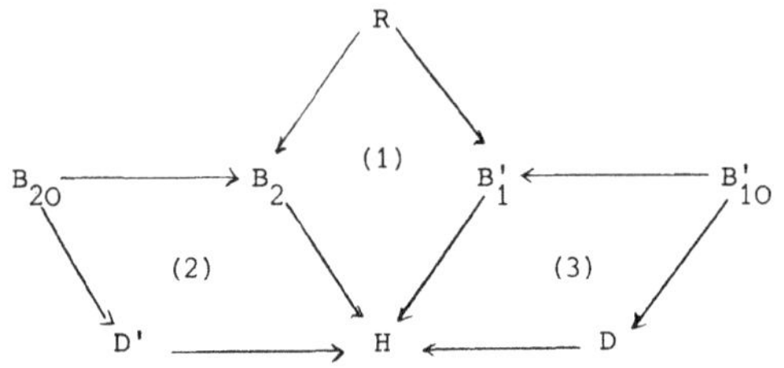

Remark:

Squares (2) and (3) automatically become PBs. Given a derivation sequence $G \Longrightarrow H \Longrightarrow X$ via fast productions (p,p') the pullback $B_2 \longleftarrow R \longrightarrow B'_1$ of $B_2 \longleftarrow H \longrightarrow B'_1$ is a relation for the pair (p,p') (called canonical relation) such that the given sequence is R-related.

Interpretation:

The relation R relates items of B'_1 and B_2 and (in the equivalence closure $\bar{R}$ of R on $B'_1 + B_2$) also items $x',y' \in B'_1$ and $x,y \in B_2$ respectively. The existence of the PO-complement B'_{10} is equivalent to the condition that $x' \neq y'$ for $x',y' \in B'_1$ are allowed to be $\bar{R}$-related only if both are gluing items. If this condition and a similar one for B_2 are not satisfied there would be no derivation sequence $G \Longrightarrow H \Longrightarrow X$ via (p,p') s.t. (1) commutes.

Commutativity of (1) means that at least the R-related items are glued together in H. The existence of $B_{20} \longrightarrow D'$ and $B'_{10} \longrightarrow D$ means that at most R-related items, or - as allowed in the independent case - common gluing points of B_2 and B'_1 are glued together in H. In order to get the bijective correspondence in our Concurrency Theorem 4.11 we also must allow diagrams (1), which are not pullbacks, and where in addition to R-related items also common gluing points of B_2 and B'_1 are glued together in H.

In the special case of independent derivations only common gluing points are allowed to be glued together. This means that at least all R-related items of B_2 and B_1 must be gluing points.

Next we will define the R-concurrent production $B_1^* \longleftarrow K^* \longrightarrow B_2^*$ of p and p' with relation R where - very roughly spoken - B_1^* consists of B_1 and the non-R-related parts of B'_1 and similar B_2^* of B'_2 and the non-R-related parts of B_2.

4.10 DEFINITION (CONCURRENT PRODUCTIONS)

Given a relation R for the pair (p,p') of fast productions(see 4.9) the R-concurrent production $p *_R p' = (B_1^* \longleftarrow K^* \longrightarrow B_2^*)$ is given by the following construction:

Step 1: In the double 3-cube below where front and bottom squares are given by Definition 4.9 let K_o, L and K'_o be constructed as pullbacks in the left, middle and right side respectively. Using the PB-properties of K_o and K'_o there are unique morphisms $L \to K_o$ and $L \to K'_o$ such that both top squares and back squares commute.

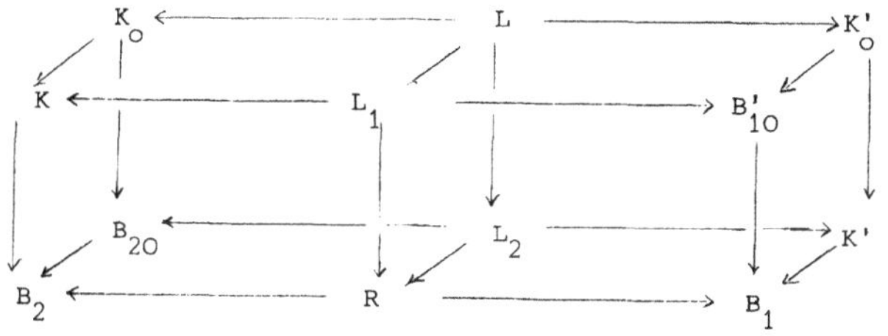

Step 2: In the double 3-cube below let $L_1 \to B_1 = L_1 \to K \to B_1$, $K_o \to B_1 = K_o \to K \to B_1$, $L_2 \to B'_2 = L_2 \to K' \to B'_2$ and $K'_o \to B'_2 = K'_o \to K' \to B'_2$. Hence we have already commutativity of the top and back squares by Step 1. Now let B_1^*, K^* and B_2^* be the pushouts in the left, middle and right side respectively such that there are unique $K^* \to B_1^*$ and $K^* \to B_2^*$ making the front and bottom squares commute.

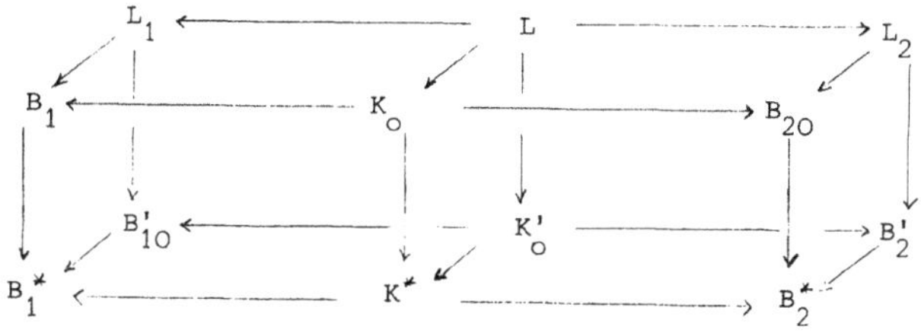

Interpretation:

B'_{10} and B_{20} are the non-R-related parts of B'_1 and B_2 together with the common gluing points L_1 (of K and R) and L_2 (of K' and R). Now K_o, L and K'_o are the intersections of K with B_{20}, L_1 with L_2, and K' with B'_{10} respectively. Hence B_1^* consists of B_1 together with the non-R-related part of B'_1 with interface L_1, dually for B_2^*, and K^* is the gluing of the subgraphs K_o and K'_o of K and K' respectively.

Now we are able to state the main theorem concerning concurrency of graph derivations:

4.11 CONCURRENCY THEOREM

Given a relation R for a pair of fast productions (p,p') and the corresponding fast R-concurrent production $p *_R p'$ there is a bijective correspondence between R-related sequences $G \overset{p}{\Longrightarrow} H \overset{p'}{\Longrightarrow} X$ via (p,p') and direct derivations $G \overset{p}{\Longrightarrow} X$ via $p *_R p'$.

Remarks:

1. In the special case $R=\emptyset$ we obtain a bijective correspondence between independent sequences $G \Longrightarrow H \Longrightarrow X$ via (p,p') and direct (parallel) derivations $G \Longrightarrow X$ via $p+p'$ as given in the PARALLELISM THEOREM 4.6.3.

2. The construction of R-concurrent productions and derivations can be iterated. Hence each derivation sequence of length $n>1$ can be reduced to a direct derivation via the corresponding iterated concurrent production.

3. The original motivation for the CONCURRENCY THEOREM in Thm. 4.2 of /AP.Eh Ro 77/ was to reduce derivation sequences such that the strong Church-Rosser property for a class P of productions can be concluded from the weak Church-Rosser property: We say that P is weak (resp. strong) Church-Rosser if for all $G \Longrightarrow H$ and $G \Longrightarrow H'$ via productions (resp. a single production) in P there exists X, $H \Longrightarrow X$, and $H' \Longrightarrow X$ via productions (resp. a single production) in P. From 4.11 it is clear that the strong Church-Rosser property follows from the weak one provided that for all p,p' in P and each relation R also the R-concurrent production $p *_R p'$ belongs to P.

4. One example for R-concurrent productions was sketched already in 4.8. A more complicated example including noninjective graph morphisms together with a proof of the CONCURRENCY THEOREM is given in /AP.Eh Ro 78a,b/. This example is reviewed in 4.12 below because the concurrent production given in Fig. 2.6 of the proceedings version /AP.Eh Ro 78a/ is not correct.

4.12 EXAMPLE

Given the direct derivations $G \Longrightarrow H$ via $p=(B_1 \longleftarrow K \longrightarrow B_2)$ in Fig. 4.4 and $H \Longrightarrow X$ via $p'=(B_1' \longleftarrow K' \longrightarrow B_2')$ in Fig. 4.5 we construct the relation $B_2 \longleftarrow R \longrightarrow B_1'$ in Fig. 4.6 as the pullback of $B_2 \longleftarrow H \longrightarrow B_1'$. Since $B_1 \longrightarrow H$ is not injective also $K \longrightarrow D$, $B_2 \longrightarrow H$ and $R \longrightarrow B_1'$ are not injective which implies (see 9.5) that the pullback R is a "generalized" intersection of B_2 and B_1' where nodes 3 and 4 are distinguished. The arcs in R as well as node 2 are "critical" because they are not mapped into (common) gluing items of B_2 and B_1' by $R \longrightarrow B_2$ resp. $R \longrightarrow B_1'$ (this means that all R-related derivation sequences $G \Longrightarrow H \Longrightarrow X$ via (p,p') are not sequential independent). By the remark in 4.9 (p,p') becomes an R-related pair of fast productions and the corresponding R-concurrent production $p *_R p' = (B_1^* \longleftarrow K^* \longrightarrow B_2^*)$ is given in the top row of Fig. 4.7. Since B_{10}', the non R-related part of B_1' consists only of the nodes colored f resp. a and L_1 of three nodes colored f,a,a the gluing B_1^* of B_1 and B_{10}' along L_1 becomes a quotient of B_1. On the other hand we obtain B_{20} from B_2 by deleting the critical arcs coming from R, but not the critical node of R because this is contained in L_2. Hence the gluing B_2^* of B_2' and B_{20} along L_2 contains B_2 and the non R-related arcs of B_2 which are those of B_{20}. Due to the CONCURRENCY THEOREM 4.11 there is exactly one direct derivation $G \Longrightarrow X$ via $p *_R p'$ given in Fig. 4.7 which corresponds to the R-related sequence $G \Longrightarrow H \Longrightarrow X$ via (p,p') in Fig. 4.4 and 4.5.

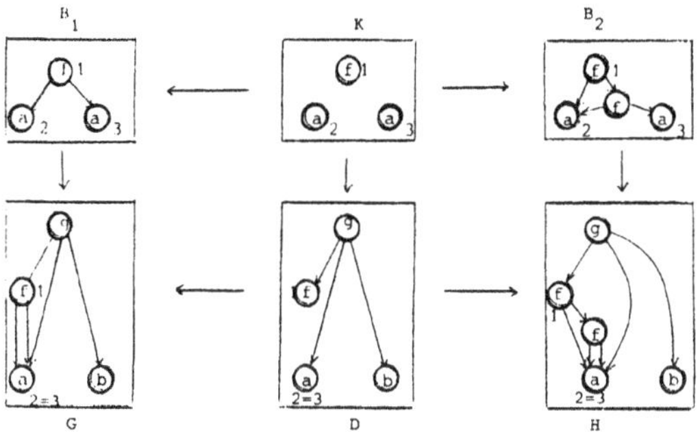

Figure 4.4

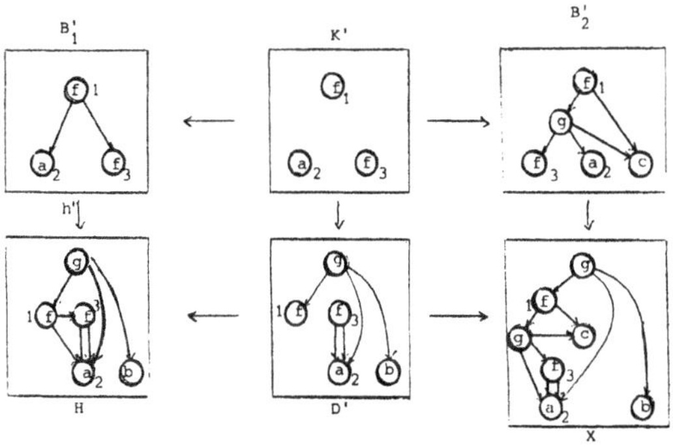

Figure 4.5

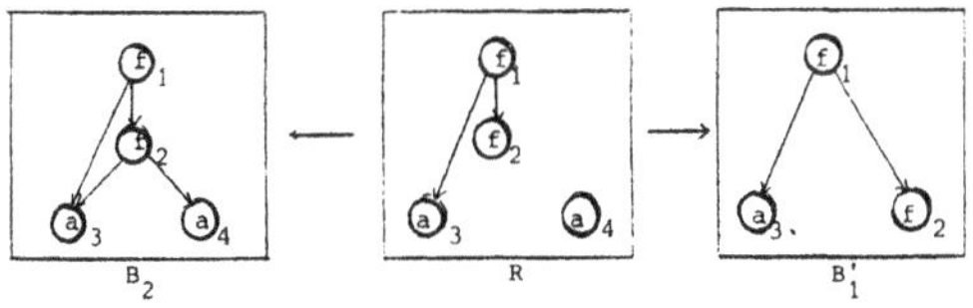

Figure 4.6

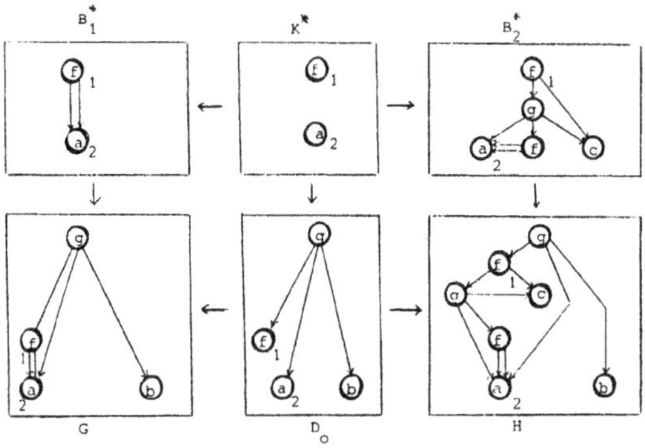

Figure 4.7

Figure 4.4 - 4.7: R-related Derivation Sequence $G \Longrightarrow H \Longrightarrow X$ via (p, p') and Corresponding Direct Derivation $G \Longrightarrow X$ via the R-concurrent Production $p *_R p'$

5. PROPERTIES OF DERIVATION SEQUENCES

In this section we want to study properties of derivation sequences $G_o \overset{*}{\Longrightarrow} G_n$. First we demonstrate a consistency property which says that there are no side effects by applying productions: each item in G_n is either already in G_o or it is an "added item" coming from the right hand side of a production. Moreover the CONSISTENCY THEOREM states the dual property: each item in G_o is either persistent up to G_n or it is deleted by the left hand side of a production. Other properties of derivation sequences we want to consider are given by the following constructions. Let $s: G_o \overset{*}{\Longrightarrow} G_n$ be a derivation sequence via $(p_1,\ldots,p_n)$ and $h_o: G_o \longrightarrow \bar{G}_o$ an injective graph morphism. Then we obtain a new sequence $\mathrm{JOIN}(s,h_o): \bar{G}_o \overset{*}{\Longrightarrow} \bar{G}_n$ via $(p_1,\ldots,p_n)$ provided that boundary items of h_o are persistent in s (JOIN-CONDITION). Vice versa given $\bar{s}: \bar{G}_o \overset{*}{\Longrightarrow} \bar{G}_n$ via $(p_1,\ldots,p_n)$ and injective $h_o: G_o \longrightarrow \bar{G}_o$ we obtain a sequence $\mathrm{CLIP}(\bar{s},h_o): G_o \overset{*}{\Longrightarrow} G_n$ via $(p_1,\ldots,p_n)$ provided that the items used in $\bar{s}$ are included in $h_o G_o$ (CLIP-CONDITION). Moreover the Embedding Theorem states that the operations JOIN and CLIP are inverse to each other. Note that the Embedding Theorem allows to cut away as much of the graphs in a derivation sequence as possible. This should be of use for implementation because most of the graph algorithms have exponential complexity. On the other hand this result is used in several applications and proofs. Another important (for implementation, applications and theory) result is the construction and uniqueness of canonical derivation sequences (which form an analogue of leftmost derivations in the string grammar case). The construction of canonical derivation sequences is based on parallel derivations and hence on the Parallelism Theorem. The operations ANALYSIS and SYNTHESIS from Thm. 4.7 can be combined to yield a SHIFT-operation which shifts a production from right to left in the derivation sequence provided that it is independent of the previous ones.

In this section we will use the following notation for step i of a derivation sequence $G_o \Longrightarrow G_1 \Longrightarrow \ldots \Longrightarrow G_n$ via $(p_1,\ldots,p_n)$

$$\begin{array}{ccccc}
B_{i1} & \xleftarrow{\;b_{i1}\;} & K_i & \xrightarrow{\;b_{i2}\;} & B_{i2} \\
{\scriptstyle g_{i-1}}\downarrow & & \downarrow & & \downarrow{\scriptstyle h_i} \\
G_{i-1} & \xleftarrow[\;c_{i1}\;]{} & D_i & \xrightarrow[\;c_{i2}\;]{} & G_i
\end{array} \qquad \text{for } i=1,\ldots,n.$$

The precise formulation of the Consistency Theorem is as follows (for the proof see /OV.De Eh 76/).

5.1 CONSISTENCY THEOREM

Given a derivation sequence $G_o \Longrightarrow G_1 \Longrightarrow \ldots \Longrightarrow G_n$ via $(p_1,\ldots,p_n)$

$$G_o + \text{ADDED ITEMS} = G_n + \text{DELETED ITEMS}$$

holds for the set of arcs and nodes (but there is no isomorphism of graphs) where

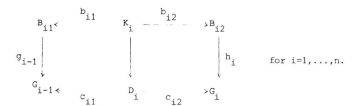

ADDED (resp. DELETED) ITEMS is the disjoint union of all ADD_i (resp. DEL_i) for $i=1,\dots,n$ with $ADD_i = g_{i-1}\, B_{i1} - g_{i-1}\, b_{i1}\, K_i$ resp. $DEL_i = h_i\, B_{i2} - h_i\, b_{i2}\, K_i$.

For the Embedding Theorem in 5.3 we need:

5.2 DEFINITION (JOIN- AND CLIP-CONDITION)

Given an injective graph morphism $h_o : G_o \longrightarrow \bar{G}_o$ we can construct the discrete subgraph BOUNDARY as defined in 3.5 and the graph CONTEXT by Lemma 3.7 leading to the following pushout $(PO)_o$. (Note that the GLUING CONDITION in Lemma 3.7 is satisfied because we have by construction K=BOUNDARY.)

$$\begin{array}{ccc} \text{BOUNDARY} & \xrightarrow{\ f_o\ } & G_o \\ \downarrow & (PO)_o & \downarrow h_o \\ \text{CONTEXT} & \xrightarrow[\ \bar{f}_o\ ]{} & \bar{G}_o \end{array}$$

The persistent points of a derivation sequence $G_o \overset{*}{\Longrightarrow} G_n$ are those which are not deleted in later steps. They can be recursively defined by

$$\text{PERSIST}(G_n) = G_n \text{ and } \text{PERSIST}(G_{i-1}) = c_{i1}\, c_{i2}^{-1}\, \text{PERSIST}(G_i)$$

for $i=1,\dots,n$. Now the

JOIN-CONDITION: $\text{BOUNDARY} \subseteq \text{PERSIST}(G_o)$

states that each item in the boundary is persistent.

This condition allows one to extend the sequence $G_o \overset{*}{\Longrightarrow} G_n$ to $\bar{G}_o \overset{*}{\Longrightarrow} \bar{G}_n$.

Conversely, if we want to restrict $\bar{G}_o \overset{*}{\Longrightarrow} \bar{G}_n$ to $G_o \overset{*}{\Longrightarrow} G_n$ then we have to define those items in $\bar{G}_o$ which are actually used in the derivation sequence by at least one of the productions. These are the left hand sides of the productions which are collected as follows:

$$\text{USE}(\bar{G}_n) = \emptyset \text{ and } \text{USE}(\bar{G}_{i-1}) = \bar{c}_{i1}\, \bar{c}_{i2}^{-1}\, \text{USE}(G_i) \cup g_{i-1}\, B_{i1}$$

for $i=1,\dots,n$. The

CLIP-CONDITION: $\text{USE}(\bar{G}_o) \subseteq h_o\, G_o$

states that the used part of $\bar{G}_o$ must be a subgraph of $h_o\, G_o$.

Now we are ready to state the Embedding Theorem which allows the construction of G_n from $\bar{G}_n$ (resp. $\bar{G}_n$ from G_n) without constructing a new derivation sequence. For the proof of various versions see /GG.Eh Pf Sc 73b/, /GG.Eh Kr 76/, /GG.Eh 77/, /GG.Kr 77a/, /GG.Eh Kr Ma Ro Wi 78/.

5.3 EMBEDDING THEOREM

1. JOIN: Given a sequence $s: G_o \overset{*}{\Longrightarrow} G_n$ via fast productions $(p_1,\dots,p_n)$ and let $h_o : G_o \longrightarrow \bar{G}_o$ be an injective graph morphism $h_o : G_o \longrightarrow \bar{G}_o$ with BOUNDARY and CONTEXT satisfying the JOIN-CONDITION.

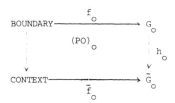

Then there exists a sequence

$JOIN(s,h_o):\bar{G}_o \stackrel{*}{\Longrightarrow} \bar{G}_n$ via $(p_1,\ldots,p_n)$

where $\bar{G}_n$ is the gluing of G_n and CONTEXT along BOUNDARY. Hence we have the following pushout $(PO)_n$

$$\begin{array}{ccc} \text{BOUNDARY} & \longrightarrow & G_n \\ \downarrow & (PO)_n & \downarrow h_n \\ \text{CONTEXT} & \longrightarrow & \bar{G}_n \end{array}$$

2. CLIP: Given a sequence $\bar{s}:\bar{G}_o \stackrel{*}{\Longrightarrow} \bar{G}_n$ via fast productions $(p_1,\ldots,p_n)$ and an injective $h_o:G_o \longrightarrow \bar{G}_o$ satisfying the CLIP-CONDITION there is a sequence

$CLIP(\bar{s},h_o):G_o \stackrel{*}{\Longrightarrow} G_n$ via $(p_1,\ldots,p_n)$

where G_n is the PO-complement in $(PO)_n$.

3. The operations JOIN and CLIP are inverses of each other meaning that

$CLIP(JOIN(s,h_o),h_o)=s$ and

$JOIN(CLIP(\bar{s},h_o),h_o)=\bar{s}$

whenever the operations are defined.

Remark:

Note that the JOIN (resp. CLIP)-CONDITION implies that there is a canonical injective graph morphism BOUNDARY$\longrightarrow G_n$ (resp. CONTEXT$\longrightarrow \bar{G}_n$) and BOUNDARY$\longrightarrow$ CONTEXT is a restriction of $h_o:G_o \longrightarrow \bar{G}_o$. Hence by pushout $(PO)_n$ we obtain an explicit gluing construction for $\bar{G}_n$ (resp. G_n). For the proof of the Embedding Theorem we refer to /GG.Kr 77a/ and /GG.Eh 77/.

5.4 EXAMPLE

Let us consider one of the derivation sequences in Fig. 4.2 to be $G_o \Longrightarrow G_1 \Longrightarrow G_2$, $\bar{G}_o$ the graph in Fig. 3.4 and $h_o:G_o \longrightarrow \bar{G}_o$ the inclusion of G_o into $\bar{G}_o$ (where colors in G_o are abbreviations for the corresponding colors in $\bar{G}_o$). In this case BOUNDARY are the two nodes colored BIB and K1 while PERSIST (G_o) is G_o except the nodes colored B1, B2 and T2 and all the adjacent arcs. Hence the JOIN-CONDITION "BOUNDARY $\subseteq$ PERSIST (G_o)" is satisfied. CONTEXT is the subgraph of $\bar{G}_o$ consisting of the nodes colored BIBLIOTHEK, LESER, LO815 and K12345 and the four arcs between these nodes. Hence by 5.3.1 we have a sequence JOIN $(s,h_o):\bar{G}_o \stackrel{*}{\Longrightarrow} \bar{G}_2$ where $\bar{G}_2$ is G_2 together with the nodes colored LESER and LO815 and the four arcs of CONTEXT.

On the other hand we can also consider one of the sequences in Fig. 4.2 as $\bar{G}_o \Longrightarrow \bar{G}_1 \Longrightarrow \bar{G}_2$, G_o to be the subgraph of $\bar{G}_o$ consisting of the bold face nodes and arcs, the node colored BIB and the two arcs from BIB to B and K respectively, and $h_o:G_o \longrightarrow \bar{G}_o$ the inclusion. Hence we have $h_o\ G_o = G_o$ and USE $(\bar{G}_o)$ is the bold face subgraph of $\bar{G}_o$ so that the CLIP-CONDITION "USE $\bar{G}_o \subseteq h_o\ G_o$" is satisfied. Applying

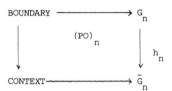

5.3.2 we obtain the sequence $CLIP(\bar{s},h_o):G_o \stackrel{*}{\Longrightarrow} G_2$ where G_2 is $\bar{G}_2$ except the nodes colored A,V,K1,T3,A3 and the adjacent arcs.

Now we proceed to the construction of canonical derivation sequences. Because there is no natural linear order in graphs the straightforward generalization of the leftmost derivations from the string case to graphs does not make sense. Based on /GG.Kr 77b/ we will use parallel derivations to construct canonical derivation sequences. Then using the Parallelism Theorem we will be able to define a SHIFT-operator, the composition of one ANALYSIS and one SYNTHESIS, which shifts an independent production one step to the left in the derivation sequence. Actually we will obtain a canonical derivation sequence if we shift each production as fas as possible to the left in the derivation sequence. Having the Parallelism Theorem this construction is straightforward. But the uniqueness of canonical derivation sequences is hard to prove (see /GG.Kr 76/, /GG.Kr 77b/). The main idea is to show a Church-Rosser property for the SHIFT operations.

5.5 DEFINITION (SHIFT-OPERATOR AND EQUIVALENT AND CANONICAL DERIVATION SEQUENCES)

Let us assume that for each derivation sequence all the productions (including parallel productions) used in that sequence are fast and have different names.

1) Let p be a production and s a derivation sequence of the form

$$s:G \stackrel{*}{\Longrightarrow} G_1 \stackrel{p_1}{\Longrightarrow} G_2 \stackrel{p+p_2}{\Longrightarrow} G_3 \stackrel{*}{\Longrightarrow} G'$$

then $SHIFT_p(S)$ is defined if p is independent of p_1 in the ANALYSIS (see Thm. 4.6.1) s' of s where

$$s':G \stackrel{*}{\Longrightarrow} G_1 \stackrel{p_1}{\Longrightarrow} G_2 \stackrel{p}{\Longrightarrow} G_2' \stackrel{p_2}{\Longrightarrow} G_3 \stackrel{*}{\Longrightarrow} G'.$$

In this case $SHIFT_p(s)$ is defined by

$$SHIFT_p(G \stackrel{*}{\Longrightarrow} G_1 \stackrel{p_1}{=\!=\!=} G_2 \stackrel{p+p_2}{\Longrightarrow} G_3 \stackrel{*}{\Longrightarrow} G') = G \stackrel{*}{\Longrightarrow} G_1 \stackrel{p_1+p}{\Longrightarrow} G_2' \stackrel{p_2}{\Longrightarrow} G_3 \stackrel{*}{\Longrightarrow} G'$$

using first the ANALYSIS- and then the SYNTHESIS-construction from the Parallelism Theorem 4.6.

Note that p_2 in s is allowed to be empty, which means $G_2 \stackrel{p}{\Longrightarrow} G_3$. Actually $SHIFT_p$ is not defined if p is the first direct derivation or p is not independent of the previous derivation p_1.

2) Two derivation sequences s and s' are called <u>equivalent</u> if s=s' or there are operators $SHIFT_{p_i}$ and derivation sequences s_i for i=0,...,n such that $s=s_o$, $s'=s_n$ and

$SHIFT_{p_i}(s_{i-1})=s_i$ or $SHIFT_{p_i}(s_i)=s_{i-1}$

(That means "equivalence of derivation sequences" is the equivalence closure of the SHIFT-relation defined above.)

3) Finally a derivation sequence s is called <u>canonical</u> if there is no production p such that $SHIFT_p(s)$ is defined.

(In other words there is no production in the sequence which is independent of the previous one in the derivation sequence.)

5.6 THEOREM (CANONICAL DERIVATION SEQUENCES)

For each derivation sequence s via fast productions there is a unique canonical sequence SHIFT(s) which is equivalent to s.

SHIFT(s) is the result of the following procedure where the productions occuring in s from left to right are $p_1, \ldots, p_n$

```
procedure SHIFT, parameter s,
begin for i:=1 step 1 until n do
    while p_i is not in the first direct derivation of s and
          p_i is independent of the previous direct derivation in s
      do s:=SHIFT_{p_i}(s)
end
```

The complete proof of this theorem is given in /GG.Kr 76/ and a condensed version in /GG.Kr 77b/ (see also /GG.Eh Kr 75b/).

5.7 EXAMPLE

Starting with Fig. 3.3 the graph in Fig. 3.4 can be derived using the following sequence of productions from Fig. 3.1.

p_1 = ADD AUTOR (KAMIDI)
p_2 = ADD VERLAG (Teubner)
p_3 = BESTELLEN(BOO1, KAMIDI, Universal Theory of Automata, Teubner)
p_4 = ADD AUTOR (Böll)
p_5 = ADD VERLAG (Luchterhand)
p_6 = BESTELLEN (BOO2, Böll, Gruppenbild mit Dame, Luchterhand)
p_7 = ADD AUTOR (Grass)
p_8 = BESTELLEN(BOO3, Grass, Der Butt, Luchterhand)
p_9 = KATALOGISIEREN(BOO3, K12345)
p_{10}= ADD LESER (LO815)
p_{11}= AUSLEIHEN (K12345, LO815)

Using the procedure SHIFT in Thm. 5.6 we obtain the following canonical derivation sequence

$$G_o \xRightarrow{p_1+p_2+p_4+p_5+p_7+p_{10}} G_1 \xRightarrow{p_3+p_6+p_8} G_2 \xRightarrow{p_9} G_3 \xRightarrow{p_{11}} G_4$$

Starting from the graph G_o in Fig. 3.3 in the first step of the canonical derivation sequence all authors, publishers and readers are added in parallel. In the second step all books are ordered in parallel, while in step 3 and 4 one book is registered and lended respectively.

6. PARALLEL GRAPH GRAMMARS

Having studied sequential graph grammars and their properties in Sections 3,4 and 5 in the following two sections we move now to the study of parallel graph grammars. Whereas sequential graph grammars generalize Chomsky-grammars parallel graph grammars generalize L-system. In /GL.Cu Li 74/ a biological motivation (models for multi-dimensional development of organisms) to study "graph L-systems" is given and a rather complex mathematical description is introduced. The first algebraic approaches to parallel graph grammars were given in /GL.Eh Rb 76/ and /GL.Eh Kr 76/ and extended in /GL.Eh 75/, /GL.Ld 78/ and /GL.Eh Ld 78/. In /GL.Eh Rb 76/ NPG (node substitution parallel graph)-grammars and HPG (handle substitution parallel graph)-grammars are studied which generalize L-Systems (without interaction) in two different ways: In NPG-grammars the basic units to be substituted are the nodes of the graphs and in HPG-grammars one substitutes the "handles" (where a handle is an arc together with its source and target node). In the next two sections we will mainly consider a special case of HPG-grammars, called simple HPG-grammars, together with a locally star gluing formula for these systems which generalize locally catenative formulas (see /GL.Ld 78/ and /GL.Eh Ld 78/. Simple HPG-grammars are a special case of the general approach to parallel graph grammars in /GL.Eh Kr 76/, where the left hand sides of the productions are arbitrary graphs (not restricted to nodes, arcs or handles).

Let us recall that a production in an OL-system is a pair $p=(a,w)$ where a is a symbol and w a string of an alphabet C. Given a string $a_1,\ldots,a_n$ and productions $p_i=(a_i,w_i)$ we obtain the direct derivation

$$a_1\cdot\ldots\cdot a_n \Longrightarrow w_1\cdot\ldots\cdot w_n$$

Replacing each symbol a_i by a handle H_i and each string w_i by a graph B_i (with designated source and target node) in parallel we arrive at simple HPG-grammars. Given a graph G consisting of handles $H_1,\ldots,H_n$ each arc a_i of H_i in G (for i=1,..,n) is replaced by the graph B_i where source and target of B_i are glued together with source and target of a_i respectively. The designation of source and target nodes in B_i, defining a discrete subgraph K_i, is given by an injective graph morphism $K_i \longrightarrow B_i$. Due to 2.2 let us start with the algorithmic description for the parallel derivation of a graph G' from graph G with arcs $a_1,\ldots,a_n$ using the gluing procedure in the introduction of Section 2:

<u>procedure</u> parallel derivation, <u>parameter</u>(G'), <u>input parameters</u>(G, $(a_i, K_i \rightarrow B_i)_{1\le i\le n}$)
<u>begin</u> G' := G
<u>for</u> i:= 1 <u>until</u> n <u>do</u>
  $D_i := G' - \{a_i\}$
  $G' := \text{gluing}(B_i, D_i, K_i \longrightarrow B_i, K_i \longrightarrow D_i)$
<u>end</u>

6.1 EXAMPLE

The following seven productions

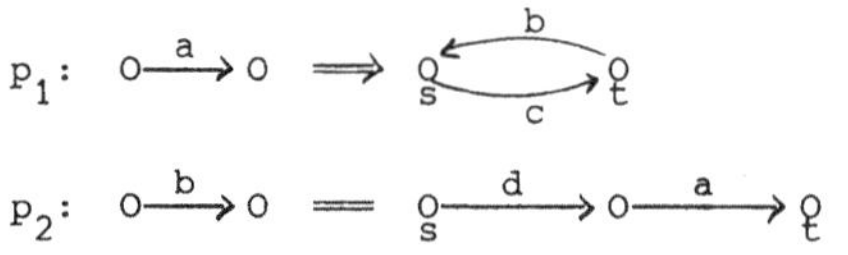

P_1: $\quad$ o $\xrightarrow{\ a\ }$ o $\quad \Longrightarrow \quad$ o$_s$ $\underset{c}{\overset{b}{\rightleftarrows}}$ o$_t$

P_2: $\quad$ o $\xrightarrow{\ b\ }$ o $\quad = \quad$ o$_s$ $\xrightarrow{\ d\ }$ o $\xrightarrow{\ a\ }$ o$_t$

P_3-P_7: $\quad$ H_i $\quad \Longrightarrow \quad$ B_i $\qquad$ for $(i=3,\ldots,7)$

with H_i a handle (o$_s$ $\longrightarrow$ o$_t$) colored c,d,e,f,g and
B_i a handle colored e,f,g,a and d respectively

are leading to the sequence of parallel derivations in Fig. 6.1 (where the numbering
(not coloring) of the nodes will be significant in Example 7.2).

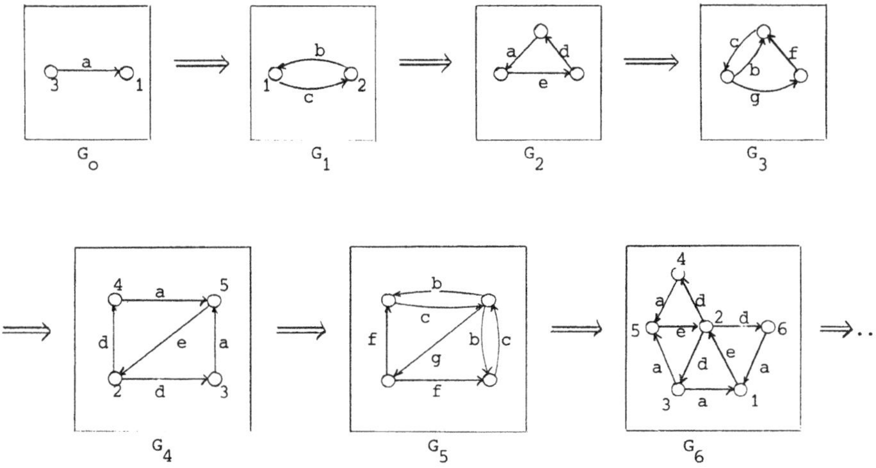

Figure 6.1: Parallel Derivation Sequence

In the derivation $G_2 \Longrightarrow G_3$, for example, the three arcs of G_2 colored a,d,e are replaced by B_1, B_4 and B_5 yielding G_3.

Now we turn to the algebraic description of the parallel derivation procedure.
Actually the derived graph G' is given by the star gluing of

$$(B_i \xleftarrow{\ K_{ij}\ } \longrightarrow B_j)_{1 \leqslant i < j \leqslant n}$$

as defined in 2.9 where the $B_1, \ldots, B_n$ are the right hand sides of the productions.
In order to get the interfaces K_{ij} of the star gluing we construct the "handle star"
HS(G) of the given graph G

$$(H_i \xleftarrow{\ K_{ij}\ } \longrightarrow H_j)_{1 \leqslant i < j \leqslant n}$$

where K_{ij} is the intersection of handles H_i and H_j in G. Since G becomes the star-gluing of HS(G) the direct derivation $G \Longrightarrow G'$ will be given by a pair of pushout-stars (cf. 2.8).

6.2 DEFINITION (HANDLE-STAR)

1) Given a color alphabet $C=(C_A,C_N)$ a handle is a (colored) graph H consisting of one arc a_o, two nodes s_o and t_o, which are source resp. target of a_o, and a triple $(c_s,c_a,c_t) \in C_N \times C_A \times C_N$ of colors for s_o, a_o and t_o respectively. Let us assume that a_o, s_o and t_o are the same for all handles so that each handle is given by a triple $(c_s,c_a,c_t) \in C_N \times C_A \times C_N$.
2) Given a graph $G=(G_A,G_N,s,t,m_A,m_N)$ we have for each arc $a_i \in \{a_1,\dots,a_n\}=G_A$ a unique handle H_i and graph morphism $H_i \longrightarrow G$ such that a_o is mapped to a_i. Now let K_{ij} the intersection (resp. pullback, see 9.5) of $H_i \longrightarrow G$ and $H_j \longrightarrow G$ in the following pullback diagram

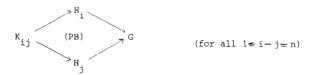

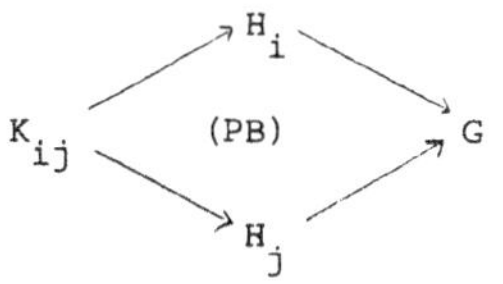

(for all $1 \le i < j \le n$)

then the handle-star of G is the following graph star (see 2.9)

$$\text{HANDLE-STAR}(G) = (H_i \longleftarrow K_{ij} \longrightarrow H_j)_{1 \le i < j \le n}$$

3) A graph G is called nondegenerate if G is nonempty, has no isolated nodes and no isolated loops.

Interpretation:

Given a nondegenerate graph G the handle-star of G is a diagrammatic decomposition of G into handles in such a way that the star gluing of this handle-star becomes G (see 6.3). This is the first step of a direct parallel derivation (see 6.5). An example will be given in 6.6.

6.3 LEMMA

For each nondegenerate graph G we have (up to isomorphism)

$$\text{STAR-GLUING}(\text{HANDLE-STAR}(G)) = G$$

For the proof see /GL.Eh Ld 78/ or /GL.Ld 78/.

Now we are able to define simple HPG-grammars. As in Section 3 we will only consider the case of "colorpreserving productions" which means that corresponding gluing items have the same color (for the "colorchanging" case see /GL.Ld 78/.

6.4 DEFINITION (HANDLE PRODUCTION AND HPG-DERIVATIONS)

1) A handle-production p is a fast graph production

$p=(H \longleftarrow K \longrightarrow B)$

where H is a handle, K a discrete graph with two nodes s_o and t_o and B a nondegenerate graph.

Remark:

Let us recall that "fast" means injectivity of $K \longrightarrow H$ and $K \longrightarrow B$. Hence B becomes a nondegenerate graph with designated nodes s(B) and t(B), called source and target of B respectively, defined as image of s_o and t_o under the graph morphism $K \longrightarrow B$.

2) Given a nondegenerate graph G with

$\text{HANDLE-STAR}(G) = (H_i \longleftarrow K_{ij} \longrightarrow H_j)_{1 \leq i < j \leq n}$

and for each $i=1,\ldots,n$ a production

$p_i = (H_i \longleftarrow K_i \longrightarrow B_i)$

we obtain a unique factorization

$K_{ij} \longrightarrow H_i = K_{ij} \longrightarrow K_i \longrightarrow H_i$.

Let for each $i=1,\ldots,n$

$K_{ij} \longrightarrow B_i = K_{ij} \longrightarrow K_i \longrightarrow B_i$

then the daughter-star of G is defined by

$\text{DAUGHTER-STAR}(G) = (B_i \longleftarrow K_{ij} \longrightarrow B_j)_{1 \leq i < j \leq n}$

Combining both constructions a direct (HPG)-derivation, written $G \Longrightarrow G'$, consists of the following two pushout-stars, the handle pushout-star $(POS)_H$ and the daughter pushout-star $(POS)_D$:

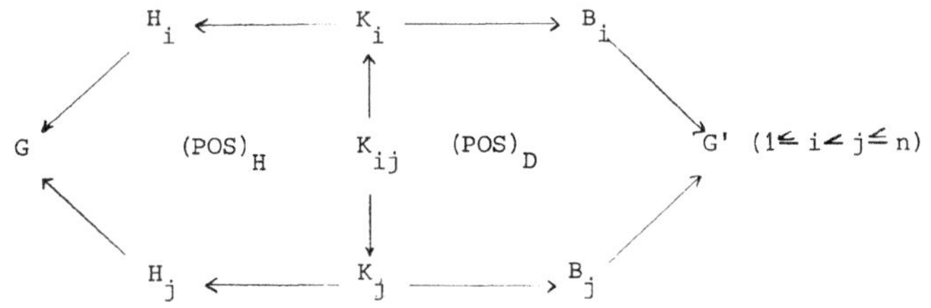

Remark:

By definition of $(POS)_H$ and $(POS)_D$ G is the star gluing of HANDLE-STAR(G) resp. G' the star gluing of DAUGHTER-STAR(G), where G and G' are unique up to isomorphism. Note that the productions p_i and p_j are explicitly included in the diagram $(POS)_H + (POS)_D$ and so the direct derivation is uniquely determined by G and the choice of $p_1,\ldots,p_n$, where we do not distinguish between isomorphic graphs.

6.5 EXAMPLE

The direct derivation $G_2 \Longrightarrow G_3$ in Example 6.1 is given by the pushout stars in Fig. 6.2 where the graph morphisms are given by the numbering of the nodes.

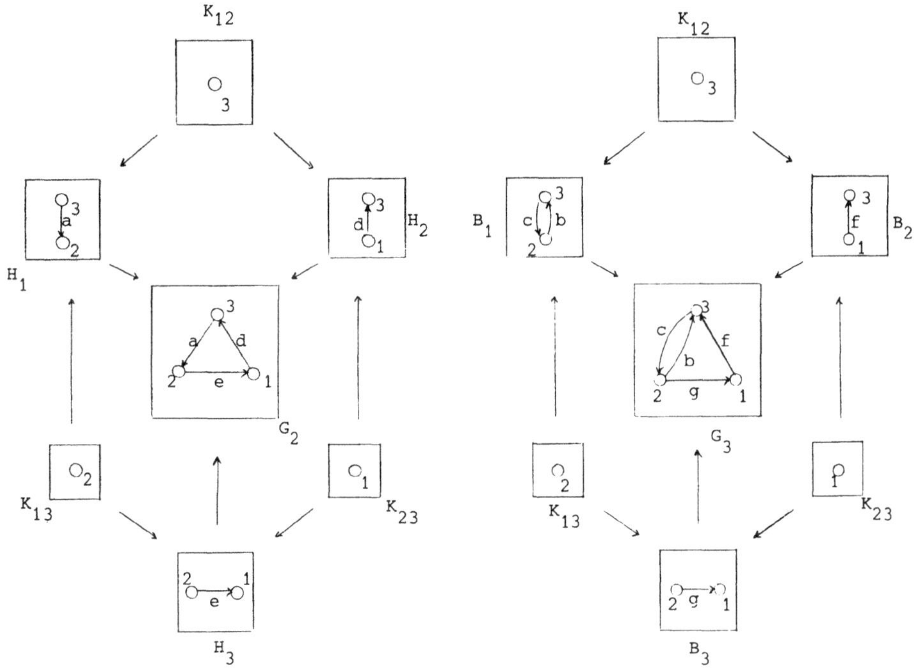

Figure 6.2: Pushout Stars $(POS)_H$ and $(POS)_D$ of a Direct HPG-Derivation

6.6 DEFINITION (SIMPLE HPG-GRAMMARS)

1) A simple handle-substitution-parallel graph-grammar, short simple HPG-grammar, $GG=(C,H\text{-}PROD,H_{ax})$ consists of
   - a color alphabet $C=(C_A,C_N)$
   - a finite set H-PROD of handle-productions $p_i=(H_i \longleftarrow K_i \longrightarrow B_i)$ $(i=1,\dots,n)$ which is deterministic, i.e. $H_i \neq H_j$ for $i \neq j$, and complete, i.e. $\{H_i/1 \leq i \leq n\} \cong C_N \times C_A \times C_N$
   - a handle H_{ax}, called axiom.
2) The graph sequence of a simple HPG-grammar is the sequence $(G_n)_{n\in\mathbb{N}_o}$ where $G_o=H_{ax}$ and $G_n \Longrightarrow G_{n+1}$ for each $n\in\mathbb{N}_o$. The set $\{G_n/n\in\mathbb{N}_o\}$ is called the graph language of the grammar.

Remarks:

Note, that determinism and completeness of H-PROD implies that for each nondegenerated G there is exactly one direct derivation $G \Longrightarrow G'$ in GG.
An example of a simple HPG-grammar was given already in Example 6.1. A description of the graph sequence in terms of a star gluing formula will be given in Example 7.2 and 7.7.

Due to 2.2 we also give an explicit set-theoretical description of HPG-derivations.

6.7 LEMMA (EXPLICIT CONSTRUCTION OF HPG-DERIVATIONS)

Given a graph G with arcs $G_A = \{a_1,\ldots,a_n\}$, corresponding handles $H_1,\ldots,H_n$ and productions $p_i=(H_i \longleftarrow K_i \longrightarrow B_i)$ for $i=1,\ldots,n$ the derived graph G' in the (uniquely determined) direct HPG-derivation $G \Longrightarrow G'$ is (up to isomorphism) given by

$$G'_A = \sum_{i=1}^{n} (B_i)_A \qquad \langle \text{disjoint union} \rangle$$

$$G'_N = G_N + \sum_{i=1}^{n} (B_i)_N - \{s(B_i),\ t(B_i)\}$$

$$\begin{aligned} s_{G'}\,a = {} & \underline{\text{if}}\ a \text{ in } B_i\ \underline{\text{then}} \\ & \quad \underline{\text{if}}\ s_{B_i}\,a = s(B_i)\ \underline{\text{then}}\ s_G\,a_i\ \underline{\text{else}} \\ & \quad\quad \underline{\text{if}}\ s_{B_i}\,a = t(B_i)\ \underline{\text{then}}\ t_G\,a_i\ \underline{\text{else}}\ s_{B_i}\,a \end{aligned}$$

$t_{G'}\,a$ is defined similar exchanging "s" and "t" simultaneously,

$m_{G'}\,x = \underline{\text{if}}\ x \in G_N\ \underline{\text{then}}\ m_G\,x\ \underline{\text{else}}\ m_{B_i}\,x$ for $x \in B_i$

The fact that G_N is a subset of G'_N in Thm. 6.6 can be used in general to define a derivation map $G_N \longrightarrow G'_N$ for each HPG-derivation $G \Longrightarrow G'$ (see /GL.Eh Ld 78/ or /GL.Ld 78/).

6.8 DEFINITION (PRODUCTION AND DERIVATION MAPS)

1) Given a handle production $p=(H \xleftarrow{h} K \xrightarrow{b} B)$ the production map on the nodes
   $MAP(p): H_N \longrightarrow B_N$
   is defined by $MAP(p) = b_N\, h_N^{-1}$

2) For each HPG-derivation $G \Longrightarrow G'$ with productions p_i the production maps $MAP(p_i)$ can be uniquely extended to a derivation map
   $MAP(G \Longrightarrow G'): G_N \longrightarrow G'_N$
   such that the following diagram commutes for $i=1,\ldots,n$

$$\begin{array}{ccc} (H_i)_N & \xrightarrow{\quad MAP(p_i)\quad} & (B_i)_N \\ \Big\downarrow & = & \Big\downarrow \\ G_N & \underset{MAP(G \Longrightarrow G')}{\dashrightarrow} & G'_N \end{array}$$

Now we will sketch briefly the concepts of HPG-, NPG- and EPG-grammars (as defined in /GL.Eh Rb 76/ and /GL.Eh 75/) and that of parallel graph grammars (based on /GL.Eh Kr 76/).

6.9 HPG-GRAMMARS

The main difference between HPG- and simple HPG-grammars is that a production in a HPG-grammar is a pair p=(H,B) consisting of a handle H and a daughter graph B, where B has no longer designated source and target nodes. The idea is to allow gluing of the daughter graphs not only in two designated nodes for each daughter graph (as it is the case in simple HPG-grammars) but the gluing in an arbitrary set K of nodes. Hence we have for each pair (B_i, B_j) of daughter graphs in an HPG-grammar at least one "connector"

$$B_i \longleftarrow K_{ij} \longrightarrow B_j$$

where K_{ij} is an arbitrary discrete graph and $K_{ij} \longrightarrow B_i$, $K_{ij} \longrightarrow B_j$ injective graph morphisms. A finite set CONNECT of all possible connectors is given in the HPG-grammar. Given a graph G with arcs $a_1,\ldots,a_n$ and corresponding handles $H_1,\ldots,H_n$ we don't construct the handle-star of G but directly a daughter-star

$$(B_i \longleftarrow K_{ij} \longrightarrow B_j)_{1 \leq i < j \leq n}$$

where $K_{ij}=\emptyset$ if a_i is not adjacent to a_j in G and $B_i \longleftarrow K_{ij} \longrightarrow B_j$ is in CONNECT if a_i is adjacent to a_j in G, i.e. $\{s_G\, a_i,\ t_G\, a_i\} \cap \{s_G\, a_j,\ t_G\, a_j\} = \emptyset$ for $i \neq j$. As before, the derived graph G' is the star gluing of the daughter star.

6.10 NPG- AND EPG-GRAMMARS

While in HPG-grammars the basic units are handles, derivations in NPG-grammars are based on node substitution. Given a graph G each node n is replaced by a daughter graph K_n and each arc from s to t in G is replaced by a "stencil" B which is a graph with designated disjoint subgraphs K_s and K_t, called source and target of the stencil B respectively, such that all nodes of B_n are either in K_s or in K_t. The stencils are glued together with the corresponding daughter graphs leading to the derived graph G'. More precisely we construct for each graph G with nodes $N_1,\ldots,N_m$, arcs $a_1,\ldots,a_n$ and corresponding handles $H_1,\ldots,H_n$ (see 6.2) a diagram QUASISTAR(G) consisting of the graphs $N_1,\ldots,N_m$, $H_1,\ldots,H_n$ and for each pair (i,j) with $1 \leq i \leq m$, $1 \leq j \leq n$ and $s_G\, a_j = N_i$ (resp. $t_G\, a_j = N_i$) the canonical graph morphism $s_{ij}: N_i \longrightarrow H_j$ (resp. $t_{ij}: N_i \longrightarrow H_j$).

Unfortunately QUASISTAR(G) is no graph star in the sense of Def. 2.9 (because different K_{ij} in 2.9 may correspond to one N_i) but the gluing of graph quasistars can be defined by a commutativity and universal property similar to those in 2.9. Especially the stargluing of QUASISTAR(G) becomes G (up to isomorphism). In QUASISTAR(G) we replace each N_i by a daughter graph K_i and each handle H_j by a stencil B_j. B_j has source (resp. target) N_i in the case $s_G\, a_j = N_i$ (resp. $t_G\, a_j = N_i$). Hence we can replace $s_{ij}: N_i \longrightarrow H_j$ (resp. $t_{ij}: N_i \longrightarrow H_j$) in QUASISTAR(G) by the corresponding canonical graph morphisms $K_i \longrightarrow B_j$. This replacement leads to a new diagram, called DAUGHTER-QUASISTAR(G), which has the same schema as QUASISTAR(G). Finally the derived graph G' of G is defined to be the gluing of DAUGHTER-QUASISTAR(G).

Generalizing the concept of stencils so that there may be nodes in the stencil not belonging to the source resp. target subgraph we obtain EPG-(edge substitution parallel graph)-grammars.

6.11 PARALLEL GRAPH-GRAMMARS

The main difference between parallel graph grammars and HPG (or NPG) grammars defined before is that the basic units to be replaced are not necessary handles (or nodes and handles as in the NPG-case) but arbitrary graphs. Hence we can take fast productions

$$p=(B_1 \longleftarrow K \longrightarrow B_2)$$

as in the sequential case where K is the discrete subgraph B_{1N}. The handle-star is replaced by the graph-star

$$(B_{1i} \longleftarrow K_{ij} \longrightarrow B_{1j})_{1 \le i < j \le n}$$

consisting of left hand sides of productions B_{1i} for i=1,...,n and discrete K_{ij} such that the gluing of the GRAPH-star is again G. Actually we will start with an injective family $B_{1i} \longrightarrow G$ of graph morphisms covering G which is pairwise disjoint on arcs and we define K_{ij} to be the intersection of B_{1i} and B_{1j} for $1 \le i < j \le n$. Then G becomes the star gluing of this intersection graph-star.

Given productions $p_i=(B_{1i} \longleftarrow K_i \longrightarrow B_{2i})$ we assume

$$K_{ij} \longrightarrow B_{1i} = K_{ij} \longrightarrow K_i \longrightarrow B_{1i}$$

such that we can define for $1 \le i < j \le n$

$$K_{ij} \longrightarrow B_{2i} = K_{ij} \longrightarrow K_i \longrightarrow B_{2i}.$$

Finally the derived graph G' becomes the star gluing of the daughter star

$$(B_{2i} \longleftarrow K_{ij} \longrightarrow B_{2j})_{1 \le i < j \le n}.$$

7. LOCALLY STAR GLUING FORMULAS

In the last section we have considered simple HPG-grammars which are generalizations of PDOL-systems. Let us recall that a PDOL-system is called dependent if each cycle in its dependence graph goes through the axiom. For each dependent PDOL-system there is a locally catenative formula $(t_1,\ldots,t_k)$ and a cut p with $p \geq \max \{t_i \ / \ i=1,\ldots,k\}$ such that the sequence $w_o,w_1,w_2,\ldots$ generated by the PDOL-system satisfies for all $n \geq p$

$$w_n = w_{n-t_1} w_{n-t_2} \ldots w_{n-t_k}$$

This formula allows to calculate w_n without using the productions of the PDOL-system explicitly (see/LS.He Rb 75/).In this section we want to extend this result to simple HPG-grammars (see /GL.Ld 78/ and /GL.Eh Ld 78/).The first step consists of defining a locally star gluing formula generalizing a locally catenative formula. This allows to define graph sequences recursively. Then we will provide (under special assumptions) the construction of locally star gluing formulas for simple HPG-grammars. In Theorem 7.4 we show that the existence of a locally star gluing formula for a simple HPG-grammar with graph sequence $G_o,G_1,G_2,\ldots$ is equivalent to the fact that for some $p>0$ G_p is the star gluing of a graph star built up by graphs $G_{p-t_1},\ldots,G_{p-t_k}$ of the sequence and suitable interface graphs K_{ij}. Using this theorem we can show in Theorem 7.6 for each "dependent" simple HPG-grammar that the corresponding graph sequence can be defined by a locally star gluing formula. For all the proofs of results in this section we refer to /GL.Eh Ld 78/ or /GL.Ld 78/. As motivation for the definition of locally star gluing formulas for graphs in 7.1 let us interprete the formula $w_n = w_{n-t_1} w_{n-t_2} \ldots w_{n-t_k}$ (given above for strings) as a star gluing construction for graphs. Due to the introduction of Section 2 each string can be considered as a totally ordered graph with arc colors corresponding to the string symbols. Then w_n becomes the star gluing in the following pushout-star where each K_i is the discrete graph of two nodes s,t such that $K_i \longrightarrow w_{n-t_i}$ maps s to the first and t to the last node of w_{n-t_i}. Moreover each K_{ij} is a single node which is mapped by $K_{ij} \longrightarrow K_i$ to t and by $K_{ij} \longrightarrow K_j$ to s, and $w_{n-t_i} \longrightarrow w_n$ is the natural embedding.

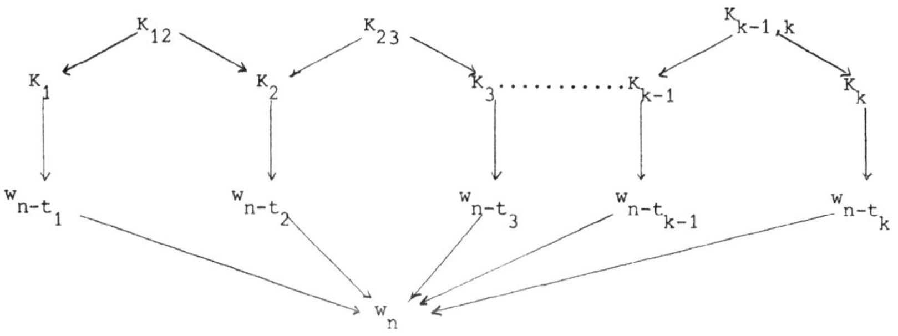

In the diagram above one part of the graph star, namely the graph star $FS=(K_i \longleftarrow K_{ij} \longrightarrow K_j)$, is the same for all $n \geq p$. Hence it can be fixed so that FS will be called fixstar. The gluing morphisms $K_i \longrightarrow w_{n-t_i}$ are formally dependent on n. But actually they can be composed $K_i \longrightarrow w_{n-t_i} = K_i \xrightarrow{i} K \longrightarrow w_{n-t_i}$ where $K_i \longrightarrow K$ is a fixed gluing morphism. In our special case we could take $K_i = K$ and $K_i \longrightarrow K$ the identity but in the general graph case we will take K to be the star gluing of the fixstar FS for $n-t_i \geq p$. Hence in our special case K becomes the discrete graph with k+1 nodes where $K_i \longrightarrow K$ maps s to the first and t to the last node in K. Finally the graph morphisms $K \longrightarrow w_{n-t_i}$ are mapping the first to the first and the last to the last node in w_{n-t_i} for $n \geq p+t_i$.

Actually we could also assume K_i to be discrete with two nodes in the graph case and this would be general enough for Theorem 7.6 where each graph uses only two gluing items. But Theorem 7.4 allows the more general case that the graphs are glued together in more than two gluing items (see /GL.Eh Ld 78/). Hence we will consider arbitrary finite discrete graphs K_i for $i=1,\ldots,k$.

7.1 DEFINITION (LOCALLY STAR GLUING FORMULA)

1) A locally star gluing formula is a triple STARFORM = (TUP, FIXSTAR, fixmor) consisting of
   - a k-tuple $TUP=(t_1,\ldots,t_k)$ of positive integers
   - a graph star $FIXSTAR=(K_i \longleftarrow K_{ij} \longrightarrow K_j)_{1 \leq i \leq j \leq k}$, called fixstar, where all the graphs K_i and K_{ij} are discrete
   - a k-tuple $fixmor=(fixmor_1,\ldots,fixmor_k)$ of graph morphisms $fixmor_i: K_i \longrightarrow K$ for $i=1,\ldots,k$, called fixed gluing morphisms, where K is the star gluing of FIXSTAR.
2) Given a locally star gluing formula STARFORM and an integer $p \geq \max\{t_i/i=1,\ldots,k\}$ a graph sequence $(G_n)_{n\in \mathbb{N}_0}$ together with graph morphisms $g_{in}: K_i \longrightarrow G_n$ for $n \geq p-t_i$ and $i=1,\ldots,k$ is called locally star glued with cut p, if, for all $n \geq p$, the following holds:
3) $G_n = \text{STAR GLUING}(G_{n-t_i} \xleftarrow{g_{i,n-t_i}} K_i \longleftarrow K_{ij} \longrightarrow K_j \xrightarrow{g_{j,n-t_j}} G_{n-t_j})_{1 \leq i < j \leq k}$ and for all $i=1,\ldots,k$ and $n \geq p$
4) $K_i \xrightarrow{g_{in}} G_n = K_i \xrightarrow{fixmor_i} K \xrightarrow{g_n} G_n$ where g_n is the unique graph morphism such that the following diagram commutes:

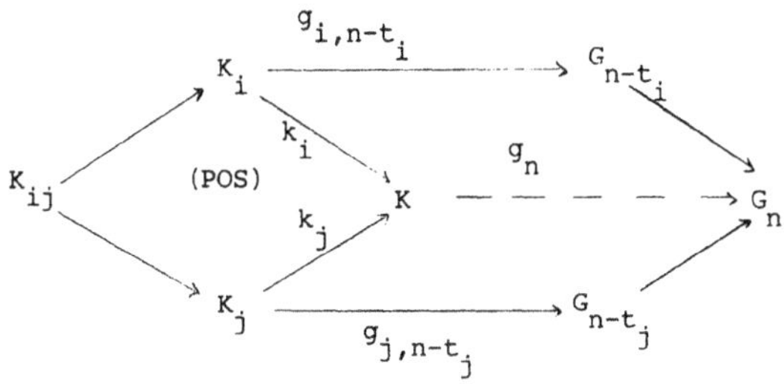

$(1 \leq i < j \leq k)$

The graph morphisms g_{in} will be called gluing morphisms of G_n.

Remark:
Note, that in general the graph morphisms $k_i : K_i \longrightarrow K$ in the POS are different from the fixed gluing morphisms $fixmor_i : K_i \longrightarrow K$, and hence $g_{in} \neq g_n \, k_i$.

Before giving a useful lemma we provide an example.

7.2 EXAMPLE
Given the locally star gluing formula STARFORM with TUP=(2,6,4), FIXSTAR in Fig. 7.1 with star gluing K= $\{1,\ldots,6\}$,

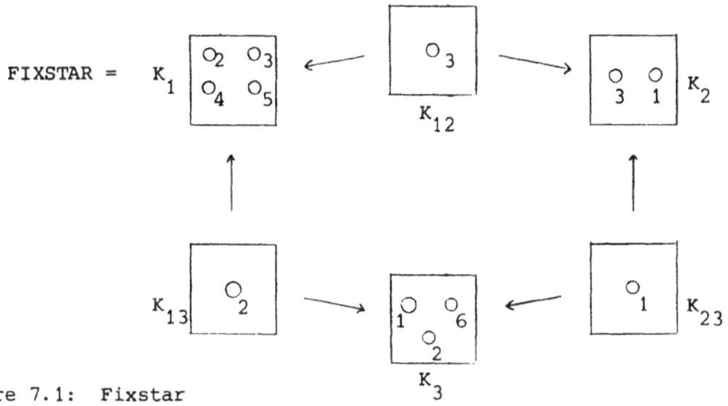

Figure 7.1: Fixstar

fixmor=$(fixmor_i : K_i \longrightarrow K)_{i=1,2,3}$ defined by

$fixmor_1 : 2 \longmapsto 3,\ 3 \longmapsto 1,\ 4 \longmapsto 5,\ 5 \longmapsto 2$

$fixmor_2 : 1 \longmapsto 1,\ 3 \longmapsto 3$

$fixmor_3 : 1 \longmapsto 3,\ 2 \longmapsto 1,\ 6 \longmapsto 2$

then the graph sequence $G_o, G_1, G_2, \ldots$ of Example 6.1 with gluing morphisms $g_{in} : K_i \longrightarrow G_n$ $(n \geq 6-t_i, i=1,2,3)$ is locally star glued with cut p=6, where g_{14}, g_{20}, g_{32} are defined by the numbering of the nodes in Fig. 7.1 and Fig. 6.1. The pushout star for G_6 according to 7.1.3) is given in Fig. 2.2 of Example 2.10 where B_i corresponds to G_{p-t_i} and $k_{ij} : K_{ij} \longrightarrow B_i$ (and similar k_{ji}) corresponds to the composition of

$K_{ij} \longrightarrow K_i$ with $g_{i,p-t_i}: K_i \longrightarrow G_{p-t_i}$ for i=1,2,3.

The graph morphism $g_6: K \longrightarrow G_6$ (by 7.1.4) and p=6) is the extension of the inclusions g_{14}, g_{20} and g_{32} and hence also an inclusion. Hence the gluing morphisms $g_{i6}: K_i \longrightarrow G_6$ are given by $g_{i6}(x) = \text{fixmor}_i(x)$ for all $x \in K_i$ and i=1,2,3.

As a matter of fact (see 7.3) it sufficies to give the graphs $G_o, \ldots, G_6$ and the gluing morphisms g_{14}, g_{15}, g_{20}, $g_{21}, \ldots, g_{25}$, $g_{32}, \ldots, g_{35}$ because all other graphs in the sequence and also the remaining gluing morphisms g_{in} can be defined recursively by 7.1.3) and 7.1.4):

7.3 LEMMA (CONSTRUCTION OF GRAPH SEQUENCES)

Given a locally star gluing formula STARFORM as in 7.1.1), an integer $p \geq \max \{ t_i / i=1,\ldots,k \}$, graphs $G_o, \ldots, G_{p-1}$ and gluing morphisms $g_{in}: K_i \longrightarrow G_n$ for $p-t_i \leq n < p$ and i=1,...,k, there exists a unique extension to a graph sequence $(G_n)_{n \in \mathbb{N}_o}$ with gluing morphisms g_{in} for $n \geq p-t_i$, i=1,...,k which is locally star glued with cut p.

Now we move to the problem of existence and construction of a locally star gluing formula for simple HPG-grammars. First we observe that there exists such a formula iff for some p>O G_p is the star gluing of graphs G_i's in the graph sequence preceding G_p.

7.4 THEOREM (EXISTENCE AND CONSTRUCTION OF LOCALLY STAR GLUING FORMULAS)

Given a simple HPG-grammar with graph sequence $G_o, G_1, G_2, \ldots$ then the following conditions (1) and (2) are equivalent:

(1) There exists a locally star gluing formula STARFORM = (TUP, FIXSTAR, fixmor), an integer p>O and gluing morphisms $g_{in}: K_i \longrightarrow G_n$ such that the sequence G_o, G_1, $G_2, \ldots$ is locally star glued with cut p.

(2) There exists an integer p>O and a graph star

$$S_p = (G_{p-t_i} \longleftarrow K_{ij} \longrightarrow G_{p-t_j})_{1 \leq i < j \leq k}$$

with $1 \leq t_i \leq p$ for i=1,...,k and discrete graphs K_{ij} such that G_p is the star gluing of S_p.

If condition (2) is satisfied the star gluing formula STARFORM and gluing morphisms g_{in} in (1) can be constructed as follows:

(3) Let TUP=$(t_1,\ldots,t_k)$ and K_i be the discrete subgraph of G_{p-t_i} consisting of all nodes such that there is a canonical factorization

$$K_{ij} \longrightarrow G_{p-t_i} = K_{ij} \longrightarrow K_i \longrightarrow G_{p-t_i}$$

Hence we obtain the following fixstar

$$\text{FIXSTAR} = (K_i \longleftarrow K_{ij} \longrightarrow K_j)_{1 \leq i < j \leq k}$$

and the gluing morphisms $g_{i,p-t_i}: K_i \longrightarrow G_{p-t_i}$.

For $p-t_i < n \leq p$ we define $g_{in}: K_i \longrightarrow G_n$ to be the derivation map $\text{MAP}(G_{p-t_i} \overset{*}{\Longrightarrow} G_n): K_i \longrightarrow (G_n)_N$ (see 6.8) followed by the inclusion $(G_n)_N \longrightarrow G_n$. Since K is the gluing of FIXSTAR and $K_i = (G_{p-t_i})_N$ we have $K = (G_p)_N$ and so $g_p: K \longrightarrow G_p$ becomes the inclusion which is bijective on nodes. Hence we can use 7.1.4) to define fixmor_i

by $g_p \circ fixmor_i = g_{ip}$ for $i=1,\dots,k$ which completes the construction of STARFORM.

Now we are able to attack the main problem: The construction of a locally star gluing formula for a "dependent" simple HPG-grammar. Similar to the string case we define:

7.5 DEFINITION (DEPENDENT)

Given a simple HPG-grammar as in 6.6 consider the following dependence graph: The nodes are all the handles and for each handle production $p=(H \longleftarrow K \longrightarrow B)$ and each handle H' of B we have an arc from H to H' in the dependence graph. Now the simple HPG-grammar is called dependent, if each cycle in the dependence graph goes through the axiom H_{ax}.

7.6 THEOREM (LOCALLY STAR GLUING FORMULAS FOR DEPENDENT SIMPLE HPG-GRAMMARS)

For each dependent simple HPG-grammar with graph sequence $G_o, G_1, G_2, \dots$ there exists a locally star gluing formula STARFORM=(TUP,FIXSTAR,fixmor) and $p>0$ such that the sequence is locally star glued with cut p, where the gluing morphisms $g_{in}: K_i \longrightarrow G_n$ are given by the derivation maps $MAP(G_{p-t_i} \overset{*}{\Longrightarrow} G_n)$ for $K_i = (G_{p-t_i})_N$, $TUP=(t_1,\dots,t_k)$, $i=1,\dots,k$ and $n>p-t_i$.

Construction:

The first part of the construction is very similar to the string case. Let p be the maximum of the length of all cycles in the dependence graph. Now we construct the "derivation tree" for the derivation sequence $G_o \Longrightarrow G_1 \Longrightarrow \dots \Longrightarrow G_p$. The nodes of the derivation tree are colored with handles and for each handle H with production $(H \longleftarrow K \longrightarrow B)$ we have arcs to the handles $H_1,\dots,H_r$ of B such that in each level n of the derivation tree we have all the handles of G_n (but not the information how to glue them to get G_n). Now for each path from the axiom H_{ax} to a leave in the derivation tree there is - in addition to the root - at least one node colored H_{ax} because of the choice of p. Hence we obtain a collection $n_1,\dots,n_k$ of nodes in the derivation tree (with distance $t_1,\dots,t_k$ from the root) such that the subtrees with root $n_1,\dots,n_k$ are covering the level p of the tree without overlapping. Due to the fact that the handles H_l $(l=1,\dots,k_i)$ of G_{p-t_i} are also handles of G_p there is a unique graph morphism $G_{p-t_i} \longrightarrow G_p$ such that $H_l \longrightarrow G_{p-t_i} \longrightarrow G_p = H_l \longrightarrow G_p$ for all $l=1,\dots,k_i$. Now let K_{ij} the intersection, or more precisely the pullback (see 9.5) in the following diagram

$$\begin{array}{ccccc} & & g_{p-t_i} & & \\ & \nearrow & & \searrow & \\ K_{ij} & & & & G_p \\ & \searrow & & \nearrow & \\ & & G_{p-t_j} & & \end{array}$$

leading to the following GRAPH-star

$$S_p = (G_{p-t_i} \longleftarrow K_{ij} \longrightarrow G_{p-t_j})_{1 \leq i < j \leq k}$$

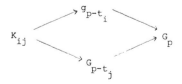

In fact the star gluing of S_p becomes G_p so that Thm. 7.4 can be applied to construct the locally star gluing formula for the graph sequence $G_o, G_1, G_2, \ldots$. By construction in 7.4 we have $K_i = (G_{p-t_i})_N$ and $g_{in}: K_i \longrightarrow G_n$ in $MAP(G_{p-t_i} \overset{*}{\Longrightarrow} G_n)$ followed by the inclusion from $(G_n)_N$ to G_n.

Remark:

In the construction above it is possible to replace the discrete graphs K_i by those having two nodes only, namely those of the axiom handle, so that g_{in} is given by $MAP(H_{ax} \overset{*}{\Longrightarrow} G_n)$ (see 6.8).

7.7 EXAMPLE

Consider the following simple HPG-grammar given in Example 6.1 where the axiom is the handle colored a.

In the dependence graph of Fig. 7.2, where each handle is represented by his arc color, the maximal length of a cycle is p=6 and each cycle goes through a such that the grammar is dependent.

The graph sequence $G_o, \ldots, G_6$ of our grammar given in Example 6.1 leads to the derivation tree in Fig. 7.2 where nodes n_1, n_2, n_3 covering level 6 have distance $t_1=2$, $t_2=6$ and $t_3=4$ from the root resepctively.

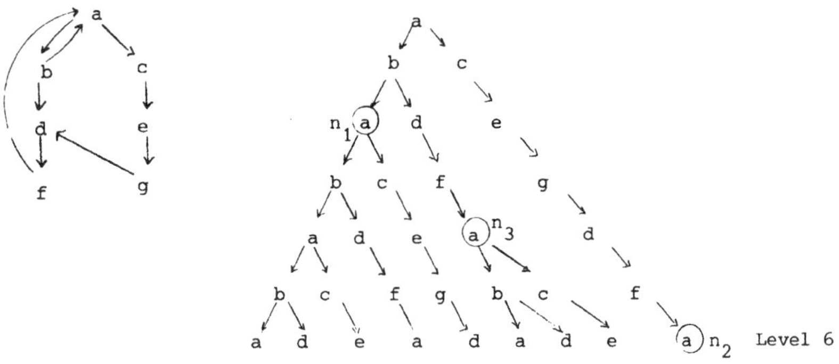

Figure 7.2: Dependence Graph and Derivation Tree of a Simple HPG-Grammar

(Note, that the numbering of the nodes is arbitrary). Next we can construct the graph morphisms $G_4 \longrightarrow G_6$, $G_o \longrightarrow G_6$ and $G_2 \longrightarrow G_6$, the discrete graphs $K_1 = (G_4)_N$, $K_2 = (G_o)_N$, $K_3 = (G_2)_N$ together with the inclusions $g_{14}: K_1 \longrightarrow G_4$, $g_{20}: K_2 \longrightarrow G_o$ and

$g_{32}:K_3 \longrightarrow G_2$ and the intersection $K_{13}=G_4 \cap G_2$, $K_{12}=G_4 \cap G_o$ and $K_{23}=G_2 \cap G_o$ in graph G_6 of Example 6.1.

Hence we obtain the locally star gluing formula STARFORM of 7.2 where $fixmor_i$ is defined by 7.1.4) for n=p and i=1,...,3. By Thm. 7.6 (resp. Thm. 7.4) the graph sequence $G_o, G_1, G_2, \ldots$ of our given simple HPG-grammar together with the gluing morphisms g_{in} defined by g_{14}, g_{20} and g_{32} (see 7.3) is locally star glued with cut p.

Let us recall that the proofs for all results in this section can be found in /GL.Eh Ld 78/ and also in /GL.Ld 78/ where a slightly more general version is treated.

8. GRAPH LANGUAGES

While in the string case the study of languages, especially hierarchies of languages, has become the central part of formal language theory, there are only few results in the graph case up to now. However, in our opinion it was more important to obtain results about derivation properties first, which can be applied in different fields of Computer Science and Biology, then to start with hierarchy problems of graph languages before it is clear which types of graph grammars defining the languages are really useful. Nevertheless there are a few results for graph languages which will be summarized in this section. Main important in this context is a Pumping Lemma for G-Type 2 and G-Type 3 graph languages which allows to extend the Chomsky hierarchy to the graph case and to rule out interesting graph languages which are not G-Type 2 resp. not G-Type 3.

8.1 PARALLEL GRAPH LANGUAGES

Considering the classes NPG, EPG and PG of graph languages generated by NPG-, EPG- and Parallel graph grammars as defined in Section 6 we have the following hierarchy

$$NPG \subsetneq EPG \subsetneq PG$$

These inclusion result are given in /GL.Eh 75/, where for strict inclusion in the first case there is given a graph language consisting of stars S_n with one center colored b and 2^n tips colored a which is EPG but not NPG. The existence of PG-languages which are not EPG follows from the decidability of the membership-problem for EPG-grammars.

The relationship between EPG, HPG and simple HPG has not been studied yet, but we would suggest

$$\text{simple HPG} \subsetneq EPG \subsetneq HPG$$

Moreover in /GL.Rb 75/ there are defined SNPG-grammars, called subgraph-matching NPG-grammars, which are introduced in analogy to the use of stencils in /GL.Cu Li 74/. It is claimed in /GL.Rb 75/ that we have

$$SNPG \subsetneq NPG$$

Of course, it is possible to extend all the different constructions for L-systems also to the graph case. Some of these extensions have been studied using other approaches to graph grammars, especially by M.Nagl (see /OV.Na 78/).

8.2 SEQUENTIAL GRAPH LANGUAGES

Let us call the class of all graph languages generated by sequential graph grammars (cf. 3.3) G-Type 0, while G-Type 1 is the class generated by those grammars where the productions $p=(B_1 \longleftarrow K \longrightarrow B_2)$ satisfy card $(B_1) \leq$ card (B_2) for card (G) being the sum of arcs and nodes in G. Further let G-Type 2 be generated by productions where B_1 consists of a single handle (arc with source and target) and K is discrete with two nodes. Finally let G-Type 3 be generated by productions with B_1 a single handle and K a single node which is mapped to the source of B_1 and a non target node of B_2.

Note, that specialization to the string case, i.e. totally ordered graphs with only one node color, yields exactly the well-known Chomsky Types. For the classes of graph languages defined above we have:

$$\text{G-Type } 3 \subsetneqq \text{G-Type } 2 \subsetneqq \text{G-Type } 1 \subsetneqq \text{G-Type } 0$$

The first two inclusion results are consequences of the Pumping-Lemma in 8.3 while the last is a consequence of the decidability of the membership problem for G-Type 1-grammars.

As mentioned in /GG.Eh Pf Sc 73b/ we can also define a 2-dimensional hierarchy of graph grammars and languages where the second dimension is the type of the graphs B_1 and B_2 in the productions, e.g. string-type, tree-type or connected-graph-type. Finally also the type of the graph morphisms may define a hierarchy. We have considered only injective and color-preserving $K \longrightarrow B_1$ and $K \longrightarrow B_2$. However, Uesu has shown in /GG.Ue 77/ that each recursively enumerable set of graphs can be generated already by "simple" graph grammars, where simple means "K discrete" and injectivity of $K \longrightarrow B_1$, $K \longrightarrow B_2$ and also of the occurrences $B_1 \longrightarrow G$ for applying the production. But the graph morphisms $K \longrightarrow B_1$ and $K \longrightarrow B_2$ are not assumed to preserve colors.

8.3 PUMPING-LEMMA

For graph languages L generated by G-Type 2 graph grammars in /GG.Kr 77a/ and /GG.Kr 78/ the following Pumping-Lemma is proved:

There are integers $p,q>0$ such that for each graph G in L with card $(G_A)>p$ there is a graph star

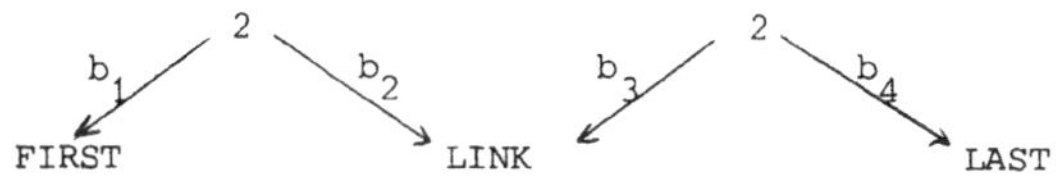

where 2 is discrete with two nodes, b_1,b_2,b_3,b_4 injective, LINK $\neq$ 2 and $\text{card}(\text{LINK}_A) + \text{card}(\text{LAST}_A) \leq q$, such that G is the star-gluing of this graph star and for each $i \geq 0$ the star-gluing G_i of the following iterated star belongs to the language L

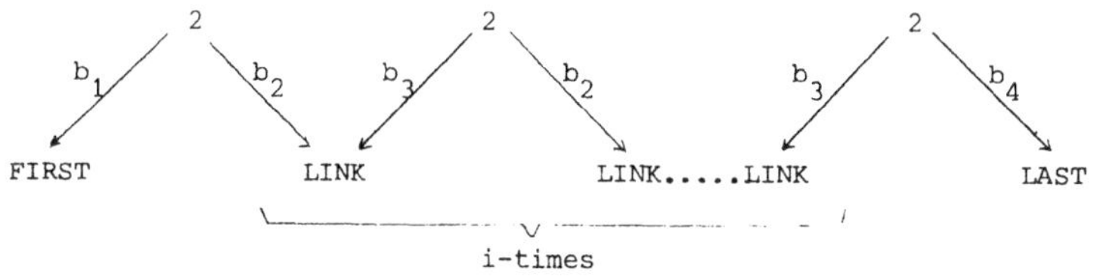

Remark:

The graph stars above are actually "graph chains" so that the gluing construction can be done by iterated pushout constructions. The interpretation of the star gluing construction is the following:

There are three subgraphs FIRST, LINK and LAST of G satisfying:
FIRST $\cup$ LINK $\cup$ LAST = G, FIRST $\cap$ LINK = 2, LINK $\cap$ LAST = 2 and FIRST $\cap$ LAST $\subseteq$ LINK

G:
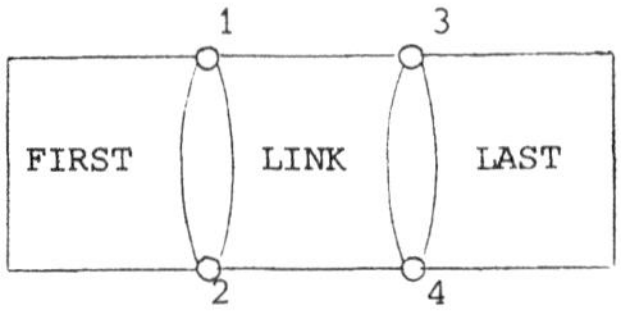

Then graph G_i has the shape

G_i:
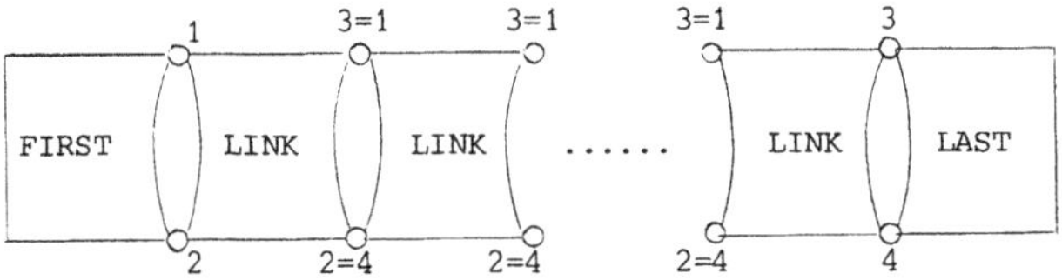

If G is a string with decomposition G=uvwxy then u together with y corresponds to FIRST, v and x to LINK and w to LAST such that G_i becomes $G_i=uv^iwx^iy$.
Hence the graph FIRST and LAST correspond to those parts of graph G generated first resp. last in the corresponding derivation sequence of G. The basic idea of the proof is similar to the string case. However, in /GG.Kr 77a/ canonical derivation sequences are used instead of derivation trees. Moreover restriction and extension of derivation sequences used in the proof for the string case become much more difficult in the graph case. They are replaced by the operations CLIP and JOIN of 5.3. Actually there is also a corresponding Pumping-Lemma for G-Type 3-languages where the graph 2 is replaced by 1, a graph with a single node.
These Pumping-Lemmas can be used to show the existence of G-Type 1-languages which are not G-Type 2 resp. of G-Type 2-languages which are not G-Type 3. A nice corollary (using some notions defined below) is the following:
A graph language L with "limited parallelism of arcs" is not of G-Type 2 (resp. G-Type 3) if there are infinitely many "at least 3-fold (resp. 2-fold) connected graphs".
By "limited parallelism of arcs" we mean that there is a constant c such that for each graph G there are at most c arcs between each pair of nodes in G. A graph is called at least n-fold connected, if each pair of nodes, which is not connected by an arc, is connected by at least n disjoint paths (where the given pair is not counted). For more details, examples and proofs see /GG.Kr 77a/ resp. /GG.Kr 78/.

9. APPENDIUM: CONCEPTS OF CATEGORY THEORY USED IN THE ALGEBRAIC THEORY OF GRAPH GRAMMARS

In the previous sections we have used notation, concepts and results of Category Theory in nearly all constructions. But we have tried to avoid categorical terminology as far as possible because most researchers in Computer Science and Biology (and also several in Mathematics!) are still not familiar with the basic constructions of Category Theory. We hope that we were able to show that the definitions, constructions and results in the Algebraic Theory of Graph Grammars are understandable without Category Theory. At least for the proofs, however, categorical techniques are highly desirable (e.g. the proof of the Church-Rosser-Property I was reduced to 1/5 of the original length using pushout composition and decomposition techniques). On the other hand Category Theory is a language which allows to speak about complex structures in a short but precise way.
In the following we will give the basic categorical concepts which are implicitly used in the previous sections. Moreover we present two typical proofs to give an idea of the proof techniques in the Algebraic Theory of Graph Grammars.
Let us point out that it is also possible to treat the theory of Graph Grammars on a higher categorical level including the cases of partial, multi and stochastic graphs. That approach given in /AP.Eh Kr 76b/, however, needs much more categorical machinery which will not be considered here. For more detailed introductions to category theory we refer to /CT.He St 73/ and /CT.Ar Ma 75/.
Let us start with the basic notion of a category:

9.1 CATEGORIES

A category $\underline{K}$ consists of a class $(\underline{K})$ of objects, for each pair $A,B \in (\underline{K})$ a set $Mor\underline{K}(A,B)$ of morphisms, written $f:A \longrightarrow B$ for $f \in Mor\underline{K}(A,B)$, and a composition

$$\circ : Mor\underline{K}(A,B) \times Mor\underline{K}(B,C) \longrightarrow Mor\underline{K}(A,C)$$

$$(f:A \longrightarrow B,\ g:B \longrightarrow C) \longmapsto (g \circ f:A \longrightarrow C)$$

for all objects $A,B,C \in \underline{K}$ such that the following axioms are satisfied:

(Associativity) $(h \circ g) \circ f = h \circ (g \circ f)$
for all morphisms f,g,h if at least one side is defined

(Identity) For each object $A \in (\underline{K})$ there is a morphism $id_A \in Mor\underline{K}(A,A)$, called identity of A, such that we have for all $f:A \longrightarrow B$ and $g:C \longrightarrow A$ with $B,C \in (\underline{K})$:
$f \circ id_A = f$ and $id_A \circ g = g$

The basic example in most of the applications is the category $\underline{SETS}$ of sets. Objects in $\underline{SETS}$ are all sets A,B,.. and morphisms are functions $f:A \longrightarrow B$ together with the usual composition and identity functions. The main example in our theory, of course, is the category $\underline{GRAPHS}_C$ of (colored) graphs with fixed color alphabet C. Objects in $\underline{GRAPHS}_C$ are colored graphs and morphisms are graph morphisms together with componentwise composition as defined in 2.2.

But there are also several other examples of categories which play an important role in Computer Science, like the category PFN of sets together with partial functions, or the category CPO of completely partially ordered sets with continuous functions, or the category $\underline{ALG}_{\Sigma}$ of Σ-algebras and Σ-homomorphisms.

Once we have objects and morphisms it makes also sense to consider commutative diagrams:

9.2 DIAGRAMS, DUALITY

Given morphisms $f:A \longrightarrow X$, $g:X \longrightarrow B$, $f':A \longrightarrow Y$, $g':Y \longrightarrow B$ the equality $g \circ f = g' \circ f'$ can be illustrated by the following commutative diagram

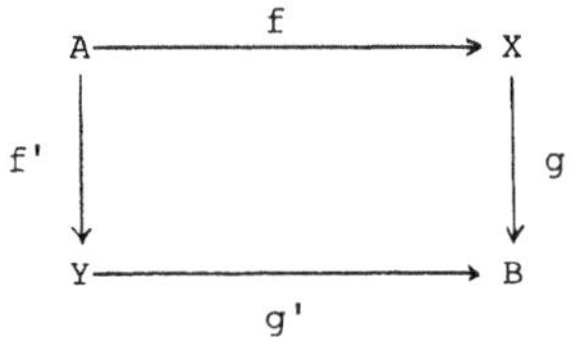

Reserving all arrows in a diagram we get the dual diagram

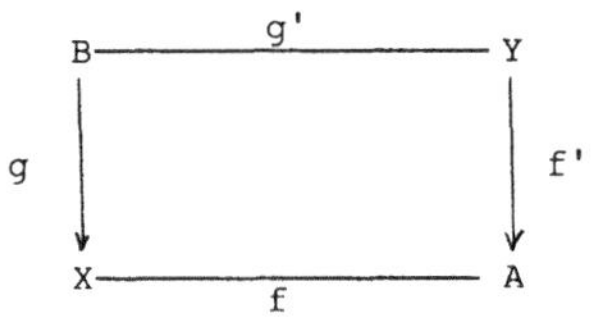

Roughly speaking this procedure allows to dualize all categorical notions and constructions, because they are defined by commutative diagrams in general. We will see that the concepts "pushout" and "pullback" are dual in this sense.

Now we are able to define the basic categorical notion in the Algebraic Theory of Graph Grammars, a pushout. Like several categorical notions it is defined by a commutative diagram of a special shape which satisfies a "universal property". Actually the pushout is characterized by this universal property uniquely up to isomorphism such that it can be used as a well-defined construction. (Note that a morphism $f:A \longrightarrow B$ in a category $\underline{K}$ is called an isomorphism if there is a morphism $g:B \longrightarrow A$ such that $g \circ f = id_A$ and $f \circ g = id_B$). In other words two pushout objects satisfying the same universal property are isomorphic. This fact follows from the definition of pushouts immediately using the universal properties of both pushout objects.

9.3 PUSHOUTS

Given morphisms $K \longrightarrow B$ and $K \longrightarrow D$ the pushout of these morphisms consists of an object G together with two morphisms $B \longrightarrow G$ and $D \longrightarrow G$ such that

(COMMUTATIVITY): The following diagram, also called pushout, is commutative

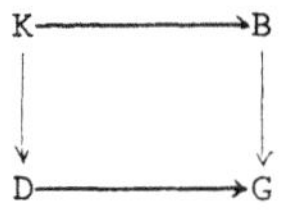

and satisfies the following

(UNIVERSAL PROPERTY): For all objects G' and morphisms B⟶ G' and D⟶ G' satisfying K⟶ B⟶ G' = K⟶ D⟶ G' there is a unique morphism G⟶ G' such that B⟶ G⟶ G' = B⟶ G' and D⟶ G⟶ G' = D⟶ G'.

This situation can be illustrated by the following diagram:

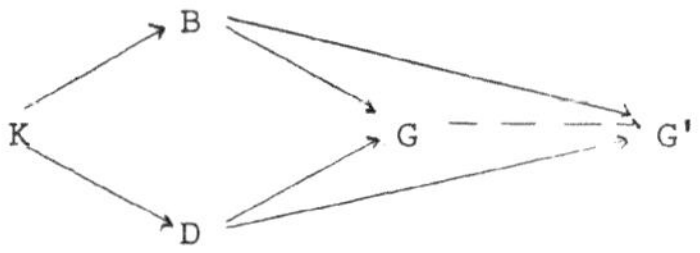

If K is an <u>initial object</u> in the category <u>K</u>, meaning that for each object K' in <u>K</u> there is exactly one morphism from K to K', then in the situation above G is called <u>coproduct</u> of B and D, written G=B+D.

In the category <u>SETS</u> the empty set is an initial object and the coproduct of B and D is the disjoint union B+D. If we have functions f:K⟶ B and g:K⟶ D the pushout G of f and g is a quotient set of B+D where for all k∈K the elements f(k) and g(k) are identified such that G can be regarded as the gluing of B and D along K. More formally G is the quotient set

$$G = B + D/_{\approx}$$

where $\approx$ is the equivalence relation generated by the relation $\sim$ defined by $f(k) \sim g(k)$ for all k∈K. The functions B⟶ G and D⟶ G in the pushout diagram are sending each element to its equivalence class.

In the category $\underline{\text{GRAPHS}}_C$ the initial object is the empty graph, the coproduct is again the disjoint union taken componentwise such that the two parts B and D become disjoint and unconnected parts of G. Given nonempty K and graph morphisms f:K⟶ B and g:K⟶ D the pushout graph G becomes the gluing of B and D as follows: For all nodes and arcs k in K the items f(k) in B and g(k) in D are glued together. More formally the pushout graph $G=(G_A, G_N, s_G, t_G, m_{GA}, m_{GN})$ is given by:

$G_A = B_A + D_A /\approx$ (<u>SETS</u> pushout for the arcs)

$G_N = B_N + D_N /\approx$ (<u>SETS</u> pushout for the nodes)

$s_q([x]) = \underline{\text{if}}\ x \in B_A\ \underline{\text{then}}\ [s_B(x)]\ \underline{\text{else}}\ [s_D(x)]$

$t_G([x]) = \underline{\text{if}}\ x \in B_A\ \underline{\text{then}}\ [t_B(x)]\ \underline{\text{else}}\ [t_D(x)]$

$m_{GA}([x]) = \underline{\text{if}}\ x \in B_A\ \underline{\text{then}}\ m_{BA}(x)\ \underline{\text{else}}\ m_{DA}(x)$

$m_{GN}([x]) = \underline{\text{if}}\ x \in B_A\ \underline{\text{then}}\ m_{BN}(x)\ \underline{\text{else}}\ m_{DN}(x)$

where $[x]$ for $x \in B_A + D_A$ means the class of x in the quotient set G_A and similar $[y]$ for $y \in B_N + D_N$ the class of y in G_N. Note, that s_G, t_G, m_{GA} and m_{GN} are well-defined functions which are uniquely determined by the universal pushout properties of G_A and G_N in <u>SETS</u>. Consider for example the following 3-cube of functions where the back and front square are pushouts in <u>SETS</u> and left and top square are commutative because f and g are graph morphisms.

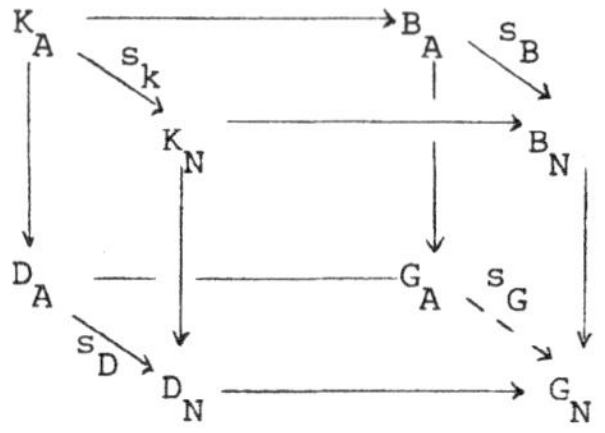

Hence we have

$$K_A \longrightarrow B_A \longrightarrow B_N \longrightarrow G_N = K_A \longrightarrow D_A \longrightarrow D_N \longrightarrow G_N$$

such that by the universal pushout properties of G_A there is a unique function $s_G : G_A \longrightarrow G_N$ making bottom and right square commutative. Using similar universal constructions for t_G, m_{GA} and m_{GN} it follows immediately that all of them are well-defined and that the pair of functions $(B_A \longrightarrow G_A,\ B_N \longrightarrow G_N)$ resp. $(D_A \longrightarrow G_A, D_N \longrightarrow G_N)$ becomes a graph morphism $B \longrightarrow G$ resp. $D \longrightarrow G$. Moreover it is easy to show the universal properties of G in $\underline{GRAPHS}_C$ using those of G_A and G_N in <u>SETS</u> (see /AP.Eh Ti 75/). The universal properties will be shown explicitly in 9.6 for the special case of Section 3.

Now we will give some fundamental properties of pushouts which are used frequently in most of the proofs:

9.4 FACT (PUSHOUT PROPERTIES)

1. Pushouts are unique up to isomorphism. More precisely, if G and G' are both pushout objects of the same morphisms $K \longrightarrow B$ and $K \longrightarrow D$ then G and G' are isomorphic.

2. Given pushout diagrams (1) and (2) below then also the composite diagram (1)+(2) is a pushout. Conversely (1)+(2) pushout and (1) pushout implies that (2) is a pushout.

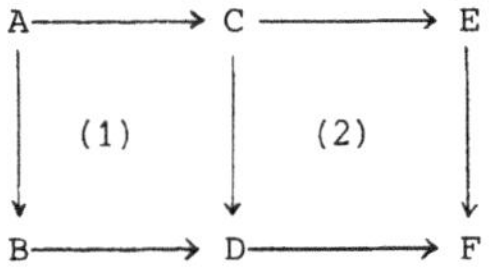

3. Unfortunately we can't have in general that (1) is a pushout if (1)+(2) and (2) are pushouts. But at least in <u>SETS</u> and $\underline{GRAPHS}_C$ this is true provided that $C \longrightarrow E$ is injective.

The proof of parts 1 and 2 is standard in category theory (see also /AP.Eh Ti 75/)

while part 3 is shown in /GG.Eh Kr 76/ and /AP.Eh Ro 76/ for example.

According to 9.2 we will now consider the dual concept of a pushout, called pullback, which is a categorical generalization of intersections, inverse images and congruence relations. We will start with the definition formally dual to that of pushouts in 9.3.

9.5 PULLBACKS

Given morphisms $B \longrightarrow K$ and $D \longrightarrow K$ the pullback, short PB, of these morphisms consists of an object G together with two morphisms $G \longrightarrow B$ and $G \longrightarrow D$ such that $G \longrightarrow B \longrightarrow K = G \longrightarrow D \longrightarrow K$, and for all objects G' and morphisms $G' \longrightarrow B$ and $G' \longrightarrow D$ satisfying $G' \longrightarrow B \longrightarrow K = G' \longrightarrow D \longrightarrow K$ there is a unique morphism $G' \longrightarrow G$ such that $G' \longrightarrow G \longrightarrow B = G' \longrightarrow B$ and $G' \longrightarrow G \longrightarrow D = G' \longrightarrow D$.

If K is a final object in K (exactly one morphism from K' to K for each K' in K) then in the situation above G is called product of B and D, written $G=B \times D$.

In the category SETS each set with one element is a final object, the product is the usual cartesian product and the pullback G of functions $f:B \longrightarrow K$ and $g:D \longrightarrow K$ is given by

$$G = \{ (x,y) \in B \times D \ / \ f(x) = g(y) \}$$

Hence in the special case f=g the set G is the equivalence relation generated by f. If $g:D \longrightarrow K$ is an inclusion G is isomorphic to the inverse image $f^{-1}(D)$, and if both $f:B \longrightarrow K$ and $g:D \longrightarrow K$ are inclusions then G is isomorphic to the intersection of B and D.

In GRAPHS_C we will only consider the case that B and D are subgraphs of K with inclusions f and g, then the pullback G is again the intersection of B and D in K.

Finally let us note that each pullback diagram

$$\begin{array}{ccc} G & \xrightarrow{h} & B \\ {\scriptstyle k}\downarrow & & \downarrow{\scriptstyle f} \\ D & \xrightarrow[g]{} & K \end{array}$$

in SETS and GRAPHS_C (but not in general categories!) with injective f and g is also a pushout with injective h and k.

Finally we will give two proofs which are typical for the Algebraic Theory of Graph Grammars. In the first case we show that the gluing construction of graphs used in Section 3 is a pushout in the category GRAPHS_C (cf. 3.2). And in the second case we use the universal properties of pushouts and pullbacks and the pushout properties in 9.4 to show the Church-Rosser-Property I of graph derivations (cf. 4.4).

9.6 PROOF OF LEMMA 2.8

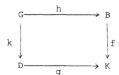

It is clear that the inclusion $c:D \longrightarrow G$ is a graph morphism but for $g:B \longrightarrow G$ we have to show $g\ s_B\ a = s_G\ g\ a$, $g\ t_B\ a = t_G\ g\ a$ for all $a \in B_A$ and $m_G\ g\ x = m_B\ x$ for all x in B. We will verify only the first equation. Let us consider three cases and use the definitions in 3.2 frequently:

<u>Case 1</u> (a = b k for some $k \in K_A$)

$$g\ s_B\ a = g\ s_B\ b\ k = g\ b\ s_K\ k = c\ d\ s_K\ k = s_G\ c\ d\ k$$
$$= s_G\ d\ k = s_G\ g\ a$$

<u>Case 2</u> ($a \notin b\ K$ and $s_B\ a \notin b\ K$)

$$g\ s_B\ a = s_B\ a = s_G\ a = s_G\ g\ a$$

<u>Case 3</u> ($a \notin b\ K$ but $s_B\ a = b\ k$ for some $k \in K_N$)

$$g\ s_B\ a = d\ k = s_G\ a = s_G\ g\ a$$

By definition of c and g we have g b = c d. Hence it remains to show the universal property of G. Let $f_1: B \longrightarrow G'$, $f_2: D \longrightarrow G'$ graph morphisms with $f_1\ b = f_2\ d$. In order to obtain $f\ g = f_1$ and $f\ c = f_2$ there is only one choice (which implies uniqueness) to define f:

$$f\ x = \underline{\text{if}}\ x \in D\ \underline{\text{then}}\ f_2\ x\ \underline{\text{else}}\ f_1\ x$$

It remains to show that $f: G \longrightarrow G'$ becomes a graph morphism. Similar to above we will only show $f\ s_G\ a = s_{G'}\ f\ a$ for $a \in G_A$. In the cases $a \in D_A$ resp. $a \in (B - b\ K)_A$ and $s_G\ a \in (B - b\ K)_N$ the required equation follows from the corresponding equations for the graph morphisms f_1 and f_2. In the remaining case we have $a \in B - b\ K$ and $s_G\ a \in D$. But by definition of s_G we have $s_G\ a = d\ k$ for $k \in K$ with $s_B\ a = b\ k$. Hence we have

$$f\ s_G\ a = f_2\ s_G\ a = f_2\ d\ k = f_1\ b\ k = f_1\ s_B\ a = s_{G'}\ f_1\ a = s_{G'}\ f\ a.$$

This completes the proof.

9.7 PROOF OF THEOREM 4.4

Due to Def. 3.1 the direct derivations $G \Longrightarrow H$ via p and $G \Longrightarrow H'$ via p' are given by the following pushouts

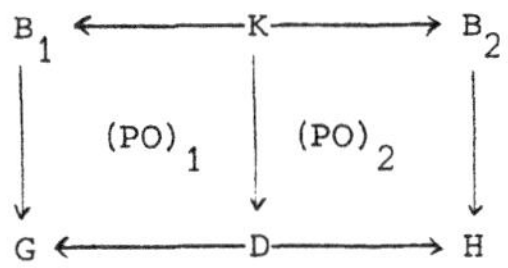

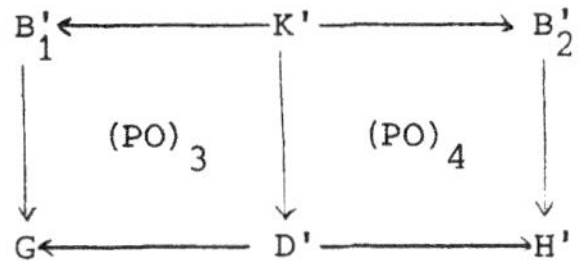

Combining $(PO)_1$ and $(PO)_3$ and using the algebraic formulation of parallel independence in Lemma 4.3 we obtain the left one of the following diagrams.

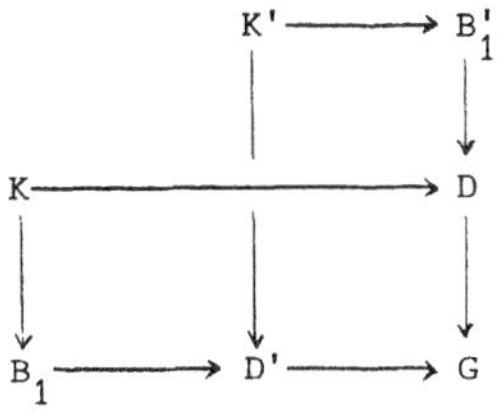

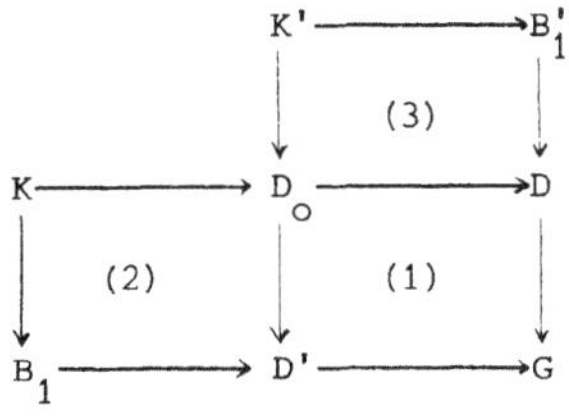

The right diagram above is obtained from the left one by constructing the pullback (1) of $D' \longrightarrow G$ and $D \longrightarrow G$ where D_o becomes the intersection of D and D'. The

universal property of the pullback (see 9.5) implies the existence of unique morphisms $K \longrightarrow D_o$ and $K' \longrightarrow D_o$ such that (2) and (3) commute and $K \longrightarrow D = K \longrightarrow D_o \longrightarrow D$, $K' \longrightarrow D' = K' \longrightarrow D_o \longrightarrow D'$. Now the pushouts $(PO)_1$ and $(PO)_3$ are decomposed by the diagrams (1) and (2) resp. (1) and (3). We will show that (1), (2) and (3) are pushouts separately:

Since $D \longrightarrow G$ and $D' \longrightarrow G$ are injective by 3.7 2) the pullback (1) is also a pushout by 9.5, and hence also (2) are (3) are pushouts by 9.4.3.

Next we will construct a similar "triple-PO-diagram" using the pushouts $(PO)_2$ and $(PO)_4$ instead of $(PO)_1$ and $(PO)_3$. That means we replace $K \longrightarrow B_1$ by $K \longrightarrow B_2$ and $K' \longrightarrow B_1'$ by $K' \longrightarrow B_2'$ in (2) and (3) and construct the pushouts (5) and (6) using the same $K \longrightarrow D_o$ and $K' \longrightarrow D_o$. Finally we construct X as pushout object in (4).

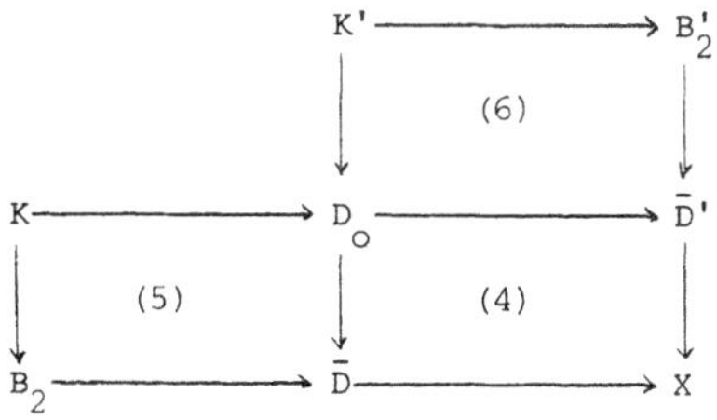

Then we observe that the pushouts $(PO)_2$ and $(PO)_4$ can be decomposed by pushout (5) resp. (6) and the decomposition of $K \longrightarrow D$ and $K' \longrightarrow D'$ shown above. The universal pushout property of (5) (resp. (6)) implies that there is $\bar{D} \longrightarrow H$ (resp. $\bar{D}' \longrightarrow H'$) such that $B_2 \longrightarrow H = B_2 \longrightarrow \bar{D} \longrightarrow H$ and diagram (7) below (resp. $B_2' \longrightarrow H' = B_2' \longrightarrow \bar{D}' \longrightarrow H'$ and (8)) commutes.

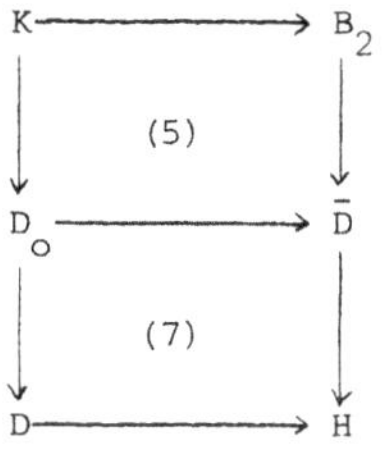

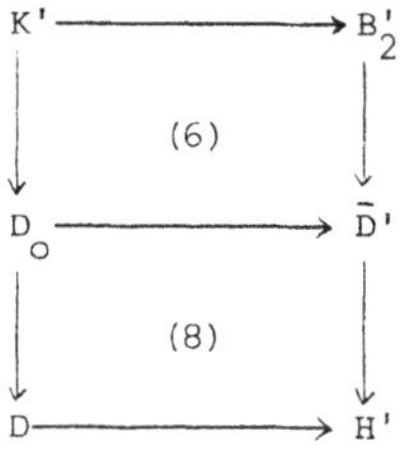

But also (7) and (8) become pushouts by Fact 9.4.2. Now we have all pushout pieces to construct the direct derivations $H \Longrightarrow X$ via p' and $H' \Longrightarrow X$ via p. In the following diagrams (3) + (7), (6) + (4), (2) + (8) and (5) + (4) are the corresponding pushouts by Fact 9.4.1.

$$
\begin{array}{ccccc}
B_1 & \longleftarrow & K' & \longrightarrow & B_2' \\
\downarrow & (3) & \downarrow & (6) & \downarrow \\
D & \longleftarrow & D_o & \longrightarrow & D' \\
\downarrow & (7) & \downarrow & (4) & \downarrow \\
H & \longleftarrow & \bar{D} & \longrightarrow & X
\end{array}
\qquad\qquad
\begin{array}{ccccc}
B_1 & \longleftarrow & K & \longrightarrow & B_2 \\
\downarrow & (2) & \downarrow & (5) & \downarrow \\
D' & \longleftarrow & D_o & \longrightarrow & \bar{D} \\
\downarrow & (8) & \downarrow & (4) & \downarrow \\
H' & \longleftarrow & \bar{D}' & \longrightarrow & X
\end{array}
$$

Finally (5) + (7) and (3) + (7) (resp. (6) + (8) and (2) + (8)) together with Lemma 4.3 imply that the sequence $G \Longrightarrow H \Longrightarrow X$ via (p,p') (resp. $G \Longrightarrow H' \Longrightarrow X$ via (p',p)) is sequentially independent. This completes the proof.

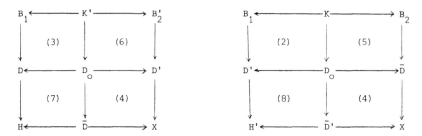

10. REFERENCES

For most of the references in this survey we have used the bibliography on graph grammars (prepared by M. Nagl). This bibliography divided into six subsections is part of this volume. These subsections are given on the following pages:

In addition we have used the following references

CT: Category Theory

/CT.Ar Ma 75/ Arbib, M.A.; Manes, E.G.: Arrows, Structures and Functors: The Categorical Imperative, Academic Press, New York, 1975

/CT.He St 73/ Herrlich, H.; Strecker G.: Category Theory, Allyn and Bacon, Rockleigh 1973

LS: L-Systems

/LS.He Rb 75/ Herman, G.T.; Rozenberg, G.: Developmental Systems and Languages, North Holland, Amsterdam, 1975

A Tutorial and Bibliographical Survey on Graph Grammars

Manfred Nagl
Universität Erlangen-Nürnberg
Lehrstuhl für Programmiersprachen
Martensstraße 3, D-852 Erlangen, Germany

ABSTRACT

In the first section we make some remarks (witout going into any details) about the main application fields of graph grammars to motivate their investigation. In section 2 and 3 we give a short and informal overview on most of the approaches for sequential and parallel graph grammars known in literature. In the last part we introduce some of the modifications and extensions enforced by several applications and give some comments on implementation of graph grammars realized so far.

1. APPLICATIONS OF GRAPH GRAMMARS

Picture and graph grammars have been introduced first for *picture processing* problems e.g. for the recognition of chromosomes, handprinted letters, bubble and fog chamber pictures of elementary particle physics (see part PA of the bibliography for references corresponding to "grammatical" or "linguistic" pattern recognition). In these fields there is no alternative to automatic picture processing. For bubble and fog chamber pictures we have no finite number of picture classes such that any picture can be related to one of these classes. Any point of a picture can be the origin of a subpicture if a disintegration takes place there. On the other hand it is possible to state recursive rules saying how subpictures are generated and how they are connected. Thus, for any class of such pictures one can give a finite set of rules, i.e. a picture grammar. A part of the picture processing problem is reduced to the problem of syntax analysis of the description of the picture by means of a picture grammar. The advantage of this method is that in the case of success of the syntax analysis one has not only a yes-no-decision but a description of the structure of the considered picture.
A picture can be described by listing its subpictures and the geometric relations between them as "is right of", "is below of", "lies within", "is connected with" etc. If we introduce for any occurrence of a subpicture a node which is labelled with the subpicture itself and if two nodes are connected by an edge, the label of which expresses a geometric relation iff the corresponding subpictures satisfy this relation,

then we get a graph with labelled nodes and edges. This graph is a description of the underlying picture and it trivially depends on the choice of primitive pictures (which are not decomposable) and geometric relations. For our picture processing problem the choice of primitive pictures correcponds directly to the capability of the available pattern recognition device.
A production of the above picture grammar replaces a subpicture of a picture by another one, more precisely: it replaces descriptions of subpictures. If we take labelled graphs for the description then a rule of the grammar replaces a subgraph by a subgraph.Thus, an important part of the problem of grammatical picture processing consists of developing a suitable graph grammar for a given class of pictures.

Since there are graphical and interactive I/O-devices for computers the question arises whether the linear notation of an algorithm by a well-formed string, i.e. a program of one of the common programming languages, is adequate to the structure of human thinking. Does this notation support the nonalgorithmic, i.e. the generative part of the development of an algorithm or can the idea of an algorithm easier be developed if one uses two-dimensional programming aids as flow-diagrams, block-diagrams, networks maps, Nassy-Shneiderman diagrams etc? The latter is important especially for nonnumeric applications with complex data structures, as these can also be graphically described. Thus one wishes to have a *two-dimensional programming language* (cf. /AP.Ch68/, /AP.DeFrSt75/, /AP.SuMaTo76/), i.e. a language which allows to program with the aid of pictures. As described above, pictures can be formalized by labelled graphs. In this case the edges rather correspond to control flow or access path than to geometrical relations. Now, for flow diagrams, block-diagrams, network maps, etc. either a graph grammar can easily be found generating all those which are correctly built up. This grammar can be used to direct the generation process, i.e. the programmer chooses the next rule to be applied from a given finite set of rules. In this manner only syntactically correct diagrams or maps can be generated. Furthermore, syntax analysis is no problem here, because the syntax tree can be stored within the generation process. The principles of modern software methodology as structured programming, stepwise refinement, modularity, etc. directly influence the shape of the generating grammar. Software experts state that most of the problems of developing algorithms arise in the design phase, i.e. before any kind of code is generated. A program or data structure denoted as a graph is some kind of code too but a code nearer to the imagination of the programmer. This is already shown by the fact that most programmers draw pictures during the design of a nontrivial piece of software.

Even if algorithms are denoted in the usual way, i.e. by programs written in common programming languages, graphs can be used to represent their logical structure. This formal model, in the sequel named program graph, has shown to be helpful for several aspect concerning theory, application, or even implementation. We want to illustrate this with some examples:

If the *semantics* of a program is to be defined *operationally*, a program graph is some kind of an abstract program notation which directly expresses syntactic as well as semantic relations. These relations cannot be directly explicated in the usual notation of a program. The specification of an operational semantics consists of the specification of an interpreter for those program graphs, which is nothing else that a graph rewriting system. Examples for this proceeding the reader can find in /GT.LuWa69/, /GT.We72/, /GT.Cu73/, /AP.Pr73/, /AP.Ra75/, /AP.Pr76/, /AP.CuFa77/, /AP.Bu78/.
To reduce the expenditure of compilation many compilers generate intermediate code today. This intermediate code can also be regarded as a graph which partly possesses the structure of a tree. Assuming this graph notation, problems of *data flow analysis* like evaluation of common subexpressions, evaluation of independent and thus parallely executable program parts, loop optimization, etc. can be precisely formulated and clearly expressed. *Code optimizing* compiling techniques can also be explicated better starting with a program graph. References for these applications are /AP.Ul73/, /AP.FaKeZu76/, /AP.Br77/ and /AP.SgSmWa77/.

Incremental or conversational *compilers* can be characterized by the following two properties: They immediately translate any input of a program increment and, furthermore, whenever a program was changed only a more less large piece containing the altered increment is recompiled. In /AP.Bu74/, /AP.Sc74/ it was shown advantageous to regard an intermediate form of the program as a graph, as the implication of a local program change on the whole program can easier be surveyed there. This program graph can be imagined as the intermediate code of above together with various references which, in a usual compiler, are stored in several lists. A change of the linear notation of the program by inserting, deleting or substituting an increment corresponds to a change of this program graph which can either be described as subgraph replacement. Even the second step of compilation, namely from this extended intermediate graph to machine code can be formalized by the use of subgraph rewriting (cf. /AP.BrBuNa77/). It should be mentioned that in the papers cited above the increments are oriented at the syntax of the underlying programming language such that the idea there is a combination of incremental compiling and syntax-directed programming.

Data bases are another application field of graph rewriting. Here the problem arises to specify the admissable structures of the data on a logical, non-physical level. For this the name data base schema is used. Graph grammars can be used for this specification (cf. /AP.EhMü74/, /AP.GoFur74/, /AP.FurMy75/, /AP.DeGh76/, /AP.Fr76/, /AP.Sc76/, /AP.NePa77/, /AP.EhKr78/, /AP.We78a/) .This is not surprising as graphs are used for schema characterization within hierarchical as well as network models.

Furthermore, there are more or less complex operations on a data base*) which have to be consistent with it, i.e.consistent with the corresponding schema. These operations can clearly and simply be formulated using subgraph replacement operations (/AP.Ea 71/, /AP.Sc76/, /AP.We78a/).
Exactly the same view of regarding data structures and their operations as an undivisible unit is the idea of *abstract data types*. Here graph rewriting can be used as a tool to specify the operations on an operational but rather abstract level (cf. /AP.Ra77/, /AP.EhKrPa78/, /AP.We78a/).
Even questions like commutativity , efficiency, and completeness of operations on *data structures in general* can be expressed adequately by the use of graph rewriting (cf. /AP.EhKr67a/, /AP.EhRo76/, /APEhRo77/, /AP.SeFur77/).

A further application of graph grammars can be found in *graph theory*.In the same way as a graph class can be characterized by inherent properties one could characterize this class by explicitly determining a graph grammar exactly generating this class. Interesting examples for that proceeding the reader can find in /GG.Mo70/, /GG.Pa72/, /GG.AbMiToTa73/, and /GG.Na74/.

Aside of the spectrum of applications regarded above lies the *development description* of simple organisms with the aid of graph grammars. Graphs can serve as a simple and precise description of the development state: The nodes of the graph correspond to cells, the different types of which are characterized by different node labels, the labelled and directed edges express biological and geometrical relations between cells. In the applications regarded above only one subgraph is replaced by another one, the rest remains unchanged. This kind of local graph rewriting we call sequential, the corresponding generative devices sequential graph rewriting systems or (sequential) graph grammars. In the development description application, however, changes and segmentations of cells take place simultaneously in the whole organism. Thus, the rewriting mechanisms for the describing graph must also be parallel, i.e. we get a nonlocal kind of graph rewriting here. The corresponding generating systems we call parallel graph rewriting systems or, synonymously, parallel graph grammars or graph L-systems, because they are a generalization of L-systems (over strings) to graphs. References for parallel rewriting and development specification are /GL.CaGrPa74/, /GL.CuLi74/, /GL.Ma74/, /GL.Na75/, /GL.CuLi76/, /GL.EhKr76/, /GL.Na76b/, and /GL.LiCu77/. The advantage of graph L-systems compared to usual L-systems is that they can model arbitrary "regular" organisms, while the latter ones are restricted to filamentous ones.

---

*) instructions of the data manipulation language as well as complex application routines using DML operations

Common to an applications we have regarded up till now (the above list of applications is not complete, some further examples are mentioned in the following paper of H. Ehrig) is the idea that *graphs* are able to *describe* structures of different fields in an *elucid* and in the same way precise way. Substructures always correspond to nodes which are labelled to say which substructure they represent, whereas directed and labelled edges express different relations beween substructures or the decomposition of substructures into further and simpler ones. Clearly, the decomposition of a structure into substructures and relations depends on the applications field and the actual problem. (Remember the pattern recognition application, where nodes usually represent primitive pictures, i.e. pictures recognizable by the underlying picture processing hardware. If a more "intelligent" hardware is chosen then the structure decomposition can be "rougher"). This includes the questions which substructures are selected, in how many levels the decomposition is realized and which relations are taken. If those decomposition parameters are layed down the translation of a structure into its describing graph and vice versa is usually no problem. Thus the modelling graph rewriting systems directly reflect the complexity of a problem at hand.

Most of the above examples correspond to local graph changes: one subgraph is replaced by another one, the rest remains unchanged. Furthermore, one has to determine how the inserted graph is embedded into the restgraph, i.e. host graph minus replaced subgraph. Above we have called this rewriting mechanism *sequential* and the corresponding generative devices sequential graph rewriting systems or (sequential) graph grammars. The various approaches to graph grammars known in literature differ mainly in the way how the *embedding transformation* is defined (cf. section 2). This embedding transformation usually is an algorithmic specification and its result in general depends on the embedding of the subgraph to be replaced. On the other hand, this embedding transformation should be applicable to any host graph which contains the subgraph to be replaced. In the biological example above, however, the whole graph is changed in one derivation step. This can be formalized by *parallel* graph rewriting: There is a partition of the underlying graph into subgraphs which are simultaneously replaced. Additionally, we have to determine here how these parallelly substituted graphs are connected. Analogously to sequential rewriting the definition of the *connection transformation* is the main criterion between the different approaches to parallel rewriting systems (cf. section 3). Special cases of parallel rewriting with respect to the complexity of the substituted graphs are *node substitution* or *edge substitution*. In the first case all single nodes are simultaneously rewritten by graphs which are joined according to the result of the connection transformation, in the second case we assume a covering of the host graph by edges (handles) which are replaced in parallel where all graphs corresponding to a node (which may be source or target of several edges) are glued together. A special case of parallel rewriting with respect to the degree of parallelism is *mixed* rewriting where more than one subgraph of the host graph is replaced in a derivation step but (as in sequential rewriting) there are invariant parts of the host graph too. The reader may have recognized that the author prefers the term (sequential, parallel or else) *graph rewriting system* instead of (sequential, parallel or else) graph grammar. The reason is that in many applications it is only the graph rewriting mechanis that is the point of interest and not the generative aspect of a grammar which starts with one or more axiom graphs, generates infinitely long or infinitely many derivation sequences where some or all graphs are regarded to belong to the language of the grammar. On the other hand, the denotation "graph grammar" is so suggestive and wide-spread that it can hardly be altered.

There are some other survey papers on graph grammars (see section OV of the following bibliography). The emphasis of this article is to give at least a vague idea of *most* of the different approaches to sequential and parallel graph grammars. Within the limited lenght an introductory survey should have this results in an *informal* way of *presentation:* We rather give an example for each approach characterizing the specific idea than formal and precise definitions.
At this time the theoretical results on graph grammars are far away from a state where a comprehensive theory includes and classifies all the different approaches and their theoretical results. That does not mean that there are no theoretical results in this field. If the reader takes into account that this topic is rather new (about nine years) and that only a rather small group of researchers worked in it then the wealth of results is quite remarkable. On the other hand there are plenty of open questions waiting for being tackled. This is especially true if one regards that most of the results of the well-developed theory of formal languages (on strings) can be examined whether they hold true in the graph case as well. Most of the papers in the graph grammar field only deal with one approach and the theoretical results following from the fundamental definitions. That is the reason for the lack of a uniform theory. A rather developed subtheory is formed by the categorical approaches, named algebraic graph grammar theory, which is in a tutorial manner presented by the next paper of this volume. Furthermore, in /GG.Na78/ a rather extensive presentation of nonalgebraic graph grammar theory is given which, however, also mainly summarizes the results of one approach. This workshop is intended to be the base of a fruitful mutual exchange of ideas on graph grammars which might possibly yield a uniform graph grammar theory in the near future.
Besides graph grammars there is another approach for the generalization of string rewriting systems: *array grammars*. The underlying structures called arrays are labelled grids, i.e. labellings of $\mathbb{Z}^2$. They are not considered in the following. Nevertheless, the bibliography contains in section AR most of the relevant refe-

rences. (Array grammars and other kinds of generalizations of string grammars are reviewed in /OV.Rf76/). Array grammars can be understood as graph grammars with two edge labels for the geometric relations "is right of " and "is below of". The problem here, however, is that each rewriting step must produce a graph representing a rectangular grid structure again.
In the next sections we give examples for the various approches to graph rewriting systems. Applications are not further investigated although a rather big part of the graph grammar activities now is devoted to application studies (cf. e.g. /AP.BaFur78/, /AP.BrBuNa77/, /AP.CuFa77/, /AP.DeGh67/, /AP.EhKr78/, /AP.EhKrPa78/, /AP.EhRo78/, /AP.FurMy75/, /AP.GoFur74/, /AP.Gö78/. /AP.Pr76/, /AP.Ra77/, /AP.Sc75/, /AP.Sc76/, /AP.We78b/). So some of the papers on graph grammars with emphasis on the application aspect, which introduced only slight modifications of other graph grammar approaches, are not mentioned in the sequel. However, the bibliography gives plenty of references (collected in section AP, and for linguistic pattern recognition in section PA). Hopefully, the development of the above mentioned spectrum of applications (and of those not mentioned here) promotes the theory of graph grammars and vice versa as it has been in the case of programming languages, especially their syntactical notation and parsing, and formal languages' theory. Finally, the author should remark that the following lists of approaches is far away from being complete even if application papers are excluded. The bibliography, however, should be complete.

2. SURVEY ON SEQUENTIAL GRAPH REWRITING SYSTEMS (GRAPH GRAMMARS)

Within a sequential rewriting step, i.e. a direct derivation step of a (sequential) graph grammar, one subgraph of a host graph is replaced by another one. As already mentioned the main problem hereby is the specification how to embed the inserted graph into the restgraph. Thus, differently from grammars on strings a *graph production* is a triple $p = (g_l, g_r, E)$ with g_l being the subgraph to be replaced *(left hand side)*, g_r being the graph which is inserted for it *(right hand side)* and E being the *embedding transformation*. The embedding transformation is the main criterion between the different graph grammar approaches and thus a big part of the following section is devoted to illustrate how this embedding transformation is differently defined by different authors.
The first papers on graph grammars have been written independently and nearly at the same time by PFALTZ/ROSENFELD /GG.PfRf69/ and SCHNEIDER /GG.Sc70/. The rapid growth of the graph grammar discipline, especially if graph grammars are understood as graph rewriting systems of arbitrary kind as we will do here, the reader can draw from the bibliography. In the sequel we roughly follow the chronological order, grouping however related papers together.

In PFALTZ/ROSENFELD /GG.PfRf69/ the embedding transformation and therefore the rewriting mechanism remains verbal, i.e. *informal*. Thus the embedding transformation is formulated like:"All edges which go into the node with label A of the left hand side are to go into the node with label B of the right hand side". May be it was this imperfection that /GG.PfRf69/ was the origin of a series of papers as e.g. /GG. Mo70/, /AP.Pr71/, /GG.RfMi72b/, /GG.AbMiToTa73/, /GG.Na73a/, /GG.BrFu74/. The underlying structures of /GG.PfRf69/ are not labelled graphs in general as indicated in the first section, but so-called *webs*. Webs are undirected graphs with node labels but without edge labels, i.e. with only one kind of (undirected) edges. The ideas of this paper, however, are easily generated to arbitrary labelled graphs as some of the subsequent papers do. In /GG.PfRf69/ many of the ideas of graph grammar research already arise which are studied in detail in later papers. That concerns the following three topics: 1.) Application of graph grammars to graph theory: For some classes of graphs as trees, forests, and transport networks web grammars are given the languages of which are exactly these graph classes. 2.) This paper is the starting point of the idea to generalize definitions from the theory of formal languages (on strings) and to check whether analogous results hold true in the graph case. This, especially, means the question of relations between different classes of graph languages generated by grammars which are successively restricted from a general form, i.e. a generalization of the CHOMSKY theory. 3.) We can find in this paper the proposal to extend productions by application conditions, which means, that a production cannot always be applied whenever the left hand side is found in the host graph but only if additionally the application condition of the production holds true for the host graph. Application conditions remain informal too in this paper. This is however true also for some later papers which take up this idea again.

The first *formal* definition of the embedding problem is due to SCHNEIDER (cf. /GG. Sc70/ and a later version in /GG.Sc71/). These papers are dealing with grammars on arbitrary labelled graphs which, however, are called n-diagrams and the corresponding grammars *n-diagram grammars* respectively. The reason for that is, that for edge labels not an arbitrary label alphabet as for node labels is assumed, but only integers in an interval from 1 to n. This difference is formally negligible as the integers from 1 to n can either be understood as an abbreviation of a label from an arbitrary finite alphabet of labels. A n-diagram is a tuple $G=(K,\varrho_1,\dots,\varrho_n,\beta)$ with K being the node set, $\varrho_i \subseteq K\times K$ the directed and labelled edges with label i, and β: $K\to \Sigma_V$ a labelling function from K into the node label alphabet Σ_V. Let $g_l \subseteq g$, i.e. g_l is a subdiagram of g,g_l being the left hand side of a production $p=(g_l,g_r,E)$, and let $In_i(g_l,g)$, $Out_i(g_l,g)$ be the set of all edges with label i going into g_l from $g-g_l$ or going out of g_l into $g-g_l$. The embedding transformation E is defined in /GG.Sc70/ as a 2n-tuple $(\pi_{-n},\dots,\pi_{-1},\pi_1,\dots,\pi_n)$

with π_{-i}, π_i either being a *relation* between the node sets K_l and K_r, i.e. $\pi_{-i} \subseteq K_l \times K_r$, $\pi_i \subseteq K_l \times K_r$, $1 \le i \le n$. The graph g' which is a direct derivation of g is defined as $(g-g_l) \cup g_r$ *) plus the following embedding edges

$$In_i(g_r,g') := \pi_{-i} \circ In_i(g_l,g)$$
$$Out_i(g_r,g') := Out_i(g_l,g) \circ \pi_i^{-1},$$

where "$\circ$" is the common composition of relations, here to be read from right to left. In Fig. 1 a host 2-diagram is given which is derived to g' by applying the production p. Nodes are drawn as circles with denotation outside and label inside the circle. From Fig. 1 we can see that this type of embedding tansformation allows a splitting or, conversely, a contraction of edges. (For the first see the incoming edge with label 1 to node 1 which is split into two 1-labelled edges into node 3 and 4 in g' while the 2-labelled edges of g are contracted to one edge in g'.)

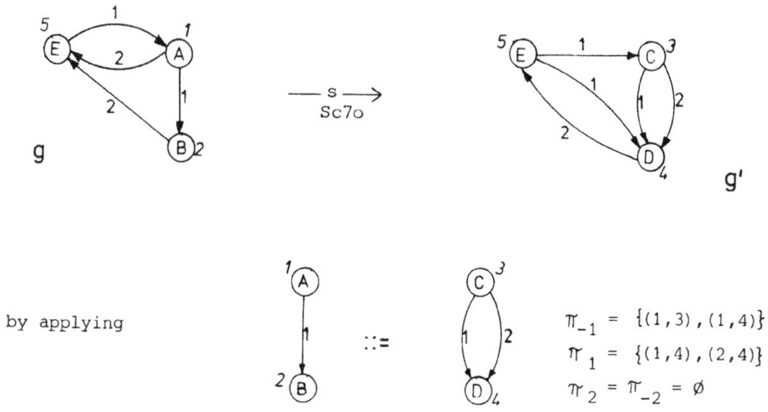

Fig.1

The reader immediately recognizes the simplicity of this approach. Equivalence classes of n-diagrams are defined as sets of n-diagrams having all exactly the same structure and differing only in the denotations for nodes, and direct derivation between classes is defined by the existence of direct derivable representatives. A n-diagram grammar is defined as a tuple consisting of a node label alphabet, Σ_v, a terminal node label alphabet, Δ_v, a finite set of productions of the above form and an axiom graph. The language of a grammar consists of all n-diagram equivalence classes with only terminal node labels derivable from the axiom class in an arbitrary but finite number of steps.

In /GG.Sc70/, /GG.Sc71/, the relations ϱ_i of each n-diagram are assumed to be *partial orderings.* **) However, this restriction has no influence on the definition

*) The node set of g_r is assumed to be disjoint with the node set of $g-g_l$.

**) This is motivated by the fact that n-diagrams have been introduced to describe geometrical structures in which relations can be assumed to be partial orderings.

of direct derivation. The result g' of such a direct sequential derivation step $g \xrightarrow{s} g'$ in general is not a n-diagram with partial orderings. In /GG.Sc72/
Sc70
necessary and sufficient conditions for productions are given such that any derivation step preserves partial orderings.
Besides a formal introduction of graph grammars the emphasis of /GG.Sc70/ is the investigation of a restricted type of grammar which is called *1-regular grammar:* The underlying structures only have one edge label (1-diagrams) and the productions are restricted in the following sense: a) The left hand side consists of a single (nonterminally labelled) node, the right hand side is a graph which has a unique maximum node (i.e. any other node of the right hand side is predecessor of this node). b) There is at most one nonterminal node within the right hand side which is the maximum node if it exists. c) The embedding transformation is built up in the way that whenever an embedding edge is to go into a node k of the right hand side, then all nodes which are successors of k have an incoming edge too. In /GG.Sc70/, /GG.Sc71/ several results are given characterizing this restricted type of grammar, especially a normal form theorem, saying, that for any 1-regular grammar an equivalent one exists, i.e. a grammar generating exactly the same language, each right hand sides of which is a primitive prefix of a graphical notation of the corresponding production as a graph (cf. Fig. 16 of section 4). That says that the productions cannot be further simplified.
/GG.Sc70/ was the origin of a series of papers on graph grammars, including algebraic graph grammar papers but also of the papers of the author.

Like /GG.PfRf69/ the paper of MONTANARI /GG.Mo70/ also deals with webs, i.e. undirected graphs with node labels but without edge labels. The embedding transformation is informal as in /GG.PfRf69/. A special case which is called *normal* is defined formally. It results in a manipulation of the embedding in the following way: For each left hand side node having embedding edges exactly one corresponding node of the right hand side is specified which after the rewriting step has exactly the same embedding edges. *) A production furthermore includes an *application condition* AC which is also informal. This condition is to be interpreted that the production can only be applied if the left hand side is contained in the host graph and AC applied to the host graph holds true. **) For embedding transformations and application conditions any recursive functions or predicates can be imagined.

---

*) In the π-approach of /GG.Sc70/ of above this means that the relations π_{-i}, π_i are one-to-one mappings.

**) In /GG.Mo70/ furthermore the possibility of *negative* application conditions is indicated. This means that the derivation step can be carried out only if some structure does not exist in the host graph.

All examples used in /GG.Mo70/, however, suggest that embedding transformations and application conditions were meant to be restricted to the direct neighbourhood of the replaced subgraph. Finally, in /GG.Mo70/ a grammar starts with a finite set of axiom graphs which, however, usually can be traced back to a single axiom graph.

Besides the languages L(G) of a grammar G which is defined as usual, /GG.Mo70/ regards *indirectly* generated sets of graphs which means the following: Let $\Delta_M \subseteq \Delta_V$ be a subset of the terminal node label alphabet. A set L of webs with node labels only from Δ_M is called to be indirectly generated by G iff any element of L is a subweb of an element g of L(G) and, furthermore, in any graph occuring in the derivation of g the number of node label symbols from $\Sigma_V - \Delta_M$ is restricted by a boundary which only depends on the number of symbols of Δ_M occuring in g.

The main part of /GG.Mo70/ is devoted to the graph theory application of graph grammars: For *various* classes of graphs the author gives *web grammars* which directly or indirectly generate these classes, e.g. for the classes of all nonseparable graphs, connected and separable graphs, planar graphs, nonseparable and planar graphs. In all these grammar examples no application conditions are used, i.e. all application conditions are either the trivial and constant condition true.

The paper of ABE/MIZUMOTO/TOYOTA/TANAKA /GG.AbMiToTa73/ is a straight continuation of /GG.Mo70/ and,therefore,also devoted to the graph theory application of web grammars. The embedding transformation is formally defined and turns out to be a restriction of the π-approach in /GG.Sc70/. *) Furthermore, grammars of embedding type normal and indirectly generated graph languages both in the sense of /GG.Mo70/ are investigated. The article contains web grammars for all Eulerian graphs and for all triple connected graphs. The embedding transformations of /GG.Sc70/, the normal embedding transformation of /GG.Mo70/ and those of /GG.AbMiToTa73/ are subclasses of a more general concept of /GG.Na73a/ introduced below.

In ROSENFELD/MILGRAM /GG.RfMi72b/ the underlying structures to be modelled are also webs which, however, in this case are loop-free and connected. The embedding transformation of any production is formally defined as a *function* $\Phi : K_l \times K_r \to 2^{\Sigma_V}$, Σ_V being the labelling alphabet for nodes, K_l and K_r the node sets of g_l and g_r respectively. A graph g' is the direct derivation of g by applying $p=(g_l, g_r, E)$ iff

RfMi.1) $g_l \subseteq g$, $g_r \subseteq g'$, $g - g_l = g' - g_r$ (as usual).

.2) For any $k \in K_l$ either all labels of neighbours in $g - g_l$ are in $\Phi(k,k')$ for some $k' \in K_r$ or the production is not applicable.

---

*) We do not mean the restriction due to the application of webs instead of arbitrary labelled graphs.

.3) For all $k_1, k_2 \varepsilon K_1$ and $k' \varepsilon K_r$ the following condition holds true:
Any neighbour of k_1 in $g - g_1$ labelled with a symbol from $\Phi(k_1,k') \cap \Phi(k_2,k')$ is also a neighbour of k_2 or the production is not applicable.

.4) If (2) and (3) hold true then g' has the following form: $g'=(g-g_1) \cap g_r$ and furthermore the following embedding edges for g_r: If $\Phi(k,k')=U$ then k' has in g' the same embedding edges as k in g, provided all neighbour node labels of k in $g-g_1$ are contained in U.

The application conditions .2) and .3) are *global* conditions in contrast to the application conditions mentioned above which are parts of productions and, therefore, can be different for different productions. Application conditions .3) can be illustrated by the following figure. Let $v' \varepsilon \Phi(k_1,k') \cap \Phi(k_2,k')$, then it is

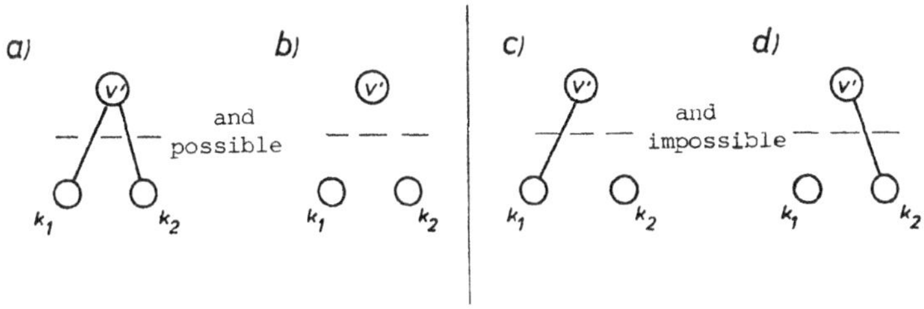

Fig. 2

Because of .2) and the exclusive use of connected graphs within productions and axiom graph it easily follows that all graphs derivable within a grammar are connected too. Let p^{-1} for $p=(g_1,g_r,\Phi)$ be defined as $p^{-1}:=(g_r,g_1,\Phi^{-1})$ where $\Phi^{-1}: K_r \times K_1 \rightarrow 2^{\Sigma_v}$ is defined by $\Phi^{-1}(k',k) = \Phi(k,k')$ for all $(k,k') \in K_1 \times K_r$. The production p^{-1} is called *inverse* production. Let $g \xrightarrow[RfMi]{s} g'$ by applying p then $g' \xrightarrow[RfMi]{s} g$ by applying p^{-1}. Now application condition .3) becomes intelligible: Assume condition .3) were false and let p be a production contracting two nodes of the left hand side to one node of the right hand side. Then application of p followed by p^{-1} would yield a situation like Fig. 2.c, or d, starting with situation of Fig. 2.a), i.e. the application of pp^{-1} does not yield the original state.

In /GG.RfMi72b/ the recognition of graph languages by *graph acceptors* is studied. A graph acceptor is an automaton with a finite number of states, one initial state q_I, one final state q_F and a rather complex transition function which-roughly sketched - allows the following transitions:

- Depending on the state q of the automation, the label A of the node k which is actually scanned by the automaton and the existence of a certain label C on a neighbour node k" the automaton changes its state, prints a new label on k and moves to k". If the neighbour label does not exist the move to the neighbour node is omitted.
- Depending on the state q, the label of the actual node, and the existence of a certain neighbour label the automaton can melt the two nodes, print a new label

on the new node and go into another state.

Depending on the state of the automaton and the label of the actual node k the automaton can split this node into two nodes k' and k" which are connected by an (undirected) edge, label these nodes and connect them with the environment of k. Depending on the labels of the environment nodes the connection is established to k' or k". The automaton changes its state, now having its input device above of k'.

A graph is *accepted* iff the automaton ends up in q_F after a finite number of states starting in state q_I on an arbitrary node of g. In the main theorem of /GG.RfMi72b/ it is claimed that for any graph grammar G in the above sense there is a graph acceptor which exactly accepts L(G) and, conversely, that for any graph acceptor there is a graph grammar the language of which is exactly the set of all graphs accepted by the automaton. The first assertion is shown by using inverse productions until the converse derivation process ends up with the axiom graph. The application of inverse productions can either be simulated by a sequence of transitions of a graph acceptor. The second direction of the proof is shown by generating symmetric graphs of the form g–○–g, g being an arbitrary graph which is connected with its duplicate along two edges. One of these graphs is used to behave as working graph of the automaton, the other one remains unchanged. The steps of the automaton are simulated as direct derivation steps of the graph grammar. Whenever the automaton reaches its final state the working graph and the additional connection node are erased. So, the grammar comes to a terminal graph iff the other duplicate is accepted by the automaton .

Two highly interesting papers dealing with special rewriting mechanisms are the works of PAVLIDIS /GG.Pa72/ and MYLOPOULOS /GG.My72/. While the first one is devoted to the graph theory application the latter one investigates the relations beween grammars and recognizing automata. The underlying structures of both are closely related to the NAPEs proposed by FEDER /PA.Fe71/. Because of the limited place for this article both papers are not further reported here.

The different approaches discussed so far have been collected and generalized by NAGL /GG.Na73a/ and /GG.Na74/. The approach given there is especially a formalization of /GG.PfRf69/ and subsequent papers and a generalization of /GG.PfRf69/ and /GG.Sc70/. It deals with arbitrary graphs with labels on nodes and edges. We introduce this approach here by the following example of Fig. 3.

The embedding transformation of a production can explicity state those nodes of the right hand side where an incoming edge is to point or where an outgoing edge is originating from. The other node cannot be specified explicitly, as it depends on the host graph. However, we can determine *expressions* within embedding transformations which, applied to nodes of the left hand side, yield nodes within the restgraph which act as source and targetnodes of incoming and outgoing edges respectively. The embedding transformation of a production $p=(g_l,g_r,E)$ consists of 2n components $l_i,r_i,1\le i\le n$, if n is the cardinality of the edge label alphabet, because of the two possible directions for any embedding edge: l_i for example yields the incoming edges of label i, r_j the outgoing edges of label j. Production p of Fig. 3 applied to graph g yields graph g'. Within l_a , a any edge label, after the semicolon the explicit (target) nodes are specified, while the explicit (source) nodes within r_a are written ahaed of the semicolon.

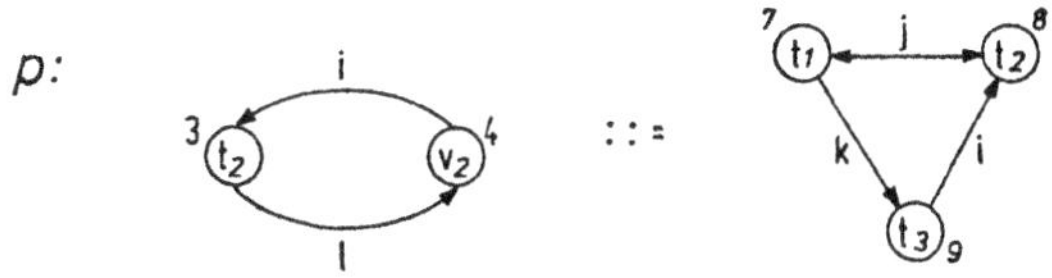

E: $l_i = (t_3 L_l R_j (3);7,8)$

$l_j = (v_3 t_1 I(4);9)$

$r_j = (7;R_j \cup L_l L_l (4,3))$

$r_k = (8;\complement R_k R_j (3))$

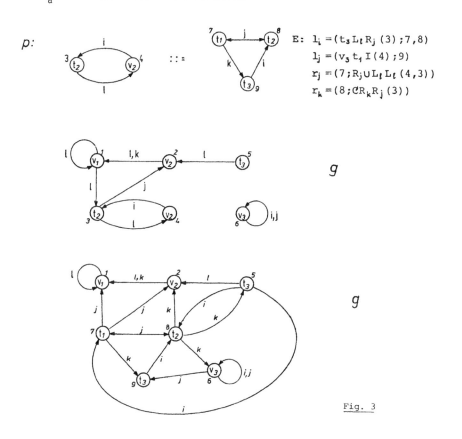

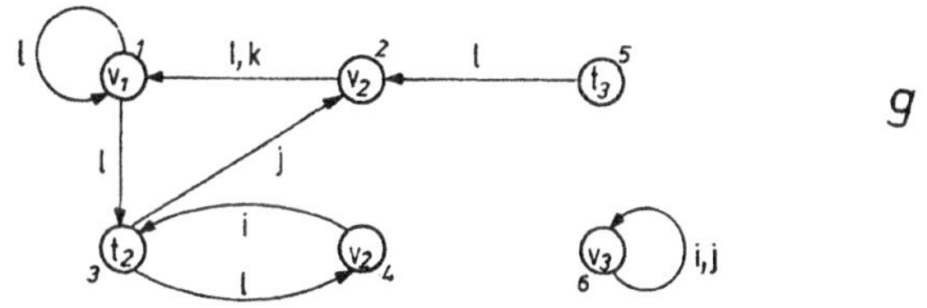

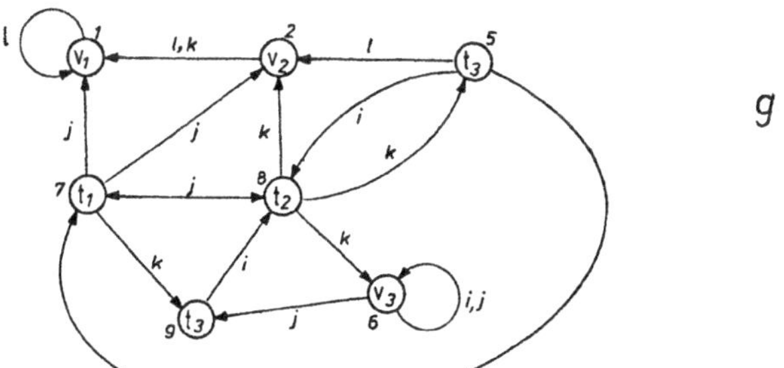

Fig. 3

So, $l_i = (t_3L_lR_j(3);7,8)$ e.g. is to be read as: Starting from node 3 of the left hand side go along an outgoing edge with label j and then along an incoming edge with label l and take only those nodes from the result the label of which is t_3. These nodes are source nodes of i-labelled edges ending in nodes 7,8 of the right hand side. The component $r_j = (7;R_j \cup L_lL_l(4,3))$ must be interpreted as: Edges with label j are to go out from node 7 of g_r to nodes determined by $R_j \cup L_lL_l(4,3)$, which must be read as: Starting from node 3 or 4 of g_l go along a chain of two incoming edges with label l or one outgoing edge with label j. For g of Fig. 3 this results in node 1 and 2. The last component specifies that outgoing edges with label k originate in node 8 of g_r and go to all nodes which cannot be reached by a chain of two outgoing edges with label j and k respectively, i.e. $\mathcal{C}$ is a component operator. Finally $l_j=(v_3t_1{}^I(4);9)$ makes use of the special operator I which yields all nodes outside the replaced subgraph *) such that $v_3t_1I(4)$ yields nodes 5 and 6. In contrast to the approaches mentioned above this approach is very powerful with respect to the manipulation of embeddings within one direct derivation step, which can already bee seen by the above example. This is due to the use of arbitrarily complex expressions which especially allow the usual set operations for nodes, the following of chains, and a selection due to node labels. These expressions are formally defined in /GG.Na73a/.

In /GG.Na73b/, /GG.Na74/, /GG.Na76/, and /GG.Na78/ a classification of productions is introduced by succesively *restricting* the form of *left and right hand sides* ranging from unrestricted over monotone (corresponding to the number of nodes), context sensitive, context free, context free in normal form, linear, regular, and regular in normal form, all being (more or less natural) extensions of the corresponding definitions in the string case. Together with two nontrivial results which have been supplied by LEVY/YUEH /GG.LeYu77/ a complete classification theory is given in /GG.Na78/ with the following hierarchy of classes of graph languages:

Na.1) $EG = UG \supset MG = CSG = CFG = CFNG \supset LG = RG = RNG$, where $EG, UG, \ldots, RNG$ are the classes of graph languages which are recursive enumerable, unrestricted,..., regular in normal form, and with the two inclusions being proper. The surprising result that the classes MG, CSG, CFG, and $CFNG$ collapse, despite of the difference in the complexity of left and right sides of corresponding grammars, is due to the fact that in all of the above classes the embedding transformation is unrestricted such that a specialization of the form of left and right hand sides can be neutralized by the complex expression mechanisms of this approach.

Another classification scheme by succesively *restricting* the complexity of *embedding transformations* (which is orthogonal to the above hierarchy) was formally introduced in /GG.Na73b/, /GG.Na74/ and extended in /GG.Na78/ ranging from "unrestricted" (with respect to the embedding transformation), over "orientation and label preserving" (olp) or alternatively over "depth1", then over "simple", "elementary", "analogous" to "invariant". Hereby "olp" means that embedding edges are not changed corresponding to orientation and label of the edge such that the outside node of the embedding edge can only be shifted to another node, whereas "depth1" means that expressions are restricted such that they only reach direct neighbours. Furthermore, "simple" stands for "olp" and "depth1", whereas "elementary" furthermore forbids the use of node selection by label within expressions. The π-approach of /GG.Sc70/ exactly corresponds to graph grammars of embedding type "elementary".

---

*) I can be built up by elementary expressions and the complement.

In embedding transformations of type "analogous" all edges of either orientation and label are treatet equally which is a restriction of "elementary" where different components are independent. Finally in "invariant" embedding transformations some nodes of the left and right hand side correspond one-to-one to each other, taking over the embedding edges without change. That is related to the normal productions of /GG.Mo70/ if one ignores the fact that the latter is restricted to webs. Regarding both hierarchies namely due to restrictions of left and right hand sides and due to embedding transformations a great number of language classes results, which is only partly investigated. For context free, linear and regular the above embedding hierarchy is developed (cf. /GG.Na73b/, /GG.Na74/, /GG.Na78/) which, however, is too complex even to be cited here. From now on we can classify the following approaches in the terminology of the above embedding hierarchy as, with respect to the embedding transformation, all graph grammar approaches can be regarded as subclasses of the expression approach.

The article of BRAYER/Fu /GG.BrFu74/ also belongs to the papers initiated by /GG.PfRf69/; it can be regarded as a subsequent paper of /GG.RfMi72b/. The underlying structures are not webs but arbitrary graphs which, however, are assumed to be loop-free and free of multiple edges between two nodes. The derivation process is a slight generalization of /GG.RfMi72b/ being below depthl of the above embedding hierarchy. Embedding edges can be reversed but not relabelled. Furthermore, an application condition is introduced which corresponds to RfMi.2) of above, but also is a generalization of it due to the application of different edge labels here. The embedding transformation is a function Φ: $K_1 \times K_r \rightarrow 2^{\Sigma_E \times \Sigma_V \times \Sigma_E}$ with Σ_V, Σ_E being the node and edge label alphabet respectively (cf. the above passage on /GG.RfMi 72b/). Let for $(k_1,k_2) \varepsilon K_1 \times K_r$ be $\Phi(k_1,k_2) = \{(a,v,b)\}$ and let k_1 not further occur in an argument of Φ. Fig.4.a) illustrated the derivation mechanism: the embedding edges of node k_1 are tansferred to node k_2 by relabelling them from a to b.

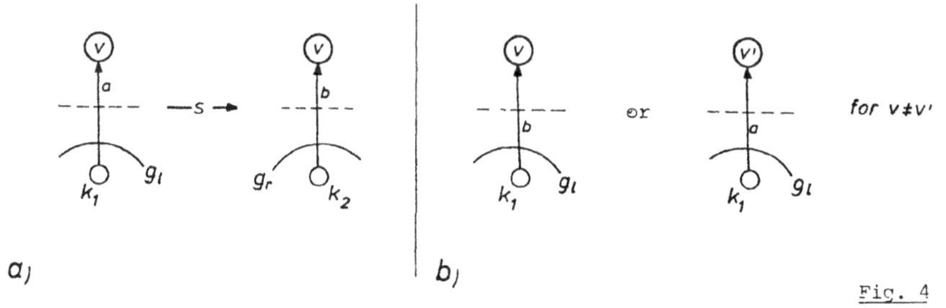

Fig. 4

The application condition says that a production is not applicable whenever the environment of a left hand side node k_1 within the host graph does not coincide with the first two components of a triple from $\Phi(k_1,k_2)$. Thus, a production with $\Phi(k_1,k_2)$ as stated above is e.g. not applicable for the host graphs of Fig.4.b).

In /GG.BrFu74/ especially *context free* graph grammars are studied which means here that the left hand side either consists of a single node and the embedding transformation cannot change edge labels, which in the embedding hierarchy is a subcase of "elementary". Furthermore /GG.BrFu74/ also contains a proof of the theorem *CSG = MG* which, however, is easier as that of /GG.Na73b/ because of the restricted embedding transformation and the application condition mentioned above. Finally, /GG.BrFu74/ contains graph acceptors for a subclass of the class of context free graph languages.

Worth noting here is a paper of RAJLICH /GG.Ra73a/ because it is one of the earlier works on moredimensional grammars and because the underlying structures are not only labelled graphs but arbitrary *relational structures*. They are defined as $S=(K,E)$, K the node set, and $E \subseteq (\Sigma_1 \times K) \cup (\Sigma_2 \times K^2) \cup .. \cup (\Sigma_n \times K^n)$, with $\Sigma := \Sigma_1 \cup \Sigma_2 \cup ... \cup \Sigma_n$ being an arbitrary alphabet. Here Σ_1 corresponds to the node label alphabet of above and Σ_2 to the edge label alphabet of labelled graphs. However, nodes and edges may be unlabelled and multiply labelled within structures. For $\Sigma_3, ..., \Sigma_n$ we have no analogy in labelled graphs. Productions are defined as pairs $p=(S_l, S_r)$, S_l, S_r either being a structure. Direct derivation $S_1 \xrightarrow[Ra]{s} S_2$ by applying a rule $p=(S_l, S_r)$ is defined that there is an injective homomorphism $e: S_l \cup S_r \rightarrow S_1 \cup S_2$ such that $S_2 = (S_1 - e(S_l)) \cup S_r$, $e(S_l) \subseteq S_1$, $e(S_r) \cap (S_1 - e(S_l)) = \emptyset$. Hereby $(S_1 - e(S_l)) \cup S_r$ does not mean that the embedding relations (as generalization of embedding edges) are omitted but they are transferred to nodes on the right hand side with the same denotation. In Fig. 5 e.g. nodes 2 and 3 of S_1 and S_2 respectively each correspond to the node with denotation 1 of the left and right hand side. If we restrict structures on unary and binary relations then we roughly get grammars on labelled graphs of embedding type "invariant". Thus the maipulation of a structure in

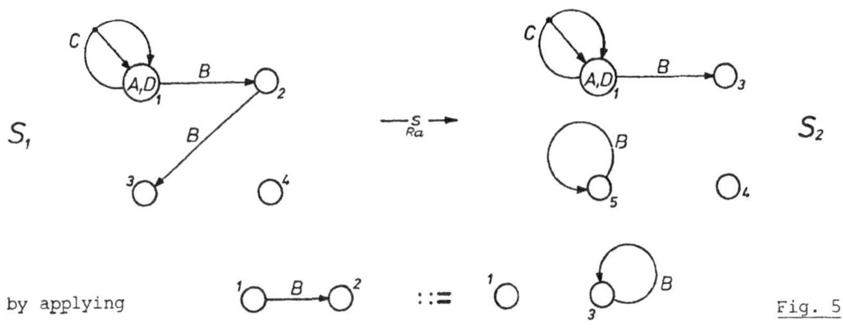

Fig. 5

a direct derivation step must completely take place wtihin the exchange of a left hand side by a right hand side. The approach of /GG.Ra73a/ has been adopted in /GG.EhKrMaRoWi78/ to the algebraic graph grammar approach. The latter will shortly be discussed now.

The central idea of the *albegraic* graph grammar approaches (cf. /GG.EhPfSc73b/, /GG.Ro75b/, /GG.ScEh76/, /GG.EhKrMaRoWi78/ and all subsequent papers) which originate from /GG.EhPfSc73a,b/ was the *generalization of the concatenation* operation on strings by a suitable operation for graphs. For that a well-known categorical construct was taken, namely the *pushout*. We give only a brief survey here as the following paper is exclusively devoted to the algebraic approach. The underlying graphs are directed and have node as well as edge labels; even multiple edges with the same direction and label between two nodes are allowed: A labelled graph over node alphabet Σ_V and edge label alphabet Σ_E is defined by $G = (V,E,q,z,m_V,m_E)$, with V being the node set, E the edge set (both finite), mappings $q,z\colon E \to V$ (source and target), and labelling functions $m_V\colon V \to \Sigma_V$, $m_E\colon E \to \Sigma_E$. A production is defined as $p = ('B \xleftarrow{'p} K \xrightarrow{p'} B')$, 'B,B' being labelled graphs, K an unlabelled graph *), 'p, p' are graph morphisms, i.e. mappings preserving the node-edge-relations. A graph H is a direct(sequential) derivation of a graph G iff there is an enlargement, i.e. an *injective* graph morphism $d\colon K \to D$ (D is partially labelled), such that the diagram of Fig. 6 commutes.

A simple example for this construction is given in Fig. 7. The morphisms 'p,p',d are indicated by the use of similar node denotations, e.g. '1 = 'p(1) etc. Roughly spoken the pushout construction means that G and H are either the disjoint union of 'B and D or B' and D respectively, in which those nodes and edges are identified which have the same preimage corresponding to the morphisms 'p,d and p',d respectively.**) Grammars and languages are usually defined. The derivation process is symmetric in the sense that $G \underset{EhPfSc}{\overset{s}{\longrightarrow}} H$ by applying p implies that $H \underset{EhPfSc}{\overset{s}{\longrightarrow}} G$ by applying p^{-1}, where p^{-1} is the same production as p, only with mutual exchange of left and right hand sides and the corresponding morphisms. Comparing this approach with the expression approach (cf. e.g. /GG. Na78/) a difference is that /GG. EhPfSc73b/ replaces subgraphs where not all edges must be found within the rule (cf. the a-edge of Fig. 7). In the above embedding hierarchy we can classify this approach approximately as "elementary" with an additional monotony with respect to embedding edges.

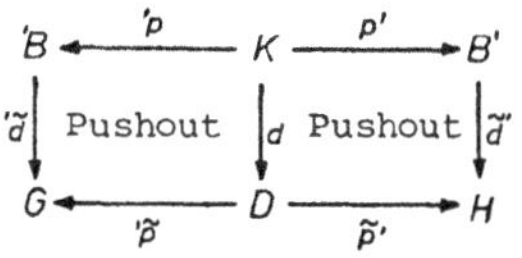

Fig. 6

---

*) If K were labelled then the gluing nodes of the left and right hand side must be labelled equally as to be seen soon, a much too strong restriction.

**) It can be shown that it is no restriction to assume that K consists of nodes only.

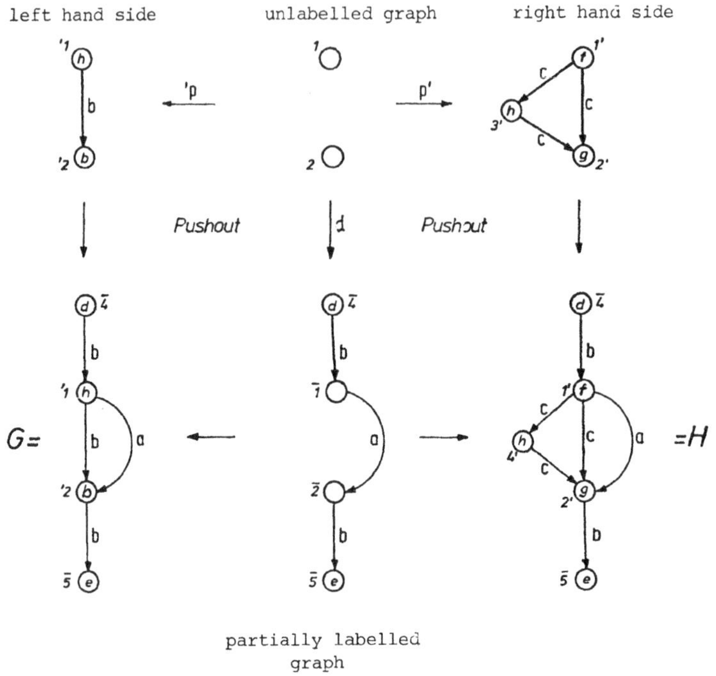

Fig. 7

The result H of a derivation step $G \xrightarrow[EhPfSc]{s} H$ by applying p depends on the choice of the enlargement. To restrict this nondeterminism in /GG.EhPfSc73b/ *grammars with enlargements* are introduced. These are graph grammars with an additional, generally infinte set of given enlargements. Furthermore, the subcase of *unique* graph grammars is studied, which are characterized, that for any left hand side of a rule being subgraph of a host graph G there is exactly one enlargement in the set of given enlargements such that G is pushout of subgraph and enlargement.
Even if the left hand side of a rule is subgraph of a host graph G it is not sure that there is a H with $G \xrightarrow[EhPfSc]{s} H$. That is because 'p specifies the nodes by which the left hand side is connected with the rest and, on the other hand, the actual embedding of the left hand side may use other nodes. For the case that 'p is injective and a special *gluing condition* holds true a derivation step is always possible and the result is unique. This condition says that source and target nodes of edges of the restgraph *) within the host are only nodes which either are not part of the left hand side or which are gluing nodes, i.e. images of nodes of K. The production of Fig. 7 has this property. If K = {1} then the gluing condition is no longer true.

*) Here we mean by restgraph the host minus left hand side together with embedding edges such that the restgraph is not really a graph but a partial graph in the sense of the next passage.

Besides of a classification with respect to left and right hand side or with respect to the embedding transformation which both have been sketched above furthermore a classification corresponding to graph theoretical properties can be regarded: 'B,B' totally ordered, 'B,B' faithful (only one edge of any label between two nodes), K without edges etc.
Furthermore, /GG.EhPfSc73b/ contains a condition guaranteeing that a derivation $G \xrightarrow[EhPfSc]{s} H$ applying p can be extended to $\overline{G} \xrightarrow[EhPfSc]{s} \overline{H}$ using the same production where $\overline{G}$ and $\overline{H}$ are graphs containing G and H respectively.

In SCHNEIDER/EHRIG /GG.ScEh76/ the above approach was generalized such that *partial graphs* are replaced. That are "graphs" where open edges are allowed, i.e. edges without source or target. Adding the missing nodes to left and right hand side this approach can be traced back to /GG.EhPfSc73b/ but this is only a theoretical consideration: The set of productions thereby is growing rapidly as for missing nodes arbitrary labels must be assumed. So, this way is unreasonable if one takes implementation into account. A production p = ('B$\xleftarrow{'p}$K$\xrightarrow{p'}$B') is defined as above with 'B,B' however being partial graphs. Even if the exchanged graphs are partial the derivation must lead from graphs to graphs. If the pushout construction shall again be used then the following conditions must hold true:

ScEh.1) All open edges of 'B and B' are images of open edges of K.

.2) If some open edges $e_1,\ldots e_j$ of K are mapped by 'p or p' on a single open edge, then the edges $e_1,\ldots e_j$ must be mapped by d: K→D on edges in which the missing nodes are identical (cf. edges 4,5 and 'p in Fig. 8).

.3) The enlargement d is an injective weak graph morphism *) **).

D is labelled in that part which is not image of d. The remarks made on /GG.EhPfSc 73b/ can be repeated here. So, similarly, for a production with injective 'p a unique direct derivative H always exists if the left hand side is subgraph and the gluing condition of above holds true.
By the extension with open edges the embedding transformation (consisting here of 'p,p', the choice of the enlargement and the diagram of Fig. 6) can treat edges of different label differently. Thus, we get here an orientation preserving subcase of depth1 embedding transformations.
In /GG.ScEh76/ so-called *convex* graph grammars are investigated. That are graph grammars where only convex enlargements d: K→D are used: If there is a chain c of edges between two nodes in the image of d then there is a chain in K too which is mapped on c by d. Such grammars preserve freeness of cycles within derivations, if the right hand side is always cycle free.

---

*) Weak graph morphism means that the image of an open edge can have a source or target.

**) However, 'p,p' must be graph morphisms.

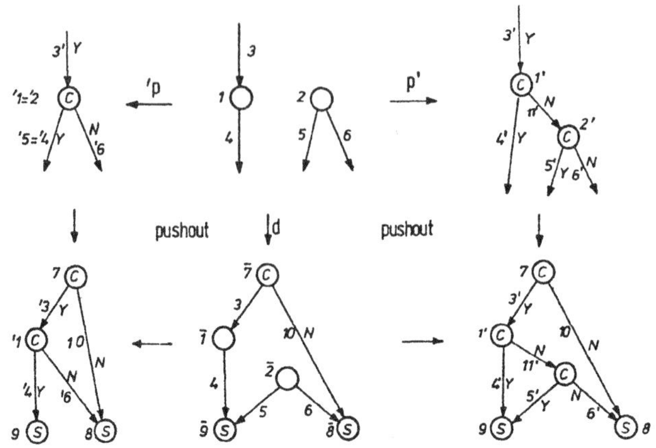

Fig. 8

A further generalization of /GG. EhPfSc73b/ is the article of ROSEN /GG.Ro75b/. Here the missing nodes of /GG.ScEh76/ are contained in the left and right hand side but they remain *unlabelled*. A production p = ('B$\xleftarrow{'p}$K$\xrightarrow{p'}$B') here consists of three partially labelled graphs 'B,K,B' and two morphisms 'p,p'. Productions fulfill the following two conditions:

Ro.1) All unlabelled edges and nodes from 'B and B' are images of edges and nodes of K.

.2) The preimage of labelled edges and nodes of 'B with respect to 'p is identical with that of B' with respect to p'.

Enlargements d: K→D are not assumed to be injective here. Direct derivation is again defined by the diagram of Fig. 6 with the following three additional conditions:

Ro.1') The labels of the image of the left hand side within the host graph must be consistent with that of 'B.

.2') If nodes (edges) a_1,a_2 of K which are mapped by 'p on labelled nodes (edges) are mapped by d on one node (edge) then the label of 'p(a_1) must be equal with that of 'p(a_2)

.3') If two nodes (edges) are mapped by 'p on one unlabelled node (edge) then their label in K must be identical.

Here again for a given G and p there can exist no graph H or more than one graphs with G $\xrightarrow[Ro]{s}$ H. If d is not injective then '$\tilde{d}$ is not injective and conversely. Therefore, the application of this approach is more complicated in the sense that not only the time-complex subgraph test must be performed but a generalized test where for the image of a graph is looked under an unknown morphism. For the special case that for a given host G and production p there exists an injective moprhism '$\tilde{d}$ which is consistent with the labels of G, i.e. that the left hand is subgraph of the host, and, furthermore, the above gluing condition holds true and, finally, .1") is valid then there is a unique H with $G \xrightarrow{s} H$:

Ro.1") If for nodes (edges) a_1, a_2^{Ro} there is $p'(a_1) = p'(a_2)$ and $'p(a_1)$ is unlabelled then these nodes (edges) are mapped by $'\tilde{d}'p$ on nodes (edges) with the same label.

Another special case besides the injective case was investigated in /GG.Ro75b/ the so-called *natural* enlargements which means in Fig. 6 that $'\tilde{p}$ is injective.

In EHRIG/KREOWSKI /GG.EhKr76a/ and ROSEN /GG.Ro75a/ CHURCH-ROSSER-theorems for graphs grammars in the sense of /GG.EhPfSc73b/ or /GG.Ro75b/ are given. That are results saying under which conditions partial derivations can be exchanged, which is desirable with respect to the definition of *canonical derivation* sequences for graph grammars as generalization of the terms leftmost or rightmost derivation of the strings case. In /GG.EhKr76a/ two CHURCH-ROSSER theorems for natural derivations ($'\tilde{p}$ is always injective) are given, which can be described informally in the following way: Let $G \xrightarrow{s} H_1$ by applying p_1, $G \xrightarrow{s} H_2$ by p_2 and $H_1 \xrightarrow{s} H_3$ by applying p_3 three direct derivation steps and let the steps $G \xrightarrow{s} H_1$, $G \xrightarrow{s} H_2$ be *parallel independent*, which means that the left hand side of p_1 is contained up to homomorphism in the enlargement D_2 and conversely. Then there is a graph $\tilde{H}$ and direct derivations $H_1 \xrightarrow{s} \tilde{H}$ by p_2, $\tilde{H}_2 \xrightarrow{s} H$ by p_1 (cf. Fig. 9). Let on the other hand $G \xrightarrow{s} H_1$ by p_1, $H_1 \xrightarrow{s} H_3$ by p_3 be *sequential independent*, i.e. the right hand side B'_1 of p_1 is contained in the enlargement D_3 of the second derivation up to homomorphism and the left hand side $'B_3$ of p_3 in D_1. Then there exists a graph H and natural derivations $G \xrightarrow{s} H_2$ by p_3, $H_2 \xrightarrow{s} H_3$ by p_1 such that these derivations are sequential independent and such that $G \xrightarrow{s} H_1$ by p_1, $G \xrightarrow{s} H_2$ by p_3 are parallel independent. Furthermore, there is a natural parallel derivation in the sense of /GG.EhKr76/ summarizing the two sequential derivations (cf. Fig. 9). The above sequential or parallel independence does not necessarily

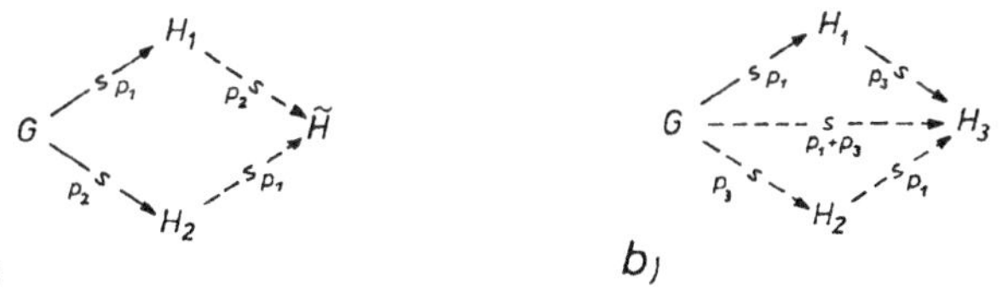

Fig. 9

demand the intersection of left hand sides to be empty. However, the intersection can only consist of gluing nodes. The collection of two sequential derivation steps by one step $G \underset{EhKr}{\xrightarrow{m}} H$ by $p_1 + p_2$ is a so-called *mixed* derivation step, i.e. an intermediate form between sequential and parallel rewriting. The second theorem is the base for the definition of canonical graph derivation sequences in /GG.Kr76/ /GG.Kr77c/. The fundamental idea is not to replace one sequential derivation by another sequential one with interchanged order of application of productions but both by the parallel derivation.

3. SURVEY ON PARALLEL GRAPH REWRITING SYSTEMS (PARALLEL GRAPH GRAMMARS, GRAPH L-SYSTEMS)

As already mentioned, the rewriting mechanism within parallel derivations is non-local as the whole host graph is rewritten in one step. Therefore if g —p→ g' there must be partitions of g and g' into left and right hand sides, more precisely into actualizations of left and right hand sides as one production may be applied more than once. Those actualizations of left and right hand sides we call *mother graphs* and *daughter graphs* respectively, corresponding to biology as the main application field of parallel graph rewriting systems (cf. /GL.CuLi77/, /GL.Ma74/, /GL.Na76b/). Additionally, the connections between the mother graphs must be specified, which can be done in various ways. This specification, called *connection transformation*, is the criterion between the different approaches. Parallel graph rewriting systems can be regarded as a generalization of L-systems to labelled graphs. Therefore, they are sometimes called graph L-systems or more shortly GL-systems. Mainly because of the difficulties arising in formally defining the connection transformation, GL-systems are much more complicated than usual L-systems (on strings) but, on the other hand, they are much better suitable to applications, as for example development description. As remarked above some papers specialize parallel graph rewriting to the subsituation of singe nodes *(node substitution* approaches) or single edges (*edge* or *handle substitution* approaches). The definitions of these papers, however, can easily adapted to the general case where arbitrary graphs are replaced.

The problem of defining the connections between daughter graphs can be tackled in two different ways, the corresponding approaches will be called explicit and implicit respectively. In *explicit* approaches there are two kinds of rules: *rewriting rules* and *connection rules* . The rewriting rules have the form $r = (g_l, g_r)$ and say which mother graphs are to be replaced by which daughter graphs, the connection rules $c = (g_e, g_{st})$ state how connections g_e between mother graphs are transformed in order to get the corresponding connections between daughter graphs. In most explicit approaches the left hand side g_e of a connection rule is a single edge *(mother edge)*, the right hand side is a bipartite graph *(stencil)* which must be embedded into the two daughter graphs which correspond to the nodes of the mother edge (see below). Representatives of the explicit approach are /GL.CuLi74/, /GL.CuLi 76/, /GL.EhRb76/, /GL.GrNa77/, /GL.Ma74/. In *implicit* approaches besides the determination, which graph is to be replaced by which one, there is additional information within productions for the connection transformation. This information can consist of expressions of the same form as the embedding transformation of /GG.Na73b/

asshown in /GL.Na75/ or it can specify morphisms for the gluing of graphs as done in /GL.EhKr76/. Typical of implicit approaches is that the additional information within one production cannot completely specify how the corresponding daughter graph is connected because a connection belongs to two daughter graphs which themselves belong to two productions. The advantage of the implicit method is that productions can have exactly the same form as in the sequential case such that the implementaion of both rewriting mechanisms is considerably facilitated. The sequential and parallel rewriting mechanisms (although using the same form of productions), however, are completely different. This is strictly analogous to the string case.
Besides parallel graph rewriting systems other models have also been used for development description: cellular automata, map rewriting systems /GL.CaGrPa74/, /GL.Ma74/, /GL.Ma76/, and globe models /GG.Ma74/. In the following we give some characterizing remarks on the different approaches on parallel graph grammars without following the chronological order.

In MAYOH/GL.Ma74/ parallel graph rewriting systems named parallel web grammars are introduced. The paper is strongly influenced by /GG.PfRf69/. The reader reminds that webs are graphs with node labels but only with one undirected kind of edges. The approach is a node-substituting one. So, in a parallel rewriting step $g \xrightarrow[Ma]{p} g'$ all nodes are simultaneously replaced by webs according to a finite set of replacement rules. The connection between either two daughter graphs g_r and g'_r which are substituted for two mother nodes k_1 and k'_1 is given by connecting each node of g_r with each node of g'_r provided k_1 and k'_1 have been connected by an edge. This yields an intermediate web g". Furthermore, there is a so-called *forbidden list* FL with $FL \subseteq \Sigma_v \times \Sigma_v$, Σ_v being the node label alphabet. From the above web g" all edges connecting daughter graphs are omitted, which have node labels of bordering nodes occuring in the forbidden list. The result is the graph g'. For this connection construction easily connection rules can be given such that /GL.Ma74/ is an explicit approach. The paper contains no results on these parallel grammars, the presentation is informal.

Most of the explicit approaches originate in CULIK/LINDENMAYER /GL.CuLi74/, /GL.CuLi76/. We first start with a slight simplification of this approach introduced in /GL.Na76b/ and then come back to /GL.CuLi74/ by discussing the differences between both approaches. Both are node substitution models which, however, can easily be extended. Typical for /GL.CuLi74/ and subsequently also for the explicit approach in /GL.EhRb76/ and /GL.Na76b/ is the way how connection rules $c = (g_e, g_{st})$ are defined. The left hand side is an edge (mother edge) which must occur as connection between two mother nodes in the graph before the parallel rewriting step is applied. The right hand side is a bipartite graph called stencil. The interplay of replacement and connection rules is shown by Fig.10, where for the reason of simplicity only two mother nodes and, consequently, only two daughter graphs are drawn. The one-node subgraphs of the graph g are replaced according to the replacement rules, i.e. by either looking for a replacement rule, the left hand side of which has exactly the same structure (node label, eventually labelled loops) as the node to be substituted. Mother edges also contain the bordering nodes together with their label

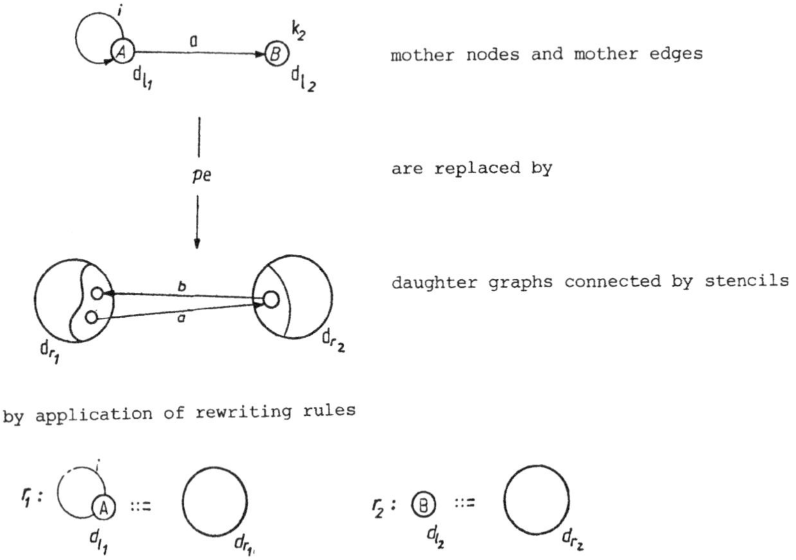

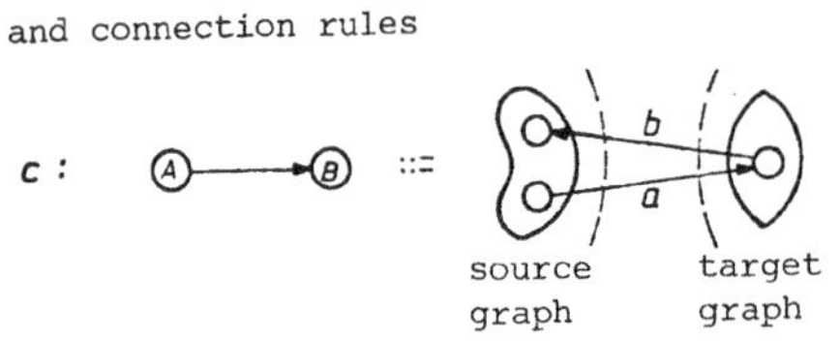

Fig. 1o

but without eventual loops. The stencil is devided into the *source graph* (the left part of the stencil) and the *target graph* (the right part) both separated by dotted lines)(. The connection between two daughter graphs is established by choosing a connection rule the left hand side of which (mother edge) is a connection between the two mother nodes and the right hand side of which (stencil) is contained in the two corresponding daughter graphs such that the source graph lies within the daughter graph corresponding to the source node of the mother edge and the target graph within the daughter graph descending from the target node. The edges between source and target graph of the stencil now interconnect the two daughter graphs. The applicability of a connection rule thus depends on two conditions: 1) The node labels of the mother edge must be identical to those of a mother node connection. 2) The source and target graph of the corresponding stencil must be embeddable into the daughter graphs. This *programming of connections* is realized in /GL.CuLi74/, /GL.CuLi76/ in a different way: In any graph there is a special node called the *environmental node* which can be imagined to be infinitely far away. Edges from or to this node are drawn as open edges, i.e. either without source or target. They are called *open hands*. Besides open hands (which may also occur within left and right hand sides) the replacement rules have the form of Fig. 10. Arbitrary derived graphs also have open hands, connection rules now look like Fig. 11.

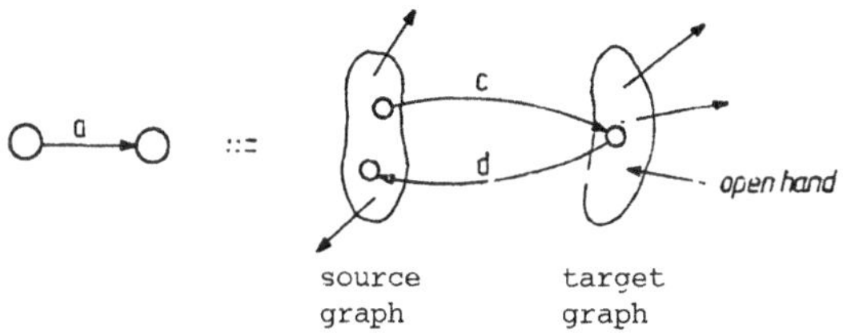

Fig. 11

Stencils usually contain open hands too. Left hand sides of connection rules are single edges which do not include the labels of the neighbour nodes. The applicability of a stencil to a pair of daughter graphs is directed in the following way:

CuLi .1) Source and target graphs must be contained in the corresponding daughter graphs.

.2) Cutting the stencil in two pieces between source and target graph we regard the separated edges as pairs of open hands which we name *matching hands*. A stencil is only applicable, if the open hands of the source and target graph and the matching hands are either additionally contained in the daughter graphs to which the stencil is to apply.

.3) Any applied stencil must be maximal, i.e. there is no larger stencil which is applicable and which contains the applied one.

Thus, the programming of connections is controlled by three conditions: embeddability of source and target graphs within daughter graphs, open/matching-hands-condition, maximality condition. The simplification in /GL.Na76b/ avoids open/matching-hands-mechanism and maximality condition.

In /GL.CuLi74/, /GL.CuLi76/ a lot of results are given concerning the relations of string L-systems to graph L-systems and the generalization of results on L-systems to GL-systems. Furthermore, recurrence systems on graphs are defined and their relations to GL-systems are studied, especially with respect to decidability. The results are extended in a recent paper /GL.CuWo78/.

The implicit approach introduced by NAGL /GL.Na75/, /GL.Na76a/ uses exactly the same definition of a production as the sequential approach of /GG.Na73a/, /GG.Na74/ which has been refereed in section 2. The definition of parallel direct derivation, of course, is different from the corresponding sequential one. We introduce here the

special case of node substitution.
In the sequential case the notion of expressions has been used to calculate nodes outside of the replaced subgraph which act as source nodes of incoming edges and target nodes of outgoing edges. This idea cannot be sustained in the parallel case as *all* nodes are rewritten in one step. However, the expression notion can be used to determine *half-edges* and we define that an edge connecting two daughter graphs is generated iff two half-edges fit together. Analogously to the edge determination in the sequential case, a half-edge is specified by an explicit and an implicit part: For incoming edges into a daughter graph the target node can be explicitly specified. We use expressions here again to calculate nodes of the host graph (before the derivation step is performed) and interpret the result in the way that the corresponding daughter graphs to those nodes are sources for edges ending within the nodes explicitly specified. Both together determine incoming half-edges. Analogously, the source nodes of outgoing edges are explicitly specified and the daughter graphs there those edges are to point to by evaluating an expression.
Let us explain this half-edge-mechanism by an example:

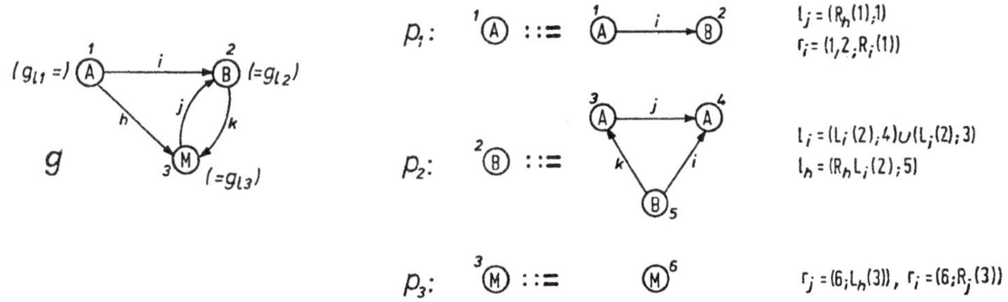

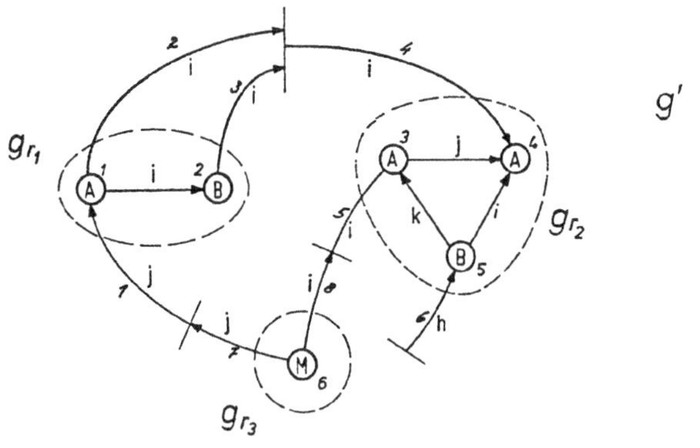

Fig. 12

All nodes of the graph g of Fig.12 are simultaneously replaced using p_1,p_2,p_3. To elucidate the half-edge-mechanism we introduce an intermediate "graph" where half-edges are denoted by inclined numbers *1*,...,*9*. The daughter graphs g_{r1},g_{r2},g_{r3} are included within dotted lines. The first component l_i of p_1 specifies that an incoming i-edge is to point to node 1 of g_{r1}. The daughter graph is specified by calculating $R_h(1)$ for graph g which yields node 3. So, g_{r3} is the source of half-edge *1* ending in node 1 of g_{r1}. Analogously, r_i of p_1 determines *2* and *3*. Finally, l_i and l_h of p_2 specify *4*,*5* and *6* respectively, r_i,r_j of p_3 the half-edges *7* and *8*. Half edges *1* and *7* fit together yielding in the derived graph g' a j-edge from 6 of g_{r3} to 1 of g_{r1}. In the same way *2*,*3* and *4* result in two i-edges from 1 or 2 to 4, *5* and *6* in an i-edge from 6 to 3. Half-edge *6* is erased as having no counterpart.

The advantage of this method is that within one direct derivation step the mechanism for programming daughter graph connections is very powerful. This can already be seen by the above example.

In /GL.Na75/, /GL.Na76a/ and /GG.Na78/ the definitions of usual L-systems are generalized to the graph case: table GL-systems (i-TGL-systems), extended GL-systems (i-EGL-systems) and finally extended i-TGL-systems (i-ETGL-systems) are introduced, the "i" either saying that it is an implicit approach. Within extended systems there is distinguished between nonterminal and terminal labels for nodes *and* edges. Comparing the corresponding language classes the following hierarchy results (cf. /GG.Na78/) with "P" standing for propagating, i.e. non-erasing:

$$\begin{array}{lccccccccc} & \textit{i-TGL} & \supset & \textit{i-GL} & & & & & & \\ & \cap & & \cap & & & & & & \\ \text{Na.2)} & \textit{i-ETGL} & \supseteq & \textit{i-EGL} & \supset & \textit{i-PEGL} & = & \textit{i-PETGL} & \supset & \textit{i-PTGL} \end{array}$$

Furthermore, the string language classes EIL and IL, understood as languages of lineary ordered graphs, are contained in *i-EGL*, ETOL,TOL,EOL are contained in *i-PEGL*. The class *i-PEGL* is identical with *CFG* (cf./GL.Na76c/,/GG.Na78/) of the sequential hierarchy Na.1), a result which has no analogon in the string case.

In GRÖTSCH /GL.Gr76/, /GL.GrNa77/ the relations of the explicit approach of /GG.Na 76b/ to that of /GG.CuLi74/ are investigated as well as the relations of both to the implicit expression approach just introduced. The results are also reported in /GG.Na78/ and /GG.GrNa78/ and are not presented here as the latter is contained in this volume.

In EHRIG/ROZENBERG /GL.EhRb76/ two different suggestions are made to define parallel rewriting systems: one node substitution approach and one handle substitution approach. The first one is a simplification of /GL.CuLi74/ also avoiding the open/ matching hands mechanism. It is an explicit approach in the above sense, i.e. connection rules are used to interconnected daughter graphs. The stencils contain here *all nodes* of the daughter graphs where they are to be embedded but *no edges*.

As a lot of "structure" is lost by forgetting the edges, the embedding procedure of stencils would become highly nondeterministic. Therefore, an *indexing technique* is introduced in /GL.EhRb76/ to make the connection between two daughter graphs unique, provided there is only one applicable connection rule. This technique is similar to a technique of /AP.Pr71/ to interrelate nonterminal nodes in the two different derivations of pair graph grammars. The mechanism shall be illustrated by the example of Fig. 13

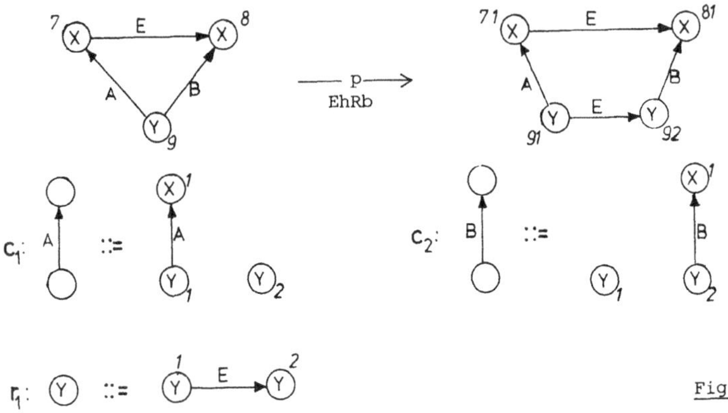

Fig.13

where we furthermore assume the existence of one identical replacement rule for the X-node and a connection rule preserving the E-edge. Starting with an axiom graph with different node denotations for different nodes the indexing technique always yields different node denotations by only extending the denotations by those of the daughter graphs. The stencil is embedded by only considering the last characters of the denotations.

The relations of this approach to /GL.CuLi74/ or the explicit approach of /GL.Na76b/ are not investigated up till now. As, however, /GL.EhRb76/ and the explicit approach of /GL.Na76b/ are simplifications of /GL.CuLi74/ the differences should not be too significant. Two remarks should be made: As already indicated in /GL.Eh Rb76/ the stencils of connection rules need not contain all nodes of the daughter graphs where they are to embed, i.e. indexing technique is possible even for "incomplete" stencils. Furthermore, the definitions of /GL.EhRb76/ could be changed without any problem such that a connection rule can also establish an edge having the converse direction of the corresponding mother edge.

The idea of the handle substitution approach of /GL.EhRb76/ is to replace all edges of a host in parallel. As this approach is a specialization of the gluing approach to be discussed below we first make some remarks on the latter one.

In EHRIG/KREOWSKI /GL.EhKr76/ the connection of daughter graphs is not established by stencils but by a generalization of the pushout-construction of Fig. 6. The approach is not restricted to node substitution and can be regarded as explicit as well as implicit approach. The basic idea is that within g and g' where $G \xrightarrow[EhKr]{p} H$ there must be coverings into subgraphs consistent with the productions. The productions here have the from

$$\pi = ('B_i \xleftarrow{k_{ij}} K_{ij}, K'_{ij} \xrightarrow{k'_{ij}} B'_i) \quad 1 \leq i \neq j \leq n, \quad K_{ij} = K_{ji}, K'_{ij} = K'_{ji}$$

where the K_{ij}, K'_{ij} are again called gluing graphs. Consistent coverings means that for any left hand side $'B_i$ and right hand side B'_i there are morphisms $u_i : 'B_i \to G$, $u'_i : B'_i \to H$, $1 \leq i \leq n$ such that G and H are either a *star gluing*, i.e. there are the following commuting diagrams (here for n=3):

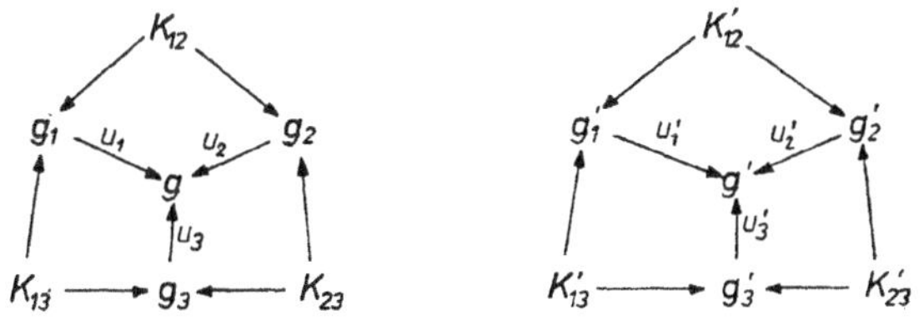

Fig. 14

More important for applications is the special case of injective morphisms, i.e. G and H are each coverings of mother graphs and daughter graphs respectively. For any two mother graphs the intersection is either empty or they are glued together along the image of the corresponding gluing graphs. The graph H then is the result of the corresponding daughter graphs with analogous gluing.

Let $G \xrightarrow[EhKr]{p} H$ and let G be covered by its edges, H by the corresponding stencils where we assume that the stencils are complete in the sense that source and target graph is either identical with the corresponding daughter where it is to be embedded. The mother edges are glued together along their common nodes, the (complete) stencils along their daughter graphs. So, a rule here plays the rôle of both a replacement and connection rule. That is, roughly decribed, the specialization of /GL.EhKr76/ which was called handle substitution approach in /GL.EhKr76/.

4. SYSTEMS FOR APPLICATIONS, PROGRAMMING, AND IMPLEMENTATION REMARKS

The headline of this section should not be understood in the sense that all graph grammar concepts regarded above are not suitable for applications. One motivation for their introduction either was theoretical, namely to consider generalizations of grammar concepts on strings. The rewriting systems we want to sketch here, however, have only been introduced to meet the requiremets of a special application. So, their theoretical investigation was a matter of secondary importance and not always delivered subsequently. The concepts we shall introduce are programmed graph grammars and two-level graph grammars. A further concept which is not regarded in the sequel is that of *pair graph grammars* introduced by PRATT /AP.Pr71/, which was motivated by the question of translations between graph structures. A pair graph grammar is a tuple (G,G') of two context free graph grammars, where with the aid of a special indexing technique for any derivation of G there is a drivation of G' and vice versa.

In a paper of UESU /GG.Ue77/ it is claimed that graph grammars of a rather restricted embedding type, namely of type analogous, are already *universal*, i.e. any recursive enumerable set of graphs can be generated by such a grammar. This implies that the use of complex embedding and connection transformations (and especially, the use of programmed or two-level concepts) does not increase the generative power, but only yields an *increase* of *efficiency* in two aspects: A programmed rewriting step or a two-level rewriting step, both assumed to be undivisible, can shorten a graph manipulation *). The second aspect, which is not independent of the first, is that both concepts in most can carry out a complex graph manipulation more evidently, which is important for the propagation of graph grammar concepts to users not always willing to learn about complicated notations.

Within graph grammar applications there are two groups: Within the first group graph grammars or graph rewriting steps are used to *formalize* topics which before have been left informal and thus a priori ambigous. Within the second group graph rewriting systems can be a *part of the implementation* provided an efficient implementation thereof exists. The latter corresponds in many cases to the existence and implementation of an efficient syntax analysis method.

The introduction of *programmed graph rewriting* is due to BUNKE /AP.Bu74/ and SCHNEIDER /AP.Sc75/ and has been formally defined in /AP.Bu78/, /GG.Na78/, and /AP.We78a/. Roughly spoken, a programmed rewriting step is nothing else than a sequence of rewriting steps (sequential, parallel, or mixed) conducted by the passing through a flow diagram, which we call *control diagram*. Operations within control diagrams are assumed either to be graph rewriting steps or calls of other control diagrams**) which are handled in the same way as procedure calls in programming languages. A programmed step can be regarded on a higher level as a single rewriting step. So, in general,again sequential, parallel, or mixed application of programmed

---

*) This speeding up takes place on a conceptual level. For any implementation such steps must be assumed to be divided into substeps (cf. the following remark about programming of graph manipulations).

**) Consisting again only of replacement steps or control diagram calls.

rewriting steps can be regarded. We restrict ourselves here to the special case indicated in Fig. 15 where all rewriting steps are sequential. Here, we have only four kinds of nodes in a control diagram: a starting node (labelled by an asterisk), halt nodes (both starting node and halt nodes labelled with comments) and two kinds of action nodes. The rectangular one is the call of another control diagram the other one, drawn hexagonal and called primitive action node is an intermediate form between a conditional jump and an assigument, namely the application of a production, if the production is applicable. The edges of control diagrams are labelled with T and F, standing for true and false respectively. Any node can either have exactly two outgoing edges labelled with T and F or an arbitrary number of outgoing T-edges. The first one we call a deterministic branching node, the second a nondeterministic one. *)

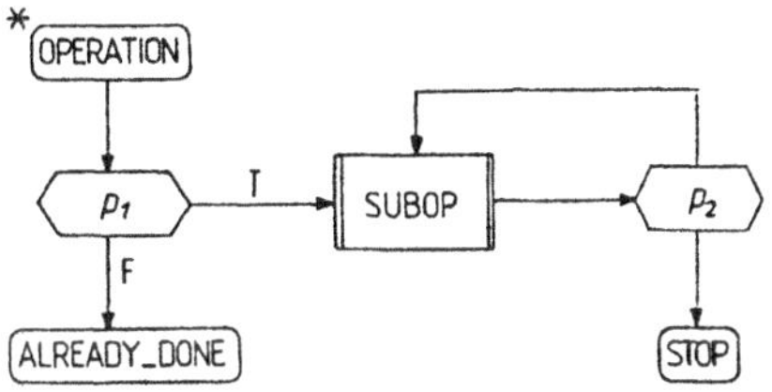

p_1, p_2 and SUBOP defined properly

Fig. 15

A control diagram call is always of the second kind. So, the p_1- node of Fig. 15 is a deterministic branching node, the p_2- node is nondeterministic and the remaining action node is a call of the subdiagram SUBOP. The semantics of a primitive action node is to apply the production it is labelled with whenever possible and to proceed along a T-exit otherwise along an F-exit. If a production is not applicable and no F-exit exists for this node, then the continuation is undefined. To avoid that a programmed step manipulates different locations of a graph the production of the entry action node of the control diagram can insert an anchoring structure (special node label, special subgraph) which is contained in all productions and which does not occur in the rest of the host graph. To increase the evidence of programming within programmed steps,productions could be extended by attaching an application condition or a negative application condition, both being graphs. The first case means, that an extended production is applicable iff the application condition is contained in the host graph in addition to the left hand side, the second case means that the negative application condition must not occur. Summing up one can say that within a programmed rewriting step rather complex graph manipu-

*) Labels of edges going out of a nondeterministic branching node are omitted within the graphical representation of control diagrams (cf. Fig. 15).

lations can clearly be formulated.
In /AP.Bu78/ programmed graph grammars are formally introduced and their relation to other graph grammar concepts, especially to /GG.Na74/ is investigated. The results are not reported here as an excerpt is contained in this volume.

Two-level-graph-grammars in a restricted form have already been introduced in /AP.Pr 71/: Here the node and edge labels are not elements of finite sets but are themselves generated by a string grammar. This kind of two-level mechanis can be imagined as the extension of the (usually finite) set of productions to an infinite set, in which only a finite number of different classes exists, if the structure of the left and right hand sides modulo labels is considered. Full two-level grammars, where the manipulation of a production is applied to left hand side, right hand side, and embedding transformation are due to GÖTTLER /AP.Gö77/. The definition of a two-level rewriting mechanism is rather simple, if a *production* is completely *denoted as* a *graph*, which especially means a graph-representation of the embedding transformation. This graph now can be manipulated in the usual way yielding actualized productions. In Fig. 16 a graphical representation of a production of embedding type 'elementary' is given, the vertical line separating left and right hand side, the dashed arrows representing the embedding transformation (cf. /AP.DeFrSt75/). In Fig. 17 the graph representation of a so-called 'local' production is given which is a subcase of the expression approach of section 2. Here the use of the complement operator within expressions is not allowed. In the lower left and right third of Fig. 17 the left and right hand side is drawn, while the upper third together with its bordering edges represents the embedding transformation. In both figures the expression notion is additionally given. Note that a graph representation of a production in the sense of Fig. 17 contains no edges between left and right hand sides. For graph representations of productions the term

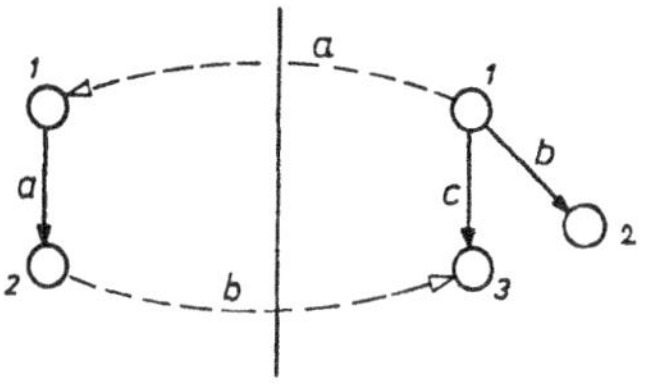

$l_b = (L_b(2);3)$
$r_a = (1;R_a(1))$

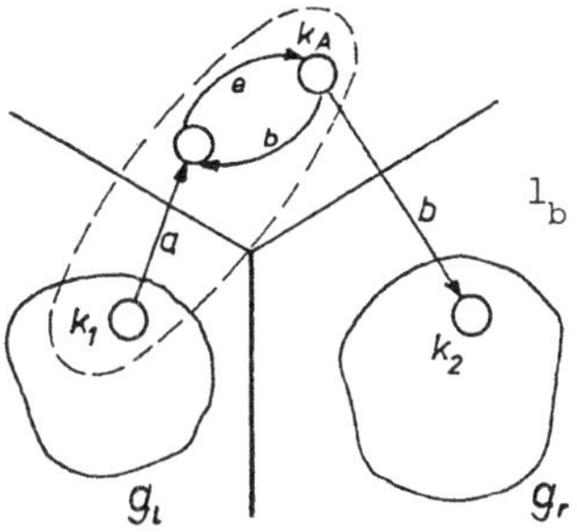

$l_b = ((L_b \cap R_e)R_a(k_1);k_2)$

Fig. 17

consistent replacement of affix string grammars can be generalized. For that we take productions with one-node left hand sides which we call metaproductions. The *actualization* of a production *) now is a mixed rewriting step on the grap notation of

*) A production to be actualized is also called hyperproduction.

the production where *all* occurences of the metaproduction's left hand side are replaced. The aprtition of the hyperproduction into left and right hand side, and
embedding transformation is not changed by the actualization. In Fig. 18 we give the
graph representation of a hyperproduction h,a metaproduction m (in the expression
notion), and the ectualization of h by m. As in a mixed rewriting step usually more
than one occurence of the left hand side of the metaproduction is replaced, we get
the half-edge mechanism between the simultaneously inserted graphs which is drawn
in Fig. 18 for the reason of lucidity.

The advantage of the two-level approach is a greater evidence: The hyperproductions
represent a *rough* version of the productions, the metaproductions moreover *refine*
this structure. Furthermore, this refinement can easily be exchanged by taking
another set of metaproductions.

hypermanipulation rule

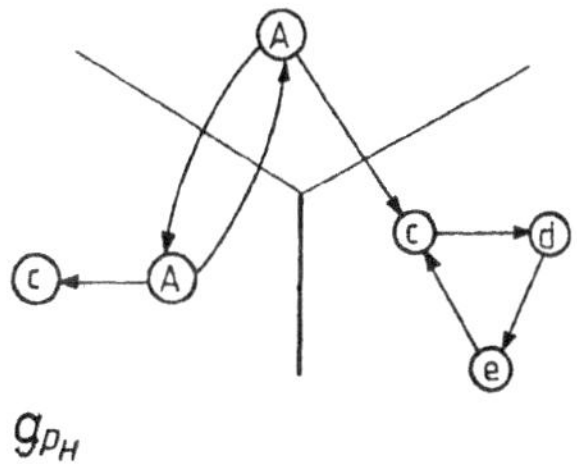

gp_H

metaproduction

p_m:

$l = (cR(1); 3) \cup (AR(1); 2)$
$r = (2; AR(1))$

$$\overset{A}{\underset{1}{\bigcirc}} \quad ::= \quad \overset{b}{\underset{2}{\bigcirc}} \longrightarrow \overset{b}{\underset{3}{\bigcirc}}$$

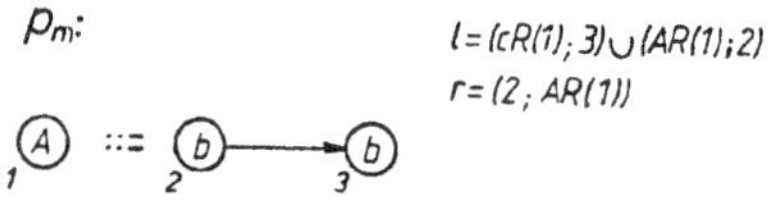

actualized production

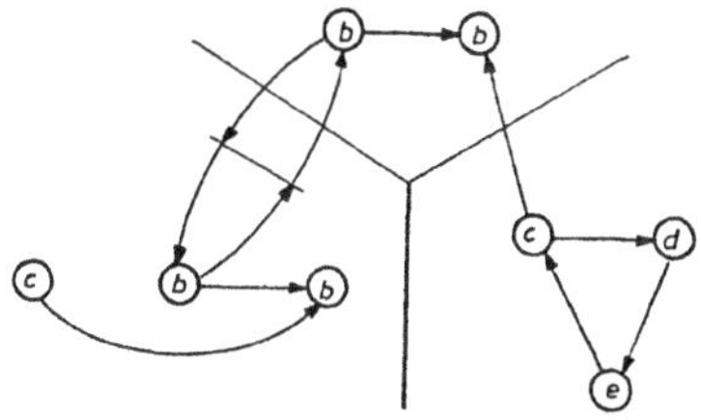

Fig. 18

The rewriting mechanisms regarded so far are nothing else than *aids* to *program* the
development of a graph. For that we got to know: (1) the exchange mechanism between
left and right hand side, (2) more or less complex ambeding or connection transformations, or the connection rules in explicit parallel approaches, (3) the distinction between terminal and nonterminal labels for nodes and edges in grammars,
(4) the programmed or the two-level mechanism.

From /GG.Ue77/ we know that graph grammars of a rather restricted embedding type
are already universal, i.e. can generate all graphs which are enumerable. So, all
programming aids are not important for the generative power but for the efficiency
with which these concepts are applied and implemented. Nevertheless, a lot of

questions of a theoretical nature remain: Which programming aid can be substituted by which other one and how can the simulation be carried out? Can the programming mechanism be replaced by the use of more complex embedding or connection transformations, how can the notion of embedding/connection transformations be simplified if a programming or two-level mechanism is added to drive the derivations, how can complex embedding/connection transformations be simplified if left and right hand sides are blown out such that they include more context, etc? Some of these questions are solved in /AP.Bu78/, namely that the programming mechanism and complex embedding transformations are mutually exchangeable.
We get a completely different point of view if the questions of *application* and *implementation* are regarded We see immediately, that the manipulation of graph structures by replacement steps of restricted embedding or connection type is completely unreasonable.Here the only programming mechanism is the exchange of subgraphs and, as the embedding/connection transformation can only hand down the embedding/connection structure, all possible environment situations must be included in the left and right hand side:The more trivial embedding and connection transformations are, the more context must be carried round. This implies great left and right hand sides and many productions, which both results in a waste of storage and computation time. This argument remains valid if one regards additionally programming and two-level mechanism. So, taking only the implementation aspect into account, the use of complex embedding/connection transformations is very efficient: Left and right hand sides can strictly be reduced with respect to size, which speeds up the subgraph test; the number of productions decreases, as the embedding/connection transformation may sum up different cases.In the same way parts *) of a control diagram can be replaced by the application of a single production.
Now, the above argumentation should not be interpreted in the sense that the programming mechanism or the two-level mechanism is either nonsense. The above argumentation completely neglects one important factor of efficiency, the time to program graph rewriting. This time can drastically be reduced using evident mechanisms. This also corresponds to the question of reliable and easy-to-change graph manipulation "programs". So, one way to combine both aspects of efficiency is the following: Start with a *structured* form of the "program" using explicit mechanisms as programmed steps, two-level mechanism etc. and then try to substitute productions, reduced with respect to the size of left and right hand side and with respect to their number. That usually implies the use of more complex embedding/connection transformations.

---

*) especially desirable for loops

The use of productions with complex embedding/connection transformations is only possible in those applications (cf. section 1) where no syntax analysis method is needed, as the only existing graph syntax analysis method up till now corresponds to a rather restricted type of (sequential) graph grammars: *precedence graph grammars* which are due to FRANCK (cf. /GG.Fr76/, /GG.Fr77/). These grammars are context free and of embedding type elementary, additionally with a monotony condition for embedding edges, saying, that no embedding edge must be deleted, and, furthermore, with a precedence condition. Precedence graph grammars are a generalization of the simple precedence grammars to graphs. The idea is to define precedence relations $\lessdot$, $\doteq$, and $\gtrdot$ for triples (v_1,a,v_2), v_1,v_2 being the label of the source and target node of an edge, a being its edge label. All triples of edges pointing to a right hand side must be contained within $\lessdot$, all edges leaving a right hand side must be within $\gtrdot$, while finally, all triples of edges being a part of a right hand side are elements of the relation $\doteq$. As the underlying rewriting mechanism neither creates nor deletes embedding edges but only transfers them, an edge going into a right hand side or leaving a right hand side must descend from an edge within a right hand side where some nodes have been replaced. Those edges and thus the triples of either relation can easily be computed.*) Within precedence graph grammars the precedence relations must be pairwise disjoint. We furthermore assume that all right hand sides of productions as well as the axiom graph are connected and that there exist neither two productions with the same right hand side. Of all these conditions precedence graph grammars must fulfill, only the restrictions corresponding to the embedding type and the precedence conditions are rather drastic. Within graphs generated by precedence grammars the next right hand side can be found by a local operation, i.e. traversing edges with increasing precedence until a precedence "hilltop" is reached.

The *implementation of* graph grammar concepts or *graph rewriting* concepts is the most recent topic within the graph grammar field. Here we have to mention /GG.Fr77/ again, where the implementation of the syntax analysis method for graph grammars is commented, which we have just explained. Other references in this context are /IM.Br76/, /IM.BrNaWe78/, /IM.Na77/ and /IM.SuMaTo76/. The first group of references deals with the expressions approach for sequential and parallel rewriting which is very powerful with respect to the manipulations of a host graph within one direct derivation step. Concerning implementation aspects this can be very efficient (cf. the above passage on programming with graph rewriting systems). This implementation is based on an associative storage (cf. /IM.EnWe74/) realized by software, i.e. by hashing techniques and complex list operations. The goal of this im-

*) In the graph case another relation $\lessdot\!\gtrdot$ is added which contains the triples of edges connecting two right hand sides, where it makes no difference which one is reduced first.

plementation is rather generality than efficiency with respect to one specific application . The author prefers to indicate future *implementation trends* than commenting the implementations cited above.
If it is not assumed that the graphs to be modelled are permanent within the primary storage of the host computer, then a paging facility must be provided which is either a part of the systems software (virtual storage) *) or has to be added, then being the base of the implementation. In /IM.EnWe74/ such a paging facility is contained as part of the associative software storage. This software storage was modified and improved, which engrossed a rather big part of the implementation expenditure. Nevertheless, it is worth while thinking of further improvements and thinking of a substitution of the software realization of the associative storage by a hardware realization or by a realization based on microprogramming (cf. /IM.Sc78/). Finally, one can coordinate the abilities of the software storage with a special application such that it meets exactly the requirements of this application. This means that all features not used are erased. All topics of this passage can be summarized by the catchword *improvement of efficiency*.
The implementation of graph rewriting at different places demands for an interaction between user and machine, i.e. the implementation should be embedded into a *dialog* environment. We want to demonstrate this by three examples: The input of all existing implementations is linear and the same holds for the output. That means that the user has to carry out two completely superfluous translation steps. As he is usually developing a graph rewriting system using graphical representations of graphs (e.g. on a sheet of paper) he has to code this by a linear representation, i.e. by a well-formed string. The same problem arises with respect to the output, where the user has to produce a graphical, two-dimensional representation from a string machine-output by hand. Assumed there were a dialog environment with a graphical display, then for the input he can immediately build up graphs and productions in a graphical form which are automatically translated to the notation expected by the implementation. Regarding the output of graphical representations of graphs, a dialog is necessary, as no existing algorithm can automatically produce an elucid graphical representation. This holds also true if a planarization algorithm is part of the output procedure as in most cases graphs are not planar and even if they were it is not sure that the planar representation is the most elucid one. In /IM.Zi77/, /IM.NaZi78/ a dialog system for this task is described. Starting with a primitive graphical representation a graph can be clearly arranged using dialog commands like: shift a node with its bordering edges, shift a node denotation , node label, edge label, deform an edge to avoid crossings etc. The final product of this dialog (which of course is a matter of taste too) can be put out by a plotter. If a graph g' is the result of a sequential derivation step then the refined version of the restgraph

---

*) which is only the case for medium size or large computers.

is contained in the primitive version of g'. Another interaction is needed if one takes into account that a production is usually applicable at different locations within a graph or that in a parallel or mixed rewriting step there are usually many ways how a partition into left hand sides can be arranged. In both cases the choice of left hand sides can hardly be left to the system if not completely arbitrary graphs shall be produced.

Finally, another future implementation goal should be to develop a *programming language for dynamic problems on graphs*. There are already a lot of existing programming languages for graph problems (cf. e.g./IM.BaReMe72/, /IM.CrMo70/, /IM.Ki72/, /IM.Kö76/, /IM.Pp76a/, /IM.SuMaTo76/) which, however, are mainly devoted to static graph problems,as the determination of a shortest path, the computation of cliques, colouring algorithms and so on. For the change of the underlying graph structure only primitive operations as adding or deleting a node or an edge are provided for. None of the existing graph programming languages has suitable operations for sequential, parallel or mixed graph rewriting. As in many applications only simple forms of embedding and connection transformations occur *) this languages should have suggestive constructs to express these special forms. Furthermore, positive and negative application conditions should be enclosed within productions. Programmed steps are easily implementable as this programming language especially contains the usual control structures of programming languages. In /IM.Bu78/ such a graph programming languages is proposed which is to be implemented in the near future.

*) especially in the unrefined and structured version (see passage on programming)

BIBLIOGRAPHY +)

The following bibliography is divided into two chapters. The first one consists of the graph grammar literature in a narrow sense, the second one contains related works. The first chapter is again divided into several sections: Overview Papers (OV), Sequential Graph Grammars (GG), Parallel Graph Grammars (GL), Applications of Graph Grammar Concepts without Linguistic Pattern Recognition (AP), Implementation of Graph Rewriting and Programming Languages for Graph Substitution Problems (IM). The second chapter contains the sections Linguistic Pattern Recognition (PA), Array Grammars (AR), Graph Theory and Applications (GT). The latter does not mean classical graphtheoretic papers but rather works related to graph rewriting and applications of graphs where, on the other hand, no graph grammar concepts are explicitly introduced. Especially the second chapter is far away from being complete. The intersection of different sections is disjoint, i.e. each paper has been classified into exactly one of the above categories which is not possible without arbitrariness. The alternative, to list all papers in lexicographic order and to attach several classification marks, however, is not very instructive for an unexperienced reader who wants to get a rough overview. Finally, it should be notet that the inclusion of a reference here is not a question of quality, i.e. no selection has been carried out. Preliminary versions of a paper as technical reports have not been omitted after the appearence of the paper in a conference proceedings or in a journal as they notify at least the chronology of the development of the graph grammar field. To elucidate the orientation the sequential order of all bibliography sections abbreviated as OV/GG/GL/AP/IM/PA/AR/GT/ is given at the bottom of each page of the following bibliography.

+) compiled by M. Nagl to whom errors and gaps should be reported.

OVERVIEW PAPERS

/OV.De76/ Denert,E./ Ehrig,H.: Mehrdimensionale Sprachen, lecture manuscript, TU Berlin 1976.

/OV.Eh75/ Ehrig,H.: Graph-Grammars: Problems and Results in View of Computer Science Applications (Extended Abstract), Techn. Report 75-21, FB Kybernetik, TU Berlin (1975).

/OV.Eh78/ Ehrig,H.: Introduction to the Algebraic Theory of Graph Grammars, Proc. International Workshop on Graph Grammars and Their Applications to Computer Science and Biology, Bad Honnef 1978,this volume.

/OV.Na78/ Nagl,M.: A Tutorial and Bibliographical Survey on Graph Grammars, Proc. International Workshop on Graph Grammars and Their Applications to Computer Science and Biology, Bad Honnef 1978, this volume.

/OV.Rf76/ Rosenfeld,A.: Array and Web Languages: An Overview, in A. Lindenmayer/G. Rozenberg (Eds.): Automata, Languages, Development, 517-529, Amsterdam: North Holland 1976.

/OV.Sc71/ Schneider,H.J.: Formal Systems for Structure Manipulations, Techn. Report 3/1/71, Informationsverarbeitung II, TU Berlin (1971).

/OV.Sc77/ Schneider,H.J.: Graph Grammars, Proc. Conf. Fund. of Comp. Theory, Poznan, Sept. 19-23, 1977, Lect. Notes in Comp. Sci. 56, 314-331, Berlin: Springer-Verlag 1977.

SEQUENTIAL GRAPH GRAMMARS

/GG.AbMiToTa73/ Abe,N. /Mizumoto,M. /Toyoda,J.-I. /Tanaka,K.: Web Grammars and Several Graphs, Journ. Comp. Syst. Sci. 7, 37-65 (1973).

/GG.BrFu74/ Brayer,J.M. /Fu,K.S.: Some Properties of Web Grammars, Techn. Report TR-EE 74-19, Purdue University (1974).

/GG.DeGh78/ Della Vigna,P. /Ghezzi,C.: Context-free Graph Grammars, Inf. Contr. 37, 2Ø7-233 (1978).

/GG.EhPfSc73a/ Ehrig,H. /Pfender,H. /Schneider,H.J.: Kategorielle Konstruktionen in der Theorie der Graph-Grammatiken, Arbeitsber. d. Inst. f. Math. Masch. u. Datenver. 6, 3, 3Ø-55 (1973).

/GG.EhPfSc73b/ Ehrig,H. /Pfender,H. /Schneider,H.J.: Graph Grammars: An algebraic approach, Proc. 14th Annual Conf. Switching a. Automata Theory, 167-18Ø (1973).

/GG.Eh73/ Ehrig,H.: Kategorielle Theorie von Automaten und mehrdimensionalen Formalen Sprachen, Techn. Report 73-21, FB 2o, TU Berlin (1973).

/GG.Eh77/ Ehrig,H.: Embedding Theorems in the Algebraic Theory of Graph-Grammars, Lect. Notes in Comp. Sci. 56, 245-255, Berlin: Springer-Verlag 1977.

/GG.EhKr75a/ Ehrig,H. /Kreowski,H.-J.: Categorical Theory of Graph-Grammars, Techn. Report 75-08, FB 20, TU Berlin (1975).

/GG.EhKr75b/ Ehrig,H. /Kreowski,H.-J.: CHURCH-ROSSER-Theorems leading to Parallel and Canonical Derivations for Graph-Grammars, Techn. Report 75-27, FB Kybernetik, TU Berlin (1975).

/GG.EhKr76/ Ehrig,H. /Kreowski,H.-J.: Contributions to the Algebraic Theory of Graph Grammars, Techn. Report 76-22, FB Kybernetik, TU Berlin (1976).

/GG.EhKrMaRoWi78/ Ehrig,H. /Kreowski,H.-J. / Maggiolo-Schettini,A. / Rosen,B.K. /Winkowski,J.: Deriving Structures from Strutures, Proc. 7th Intern. Symp. on Math. Found. of Comp. Science, Zakopane (1978).

/GG.EhRo77/ Ehrig,H. /Rosen,B.K.: Reduction of Derivation Sequences, private communication (1977).

/GG.EhTi75/ Ehrig,H. /Tischer,K.-W.: Development of Stochastic Graphs, Proc. Conf. on Unformly Structured Automata Theory and Logic, Tokyo, 1-6 (1975).

/GG.Fr76/ Franck,R.: PLAN2D - Syntactic Analysis of Precedence Graph Grammars, Proc. 3rd ACM Symp. on Principles of Programming Languages, Atlanta, 134-139 (1976).

/GG.Fr77/ Franck,R.: Precedence Graph Grammars: Theoretical Results and Documentation of an Implementation, Techn. Report 77-10, FB 2o, TU Berlin (1977).

/GG.He75/ Heibey,H.W.: Ein Modell zur Behandlung Mehrdimensionaler Strukturen unter Beruecksichtigung der in ihnen definierten Lagerelationen, Report no 15, University of Hamburg (1975).

/GG.Kr76/ Kreowski,H.-J.: Kanonische Ableitungssequenzen fuer Graph-Grammatiken, Techn. Rep. 76-26, FB Kybernetik, TU Berlin (1976).

/GG.Kr77a/ Kreowski,H.-J.: Ein Pumping Lemma fuer kanten-kontextfreie Graph-Sprachen, Techn. Rep. 77-15, FB 2o, TU Berlin (1977).

/GG.Kr.77b/ Kreowski,H.-J.: Transformations of Derivation Sequences in Graph-Grammars, Lect. Notes Comp. Sci. 56, 275-286, Berlin: Springer-Verlag 1977.

/GG.Kr77c/ Kreowski,H.-J.: Manipulationen von Graphenmanipulationen, Dissertation, FB Informatik, TU Berlin (1977).

/GG.Kr78/ Kreowski,H.-J.: A Pumping Lemma for Context-free Graph Languages, Proc. Int. Workshop on Graph Grammars and Their Application to Computer Science and Biology, Bad Honnef 1978, this volume.

OV/GG/GL/AP/IM/PA/AR/GT

/GG.LeYu77/ Levy,L.S. /Yueh,K.: On Labelled Graph Grammars, private communication (1977).

/GG.Mi72/ Milgram,D.: Web Automata, Comp. Science Center Techn. Rep. TR-72-182, University of Maryland (1972).

/GG.Mo70/ Montanari,U.G.: Separable Graphs, Planar Graphs and Web Grammars, Inf. Contr. 16, 243-267 (1970).

/GG.My71/ Mylopoulos,J.: On the relation of graph automata and graph grammars, Techn. Report no 34, Comp. Science Dpt., University of Toronto (1971).

/GG.My72/ Mylopoulos,J.: On the Relation of Graph Grammars and Graph Automata, Proc. 11th Conf. Switching and Automata Theory, 108-120 (1972).

/GG.Na73a/ Nagl,M.: Eine Praezisierung des Pfaltz/Rosenfeldschen Produktionsbegriffs bei mehrdimensionalen Grammatiken, Arbeitsber. d. Inst. f. Math. Masch. u. Datenver. 6, 3, 56-71, Erlangen (1973).

/GG.Na73b/ Nagl,M.: Beziehungen zwischen verschiedenen Klassen von Diagramm-Sprachen, Arbeitsber. d. Inst. f. Math. Masch. u. Datenver. 6, 3, 72-93 (1973).

/GG.Na74/ Nagl,M.: Formale Sprachen von markierten Graphen, Arbeitsber. d. Inst. f. Math. Masch. u. Datenver. 7, 4, Erlangen (1974).

/GG.Na76/ Nagl,M.: Formal Languages of Labelled Graphs, Computing 16, 113-137 (1976).

/GG.Na78/ Nagl,M.: Graph-Ersetzungssysteme: Theorie, Anwendungen, Implementierung, Habilitationsschrift, University of Erlangen (1978).

/GG.NgBa76/ Ng,P.A. /Bang,S.Y.: Toward a Mathematical Theory of Graph-generative Systems and its Applications, Information Sciences 11, 223-250 (1976).

/GG.NgYe75/ Ng,P.A. /Yeh,R.T.: Graph walking automata, Proc. Int. Symp. on Math. Found. of Comp. Science, Marianski Lazne, Czechoslowakia, Lect. Notes in Comp. Sci. 32, 330-336, Berlin: Springer-Verlag 1975.

/GG.OD76/ O'Donell,M.J.: Reduction Strategies in Subtree Replacement Systems, Ph. D. Thesis, Comp. Sci. Dpt., Cornell University, Ithaca (1976).

/GG.Pa72/ Pavlidis,T.: Linear and Context-free Graph Grammars, Journ. ACM 19, 1, 11-23 (1972).

/GG.PfRf69/ Pfaltz,J.L. /Rosenfeld,A.: Web Grammars, Proc. Int. Joint Conf. Art. Intelligence, Washington, 609-619 (1969).

/GG.Ra73a/ Rajlich,V.: Relational Structures and Dynamics of Certain Discrete Systems, Proc. Conf. Math. Found. of Comp. Science, High Tatras, Sept. 3-8, Czechoslowakia, 285-292 (1973).

/GG.Ra73b/ Rajlich,V.: On oriented hypergraphs and dynamics of some discrete systems, Proc. 3rd GI Annual Conference, Lect. Notes Comp. Sci. 1, 70, Berlin: Springer-Verlag 1973.

/GG.Ra74/ Rajlich,V.: Dynamics of certain discrete systems and self-reproduction of patterns, Proc. Conf. Biol. Motivated Automata Theory, Mc Lean, Virginia, 192-198 (1974).

/GG.Ra75/ Rajlich,V.: Dynamics of Discrete Systems and Pattern Reproduction, Journ. Comp. Syst. Sci. 11, 2, 186-202 (1975).

/GG.Ro73/ Rosen,B.K.: Tree-manipulating systems and Church-Rosser theorems, Journ. ACM 20, 160-187 (1973).

/GG.Ro75a/ Rosen,B.K.: A Church-Rosser Theorem for Graph Grammars, SIGACT News 7, 3, 26-31 (1975).

/GG.Ro75b/ Rosen,B.K.: Deriving Graphs from Graphs by Applying a Production, Acta Informatica 4, 337-357 (1975).

/GG.Rf71/ Rosenfeld,A.: Isotonic Grammars, Parallel Grammars, and Picture Grammars, Machine Intelligence 6, 281-294 (1971).

/GG.Rf74/ Rosenfeld,A.: Networks of Automata: Some Applications, Techn. Rep. TR-321, Computer Science Center, University of Maryland, College Park (1974).

/GG.RfMi72a/ Rosenfeld,A. /Milgram,D.: Web Automata and Web Grammars, Techn. Rep. TR-181, Computer Science Center, University of Maryland (1972).

/GG.RfMi72b/ Rosenfeld,A. /Milgram,D.: Web Automata and Web Grammars, Machine Intelligence 7, 307-324 (1972).

/GG.Sc70/ Schneider,H.J.: Chomsky-Systeme fuer partielle Ordnungen, Arbeitsber. d. Inst. f. Math. Masch. u. Datenver. 3, 3, Erlangen (1970).

/GG.Sc71/ Schneider,H.J.: Chomsky-like Systems for Partially Ordered Symbol Sets, Techn. Rep. 2/2/71, Informationsverarbeitung II, TU Berlin (1971).

/GG.Sc72/ Schneider,H.J.: A necessary and sufficient condition for Chomsky-productions over partially ordered symbol sets, Lect. Notes in Econ. and Math. Syst. 78, 90-98 (1972).

/GG.ScEh76/ Schneider,H.J. /Ehrig,H.: Grammars on Partial Graphs, Acta Informatica 6, 2, 297-316 (1976).

/GG.ShMiRo73/ Shah,A.N. /Milgram,D. /Rosenfeld,A.: Parallel Web Automata, Techn. Rep. TR-231, Comp. Science Center, University of Maryland (1973).

/GG.Sk71/ Shank,H.S.: Graph property recognition machines, Math. Systems Theory 5, 45-50 (1971).

/GG.St77a/ Staples,J.: Computation on graph-like expressions, Techn. Rep. 2/77, Dpt. Math. & Comp. Sci., O.I.T., Brisbane (1977).

/GG.St77b/ Staples,J.: Optimal evaluations of graph-like expressions, Techn. Rep. 2/78, Dpt. Math. & Comp. Sci., O.I.T., Brisbane (1978).

/GG.Ue77/ Uesu,T.: A system of graph grammars which generates all recursively enumerable sets of labelled graphs, private communication (1977).

PARALLEL GRAPH GRAMMARS (GRAPH-L-SYSTEMS)

/GL.CaGrPa74/ Carlyle,J.W. /Greibach,S.A. /Paz,A.: A two-dimensional generating system modelling growth by binary cell division, Proc. 15th Conf. Switching and Automata Theory, 1-12 (1974).

/GL.CuLi74/ Culik,K.II. / Lindenmayer,A.: Parallel Rewriting on Graphs and Multidimensional Development, Techn. Rep. CS-74-22, University of Waterloo, Canada (1974).

/GL.CuLi76/ Culik,K.II. /Lindenmayer,A.: Parallel Rewriting on Graphs and Multidimensional Development, Int. Journ. of Gen. Systems 3, 53-66 (1976).

/GL.Cu74/ Culik,K.II: Weighted Growth Functions of DOL-Systems and Growth Functions of Parallel Graph Rewriting Systems, Techn. Rep. CS-74-24, University of Waterloo, Canada (1974).

/GL.CuWo78/ Culik,K.II /Wood,D.: A Mathematical Investigation of Parallel Graph OL-Systems, Private communication (1978).

/GL.Eh75/ Ehrig,H.: An Approach to Context-free Parallel Graph-Grammars, Techn. Rep. 75-30, FB 2o, TU Berlin (1975).

/GL.EhKr76/ Ehrig,H. /Kreowski,H.-J.: Parallel Graph Grammars, in A. Lindenmayer /G. Rozenberg (Eds.): Automata, Languages, Development, 425-442, Amsterdam: North Holland 1976.

/GL.EhLd78/ Ehrig,H. /Liedtke,A.: Locally Star-Gluing Formulas for a Class of Parallel Graph Grammars, Proc. Int. Workshop on Graph Grammars and Their Applications to Computer Science and Biology, this volume.

/GL.EhRb76/ Ehrig,H. /Rozenberg,G.: Some Definitional Suggestions for Graph Grammars, in A. Lindenmayer/ G. Rozenberg(Eds.): Automata, Languages, Development, 443-468, Amsterdam: North Holland 1976.

/GL.Gr76/ Groetsch,E.: Vergleichende Studie ueber parallele Ersetzung auf markierten Graphen, Arbeitsber.d. Inst. f. Math. Masch. u. Datenver. 9, 6, 1-152 (1976).

/GL.GrNa77/ Groetsch,E. /Nagl,M.: Comparison between Explicit and Implicit Graph L-Systems, Arbeitsber. d. Inst. f. Math. Masch. u. Datenver. 10, 8, 5-24, Erlangen (1977).

/GL.GrNa78/ Groetsch,E. /Nagl,M.: Explicit versus Implicit Parallel Rewriting on Graphs, Proc. Int. Workshop on Graph Grammars and Their Applications to Computer Science and Biology, this volume.

/GL.JoLe74/ Joshi,A.K. /Levy,L.S.: Developmental Tree Adjunct Grammars, Proc. Conf. Biologically Motivated Automata Theory, 59-62, Record MITRE Corp., Virginia (1974).

/GL.Ld78/ Liedtke,A.: Lokale Sternverklebungen in der Algebraischen Theorie paralleler Graph-Grammatiken, Diplomarbeit, TU Berlin (1978).

/GL.LiCu77/ Lindenmayer,A. /Culik,K.II: Growing Cellular Systems: Generation of Graphs by Parallel Rewriting, to appear in Int. Journ. Gen. Systems.

/GL.Ma74/ Mayoh,B.H.: Multidimensional Lindenmayer Organisms, Lect. Notes in Comp. Sci. 15, 302-326, Berlin: Springer-Verlag 1974.

/GL.Ma76/ Mayoh,B.H.: Another Model for the Development of Multidimensional Organisms, in A. Lindenmayer/ G. Rozenberg (Eds.): Automata, Languages, Developmet, 469-486, Amsterdam: North Holland 1976.

/GL.Na75/ Nagl,M.: Graph Lindenmayer-Systems and Languages, Arbeitsber. d. Inst. f. Math. Masch. u. Datenver. 8, 1, 16-63, Erlangen (1975).

/GL.Na76a/ Nagl,M.: On a Generalization of Lindenmayer-Systems to Labelled Graphs, in A. Lindenmayer/ G. Rozenberg (eds.): Automata, Languages, Development, 487-508, Amsterdam: North Holland 1976.

/GL.Na76b/ Nagl,M.: Graph Rewriting Systems and Their Application in Biology, Lect. Notes in Biomathematics 11, 135-156, Berlin: Springer-Verlag 1976.

/GL.Na76c/ Nagl,M.: On the Relation between Graph Grammars and Graph Lindenmayer-Systems, Arbeitsber. d. Inst. f. Math. Masch. u. Datenver. 9, 1, 3-32, Erlangen (1976).

/GL.Na77/ Nagl,M.: On the Relation between Graph Grammars and Graph L-Systems, Proc. Int. Conf. Fundamentals of Computation Theory, Poznan, Poland, Sept. 19-32, Lect. Notes Comp. Sci. 56, 142-151, Berlin: Springer-Verlag 1977.

/GL.Nv76/ Nguyen van Huey: Graph-Lindenmayer-Systeme, Diplomarbeit, University of Dortmund (1976).

/GL.Re76/ Reusch,P.J.A.: Generalized Lattices as fundamentals to retrieval models, multidimensional developmetal systems, and the evaluation of fuzziness, Informatik-Berichte 10, University of Bonn (1976).

/GL.Rb75/ Rozenberg,G.: A Definitional Suggestion for Parallel Graph Rewriting Systems, Techn. Rep. LOCOS 27, University of Utrecht (1975).

/GL.Wm76/ Weckmann,H.D.: Mehrdimensionale Parallele Ableitungssysteme - basierend auf markierten Hypergraphen - und ihre Anwendungsmoeglichkeiten, Informatik-Berichte 11, University of Bonn (1976).

APPLICATION OF GRAPH GRAMMATICAL CONCEPTS (WITHOUT LINGUISTIC PATTERN RECOGNITION)

/AP.BaFur78/ Barroso,P.B. /Furtado,A.L.: Implementing a data definition facility driven by graph grammars, to appear in J. of Comp. Languages.

/AP.Br77/ Brendel,W.: Maschinencode-Erzeugung bei inkrementeller Compilation, Arbeitsber. d. Inst. f. Math. Masch. u. Datenver. 10, 8, 24-120 (1977).

/AP.BrBuNa77/ Brendel,W. /Bunke,H. /Nagl,M.: Syntaxgesteuerte Programmierung und inkrementelle Compilation, Informatik-Fachberichte 10, 57-74, Berlin: Springer-Verlag 1977.

/AP.Bu74/ Bunke,H.: Beschreibung eines syntaxgesteuerten inkrementellen Compilers durch Graph-Grammatiken, Arbeitsber. d. Inst. f. Math. Masch. u. Datenver. 7, 7, Erlangen (1974).

/AP.Bu78/ Bunke,H.: Ein Ansatz zur Beschreibung von Programmiersprachen mit expliziten Parallelismen, Dissertation to appear.

/AP.Ch68/ Christensen,C.: An example of the manipulation of directed graphs in the AMBIT/G programming language, in Klerer/ Reinfelds (Eds.): Interactive Systems for Applied Mathematics, New York: Academic Press 1968.

/AP.CuFa77/ Culik,K.II /Farah,M.: Linked forest manipulation systems, a tool for computational semantics, Techn. Rep. CS-77-18, University of Waterloo (1977).

/AP.DeGh76/ Della Vigna,P.L. /Ghezzi,C.: Dta Structures and Graph Grammars, Lect. Notes Comp. Sci. 44, 130-145, Berlin: Springer-Verlag 1976.

/AP.DeFrSt75/ Denert,E. /Franck,R. /Streng,W.: PLAN2D - Toward a Two-dimensional Programming Language, Lect. Notes Comp. Sci. 26, 202-213, Berlin: Springer-Verlag 1975.

/AP.Ea71/ Earley,J.: Toward an Understanding of Data Structures, Comm. ACM 14, 10, 617-627 (1971).

/AP.EcLo78/ Erich, H.D. /Lohberger,V.G.: Parametric specification of abstract data types, parameter substitution, and graph replacements, Proc. Workshop WG 78 on Graphtheoretic Concepts in Computer Science, to appear in the series Applied Computer Science.

/AP.EhKr76a/ Ehrig,H. /Kreowski,H.-J.: Parallelism of Manipulations in Multidimensional Information Structures, Lect. Notes Comp. Sci. 45, 284-293, Berlin: Springer-Verlag 1976.

/AP.EhKr76b/ Ehrig,H. /Kreowski,H.-J.: Categorical Theory of Graphical Systems and Graph Grammars, Lect. Note Econ. Math. Syst. 131, 323-351 (1976).

/AP.EhKr76c/ Ehrig,H. /Kreowski,H.-J.: Algebraic Graph Theory Applied in Computer Science, Proc. Conf. Categorical and Algebraic Methods in Comp. Sci. and Syst. Theory, Haus Ahlenberg, Dortmund (1976).

/AP.EhKr78/ Ehrig,H. /Kreowski,H.-J.: Algebraic Theory of Graph Grammars Applied to Consistency and Synchronization in Data Bases, Proc. Workshop WG 78 on Graphtheoretic Concepts in Computer Science, to appear in the seiries Applied Computer Science.

/AP.EhKrPa77/ Ehrig,H. /Kreowski,H.-J. /Padawitz,P.: Some Remarks Concerning Correct Specification and Implementation of Abstract Data Types, Techn. Rep. 77-13, FB 20, TU Berlin (1977).

/AP.EhKrPa78/ Ehrig,H. /Kreowski,H.-J. /Padawitz,P.: Stepwise Specification and Implementation of Abstract Data Types, Proc. 5th ICALP, Udine (1978).

/AP.EhMu74/ Ehrig,H. /Mueller,F.: Graph-Grammar Formalization and Manipulation of Data Structures in the CODASYL-Report, Abstract, TU Berlin (1974).

/AP.EhRo76/ Ehrig,H. /Rosen,B.K.: Commutativity of Independent Transformations on Complex Objects, IBM Research Rep. RC 6251 (1976), to appear in Acta Informatica.

/AP.EhRo77/ Ehrig,H. /Rosen,B.K.: The Mathematics of Record Handling, Lect. Notes Comp. Sci. 52, 206-220, Berlin: Springer-Verlag 1977.

/AP.EhRo78a/ Ehrig,H. /Rosen,B.K.: Concurrency of Manipulation in Multidimensional Information Structures, Proc. 7th Int. Symp. on Math. Found. of Comp. Sci., Zakopane (1978).

/AP.EhRo78b/ Ehrig,H. /Rosen,B.K.: Concurrency of Manipulation in Multidimensional Information Structures, Techn. Rep. 78-13, FB 20, TU Berlin (1978).

/AP.EhTi74/ Ehrig,H. /Tischer,K.-W.: Graph-Grammars for the Specification of Organisms, Proc. Conf. on Biologically Motivated Automata Theory, 158-165, Record MITRE Corp., Virginia, (1974).

/AP.EhTi75/ Ehrig,H. /Tischer,K.-W.: Graph grammars and Applications to Specialization and Evolution in Biology, Journ. Comp. Syst. Sci. 11, 212-236 (1975).

/AP.ErGu77/ Ershov,A.P. /Grushefsky,N.V.: An implementation oriented method for describing algorithmic languages, Inf. Proc. 77, 117-122, Amsterdam: North Holland 1977.

/AP.FaKeZu76/ Farrow,R. /Kennedv,K. /Zucconi,L.: Graph Grammars and Global Program Data Flow Analysis, Proc. 17th Ann. Symp. on Foundation of Computer Science, Houston (1976).

/AP.Fr76/ Fruehauf,T.: Formale Beschreibung von Informationsstrukturen mit Hilfe von Graphersetzungsmechanismen, Arbeitsber. d. Inst. f. Math. Masch. u. Datenver. 9, 1, 33-125, Erlangen (1976).

/AP.Fur76/ Furtado,A.L.: Characterizing sets of data structures by the connectivity relation, Int. Journ. Comp. Inf. Sci. 5, 2, 89-108 (1976).

/AP.FurMy75/ Furtado,A.L. /Mylopoulos,J.: Using graph grammars to define sets of digraphs, Techn. Rep. 1/75-PUC/RJ, Pontificia Universidade Catolica do Rio de Janeiro (1975).

/AP.Gö77/ Goettler,H.: Zweistufige Graphmanipulationssysteme fuer die Semantik von Programmiersprachen, Arbeitsber. d. Inst. f. Math. Masch. u. Datenver. 10, 12, Erlangen (1977).

/AP.Gö78/ Goettler,H.: Semantical dsecription by two-level graph-grammars for quasihierarchical graphs, Proc. Workshop WG 78 on Graphtheoretical Concepts in Computer Science, to appear in the series Applied Computer Science.

/AP.GoFur74/ Gotlieb,C.C. /Furtado,A.L.: Data Schemata Based on Directed Graphs, Techn. Rep. 70, Comp. Sci. Dpt., University of Toronto (1974).

/AP.Ho65/ Holt,A.W.: n-Theory, a mathematical method for the description and analysis of discrete finite information systems, Applied Data Research Inc. (1965).

/AP.Kr78/ Kreowski,H.-J.: Anwendungen der Algebraischen Theorie von Graph-Grammatiken auf Konsistenz und Synchronisation in Datenbanksystemen, Techn. Rep. 78-15, FB Informatik, TU Berlin (1978).

/AP.Kn74/ Kron,H.H.: Practical subtree replacement systems, M.S. Thesis, University of California, Santa Cruz (1974).

/AP.Kn78/ Kron,H.H.: Template Overlaps i Tree Manipulation Systems, Proc. Workshop WG 78 on Graphtheoretic Concepts in Computer Science, to appear in the series Applied Computer Science.

/AP.Ne77/ Negraszus-Patan,G.: Anwendungen der algebraischen Graphentheorie auf die formale Beschreibung und Manipulation eines Datenbankmodells, Diplomarbeit, FB 20, TU Berlin (1977).

/AP.Pa78/ Padawitz,P.: Church-Rosser-Eigenschaften von Graph-Grammatiken und Anwendungena auf die Semantik von LISP, Diplomarbeit, FB 2o, TU Berlin (1978).

/AP.Pr71/ Pratt,T.: Pair Grammars, Graph Languages and String-to-Graph Translations, Journ. Comp. Syst. Sci. 5, 560-595 (1971).

/AP.Pr73/ Pratt,T.: A formal definition of ALGOL 60 using hierarchical graphs and pair grammars, Techn. Rep. TSN-33, University of Texas Comp. Center, Austin (1973).

/AP.Pr75/ Pratt,T.: A theory of programming languages, Part I, Techn. Rep. CCSN-41, University of Texas Computation Center, Austin (1975).

/AP.Pr76/ Pratt,T.: Application of formal grammars and automata to programming language definition, in R.T. Yeh (Ed.): Applied Computation Theory, Englewood Cliffs: Prentice Hall 1976.

/AP.Ra75/ Rajlich,V.: Relational Definition of Computer Languages, Proc. Conf. Math. Found. Comp. Sci. 1975, Lect. Notes Comp. Sci. 32, 362-376, Berlin: Springer-Verlag 1975.

/AP.Ra77/ Rajlich,V.: Theory of Data Structures by Relational and Graph Grammars, Proc. ICALP Turku, Lect. Notes Comp. Sci. 52, 391-411, Berlin: Springer-Verlag 1977.

/AP.Ra79/ Rajlich,V.: Theory of computing machines, to be published in Czech by SNTL, Prague (1979).

/AP.Ri77/ Ripken,K.: Formale Beschreibung von Maschinen, Implementierungen und optimierender Maschinencode-Erzeugung aus attributierten Programmgraphen, Dissertation, Techn. Rep. TUM-Info-7731, Muenchen (1977).

/AP.Sc75/ Schneider,H.J.: Syntax-directed Description of Incremental Compilers, Lect. Notes Comp. Sci. 26, 192-201, Berlin: Springer-Verlag 1975.

/AP.Sc76/ Schneider,H.J.: Conceptual data base description using graph grammars, in H. Noltemeier (Ed.): Graphen, Algorithmen, Datenstrukturen, Applied Computer Science 4, 77-98, Muenchen: Hanser Verlag 1976.

/AP.SeFur77/ Sevcik,K.C. /Furtado,A.L.: Complete and compatible sets of update operations, Techn. Rep. 26/77 PUC/RJ, Pontificia Universidade Catolica do Rio de Janeiro (1977).

/AP.SgSmWa77/ Siegmund,N. /Schmitt,R. /Wankmueller,F.: Abaenderung von Programmen als Anwendung des Einbettungsproblems fuer Graphen, Techn. Rep. 42/77, Abt. Informatik, University of Dortmund (1977).

/AP.St78/ Steiner,S.: Untersuchungen ueber die gleichzeitige Ausfuehrung von Operationen in Datenbankmodellen unter Verwendung der Algebraischen Graphentheorie, Diplomarbeit, FB Informatik, TU Berlin (1978).

/AP.Si74/ Siromoney,G. and R.: Radial Grammars and Biological Systems, Proc. Conf. Biologically Motivated Automata Theory, 92-96, Record MITRE Corp. Virginia (1974).

/AP.St75/ Staples,J.: Church-Rosser Theorems for replacement systems, Lect. Notes Comp. Sci. 45, 291-307, Berlin: Springer-Verlag 1975.

/AP.St77a/ Staples,J.: Optimal reduction in replacement systems, Bull. Austr. Math. Soc. 16, 341-349 (1977).

/AP.St77b/ Staples,J.: A class of replacement systems with simple optimality theory, Bull. Austr. Math. Soc. 17, 335-350 (1977).

/AP.St78a/ Staples,J.: Speeding up subtree replacement systems, Techn. Rep. 3/78, Dpt. Math. & Comp. Sci., Q.I.T., Brisbane (1978).

/AP.St78b/ Staples,J.: Efficient combinatory reduction, submitted for publication.

/AP.St78c/ Staples,J.: A lambda calculus with naive substitution, submitted for publication.

/AP.Ul73/ Ullman,J.D.: Fast Algorithms for the Elimination of Common Subexpressions, Acta Informatica 2, 191-214 (1973).

/AP.We78a/ Weber,D.: Datengraphen und deren Transformation: Ein Konzept zur Spezifikation von Datentypen, Arbeitsbericht d. Inst. f. Math. Masch. u. Datenver. 11, 8, Erlangen (1978).

/AP.We78b/ Weber,D.: Transformation Programs for Data Graphs, a Tool for Specifying, Verifying and Implementing Data Types, Proc. Workshop WG 78 on Graphtheoretic Concepts in Computer Science, to appear in the series Applied Computer Science.

IMPLEMENTATION OF GRAPH REWRITING AND PROGRAMMING LANGUAGES FOR GRAPH PROBLEMS

/IM.An76/ Anthonisse,J.M.: A Graph Defining Language and its Implementation and Applications, in U. Pape (Ed.): Graphen-Sprachen und Algorithmen auf Graphen, Applied Computer Science 1, 127-130, Muenchen: Hanser Verlag 1976.

/IM.Ba74/ Basili,V.R.: Sets and graphs in GRAAL, Proc. 27th ACM National Conf., 289-296 (1974).

/IM.Ba76/ Basili,V.R.: Some Supplementary Notes on the Graph Algorithmic Language GRAAL, in U. Pape (Ed.): Graphen-Sprachen und Algorithmen auf Graphen, Applied Computer Science 1, 31-48, Muenchen: Hanser Verlag 1976.

/IM.BaReMe72/ Basili,V.R. /Reinbold,W.C. /Mesztenyi,C.K.: On a Programming Language for Graph Algorithms, BIT 12, 220-241 (1972).

/IM.Br76/ Brendel,W.: Implementierung von Graph-Grammatiken, Arbeitsber. d. Inst. f. Math. Masch. u. Datenver. 9, 1, 126-237, Erlangen (1976).

/IM.BrNaWe78/ Brendel,W. /Nagl,M. /Weber,D.: Implementation of Sequential and Parallel Graph Rewriting Systems, in J. Muehlbacher (Ed.): Datenstrukturen, Graphen, Algorithmen, Applied Computer Science 8, 79-106, Muenchen: Hanser Verlag 1978.

/IM.Bu78/ Bulin,K.: Entwurf einer Programmiersprache fuer Graphenprobleme und ihres Praecompilers, Diplomarbeit, University of Erlangen (1978).

/IM.CrMo70/ Crespi-Reghizzi,J. /Morpurgo,R.: A Language for Treating Graphs, Comm. ACM 13, 5, 319-323 (1970).

/IM.EaCa71/ Earley,J. /Caizergues,P.: VERS Manual, Comp. Sci. Dpt. University of California, Berkeley (1971).

/IM.EnWc74/ Encarnacao,J. /Weck,G.: Eine Implementierung von DATAS (Datenstrukturen in assoziativer Speicherung), Techn. Rep. A 74-1, University of Saarbruecken (1974).

/IM.FrPr71/ Friedman,D. /Pratt,T.: A Language Extension for Graph Processing and its Formal Semantics, Comm. ACM 14, 460-467 (1971).

/IM.Ha74/ Hansal,A.: Software Devices for Processing Graphs Using PL/I Compile Time Facilities, Inf. Proc. Letters 2, 171-179 (1974).

/IM.Ja76/ Jahn,B.: Eine Studie zur Implementierung von Graph-Grammatiken unter Verwendung von Assoziativverarbeitung, Arbeitsber. d. Inst. f. Math. Masch. u. Datenver. 9, 6, 153-260, Erlangen (1976).

/IM.Ki72/ King,C.A.: A Graph-Theoretic Programming Language, in R.C. Read (Ed.): Graph Theory and Computing, 63-75, New York: Academic Press 1972.

/IM.Kö76/ Köpke,F.: GALA - Eine Sprache zur Erzeugung und Manipulation von intepretierten Graphen, in U. Pape (Ed.): Graphen-Sprachen und Algorithmen auf Graphen, Applied Computer Science 1, 117-126, Muenchen Hanser Verlag 1976.

/IM.Na77/ Nagl,M.: Implementation of Parallel Rewriting on Graphs Arbeitsber. d. Inst. f. Math. Masch. u. Datenver. 10, 8, 121-154, Erlangen (1977).

/IM.NaZi78/ Nagl,M. /Zischler,H.: A Dialog for the Graphical Representation of Graphs, Proc. Workshop WG 78 on Graphtheoretic Concepts in Computer Science, to appear in the series Applied Computer Science.

/IM.Pp76a/ Pape,U.: A Model of a High Level Design Language for Graph Algorithms, Techn. Rep. 75-29, TU Berlin (1976).

/IM.Pp76b/ Pape,U.: Datenstrukturen fuer Mengen in Algorithmen auf Graphen, in H. Noltemeier (Ed.): Graphen, Algorithmen, Datenstrukturen, Applied Computer Science 4, 99-122, Muenchen: Hanser Verlag 1976.

/IM.Sc78/ Schneider,H.J.: Implementation of graph grammars using a pseudo-associative memory, in J. Muehlbacher (Ed.): Datenstrukturen, Graphen, Algorithmen, Applied Computer Science 8, 63-78, Muenchen: Hanser Verlag 1978.

/IM.SuMaTo76/ Sugito,Y. /Mano,Y. /Torii,K.: Ona two-dimensional graph manipulation language GML, Transact. of the IECE of Japan, vol. J59-D, 9, 597-604 (1976).

/IM.Wo69/ Wolfberg,M.: An Interactive Graph Theory System, Doctoral Thesis, University of Pennsylvania, Techn. Rep. 69-25, Philadelphia (1969).

/IM.Zi77/ Zischler,H.: Entwurf eines Dialogsystems zum Ausgeben von Graphen, Studienarbeit, University of Erlangen (1977).

LINGUISTIC PATTERN RECOGNITION

/PA.An68/ Anderson,R.H.: Syntax-directed Recognition of Hand-printed Two-dimensional Mathematics, in Klerer/Reinfelds (Eds.): Interactive Systems for Exp. Applied Mathematics, 436-459, New York: Academic Press 1868.

/PA.Ba71/ Banerji,R.B.: Some Linguistic and Statistical Problems in Pattern Recognition, Pattern Rec. 3, 409-419 (1971).

/PA.BiFe72/ Biermann,A.W. /Feldman,J.A.: A Survey of Results in Grammatical Inference, in S. Watanabe (Ed.): Frontiers of Pattern Recognition, New York: Academic Press 1972.

/PA.BrFu75/ Brayer,J.M. /Fu,K.S.: Web Grammars and Their Application to Pattern Recognition, Techn. Rep. TR-EE-75-1, Purdue University, West Lafayette (1975).

/PA.Ch71/ Chang,S.-K.: Picture Processing Grammars and its Applications, Inf. Sciences 3, 121-148 (1971).

/PA.ChiRi72/ Chien,Y.T. /Ribak,R.: A New Data Base for Syntax-directted Pattern Analysis and Recognition, IEEE Trans. on Comp. 21, 790-801 (1972).

/PA.ChoFu76/ Chou,S.M. /Fu,K.S.: Inference for Transition Network Grammars, Proc. 3rd Int. Joint Conf. on Pattern Recognition, Coronado, California (1976).

/PA.Cl69/ Clowes,M.: Pictorial Relationships - A Syntactical Approach, Mach. Int. 4, 361-383 (1969).

/PA.Ev68/ Evans,T.G.: A Grammar-cotrolled Pattern Analyser, Inf. Proc. 68, vol. II, 1592-1598 (1968).

/PA.Ev71/ Evans,T.G.: Grammatical inference techniques in pattern analysis, Software Engineering 2, 183-202 (1971).

/PA.Fe71/ Feder,J.: Plex Languages, Inf. Sciences 3, 225-241 (1971).

/PA.Fu72/ Fu,K.S.: On syntactical pattern recognition and stochastic languages, in S. Watanabe (Ed.): Frontiers of Pattern Recognition, 113-137, New York: Academic Press 1972.

/PA.Fu74/ Fu,K.S.: Syntactic Methods in Pattern Recognition, New York: Academic Press 1974.

/PA.Fu76/ Fu,K.S. (Ed.): Applications of Syntactic Pattern Recognition, New York: Springer-Verlag 1976.

/PA.Fu77/ Fu,K.S. (Ed.): Syntactic Pattern Recognition, application, communication and cybernetics, Lect. Notes Comp. Sci. 14, Berlin: Springer-Verlag 1977.

/PA.Fu/ Fu,K.S.: Linguistic approach to pattern recognition, in R.T. Yeh (Ed.): Applied Computation Theory, Analysis, Design, Modelling, 106-149, Englewood Cliffs: Prentice Hall.

/PA.FuBh73/ Fu,K.S. /Bhargava,B.K.: Tree Systems for Syntactic Pattern Recognition, IEEE Trans. on Computers C-22, no 12, 1087-1099 (1973).

/PA.FuBo75/ Fu,K.S. / Booth,T.L.: Grammatical inference - Introduction and Survey, Part I, Part II, IEEE Trans. Syst. Man Cybern., vol. SMC-5, 95-111 and 409-423 (1975).

/PA.FuSw71/ Fu,K.S. /Swain,P.H.: On syntactic pattern recognition, in I.T. Ton (Ed.): Software Engineering, New York: Academic Press 1971.

/PA.Ki64/ Kirsch,R.A.: Computer Interpretation of English Text and Picture Patterns, IEEE-Trans. EC-13, 363-376 (1964).

/PA.LuFu76/ Lu,S.Y. /Fu,K.S.: Structure-Preserved error-correcting tree automata for syntactic pattern recognition, Proc. 1976 IEEE Conf. on Decision and Control, Clearwater, Florida.

/PA.MiSh67/ Miller,W.F. /Shaw,A.C.: A Picture Calculus, in: Emerging Concepts of Computer Graphics, Univ. Illinois Conference, 101-121 (1967).

/PA.MiSh68/ Miller,W.F. /Shaw,A.C.: Linguistic Methods in Picture Processing - A Survey, Proc. AFIPS 1968 FJCC, vol. 33, I, 279-290.

/PA.My72/ Mylopoulos,J.: On the Application of Formal Languages and Automata Theory to Pattern Recognition, Pattern Rec. 4, 37-51 (1972).

/PA.Ns64/ Narasimhan,R.: Labelling Schemata and Syntactic Description of Pictures, Inf. Contr. 7, 151-179 (1964).

/PA.Ns66/ Nrasimhan,R.: Syntax-directed Interpretation of Classes of Pictures, Comm. ACM 9, 166-173 (1966).

/PA.NsClEv69/ Narasimhan,R. /Clowes,M. /Evans,T.G.: Survey on Picture Processing with Linguistic Approach, in A. Graselli (Ed.): Automatic Interpretation and Classification of Images, New York: Academic Press 1969.

/PA.NsRe71/ NarasimhanR. /Reddy,V.S.N.: A Syntax-aided Recognition Scheme for Handprinted English Letters, Pattern Rec. 3, 345-361 (1971).

/PA.Pf72/ Pfaltz,J.L.: Web Grammars and Picture Description, Comp. Graphics and Image Processing 1 (1972).

/PA.Rf73/ Rosenfeld,A.: Progress in Picture Processing 1969-71, Computing Surveys 5, 2, 81-108 (1973).

/PA.RfSg71/ Rosenfeld,A. /Strong,J.P.: A grammar for maps, Software Engineering 2, 227-239 (1971).

/PA.Sb72/ Schwebel,J.C.: A Graph-Structure Transformation Model for Picture Parsing, UIUCDCS-R-72-514, Dpt. Comp. Sci., University of Illinois, Urbana (1972).

/PA.Sh69/ Shaw,A.C.: A Formal Description Scheme as a Basis for Picture Processing Systems, Inf. Contr. 14, 9-52 (1969).

/PA.Sh70/ Shaw,A.C.: Parsing of Graph-Representable Picyuers, Journ. ACM 17, 3, 453-481 (1970).

/PA.SyGi72/ Stiny,G. /Gips,J.: Shape grammars and the generative specification of painting and sculpture, Proc. IFIP-Congress 1971, 1460-1465, Amsterdam: North Holland 1972.

/PA.SwFu70/ Swain,P.H. /Fu,K.S.: Nonparametric and Linguistic Approaches to Pattern Recognition,Techn. Rep. TR-EE-70-20, Purdue University, West Lafayette (1970).

/PA.Uh71/ Uhr,L.: Flexible Linguistic Pattern Recognition, Pattern Rec. 3, 361-383 (1971).

/PA.Wa71/ Watanabe,S.: Ungrammatical Grammar in Pattern Recognition, Pattern Rec. 3, 4, 385-408 (1971).

/PA.WtBe71/ Watt,A.H. /Beurle,R.L.: Recognition of hand-printed numerals reduced to graph-representable form, 2nd Int. Joint Conf. Art. Int., 322-332 (1971).

ARRAY GRAMMARS AND ARRAY AUTOMATA

/AR.Cd68/ Codd,E.F.: Cellular Automata, New York: Academic Press 1968.

/AR.Co69/ Cole,S.N.: Real-time Computation by n-Dimensional Iterative Arrays of Finite State Machines, IEEE Trans. on Computers, vol. C-18, 349-365 (1969).

/AR.Da70/ Dacey,M.F.: The Syntax of a Triangle and some other Figures, Pattern Rec. 2, 1, 11-31 (1970).

/AR.Da71/ Dacey,M.F.: Poly - A Two-Dimensional Language for a Class of Polygons, Pattern Rec. 3, 197-208 (1971).

/AR.IoNk78/ Inone,K. /Nakamura,A.: Two-dimesional Multipass On-line Tesselation Acceptors, Techn. Rep. TR-628, University of Maryland (1978).

/AR.MeRf73/ Mercer,A. /Rosenfeld,A.: An Array Grammar Programming System, Comm. ACM 16, 406-410 (1973).

/AR.Rd71/ Rosendahl,M.: Zur Beschreibung mehrdimensionaler Zeichenketten durch formale Sprachen, Dissertation, GMD Techn. Rep. 76, Bonn (1971).

/AR.Rf73/ Rosenfeld,A.: Array grammar normal forms, Inf. Contr. 23, 173-182 (1973).

/AR.Rf78/ Rosenfeld,A.: Array Grammars, Techn. Rep. TR-629, University of Maryland (1978).

/AR.SiSiKt/ Siromoney,G. and R. /Krithivasan,K.: Picture languages with array rewriting rules, Inf. Contr. 22, 447-470 (1973).

/AR.Sm70/ Smith,A.R. III: Cellular Automata and Formal Languages, Proc. 11th Conf. Switching and Automata Theory, 216-224 (1970).

/AR.Sm71/ Smith,A.R. III: Two-dimensional Formal Languages and Pattern Recognition by Cellular Automata, Proc. 12 Conf. Switching and Atomata Theory, 144-152 (1971).

/AR.Sm76/ Smith,A.R. III: Introduction to and survey of polyautomata theory, in A. Lindenmayer/G. Rozenberg (Eds.): Automata, Languages,Development, 405-424, Amsterdam: North Holland 1976.

/AR.YaAm69/ Yamada,H. /Amoroso,S.: Tesselation Automata, Inf. Contr. 14, 299-317 (1969).

GRAPH THEORY AND APPLICATIONS

/GT.Al78/ Altmann,W.: Beschreibung von Programmoduln zum Entwurf zuverlaessiger Softwaresysteme, Dissertation, Erlangen (1978).

/GT.BaTu73/ Basili,V.R. /Turner,A.J.: A Hierarchical Maschine Model for the Semantics of Programming Languages, ACM SIGPLAN Notices 8, 11, (1973).

/GT.BeOlWe77/ Bergstra,J.A. /Ollongren,A. /van der Weide,Th.P.: An axiomatization of the relational data objects.

/GT.BeGoOlTeWe78/ Bergstra,J.A. /Goeman,H.J.M. /Ollongren,A. /Terpstra, G.A. /van der Weide,Th.P.: Axioms for multilevel objects, submitted for publication in Fundamenta Informaticae.

/GT.CoGo70/ Corneil,D.G. /Gotlieb,C.C.: An Efficient Algorithm for Graph Isomorphism, Journ. ACM 17, 51-64 (1970).

/GT.Cu71/ Culik,K.: Combinatorial problems in the theory of complexity of algorithmic nets without cycles for simple computers, Aplikace Mathematiky 16, 3, 188-202 (1971).

/GT.Cu73/ Culik,K. II: A model for the formal definition of programming languages, Int. Journ. of Comp. Math., Section A, 3, 315-345 (1973).

/GT.CuMa76/ Culik,K. II /Maurer,H.A.: String Representation of Graphs, Techn. Rep. 50, Inst. f. Ang. Inf. u. Form. Beschreibungsverf., University of Karlsruhe, to appear in Int. J. of Comp. Math. (1976).

/GT.CuMa77/ Culik,K. II/Maurer,H.A.: Linearizing selector-graphs and applications thereof, Angewandte Informatik 9, 386-394 (1977).

/GT.Ed76/ Eden,B.N.: Ein Heuristisches Verfahren zur Distriktermittlung in bewerteten Graphen und seine Anwendungen auf die Berechnung von Schuleinzugsbereichen, Dissertation, TU Berlin (1976).

/GT.GeLa73/ Genrich,H.J. /Lautenbach,K.: Synchronisationsgraphen, Acta Informatica 2, 143-161 (1973).

/GT.GoOlWe78/ Goeman,H.J.M. /Ollongren,A. /van der Weide,Th.P.: Axiomatiek van datastrukturen, Colloquium Capita Datastructuren, MC Syllabus 37, Math. Centre Amsterdam, 85-98 (1978).

/GT.Hu73/ Huang,J.C.: A Note on Information Organization and Storage, Comm. ACM 16, 7, 406-410 (1973).

/GT.Kn71/ Knődel,W.: Ein Verfahren zur Feststellung der Isomorphie von endlichen zusammenhaengenden Graphen, Computing 6, 329-334 (1971).

/GT.Li72/ Liebermann,R.N.: Topologies on directed graphs, Techn. Rep. TR-214, University of Maryland (1972).

/GT.LuWa69/ Lucas,W. /Walk,K.: On a formal description of PL/I, Ann. Rev. Aut. Progr. 6, 3, 105-182 (1969).

/GT.Nu72/ Nutt,G.J.: Evaluation Nets for Computer System Performance Analysis, Proc. FJCC, 279-286 (1972).

/GT.Ol76/ Ollongren,A.: A new look at abstract data structures, IBM Lab. Vienna, Techn. Rep. TR.25.147 (1976).

/GT.Pe62/ Petri,C.A.: Kommunikation mit Automaten, Techn. Rep. IIM 2, University of Bonn (1962).

/GT.Pf71/ Pfaltz,J.L.: Convexity in directed graphs, Journ. Combin. Theory 10, 2, 143-162 (1971).

/GT.Pf72/ Pfaltz,J.L.: Graph Structures, J. ACM 19, 3, 411-422 (1972).

/GT.Pf75/ Pfaltz,J.L.: Representing Graphs by Knuth Trees, J. ACM 22, 3, 361-366 (1975).

/GT.Pr69/ Pratt,T.W.: A Hierarchical graph model of the semantics of programs, Proc. SJCC, 813-825 (1969).

/GT.Ro76/ Rosen,B.K.: Correctness of Parallel Programs: The Church-Rosser Approach, Theor. Comp. Sci. 2, 183-207 (1976).

/GT.Ro77/ Rosen,B.K.: Arcs in graphs are not pairs of nodes, SIGACT News 9, 3, 25-27 (1977).

/GT.RzTh75/ Rozenberg,A.L. /Thatcher,J.W.: What is a multilevel array?, IBM Journ. of Research and Development 19, 2, 163-169 (1975).

/GT.SaSu64/ Salton,G. /Sussengut,E.H.: Some flexible information retrieval systems using structure matching procedures, AFIPS Proc. SJCC 25, 587-597, Washington (1964).

/GT.St75/ Streng,W.: PLAN2D - Semantik einer zeidimensionalen Programmiersprache, Dissertation, FB Kybernetik, TU Berlin (1975).

/GT.Un64/ Unger,S.H.: GIT - a heuristic program for tesing pairs of directed line graphs for isomorphism, Comm. ACM 7, 1, 26-34 (1964).

/GT.WaSo73/ Walker,S.A. /Strong,H.R.: Characterization of flowchartable Recursions, J. Comp. Syst. Sci. 7, 404-447 (1973).

/GT.We73/ Weber,D.: Ein Test der Einbettbarkeit von Graphen, Arbeitsber. d. Inst. f. Math. Masch. u. Datenver. 6, 3, 154-190, Erlangen (1973).

/GT.Wg72/ Wegner,P.: The Vienna Definition Language, Computing Surveys 4, 1 (1972).

/GT.WgHo78/ Wegner,E. /Hopmann,C.: Semantics of a Language for Describing Systems and Processes, Techn. Rep. IST 36, GMD Bonn(1978).

/GT.Wo75/ Wolfberg,M.S.: Fundamentals of the AMBIT/L List Processing Language, ACM SIGPLN Notices 7, 10, 66-75 (1975).

/GT.Ya60/ Yanow,I.I.: The logical schemes of algorithms, Probl. Cybernetics 1, 82-140 (1960).

OV/GG/GL/AP/IM/PA/AR/GT

International Workshop on Graph Grammars and their Applications to Computer Science and Biology, October 30-November 3, 1978, Bad Honnef, West Germany.

PARTIALLY-ADDITIVE MONOIDS, GRAPH-GROWING, AND THE ALGEBRAIC SEMANTICS OF RECURSIVE CALLS[1]

M. A. Arbib
Computer and Information Science

E. G. Manes
Mathematics Department
University of Massachusetts
Amherst, MA 01003, USA

(Abstract)

The way in which Pfn (sets and partial functions) provides a setting for the semantics of deterministic programs [and Rel (sets and relations) provides a setting for the semantics of nondeterministic programs] has led us to axiomatize the notion of a partially-additive monoid. We show that programs incorporating procedure calls may be represented by graph grammars, with one non-terminal and production for each distinct procedure (including the program itself). Program execution may be construed as a process of interpretation of graphs obtained by repeated graph substitution. We show that the resultant interpretive semantics yields the same result as our theory of the canonical fixpoint for abstract recursion schemes introduced in an earlier paper.

1. Abstract Recursion Schemes: The Canonical Fixpoint.

Consider, for concreteness, the flow diagram (1) where at any defined stage of the computation, the state lies in some fixed data set D.

1

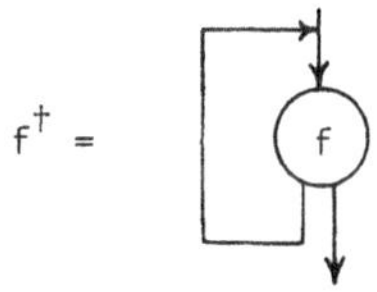

Thus f is to be interpreted as a map $D \longrightarrow 2\cdot D$ (where $2\cdot D$ is the disjoint union $\{(d,1) : d\in D\} \cup \{(d,2) : d\in D\}$ of 2 copies of D), while the iterate of f is to be interpreted as a partial function (the computation may get 'stuck in the loop') $f^\dagger: D \longrightarrow D$. This iterate may be viewed as a fixed point of h where

2

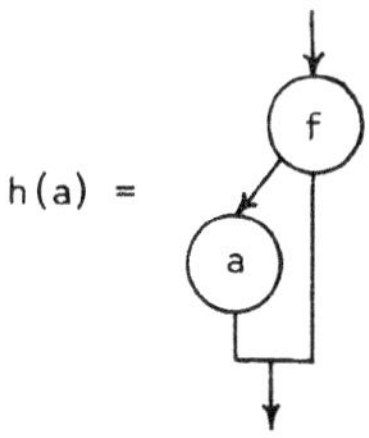

In [3] we have shown how each such fixed point equation gives rise to an abstract recursion scheme, and we have shown that a unique canonical fixpoint can be assigned to these schemes. Our aim in the present paper is to provide an

[1] The research reported in this paper was supported in part by the National Science Foundation under grant MCS 76-84477.

interpretive semantics and show that it does indeed provide the canonical fixpoint. First, we must devote the present section to the exposition of basic concepts from [3].

We stress (following [2]) partially-additive structure. Our a's lie in Pfn(D,D), the space of partial functions from the set D to itself. On Pfn(D,D) we may define a partial addition for families $(f_i : i \in I)$ by saying that Σf_i is defined only if the domains of the f_i are disjoint, and we then have

3
$$(\Sigma f_i)(x) = \begin{cases} f_j(x) & \text{if } x \in \text{dom}(f_j) \\ \text{undefined} & \text{if no such } j \text{ exists.} \end{cases}$$

Given a test $p: D \longrightarrow \{\text{true}, \text{false}\}$, we may define partial functions in Pfn(D,D) $p_t(d) = d$ with domain $\{d : p(d) = \text{true}\}$ and $p_f(d) = d$ with domain $\{d : p(d) = \text{false}\}$. In this framework, the conditional if p then f else g is written as $f \cdot p_t + g \cdot p_f$, as diagrammed in 4. This sum puts 'the different possible paths in a test' in the abstract language. Conversely, any sum can be thought of as a generalized conditional.

4
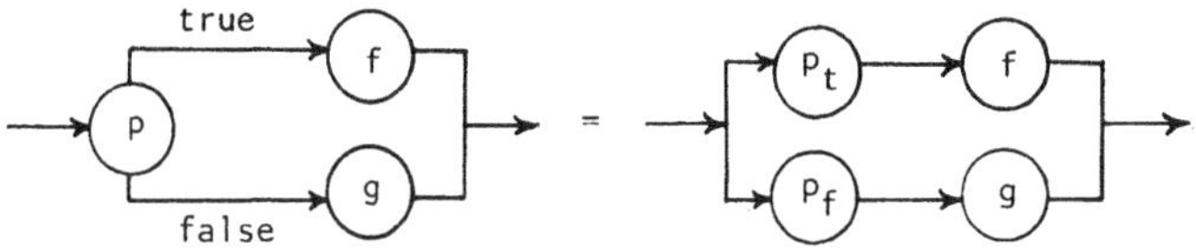

We turn now to an axiomatization of (Pfn(D,D),Σ).

5 Definition [2]. An ω-complete partial abelian monoid (henceforth, partially-additive monoid, for short) is a pair (A,Σ) where A is a set and Σ is a partial operation on countable (i.e. finite or denumerable) sequences in A subject to the following axioms:

Partition-associativity axiom: If the countable set I is partitioned into $(I_j : j \in J)$ then for each family $(a_i : i \in I)$ in A,

$$\Sigma(a_i : i \in I) = \Sigma(\Sigma(a_i : i \in I_j) : j \in J)$$

in the sense that the left side is defined iff the right side is defined and then the values are equal.

Limit axiom: If $(a_i : i \in I)$ is a countable family in A and if $\Sigma(a_i : i \in F)$ is defined for every finite subset F of I, then $\Sigma(a_i : i \in I)$ is defined.

Unary sum axiom: For one-element families, Σa is defined, and Σa = a.

Since the unary-sum axiom ensures that some sums exist, I_j may be empty and in the partition-associativity axiom, it follows that the empty sum is defined and provides an additive zero which we denote 0 or ⊥.

For examples of partially-additive monoids see [2]. Here we note that non-deterministic semantics is obtained if we replace Pfn(A,B) by Rel(A,B) -- relations from A to B -- with sum being union, and thus, in this case, totally additive.

While partially-additive semantics was intended to be disjoint from the Scott theory [7], it is worth noting that an ω-cpo (ω-complete partially-ordered set with minimal element) is a partially-additive monoid if ΣS is defined as sup(S) if S is a countable chain and is undefined otherwise.

Returning to 2, note that it may be rewritten as

6

$h(a) =$ 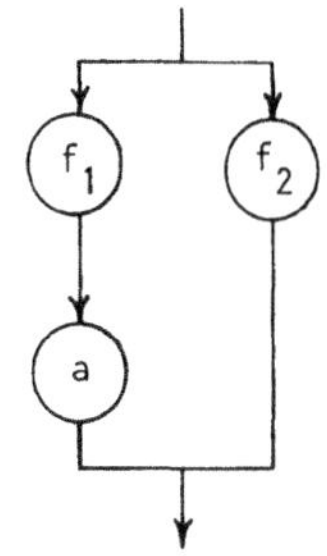 $= a \cdot f_1 + f_2.$

Here we have broken $f: D \longrightarrow 2 \cdot D$ into disjoint pieces f_j, $j = 1,2$, where

$$f_j(d) = \begin{cases} d' & \text{if } f(d) = (d',j) \\ \text{undefined} & \text{if no such } d' \text{ exists} \end{cases}$$

and exploited this disjointness to write h(a) as the well-defined sum $a \cdot f_1 + f_2$ -- the first term corresponding to '1-substitution paths' and the second to '0-substitution paths'. More generally, any such definition can be broken into a sum of disjoint paths, and then we may aggregate those paths which involve the same number n of substitutions. This leads us to consider Ω-algebras for the fixed label set Ω which has one operator symbol, namely ω_n, for each integer $n \geq 0$. ω_n is the abstract operator to be interpreted as 'substitution in all n-variable paths'. An Ω-algebra is a pair (A,H) where A is a set, and H is a family of functions $H_n: A^n \longrightarrow A$ one for each $n \geq 0$. An Ω-algebra homomorphism $\phi: (A,H) \longrightarrow (A',H')$ is a map $A \longrightarrow A'$ satisfying $\phi H_n(a_1,\ldots,a_n) = H'_n(\phi a_1,\ldots,\phi a_n)$ for all $n \geq 0$ and $(a_1,\ldots,a_n) \in A^n$.

7 Definition. An abstract recursion scheme is (A,Σ,H) where (A,Σ) is a partially-additive monoid and (A,H) is an Ω-algebra subject to the two conditions:

(i) Each H_n is n-additive, i.e. for each n countable subsets $S_1,\ldots,S_n$ of A for which each $\Sigma S_j = \Sigma(s : s \in S_j)$ is defined, we have

$$H_n(\Sigma S_1,\ldots,\Sigma S_n) = \Sigma(H_n(s_1,\ldots,s_n) : s_j \in S_j)$$

so that the right-hand side is defined. (We take '0-additive' = 'constant'.)

(ii) $h(a) = \sum_n H_n(a,\ldots,a)$ is defined for all $a \in A$.

A fixpoint of (A,Σ,H) is an a in A such that $ha = a$.

To recapture our iteration example 6 where $h(a) = f_2 + a \cdot f_1$ we take

$A = \underline{Pfn}(D,D)$

$H_0 = f_2$

$H_1(a) = a \cdot f_1$

$H_n = 0$ (i.e. every $H_n(a_1,\ldots,a_n)$ is undefined) for all $n \geq 2$

and we do indeed have that

$$h(a) = H_0 + H_1(a) + 0 + 0 + \ldots = f_2 + a \cdot f_1$$

is defined for every a in A.

For a 'more generic' example of a recursive definition consider one which involves two procedure calls.

8

x = 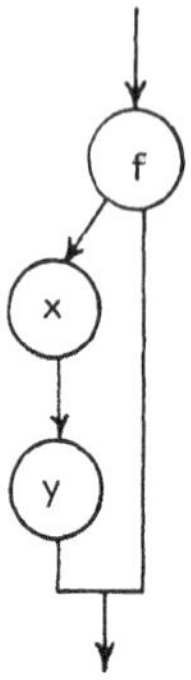

y = 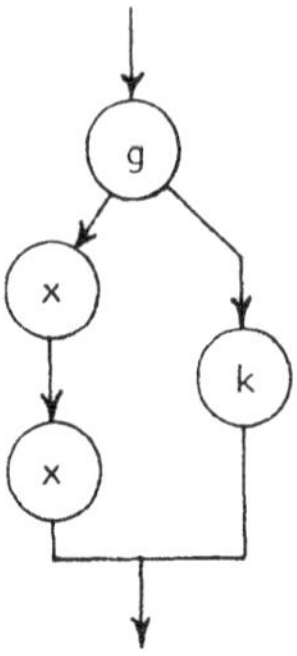

Here we take $A = \underline{\underline{Pfn}}(D,D) \times \underline{\underline{Pfn}}(D,D)$ which inherits a partially-additive structure from $\underline{\underline{Pfn}}(D,D)$ under componentwise partial-addition. Decomposing f into f_1 and f_2 and g into g_1 and g_2 as before, we then rewrite 8 as

$$x = y\cdot x\cdot f_1 + f_2, \quad y = x\cdot x\cdot g_1 + k\cdot g_2.$$

We thus set

9
$$H_0 = (f_2, k\cdot g_2)$$
$$H_1(a_1,a_2) = (0,0)$$
$$H_2((a_1,a_2),(a_1',a_2')) = (a_2'\cdot a_1\cdot f_1,\ a_1'\cdot a_1\cdot g_1)$$
$$H_n = 0 \qquad \text{for } n\geq 3$$

and each H_n is clearly n-additive (but not symmetric). Again, the disjointness of the paths in 8 ensures that for each $a = (a_1,a_2) \in A$,

$$h(a) = \Sigma H_n(a,\ldots,a) = (a_2\cdot a_1\cdot f_1 + f_2,\ a_1\cdot a_1\cdot g_1 + k\cdot g_2)$$

is well-defined, and that a fixed-point of this h is indeed what we seek in providing a semantics for the recursive procedure calls of 8.

The general situation is thus clear. Given a simultaneous definition of m procedures, the A of the corresponding abstract recursion scheme has the form of an m-fold Cartesian product of partially-additive monoids; while the j-th component of the corresponding H_n represents the sum of the semantics of all those paths in the flow diagram defining the j-th procedure which involve exactly n occurrences of the to-be-defined procedures.

10 Definition. A homomorphism $\phi: (A,\Sigma) \longrightarrow (A',\Sigma')$ of partially-additive monoids is a function $\phi: A \longrightarrow A'$ which preserves sums in the sense that if ΣS is defined then $\Sigma'\{\phi(s) : s\in S\}$ is defined and equals $\phi(\Sigma S)$. A scheme homomorphism is a simultaneous partially-additive monoid and Ω-algebra homomorphism.

Such $\phi: (A,\Sigma,H) \longrightarrow (A',\Sigma',H')$ satisfies

$$\begin{aligned}
\phi ha &= \phi\Sigma H_n(a,\ldots,a) \\
&= \Sigma'\phi H_n(a,\ldots,a) && \text{since } \phi \text{ is a partially-additive homomorphism} \\
&= \Sigma' H_n'(\phi a,\ldots,\phi a) && \text{since } \phi \text{ is an } \Omega\text{-algebra homomorphism} \\
&= h'\phi a.
\end{aligned}$$

11 Observation. Any scheme homomorphism preserves fixpoints: If $ha = a$, then $h'\phi a = \phi ha = \phi a$. □

12 Definition [3]. A canonical fixpoint α is an assignment of a fixpoint $\alpha_{A,\Sigma,H} = h\alpha_{A,\Sigma,H}$ in A to each abstract recursion scheme (A,Σ,H) in such a way that for every scheme homomorphism $\phi: (A,\Sigma,H) \longrightarrow (A',\Sigma',H')$ we have

$$\phi\alpha_{A,\Sigma,H} = \alpha_{A',\Sigma',H'} .$$

Let now L be the set of those Ω-trees all of whose leaves are ω_0. This L is the abstract expression of the result of all possible iterated substitutions, starting with ω_0 which represents the result of 'replacing all occurrences of variables by 0' thus nulling out all paths save those containing no variables. Note that this is done at a level of abstraction which relieves us of keeping track of any specific path structure. We now show how L interprets to yield a fixpoint for any abstract recursion scheme (A,Σ,H) and then observe that the fixpoints so obtained constitute the unique canonical fixpoint.

The main result of [3] is the following:

13 Theorem. For each abstract recursion scheme (A,Σ,H), the following sum

$$\psi_{A,\Sigma,H}(L) = \Sigma(s^{\#} : s\in L)$$

is well-defined, where $s^{\#}$ is the evaluation of s obtained on interpreting each ω_n by $H_n: A^n \longrightarrow A$. Moreover, there is a unique canonical fixpoint, and it is given by assigning $\psi_{A,\Sigma,H}(L)$ in A to each abstract recursion scheme.

Proof: See [3, Theorem 3.10]. □

14 Example. In our iteration example 6, we have $H_0 = f_2$; $H_1(a) = a\cdot f_1$; $H_n = 0$ for $n\geq 2$. In this case, then, the only trees in L that have a non-zero interpretation under ψ are those of the form $s_n = \omega_1^n\omega_0$. This yields the fixpoint

$$\psi(L) = \Sigma(s^{\#} : s\in L) = \Sigma(s_n^{\#} : n\geq 0) = \sum_{n\geq 0} f_2 f_1^n$$

with one term $f_2 f_1^n$ for each distinct 'n times round the loop' or 'n successive unary substitutions'.

Similarly, for our example 8 in which no more than two variables occur along any path, we may restrict attention to trees composed from ω_0, ω_1 and ω_2. Using $H_0 = (f_2, k\cdot g_2)$; $H_1(a_1,a_2) = (0,0)$; $H_2((a_1,a_2),(a_1',a_2')) = (a_2'\cdot a_1\cdot f_1, a_1'\cdot a_1\cdot g_1)$ we may, for example, evaluate $\omega_2[\omega_0,\omega_0]$ to yield $(kg_2f_2f_1, f_2f_2g_1)$ as one term (there is a term for every $(\omega_0,\omega_1,\omega_2)$-tree) of the countable sum which yields the semantics of 8. Note that the general result of the first half of Theorem 13 assures us that this sum is indeed well-defined.

We may say a fixpoint equation is linear if it yields $H_n = 0$ for $n\geq 2$. Backus [4, p. 629] claims that "the question of the existence of simple expansions that 'solve' 'quadratic' and higher order equations remains open." We offer a possible solution. The collection of n's for which H_n is non-zero determines which ω-trees t must provide terms $\psi(t)$ for the expansion which constitutes the solution of $h(a) = a$; we then exploit identities or seek an exhaustive subset (see [3] for worked out examples) to simplify the solution by algebraic manipulation.

2. Σ-DOAGs: The Program Interpretation.

Consider the 'generalized conditional'

1

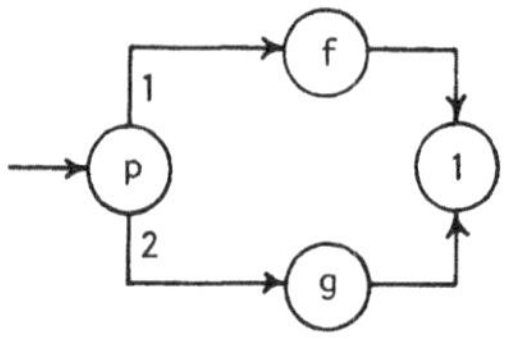

where we use the leftmost arrow to designate the entry point, and the node (1) to indicate the first (and in this case, the only) exit. We order the successors to each node -- just as we distinguish the 'true-line' and 'false-line' from a test in 1.4. We now introduce the notion of a DOAG to characterize the type of acyclic graph which underlies 1 -- a Σ-DOAG [1] is then a DOAG which is suitably labelled. Here (Σ,ν) is an operator domain, i.e. a set equipped with an arity function $\nu\colon \Sigma \longrightarrow \underline{N}$.

2 Definition. A directed ordered graph Γ is a map $\Gamma\colon V \longrightarrow V^*$. V is called the set of vertices of Γ. We often write $({}^1v, {}^2v, \ldots, {}^{n(v)}v)$ for $\Gamma(v)$, and call ${}^jv$ a successor for v. v is called initial if v is not a successor of any v' in V. v is called terminal if it has no successors, i.e. $\Gamma(v) = \Lambda$, the empty string. Defining loops in the obvious way, we say that a directed ordered graph is a DOAG (directed ordered acyclic graph) if there are no loops.

One word of caution. The above definition 'reverses the arrows' from the definition given in [1]. (If we think of a tree as interpreted by term evaluation then the arrows go 'rootward'; if we interpret it as a flow diagram, as we do in this paper, the arrows go 'leafward'.) Again, the next definition varies from [1] in that (what we here call) terminal nodes are no longer labelled with elements of Σ.

3 Definition. A Σ-DOAG is a pair (Γ,h) where $\Gamma\colon V \longrightarrow V^*$ is a DOAG and $h\colon V \longrightarrow \Sigma\cup\underline{N}$ subject to

(i) $n(v) = \nu(h(v))$ if $h(v) > 0$;

(ii) If Γ has p terminal nodes $v_1,\ldots,v_p$, then h labels them $1,\ldots,p$ in some order. If the terminal node v satisfies $h(v) = j$, we refer to v as the j-th exit node of (Γ,h).

Arbib and Give'on [1] interpret (Γ,h) via a Σ-algebra (Q,δ): for each σ in Σ, δ supplies a map $\delta_\sigma\colon Q^{\nu(\sigma)} \longrightarrow Q$. We here interpret each Σ-DOAG via a Σ-coalgebra (D,θ) in Pfn: for each σ in Σ, θ supplies a partial function $\theta_\sigma\colon D \longrightarrow \nu(\sigma)\cdot D$, where $n\cdot D$ is the n-fold copower of D. In our motivating categories Pfn and Rel, $n\cdot D$ as the disjoint union of n copies of D, whose typical element is (d,j), with d in D and $1\le j\le n$, 'the occurrence of d in the j-th copy of D. We then regard D as a data type fixed throughout the computation. Then if $\theta_\sigma(d) = (d',j)$, we view this as meaning "If computation enters node v, where $h(v) = \sigma$, with data d, then d is transformed to d', and control is transferred to the j-th successor of v." For example, a conditional $p\colon D \longrightarrow \{\underline{true},\underline{false}\}$ corresponds to the map $\hat{p}\colon D \longrightarrow 2\cdot D$ where

$$\hat{p}(d) = \begin{cases} (d,1) & \text{if } p(d) = \underline{true} \\ (d,2) & \text{if } p(d) = \underline{false}. \end{cases}$$

This style of program interpretation is essentially that of Elgot [5] (though we here dispense with the apparatus of algebraic theories). What will be new here will be the extension of this formalism from flow diagrams to programs with recursive procedure calls.* But first we must see how the interpretation of each node yields an interpretation of an arbitrary Σ-DOAG.

4 Definition. Given a DOAG Γ, we associate a level with each node as follows:

$\underline{\text{level}}(v) = 0$ iff v is terminal

$\underline{\text{level}}(v) = \underline{\max}(\underline{\text{level}}(^j v) : 1 \le j \le n(v)) + 1$ otherwise

We have [1, Lemma 1.8]:

Lemma. For a finite DOAG Γ, there is a finite number d_Γ, the depth of Γ, such that each node of Γ has level k for some $k \in \{0,1,\ldots,d_\Gamma\}$; for every such k there is a node with that level; and v is terminal if (but not only if, in general) it has level d_Γ. □

This lemma justifies the inductive step in our definition 6, below, of the semantics of flow diagrams. First, for motivation consider

5

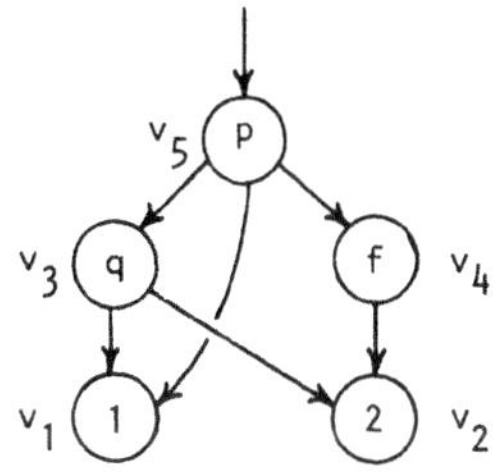

$h(v_5) = p$

$h(v_3) = q; \quad h(v_4) = f$

Since the graph has two exit nodes, we interpret each node v by a map $\theta_v: D \longrightarrow 2 \cdot D$ where $\theta_v(d) = (d',j)$ means "if we enter node v with data d, we exit from the entire program with data d' via exit j." Clearly, then, $\theta_{v_1} = in_1: D \longrightarrow 2 \cdot D$, $d \mapsto (d,1)$ and $\theta_{v_2} = in_2$, $d \mapsto (d,2)$. Let $q = in_1 q_1 + in_2 q_2$: $D \longrightarrow 2 \cdot D$ (recall 1.6) and let $p = in_1 \cdot p_1 + in_2 \cdot p_2 + in_3 \cdot p_3$: $D \longrightarrow 3 \cdot D$. Then

$\theta_{v_3} = \theta_{v_1} \cdot q_1 + \theta_{v_2} \cdot q_2$ (i.e. do q_1 then go to v_1; or do q_2 then go to v_2)

$= in_1 \cdot q_1 + in_2 \cdot q_2 = q: D \longrightarrow 2 \cdot D.$

$\theta_{v_4} = \theta_{v_2} \cdot f = in_2 \cdot f: \quad D \longrightarrow 2 \cdot D.$

$\theta_{v_5} = \theta_{v_3} \cdot p_1 + \theta_{v_1} \cdot p_2 + \theta_{v_4} \cdot p_3$ (i.e. do p_1 then go to v_3; or do p_2 and go to v_1; or do p_3 then go to θ_{v_4})

$= q \cdot p_1 + in_1 \cdot p_2 + in_2 \cdot f \cdot p_3: \quad D \longrightarrow 2 \cdot D.$

6 Definition. Given a Σ-DOAG (Γ,h) with p exit nodes and a Σ-coalgebra (D,θ), we associate with each node v of Γ a map $\theta_v: D \longrightarrow p \cdot D$ by the following inductive definition:

(i) If $\underline{\text{level}}(v) = 0$ and $h(v) = j$, $1 \le j \le p$, then

$$\theta_v = in_j: D \longrightarrow p \cdot D.$$

---

* Another generalization has us associate a (possibly different) data type with each edge, so that a σ may be interpreted as a map $D \longrightarrow D_1 + \ldots + D_n$. In this setting, we can handle declarations, etc. But these details would obscure the basic 'graph-growing' of procedure calls, and so are not included in the present paper.

(ii) If $\Gamma(v) = (v_1,\ldots,v_n)$ with θ_{v_i} already defined for $1\le i\le n$, then

$$\theta_v = \Sigma\, \theta_{v_i}\, \theta_i : \quad D \longrightarrow p\cdot D$$

where $\theta_{h(v)} = \Sigma\, in_i \theta_i : \; D \longrightarrow n\cdot D.$

In particular, we associate a partial function $D \longrightarrow p\cdot D$ with each designated entry point of the flow diagram. In what follows, we will usually designate a single node v_0 as entry node. Only those nodes reachable from v_0 (i.e. $v = v_0$ or $v_0 < v$) will then play any role in our study of program semantics.

3. Recursive Programs: Graph-Growth Semantics.

In algebraic theories (see Manes [6] for a textbook treatment), it is common to append a set of nullary variables to the operator domain. But, as can be seen by inspecting 1.8, in modelling procedure calls the variables themselves constitute an operator domain (X,k) with one non-nullary symbol of appropriate arity for each procedure. An $(X+\Sigma)$-DOAG is then a flow diagram in which either an interpreted symbol in Σ or a procedure symbol in X may label a node. We will order the variables in X as $x_1,\ldots,x_r$, with the convention that x_1 labels that procedure which is the program under consideration.

1 Definition. A program with procedures X is a triple $\mathbf{P} = (\mathbf{G},D,\theta)$ where (D,θ) is a Σ-coalgebra and, for each $1\le j\le r$, G_j is a one-entry, n_j-exit $(X+\Sigma)$-DOAG, where n_j is the arity of x_j. We may often view $\mathbf{G}$ as a display $x_j = G_j$, $1\le j\le r$.

We specify the simple form of graph replacement required:

2 Definition. Let G be an $(X+\Sigma)$-DOAG, let v be a node labelled with x_j, and let G' be a one-entry s-exit $(X+\Sigma)$-DOAG, with entry node w and terminal nodes $w_1,\ldots,w_s$ (where $s = n_j$) in that order. Then $G^v_{G'}$, the substitution of G' for v in G, is obtained by

(i) Deleting v and all edges adjoining it from G.

(ii) Taking a copy of G' whose vertices are disjoint from those of G, and deleting the terminal nodes $w_1,\ldots,w_s$, and all edges adjoining them.

(iii) For each vertex u in G and j such that ${}^j u = v$, set w to be the j-th successor of u in $G^v_{G'}$.

(iv) For each vertex u in G_j and i such that ${}^i u = w_j$, some j, $1\le j\le s$, set ${}^j v$, the j-th successor of v in G, to be the i-th successor of u in $G^v_{G'}$.

3 Example.

Let G =

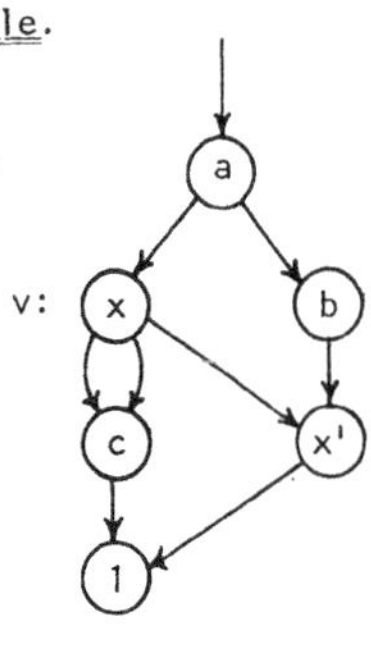

and G' =

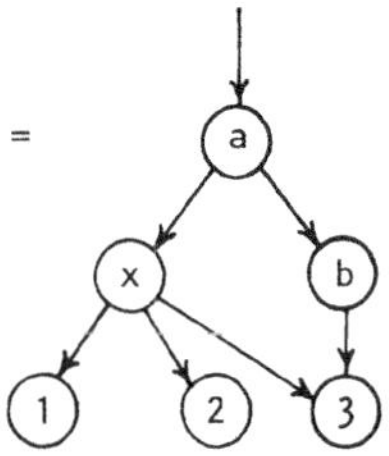

Then $G^v_{G'}$ =

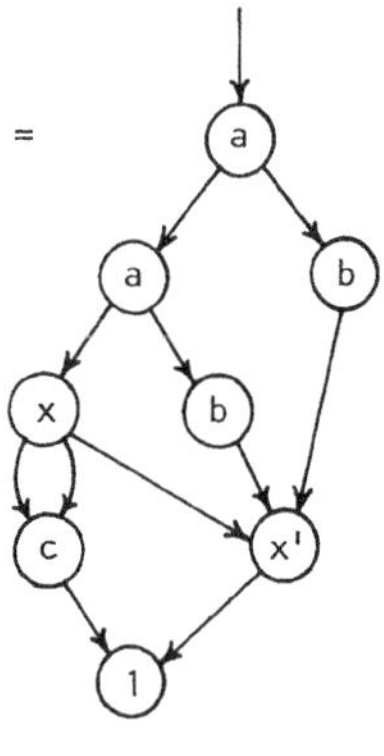

In Section 1, we saw how each such 'program with procedures' yields a canonical fixpoint. In this section, we now specify the computation performed by such a program with a given Σ-coalgebra (D,θ) as interpretation. We will then show that this interpretive semantics yields the same result as the canonical fixpoint. The basic idea of the interpretive semantics is this: At each stage, computation is at a node with some data value d. If the node is a Σ-node we transform d and transfer control as specified by θ. However, if the node is an X-node, x_j, we replace x_j by G_j and then proceed as before.

4 Definition. Let us be given a program **P** with procedures $\mathbf{G} = (x_j = G_j : 1 \le j \le r)$ together with a Σ-coalgebra (D,θ). Then a computation state for $(\mathbf{G},D,\theta)$ is a triple (G,d,v) where G is an $(X+\Sigma)$-DOAG, d is in D, and v is a vertex of G. Let **Q** be the set of all such computation states. We say (G,d,v) is terminal if v is a terminal vertex of G. We define a next-state function $\delta: \mathbf{Q} \longrightarrow \mathbf{Q}$ by the rule

(i) If vertex v of G is labelled by σ in Σ, and if $\theta_\sigma(d) = (d',j)$ then $\delta(G,d,v) = (G,d',v')$, where v' is the j-th successor of v in G. If $\theta_\sigma(d)$ is undefined, then $\delta(G,d,v)$ is undefined.

(ii) If vertex v of G is labelled by x_j in X, then $\delta(G,d,v) = (G',d,v')$ where $G' = G^v_{G_j}$, and v' is the entry node of the disjoint copy of G_j that replaced v in forming G'.

(iii) If v is terminal, then $\delta(G,d,v)$ is undefined.

Let v_i be the entry node of G_i. Then the computation of G_i with initial data d is a sequence of computation states

$$q_0, q_1, q_2, \ldots$$

such that $q_0 = (G_i,d,v_i)$, $q_{t+1} = \delta(q_t)$ for each $t \ge 0$, and which is either infinite, or ends in a nonterminal state q for which $\delta(q)$ is undefined, or is terminating, i.e. is of the form $q_0, q_1, \ldots, q_n$ with q_n terminal. In the last case, let $q_n = (\hat{G},\hat{d},\hat{v})$ where $\hat{d}$ is in D, and $\hat{v}$ is the j-th exit node of $\hat{G}$. We then set $\phi^{\mathbf{P}}_i(d) = (\hat{d},j)$. In the two former cases, $\phi^{\mathbf{P}}_i(d)$ is undefined. $\phi^{\mathbf{P}}_i$ is a partial function $D \longrightarrow n_j \cdot D$ where n_j is the number of exit nodes of G_j.

5 Example. Consider the program x =

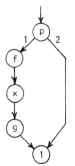

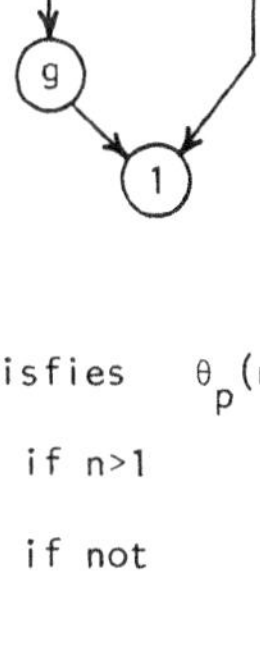

where the interpretation is $(\theta,\underline{N})$ with

$$\theta_p : \underline{N} \longrightarrow 2\cdot\underline{N} \quad \text{satisfies} \quad \theta_p(n) = \begin{cases} (n,1) & \text{if } n>1 \\ (n,2) & \text{if } n\le 1 \end{cases}$$

$$\theta_f(n) = \begin{cases} n-2 & \text{if } n>1 \\ \text{undefined} & \text{if not} \end{cases}$$

$$\theta_g(n) = n+1.$$

This corresponds to the recursive program definition:

f(n): <u>if</u> n>1 <u>then</u> n := n-2; f(n); n := n+1.

The evaluation of $\phi^P(3)$ is shown in Figure 1, where we place the current d against the current v of the current graph G. Since the last computation state is terminal, we see that $\phi^P(3) = 2$.

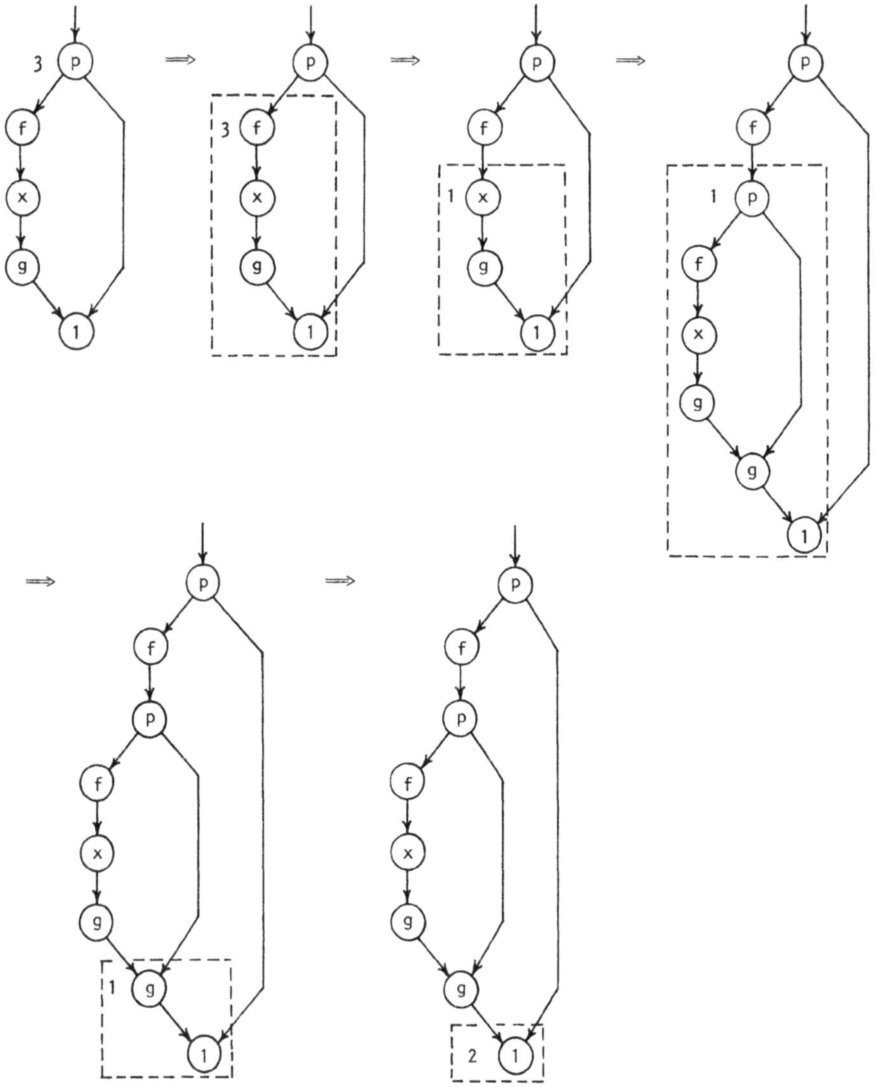

Figure 1

Note that, as far as computing any $\phi_i^{\mathbf{P}}$ is concerned, we may replace (G,d,v) at each stage by (G_v,d,v) where G_v comprises that portion of G reachable from v (so that the nodes are v and all v' such that $v < v'$ in G). This provides the minimal information that must be preserved in computing a value of $\phi_i^{\mathbf{P}}$ according to the prescription **P**. The dashed boxes in the above states indicate the storage economy obtained by this strategy.

Consider again a set of variables X with corresponding $(X+\Sigma)$-DOAGs G_j, with G_j being one-entry and n_j-exit, where n_j is the arity of x. Fix a Σ-coalgebra (D,θ). Now suppose we interpret each x_j by a partial function $f_j : D \longrightarrow n_j \cdot D$. Then we can form an $(X+\Sigma)$-coalgebra $(D,\theta+f)$, where $(\theta+f)_\sigma = \theta$, $(\theta+f)_{x_j} = f_j$. Then all nodes of the $(X+\Sigma)$-DOAGs G_j are interpreted, and we may evaluate their entry nodes to yield the partial functions

$$g_j : D \longrightarrow n_j \cdot D.$$

Let $A_j = \underline{\underline{\mathrm{Pfn}}}(D, n_j \cdot D_j)$ for $1 \le j \le r$, and let $A_X = A_1 \times \ldots \times A_r$. By the above passage $(f_1,\ldots,f_r) \mapsto (g_1,\ldots,g_r)$, we have that $\mathbf{P}$ induces a functional

6 $$h_{\mathbf{P}} : A_X \longrightarrow A_X$$

which is the h of the abstract recursion scheme associated with $\mathbf{P} = (G,D,\theta)$ in the manner of Section 1. The unifying theorem of this paper is then:

7 Theorem. For each program $\mathbf{P} = (G,D,\theta)$ with procedures X, the vector $\phi^{\mathbf{P}} = (\phi_1^{\mathbf{P}},\ldots,\phi_r^{\mathbf{P}})$ in A_X is the canonical fixpoint of $h_{\mathbf{P}}$.

Proof: We first prove that the canonical fixpoint is contained in $\phi^{\mathbf{P}}$:

Basis Step: Clearly the interpretation of the one-node tree ω_0 has an interpretive semantics: it is $\phi_j^{\mathbf{P}}$ for those d which lie in the domain of the variable-free paths for G_j.

Induction Step: Suppose that $p_1,\ldots,p_k$ are trees which have an interpretive semantics. Then $\omega_k[p_1,\ldots,p_k]$ is interpreted via taking the subcollection of entry-exit paths obstructed by k calls, and using the appropriate component of p_j in replacing the j-th occurrence of a variable in the path.

Conversely, any actual $\phi_i^{\mathbf{P}}(d)$ is obtained by a process which involves a finite number of substitutions -- and this lets us define the tree (part of the canonical fixpoint) which returns the same value. (Note that, in general, the tree which returns the value of $\phi_i^{\mathbf{P}}(d)$ will not be the tree that returns the value of $\phi_{i'}(d)$ for $i' \neq i$.) □

References

[1] M. A. Arbib and Y. Give'on: Algebra automata I: Parallel programming as prolegomenon to the categorical approach, Information and Control 12 (1968), 331-345.

[2] M. A. Arbib and E. G. Manes: Partially-additive categories and computer program semantics, COINS Technical Report 78-12, Department of Computer and Information Science, University of Massachusetts, Amherst, MA 01003 (1978), 39 pp.

[3] M. A. Arbib and E. G. Manes: Abstract theory of recursive calls, COINS Tech. Report 78-18, Department of Computer and Information Science, University of Massachusetts, Amherst, MA 01003 (August 1978).

[4] J. W. Backus: Can programming be liberated from the Von Neumann style? A functional style and its algebra of programs, Communications of the ACM **21** (1978), 613-641.

[5] C. C. Elgot: Algebraic theories and program semantics, in Symposium on Semantics of Algorithmic Languages, (E. Engeler, Ed.), Springer Lecture Notes in Mathematics, **188** (1971), 77-88.

[6] E. G. Manes: Algebraic Theories, Springer-Verlag (1976).

[7] D. Scott: The lattice of flow diagrams, in Symposium on Semantics of Algorithmic Languages, (E. Engeler, Ed.), Springer Lecture Notes in Mathematics, **188** (1971), 311-366.

REWRITING SYSTEMS AS A TOOL FOR RELATIONAL DATA BASE DESIGN

Carlo Batini, Alessandro D'Atri
Istituto di Automatica, Università di Roma
Via Eudossiana 18-00184 ROMA (Italy)

ABSTRACT

Methodologies for relational data base design have been extensively studied in the literature, mainly with regard to functional dependencies. Rewriting systems may be used as a formal tool to express transformations between refinements of the model in the design process.

In this paper we present a formalism based on hypergraphs and hypergraph grammars to investigate the advantages of a top-down design of a relational data model.

Classes of grammars whose associated languages respect meaningful properties are investigated.

1. INTRODUCTION

The aim of this paper is to define methodologies for the design of the conceptual scheme of a data base (DB).

We are mainly concerned in the following with the relational model of data. This model has been in the last years extensively studied for its advantages with respect to hyerarchical and network models (see [10],[23]).

As in software design, we think that also in database methodologies advantages arise with a top-down approach in documentation, maintenance and modifiability of the design.

Such goals are especially relevant in the n-ary relational model (see [6],[8],[9] for the basic definitions and properties of the n-ary model).

In the design of a n-ary scheme a normalization step is needed, whose final result is a DB in which undesirable anomalies in the updating process are eliminated.Several different normal forms have been defined (see [23]). In the literature two approaches to obtain schemes in normal form are proposed (see [11],[14],[24]).

In a first approach (called in [14] "decomposition approach") an initial set of relation schemes along with a set of functional dependencies is initially given. Afterwards, the set of relation schemes is replaced by one in normal form.

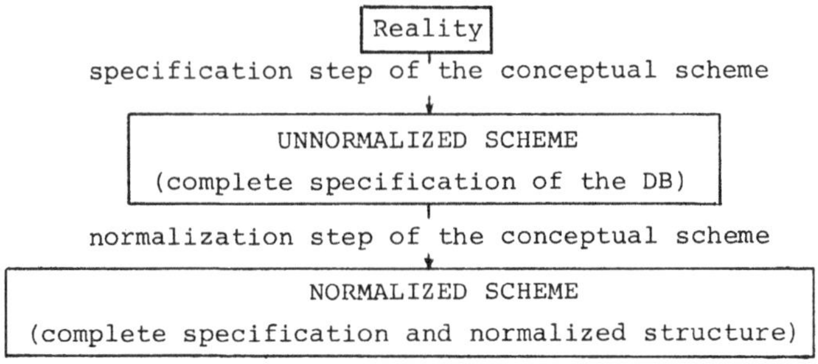

In the "synthetic approach" (see [14]) attributes and functional dependencies are initially extracted from reality; a further "synthesis" on functional dependencies produces the normalized scheme.

Both the approaches proceed by initially specifying the complete conceptual content of the DB and afterwards producing a normalized scheme. A top-down design allows to join the two steps. A conceptual scheme can be initially specified at a very abstract level: the conceptual content of the scheme can be refined step by step, finally obtaining the complete scheme. A normalized scheme can be obtained at every expansion step if derivation rules are suitably restricted.

Such an approach increases also the quality of documentation and the changeability of the DB.

We use in our approach hypergraphs to formally represent sets of n-ary relations (as a related work see [1], in which labelled graphs are used to represent binary relations) and hypergraph grammars as a formal tool to describe and investigate the top-down approach to relational data base schemes design.

This paper is organized as follows.

In Section 2 the type of hypergraphs we need to represent "statically" functional dependencies in relational data base schemes is defined and, to show the adequacy of the model, four different equivalences in the class of such hypergraphs are stated.

Then in Section 3 through the formalism of hypergraph grammars methodologies for top-down design of schemes are investigated. Using such formal framework we characterize classes of grammars whose associated derivations respect meaningful properties: for instance, guarantee a fixed degree of normalization in the generated hypergraphs.

2. HYPERGRAPH REPRESENTATION OF FUNCTIONAL DEPENDENCIES

2.1. *Basic definitions*

We want to represent sets of relations together with functional dependencies between the attributes in the formalism of hypergraphs.

Initially we are not interested to give names to such attributes.

Definition 2.1. A *pattern hypergraph* (PH) is a pair $\langle N,S \rangle$ where:

a. N is a finite set of nodes.

b. $S \subseteq (P(N) - \emptyset) \times P(N)$ (where $P(N)$ is the power set of N) is a nonempty set of directed surfaces.

Since we want to give names to the attributes we have to label the nodes.

Definition 2.2. A *node labelled hypergraph* is a 4-pla $\langle N,\Sigma,\varphi,S \rangle$ where:

a. N is finite set of nodes.

b. Σ is a finite set of labels.

c. $\varphi : N \rightarrow \Sigma$ is a function from nodes to labels.

d. $S \subseteq (P(N) - \emptyset) \times P(N)$ is a nonempty set of directed surfaces.

We call in the following *table* (T) a maximally connected subhypergraph of a labelled hypergraph. With $\Sigma(T)$ ($\Sigma(s)$) we mean the set of labels of table T (surface s).

Definition 2.3. A *Data Base Hypergraph* (DBH) is a labelled hypergraph such that no two nodes can have the same label in any table.

Example 2.1. The n-ary scheme defined by the two relations

Student (Student #, Course #, Grade, Student Age)

Course (Course #, Course Credit)

may be represented as a DBH where:

$N = \{1,2,3,4,5,6\}$

Σ = {Student#, Course#, Grade, Student Age, Course Credit}

φ = {(1, Student#), (2, Course#), (3, Grade), (4, Student Age), (5, Course#), (6, Course Credit)}

$S = \{(1,2;3),(1;4),(2;2),(5;6)\}$

Graphically (see fig.1) we may represent functional dependencies by surfaces in which arrows point to nodes representing functionally dependent attributes (*non key* nodes in the following; we call *key nodes* the keys of functional dependencies). We call *all key surface* a surface with empty set of non key nodes.

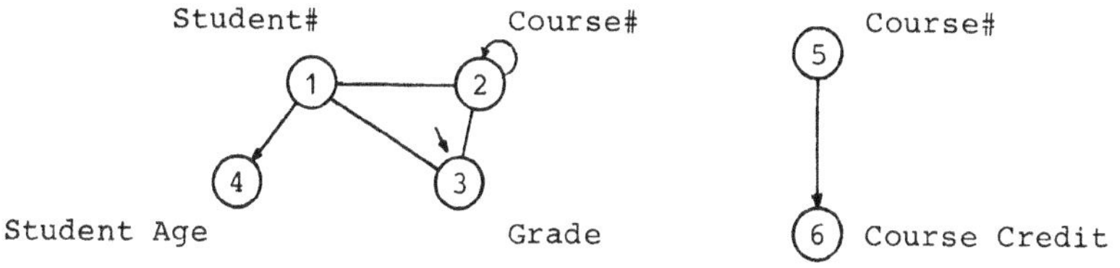

fig. 1

Remark. In the interpretation in terms of relational schemes, to every relation in the scheme a table corresponds. As it can be noticed we do not represent in our formalism names of relations.

Notice also that the same label may be associated to nodes in different tables. For this reason we have to distinguish between names of nodes and labels ⊠

3.2. *Adequacy of the formalism. Equivalences in the class of Data Base Hypergraphs.*

In this section we investigate the adequacy of the formalism to represent the n-ary relational model of data. We start defining semantically meaningful equivalences in the class of DBHs.
In the following $\mathcal{H}$ denotes the set of all DBHs.

Definition 2.4. Given two DBHs $H_1 = \langle N_1, \Sigma_1, \varphi_1, S_1 \rangle$ and $H_2 = \langle N_2, \Sigma_2, \varphi_2, S_2 \rangle$ we say that H_1 is 1-equivalent to H_2 ($H_1 \overset{1}{\equiv} H_2$) if $\exists \psi : N_1 \rightarrow N_2$ bijective such that:

a. $\forall n \in N_1 \quad \varphi_1(n) = \varphi_2(\psi(n))$

b. $\forall (r_1', r_1'') \in S_1 \; \exists! (r_2', r_2'') \in S_2$ (and viceversa):

  b1. $r_2' = \bar{\psi}(r_1')$ and $r_2'' = \bar{\psi}(r_1'')$

  b2. $\bar{\varphi}_2(r_2') = \bar{\varphi}_1(r_1')$ and $\bar{\varphi}_2(r_2'') = \bar{\varphi}_1(r_1'')$

where $\bar{\varphi}$ and $\bar{\psi}$ are the set extensions of φ and ψ.

Example 2.2. The DBHs

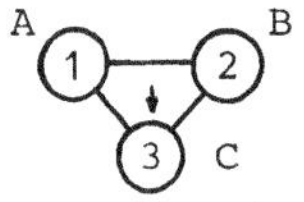

and

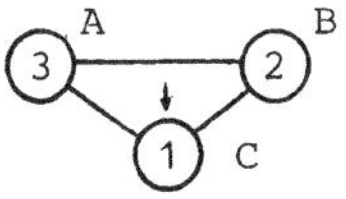

are 1-equivalent.
For our purposes, we are not interested in distinguishing among two 1-equivalent DBHs. So, names of nodes are irrelevant and from now on we omit such names in our graphical representation of DBHs.
Now, come back to fig. 1. The functional dependency (2;2) is not meaningful. Such dependencies are usually called *trivial dependencies*. Furthermore, we call *derivable* the dependencies logically implied by other dependencies (for instance, transitive dependencies).
We need in our formalism a new kind of equivalence that "filters" trivial and derivable dependencies.

Definition 2.5. Given two DBHs, $H_1 = \langle N_1, \Sigma_1, \varphi_1, S_1 \rangle$ and $H_2 = \langle N_2, \Sigma_2, \varphi_2, S_2 \rangle$ we say that $H_1 \leq H_2$ if:

1) $H_3 = \langle N_3, \Sigma_3, \varphi_3, S_3 \rangle$ exists 1-equivalent to H_1 such that $N_2 = N_3$, $\Sigma_2 = \Sigma_3$, $\varphi_2 = \varphi_3$ and $S_2 = S_3$ or $S_2 = S_3 \cup \{R\}$ with $R \in (P(N_3) - \emptyset) \times P(N_3)$

defined according to one of the following rules, that can be applied only among nodes of the same table:

a. $n \in N_3 \Rightarrow R = (n,n)$

b. $(r_1,r_2),(r_2,r_3) \in S_3 \Rightarrow R = (r_1,r_3)$

c. $(r_1,r_2) \in S_3,\ n \in N_3 \Rightarrow R = (r_1 \cup \{n\},r_2)$

d. $(r_1,r_2) \in S_3,\ n \in N_3 \Rightarrow R = (r_1,r_2 - \{n\})$

e. $(r_1,r_2),(r_3,r_4) \in S_3 \Rightarrow R = (r_1 \cup r_3, r_2 \cup r_4)$

or

2) There exists H such that $H_1 \leq H$ and $H \leq H_2$.

Fact 2.1. $\leq$ induces a partial order over $\mathcal{H}/\overset{1}{\equiv}$.

Definition 2.6. Given $H_1,H_2 \in \mathcal{H}$ we say that $H_1 \overset{2}{\equiv} H_2$ if $H_1 \leq H_2$ or $H_2 \leq H_1$ or $\exists H_3 : H_1 \overset{2}{\equiv} H_3 \wedge H_3 \overset{2}{\equiv} H_2$.

Example 2.3. The following DBHs are pairwise 2-equivalent.

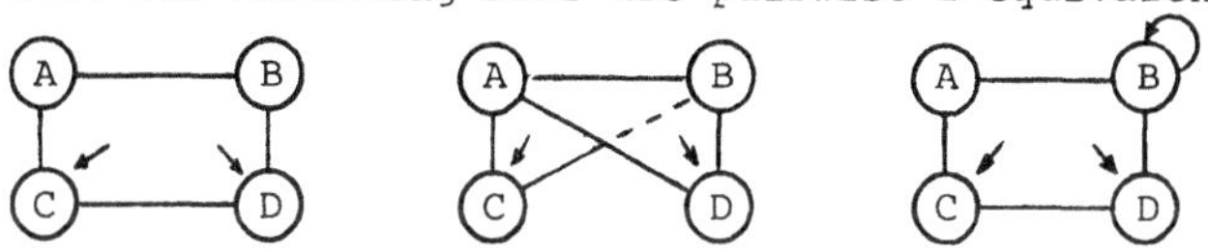

We want now to characterize the maximal elements under $\leq$.
This problem has been studied with different formalisms (see [3] and [11]).

Definition 2.7. We call *complete DBH* associated to a $\overset{2}{\equiv}$ class every maximal element (mod $\overset{1}{\equiv}$) in the partial order $\leq$.

In [5] the following theorem is proved.

Theorem 2.1. Every $\overset{2}{\equiv}$ class has a unique complete DBH. It may be obtained from any element H of the class applying to H rules a,b,c,d,e of definition 2.5 in any order (until no such rule can be applied).

Notice that Definitions 2.4,2.5,2.6,2.7 can be easily extended to pattern hypergraphs. We want now to show how the concept of normalization is represented in our formalism. We start from a generalized definition of normalization. Intuitively $H_1 \in \mathcal{H}$ is a normalization of $H_2 \in \mathcal{H}$ if two surfaces in the same table in H_1 are splitted in different tables in H_2.

Definition 2.8. Given $H_1,H_2 \in \mathcal{H}$ we say that H_2 *NORM* H_1 if $H_3 \in \mathcal{H}$ exists such that:

a. $H_3 \overset{2}{\equiv} H_1$

b. $\exists h:S_2 \to S_3$ bijective such that $(r_3',r_3'')=h\left[(r_2',r_2'')\right]$ implies $\bar{\varphi}_2(r_2') = \bar{\varphi}_3(r_3') \wedge \bar{\varphi}_2(r_2'') = \bar{\varphi}_3(r_3'')$.

Definition 2.9. Given $H_1, H_2 \in \mathcal{H}$ we say that $H_1 \overset{3}{\equiv} H_2$ if H_1 *NORM* H_2 or H_2 *NORM* H_1 or $\exists H_3 \in \mathcal{H}$ such that $H_1 \overset{3}{\equiv} H_3 \wedge H_3 \overset{3}{\equiv} H_2$.

Example 2.4. The three DBHs of fig. 2 are 3-equivalent. Moreover, H_3 *NORM* H_2 *NORM* H_1.

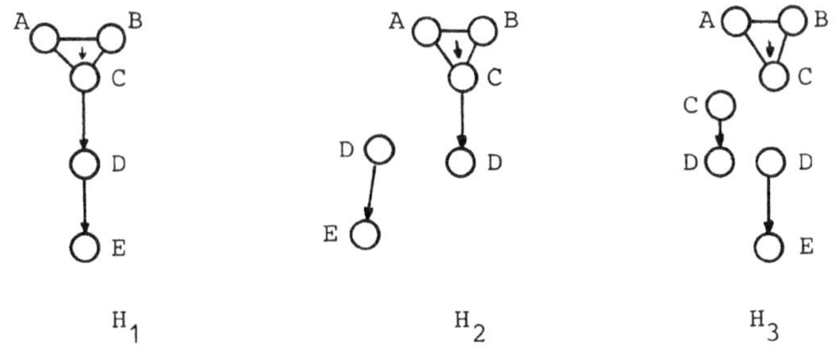

fig. 2

We are now able to give in our formalism the definitions of primary key and first, second, third and Boyce Codd normal form (1NF,2NF,3NF,BCNF) that we use in the following and can be easily seen equivalent to those appeared in the literature.

The definition 2.3 of DBH implies 1NF.

Let T be a table and T_c its complete DBH. Any minimal set of nodes that is key in a surface S incident to all the nodes of T_c is said *Primary key* of T. A set of nodes in a table is said *nonprime* if no node in the set is a member of any primary key.

$H \in \mathcal{H}$ is said *in 2NF* if for any table in H no surface exists whose non key nodes are nonprime and keynodes are a proper subset of a primary key.

$H \in \mathcal{H}$ is said *in 3NF* if it is in 2NF and, for any table in H, no pair of surfaces $S_1 = \{k_1, nk_1\}$, $S_2 = \{k_2, nk_2\}$ exists such that:

a. k_1 is a primary key.

b. $nk_1 = k_2$

c. k_2 is not a primary key and nk_2 is nonprime.

We will not deal with DBHs in BCNF with non disjoint primary keys,like the following:

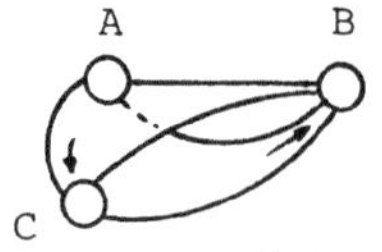

that generally do not correspond to meaningful situations in the real world. Such a choiche allows a definition of BCNF suitable for our purposes.

Definition 2.10. $H \in \mathcal{H}$ is said *in BCNF* if any table in H is 2-equivalent to one belonging to the following classes:

C1. 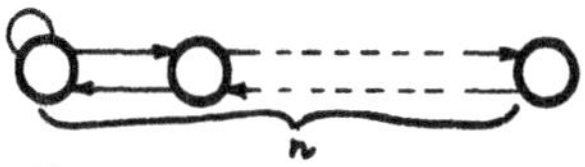 with $n \geq 1$

C2. 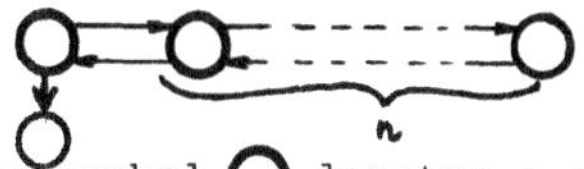 with $n \geq 0$

where symbol ○ denotes a nonempty set of nodes and symbol ∩ denotes an all key surface. So, for instance,

is the compact notation for

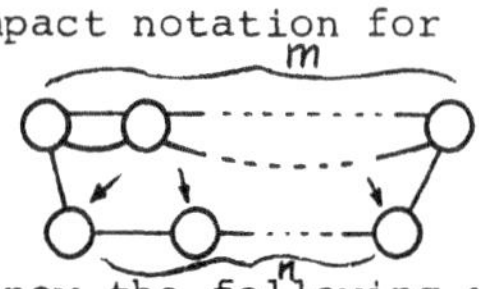

with $m,n \geq 1$

We define now the following relation between DBHs:

$\underset{2\ 3}{\subseteq} = \left\{ (H_1,H_2) \in \mathcal{H}^2 / H_1 \text{ is in 2NF} \wedge H_2 \text{ is in 3NF and is a normalization of } H_1 \right\}.$

Fact. 2.2. $\underset{2\ 3}{\subseteq}$ is contained in NORM.

The proof is simply obtained building a mapping h (see *Definition* 2.8) that "breaks" at least the tables in which a transitive dependency appears.

Similarly, we can define relations $\underset{1\ 2}{\subseteq}$, $\underset{1\ 3}{\subseteq}$,..., all contained in NORM.

We may call *DBH's Schema* any element of $\mathcal{H}/\overset{3}{\equiv}$. Two DBHs in the same schema are defined over the same alphabet and "describe" the same piece of world.

We define finally a fourth type of equivalence between DBHs.

Definition 2.11. Given H_1 and $H_2 \in \mathcal{H}$ we say that $H_1 \overset{4}{\equiv} H_2$ if $H_3 \in \mathcal{H}$ exists such that $H_1 \overset{3}{\equiv} H_3$ and:

$\exists h : \Sigma_2 \to \Sigma_3$ bijective such that

$\forall n_2 \in N_2 \exists n_3 \in N_3 : \varphi_2(n_2) = h(\varphi_3(n_3))$.

Intuitively, two DBHs are 4-equivalent when they represent two "pieces of reality" that differ only in the names of the attributes and are characterized by the same set of functional dependencies.

The following DBHs are 4-equivalent:

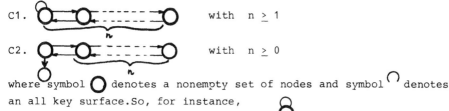

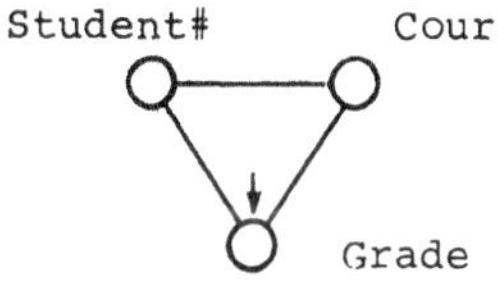

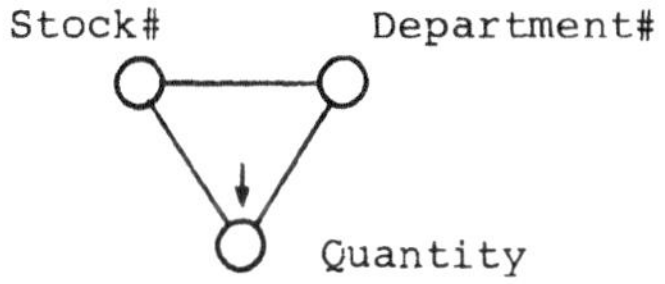

Remark. Notice that 1-equivalence implies 2-equivalence, 2-equivalence implies 3-equivalence and 3-equivalence implies 4-equivalence ☒

The four equivalences we have defined show that in our model it is possible to represent in a formal and uniform way the theory of functional dependencies and normalizations (see [5] for a more detailed investigation).

3. HYPERGRAPH GRAMMARS REPRESENTATION OF TOP-DOWN DESIGN RULES FOR RELATIONAL DATA BASE SCHEMES.

3.1. *Introduction*

We extend now the formalism of Data Base Hypergraphs to define a tool for their top-down design, in order to investigate methodologies for relational data base schemes design.
Grammars for labelled graphs were originally defined in [17]. Since than this formalism has been extended in several ways: graphs have been replaced by multigraphs [16], mwebs [15], arbitrary relational structures [18], and can be labelled in the nodes, arcs or surfaces. Such grammars differ in their generative power and in the way the "embedding" in the application of productions is performed (see also [16],[17],[19]). More recently, algebraic methods have been introduced in the theory of graph grammars with powerful results (see [12],[13]). Our goal is to define hypergraph grammars suited to represent the design of a data base scheme.

3.2. *The formalism of hypergraph grammars*

In the following a Data Base Hypergraph and a Pattern Hypergraph are said *atomic* if $|S| = 1$. An atomic DBH is said to *match* a PH if their unique surface are isomorphic.
With T_γ we mean the table in which the DBH γ occurs.

Definition 3.1. We define *production* a triple $\langle \alpha,\beta,h \rangle$ where:

a. α is an atomic PH.

b. β is a PH.

c. h is a function that maps nodes of α into sets of nodes of β such that:

c1. a table exists in β (that we call *link table*) that includes the codomain of h.

c2. for every pair of nodes of α the corresponding elements in the codomain of h are disjoint.

In the following we represent a production as in the diagram:

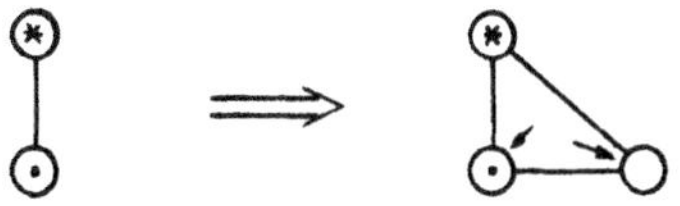

in which the same symbols mark nodes of α and β that are in the correspondence defined by h.

Definition 3.2. A *DBH's grammar* is a triple G = ⟨V,S,P⟩ where:

a. V is an alphabet of labels.

b. S is a set of starting DBHs with labels in V.

c. P is a set of productions.

Definition 3.3. Let H_1, H_2 be two DBHs with labels in V. We say that H_2 is *directly derivable* from H_1 in the grammar G = ⟨V,S,P⟩ and write

$$H_1 \xrightarrow{G} H_2$$

if a production p = ⟨α,β,h⟩ exists in G and an atomic DBH γ exists, subhypergraph of H_1, such that γ matches α and H_2 can be obtained from H_1 with the following steps:

a. join β to $H_1 - \gamma$, making use of function h to expand nodes in $H_1 - \gamma$ common to γ.

b. Assign labels to nodes in β: labels for the link table must be in $V - \Sigma(T_\gamma - \gamma)$.

Given $H, H^* \in \mathcal{H}$ we say that H^* is *derivable* from H in the grammar G if a finite chain of DBHs $H_o, H_1, \dots, H_n$ exists such that $H_o = H$, $H_n = H^*$ and $H_o \xrightarrow{G} H_1 \xrightarrow{G} \dots \xrightarrow{G} H_{n-1} \xrightarrow{G} H_n$.

Example 3.1. Fig. 3 and 4 show a DBH and a production:

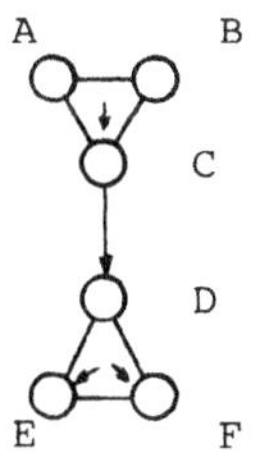

fig. 3

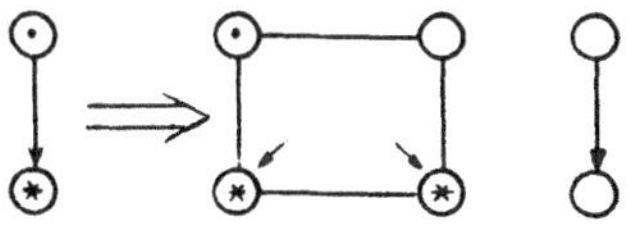

fig. 4

Fig. 5 shows the expanded DBH when the production is applied to surface

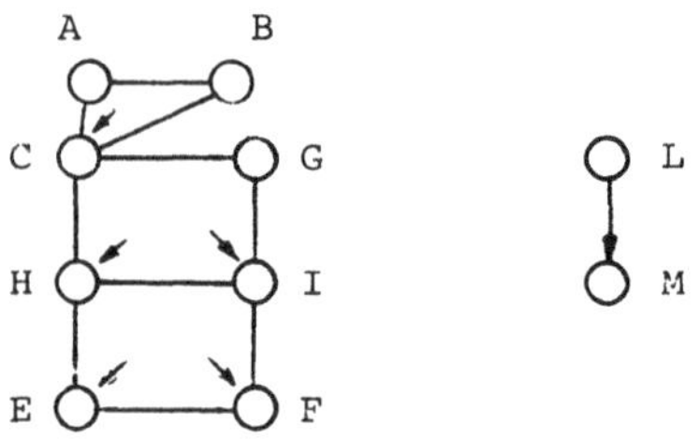

fig. 5

Definition 3.4. Given a grammar G we define language associated to G (L(G)) the set of DBHs such that a derivation exists from the starting DBHs to every element in L(G).

We now want to investigate how, suitably restricting the class of productions, we can characterize grammars and languages with meaningful properties with respect to DB design. A first restriction is necessary to keep memory during the DB design (i.e. in our formalism during the generation of an element of L(G)) of implied transitive dependencies.

Example 3.2. Fig. 6 shows a DBH and a production:

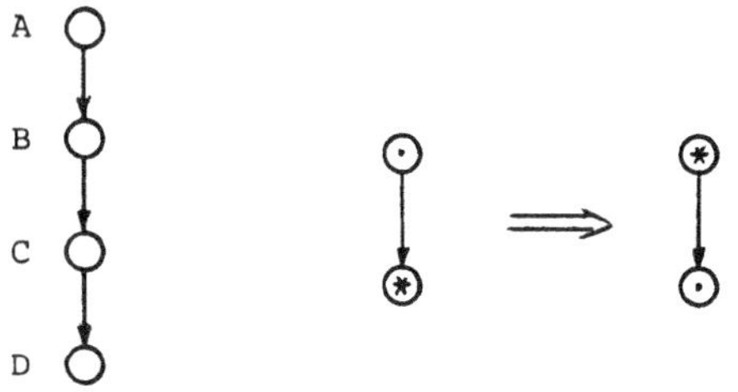

fig. 6

Fig. 7 shows the expanded DBH when the production is applied to surface

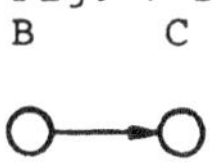

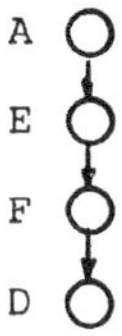

fig. 7

We may obtain surface A  D by means of def. 2.5 from the starting hypergraph but not from the expanded one.

Definition 3.5. Given H ∈ $\mathcal{H}$ and a production p we say that p is *correctly applicable to* H if for any H' directly derivable from H all the surfaces of the complete DBH associated to H not including nodes of the atomic DBH to be expanded are also included in the complete DBH

associated to H'.
Given a production p, p is said *correctly applicable* if for any $H \in \mathcal{H}$, p is correctly applicable to H.

Theorem 3.1. A production $p = \langle \alpha, \beta, h \rangle$ is correctly applicable if a surface S exists in the complete DBH associated to β such that key nodes of α are mapped in key nodes of S and non key nodes are mapped in non key nodes of S.

Proof. Given any $H \in \mathcal{H}$ we need only prove the theorem for surfaces of the complete DBH associated to H that represent transitive dependencies (rule b in def. 2.5).
Such surfaces may be partitioned in two sets:

a. surfaces obtained making use of surface α in the application of rule b in def. 2.5.
   Such surfaces may be obtained in the complete DBH associated to any direct derivation of H via p making use of surface S instead of surface α in rule b.

b. All the other surfaces: are obtained in the same way in any direct derivation ⊠

In the following we consider only correctly applicable productions.

Finally, we say that a production $p = \langle \alpha, \beta, h \rangle$ is *key preserving* if the key of α is mapped in one of the primary keys of β. We call *key preserving grammar* a grammar whose productions are all key preserving.

3.3. *Characterization of meaningful classes of grammars*

We are now interested in applying our formalism to investigate methodologies for relational data base design. Formally, given a class C of DBHs that satisfies a property p, we are looking for classes of grammars such that their associated languages are contained in (or are equal to) C.
Notice that property p may be quite general; for instance, in the relational interpretation:

1) every element in C respects a fixed degree of normalization;
2) every element in C is an independent realization (see [21]) of an associated element of another class C'.
3) for every element in C there is a complexity bound on the number of canonical operators (see [7]) necessary to express meaningful classes of queries.

In the following, we point our attention on the problem of normalization.

Given a grammar G, whose set $\mathcal{S}$ of starting DBHs has a certain normalization degree, it is not possible in general, imposing for every production $p = \langle \alpha, \beta, h \rangle$ only restrictions on the normalization degree of α and β, to obtain for $L(G)$ the same normalization degree of $\mathcal{S}$. For example, a grammar G exists whose unique production has β in 3NF, such that $L(G)$ is not a 2NF-Language (i.e. a language whose DBHs are in 2NF).

Infact, with two applications of production

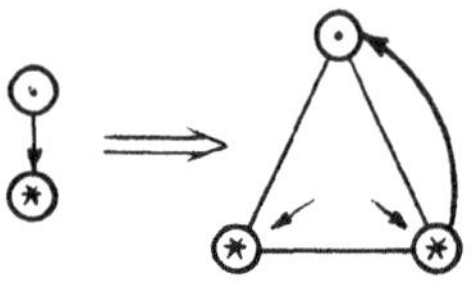

we may derive in two steps the following DBH

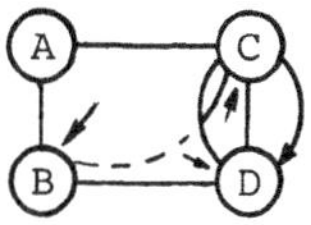

which is not in 2NF.

We show now a sufficient condition for a grammar G to generate a 2NF-Language.

Definition 3.6. Given $H \in \mathcal{H}$ and two of its surfaces s' and s" we say that $s' \leq s''$ if:

a. s' = s" or

b. a set S^* of surfaces $s_1, s_2, \ldots, s_n$ exists in H such that $s'' \in S^*$ and any key node of s' is a nonkey node of at least one surface in S^* or

c. s"' exists in H such that $s' \leq s'''$ and $s''' \leq s''$.

We say that $H \in \mathcal{H}$ is an *ordered DBH* (ODBH) if for any table in H the relation $\leq$ is a partial order with a unique maximal element.

The following is an ordered DBH:

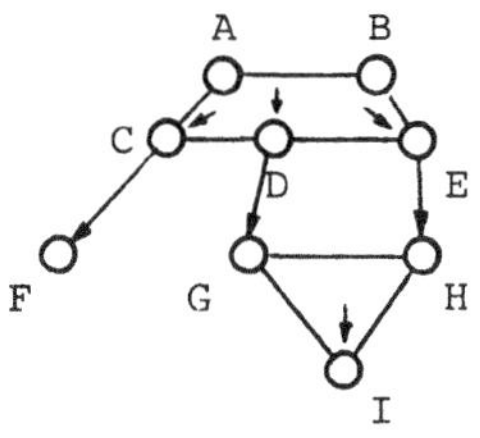

Lemma 3.1. Every ordered DBH is in 2NF.

Proof. For every table, the primary key of the table is unique and is the key of the maximal element in $\leq$. Now, if an ODBH exists not in 2NF, then in one of its tables a surface must exist whose key nodes are a proper part of the primary key of the table. So, the maximal element cannot be unique ☒

Theorem 3.2. Given a grammar G, $L(G)$ is a 2NF-Language if the starting DBHs are ODBHs and for every production $p = \langle \alpha, \beta, h \rangle$ p is key preserving and β is an ODBH.

Proof. Let $H_1 \in \mathcal{H}$ be an ODBH and $g(H_1)$ be the graph whose nodes represent the surfaces of H_1 and edges connect nodes representing surfaces in relation $\leq$.
When a production $p = \langle \alpha, \beta, h \rangle$ is applied to H_1 and a DBH H_2 is derived, $g(H_2)$ has the following structure:

a. Any node $\gamma \geq \alpha$ in $g(H_1)$ is in $g(H_2)$ $\geq$ to any node in $g(\beta)$, according to the ordering in β and the key preserving property of p.

b. Any node $\delta \leq \alpha$ in $g(H_1)$ is in $g(H_2)$ $\leq$ to any node in $g(\beta)$ representing surfaces in one of the following sets:
   b1. surfaces with at least one non key node in the codomain of h.
   b2. surfaces in $g(\beta)$ that are $\geq$ to at least one surface in b1.

c. All other edges in $g(H_1)$ are unchanged in $g(H_2)$.

So, the partial order is preserved.
The key preserving property of p guarantees the uniqueness of maximal element for every table in H_2.
Finally, lemma 3.1 guarantees that $L(G)$ is a 2NF-Language ☒

With regard to BCNF-Languages, we want to characterize a class of grammars that allows to generate, for any given DBH in BCNF, a 2-equivalent one. Related work may be found in [22].

Definition 3.7. A grammar G is said BCNF-canonical if its starting DBHs are atomic and all key and its productions belong to the following classes:

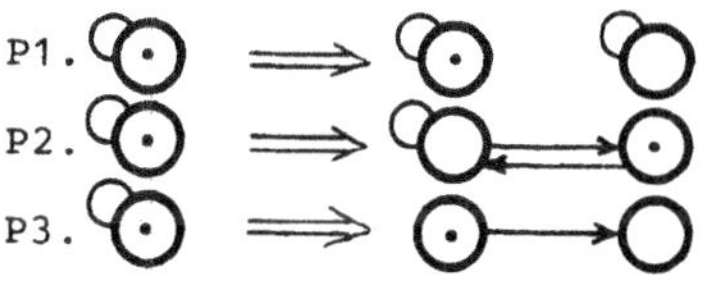

Theorem 3.3. Given any BCNF-canonical grammar G, $L(G)$ is a BCNF-Language. Given any $H \in \mathcal{H}$ in BCNF, a BCNF-canonical grammar G and $H' \overset{2}{\equiv} H$ exist such that $H' \in L(G)$.

Proof of the first part. The starting DBHs are in class C1 of Def.2.10. Class C1 is closed with respect to rules P1 and P2. Rule P3 is applicable only once and changes members of C1 into members of C2.

Proof of the second part. Any $H \in \mathcal{H}$ in classes C1 and C2 Def. 2.10 may be obtained in the following way:
1) Use initially P1 to create starting DBHs for all the tables in H.

2) Any DBH in class C1 is generated with n applications of rule P2.
3) Any DBH in class C2 may be obtained by a DBH in class C1 applying once rule P3 ⊠

Finally, we notice that a top-down generation of a DB scheme has positive effects also when the set of functional dependencies changes, in consequence of changes in the laws of real world.
Such change corresponds in our formalism to creating new surfaces and/or deleting existing ones.
If the desired normalization degree is lost, it can be newly obtained deleting the part of the syntactic tree effected by the change and expanding it again, as in top-down programming techniques.

4. CONCLUSIONS

In this paper we have studied the adequacy of the concept of Data Base hypergraph to model functional dependencies in relational schemes. In particular we have formalized several reductions and equivalences among DBHs and we have given conditions on DBH grammars that insure to generate normalized relational schemes.
Further research is being devoted to study how stronger is the generative power of DBH grammars if we make use of the concept of nonterminal objects and if we extend the power of the rewriting rules by allowing context sensitive productions.

ACKNOWLEDGEMENTS

We are indebted to Giorgio Ausiello for his stimulating comments and suggestions.

REFERENCES

[1] ABRIAL J.R.: *Data Semantics*, Data Base Management, North Holland (1974).

[2] AIELLO CARLUCCI L., MONTANARI U.: *Toward a formal definition of the control in Structured Programs*. Proc. 2nd Intern.Symp. on Math. Found. of Comp. Science, Springer Verlag (1973).

[3] ARMSTRONG W.W.: *Dependency structures of data base relationships*. Proc. of IFIP, North Holland (1974).

[4] BATINI C., D'ATRI A.: *Un formalismo per il progetto di Basi di Dati relazionali*. Proc. of Congresso AICA, (1976).

[5] BATINI C., D'ATRI A.: *On the hypergraph model of functional dependencies*. Techn.Report, Ist.di Automatica, Università Roma (1978).

[6] CODD E.F.: *A Relational model of data for large shared data banks*.CACM 13 (1970).

[7] CODD E.F.: *A Data Base sublanguage founded on the relational calculus*. Proc. ACM SIGFIDET Workshop on Data Description, Access and Control (1971).

[8] CODD E.F.: *Further normalization of the data base relational model*. Data Base Systems, Prentice Hall (1972).

[9] CODD E.F.: *Recent investigation in Relational Data Base Systems*. Proc. of IFIP, North Holland (1974).

[10] DATE C.J.: *An Introduction to Data Base Systems*.Addison Wesley (1977).

[11] DELOBEL C., CASEY R.C.: *Decomposition of Data Bases and the theory of Boolean Switching Functions*.IBM Journal Res.Dev. 17 (1973).

[12] EHRIGH M., KREOWSKY M.: *Algebraic Graph Theory Applied in Computer Science*. Conference on Algebraic and Categorical Methods in Computer Science and Systems Theory, Hans Ahlenberg, Dortmund (1976).

[13] EHRIGH M., KREOWSKI H.J., MAGGIOLO SCHETTINI A., ROSEN B.K., WINKOWSKI J.: *Deriving Structures from Structures*. Proc. 7th Intern. Symp. on Math. Found. of Comp. Science, Springer Verlag (1978).

[14] FAGIN R.: *The decomposition versus the synthetic approach to Relational Database Design*. IBM Journal Res. Dev., (1977).

[15] MONTANARI U.: *Separable graphs, planar graphs and web grammars*. Information and Control , 16 (1970).

[16] NAGL M.: *Formal Languages of labelled graphs*. Computing 16 (1976).

[17] PFALZ J.L., ROSENFELD A.: *Web Grammars*. 1st Int. Joint Conf. on Art. Intelligence, Washington (1969).

[18] RAJLICH V.: *Relational Structures and Dynamics of Certain Discrete Systems*. Proc. Conf. Math. Found of Comp.Science. High Tatras, Czechoslovakia (1973).

[19] ROSEN B.K.: *Deriving Graphs from Graphs by Applying a Production*. Acta Informatica, 4 (1975).

[20] ROSENFELD A., MILGRAM D.: *Web Automata and Web Grammars*. Machine Intelligence , 7 (1972).

[21] RISSANEN J.: *Independent Components of Relations.* ACM Trans. on Database Systems, 2 (1977).

[22] SHARMAN G.: *A constructive definition of third normal form.* Proc. ACM SIGMOD Int. Conf. on the Management of Data (1976).

[23] TSICHRITZIS D.: *Data Base Management Systems.* Academic Press (1977).

[24] WANG C.Q., WEDEKIND M.M.: *Segment Synthesis in Logical Data Base Design.* IBM Journal Res. Dev. 19 (1976).

PROGRAMMED GRAPH GRAMMARS

Horst Bunke, Lehrstuhl für Informatik 5 (Mustererkennung)
Universität Erlangen-Nürnberg, Martensstr.3, 8520 Erlangen

1. Introduction

Programmed string grammars have been introduced by Rosenkrantz in 1969 [7]. Their idea is to add a control mechanism for the order of productions to be applied. This concept was recently generalized by several authors to graph grammars (cf.[0,9]). Their primary motivation was to develop a convenient tool for some application fields, where rather complex graph manipulations are needed, as data base description [9], semantics of programming languages [3,5], or incremental compiling [0,2]. In these topics, the advantage of a programmed approach is an increase of evidence, i.e. a complex graph manipulation step can be formulated in a structured and suggestive way. The aim of this paper is to formally introduce programmed graph grammars (pr-gg's) and to investigate their generative power.

The various approaches to non-programmed graph grammars (gg's) known in literature differ mainly in the way how the embedding transformation is defined (for a survey see [6]). A very powerful model is presented in [5]. The gg's of [5] are called exp-gg's in the following because the main characteristic of this approach is the representation of the embedding component of a production by well formed expressions. Most of the other models are based on embedding transformations of a more simple type. Adding explicit control by programming, we also choose simple embedding transformations for the underlying graph rewriting steps.

The main result of this paper is the equivalence of pr-gg's and exp-gg's. Clearly, nobody would expect a decrease of generative power by augmenting gg's with a programming mechanism. At the other hand, it is shown in the paper of Uesu [10] that any recursively enumerable set of graphs can be already generated by a non-programmed gg using embedding transformations of rather simple type, as e.g. defined in [4]. In contrast to [10], the proofs in this paper are performed in constructive way, i.e. procedures are given for transforming a exp-gg into an equivalent pr-gg and vice versa. Therefore, this paper can be considered as a connecting link between gg's using complex embedding transformations (as e.g. exp-gg's) and those restricting the embedding transformation to simpler forms.

Furthermore, monotone and context free pr-gg's will be introduced and their relations to the corresponding classes of graph languages defined in [5] will be studied.

The results presented in the following are part of a forthcoming work [1] where the subject is treated in more detail. Only a rough idea of the proofs to the theorems can be given here and some crucial points must be omitted. These points, however, are more of technical interest and only understandable to the reader particularly familiar with the techniques inherent to the approaches used here. Neglecting these difficulties thus results in a more compact representation of the proofs featuring the main ideas without digression into too many details.

2. Definition of pr-gg's

The first definitions are taken up to some slight differences from [8].

Def. 2.1 : Let V, W be alphabets for node and edge labels. A labelled graph over (V,W) is a tuple

$g = (K,(\rho_w)_{w\in W},\beta)$ where

1) K is a finite set, the set of nodes

2) $\rho_w \subseteq K \times K$ are relations over K x K for every $w\in W$

3) $\beta: K \longrightarrow V$ is a function called the labelling function

We interprete every pair $(k,k')\in\rho_w$ as a directed edge from node k to node k' labelled with the symbol $w\in W$. Let $\Gamma(V,W)$ denote the set of all labelled graphs over (V,W) and g_ε the empty graph, i.e. the graph with an empty set of nodes.

Def. 2.2 : Let $g,g'\in\Gamma(V,W)$. g' is called subgraph of g (abbr. $g'\subseteq g$) iff

1) $K'\subseteq K$

2) $\rho'_w = \rho_w \cap (K' x K')$ for every $w\in W$

3) $\beta' = \beta\restriction K'$

Def. 2.3 : Let $g,g'\in\Gamma(V,W)$. g and g' are called isomorphic (abbr. $g\cong g'$) iff there exists a bijective mapping $f:K \longrightarrow K'$ with $(k_1,k_2)\in\rho_w \Longleftrightarrow (f(k_1),f(k_2))\in\rho'_w$ for any $k_1,k_2\in K$ and $w\in W$. g and g' are called equivalent (abbr. $g\equiv g'$) iff $g\cong g'$ and, additionally, $\beta=\beta'\circ f$.

In the following we identify equivalent graphs. In this way we eliminate the trivial differences arising from the arbitrary choice of the node denotations.

Def. 2.4 : Let $g,g'\in\Gamma(V,W)$ and $g'\subseteq g$. The difference g-g' is given by the graph

$g''=(K'',(\rho''_w)_{w\in W},\beta'')$ where

1) $K'' = K-K'$

2) $\rho''_w = \rho_w \cap (K'' x K'')$

3) $\beta'' = \beta\restriction K''$

Def. 2.5 : Let $g,g'\in\Gamma(V,W)$ and $g'\subseteq g$. We define

$In_w(g',g) := \rho_w \cap ((K-K') x K')$

$Out_w(g',g) := \rho_w \cap (K' x (K-K'))$

$In_w(g',g)$ is the set of all w-labelled edges originating in g-g' and terminating in g'. $Out_w(g',g)$ is the set of all edges in the opposite direction. The union of all edges between g-g' and g' is called the embedding of g' in g.

Def.2.6 : Let V,W be alphabets. A production over (V,W) is a 3-tuple $p = (g_l, g_r, E)$ where

1) $g_l, g_r \in \Gamma(V,W) \wedge g_l \neq g_\varepsilon$

2) $E = (L_w, R_w)_{w \in W} \wedge L_w \subseteq K_l \times K_r \wedge R_w \subseteq K_r \times K_l$

g_l and g_r are called the left-hand and right-hand side respectively. E is called the embedding transformation. By means of L_w and R_w the embedding of g_l in g is transformed into that of g_r in the derived graph g'. Productions of the above form are called unrestricted.

Def.2.7 : Let $p = (g_l, g_r, E)$ be a production and $g, g' \in \Gamma(V,W)$. g' is directly derivable from g by p (abbr. $g \xrightarrow[p]{} g$) iff

1) $g_l \subseteq g \wedge g_r \subseteq g' \wedge g - g_l = g' - g_r$

2) $In_w(g_r, g') = L_w \circ In_w(g_l, g) \wedge Out_w(g_r, g') = Out_w(g_l, g) \circ R_w \ (\forall w \in W)$

The reader can find some theorems resulting from the above definitions in [8].

Def.2.8 : Let P be a set of productions. A control diagram over P is a graph $C = (K_C, (\rho_{C,Y}, \rho_{C,N}), \beta_C)$ where the nodes are labelled with symbols of $P \cup \{START, STOP\}$ and the edges are labelled with symbols of {Y,N} standing for YES and NO. Furthermore, the following conditions hold true:

1) there exists exactly one node $k_{START} \in K_C$ with $\beta_C(k_{START}) = START$

2) there exists exactly one node $k_{STOP} \in K_C$ with $\beta_C(k_{STOP}) = STOP$

3) there exists no edge terminating at the node k_{START}

4) there exists no edge originating at the node k_{STOP}.

The control diagram is the crucial point of the approach presented here, because it programs the order in which productions are to be applied. A more detailled explanation is given by the following definitions and remarks.

Def.2.9 : A programmed graph grammar (pr-gg) is a 5 tuple G = (V,W,P,S,C) where

1) V,W are alphabets for labelling the nodes and edges, respectively

2) P is a finite set of productions over (V,W)

3) $S \in \Gamma(V,W)$ is called initial graph, $S \neq g_\varepsilon$

4) C is a control diagram over P

No distinction between terminal and nonterminal labels is made within pr-gg's. The reader should recognize that a control diagram is a powerful tool to control the order of production applications including the termination of a derivation sequence.

Def.2.10 : Let $g, g' \in \Gamma(V,W)$, G pr-gg, $k, k' \in K_C$, $p = (g_l, g_r, E)$ with $\beta_C(k) = p$. The pair (g',k') is directly programmed derivable from (g,k) (abbr. $(g,k) \xrightarrow{prog} (g',k')$) iff

either $g \xrightarrow[p]{} g' \wedge (k,k') \in \rho_{C,Y}$

<u>or</u> $g_1 \not\Rightarrow g \wedge g = g' \wedge (k,k') \in \rho_{C,N}$

In the following $\xrightarrow{prog^*}$ denotes the reflexive and transitive closure of the relation $\xrightarrow{prog}$.

<u>Def.2.11 :</u> Let be G pr-gg. The <u>language</u> generated by G is given by

$$\mathcal{L}(G) := \{g \mid g \in \mathcal{T}(V,W) \wedge (\exists k \in K_C)\ ((S,k) \xrightarrow{prog^*} (g,k_{STOP}) \wedge (k_{START},k) \in \rho_{C,Y})\}.$$

$k_{START}(k_{STOP})$ denotes in the above definition the unique node of the control diagram of G labelled with the symbol START (STOP). In order to elucidate the derivation mechanism of a pr-gg, one may imagine the following procedure: Consider at any moment t a pair consisting of a graph g and a node k of the control diagram. Start with the initial graph S and a node k of the control diagram which is a direct Y-successor of the node k_{START}. Try the application of the production $p = \beta_C(k)$ to the graph g according to Def.2.7. Consider at time t + 1 a graph g' with $g \xrightarrow{p} g'$ and a node k' of the control diagram with $(k,k') \in \rho_{C,Y}$ if p is applicable to g at time t. We have to consider the graph g and a node k" of the control diagram with $(k,k") \in \rho_{C,N}$ at time t + 1 if the application of p fails. In other words, we track a path of the control diagram and try at every node the application of the corresponding production. We leave a node along an outgoing Y-edge (N-edge) if the application was (not) successful. The derivation sequence stops and an element of the language in question is generated when the STOP-node of the control diagram is reached. For all other cases, e.g. the absence of an outgoing Y-edge (k,k') if the application of $p = \beta_C(k)$ was successful, the continuation of the derivation sequence is not defined, i.e. no element of $\mathcal{L}(G)$ will be generated.

It should be mentioned that the above definitions are not the only possible way to introduce pr-gg's. For example, an alternative definition is given in [5], but the reader may easily ascertain that this approach is properly contained in the model presented here.

<u>Def.2.12 :</u> Let G,G' be gg's or pr-gg's of any type. G and G' are called <u>equivalent</u> iff they generate the same language.

<u>Def.2.13 :</u> Let $p = (g_l, g_r, E)$ be a (unrestricted) production. p is called <u>monotone</u> iff $|K_l| \leq |K_r|$. p is called <u>context free</u> iff it is monotone and $|K_l| = 1$.

<u>Def.2.14 :</u> A pr-gg is called unrestricted (monotone, context free) iff all productions are of corresponding type. A subset $L \subseteq \mathcal{T}(V,W)$ is called a programmed graph language of one of the above types iff there exists a pr-gg G of corresponding type with $L = \mathcal{L}(G)$.

3. Simulation of ex-gg's by pr-gg's

The aim of section 3 and 4 is to show the equivalence between exp-gg's and pr-gg's. The main differences between the two models are briefly mentioned in the following.

For any formal definition concerning exp-gg's the reader is referred to [5].

We distinguish in the exp-gg model between terminal and nonterminal labels for nodes as well as for edges. Furthermore, very powerful operations for the transformation of the embeddings are possible. Conversely, a rather simple approach to embedding is used within pr-gg's, and there is no distinction between terminal and nonterminal labels in this model. However, we can use the tool of programming to control the order in which productions are to be applied.

Theorem 3.1 : For any monotone exp-gg $G = (\Sigma_V, \Sigma_E, \Delta_V, \Delta_E, do, P, \xrightarrow{S})$ there exists an equivalent monotone pr-gg $G' = (V', W', P', S', C')$.

Outline of the proof: The proof is performed in a constructive manner. In the first part productions $p_i^{(1)}, \ldots, p_i^{(n_i)} \in P'$ and fragments of the control diagram C' are constructed for the simulation of any exp-production $p_i \in P$. The second part aims at the simulation of the complete exp-gg G and is based on the constituents constructed in the first part. Because the formal proof is rather extensive [1], only an outline, guided by an example, can be presented here.

Part 1 : (Simulation of a single exp-production $p \in P$).

Consider the exp-production p of Fig.1 and the graph g of Fig.2. The graph g' of Fig.3 is obtained by applying p to g. In the following we simulate the step which leads from g to g' by the application of a programmed sequence of pr-productions which are all of the form demanded in Def.2.6. The simulation consists of four steps.

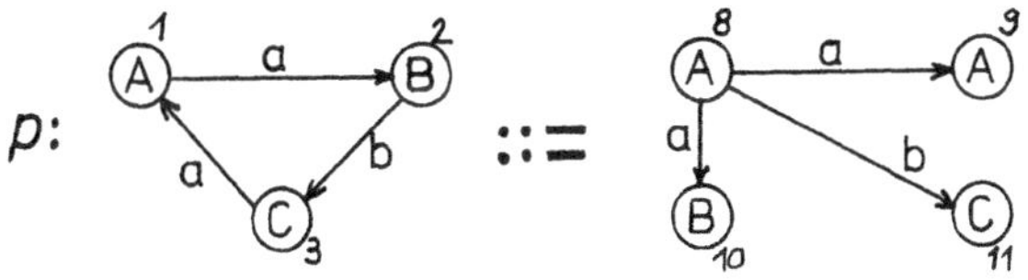

$E:\ l_a = (R_a P_a(2);9) \cup (R_a R_a(3);11) \cup (YR_b(2);8)$

Fig.1

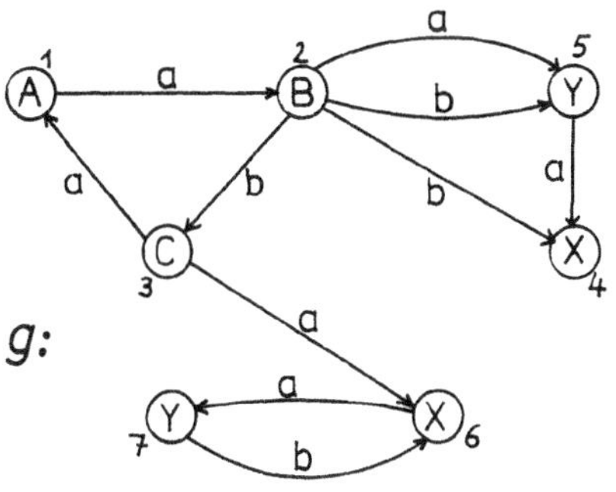

Fig.2

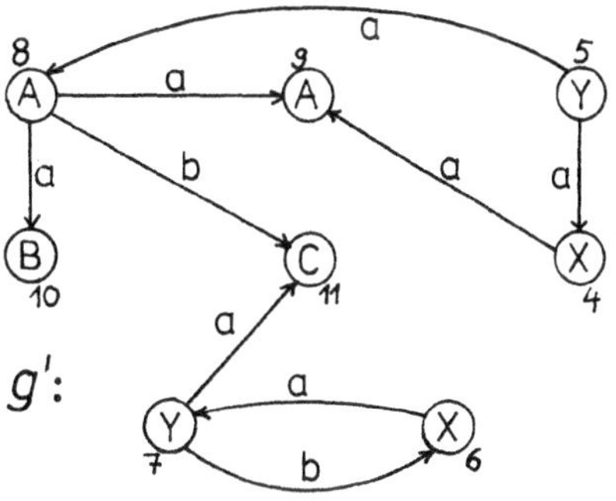

Fig.3

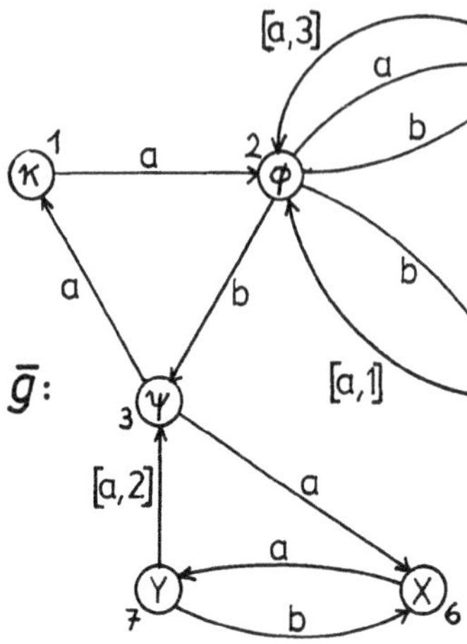

Fig.4

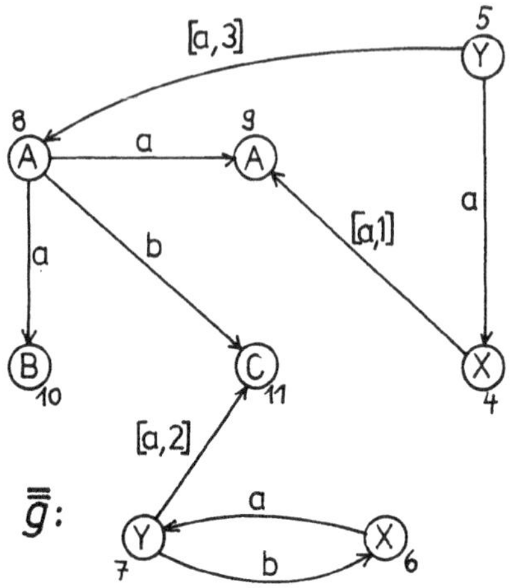

Fig.5

I) Relabelling the nodes of the left-hand side in the graph g by unique labels. This can be done by a single production $p^{(1)}$ which replaces, for example, the labels A,B,C in the graph g of Fig.2 by κ,ϕ,ψ, respectively.

II) Now the embedding expressions occurring in p are "evaluated". The result of this procedure is shown in Fig.4. (Note that the labels A,B,C have been replaced by the labels κ,ϕ,ψ in step I). In order to get the graph of Fig.4 the embedding component*) $l_a = (R_aR_a(2);9) \cup (R_aR_a(3);11) \cup (YR_b(2);8)$ is decomposed into three constituents $expr_1 = (R_aR_a(2);9)$, $expr_2 = (R_aR_a(3);11)$, $expr_3 = (YR_b(2);8)$. Then productions which insert an edge labelled with [a,i] (i=1,2,3) between the argument node and the result node(s) of $expr_i$ are to be applied in a programmed order. An algorithm for the construction of these productions including the order of application is given in [1]. We consider here only a basic step of the whole procedure: the "evaluation" of the "atomic" subexpression $l_a = (R_a(2);9)$ of $l_a = (R_aR_a(2);9)$ which can be done by the production of Fig.6, where N stands for any node label and where the embedding is transformed identically.

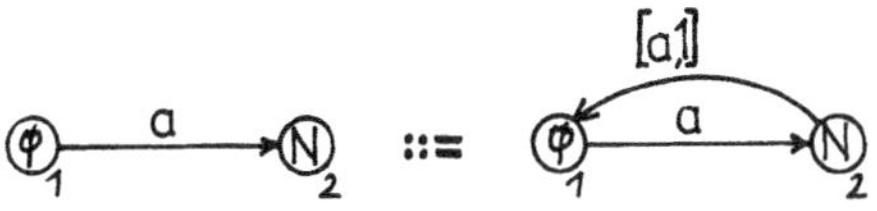

$E: L_w = \{(1,1),(2,2)\} = R_w$ for any $w \in W$

Fig.6

In order to treat the given embedding expression l_a, the "atomic" subexpressions are expanded successively to more complex expressions and the nodes within the range of every expression occurring thus are determined by means of programmed application of productions until the whole expression l_a is exploited.

III) The subgraph of $\bar{g}$ in Fig.4 fixed by the nodes with labels κ,ϕ,ψ must be replaced by the right-hand side of p. For that we need only a single production identically to p up to the labels κ,ϕ,ψ of the left-hand side and the embedding which is easily

* The reader not familiar with the expression notion of [5] is referred to Fig.3 and the corresponding text within the introductory paper [6] contained in this volume.

obtained from the embedding component of p by erasing in $expr_1$, $expr_2$ and $expr_3$ the operators R_aR_a, R_aR_a and YR_b. In our example we get the embedding components $L_{[a,1]} = \{(2,9)\}$, $L_{[a,2]} = \{(3,11)\}$, $L_{[a,3]} = \{(2,8)\}$. The result of step III is given in Fig.5.

IV) The only task which remains to do is to change the labels [a,i] in the graph $\bar{\bar{g}}$ of Fig.5 to "a" (i=1,2,3) by application of suitable productions. Finally, we get the graph g' of Fig.3 and the simulation of p is complete.

Part 2 : (Simulation of the complete exp-ggG):

Besides the productions constructed in part 1 we need productions for testing whether there exist nonterminal labels in the derived graph. Nonterminal edge labels as well as node labels must be taken into consideration.

Then the pr-gg G' is defined in the following way:

$V' := \Sigma_V \cup L_V$ where L_V consists of the auxiliary node labels $\kappa, \phi, \psi, \ldots$ introduced in part 1

$W' := \Sigma_E \cup L_W$ where L_W consists of the auxiliary edge labels [w,i] introduced in part 1

P' consists of all productions constructed in part 1 und 2

$S' := d_0$

C' is constructed as indicated in Fig.7 where the dots are drawn in order to simplify the graphical representation and may not be regarded as nodes in the sense of Def.2.8.

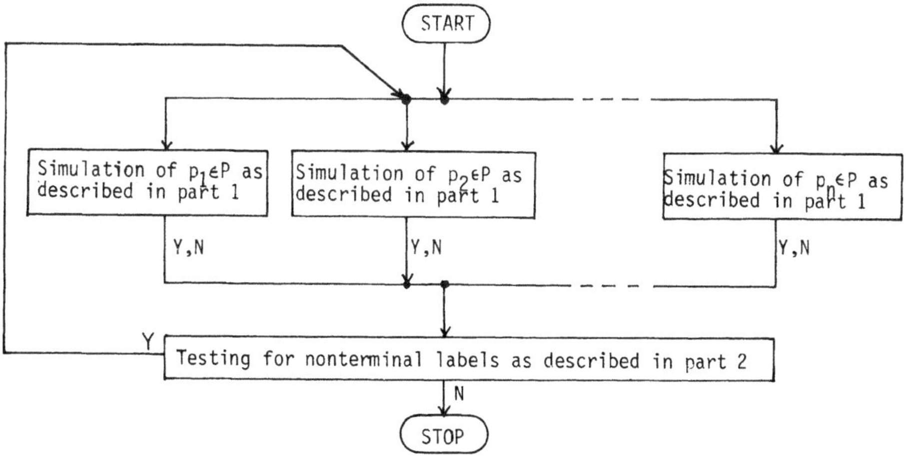

Fig.7

4. The simulation of pr-gg's by exp-gg's

An ex-gg has to be constructed where the rules are forced to be applied in an order compatible with the control diagram of the given pr-gg. In order to simlify this task we define a special attribute for pr-gg's:

Def.4.1 : A pr-gg $G = (V,W,P,S,C)$ is called pivotal iff

1) $V = V_1 \cup V_2$
2) There exists exactly one node of the initial graph S labelled with an element of V_2 (pivotal node of S)
3) For every production holds: there exists exactly one node of the left-hand side labelled with an element of V_2 (pivotal node of the left-hand side), and there exists exactly one node of the right-hand side labelled with an element of V_2 (pivotal node of the right-hand side).

It follows immediately from this definition that every graph g derivable by means of a pivotal pr-gg contains exactly one node labelled with an element of V_2 (pivotal node of g). The application of any production is always bound to a subgraph containing the pivotal node.

Lemma 4.2 : For any monotone pr-gg there exists an equivalent one which is pivotal monotone and programmed.

The proof is given in [1]. The idea is to introduce dummy productions which don't change a graph but allow the transfer of the pivotal node to any other node. In this way the application of productions in any part of g can be simulated.

Because of Lemma 4.2 we can restrict our considerations in the sequel to pivotal monotone pr-gg's.

Theorem 4.3 : For any pivotal monotone pr-gg $G = (V,W,P,S,C)$ there exists an equivalent monotone exp-gg $G' = (\Sigma'_V, \Sigma'_E, \Delta'_V, \Delta'_E, do', P', \xrightarrow{S})$.

Outline of the proof: The most important task is to force the productions of G' to be applied in an order compatible with the control diagram. For that reason we expand the label v of the pivotal node of every actual graph to a pair label $(v,k) \in V \times K_C$ where we keep the current control diagram node k in the second component. By changing this second component using rewriting steps of G' we simulate the tracking of the paths of the control diagram within G . Because the pivotal node is affected in each rewriting step (cf. Def. 4.1) the updating of the current control diagram node is ensured.

In the sequel the components of G' will be defined in terms of constituent parts of G:

$\Delta'_V := V$

$\Delta'_E := W$

$\Sigma'_E - \Delta'_E$: = {n} where $\{n\} \cap \Delta'_E = \emptyset$, i.e. in G' we have only one nonterminal edge label

$\Sigma'_V - \Delta'_V$: = V x K_C, i.e. nonterminal node labels are those having the location of the control diagram as second component

$d\acute{o}$: replace in S the label v of the pivotal node by $(v, k_{START}) \in V \times K_C$

P' is obtained in 3 steps:

I) For any edge of the control diagram C originating at the START-node k_{START} and terminating at any node k construct a production as shown in Fig.8. (v, k_{START}) is equal to the label used for the construction of $d\acute{o}$ as described above. According to Def.2.11 these productions ensure that the simulation starts with a node of the control diagram which is a direct successor of k_{START}.

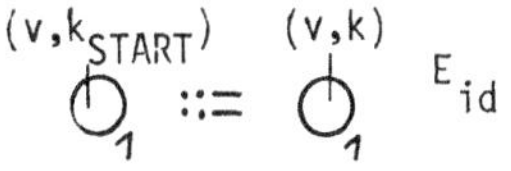

Fig.8

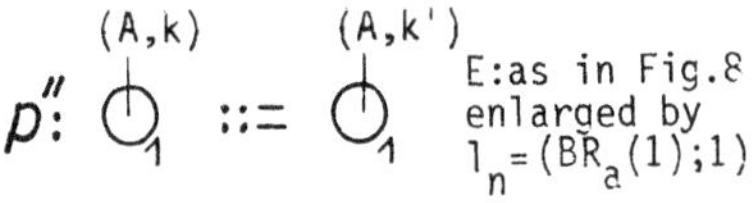

Fig.9

II) Consider every remaining Y-edge (k,k') of the control diagram and change the production p = (g_l, g_r, E) belonging to node k, i.e. $\beta_C(k) = p$, in the following way:

- replace the label v_l of the pivotal node of g_l by (v_l, k)
- replace the label v_r of the pivotal node of g_r by (v_r, k') if $k' \neq k_{STOP}$

Let p' be the result of the above changes. Obviously, before the application of p' we keep the node k as current control diagram node in the second component of the (only) pair label in the underlaying graph. The application of p' causes together with the replacement of the left-hand side by the right-hand side the replacement of the current control diagram node k by k'. In this manner the step along the Y-edge from node k to node k' in the control diagram is simulated. For $k' = k_{STOP}$ the nonterminal pair label is erased. Therefore, no production of P' is applicable and the simulation stops.

III) The method of II) does not work for the simulation of tracking a N-edge (k,k') in the control diagram. We have to construct a seperate production for every such edge which changes the current control diagram node in the second component of the pair label from k to k'. An example is given in Fig.9 where the symbol A stands for any element of V and the embedding component may be neglected for a moment. The problem which arises here is to prevent the application of the production p" of Fig.9 if the production p' of part II) which belongs to the node k is applicable. In this case p' must be applied and a control diagram node $\tilde{k}$ reachable by a Y-edge from k must be considered next. The false application of p" cannot be prohibited explicitly in the exp-gg G' but a nonterminal edge can be inserted in this case by means of the embedding component of p". If we enlarge the embedding components of all productions constructed up till now so that such a nonterminal edge will never be erased, no

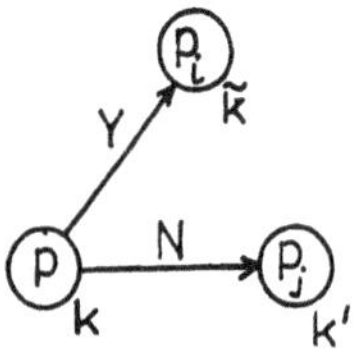

Fig.10

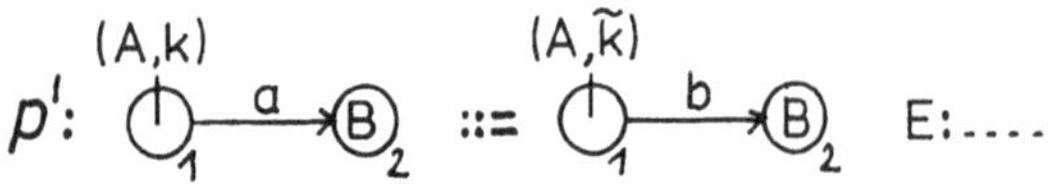

Fig.11

graph belonging to $\mathcal{L}$(G') can be derived from a graph containing a nonterminal edge. Thus, the tracking of an N-edge (k,k') in the control diagram is simulated if and only if the production p' of part II) belonging to k is not applicable. In order to complete the example of Fig.9 consider the part of the control diagram represented in Fig.10. Here p is the production belonging originally to node k of the control diagram, i.e. $\beta_C(k)$ = p. Let p' of Fig.11 be the production obtained from p by applying the procedure described in II). The embedding component of p' may be arbitrary in this example. The expression l_n=(BR_a(1);1) of E in Fig.9 causes the insertion of a nonterminal edge labelled with n if and only if the left-hand side of p' exists (i.e. p' is applicable) at the moment when p" is applied.

Some more productions are necessary, when the left-hand side of p' contains more than two nodes. The construction and verification of these productions is a nontrivial task based on some very special properties inherent to the expression formalism of [5]. In order to avoid a digression into this topic the reader is referred for the remainder of the proof to [1].

5. Context free pr-gg's

Whereas the class of graph languages generated by monotone exp-gg's is equal to the class generated by context free exp-gg's (cf.[5]), we get a different result for pr-gg's.

Theorem 5.1 : The class of monotone programmed graph languages properly contains the class of context free programmed graph languages.

Proof : The graph language M of Fig.12 is monotone programmed but not context free programmed.

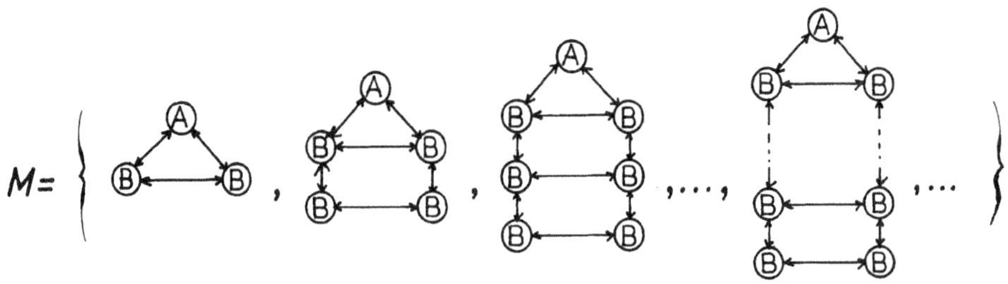

Fig.12

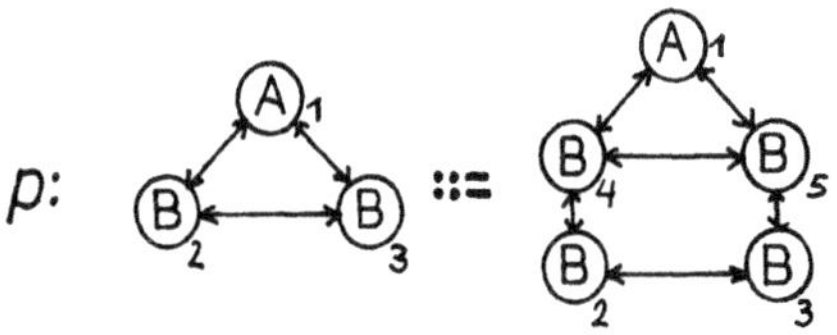

E: L= {(2,2), (3,3)} = R

Fig.13

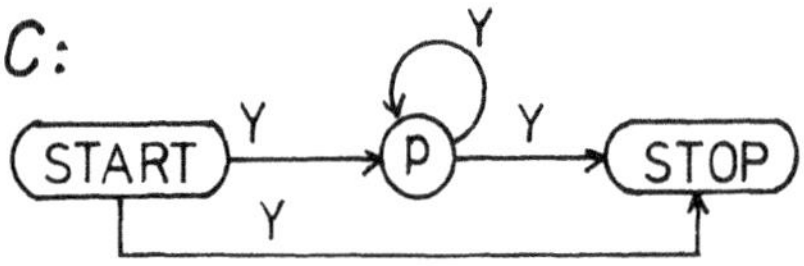

Fig.14

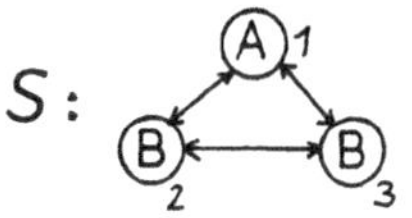

Fig.15

1) The monotone pr-gg G = (V,W,S,P,C), where V = {A,B}, |W|=1, P = {p} and p,S,C are given in Fig.13,14,15 respectively, generates M.*)
2) We have to show that there exists no context free pr-gg G with $\mathcal{L}(G)$ = M. The formal proof is given in [1] by contradiction. From Def.2.7 follows immediately that after the application of any context free pr-production p either there exists no edge between a node k of g_r and $g'-g_r$ or k is connected by an edge with every node of $g'-g_r$ which was connected to the node of the left-hand side before the application of p. To overcome this weakness, one cannot use the tool of programming. Because only one node can occur in the left-hand side of a context free pr-production, the explicit manipulation of edges is not possible. These are the crucial points which lead for our special language M to the contradiction mentioned above.

6. Summary

Let [enum], [exp-i] and [pr-i] denote the class of recursively enumerable, typ-i expression and typ-i programmed graph languages respectively. The following hierarchy is known from [5]:

[enum] = [exp-unrestricted] $\supsetneqq$ [exp-monotone] = [exp-context free]

The proof of section 3 holds true also for unrestricted productions, so

[enum] = [exp-unrestricted] $\subseteqq$ [pr-unrestricted].

At the other hand, from Def.2.11 it follows immediately that

[pr-unrestricted] $\subseteqq$ [enum].

Summarizing these results including the theorems of section 3, 4 and 5 we get the

Corollary 6.1 : The following diagram of relations holds true:

$$
\begin{array}{lccccc}
 & [\text{pr-unrestricted}] & \supsetneqq & [\text{pr-monotone}] & \supsetneqq & [\text{pr-context free}] \\
[\text{enum}] \begin{smallmatrix} /\!\!/ \\ \\ \backslash\!\!\backslash \end{smallmatrix} & \text{\rotatebox{90}{$=$}} & & \text{\rotatebox{90}{$=$}} & & \cap\!\!\!\!\!\not\; \\
 & [\text{exp-unrestricted}] & \supsetneqq & [\text{exp-monotone}] & = & [\text{exp-context free}]
\end{array}
$$

Acknowledgement

The author would like the thank M.Nagl for many helpful remarks and suggestions in preparing this paper.

*) As there is only one edge label it is omitted in the graphical representation of Fig.13-15.

References

[0] BUNKE,H.: Beschreibung eines syntaxgesteuerten inkrementellen Compilers durch Graph-Grammatiken, Arbeitsbericht des Instituts für Math.Masch.u. Datenverarbeitung 7, 7, Erlangen 1974

[1] BUNKE,H.: Sequentielle und parallele programmierte Graph-Grammatiken, Dissertation to appear

[2] BRENDEL,W./BUNKE,H./NAGL,M.: Syntaxgesteuerte Programmierung und inkrementelle Compilation, Informatik-Fachberichte 10, 55-74, Berlin, Springer-Verlag, 1977

[3] CULIK,K.II/FARAH,M.: Linked forest manipulation systems, a tool for computational semantics, Techn.Rep.CS-77-18, University of Waterloo, 1977

[4] EHRIG,H.: Introduction to the Algebraic Theory of Graph Grammars, this volume

[5] NAGL,M.: Graph-Ersetzungssysteme: Theorie, Anwendungen, Implementierung, Habilitationsschrift, University of Erlangen, 1978

[6] NAGL,M.: A Tutorial and Bibliographical Survey on Graph Grammars, this volume

[7] ROSENKRANTZ,D.J.: Programmend Grammars and Classes of Formal Languages, JACM 16, 1969, 107-131

[8] SCHNEIDER,H.J.: Chomsky-Systeme für partielle Ordnungen, Arbeitsbericht des Instituts für Math.Masch.und Datenverarbeitung 3, 3, Erlangen, 1970

[9] SCHNEIDER,H.J.: Conceptual data base description using graph grammars, in H. Noltemeier (Ed.): Graphen, Algorithmen, Datenstrukturen, Applied Computer Science 4, 77-98, München, Hauser-Verlag, 1976

[10] UESU,T.: A system of graph grammars which generates all recursively enumberable sets of labelled graphs, private communication 1977

Shortest Path Problems and Tree Grammars: An Algebraic Framework.

by Alfonso Catalano, Stefania Gnesi and Ugo Montanari
Istituto di Scienze dell'Informazione, University of Pisa, Italy.

1. Introduction

Some interesting, recent results concern the equivalence between the operational and the denotational semantics of recursive programs [1], in particular nondeterministic programs [2]. A recursive definition in the operational approach, is considered first as a recursive schema, i.e. a grammar which can generate a (possibly) infinite tree or a set of trees. Every tree is a symbolic expression built up in terms of the elementary operations available in the programming language. Such trees can then be evaluated yielding a result. The same result can be obtained, in the denotational approach, by first evaluating the schema, obtaining the original program now considered as a system of equations in a suitable algebra, and then finding the minimal fixpoint of the system. The whole process can be completely described in simple algebraic terms if we consider also the recursive schema as a system of equations whose unknowns are sets of trees: The above equivalence result can be expressed in terms of commutativity of the fixpoint operation and of the evaluation homomorphism.

In this paper, a similar paradigm is applied to regular tree grammars (the symbolic schemata) and to the so-called functional equations of dynamic programming (the interpreted counterpart). An interesting aspect of this construction is that the union operation on sets of trees is interpreted as the minimum operation on real numbers. The commutativity result we prove in the paper has practical applications, since it allows to use efficient graph searching techniques on combinatorial problems expressed in the framework of dynamic programming.

2. Trees and tree grammars

In this section we recall some basic concepts and introduce an operational semantics for tree grammars. Our tree domain is essentially CT_Σ as defined in [1]. In short, given a ranked alphabet Σ (i.e. a family $\Sigma_i, i \in \omega$ of alphabets, indexed by the natural numbers), a Σ-tree is a partial function

$$t : \omega^* \to \Sigma$$

such that for all $u \in \omega^*$ and $i \in \omega$

a) $ui \in def(t)$ implies $u \in def(t)$;

b) $ui \in def(t)$ implies $t(u) \in \Sigma_n$ and $i < n$ for some $n > 0$, where $def(t)$ is the definition domain of partial function t.

The set CT_Σ of all such trees is ordered according to the standard order of partial functions, namely

$$t' \subseteq t'' \text{ iff } def(t') \subseteq def(t'') \text{ and } \forall u \in def(t') \text{ we have } t'(u)=t''(u)$$

If $t' \subseteq t''$ we say that t' approximates t''. If t' does not approximate any other tree, t' is called maximal. It is easy to see that with this definition CT_Σ is a complete partial order, namely is has a minimum (the everywhere undefined function) and every chain has a least upper bound. The set of all Σ trees with finite definition domain is called

T_Σ.

A regular tree grammar is a quadruple $G = (\Sigma, V, P, S)$ where Σ is a ranked alphabet of terminal symbols;
V is a set of nonterminal symbols; let Σ' be a ranked alphabet such that $\Sigma'_i = \Sigma_i$ for $i \neq 0$ and $\Sigma'_0 = \Sigma_0 \cup V$;
$P \subseteq V \times T_{\Sigma'}$ is a nonempty set of productions;
$S \in V$ is an initial symbol.

We can now define over $CT_{\Sigma'}$ the immediate derivability relation $\rightarrow$:

$t' \rightarrow t''$ iff for all $u \in def(t') \cap def(t'')$ such that $t'(u) \notin V$ we have $t'(u) = t''(u)$; and for all $u \in def(t'')$ such that $t'(u) = A \in V$ there exist a production (A, t) such that for all i such that $ui \in def(t'')$ we have $t''(ui) = t(i)$.

Note that if $t \rightarrow t'$ and $t'' \sqsubseteq t'$ then also $t \rightarrow t''$. Informally the trees immediately derivable from a tree t are those which can be obtained by replacing in parallel all nonterminals of t using productions of the grammar, and by all their approximations.

The language of trees generated by a regular tree grammar G is defined as follows

$$L(G) = \{ t \mid t \in T_\Sigma , \ \{(\lambda, S)\} \rightarrow^* t \}$$

where $\rightarrow^*$ is as usual the transitive closure of $\rightarrow$. In what follows we are interested also in infinite trees, and thus we define the closed language $CL(G)$ generated by G as the union of $L(G)$ and of all trees in CT_Σ which are least upper bounds of chains of trees in $L(G)$.

As an example let us consider the following grammar $G = (\Sigma, V, P, S)$, where

$$\Sigma_0 = \{a_1\}, \quad \Sigma_1 = \{b_1, b_2\}, \quad \Sigma_2 = \{c_1, c_2\}, \quad \Sigma_3 = \Sigma_4 = \dots = \emptyset$$

$$V = \{S, B, C, D\}$$

(2.1) $$P = \left\{ \begin{array}{lll} S \rightarrow a_1 ; & S \rightarrow b_1(S), & S \rightarrow c_1(S, B); \\ B \rightarrow b_2(C); & B \rightarrow c_2(\bot, b_1(D)) ; & \\ C \rightarrow B & & \end{array} \right\}$$

To separate the members of a production we use the symbol $\rightarrow$; and to represent trees we use the familiar functional notation. For instance, $c_2(\bot, b_1(D))$ stays for the partial function $t: \omega^* \rightharpoonup \Sigma$

$$t = \{(\lambda, c_2), (1, b_1), (10, D)\}$$

A grammar G is in normal form iff the right members of all productions are of type $f(A_1, A_2, \dots, A_n)$, where $f \in \Sigma_n$ and $A_1, A_2, \dots, A_n \in V$.

Given any grammar G, it is always possible to find an equivalent grammar G' (i.e. such that $L(G') = L(G)$) in normal form. In fact we can first eliminate all productions of the type $A \rightarrow B$ using the corresponding well known algorithm for context free grammars. Then we can decompose all trees deeper than one which appear in right members of productions by introducing new nonterminals. For instance the grammar (2.1) would generate a new grammar $G' = (\Sigma, V', P', S)$, where

$$V' = \{S, B, D, E, F\}$$

$$P' = \{ S \rightarrow a_1 ; \quad S \rightarrow b_1(S) ; \quad S \rightarrow c_1(S, B);$$

(2.2) $B \to b_2(B)$; $B \to c_2(E,F)$;
$F \to b_1(D)$ |

Given a grammar in normal form, it can be easily represented using a labeled AND-OR graph [8,3]. For instance in our example we would have

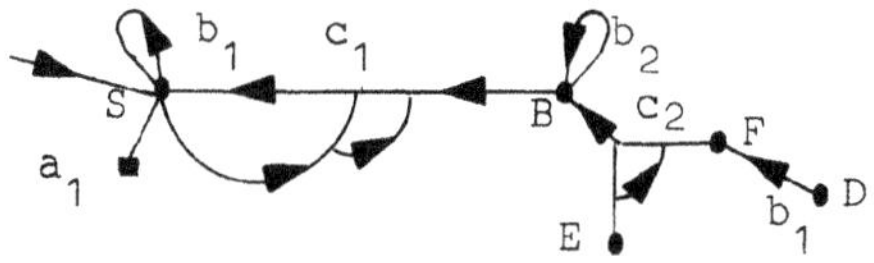

Fig.1

More precisely, the labeled AND-OR graph corresponding to a grammar G in normal form is an hypergraph whose nodes correspond to nonterminals, and an hyperarc $(A,A_1,A_2,\ldots, A_n)$ exists and is labeled with σ iff $A \to \sigma(A_1,A_2,\ldots,A_n)$ is a production of G. Furthermore, an AND-OR graph has a root node corresponding to the initial symbol of G.

An AND-OR tree (namely an AND-OR graph where every node is first node of at most one hyperarc, every node except the root node is nonfirst node of exactly one hyperarc, and the root node is nonfirst node of no hyperarc) can properly represent a tree, and viceversa. For instance, the AND-OR tree

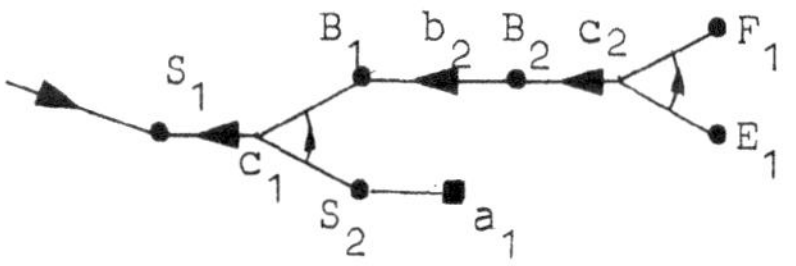

Fig.2

corresponds to $c_1(a_1,b_2(c_2(\bot,\bot)))$, or in partial function form, to

$$t = \{\{\bot, c_1\}, \{0, a_1\}, \{1,b_2\}, \{10,c_2\}\}.$$

Given a finite AND-OR graph H and a possibly numerably infinite AND-OR tree T, we say that T is a generalized path (g-path) of H iff there exists a homomorphism mapping T into H. More precisely, T and H must be labeled with the same alphabet and a function h must exist mapping nodes of T into nodes of H such that if an hyperarc $(A,A_1,\ldots,A_n)$ exists in T and is labeled with σ, then an hyperarc $(h(A),h(A_1),\ldots,h(A_n))$ labeled with σ must also exist in H. Furthermore, h must map the root of T into the root of H.

As emphasized by the name, the concept of a g-path of an AND-OR graph can be seen as an extension of the concept of path of an ordinary graph (and in fact reduces to it if $\Sigma_i=\emptyset$ for $i \neq 1$). For instance, the AND-OR tree in Fig.2 is a g-path of the AND-OR graph in Fig.1. Infact the following, suitable function h exists

$h(S_1)=h(S_2)=S$; $h(B_1)=h(B_2)=B$

$h(E_1)= E$; $h(F_1) = F$.

Trees generated by a grammar and g-paths of the corresponding AND-OR graph are related by the following theorem.

Theorem 2.1 : Let G be a regular tree grammar in normal form and let H be the corresponding AND-OR graph. Then CL(G) (L(G)) consists of trees corresponding to all (finite) g-paths of H.

Proof. Finite case. Given a g-path, its homomorphism function h provides immediately a derivation for the corresponding tree in G. Viceversa, given a tree and its derivation in G, the nonterminals which the leaves of the intermediate trees in the derivation have been labeled with, define a proper function h for the corresponding AND-OR tree. Infinite case. All finite subtrees of an infinite g-path of H are g-paths of H. Viceversa, given a chain of finite trees, the homomorphism functions of the corresponding AND-OR trees are also a chain and define as a limit the homomorphism function of an infinite g-path of H. ∎

The above theorem allows to interpret the operational semantics of a regular tree grammar as the generation of all g-paths of the corresponding AND-OR graph.

3. The denotational semantics of regular tree grammars.

The construction reported in this section follows almost exactly the guideline exposed in [1]. Our goal is to interpret a regular grammar as a system of equations whose unknowns are languages of trees, to solve it using fixpoint theory and to prove that the obtained solution for the initial symbol coincides with the language generated by the grammar according to the definition given in the previous section.

We first need some definitions. Let A be an algebra (i.e. a set with operations) and let I be the set of its elements. Set I is called the carrier of A. Here we consider for simplicity only one-sorted algebras, but the extension of our results to many-sorted algebras would be trivial. Let us then assume over I a partial order $\sqsubseteq$. Algebra A is called continuous iff the following properties are satisfed.

i) The carrier I of A is a complete partial order (cpo), namely every chain $x_0 \sqsubseteq x_1 \sqsubseteq x_2 \sqsubseteq \dots \quad x_i \in I$, $i = 0,1,2,\dots$ has a least upper bound $\bigsqcup_{i=0}^{\infty} x_i = \bar{x} \in I$; and a bottom element $\perp$ exists, namely $\forall x \in I$, $\perp \sqsubseteq x$;

ii) every (elementary) operation of A is a monotone, continuous function. Namely, if σ_A is an n-adic operation of A, then (monotonicity)
$x_k' \sqsubseteq x_k''$ implies $\sigma_A(x_1,\dots,x_k',\dots,x_n) \sqsubseteq \sigma_A(x_1,\dots,x_k'',\dots,x_n)$

and (continuity)
$$\bigsqcup_{i=0}^{\infty} \sigma_A(x_1,\dots,x_k^i,\dots,x_n) = \sigma_A(x_1,\dots,\bigsqcup_{i=0}^{\infty} x_k^i,\dots,x_n), \quad x_k^0 \sqsubseteq x_k^1 \sqsubseteq \dots$$

Given a continuous algebra A it is possible to obtain its derived operations by composing its elementary operations. It is easy to see that also derived operations are monotone, continuous functions. Let us now write a system of equations in A

$$(3.1) \qquad \left| \begin{array}{l} x_1 = \tau_1 \ (x_1,x_2,\dots,x_n) \\ x_2 = \tau_2 \ (x_1,x_2,\dots,x_n) \\ \dots \\ x_n = \tau_n \ (x_1,x_2,\dots,x_n) \end{array} \right.$$

Where x_i, $i=1,\dots,n$ are variables over I and τ_i are (derived) operations. If we define a partial order over tuples of I

$(x_1', \ldots, x_k', \ldots x_n') \sqsubseteq (x_1'', \ldots, x_k'', \ldots, x_n'')$ iff $x_k' \sqsubseteq x_k''$, $k=1,\ldots,n$

we can apply the fixpoint theorem. Namely, system (3.1) has a least solution $(\bar{x}_1, \ldots, \bar{x}_n)$ which is the least upper bound of the chain of n-tuples $(x_1^i,\ldots,x_n^i)^n$ $i = 0,1,\ldots$ obtained by starting with $x_k^0 = \perp$, $k=1,\ldots,n$ and by iteratively applying the operators in the right member of the equations:

$$x_k^{i+1} = \tau_k (x_1^i, \ldots, x_n^i), \qquad k=1,\ldots,n$$

Going back to regular tree grammars, let Σ be a ranked alphabet, and let us define a suitable algebra A as follows. The carrier I_L of A_L consists of all languages (i.e. sets) of finite trees over Σ, with the following restrictions :

i) Prefix property: if a language contains a tree t, then it must also contain all trees t' such that $t' \sqsubseteq t$;

ii) all languages must contain the empty tree $\perp = \{ \}$. In other words the empty language does not belong to I_i.

Algebra A_L has as many elementary operations as are the symbols in the ranked alphabet Σ, plus the union operation. The result of applying the operation σ_L $(\sigma \in \Sigma_m)$ to the m elements $L_1,L_2,\ldots,L_m \in I_L$ is defined as follows :

$$\sigma_L(L_1,L_2,\ldots,L_m) = \left\{ \sigma(x_1,x_2,\ldots,x_m) \mid x_i \in L_i,\ i=1,\ldots m \right\} \cup \{\perp\}$$

Notice that the resulting language satisfies restrictions i) and ii). Notice also that the union operation commutes with any operation σ_L, namely

$$\sigma_L(L_1,\ldots,L_k' \cup L_k'', \ldots,L_n) = \sigma_L(L_1,\ldots,L_k',\ldots L_m) \cup \sigma_L(L_1,\ldots,L_k'',\ldots L_m).$$

As a consequence, if we consider a composed expression for a derived operation T, we can always bring to the outermost level the union operations (if any). Thus algebra A_L has as many derived operations as are the finite unions of finite tres over Σ'. Every tree is interpreted as the composition of the elementary operations corresponding to its terminal symbols and the nonterminal symbols are interpreted as variables. For example the operation

$$a_1 \cup b_1 (\perp) \cup c_1(S,c_2 (S, b_1 (D)))$$

denotes a function $f_L : I_L^2 \to I_L$ defined as follows :

$$f_L(L_S,L_D)=\{a_1,\perp ,b_1 (\perp),c_1 (S_1,c_2(S_2,b_1(D))), c_1(S_1,c_2(S_2,\perp)), c_1(S_1,\perp) \mid S_1,S_2 \in L_S, D \in L_D \}.$$

Notice that if a variable appears more then once in the same tree, different elements of the corresponding language can be substituted to different occurrences of the variable (for the implications of the two possible ways of substituting, see [4]).

Algebra A_L can now be given an ordering relation: Simply set inclusion among languages of trees. Thus the language $\{\perp\}$ is the bottom element of the partial order (we will denote it simply as $\perp$, whenever no confusion is possible) and, since every chain has a least upper bound (just the set union of all trees in the chain) then the carrier I_L is a complete partial order. Furthermore it is easy to see that all elementary

operations are monotone, continuous functions.
Therefore algebra A_L is a continuous algebra. We can now interpret, a regular tree grammar as a system of equations as follows. The unknowns correspond to the nonterminals of the grammar. All productions with the same left member give rise to a single equation. Its left member is the language denoted by the common nonterminal and the derived operation in its right member corresponds to the union of the right members of the productions. Nonterminals which never occur as left members of productions are equated to the bottom $\perp$ of the partial order.

For instance the grammar (2.1) gives rise to the following system of equations:

$$\left|\begin{array}{l} S = a_1 \cup b_1(S) \cup c_1(S,B) \cup \perp \\ B = b_2(C) \cup c_2(\perp, b_1(D)) \cup c_2(\perp, \perp) \cup \perp \\ C = B \\ D = \perp \end{array}\right.$$

The language which is the minimal solution of the system of equations corresponding to a grammar G for the unknown corresponding to the initial symbol S, will be called $\bar{L}(G)$.

As an example we take grammar (2.2), which corresponds to the following system of equations:

$$(3.2)\quad \left|\begin{array}{l} S = a_1 \cup b_1(S) \cup c_1(S,B) \cup \perp \\ B = b_2(B) \cup c_2(E,F) \cup \perp \\ F = b_1(D) \cup \perp \\ D = E = \perp \end{array}\right.$$

We clearly have $\bar{D} = \bar{E} = \perp$ and $\bar{F} = \{b_1(\perp); \perp\}$, thus we apply the iterative algorithm only to the two first equations. We start with a pair of bottom elements,

$$\left|\begin{array}{l} S_0 = \perp \\ B_0 = \perp \end{array}\right.$$

and at the first and second iteration we get

$$\left|\begin{array}{l} S_1 = \{a_1;\ b_1(\perp);\ c_1(\perp,\perp); \perp\} \\ B_1 = \{b_2(\perp);\ c_2(\perp,\perp); \perp\} \end{array}\right.$$

$$\left|\begin{array}{l} S_2 = \{a_1; b_1(a_1); b_1(\perp); b_1(c_1(\perp,\perp)); b_1(\perp); c_1(a_1, b_2(\perp)); c_1(a_1, c_2(\perp,\perp)); \\ \quad c_1(a_1,\perp); c_1(b_1(\perp), b_2(\perp)); c_1(b_1(\perp), c_2(\perp,\perp)); c_1(b_1(\perp), \perp); \\ \quad c_1(c_1(\perp,\perp), b_2(\perp)); c_1(c_1(\perp,\perp), c_2(\perp,\perp)); c_1(c_1(\perp,\perp), \perp); \\ \quad c_1(\perp, b_2(\perp)); c_1(\perp, c_2(\perp,\perp)); c_1(\perp,\perp); \perp\} \\ B_2 = \{b_2(b_2(\perp)); b_2(c_2(\perp,\perp)); b_2(\perp); c_2(\perp, b_1(\perp)); c_2(\perp,\perp); \perp\} \end{array}\right.$$

Whe can now prove the following lemma and theorem.

<u>Lemma 3.1</u>. Let G be a regular tree grammar and let L_n^X be the set of all Σ trees which can be generated from the nonterminal X using

the productions of $\bar{G}$ in at most n immediate derivation steps, n=1,2,..; $X \in V$. Furthermore, let $\bar{L}_n^X$ be the language which can be obtained as value of X at the n-th step of the iterative algorithm when applied to the solution of the system of equations corresponding to G. We have

$$L_n^X = \bar{L}_n^X \qquad n=1,2,\ldots; \qquad X \in V$$

Proof. By induction. When n=1, both languages consist of all Σ trees which can be obtained from the right members of all productions having X as left member, by replacing all nonterminal symbols with $\perp$; and of all their approximations. Let us now assume $L_{n-1}^X = \bar{L}_n^X$. Then a derivation sequence will exist

$$\{(\lambda,X)\} = u_o \to u_1 \to \ldots \to u_n \equiv v \equiv t, \qquad 0 < m \leqq n$$

where u_i, i=0,1,...,n is a sequence of Σ trees such that every tree can be obtained by the preceding one by replacing all nonterminals using grammar productions. Namely, no approximation is performed during the derivation process, but only at the end of it. Here, v is obtained from u_n by replacing all nonterminals with $\perp$, and t is a further approximation of v. Since u_1 is obtained from $\{(\lambda,X)\}$ in one step, it must be the right member of some production, namely

$$u_1 = t_X\ (X_1, X_2, \ldots, X_k)$$

Since v is obtained from u_1 by successive replacements, it must be of the form

$$v = t_X\ (t_1, t_2, \ldots, t_k)$$

where t_j, j = 1,...,k are Σ trees. Looking at suitable subtrees of the trees in the sequence u_i, i=0,1,...,m it is thus possible to reconstruct derivation sequences of length at most n-1, 0<m$\leqq$n, from $\{\lambda, X_j\}$ to t_j, j = 1,...,k. Therefore we have

$$t_j \in L_{n-1}^{X_j} \qquad j = 1, \ldots, k$$

and, due to the induction hypothesis,

$$t_j \in \bar{L}_{n-1}^{X_j} \qquad j = 1, \ldots, k$$

On the other hand, from the defining equation for X we get

$$\bar{L}_n^X \supseteq t_X\ (\bar{L}_{n-1}^{X_1}, \ldots, \bar{L}_{n-1}^{X_k})$$

and thus

$$v = t_X\ (t_1, t_2, \ldots, t_k) \in \bar{L}_n^X$$

Finally since all elements of I_L have the prefix property, we have

$$t \in \bar{L}_n^X$$

and thus we have proved

$$L_n^X \subseteq \bar{L}_n^X$$

Simply reversing the above argument we can prove that $L_n^X \subseteq L_n^X$, and thus we have

$$L_n^X = \bar{L}_L^X$$ ∎

Theorem 3.1 (Equivalence of the operational and denotational semantics for a regular tree grammar G). We have

$$L(G) = \bar{L}(G)$$

Proof : This result follows directly from lemma 3.1 if we notice that

$$L(G) = \bigcup_{i=1}^{\infty} L_n^S$$

and

$$\bar{L}(G) = \bigcup_{i=1}^{\infty} \bar{L}_n^S$$

■

4. The functional equations of dynamic programming

In this section we introduce a new algebra A_R, which allows to write the so-called functional equations, namely the standard way of stating combinatorial problems in discrete deterministic dynamic programming [5].

Algebra A_R has one carrier, I_R , defined as the real numbers with the usual ordering plus a "bottom" element, $+\infty$, to obtain a complete partial order (when seen "upside down"). Also the elementary operations on A_R have the same name that on A_L, i.e. they are denoted by the symbols of the ranked alphabet Σ , plus the union operation . A function $\sigma_R : I_R^n \to I_R$, where $\sigma \in \Sigma_n$, must be a monotone, continuous from above function. Namely we must have

$$x_k' \geq x_k'' \quad \text{implies} \quad \sigma_R(x_1, \ldots, x_k', \ldots, x_n) \geq \sigma_R(x_1, \ldots, x_k'', \ldots x_n)$$

and

$$\lim_{x_k \to \bar{x}_k, x_k > \bar{x}_k} \sigma_R(x_1, \ldots, x_k, \ldots, x_n) = \sigma_R(x_1, \ldots, \bar{x}_k, \ldots, x_n)$$

These properties imply that function σ_R is a monotone, continuous function also in the complete partial order defined above.

The interpretation of the union operation is here the minimum operation, and we will thus write indifferently the simbols $\cup$ and min. We clearly have

$$x' \geq x'' \quad \text{implies} \quad \min(x', y) \geq \min(x'', y)$$

and

$$\lim_{x \to \bar{x}} \min(x, y) = \min(\bar{x}, y)$$

and thus also min is a monotone continuous function. Therefore we can conclude that also A_R is a continuous algebra.

Let us now consider a system of equations in the algebra A_R. Since the min operation commutes with all the operations (they are monotone) we assume, as we did for A_L, to have min operations only at the outermost level of the derived operators in the right members of equations. For example :

$$(4.1) \quad \left| \begin{array}{l} x = \min(a_1, b_1(x), c_1(x,y)) \\ y = \min(b_2(y), c_2(v,z)) \\ z = b_1(u) \\ u = v = +\infty \end{array} \right.$$

where

$a_1 = 5$

$b_1(x) = \frac{x}{2} + 2$

$b_2(x) = \text{if } x=1 \text{ then } 1 \text{ else } 2 - \frac{1}{x}$

$c_1(x,y) = \frac{x}{2} + y$

$c_2(x,y) = x + y$

Equations of this type are called functional equations in the dynamic programming context. It is well known [5] that they can be solved iteratively starting from an initial value of $+\infty$ for the variables. Of course in our framework this is a consequence of the fixpoint theorem, since, as we showed, algebra A_R is continuous. In our example we have $z=u=v=+\infty$, and for the remaining variables we get

$$\begin{cases} x = \min\left(5, \frac{x}{2} + z, \frac{x}{2} + y\right) \\ y = \text{if } y = 1 \text{ then } 1 \text{ else } 2 - \frac{1}{y} \end{cases}$$

$$\begin{cases} x_o = +\infty \\ y_o = +\infty \end{cases} \quad \begin{cases} x_1 = 5 \\ y_1 = 2 \end{cases}$$

$$\begin{cases} x_1 = 4,5 \\ y_2 = 1,5 \end{cases} \quad \cdots \quad \begin{cases} \bar{x} = 2 \\ \bar{y} = 1 \end{cases}$$

5. From regular tree grammars to functional equations

In this section we will show the connections between regular tree grammars and functional equations. We first need to introduce some concepts.

Let A and B be two continuous algebras, let I_A and I_B be their carriers (as we already pointed out, we consider one-carrier algebras for simplicity, but our result can be easily extended) and let A and B have the same signature (i.e. the same operation names). A function $h: I_A \to I_B$ defines a homomorphism from A to B iff for every zeradic function (i.e. for every constant) name a, we have

(5.1) $\quad h(a_A) = a_B$

and for every n-adic function name σ, $n=1,2,\ldots,m$, we have

(5.2) $\quad h(\sigma_A(x_1,x_2,\ldots,x_n)) = \sigma_B(h(x_1), h(x_2),\ldots,h(x_n))$.

A homomorphism is called strict if it maps bottom into bottom

(5.3) $\quad h(\bot_A) = \bot_B$

and it is called monotone if it preserves the partial orders of A and B

(5.4) $\quad x \sqsubseteq_A y \quad$ implies $\quad h(x) \sqsubseteq_B h(y)$.

A monotone homomorphism is called continuous iff it preserves the limits of chains

$$(5.5) \qquad h\left(\bigsqcup_{i=0}^{\infty}{}_A\, x_i\right) = \bigsqcup_{i=0}^{\infty}{}_B\, h(x_i) \quad , \qquad x_0 \sqsubseteq x_1 \sqsubseteq \ldots$$

We can now prove the following theorem, which is a generalization of a result by Goguen [1].

Theorem 5.1 . Let A and B be continuous algebras and let h be a strict, continuous homomorphism from A to B. Let

$$x_k = \tau_k^A (x_1, x_2, \ldots, x_n) \qquad k=1,\ldots,n$$

be a system of equations in algebra A and let $\bar{x}_k^A$ be its least solution ; let

$$x_k = \tau_K^B (x_1, x_2, \ldots, x_n) \qquad k=1,\ldots,n$$

be the corresponding system of equations in algebra B, obtained by replacing in the right members of equations the operations of A with operations of B with the same name and let $\bar{x}_k^B$ be its least solution. We have

$$h(\bar{x}_k^A) = \bar{x}_k^B \quad , \qquad k=1, \ldots, n .$$

Proof. Let $((x_1^{A,0}, \ldots x_n^{A,0}), (x_1^{A,1}, \ldots, x_n^{A,1}), \ldots)$ and $((x_1^{B,0}, \ldots, x_n^{B,0}), (x_1^{B,1}, \ldots x_n^{B,1}), \ldots)$ be the approximating chains for $\bar{x}_k^A$ and $\bar{x}_k^B$ obtained in A and B by applying the fixpoint theorem. We will prove that

$$h(x_k^{A,i}) = x_k^{B,i} \qquad k = 1, \ldots, n ; \qquad i = 0,1,\ldots$$

Infact we have

$$h(x_k^{A,0}) = h(\perp_A) = \perp_B = x_k^{B,0} \qquad k = 1, \ldots, n$$

since h is strict and if we assume

$$h(x_k^{A,i}) = x_K^{B,i} \qquad k=1,\ldots,n$$

we have also

$$h(x_k^{A,i+1}) = h(\tau_k^A(x_1^{A,i}, \ldots, x_n^{A,i})) = \tau_k^B(h(x_1^{A,i}), \ldots, h(x_n^{A,i})) =$$

$$= \tau_k^B (x_1^{B,i}, \ldots, x_n^{B,i}) = x_k^{B,i+1} \quad , \qquad k=1,\ldots,n.$$

Finally, since h is continuous, it preserves also the limits of the approximating chains, namely

$$h(\bar{x}_k^A) = h\left(\bigsqcup_{i=0}^{\infty}{}_A\, x_k^{A,i}\right) = \bigsqcup_{i=0}^{\infty}{}_B\, h(x_k^{A,i})$$

$$= \bigsqcup_{i=0}^{\infty}{}_B\, x_k^{B,i} = \bar{x}_k^B \quad , \qquad k=1, \ldots, n$$

■

Let us now apply theorem 5.1 to algebras A_L and A_R introduced in sections 3 and 4. We propose the following function h . Given a language L of Σ trees belonging to I_L

i) for every tree in L, interpret every symbol σ on the nodes as the operation σ_R and evaluate the tree. The empty tree evaluates to $+\infty$. Let us call g this function, which given a L returns a set of values belonging to I_R;

ii) take the greatest lower bound of all values obtained in i). Thus $h(L)=glb(g(L))$.

Notice that for the operation symbols belonging to Σ, A_L acts as the initial algebra and h as the evaluation homomorphism [1]. Thus for such operations conditions (5.1) and (5.2) are clearly satisfied. For the union-min operation (5.2) is also valid :

$$h(L_1 \cup L_2) = glb(g(L_1 \cup L_2)) = glb\ (g(L_1) \cup g(L_2)) =$$
$$= \min\ (glb(g(L_1)),\ glb(g(L_2))) = \min\ (h(L_1), h(L_2))$$

Thus h is a homomorphism. Furthermore, (5.3) is satisfied, since

$$h(\perp_L) = glb(g(\perp_L)) = glb\ (\{+\infty\}) = +\infty = \perp_R$$

Therefore h is strict. Moreover (5.4) is satisfied since

$$L_1 \sqsubseteq_A L_2 \text{ implies } L_1 \subseteq L_2 \text{ implies } g(L_1) \subseteq g(L_2) \text{ implies}$$
$$glb(g(L_1)) \geq glb\ (g(L_2)) \text{ implies } h(L_1) \sqsubseteq h(L_2)$$

Thus h is monotone. Finally (5.5) is satisfied, since

$$h(\bigsqcup_{i=0}^{\infty}{}_A L_i) = glb\ (g \bigcup_{i=0}^{\infty} Li) = glb\ (\bigcup_{i=0}^{\infty} g(Li) =$$
$$= glb_{i=0}^{\infty}\ (glb(g(L_i))) = \bigsqcup_{i=0}^{\infty}{}_B\ h(Li), \quad L_o \sqsubseteq L_1 \sqsubseteq \ldots$$

Therefore h defines a strict, continuous homomorphism and theorem (5.1) can be applied.

A system of operations in algebra A_L correspond to a regular tree grammar, and its solution for the initial symbol S, by Theorem 3.1, is exactly the language generated by the grammar. Applying function h to such a language means to evaluate the "cost" of every tree and to take the cost of the "cheapest" tree (or the glb of the costs of all trees, if no cheapest tree exists). Alternatively, the same value can be obtained by first applying function h to the grammar, thus getting a system of functional equations, and then solving the system for the unknown corresponding to the initial symbol S. In short, if we see homomorphism h as an interpretation, we can state our main result as the commutativity of the following diagram

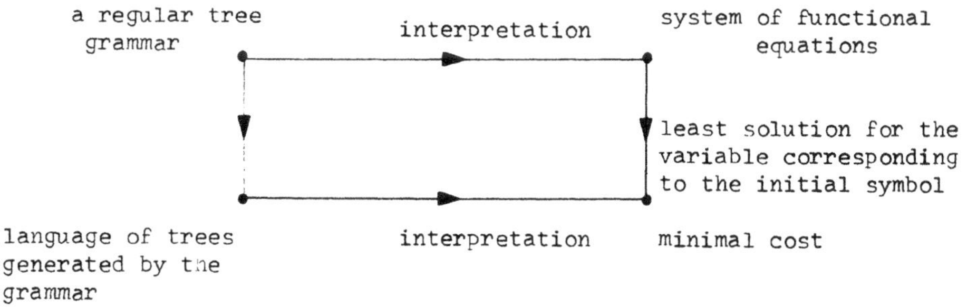

As an example, we see that the system of functional equations (4.1) can be obtained by interpreting the grammar (3.2). Since the diagram commutes not only for the fixpoint, but also for all elements in the chains, we can check that in the iterative solutions of (3.2) and (4.1) we have

$$h(S_1) = glb(g(S_1)) = glb(5, \infty) = 5 = x_1$$
$$h(B_1) = glb(g(B_1)) = glb(2, \infty) = 2 = y_1$$

$$h(S_2) = glb(5, 4.5, \infty) = 4.5 = x_2$$
$$h(B_2) = glb(1.5, 2, \infty) = 1.5 = y_2$$

The minimal cost $\bar{x} = 2$ is here achieved by the following infinite tree

$$c_1(c_1(c_1(\ldots), b_2(b_2(\ldots))), b_2(b_2(\ldots)))$$

6. Conclusions

The commutativity result stated in section 5 was already mentioned in the literature, to our knowledge only for special cases. In [6] Karp and Held proved the result for string grammars (i.e. in the monadic case where $\Sigma_2 = \Sigma_3 = \ldots = \emptyset$) under the restriction that a cheapest finite string exists. In [7] Martelli and Montanari eliminate this restriction, but require that all functions be infinite-preserving (namely $\sigma(+\infty) = +\infty$; notice that $b_2(x)$ in our example is not infinite preserving). In [8] they extend the result to tree grammars, still in the infinite-preserving case. The general case is achieved in this paper by a suitable definition of tree grammar, which guarantees the prefix property and the non-emptyness of the generated language.

There are interesting practical applications in conjunction with theorem 2.1. In fact, the trees generated by a grammar are there shown to correspond to generalized paths in an AND-OR graph and thus our result states the equivalence of solving a system of functional equations and of searching for the cheapest generalized path in an (interpreted) AND-OR graph. Thus efficient graph-searching techniques like the Djkstra-Knuth algorithm [9] or the heuristically guided search algorithms [10] can be directly applied to combinatorial problems stated in the dynamic programming framework In [3] we have an example of an important practical problem, optimal decision table conversion, which has been solved more efficiently using heuristically guided search than using standard dynamic programming techniques.

References

[1] Goguen, J.A., Thatcher, J.W., Wagner, E.G. and Wright, J.B., Initial Algebra Semantics and Continuous Algebras, J.Assoc.Comput.Mach.24, 1977, 68-95.

[2] Arnold, A. and Nivat, M., Non Deterministic Recursive Program Schemes, Fundamentals of Computation Theory 1977, Lecture notes in Computer Science n°56, Springer Verlag (1977), 12-21.

[3] Martelli, A. and Montanari, U., Optimizing Decision Trees Through Heuristically Guided Search, Technical Report S-77-33, Computer Science Dept., Univ.of Pisa ; also Comm.of the ACM, in press.

[4] Engelfriet, J. and Schmidt, E.M., IO and OI, Daimi Report PB 47, University of Aarhus, Danmark (1975).

[5] Bellman, R.E., Dynamic Programming, Princeton University Press,

Princeton, N.J. 1957.

[6] Karp, R.M. and Held, M., Finite State Processes and Dynamic Programming, SIAM J.Appl. Math., 15, 1957.

[7] Martelli, A. and Montanari, U., On the Foundation of Dynamic Programming, Topics in Combinational Optimization (S.Rinaldi ed.), Springer Verlag, 1975, 145-163.

[8] Martelli, A. and Montanari, U., Programmazione Dinamica e Punto Fisso, Atti del Convegno di Informatica Teorica, Mantova, November 1974.

[9] Knuth, D.E. , A Generalization of Dijkstra's Algorithm, Information Processing Letters, February 1977, 1-4.

[10] Martelli, A. and Montanari, U., From Dynamic Programming to Search Algorithms with Functional Costs, Proc.Fourth Int.Joint Conf.on Artificial Intelligence, Tbilisi, September 1975, 345-350.

CONSTRUCTING SPECIFICATIONS OF ABSTRACT DATA TYPES BY REPLACEMENTS

H.-D. Ehrich / V.G. Lohberger

Abteilung Informatik, Universität Dortmund
Postfach 5oo5oo, 46oo Dortmund 5o, West Germany

Abstract - Categories of specifications, equational specifications, and partially labelled partial specifications of abstract data types are shown to have pushouts. These results allow us to carry over the machinery of graph replacement to specifications. We give some examples. Parametrization is considered as an important special case of replacement.

1. Introduction

In the development of programs and program systems, the initial specification phase is of increasing importance. It is essential to have a clean, unique, complete, and implementation independent description of what the system is intended to do in order to cope with many problems of reliability. Such a specification is not only necessary as a documentation and communication basis for the programmer team. Also, logical errors can be detected and debugged in an early state, seperate from implementation errors occuring later in the implementation process. Moreover, implementations or implementation steps can be matched against the requirements of the specification, thus controlling the correctness of the program development. The role of specification and the related concept of modularity has been studied by Parnas [19] , Liskov and Zilles [16] and others.

There is a great need for formal methods to support these tasks. Program modules have been modelled by abstract data types [16, 13] , i.e. by sets of operations on various domains interrelated in a certain way. Mathematically speaking, abstract data types are abstract algebraic structures. To specify the desired properties of a program module means to specify a class of abstract data types, and this means to give a presentation of a class of algebraic structures.

There are well approved methods in algebra and logic to give presentations and investigate the structure of their models. Equational presentations and corresponding classes of algebras are especially well understood [1, 2, 4, 5, 6, 9, 11, 12, 18] . Specifications consist of a set of sorts, a set of operation symbols with information about their domains and codomains, a set of predicates with information about their domains, and a collection of conditions or axioms.

We give some introductory examples that may serve to illustrate the basic ideas. In our examples, we use a somewhat ad hoc notation which can be viewed to be an informal algebraic specification language.

Example 1.1: The natural numbers with their ordering relation can be specified as follows.

Sorts: nat
Ops: $0: \longrightarrow nat$
succ: $nat \longrightarrow nat$

Preds: $\leq : nat \times nat$
Conds: $x \leq succ(x)$
$x \leq x$
$x \leq y \wedge y \leq z \Rightarrow x \leq z$
$x \leq y \wedge y \leq x \Rightarrow x = y$
$x \leq y \vee y \leq x$

Example 1.2: The interval 1 to 10 of natural numbers will be used in the next example.

Sorts: [1:10]

Ops: 1, 2, 3, 4, 5, 6, 7, 8, 9, 10: $\rightarrow$ [1:10]

suc : [1:10] $\longrightarrow$ [1:10]

Preds: $\lesssim$: [1:10] $\times$ [1:10]

Conds: $1 \lesssim 2,\ 2 \lesssim 3,\ \ldots,\ 9 \lesssim 10,$ $\quad x \lesssim y \wedge y \lesssim x \Longrightarrow x = y$

$x \lesssim x$ $\quad x \lesssim y \vee y \lesssim x$

$x \lesssim y \wedge y \lesssim z \Longrightarrow x \lesssim z$ $\quad$ suc (1)=2, ..., suc(9) = 10

Example 1.3: We give a specification of an array with the components consisting of the sorts, ops, preds, and conds of the previous examples plus the following:

Sorts: array

Ops: new: $\longrightarrow$ array

. [.] :=. : array $\times$ [1:10] $\times$ nat $\longrightarrow$ array

. [.] : array $\times$ [1:10] $\longrightarrow$ nat

Conds: new [i] = 0/(a [i] := n) [j] = if i eq j then n else a [j] fi

Intuitively speaking, a [i] := n assigns value n to the i-th component of array a, while a[i] denotes the value stored in that component.

Example 1.4.: We extend the previous example by an operation sorting a given array. The following operations and conditions are added to those of the previous example.

Ops: sort: array $\longrightarrow$ array

Conds: $i \lesssim j \Rightarrow$ sort(a) [i] $\leq$ sort(a) [j]

$(\exists P)$ [$(\forall i)$ a[P(i)] = sort(a) [i]

$\wedge$ (P(i) = P(j) $\Rightarrow$ i = j) $\wedge$ $(\forall i)$ $(\exists j)$ P(j) = i]

The first condition expresses what it means for an array to be sorted, and the second condition expresses that the contents of the array may not be changed but only permuted. If we would like to restrict ourselves to equational specifications where the conditions are just sets of equations, we could do so by viewing predicates π : x as operations π : x $\longrightarrow$ bool, where bool has two constants, true and false, equipped with appropriate boolean operations. The first three examples are easily rewritten in equational form, but there seems to be no way to express the idea of sorting by equations as conveniently as example 1.4 does.

One possivility is to use an auxiliary operation

sort1 : array $\times$ [1:10] $\longrightarrow$ array

and express the algorithm of bubble sort by the following equations:

sort(a) = sort1(a,1)

sort1(a,i) = if i =10 then a else

if a [i] $\leq$ a[suc(i)] then sort1(a,suc(i)) else sort1(a',1) fi fi

where a' = (a[suc(i)] := a[i]) [i] := a[suc(i)].

We feel that example 1.4 gives a more adequate and easier to understand description of what sorting means.

Although the expressive power of equational specification is principally sufficient for all practical cases [2, 17], convenience requires more comfortable specification language. In the present paper, we therefore use second-order predicate calculus.

With increasing complexitiy of program systems, the design process of specifications must be given more and more attention. A structured and modular approach to specification design requires means to manipulate pieces of specifications, put them together, and consistently replace parts of them. For example, it is very convenient to give specifications with formal parts, socalled parametric specifications, where the formal parts can be replaced by different actual specifications [6, 7]. Other types of replacement operations occur when specifications are to be modified, e.g. to remove errors or to adapt the system to changed user needs [7].

In the field of graph grammars, methods and tools for handling replacement operations on graphs have been successfully developed and applied to various situations. The purpose of this paper is to demonstrate that these ideas can be carried over to tackle some problems of specification design.

In the categorical approach to graph grammars, the mechanisms of graph rewriting have been formalized by means of pushouts in the category graph of graphs [10, 20, 21]. It has been realized that these mechanisms can be applied to any structures forming a category with pushouts [8]. Therefore, we investigate the existence of pushouts in various related categories of specifications. The usefulness of rewritings on these specifications is demonstrated by examples. The techniques and results carry over to partially labelled partial specifications, which suit better to applications. Here, we refer to [21].

In a certain sense, specifications can be viewed as graphs enriched by conditions Conversely, if we forget about the conditions, we get the socalled syntax graph of a specification. Thus, there are forgetful functors from specification categories to corresponding graph categories. It is shown that these functors respect pushouts. Therefore, specification rewritings effect corresponding graph rewritings on the syntax graphs.

Parametric specifications can be considered as special cases of rewriting rules, giving the rules how the formal parameter is substituted by the actual parameter. We illustrate by an example how parametric specifications and corresponding specification productions can be used in the editing process of specifications.

2. Categories of specifications and their graphs

Let S be a set of sorts. S^* and S^+ denote the sets of words resp. nonempty words over S. Elements $x \in S^*$ will be called sorts, too. A signature over S is a mapping $\Omega : \bar{\Omega} \to S$. Mappings into a sort set S are called S-sorted sets or simply sorted sets, if the sort set is clear from the context. Thus, a signature Ω is an S^+-sorted set, and its elements are called operations. If $\omega \mapsto xs$ is in Ω, $x \in S^*$, $s \in S$, we call x the domain sort and s the codomain sort of $\omega \mapsto xs$ (or just of ω). A codomain sort always has word length 1. Ω determines two mappings: ${}^\circ\Omega : \omega \mapsto x$ and $\Omega^c : \omega \mapsto s$ for each $\omega \longmapsto xs$ in Ω, the domain resp. codomain mappings.

We assume that the reader is familiar with the category graph of graphs [10, 20, 21]. A signature Ω will sometimes be considered to be that graph with nodes S^*, edges $\bar{\Omega}$, source function ${}^\circ\Omega$, and target function Ω°. Signature morphisms $f : \Omega_1 \to \Omega_2$ are those graph morphismus $f = (h,g)$ $h : S_1^* \longrightarrow S_2^*$, $g : \bar{\Omega}_1 \to \bar{\Omega}_2$, where h is a length preserving string homomorphism. Thus, h is completely determined by its restriction to S_1 and S_2, also denoted by $h : S_1 \longrightarrow S_2$.
If $\Omega_i : \bar{\Omega}_i \longrightarrow S_i^+$, $i = 1,2$, the morphism condition is equivalent to $\Omega_1 h = g\Omega_2$ (we write function composition and application from left to right, e.g. xf and xfg instead of the more conventional f(x) and gf(x).) Let sign be the subcategory of graph consisting of all signatures and its morphisms. The following result carries over form graph.

Theorem 2.1: sign has pushouts.

Proof: We do not give the complete proof since it parallels that in the graph case [10, 20, 21]. For later reference, we give the pushout construction in sign.

Let $f_1: \Omega_1 \longrightarrow \Omega_2$, $f_2: \Omega_1 \longrightarrow \Omega_3$ be morphisms in sign. We construct Ω_4, $f_3: \Omega_2 \rightarrow \Omega_4$, $f_4: \Omega_3 \rightarrow \Omega_4$ such that fig.1(1) is a pushout: let $\Omega_i: \bar{\Omega}_i \rightarrow S_i^+$ and $f_i = (h_i, g_i)$ for

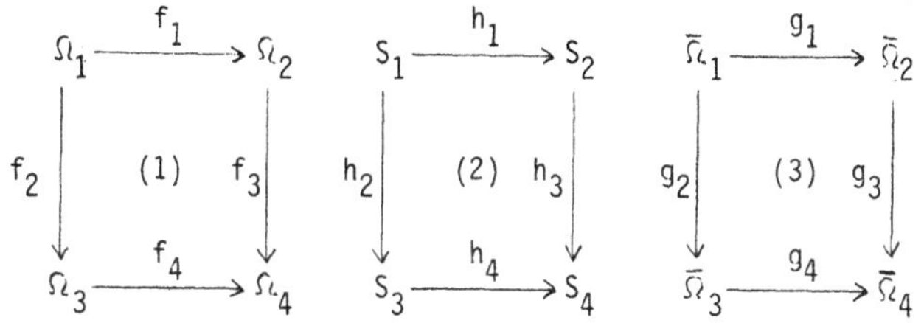

figure 1

$i=1, 2, 3, 4$, and let h_3, h_4 and g_3, g_4 be given such that the diagrams in fig.1(2) and (3) are pushouts in the category set of sets. Due to the definition of morphisms in sign, the diagram in fig.2 is commutative. The upper quadrangle coincides with fig1(3), i.e. it is a pushout. Thus, there is a unique mapping $\Omega_4: \bar{\Omega}_4 \rightarrow S_4^+$ making the whole diagram in fig.2 commutative. ///

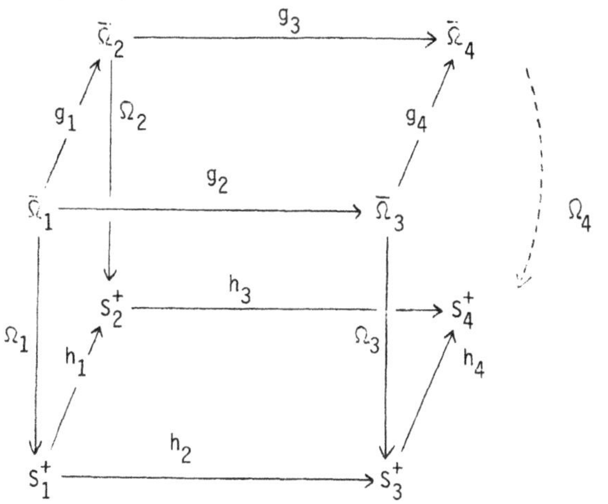

figure 2

Now we continue to develop our specification language. Given a sort set S, let $\Pi: \bar{\Pi} \rightarrow S^*$ be an S^*-sorted set of predicates. If $\pi \mapsto x$ is in Π, x is called the domain of the predicate. We suppose that an S-sorted set $V_i: \bar{V}_i \rightarrow S$ of individual variables is given, together with an S^*-sorted set $V_\pi : \bar{V}_\pi \longrightarrow S^*$ of predicate variables and an S^+-sorted set $V_\omega : \bar{V}_\omega \longrightarrow S^+$ of operation variables. Let $V = V_i \cup V_\pi \cup V_\omega$.

Let a sort set S, a signature Ω, predicates Π and variables V_i, V_π , V_ω over S be given, and let all these sets be disjoint. Terms and formulae are now constructed as usual in sorted second-order predicate calculus with equality [14]. We shortly introduce our notation.

The S^*-sorted set T of terms (including term n-tuples) is given as follows:

Definition 2.2: $v \mapsto s \in V_i \succ \langle v \rangle \mapsto s \in T$

$\langle \tau_1 \rangle \mapsto x,\ \langle \tau_2 \rangle \mapsto y \in T \succ \langle \tau_1, \tau_2 \rangle \mapsto xy \in T$

$\omega \mapsto xs \in \Omega,\ \langle \tau \rangle \mapsto x \in T \succ \langle [\langle \tau \rangle \mapsto x]\omega \rangle \mapsto s \in T$

$F \mapsto xs \in V_\omega,\ \langle \tau \rangle \mapsto x \in T \succ \langle [\langle \tau \rangle \mapsto x] F \rangle \mapsto s \in T$

$\varphi \in \Lambda, \langle \tau_1 \rangle \mapsto x,\ \langle \tau_2 \rangle \mapsto x \in T \succ$

$\langle \text{if } \varphi \text{ then } \langle \tau_1 \rangle \mapsto x \text{ else } \langle \tau_2 \rangle \mapsto x \text{ fi} \rangle \mapsto x \in T$

Here, Λ is the set of formulae defined as follows:

Definition 2.3: true, false $\in \Lambda$

$\langle \tau_1 \rangle \mapsto x,\ \langle \tau_2 \rangle \mapsto x \in T \succ \tau_1 = \tau_2 \in \Lambda$

$p \mapsto x \in \Pi, \langle \tau \rangle \mapsto x \in T \succ p(\tau) \in \Lambda$

$P \mapsto x \in V_\pi, \langle \tau \rangle \mapsto x \in T \succ P(\tau) \in \Lambda$

$\varphi_1, \varphi_2, \varphi_3 \in \Lambda \succ$ IF φ_1 THEN φ_2 ELSE φ_3 FI $\in \Lambda$

$\varphi \in \Lambda,\ (v \mapsto x) \in V \succ ((\forall v)\varphi) \in \Lambda$

As usual we will use some deviations from the strong syntactical rules of notation in order to increase readability. Especially, we will omit the sort part $\mapsto x$ whenever it is clear from the context. Furthermore, we will use the notational abbreviations $\neg\varphi$, $\varphi_1 \vee \varphi_2$, $\varphi_1 \wedge \varphi_2$, $\varphi_1 \Rightarrow \varphi_2$, etc. for the conventional boolean operations that are easily expressible by IF-THEN-ELSE-FI. Another conventional notation is $((\exists v)\varphi)$ for $\neg((\forall v)\neg\varphi)$.

The set Λ of formulae is called the (object) language of S, Ω, Π. We write $\Lambda(S, \Omega, \Pi)$ in order to express the underlying items explicitely. The variable sets are assumed to be fixed in the sequel. If we take only the first two lines of definition 2.3, we get a subset of Λ, called the equational language of S, Ω and denoted by H(S, Ω). We will not explain the semantics of these languages in detail but adopt the usual conventions (see, e.g.[14] or any text book on logic).

Now we have the tools to give a precise definition of specification.

Definition 2.4: A specification is a quadruple $D = \langle S, \Omega, \Pi, C \rangle$ where S is a set of sorts, Ω is a signature over S, Π is an S^*-sorted set of predicates, and $C \subset \Lambda(S, \Omega, \Pi)$ is a set of conditions. The specification is called equational iff $C \subset H(S, \Omega)$.

In equational specifications, Π is empty. Therefore we write $D = \langle S, \Omega, C \rangle$ if we have an equational specification. The signature Ω - viewed as a graph - is called the graph of the specification.

Definition 2.5: A model (or interpretation) of D is given by

(1) an S^*-sorted set A: $\bar{A} \to S^*$ with the properties

(1.1) $xA^{-1} \neq \emptyset$

(1.2) $(xy)A^{-1} = xA^{-1} \times yA^{-1}$

} for all $x, y \in S^*$

(2) an assignment of a function $\bar{\omega}: xA^{-1} \to sA^{-1}$ to each operation $\omega \mapsto xs \in \Omega$

(3) an assignment of a relation $\bar{\pi} \subset xA^{-1}$ to each predicate $\pi \mapsto x \in \Pi$. Equality must be interpreted by a congruence relation on A.

(4) C is satisfied (i.e. each formula in C evaluates to true when assigning

arbitrary values of appropriate sorts to the free variables).

Definition 2.6: Let $D=\langle S,\Omega,\Pi,C\rangle$ be a specification, and let $B_1, B_2 \subset \Lambda := \Lambda(S,\Omega,\Pi)$.

$B_1 \models_\Lambda B_2$ means that B_2 is a logical consequence of B_1, i.e. B_2 is satisfied in each model of $\langle \Lambda, B_1\rangle$. We shortly write $D \models B$ instead of $C \models_\Lambda B$.

Specifications can be related by specification morphisms in a natural way. Let $D_i=\langle S_i, \Omega_i, \Pi_i, C_i\rangle$, i=1, 2, be specifications, $f'=(h, g_\omega): \Omega_1 \rightarrow \Omega_2$ be a signature morphism, and $g_\pi : \overline{\Pi}_1 \rightarrow \overline{\Pi}_2$ be a mapping such that $\Pi_1 h = g_\pi \Pi_2$. The triple $f=(h,g_\omega,g_\pi)$ can then be extended to a mapping

$$\hat{f}: \Lambda_1 \rightarrow \Lambda_2 ,$$

where $\Lambda_i=\Lambda(S_i,\Omega_i,\Pi_i)$, i=1, 2, by replacing each occurrence of a sort x by xh, of an operation symbol ω by ωg_ω, and of a predicate symbol π by πg_π. (Without restricting generality, we assume that there are variables $(v \mapsto xh)$ for each variable $(v \mapsto x)$.)

Definition 2.7: A specification morphism $f:D_1 \rightarrow D_2$ is a triple $f=(h,g_\omega,g_\pi)$ with the properties

(1) $f'=(h,g_\omega)$ is a signature morphism, $f': \Omega_1 \rightarrow \Omega_2$

(2) $g_\pi : \overline{\Pi}_1 \rightarrow \overline{\Pi}_2$ satisfies $g_\pi \Pi_2 = \Pi_1 h$

(3) for each formula $B \in \Lambda_1$, if $D_1 \models B$, then $D_2 \models B\hat{f}$.

Composition of specification morphisms is defined by composition of the constituent mappings, separately for each component. It is easily checked that the criteria of a category are satisfied.

Definition 2.8: The category of specifications is denoted by spec. By $\text{spec}^=$ we denote the full subcategory of equational specifications.

We are now ready to prove our main result: spec and $\text{spec}^=$ inherit the existence of pushouts from their signatures sign. Let Γ, $\Gamma^=$ be the forgetful functors Γ:spec $\rightarrow$ sign resp. $\Gamma^=$: $\text{spec}^= \rightarrow$ sign sending each specification to its signature (considered as a graph).

Theorem 2.9: spec and $\text{spec}^=$ have pushouts. Γ and $\Gamma^=$ respect pushouts.

Proof: Let $f_1:D_1 \rightarrow D_2$ and $f_2:D_1 \rightarrow D_3$ be specification morphisms in spec. We construct D_4, $f_3:D_2 \rightarrow D_4$ and $f_4:D_3 \rightarrow D_4$ as follows (cf. figures 1 and 2).

Let $f_i=(h_i,g_i^\omega, g_i^\pi)$, $f_i' =(h_i,g_i^\omega)$, $D_i=\langle S_i, \Omega_i, \Pi_i, C_i\rangle$, i=1, 2, 3, 4.
We define Ω_4, f_3', f_4' to be the pushout of f_1' and f_2' in sign (cf. theorem 2.1) and Π_4', g_3^π, g_4^π to be the pushout of g_1^π, g_2^π in set. $\Pi_4: \Pi_4' \rightarrow S_4^*$ is then obtained in the same unique way as Ω_4 in the proof of theorem 2.1 (cf. fig.2). Conditions C_4 are defined as follows: $C_4=\{B\hat{f}_3 \mid D_2 \models B\} \cup \{B\hat{f}_4 \mid D_3 \models B\}$ (or any set of formulae that is logically equivalent).

We claim that D_4, f_3, f_4 constructed this way form a pushout of f_1, f_2 in spec. In order to prove this, let D_5, $f_5:D_2 \rightarrow D_5$, $f_6:D_3 \rightarrow D_5$ be such that $f_1f_5=f_2f_6$. It follows that $f_1'f_5'=f_2'f_6'$ and $g_1^\pi g_5^\pi=g_2^\pi g_6^\pi$, and thus there is exactly one $f_7': \Omega_4 \rightarrow \Omega_5$

and exactly one $g_7^{\pi}: \bar{\Pi}_4 \longrightarrow \bar{\Pi}_7$ such that $f_3'f_7'=f_5'$, $f_4'f_7'=f_6'$ resp. $g_3^{\pi}g_7^{\pi}=g_5^{\pi}$, $g_4^{\pi}g_7^{\pi}=g_6^{\pi}$. Therefore there is at most one morphism $f_7:D_4 \longrightarrow D_5$ in spec satisfying $f_3f_7=f_5$ and $f_4f_7=f_6$, namely $f_7=(f_7',g_7^{\pi})$. That f_7 is in fact a morphism in spec follows from the definition of C_4: if $D_4 \models B$, we have $B=B'\hat{f}_3$ and $D_2 \models B'$ or $B=B'\hat{f}_4$ and $D_3 \models B'$. In the first case, we have $D_5 \models B'\hat{f}_5$ since f_5 is a morphism. Obviously, $B'\hat{f}_5=B'(\hat{f}_3\hat{f}_7)=(B'\hat{f}_3)\hat{f}_7=B\hat{f}_7$. The second case is proven in the same way.

Pushouts in $spec^=$ are constructed in the same way. That Γ and $\Gamma^=$ respect pushouts is clear from the definition. ///

If we consider other languages of logic, e.g. first-order predicate calculus, propositional calculus etc., similar results hold and can be proven in the same way. The main drawback of the above construction is the rather clumsy set of conditions C_4. It can be shown, however, that simplifications are possible: condition (3) of definition 2.7 can be replaced by $D_2 \models C_1\hat{f}$, and C_4 can then be defined in the above proof to be simply $C_4=C_2\hat{f}_3 \cup C_3\hat{f}_4$. The verification of these propositions requires a little bit heavier machinery, and we cannot give the details here.

3. Labelled and partial specifications

To use specifications and specification productions in practical situations, as [3] do with graphs, it is desirable to generalize the tools developed so far, to include labels and partiality.

The symbols that we used for sorts and operations in specifications, until now, are only a notational means to identify the different items in the specifications. We see that the morphisms do not care about these notations. On the other hand we feel that these names, although sometimes called "syntactical sugar", play an essential part as a guide through large specifications, and we should provide for taking these names to be part of the structure and to be respected by morphisms. In conjunction with partiality, we can have the possibility to alter these names, but these alterations must be made explicit and are formally contained in the calculus and not mere arbitrary notation, as we shall learn from the examples. For these purposes we need a globally defined set of labels.

[21] give a motivation for the use of partial graphs which we accept also for specifications: if we want to describe syntactic operations by these formalisms, operations that replace only parts of graphs, it would in general not be a natural thing to add unnecessary information, e.g. context to make the occurring partial graphs or specifications total, and to increase at the same time the number of replacement rules, since there are many possibilities to make these graphs or specifications total. Instead, we should be able to express handling of partial specifications directly.

To give an example, let us think of the specification of our array with natural numbers as entries and a finite subset of natural numbers as keys. Imagine that the above array of nat specification is supplied with labels "array", "nat", "new", etc., such that we have a labelled specification with explicit labels. Now, we want to alter the specification by deleting nat and inserting int for nat. The names (labels) of all items not directly affected by this substitution shall be maintained. This can be expressed by the production of figure 3. It is obvious how 'p and p' shall map ('p: key$\mapsto$nat, s$\mapsto$succ, etc.; p' analogously). The labelling is expressed by the symbol $\underline{l}$.

Here, the gluing specification has no labels. That is why there are no labels to be respected by the morphisms 'p and p' and so the production can alter the labels as required. It is obvious how the specification of example 1.3 has to be supplemented by labels. On the other hand, the application of the production must care for saving the labels of the old specification which are not affected.

We need not emphasize the fact that there are possibilities to handle labelling implicitely when writing down a specification, thus simplifying the work of writing specifications in a practical situation. Here, the explicit handling suits to the formal treatment.

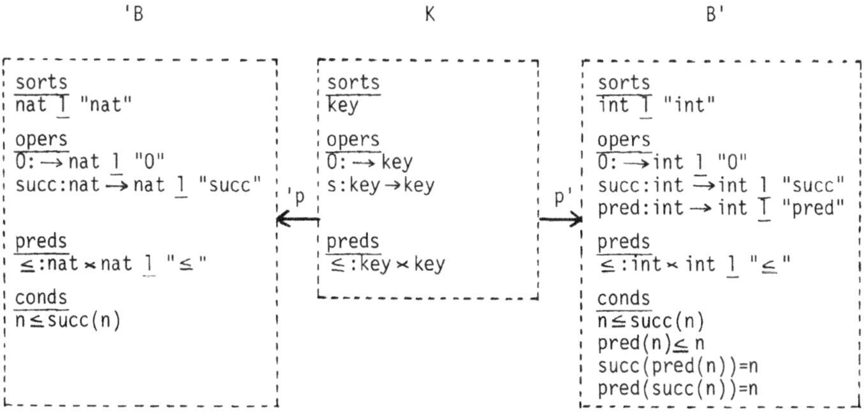

Figure 3: production to substitute nat by int

Guided by the definitions of total specifications in section 2, by our intuition (example), and definitions of partially labelled partial graphs [21], we give the following precise formulation:

Definition 3.1: The category spec-, called the category of partially (L_S, L_Ω, L_Π) -labelled specifications, has objects $D=\langle S, \Omega, \Pi, C, \lambda\rangle$, where S, Ω, Π, C are items as in the definition of spec, except of the requirement that $^\circ\Omega$, Ω°, need only be partial pappings, but those operations and predicates occurring in C must be total; and $\lambda=(\lambda_S, \lambda_\Omega, \lambda_\Pi)$ is a triple of three partial mappings $\lambda_S: S^* \to L_S$, $\lambda_\Omega: \Omega \to L_\Omega$, $\lambda_\Pi: \Pi \to L_\Pi$, and this category has morphisms $f:D_1 \to D_2$, $f=(h, g_\omega, g_\pi)$ which obey the same laws as in spec but additionally the labelling of sorts, operations, and predicates is transported by morphisms if it is defined.

In [21], the respective morphisms for graphs are called "weak morphisms".

Theorem 3.2: spec- has pushouts.

proof: The argument is as with spec, although we must be careful with some of the arrows because of the partiality of the involved mappings. ///

In analogy to the discussion of the last section, the same result holds for the subcategories of spec- determined by a special calculus, as e.g. equational calculus or first order predicate calculus. A pushout diagram in such a specification category implies a pushout diagram in the underlying graph-category, i.e. we have a forgetful functor from the specification catagory to the graph category respecting pushouts.

We hint further that it is useful for practical situations to be sure that applying a production to a total specification yields a total specification, even if this production consists of partial specifications. [21] give sufficient criteria for this problem in the graph case, which carry over to the spec case.

We give an example in figure 4 to demonstrate that it is conveniently possible to use productions for relabelling of operations. Here, the partiality of operations provides the economy of specifying not more than required. This production can be applied to any specification where we find an analysis pushout. Obviously, all other labels of the analysed specification are saved via the pushout-complement.

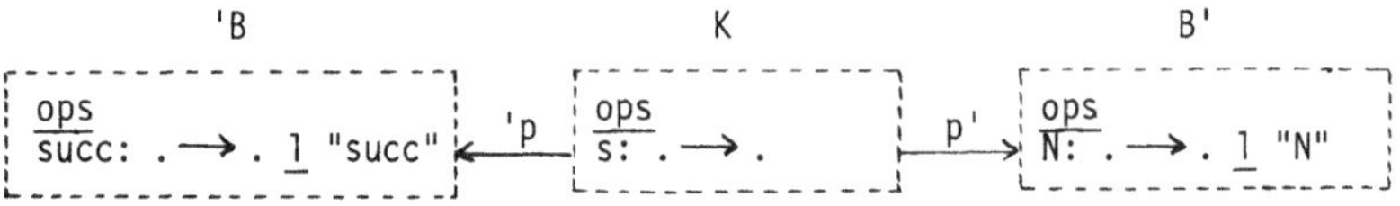

Figure 4: production to relabel the successor operation

4. Parametric specifications

Parametric specifications are a very convenient means for the specification process. We do not care about semantical problems of parametric specifications cf.[15], but discuss a more syntactically oriented treatment following [7]. To give an example, the concept of an array is rather independent of the type of its entries and keys. The only requirement is that there should be an "eq"-relation on keys and a constant entry serving as the value of new(i). Thus we would like to give specifications as follows.

Example 4.1: The parametric specification of array(key, entry) is:

params key, entry, eq, 0

sorts array, key, entry

ops 0 : ⟶ entry
new: ⟶ array
.[.]:=. : array × key × entry ⟶ array
.[.] : array × key ⟶ entry
if.then.else.fi : bool × entry×entry ⟶ entry

preds eq : key × key

conds new[i] = 0
(a[i]:=n)[j] = if i eq j then n else a[j] fi

We denote the formal parameter part by the params symbol. In spec-, an embedding will serve for this purpose. A parameter assignment should map formal parameters to actual parameters which suit in type and behaviour. So, assignments are well modelled by morphisms. To apply a parametric specification to an actual parameter is intended to substitute the formal parameter specification by the actual parameter specification and this is done by the pushout construction.

Definition 4.2: A parametric specification p:F ⟶P is an embedding in spec-. A parameter assignment for p:F ⟶P is a morphism f:F ⟶A. The result of the application of the parametric specification p:F⟶P to the actual parameter A via f:F ⟶A is the pushout-object of the pushout of p and f.

In our examples with arrays, 1.3 and 4.1, we have:

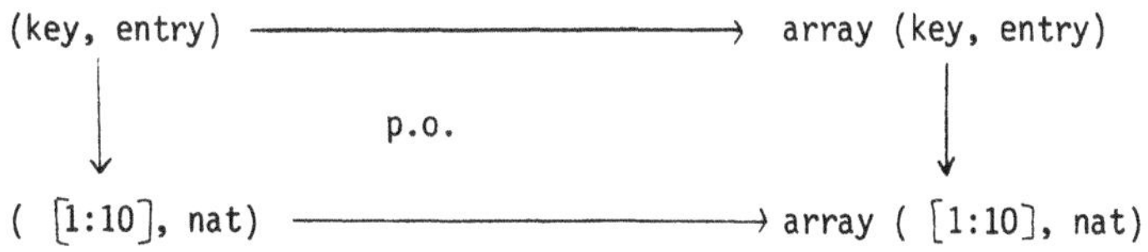

Not that the actual parameter A can itself be a parametric specification $q : E \longrightarrow A$ with a formal parameter part E. Thus, sequences of applications of parametric specifications can be constructed. The following result for spec = [6,7] carries over to spec and spec -:

Theorem 4.3: The application of parametric specifications to parametric specifications is associative.

When we have a parametric specification, we can use it as well as a production by duplicating the parameter. The idea is demonstrated by figures 5 und 6.

params $d, \leq$

sorts d

preds $\leq : d \times d$

conds $x \leq x$
$x \leq y \wedge y \leq z \Longrightarrow x \leq z$
$x \leq y \wedge y \leq x \Longrightarrow x = y$
$x \leq y \vee y \leq x$

Figure 5: Parametric specification of a total ordering

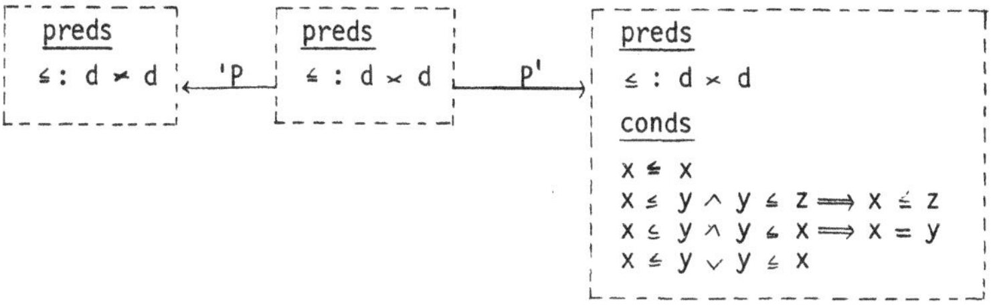

Figure 6: Production to generate total orderings

Taking parametric concepts, supplementing them to productions, and storing these productions in a library is a promising tool for editing specifications. Using the production of figure 6, when we want to specify any situation where a total ordering is involved, we need only give the few axioms that determine the specific ordering. For example, for natural numbers we need only give

sorts: nat
ops: $0 : \longrightarrow nat$
succ: nat $\longrightarrow$ nat
preds: $\leq$: nat $\times$ nat
conds: $x \leq succ(x)$

Applying the production of figure 6 to this specification, the ordering axioms are inserted, and we get the specification of example 1.1.

We can imagine that for more complex concepts there may be a considerable economy in using parametric specifications as replacement rules or productions.

5. References

1. ADJ (Goguen, J.A.-Thatcher, J.W.-Wagner, E.G.):
   An initial algebra approach to the specification, correct ness, and implementation of abstract data types. Current Trends in Programming Methodology IV, ed. by R. Yeh, Prentice Hall, New Jersey 1977

2. ADJ (Thatcher, J.W.-Wagner, E.G.-Wright, J.B.):
   Data type specification, parametrization, and the power of specification technigues. Proc-Sigact Annual Symp. Theory Comp., 1978

3. Brendel, W.-Bunke, H.-Nagl, M.:
   Syntaxgesteurte Programmierung und inkrementelle Compilation. Proc. GI-7. Jahrestagung, Informatik Fachberichte 10, 57-73, Springer Berlin 1977

4. Burstall, R.M.-Goguen, J.A.:
   Putting theories together to make specifications. Proc. 5th IJCAI 77, MIT, Cambridge, Mass. 1977

5. Ehrich, H.-D.:
   Extensions and implementations of abstract data type specifications. Proc. MFCS'78, ed. by J. Winkowski, Lecture Notes in Computer Science, Vol. 64, Springer-Verlag, Berlin 1978, 155-164

6. Ehrich, H.-D.:
   On the theory of specification, implementation , and parametrization of abstract data types. To be published

7. Ehrich, H.-D.-Lohberger, V.G.:
   Parametric specification of abstract data types, parameter substitution, and graph replacements. Proc. Workshop "Graphentheoretische Konzepte in der Informatik", Applied Comp. SC., Carl Hanser Verl., Muenchen-Wien 1978

8. Ehrig, H.-Kreowski, H.-J.-Maggiolo-Schettini, A.-Rosen, B.K.- Winkowski, J.:
   Deriving structures from structures. Proc. MFCS 1978, ed. by J. Winkowski, Lecture Notes in Computer Science, Vol. 64. Springer-Verlag, Berlin 1978, 177-19o

9. Ehrig, H.-Kreowski, H.-J.-Padawitz, P.:
   Stepwise specification and implementation of abstract data types. Proc. 5th Intern Colloq. on Automata, Languages, and Programming, Venice 1978

1o. Ehrig, H.-Pfender, M.-Schneider, H.-J.:
   Graph-Grammars-an algebraic approach. Proc. Conf. Switch. Automata Theory 1973, 167-18o

11. Goguen, J.A.:
   Correctness and eqivalence of data types. In: Proc. Conf. on Alg. Syst. Th., Udine, Lecture Notes In Comp. SC., Springer-Verl., Berlin 1975

12. Goguen, J.A.:
   Abstract errors for abstract data types. In: Proc. Conf. on Formal Description of Programming Languages, Ed. by E.J. Neuhold, North-Holland Publ. Company, Amsterdam 1976

13. Guttag, J.V.:
The specification and application to programming of abstract data types. Techn. Report CSRG-59, Univ. of Toronto 1975

14. Kreisel, G.-Krivine, J.L.:
Modelltheorie, Springer, Berlin 1972

15. Lehmann , D.-J.-Smyth, M.B.:
Data types. Proc. 18th IEEE Symp. on Foundations of Computing. Providence R.I., 1977, 7-12

16. Liskov, B.-H.-Zilles, S.N.:
Specification Tehcniques for data abstractions. IEEE Transact. Softw.-Eng., Vol. SE-1 (1975), 7-19

17. Majster, M-E.:
Data types, abstract data types and their specification problem. Report TUM-INFO-774o, Techn. Univ. Muenchen, 1977

18. Manes, E.G.:
Algebraic Theories. Springer-Verl., New York 1976

19. Parnas, D.L.:
A technique for module specification with examples. Comm. ACM 15 (1972) 33o-336

2o. Rosen, B.K.:
Deriving Graphs from Graphs by applying a production. Acta Informatica 4, 337-357 (1975)

21. Schneider, H.J.-Ehrig, H.:
Grammars on partial graphs. Acta Inf. 6, 297-316 (1976)

DECOMPOSITION OF GRAPH GRAMMAR PRODUCTIONS AND DERIVATIONS

Hartmut Ehrig
Fachbereich Informatik
Techn. Universität Berlin
1000 Berlin 10, Germany

Barry K. Rosen
Computer Science Dept.
IBM Research Center
Yorktown Heights, N.Y.10598
U.S.A.

(January 1979)

Key Words: Decomposition, Graph Grammars, Concurrency, Applications of Category Theory to Graph Grammars

ABSTRACT:

Given a production p^* in a graph grammar we consider the problem to find all productions p and p' and all dependency relations R between p and p' such that p^* is equal to the concurrent production $p*_R p'$. In view of the Concurrency Theorem - shown in an earlier paper - this means that there is a bijective correspondence between direct derivations $G \Longrightarrow X$ via p^* and R-related derivations $G \Longrightarrow H \Longrightarrow X$ via (p,p'). We are able to give a general procedure for the decomposition of $p^*=p*_R p'$ which leads to all possible decompositions at least in the case of injective relations R. An important application of this decomposition theorem is the problem to find all possible decompositions of manipulation rules into atomic manipulation rules of a data base system. The theorem is proved within the framework of the algebraic theory of graph grammars using pushout and pullback techniques.

1. INTRODUCTION

In our paper /ER 78/ we have shown the following result: Given a sequence of graph grammar productions together with dependence relations, we are able to construct a single concurrent production with the following property: Each application of the sequence of productions to a graph - such that the dependence relations are respected - can be performed in a single step applying the concurrent production to the same graph. Moreover, this becomes a bijective correspondence between such derivation sequences and direct derivations via the concurrent production.

Presenting this result at several places we were manily asked the following two questions:

1. Why do you call the resulting single production "concurrent"?
2. What about the inverse result for the decomposition of productions?

The main reason for using the notion "concurrent" is that applying the concurrent production $p*_R p'$ we can execute the relevant parts of p and p' at the same time and hence concurrently, although p and p' are not necessarily applicable in parallel. Parallel application implies also application in arbitrary order while concurrent

application allows only one sequentialization in general. In this sense concurrency generalizes parallelism. But we could have used also the name "composite" production where, however, the composition is parameterized by the dependence relation.
With respect to the second question we were not able to give a definite answer at that time. People, especially from data base systems, convinced us that this decomposition problem is interesting in several applications. Especially the problem to find all possible decompositions of manipulation rules into atomic manipulation rules of a data base system. As shown by several authors (e.g. /Fu 78/, /BA 78/, /EK 78/, /Ne 77/, /St 78/) manipulation rules in data base systems can be formalized using productions or sequences of productions in a graph grammar. Hence the data base problem reduces to the problem of decomposition of productions.
This was the main motivation for the present paper. We are able to give a general procedure for the decomposition of a given production which leads to all possible decompositions at least in the case of injective relations. This result is prepared and stated in Section 3 and proved in Section 4. Some basic notions from the theory of graph grammars are reviewed in Section 2. For more details we refer to our tutorial survey /Eh 78/.

2. PRODUCTIONS, DERIVATIONS AND CONCURRENCY

Following /Eh 78/ a production $p=(B_1 \xleftarrow{b_1} K \xrightarrow{b_2} B_2)$ consists of a pair of graphs (B_1, B_2), an auxiliary interface graph K and a pair of graph morphisms $b_1:K \longrightarrow B_1$ and $b_2:K \longrightarrow B_2$ in the category of colored graphs and color-preserving graph morphisms.
A production is called fast if b_1 and b_2 are injective.

Given a production $p=(B_1 \xleftarrow{b_1} K \xrightarrow{b_2} B_2)$ and a graph morphism $d:K \longrightarrow D$, where D may be called the environment with interface d(K), we obtain a direct derivation $G \overset{p}{\Longrightarrow} H$ when G and H are the pushout objects in the following diagrams

$$\begin{array}{ccccc}
B_1 & \xleftarrow{b_1} & K & \xrightarrow{b_2} & B_2 \\
g\downarrow & (1) & \downarrow d & (2) & \downarrow h \\
G & \xleftarrow[c_1]{} & D & \xrightarrow[c_2]{} & H
\end{array}$$

constructed in the category of colored graphs.
We will often use the short notations PO and PB for pushouts and pullbacks respectively (/AM 75/). Moreover we will use a sequential notation for squares if the notation of morphisms is not essential, e.g. PO (1) above will be cited as KB_1DG or KDB_1G.

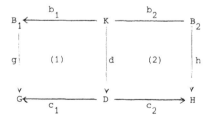

Let us explain the effect of POs (1) and (2) above:
The graph G becomes the gluing of B_1 and environment D glued together in the "gluing points" $b_1(k)$ in B_1 and d(k) in D for all "gluing points" k in K. Similarily, H becomes the gluing of B_2 and D (along K) such that H is obtained from G by replacing B_1 by B_2, or more precisely the occurence $g(B_1)$ of p in G by the occurence $h(B_2)$ of p in H. Actually we often have the situation that the production and a graph G together with $g:B_1 \longrightarrow G$ is given but not $d:K \longrightarrow D$. In this case we first have to construct the "pushout complement" $K \xrightarrow{d} D \xrightarrow{c_1} G$ of $K \xrightarrow{b_1} B_1 \xrightarrow{g} G$ such that (1) becomes PO and in a second step the PO (2) from d and b_2. Note, that for injective b_1 there is a unique PO-complement iff the "gluing condition" given in 3.5 of /Eh 78/ is satisfied.

EXAMPLE 1

The diagram in Fig. 2.1 shows a direct derivation of graphs $G \overset{p}{\Longrightarrow} H$ and $H \overset{p'}{\Longrightarrow} X$ in Fig. 2.2 where corresponding gluing points have same numbers. The productions p and p', given in the top of Fig. 2.1 and Fig. 2.2 respectively correspond to a pair of recursive definitions

f(u,v)=f(u,f(u,v))

f(u',v')=f(g(u',v',c)c)

applied to actual parameters u=v=u'=a and v'=f.

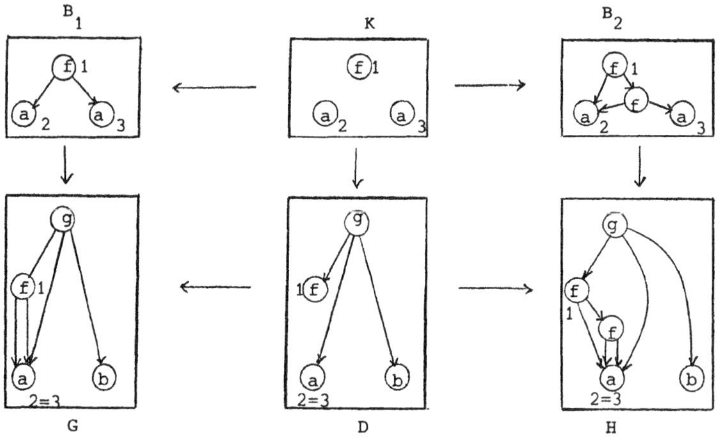

Figure 2.1: Direct derivation $G \overset{p}{\Longrightarrow} H$

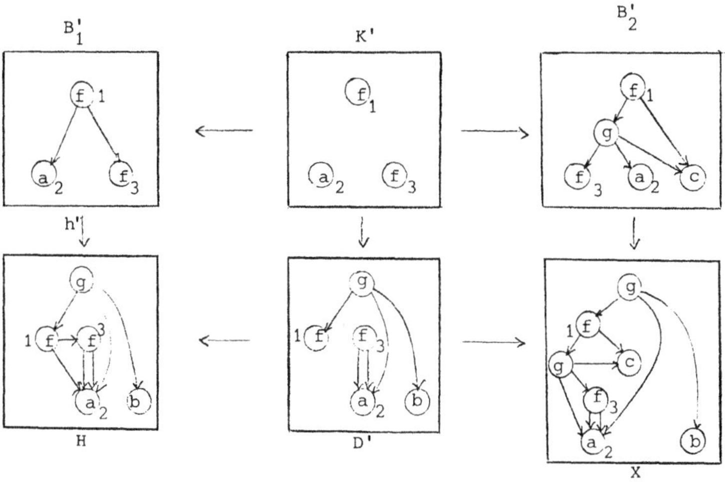

Figure 2.2: Direct derivation $H \overset{p'}{\Longrightarrow} X$

Note, that in the derivation sequence $G \overset{p}{\Longrightarrow} H \overset{p'}{\Longrightarrow} X$ p and p' are not independent in the sense of /EK 76a/ because the intersection of the occurences of p and p' in H contains two edges which are not in the image of K and K'. This intersection, or more precisely the categorical intersection, which is the usual one for injective h and h', is given by the pullback (PB) $B_2 \longleftarrow R \longrightarrow B_1'$ of h and h'. This PB defines a relation R for the pair of productions (p, p') given in Fig. 2.3 such that the derivation sequence is R-related. The general definition will be given below.

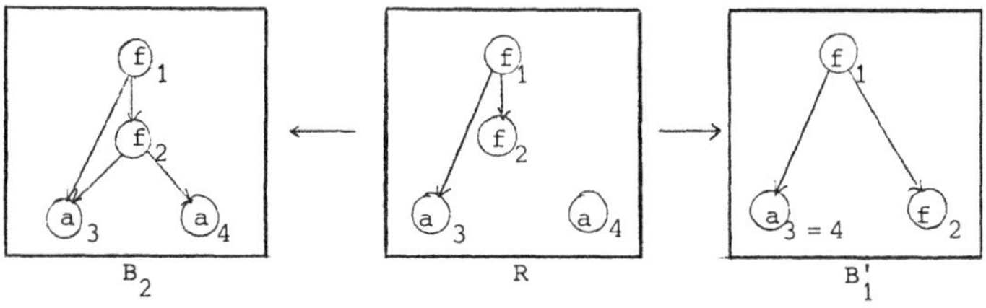

Fig. 2.3: A relation R for the pair (p, p') in Fig. 2.1 and 2.2

In general a <u>relation</u> R for a pair of fast productions (p, p') is a pair of graph morphisms $B_2 \longleftarrow R \longrightarrow B_1'$ satisfying the following condition and a similar one for B_2: If two items $x' \neq y'$ in B_1' are in relation with respect to the closure $\bar{R}$ of R on $B_1'+B_2$ then both are gluing points of B_1'.

Especially this condition is satisfied if the graph morphisms $R \longrightarrow B_2$ and $R \longrightarrow B_1'$ are injective. In this case the relation is called injective.

Given a relation R for (p, p') a derivation sequence $G \Longrightarrow H \Longrightarrow X$ via (p, p') is called R-related if all R-related items of B_2 and B_1' (and in addition at most common gluing items of B_2 and B_1') are glued together in H.

In this case the R-concurrent production $p *_R p' = (B_1^* \longleftarrow K^* \longrightarrow B_2^*)$ of $p = (B_1 \longleftarrow K \longrightarrow B_2)$ and $p' = (B_1' \longleftarrow K' \longrightarrow B_2')$ is given in the following way:

B_1^* consists of B_1 and the non-R-related parts of B_1' and similar B_2^* consists of B_2' and the non-R-related parts of B_2. In more detail: Let B_{10}' and B_{20} the non-R-related parts of B_1' and B_2 together with the common gluing points L_1 (of K and R) and L_2 (of K' and R). Now let K_o, L and K_o' the intersections of K with B_{20}, L_1 with L_2, and K' with B_{10}' respectively. Then B_1^* is the gluing of B_1 and B_{10}' a long L_1, B_2^* the gluing of B_2' and B_{20} along L_2, and K^* the gluing of K_o and K_o' along L.

In other words $p *_R p'$ is the gluing of the restricted productions $p_o = (B_1 \longleftarrow K_o \longrightarrow B_{20})$ and $p_o' = (B_{10}' \longleftarrow K_o' \longrightarrow B_2')$.

For the formal versions of the defintions above we refer to /ER 78/ or /Eh 78/. Let us illustrate the last construction with the following example:

EXAMPLE 2

Given the R-related pair of productions (p, p') from Example 1 the corresponding R-concurrent production $p^* = p *_R p'$ is given by the top row in Fig. 2.4

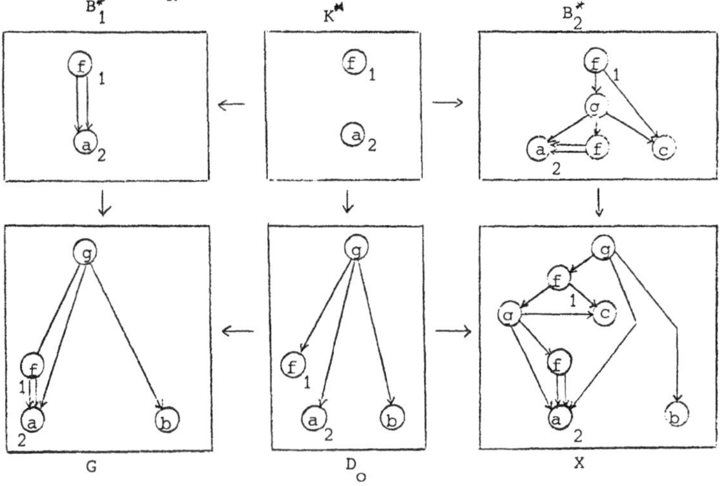

Fig. 2.4: Derivation $G \Longrightarrow X$ via the R-concurrent production

Actually B_1^* consists of the items of B_1 while the non-R-related part of B_1' is empty. However, the gluing procedure for B_1^* implies that the leaves of B_1 are glued together in B_1^*. On the other hand B_2^* consists of the items of B_2' together with non-R-related

parts of B_2 which are the two arcs between the nodes colored f and a.
Note that the top tow of Fig. 2.6 in /ER 78/ (proceedings version) does not show the R-concurrent production but the parallel production $p_o+p_o'=(B_1+B_{10}'\longleftarrow K_o+K_o'\longrightarrow B_{20}+B_2')$.

Finally let us review the main result of /ER 78/:

CONCURRENCY THEOREM

Given a relation R for a pair of fast productions (p, p') and the corresponding fast R-concurrent production $p^*=p*_Rp'$ there is a bijective correspondence between R-related sequences $G\Longrightarrow H\Longrightarrow X$ via (p, p') and direct derivations $G\Longrightarrow X$ via p^*.

3. DECOMPOSITION OF PRODUCTIONS

In this section we consider the problem to decompose a given production p^* into productions p and p' and a relation R such that p^* becomes the R-concurrent production $p*_Rp'$. Given the R-related pair (p, p') of productions $p*_Rp'$ was constructed by first restricting $p=(B_1\longleftarrow K\longrightarrow B_2)$ and $p'=(B_1'\longleftarrow K'\longrightarrow B_2')$ to $p_o=(B_1\longleftarrow K_o\longrightarrow B_{20})$ and $p_o'=(B_{10}'\longleftarrow K_o'\longrightarrow B_2)$ and then gluing p_o and p_o' to obtain $p*_Rp'$. Vice versa given p_o and p_o' and the relation R we will be able to construct p and p' as "R-extended" productions of p_o and p_o' respectively. It remains the problem to find p_o, p_o' and R provided that p^* is given. Actually we will be able to take arbitrary productions p_o and p_o' which are "preimage" productions of p^* and both together are "covering" p^*. Moreover we can take an arbitrary relation R provided that R is an extension of R_o where R_o is the "overlapping" of p_o and p_o' with respect to p^*.

Before we give the decomposition theorem we will start with the exact definitions of the notions introduced above:

DEFINITION 1

1. Given a fast production $p^*=(B_1^*\longleftarrow K^*\longrightarrow B_2^*)$ a fast production $p_o=(B_1\longleftarrow K_o\longrightarrow B_{20})$ together with graph morphisms $B_1\longrightarrow B_1^*$, $K_o\longrightarrow K^*$, $B_{20}\longrightarrow B_2^*$ is called <u>preimage production</u> of p^* if the diagrams (1) and (2) below are pullbacks

$$\begin{array}{ccccc}
B_1 & \longleftarrow & K_o & \longrightarrow & B_{20} \\
\downarrow & (1) & \downarrow & (2) & \downarrow \\
B_1^* & \longleftarrow & K^* & \longrightarrow & B_2^*
\end{array}$$

2. Two preimage productions p_o and $p_o'=(B_{10}'\longleftarrow K_o'\longrightarrow B_2')$ of p^* are called <u>covering</u> (resp. injective covering) of p^* if

$B_1\longrightarrow B_1^*\longleftarrow B_{10}'$ and $B_2\longrightarrow B_2^*\longleftarrow B_{20}$ are pushout pairs
(resp. injective pushout pairs).

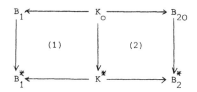

3. Let L_1 and L_2 be the pullbacks of the pushout pairs above and L the pullback of $K_o \longrightarrow K^* \longleftarrow K'_o$. Then there are unique graph morphisms $L \longrightarrow L_1$ and $L \longrightarrow L_2$ making the 3-cubes in Fig. 3.1 commutative and the pushout R_o of these morphisms is called <u>overlapping</u> of p_o and p'_o.

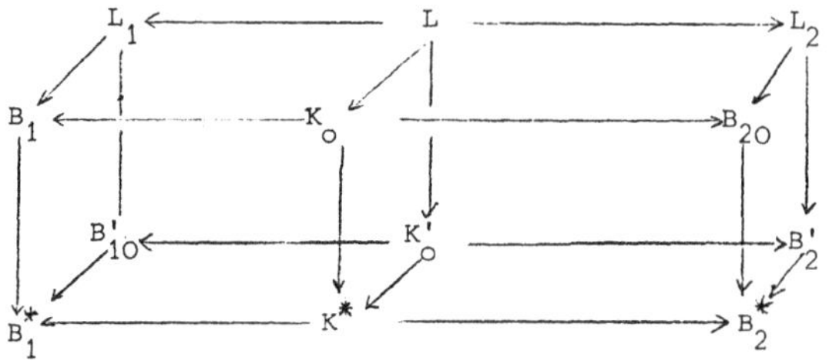

Fig. 3.1: Covering of production $p^*=(B^*_1 \longleftarrow K^* \longrightarrow B^*_2)$

4. Given an injective graph morphism $R_o \longrightarrow R$, called <u>extension</u> of R_o, a production $p=(B_1 \longleftarrow K \longrightarrow B_2)$ (resp. $p'=(B'_1 \longleftarrow K' \longrightarrow B'_2)$ is called <u>R-extension</u> of p_o (resp. p'_o) if B_2 is the gluing of B_{20} and R along L_2 (resp. B'_1 the gluing of B'_{10} and R along L_1).

To find a pair of preimage productions which is covering p^* the following lemma is usefull:

<u>LEMMA 1</u>

1. Given a fast production $p^*=(B^*_1 \overset{b^*_1}{\longleftarrow} K^* \overset{b^*_2}{\longrightarrow} B^*_2)$ and graph morphisms $f_1:B_1 \longrightarrow B^*_1$, $f_2:B_{20} \longrightarrow B^*_2$ then f_1 and f_2 can be extended (uniquely up to isomorphisms) to a preimage production $p_o=(B_1 \longleftarrow K_o \longrightarrow B_{20})$ iff there is an isomorphism $b:f_1^{-1}b^*_1K^* \xrightarrow{\sim} f_2^{-1}b^*_2K^*$ such that $f_2\, bx=b^*f_1x$ for all x in the domain of b where b^* is the isomorphism $b^*:b^*_1K^* \xrightarrow{\sim} b^*_2K^*$ defined by $b^*x=b^*_2b^{*-1}_1x$ for all x in the domain of b^*.

2. Two preimage productions p_o and p'_o of p^* with graph morphisms $f_1:B_1 \longrightarrow B^*_1$, $g_1:B'_{10} \longrightarrow B^*_1$ and $f_2:B_{20} \longrightarrow B^*_2$, $g_2:B'_2 \longrightarrow B^*_2$ are a covering of p^* iff we have:

(i) f_1 is injective up to g_1
(i.e. $f_1x=f_1y$ for $x \neq y$ implies $f_1x \in g_1B'_{10}$)

(ii) g_1 is injective up to f_1

(iii) (f_1,g_1) is jointly surjective
(i.e. for all z in B^*_1 there is either x in B_1 with $f_1x=z$ or y in B'_{10} with $g_1y=z$)

and similar conditions for f_2 and g_2.

REMARK: To find a preimage covering of p^* in practical cases we can start with fairly arbitrary graph morphisms $f_1:B_1 \longrightarrow B_1^*$ and $g_2:B_2' \longrightarrow B_2^*$ and then construct $g_1:B_{10}' \longrightarrow B_1^*$ and $f_2:B_{20} \longrightarrow B_2^*$ such that the conditions of Lemma 1 are satisfied. In fact there are weak necessary and sufficient conditions for f_1 and g_2 such that they can be extended to a preimage covering of p^*. The first necessary condition for f_1 and g_2 is that for each x in K^* either b_1^*x is in f_1B_1 or b_2^*x is in g_2B_2'. The second one is that b^*-images of boundary points with respect to f_1 are in g_2B_2' and the dual for f_1B_1. For injective coverings these both conditions are already sufficient.

EXAMPLE 3

Given the production p^* in the bottom row of Fig. 3.2 we consider the graph morphisms f_1, g_1, f_2 and g_2. Actually the conditions of Lemma 1 are satisfied such that the graph morphisms can be extended uniquely to a pair of preimage productions covering p^* which are given in Fig. 3.2. Note that the covering is not injective because $f_2(2) = f_2(3)$.

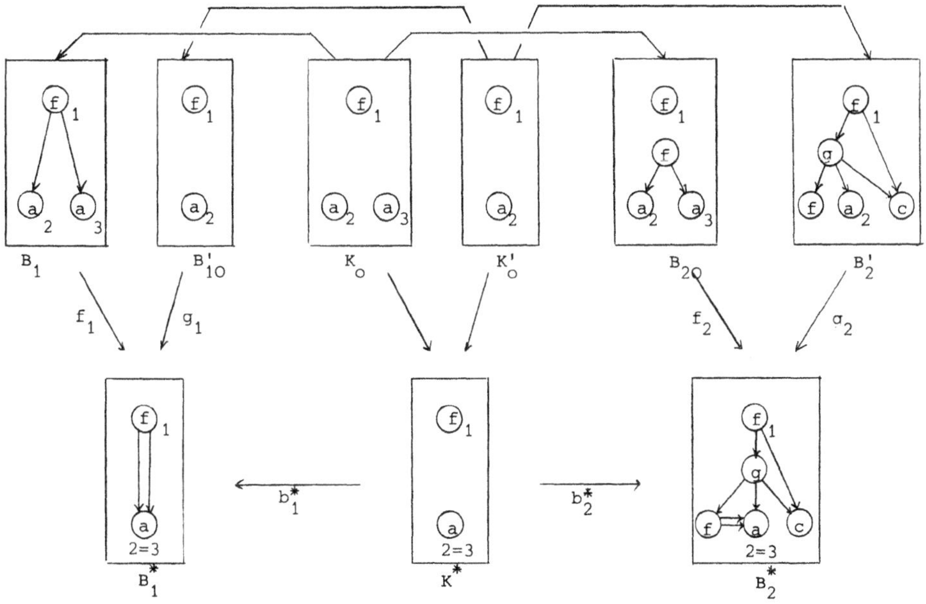

Fig. 3.2: A pair of preimage productions covering p^*

Starting with p^* and f_1, g_2 only, the necessary conditions mentioned in the remark above are satisfied. Constructing K_o as pullback of f_1 and b_1^* we can find B_{20} as "union" of K_o and the subgraph generated by $B_2^* - g_2B_2'$ which implies that the second node colored f is in B_{20}. Similar the pullback K_o' of g_2 and b_2^* leads to B_{10}'.

Now we will state the main theorem of this paper:

DECOMPOSITION THEOREM

1. Given a fast production $p^* = (B_1^* \leftarrow K^* \rightarrow B_2^*)$. Then there is for each pair of preimage productions (p_o, p_o') covering p^* with overlapping R_o and for each extension $R_o \rightarrow R$ a uniquely determined decomposition

$$p^* = p *_R p'$$

where p and p' are uniquely determined R-extended productions of p_o and p_o' respectively, the relation between p and p' is uniquely determined by R, and $p *_R p'$ is the R-concurrent production of p and p'.

2. Moreover if the covering of p^* by p_o and p_o' is injective the relation between p and p' becomes injective and p,p' fast and all decompositions of $p^* = p *_R p'$ with injective relation R between fast productions p and p' can be obtained by the construction above.

REMARKS:

1. The preimage productions p_o and p_o' covering p^* do not provide a decomposition of p^* in general due to the following Lemma 2.

2. It is still open whether we obtain all decompositions also in the general case and not only for injective relations R. The injective case, however, is sufficient for most applications.

LEMMA 2

Given a pair of preimage productions (p_o, p_o') covering p^* with overlapping R_o and an R-extension $R_o \rightarrow R$ such that $p^* = p *_R p'$ then the following conditions are equivalent:

(i) $p = p_o$ and $p' = p_o'$

(ii) p_o and p_o' are parallel independent with respect to B_1^* and B_2^* and $R = R_o$, i.e. we have for the pullbacks L_1 of f_1 and g_1, L of $K_o \rightarrow K^*$ and $K_o' \rightarrow K^*$, and L_2 of f_2 and g_2 $L_1 = L = L_2 = R_o = R$.

Parallel decompositions are obtained in the following case:

COROLLARY 1

If the pullbacks L_1 of f_1 and g_2 and L_2 of f_2 and g_2 are both empty then we obtain a parallel decomposition $p^* = p_o + p_o'$ in the case $R = R_o = \emptyset$.

The decomposition of productions leads also to a decomposition of the corresponding direct derivation using the CONCURRENCY THEOREM:

COROLLARY 2

Given a decomposition $p^* = p *_R p'$ then there is a bijective correspondence between direct derivations $G \Rightarrow X$ via p^* and R-related sequences $G \Rightarrow H \Rightarrow X$ via (p,p').

Finally we will give an example:

EXAMPLE 4

Given a pair of preimage productions (p_o, p_o') covering p^* of Example 3 and the extension $R_o \longrightarrow R$ of the overlapping R_o in Fig. 3.3

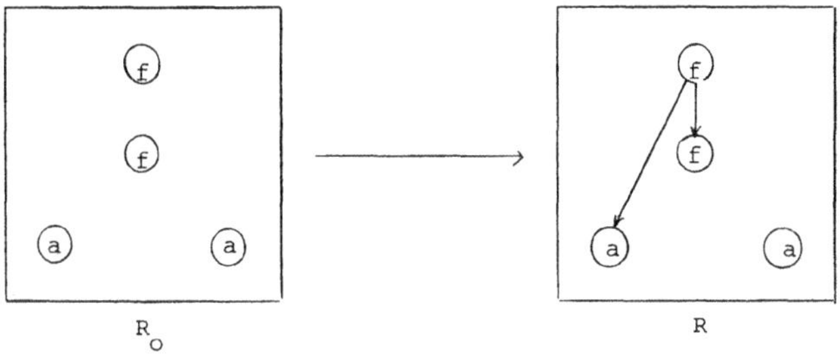

Fig. 3.3: Extension R of the overlapping R_o

then the R-extended productions p and p' of p_o and p_o' are given in the top row of Fig. 2.1 and Fig. 2.2 respectively. The corresponding relation R between p and p' is given in Fig. 2.3 such that we obtain the decomposition $p^* = p *_R p'$. Corresponding derivations due to Corollary 2 are given in Fig. 2.1 - 2.4.

4. PROOFS

In this section we give the proofs of all the results of Section 3. The main part is the proof of the DECOMPOSITION THEOREM which is based on the construction of R-concurrent productions and some pushout and pullback lemmas which are given in /ER 78/ and /EK 76/.

PROOF OF LEMMA 1

1. If diagrams (1) and (2) in Definition 1.1 are pullbacks then we have $f_1^{-1} b_1^* K^* \cong K_o \cong f_2^{-1} b_2^* K^*$ defining the isomorphism b. Commutativity of (1) and (2) and injectivity of the bottom and hence also the top morphisms implies $f_2 bx = b^* f_1 x$ for all x in $f_1^{-1} b_1^* K^*$. Vice versa let $K_o = f_1^{-1} b_1^* K^*$ such that (1) becomes pullback. Then define $K_o \longrightarrow B_{20}$ to be b followed by the inclusion into B_{20} which makes (2) pullback using $f_2 bx = b^* f_1 x$.
2. Follows directly from the characterization of pushout pairs in /EK 76b/.

PROOF OF THE DECOMPOSITION THEOREM

Part 1 of the proof: Given p^* and a pair of preimage productions (p_o, p_o') covering p^* with overlapping R_o we have already the double-3-cube in Fig. 3.1. Note that the pullback $L_1 B_1 B_{10}' B_1^*$ (and similar $L_2 B_2 B_{20} B_2^*$) is also a pushout because $B_1 \longrightarrow B_1^* \longrightarrow B_{20}'$ is a pushout-pair (see PB-PO Lemma in /EK 76b/). Moreover, all sequences in Fig. 3.1 are pullback by the 3-CUBE-PB-LEMMA in /ER 78/, $LK_o K_o' K^*$ is a pushout by the 3-CUBE-PO-LEMMA in /ER 78/, and $K_o \longrightarrow B_1$, $K_o \longrightarrow B_{20}$, $K_o' \longrightarrow B_{10}'$, $K_o' \longrightarrow B_2'$, $L \longrightarrow L_1$, $L \longrightarrow L_2$ are injective because they are opposite to injective morphisms in a pullback.

Now we are going to construct the R-extended productions p and p' from p_o and p_o' using the extension $R_o \longrightarrow R$ given by assumption. Let $L_1 \longrightarrow R = L_1 \longrightarrow R_o \longrightarrow R$ and $L_2 \longrightarrow R = L_2 \longrightarrow R_o \longrightarrow R$ where all morphisms are injective. $LL_1L_2R_o$ is pushout by definition of R_o and hence also pullback because $L \longrightarrow L_1$ is injective. Since $R_o \longrightarrow R$ is also injective this implies that LL_1L_2R is also pullback (but no longer a pushout for nonisomorphic extensions $R_o \longrightarrow R$). Let us construct K, K', B_2 and B_1' as pushouts in LL_1K_oK, $LL_2K_o'K'$, $L_2RB_{20}B_2$ and $L_1RB_{10}'B_1'$ respectively. Then there are unique $K \longrightarrow B_2$ and $K' \longrightarrow B_1'$ such that the left and the right cube in Fig. 4.1 commutes respectively.

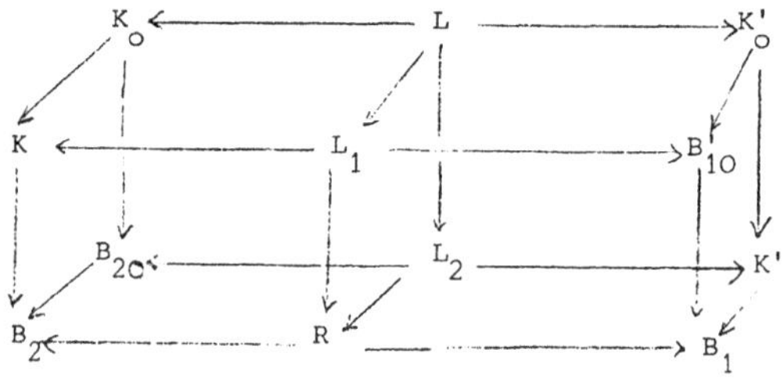

Fig. 4.1: Construction of R-extended productions p and p'

Using the pushout properties of K and commutativity of $LL_1K_oB_1$ we obtain a unique $K \longrightarrow B_1$ such that $L_1 \longrightarrow B_1 = L_1 \longrightarrow K \longrightarrow B_1$ and $K_o \longrightarrow B_1 = K_o \longrightarrow K \longrightarrow B_1$. Hence we have the production $p = (B_1 \longleftarrow K \longrightarrow B_2)$ which is an R-extension of p_o. Similar we obtain $K' \longrightarrow B_2'$ and hence an R-extended production $p' = (B_1' \longleftarrow K' \longrightarrow B_2')$ of p_o'.

We will show that all squares in Fig. 4.1 are pullback. Injectivity of $L \longrightarrow L_1$ in the pushout LL_1K_oK implies that it is also a pullback and $K_o \longrightarrow K$ injective. Similar $LL_2K_o'K'$, $L_2RB_{20}B_2$ and $L_1RB_{10}'B_1'$ become pullbacks and $K_o' \longrightarrow K'$, $B_{20} \longrightarrow B_2$, and $B_{10}' \longrightarrow B_1'$ injective.

In order to show that L_1KRB_2 is pullback and $K \longrightarrow B_2$ injective let us consider for a moment Fig. 4.1 with R replaced by R_o and hence B_2 replaced by $(B_2)_o$. Then the 3-CUBE-INJECTIVITY-LEMMA applied to the left 3-cube in the modified Fig. 4.1 with front $L_2R_oB_{20}(B_2)_o$ implies that $K \longrightarrow (B_2)_o$ is injective. The SPECIAL 3-CUBE-PB-LEMMA applied to the same 3-cube with front $K_oKB_{20}(B_2)_o$ implies that $L_1KR_o(B_2)_o$ is pullback using that $K \longrightarrow (B_2)_o$ is injective and $LL_1L_2R_o$ pushout. Now let B_2 pushout in $R_oR(B_2)_oB_2$ such that B_2 becomes pushout in $L_2RB_{20}B_2$ as constructed in Fig. 4.2. But injectivity of $R_o \longrightarrow R$ implies that $R_oR(B_2)_oB_2$ is also pullback. Hence L_1KRB_2 is a composition of pullbacks and hence also pullback (where uniqueness of $K \longrightarrow B_2$ constructed in Fig. 4.2 implies $K \longrightarrow B_2 = K \longrightarrow (B_2)_o \longrightarrow B_2$). Note that injectivity of $R_o \longrightarrow R$ implies that of $(B_2)_o \longrightarrow B_2$ and hence that of $K \longrightarrow B_2$.

Now we consider again the original left 3-cube in Fig. 4.1 with front $L_2RB_{20}B_2$. Applying the SPECIAL 3-CUBE-PB-LEMMA we see that $K_oKB_{20}B_2$ is pullback.

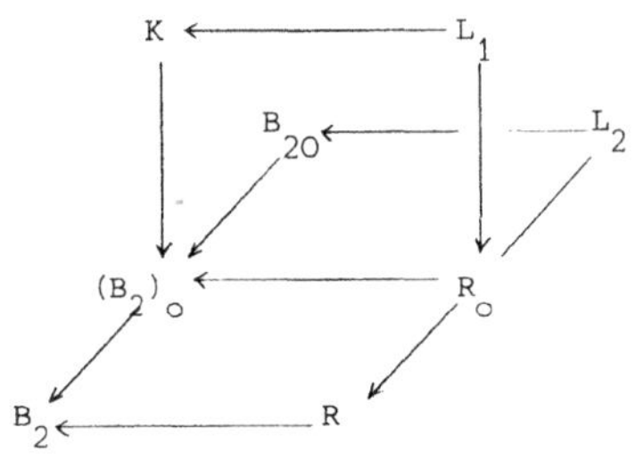

Fig. 4.2: Pullback property of L_1KRB_2

Dually $L_2K'RB_1'$ and $K_o'K'B_{10}'B_1'$ become pullback and $K' \longrightarrow B_1'$ injective in the right 3-cube of Fig. 4.1. Hence all squares in Fig. 4.1 are pullbacks and we have the following pushouts by construction:

LL_1K_oK, $LL_2K_o'K'$, $L_2RB_{20}B_2$, $L_1RB_{10}'B_1'$

This shows that $B_2 \longleftarrow R \longrightarrow B_1'$ is a relation for the pair (p, p'). On the other hand the R-concurrent production $p*_Rp'$ is defined (see Def. 2 of /ER 78/) by starting with the front and bottom squares in Fig. 4.1 and constructing K_o, L and K_o' as pullbacks in the left middle and right side respectively which were shown to be pullbacks in our case. The construction of $p*_Rp'$ is finished in Fig. 3.1 defining $L_1 \longrightarrow B_1 = L_1 \longrightarrow K \longrightarrow B_1$, $K_o \longrightarrow B_1 = K_o \longrightarrow K \longrightarrow B_1$ (similar $L_2 \longrightarrow B_2'$ and $K_o' \longrightarrow B_2'$) and B_1^*, K^* and B_2^* to be pushouts in the left, middle and right side respectively. Again these properties were shown above in our construction such that the R-concurrent production $p*_Rp'$ coincides with our given production p^* leading to the desired decomposition $p*_Rp'$.

(Note, that we have not shown that p and p' are fast. We only have shown the injectivity of $K \longrightarrow B_2$ and $K' \longrightarrow B_1'$. But $K \longrightarrow B_1$ and $K' \longrightarrow B_2$ become also injective iff $B_{10}' \longrightarrow B_1^*$ is injective up to $K^* \longrightarrow B_1^*$ and $B_{20} \longrightarrow B_2^*$ injective up to $K^* \longrightarrow B_2^*$ respectively.)

Part 2 of the proof: Now let us assume that $B_1 \longrightarrow B_1^*$, $B_{10}' \longrightarrow B_1^*$, $B_{20} \longrightarrow B_2^*$, and $B_2' \longrightarrow B_2^*$ are injective. Then all morphisms in Fig. 3.1 and in Fig. 4.1 become injective, especially the relation $B_2 \longleftarrow R \longrightarrow B_1'$. In this case also $K \longrightarrow B_1$ (and similar $K' \longrightarrow B_2'$) is easily shown to be injective using that of $L_1 \longrightarrow B_1$ and the pullback property of $LL_1K_oB_1$. Hence p and p' are fast.

Vice versa starting with fast productions p, p' and injective relation $B_2 \longleftarrow R \longrightarrow B_1'$ also all morphisms in Fig. 4.1 and 3.1 become injective. Hence also the covering of p^* becomes injective.

It remains to be shown that each decomposition of $p^* = p*_Rp'$ with injective relation can be obtained by the construction of part 1. That means we have to show that Fig. 3.1 and Fig. 4.1 as constructed in the definition of R-concurrent productions remain unchanged during the decomposition construction. In Fig. 3.1 we have assumed K_o and K'_o to be double pullbacks and constructed L_1, L and L_2 as pullbacks. Now we have to show these pullback properties in the injective case. First of all the injective pushouts $L_1B_1B'_{10}B^*_1$, $LK_oK'_oK^*$ and $L_2B_{20}B'_2B^*_2$ are also pullbacks. To show that $K_oK^*B_1B^*_1$ (and similar the other squares with K_o and K'_o mentioned above) is pullback we use the following lemma which is easily proved:

If the composition of commutative squares is pullback, the first one pushout and all morphisms injective, then the second square is pullback. (Note, that we can also show the double pullback properties of K_o and K'_o in the noninjective case of part 1. But the proof is more difficult.)

In Fig. 4.1 we have constructed K, K', B_2 and B'_1 as pushouts in our decomposition construction. But the corresponding squares are also pushouts in the construction for the R-concurrent production. Moreover each injective pullback LL_1L_2R can be obtained by extending an injective pushout $LL_1L_2R_o$ by an injective morphism $R_o \longrightarrow R$.

Hence we have shown that given an injective R-related pair of fast productions remains unchanged if we decompose the corresponding R-concurrent production. This was to be shown.

(Note, that in the noninjective case of part 1 we are not sure whether L_1, L and L_2 are necessarily pullbacks of the left, middle and right hand side in Fig. 3.1.)

PROOF OF LEMMA 2

First of all let us note that L is constructed as pullback in $LK_oK'_oK^*$. But injectivity of $K^* \longrightarrow B^*_1$ implies that also $LK_oK'_oB^*_1$ is pullback. Now we have by construction of the R-extended productions in the DECOMPOSITION THEOREM:

(i) $p=p_o$ and $p'=p'_o$

$\Longleftrightarrow$ $K=K_o$, $K'=K'_o$, $B_2=B_{20}$ and $B'_1=B'_{10}$

$\Longleftrightarrow$ $L=L_1$, $L=L_2$, $L_2=R$ and $L_1=R$

$\Longleftrightarrow$ $L=L_1=L_2=R=R_o$, i.e.

(ii) p_o and p'_o are parallel independent with respect to B^*_1 and B^*_2 and $R=R_o$.

PROOF OF COROLLARY 1

$L_1=\emptyset=L_2$ implies $L=\emptyset$ and $R_o=\emptyset$ and hence $B^*_1=B_1+B'_{10}$, $K^*=K_o+K'_o$ and $B^*_2=B_{20}+B'_2$. For $R=R_o=\emptyset$ this implies $p=p_o$ and $p'=p'_o$ by Lemma 2 and hence by the DECOMPOSITION THEOREM $p^*=p *_R p'=p_o *_R p'_o=p_o+p'_o$.

Finally let us mention that the proof of Corollary 2 follows immediately from the CONCURRENCY THEOREM which is proved in /ER 78/.

5. REFERENCES

/AM 75/ Arbib, M.A.; Manes, E.G.: Arrows, Structures and Functors: The Categorical Imperative, Academic Press, New York, 1975

/BA 78/ Batini, C.; D'Atri, A.: Rewriting Systems as a Tool for Relational Data Base Design, Proc. International Workshop on Graph Grammars and Their Applications to Computer Science and Biology, Bad Honnef 1978, this volume

/Eh 78/ Ehrig, H.: Introduction to the Algebraic Theory of Graph Grammars, Proc. International Workshop on Graph Grammars and Their Applications to Computer Science and Biology, Bad Honnef 1978, this volume

/EK 76/ Ehrig, H.; Kreowski, H.-J.: Contributions to the Algebraic Theory of Graph Grammars, Techn. Report 76-22, FB 20, TU Berlin (1976), to appear in Math. Nachr.

/EK 78/ --: Algebraic Theory of Graph Grammars Applied to Consistency and Synchronization in Data Bases, Proc. Workshop WG 78 on Graphtheoretic Concepts in Computer Science, to appear in the series Applied Computer Sci.

/ER 78/ Ehrig, H.; Rosen, B.K.: Concurrency of Manipulations in Multidimensional Information Structures, Techn. Rep. 78-13, FB 20, TU Berlin (1978), short version in Proc. MFCS'78, Springer Lect. Notes Comp. Sci(64), 165-176 (1978)

/Fu 78/ Furtado, A.L.: Transformations of Data Base Structures, Proc. International Workshop on Graph Grammars and Their Applications to Computer Science and Biology, Bad Honnef 1978, this volume

/Ne 77/ Negraszus-Patan, G.: Anwendungen der algebraischen Graphentheorie auf die formale Beschreibung und Manipulation eines Datenbankmodells, Diplomarbeit, FB 20, TU Berlin (1977)

/St 78/ Steiner, S.: Untersuchungen über die gleichzeitige Ausführung von Operationen in Datenbankmodellen unter Verwendung der Algebraischen Graphentheorie, Diplomarbeit FB 20, TU Berlin (1978)

LOCALLY STAR GLUING FORMULAS FOR A CLASS OF PARALLEL GRAPH GRAMMARS

Hartmut Ehrig
Axel Liedtke

TU Berlin, FB Informatik
Otto-Suhr-Allee 18/20, 1000 Berlin 10
Germany

ABSTRACT

The construction of locally catenative formulas for PDOL-systems is generalized to graphs. Concatenation in the string case becomes star gluing (a special colimit construction known from category theory) of graphs which is the basic concept in the algebraic approach to parallel graph grammars. We consider the special class of simple handle-substitution-parallel-graph-grammars (simple HPG-grammars). The main results are the construction of a locally star gluing formula for simple HPG-grammars resp. dependent simple HPG-grammars. That means there is a cut p such that for all $n \geq p$ the graphs G_n in the graph sequence of the grammar can be constructed as a star gluing of graphs G_{n-t_i} with $1 \leq t_i \leq p$ for $i=1,\dots,k$.

1. INTRODUCTION

Parallel graph grammars and especially simple HPG-grammars are introduced in Section 6 of the survey paper /Eh 78/ in this volume. They are based on the concepts of parallel graph grammars given in /Eh Kr 76/, /Eh Rb 76/ and especially /Ld 78/. The main results of this paper are motivated and formulated already in Section 7 of /Eh 78/ but without proofs. In this paper we repeat the basic definitions and results without further motivation but we give the proofs of the results and some additional thechnical lemmas. For more details and a slightly more general treatment we refer to /Ld 78/. For a generalization of recurrence systems from strings to graphs we refer to /Cu Li 76/. Moreover it is shown how to construct for each parallel graph grammar (more precisely PGOL-system) a recurrence system on graphs generating the same graph language.
The reader is assumed to be familiar with the basic concepts of Category Theory used

in the Algebraic Theory of Graph Grammars as given in the Appendium of /Eh 78/ and the notation of graphs and graph morphisms as given in Section 2 of /Eh 78/. For further motivation we suggest Sections 6 and 7 of /Eh 78/ as well as the theory of locally catenative formulas in the string case as given in /He Rb 75/.

We start with the basic gluing concept for parallel graph grammars which generalizes the pushout construction used in the sequential case.

2. DEFINITION (STAR GLUING AND PUSHOUT-STAR)

A graph star of degree $n \geq 1$ is a diagram

$$S=(B_i \longleftarrow K_{ij} \longrightarrow B_j)_{1 \leq i<j \leq n}$$

consisting of graphs $B_1,\ldots,B_n$, called gluing graphs, and $K_{12},\ldots,K_{n-1,n}$ called interface graphs, and graph morphisms $k_{ij}:K_{ij} \longrightarrow B_i$ resp. $k_{ji}:K_{ij} \longrightarrow B_j$. In the case n=1 we only have the single graph B_1 and for n=2 we have a pair of graph morphisms $K_{12} \longrightarrow B_1$ and $K_{12} \longrightarrow B_2$.

Given a star $S=(B_i \longleftarrow K_{ij} \longrightarrow B_j)_{1 \leq i<j \leq n}$ a graph G together with graph morphisms $B_i \longrightarrow G$ for $i=1,\ldots,n$ is called star gluing of S or pushout-star of S, POS for short, if we have:

1. (Commutativity): $K_{ij} \longrightarrow B_i \longrightarrow G = K_{ij} \longrightarrow B_j \longrightarrow G$ for all $i<j$, and
2. (Universal Property): For all graphs G' and graph morphisms $B_i \longrightarrow G'$ satisfying $K_{ij} \longrightarrow B_i \longrightarrow G' = K_{ij} \longrightarrow B_j \longrightarrow G'$ for all $i<j$ there is a unique graph morphism $G \longrightarrow G'$ such that $B_i \longrightarrow G \longrightarrow G' = B_i \longrightarrow G'$ for all $i=1,\ldots,n$ in the following diagram:

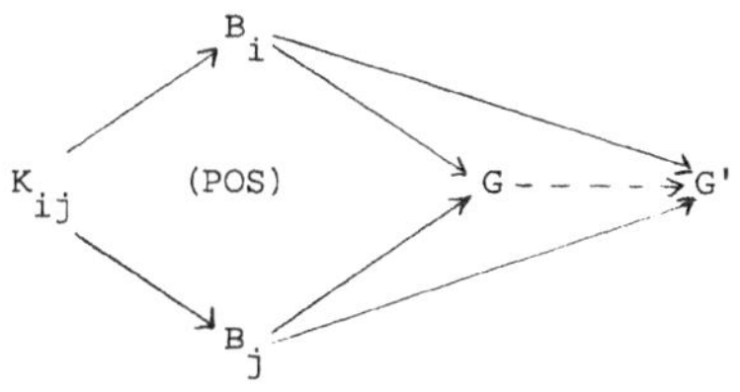

Also the diagram (POS) above is referred to a pushout-star which has in the case n=3 the following shape:

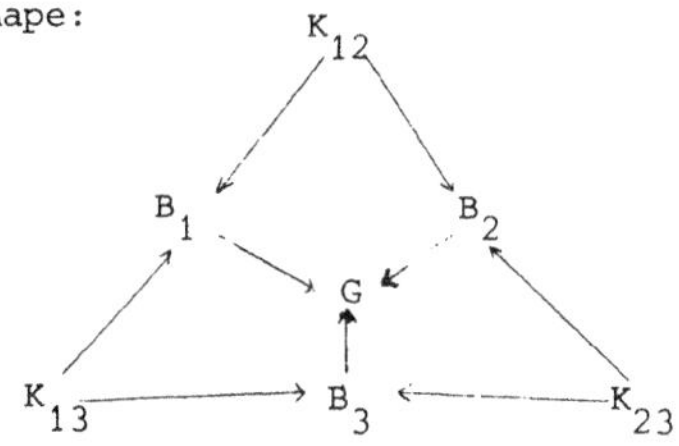

The graph G, written G=STARGLUING(S), is uniquely determined up to isomorphism and we will not distinguish between isomorphic graphs.

The pushout-star (POS) is called locally pullback if for each (i,j) the (i,j) component of (POS) is pullback.

Now we turn to the algebraic description of the parallel derivation procedure. Actually the derived graph G' is given by the star gluing of

$$(B_i \longleftarrow K_{ij} \longrightarrow B_j)_{1\leq i<j\leq n}$$

as defined in 2 where the $B_1,\ldots,B_n$ are the right hand sides of the productions. In order to get the interfaces K_{ij} of the star gluing we construct the "handle star" HS(G) of the given graph G

$$(H_i \longleftarrow K_{ij} \longrightarrow H_j)_{1\leq i<j\leq n}$$

where K_{ij} is the intersection of handles H_i and H_j in G. Since G becomes the star-gluing of HS(G) the direct derivation $G \Longrightarrow G'$ will be given by a pair of pushout-stars.

3. DEFINITION (HANDLE-STAR)

1. Given a color alphabet $C=(C_A,C_N)$ a handle is a (colored) graph H consisting of one arc a_o, two nodes s_o and t_o, which are source resp. target of a_o, and a triple $(c_s,c_a,c_t)\in C_N \times C_A \times C_N$ of colors for s_o, a_o and t_o respectively. Let us assume that a_o, s_o and t_o are the same for all handles so that each handle is given by a triple $(c_s,c_a,c_t)\in C_N \times C_A \times C_N$.
2. Given a graph $G=(G_A,G_N,s,t,m_A,m_N)$ we have for each arc $a_i\in \{a_1,\ldots,a_n\} = G_A$ a unique handle H_i and graph morphism $H_i \longrightarrow G$ such that a_o is mapped to a_i. Now let K_{ij} the intersection (resp. pullback of $H_i \longrightarrow G$ and $H_j \longrightarrow G$ in the following pullback diagram (where all the K_{ij} are discrete)

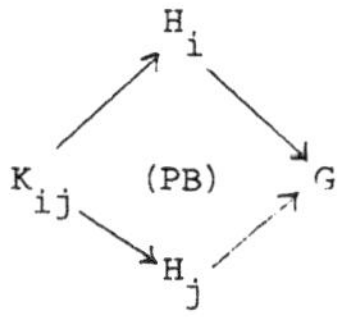

(for all $1\leq i<j\leq n$)

then the handle-star of G is the following graph star

$$\text{HANDLE-STAR}(G) = (H_i \longleftarrow K_{ij} \longrightarrow H_j)_{1\leq i<j\leq n}$$

3. A graph G is called nondegenerate if G is nonempty, has no isolated nodes and no isolated loops.

4. LEMMA

For each nondegenerate graph G we have

$$\text{STAR-GLUING (HANDLE-STAR}(G)) = G$$

(where isomorphic graphs are not distinguished).

Proof: Let $(H_i \longleftarrow K_{ij} \longrightarrow H_j)_{1\leq i<j\leq n}$ the handle-star of G with graph morphisms $c_i: H_i \longrightarrow G$ and G' the pushoutstar (POS) of the handle-star with graph morphisms $u_i: H_i \longrightarrow G'$ for i=1,...,n. We have to show $G' \cong G$. Using the universal property of (POS) there is a unique graph morphism $f: G' \longrightarrow G$ such that $f \circ u_i = c_i$ for i=1,...,n in the following diagram

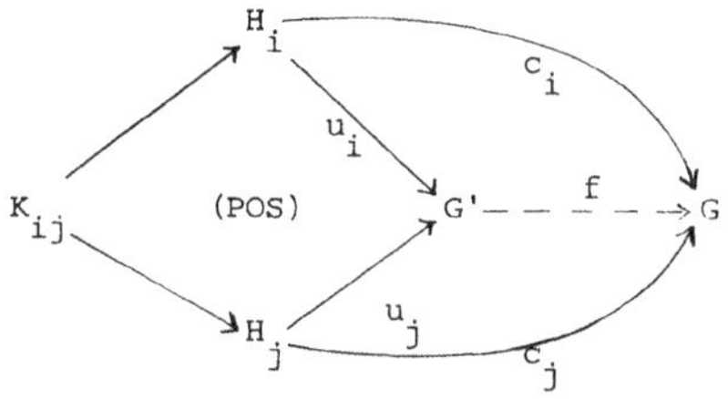

Since G is nondegenerate each item in G has a preimage in H_i under c_i for some i such that f becomes surjective. Moreover the graph morphism $f=(f_A, f_N)$ is injective and hence an isomorphism of G' and G because f_A and f_N are injective due to the following reasoning: The graphs K_{ij} are discrete such that G' can be assumed to have the arcs $a_1, \ldots, a_n$ of G and $f_A: G'_A \longrightarrow G_A$ is the inclusion. But also f_N is injective because G has no isolated loops which would imply a noninjective c_i but injective u_i for some i.□

Now we are able to define simple HPG-grammars. As in /Eh 78/ we will only consider the case of "colorpreserving productions" which means that corresponding gluing items have the same color (for the "colorchanging" case see /Ld 78/).

5. DEFINITION (HANDLE PRODUCTION AND HPG-DERIVATIONS)

1. A handle-production p is a fast graph production

   $p = (H \longleftarrow K \longrightarrow B)$

   where H is a handle, K a discrete graph with two nodes s_o and t_o and B a nondegenerate graph. The graph morphisms $K \longrightarrow H$, $K \longrightarrow B$ are injective since p is fast.
2. Given a nondegenerated graph G with

   $\text{HANDLE-STAR}(G) = (H_i \longleftarrow K_{ij} \longrightarrow H_j)_{1\leq i<j\leq n}$

   and for each i=1,...,n a production

   $p_i = (H_i \longleftarrow K_i \longrightarrow B_i)$

   we obtain a unique factorization

   $K_{ij} \longrightarrow H_i = K_{ij} \longrightarrow K_i \longrightarrow H_i.$

   Let for each i=1,...,n

   $K_{ij} \longrightarrow B_i = K_{ij} \longrightarrow K_i \longrightarrow B_i$

   then the daughter-star of G is defined by

   $\text{DAUGHTER-STAR}(G) = (B_i \longleftarrow K_{ij} \longrightarrow B_j)_{1\leq i<j\leq n}.$

Combining both constructions a direct (HPG)-derivation, written $G \Longrightarrow G'$, consists of the following two pushout-stars, the handle pushout-star $(POS)_H$ and the daughter pushout-star $(POS)_D$:

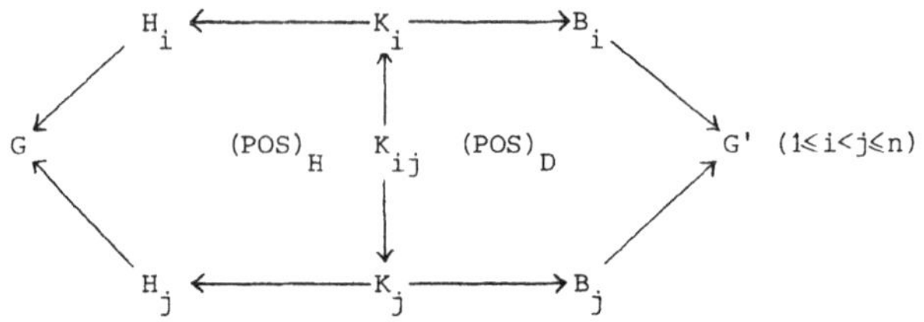

Remark: By definition of $(POS)_H$ and $(POS)_D$ G is the star gluing of HANDLE-STAR(G) resp. G' the star gluing of DAUGHTER-STAR(G) and also G' is nondegenerate (see /Ld 78/).

6. DEFINITION (SIMPLE HPG-GRAMMARS)

1. A simple handle-substitution-parallel graph-grammar, short simple HPG-grammar, $GG=(C,H\text{-}PROD,H_{ax})$ consists of
   - a color alphabet $C=(C_A,C_N)$
   - a finite set H-PROD of handle-productions $p_i=(H_i \longleftarrow K_i \longrightarrow B_i)$ (i=1,...,n) which is deterministic, i.e. $H_i \neq H_j$ for $i \neq j$, and complete, i.e. $\{H_i/1 \leq i \leq n\} \cong C_N \times C_A \times C_N$
   - a handle H_{ax}, called axiom.
2. The graph sequence of a simple HPG-grammar is the sequence $(G_n)_{n \in \mathbb{N}_0}$ where $G_0=H_{ax}$ and $G_n \Longrightarrow G_{n+1}$ for each $n \in \mathbb{N}_0$. The set $\{G_n/n \in \mathbb{N}_0\}$ is called the graph language of the grammar.

Remarks: Note, that determinism and completeness of H-PROD implies that for each nondegenerated G there is exactly one direct derivation $G \Longrightarrow G'$ in GG.

7. DEFINITION AND LEMMA (PRODUCTION AND DERIVATION MAPS)

1. Given a handle production $p=(H \overset{h}{\longleftarrow} K \overset{b}{\longrightarrow} B)$ the production map on the nodes $MAP(p):H_N \longrightarrow B_N$, written $MAP(p):H \dashrightarrow B$, is defined by $MAP(p)=b_N \circ h_N^{-1}$.
2. For each HPG-derivation $G \Longrightarrow G'$ with productions p_i the production maps MAP(p) can be uniquely extended to a derivation map $MAP(G \Longrightarrow G'):G_N \longrightarrow G'_N$, written $MAP(G \Longrightarrow G'):G \dashrightarrow G'$, such that the following diagram commutes for i=1,...,n.

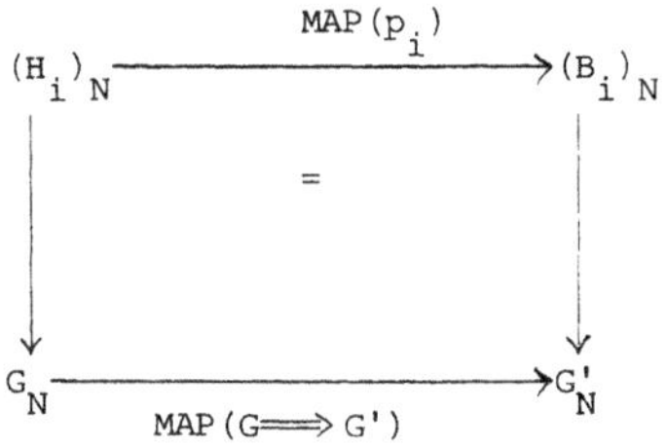

The derivation map $MAP(G\overset{*}{\Longrightarrow}G')$ is defined as the composition of the derivation maps for the corresponding direct derivations.

Proof: Given the handle star $(H_i \longleftarrow K_{ij} \longrightarrow H_j)_{1\leq i<j\leq n}$ of G and the daughter-star $(B_i \longleftarrow K_{ij} \longrightarrow B_j)_{1\leq i<j\leq n}$ we have

$$
\begin{aligned}
(K_{ij})_N \longrightarrow (B_i)_N &= (K_{ij})_N \longrightarrow (K_i)_N \xrightarrow{b_i} (B_i)_{N-1} \\
&= (K_{ij})_N \longrightarrow (K_i)_N \xrightarrow{h_i} (H_i)_N \xrightarrow{h_i} (K_i)_N \xrightarrow{b_i} (B_i)_N \\
&= (K_{ij})_N \longrightarrow (H_i)_N \xrightarrow{MAP(p_i)} (B_i)_N
\end{aligned}
$$

and so by the universal property of the star gluing G_N in SETS (which is the same as in GRAPHS replacing graphs and graph morphisms by sets and maps) we have a unique map $G_N \longrightarrow G'_N$ making the following diagram commutative

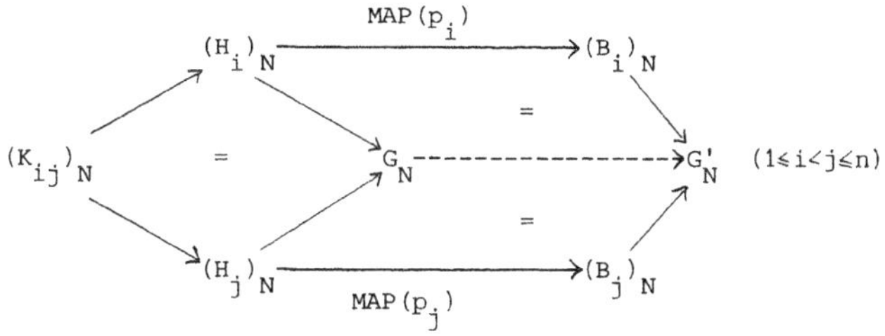

We have briefly reviewed the basic definition for simple HPG-grammars. For more motivation and examples we refer to /Eh 78/. Before we define locally star gluing formulas let us give three technical lemmas for pushout-stars which are basic for the proofs of the main results (cf. 13. and 15.). In the first lemma we show that each pushout-star can be reduced to a locally pullback one.

8. LEMMA (PULLBACK-PROPERTIES OF PUSHOUT-STARS)

1. For each pushout-star $(POS)_1$ in the diagram below there is a pushout-star $(POS)_2$ where the graph morphisms $H_i \longrightarrow G$ $(i=1,\ldots,n)$ are the same but which is locally pullback.

2. Given in addition to 1. for all i=1,...,n graph morphisms $H_i \longrightarrow B_i$ and

$$G^1 = \text{STAR-GLUING}(B_i \longleftarrow H_i \longleftarrow L_{ij} \longrightarrow H_j \longrightarrow B_j)_{1 \leq i < j \leq n}$$

$$\bar{G}^1 = \text{STAR-GLUING}(B_i \longleftarrow H_i \longleftarrow \bar{L}_{ij} \longrightarrow H_j \longrightarrow B_j)_{1 \leq i < j \leq n}.$$

Then G^1 and $\bar{G}^1$ are isomorphic.

3. If all graph morphisms $H_i \longrightarrow B_i$ are injective, the pushout-star $(POS)_3$ for $\bar{G}^1$ in 2. is locally pullback.

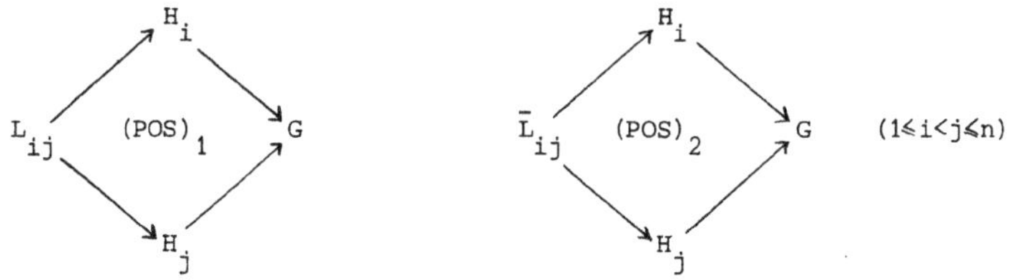

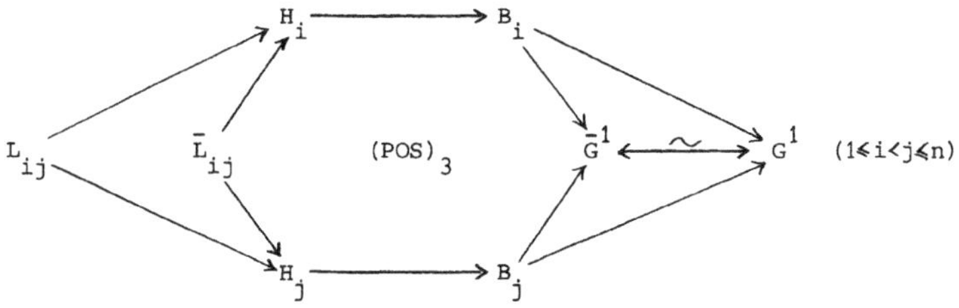

Proof: We only give an explicit proof for part 1. The other two parts can be proved by using also the universal properties of pullbacks and pushout-stars. Given $(POS)_1$ let $\bar{L}_{ij}$ the pullback of $H_i \longrightarrow G$ and $H_j \longrightarrow G$ such that there is a unique graph morphism $L_{ij} \longrightarrow \bar{L}_{ij}$ for each pair (i,j) making the left triangles in the following diagram commutative

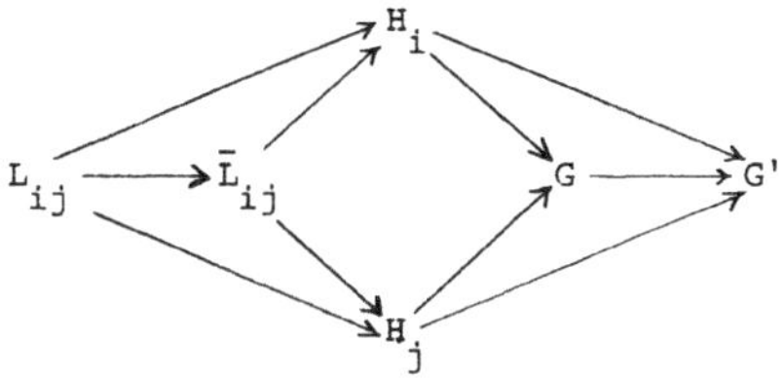

In order to show that $(POS)_2$ is a pushout-star let us assume to have a graph G' and graph morphisms $H_i \longrightarrow G'$ (i=1,...,n) satisfying $\bar{L}_{ij} \longrightarrow H_i \longrightarrow G' = \bar{L}_{ij} \longrightarrow H_j \longrightarrow G'$ for $1 \leq i < j \leq n$. This implies $L_{ij} \longrightarrow H_i \longrightarrow G' = L_{ij} \longrightarrow H_j \longrightarrow G'$ such that by the universal property of $(POS)_1$ there is a unique graph morphism $G \longrightarrow G'$ making the right triangles commutative. Hence also $(POS)_2$ is a pushout-star. □

In the following lemma we show how to refine a pushout-star for G if the gluing graphs B_i in the graph-star are star gluings itself.

9. LEMMA (REFINEMENT OF PUSHOUT-STARS)

Given a graph G a graph-star $S=(B_p \leftarrow K_{pq} \longrightarrow B_q)_{1\leq p<q\leq k}$ such that

G=STAR-GLUING(S) and pushout-star $(POS)_G$ is locally pullback,

and for each p=1,...,k a graph-star $S_p=(H_i \longleftarrow L_{ij} \longrightarrow H_j)_{m_{p-1}\leq i<j\leq m_p}$ with $0=m_0\leq m_1\leq \ldots \leq m_k=m$ and

B_p=STAR-GLUING(S_p) with pushout-star $(POS)_p$.

Then we have a "refined" graph-star $S_{ref}=(H_i \longleftarrow L_{ij} \longrightarrow H_i)_{1\leq i<j\leq m}$ such that

G=STAR-GLUING(S_{ref})

where for i<j in $I_p=\{m_{p-1}+1,\ldots,m_p\}$ $(H_i \longleftarrow L_{ij} \longrightarrow H_j)$ is the same as in S_p and for p<q and $j\in I_p$, $r\in I_q$ $(H_j \longleftarrow L_{jr} \longrightarrow H_r)$ is defined by the following pullback

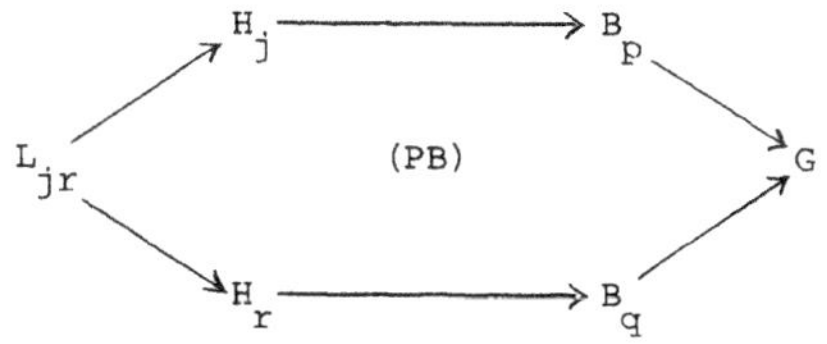

and $H_j \longrightarrow B_p$, $H_r \longrightarrow B_q$, $B_p \longrightarrow G$, $B_q \longrightarrow G$ are the graph morphisms from the pushout-stars $(POS)_p$, $(POS)_q$, and $(POS)_G$ respectively.

<u>Proof:</u> We have to show that G is the star-gluing of S_{ref} where $H_i \longrightarrow G = H_i \longrightarrow B_p \longrightarrow G$ for $i\in I_p$.
The commutativity $L_{ij} \longrightarrow H_i \longrightarrow G = L_{ij} \longrightarrow H_j \longrightarrow G$ for all $1\leq i<j\leq m$ follows from that in the pushout-stars $(POS)_p$ for p=1,...,k and from the definition of L_{jr} above. To show the universal property assume that we have $H_i \longrightarrow G'$ for i=1,...,m satisfying $L_{ij} \longrightarrow H_i \longrightarrow G' = L_{ij} \longrightarrow H_j \longrightarrow G'$. For each p we use the universal property of $(POS)_p$ to obtain a unique graph morphism $B_p \longrightarrow G'$ satisfying $H_i \longrightarrow B_p \longrightarrow G' = H_i \longrightarrow G'$ for all $i\in I_p$. For each pair (p,q) with p<q we will show $K_{pq} \longrightarrow B_p \longrightarrow G' = K_{pq} \longrightarrow B_q \longrightarrow G'$. Since $(POS)_G$ is locally pullback there is for each (j,r) with $j\in I_p$ and $r\in I_q$ a unique graph morphism $L_{jr} \longrightarrow K_{pq}$ such that (1) and (2) in the following diagram commutes.

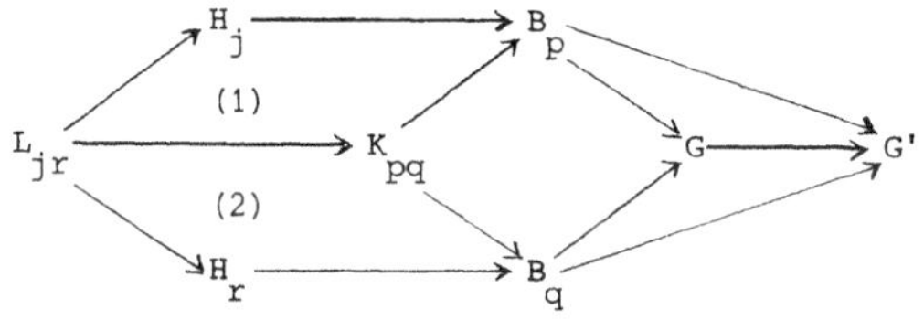

From the pushout-stars $(POS)_p$ and $(POS)_q$ and the pullback properties of K_{pq} it follows that each item in K_{pq} has a preimage in L_{jr} for some (j,r). Hence $L_{jr} \longrightarrow H_j \longrightarrow B_p \longrightarrow G' = L_{jr} \longrightarrow H_r \longrightarrow B_q \longrightarrow G'$ implies $K_{pq} \longrightarrow B_p \longrightarrow G' = K_{pq} \longrightarrow B_q \longrightarrow G'$. Hence we have a unique $G \longrightarrow G'$ with $B_p \longrightarrow G \longrightarrow G' = B_p \longrightarrow G'$ for $p=1,\dots,k$ using the universal properties of $(POS)_G$. But this implies also $H_i \longrightarrow B_p \longrightarrow G' = H_i \longrightarrow G'$ for $i=1,\dots,m$. Moreover $G \longrightarrow G'$ is unique with respect to this property because it is unique with respect to $B_p \longrightarrow G \longrightarrow G' = B_p \longrightarrow G'$ for all $p=1,\dots,k$ and the uniqueness properties of $(POS)_p$.□

In the last lemma we show how to obtain a derived pushout-star $(POS)_{G'}$ for a derived graph G' of G from a (general) pushout-star $(POS)_G$ for G. In Definition 5.we only have the special case of one derivation step and assuming that $(POS)_G$ is the handle-star of G.

10. LEMMA (DERIVATION OF PUSHOUT-STARS)

Let G be a graph in the graph sequence of a simple HPG-grammar and $S=(B_p \longleftarrow K_{pq} \longrightarrow B_q)_{1 \le p < q \le k}$ a graph-star with discrete K_{pq} and nondegenerate B_p such that

$G=$STAR-GLUING(S) with locally pullback pushout-star $(POS)_G$.

Moreover let B_p^n the derived graph of B_p after n steps with derivation map $MAP(B_p \overset{*}{\Longrightarrow} B_p^n): B_p \dashrightarrow B_p^n$. Then we have a "derived" graph-star $S^n=(B_p^n \longleftarrow K_{pq} \longrightarrow B_q^n)_{1 \le p < q \le k}$ such that

$G^n=$STAR-GLUING(S^n)

where G^n is the derived graph of G in n steps and $K_{pq} \longrightarrow B_p^n$ is the composition $K_{pq} \longrightarrow B_p \dashrightarrow B_p^n$. (Note, that this composition is well-defined because K_{pq} is discrete, but the notation does not take into account the inclusions $(B_p)_N \longrightarrow B_p$ and $(B_p^n)_N \longrightarrow B_p^n$.)

<u>Proof:</u> First we assume n=1. For each $p=1,\dots,k$ let S_p be the handle-star of B_p (using the same notation as in Lemma 9) such that by Lemma 4 we have $B_p=$STAR-GLUING(S_p). For the refined graph-star S_{ref} of Lemma 9 we have $G=$STAR-GLUING(S_{ref}). On the other hand $H_1,\dots,H_m$ are exactly the handles of G and $H_i \longrightarrow B_p \longrightarrow G$ for $i \in I_p$ the corresponding graph morphisms because the K_{pq} in graph-star S are discrete. Unfortunately the L_{ij} in S_{ref} are not necessary the same as the pullbacks $\bar{L}_{ij}$ of $H_i \longrightarrow G$ and $H_j \longrightarrow G$. (We have only $L_{jr}=\bar{L}_{jr}$ for $j \in I_p$ and $r \in I_q$ for $p \neq q$ by definition of L_{jr} in Lemma 9.) These $\bar{L}_{ij}$ are used in HANDLE-STAR$(G)=(H_i \longleftarrow \bar{L}_{ij} \longrightarrow H_j)_{1 \le i < j \le m}$ and because of its pullback properties there are unique graph morphisms $L_{ij} \longrightarrow \bar{L}_{ij}$ such that $L_{ij} \longrightarrow \bar{L}_{ij} \longrightarrow H_i = L_{ij} \longrightarrow H_i$ for all (i,j).

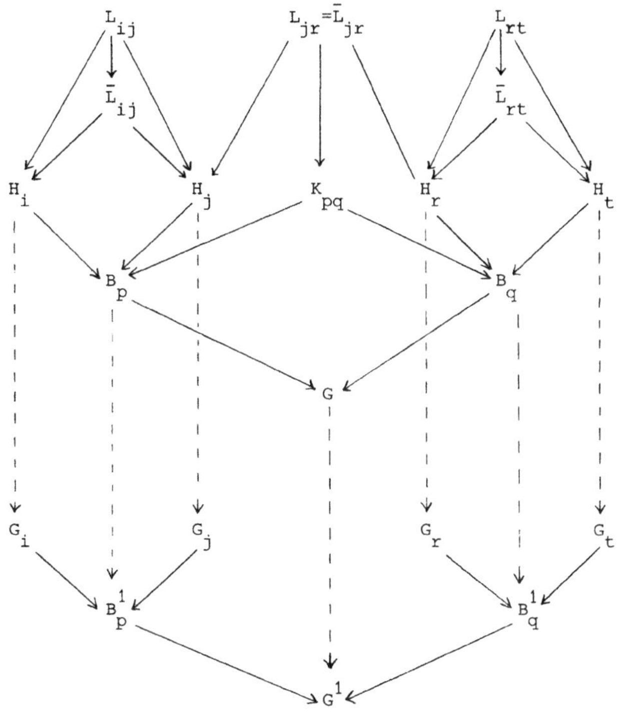

Due to Definitions 5. and 7. let $S_p^1=(G_i \dashleftarrow H_i \longleftarrow L_{ij} \longrightarrow H_j \dashrightarrow G_j)_{m_{p-1}<i<j\leq m_p}$ the daughter-star of B_p such that B_p^1=STAR-GLUING(S_p^1) for all p=1,...,k. On the other hand the daughter-star of G is $\bar{T}=(G_i \dashleftarrow H_i \longleftarrow \bar{L}_{ij} \longrightarrow H_j \dashrightarrow G_j)_{1\leq i<j\leq m}$ such that we have for the derived graph G^1 of G G^1=STAR-GLUING($\bar{T}$). We will show that G^1 is also the star-gluing of $T=(G_i \dashleftarrow H_i \longleftarrow L_{ij} \longrightarrow H_j \dashrightarrow G_j)_{1\leq i<j\leq m}$. Actually the graph-stars $\bar{T}$ and T are built up from the graph-stars HANDLE-STAR(G) and S_{ref} respectively extended by the same production maps $H_i \dashrightarrow G_i$. By Lemma 4. we have STAR-GLUING(HANDLE-STAR(G))=G because each graph in a graph sequence is non-degenerate, and we have shown above G=STAR-GLUING(S_{ref}). Using the universal properties of STAR-GLUING(T) and STAR-GLUING($\bar{T}$) we can show that both are isomorphic such that we also have G^1=STAR-GLUING(T) (see Lemma 8.2). Now let us apply Lemma 9 to graph-stars $S^1=(B_p^1 \dashleftarrow B_p \longleftarrow K_{pq} \longrightarrow B_q \dashrightarrow B_q^1)_{1\leq p<q\leq k}$ and S_p^1 defined above for p=1,...,k leading to the "refined" graph-star $S^1_{ref}=(G_i \dashleftarrow H_i \longleftarrow L_{ij} \longrightarrow H_i \dashrightarrow G_j)_{1\leq i<j\leq m}$. Hence we have by Lemma 9 STAR-GLUING(S^1)=STAR-GLUING(S^1_{ref}). Note that we can apply Lemma 9 because $(POS)_G$ locally pullback and $B_p \dashrightarrow B_p^1$ injective implies by Lemma 8.3 that also the pushout-star of S^1 is locally pullback. Moreover we can use the same L_{jr} as in the graph-star T because the L_{jr} are also pullbacks of the graph morphisms

$G_j \longrightarrow B_p^1 \longrightarrow G^1$ and $G_r \longrightarrow B_q^1 \longrightarrow G^1$. This pullback property of L_{jr} can be shown applying Lemma 8.3 to the handle-star of G and using the universal properties of B_p^1 (resp. B_q^1) to show $G_j \longrightarrow G^1 = G_j \longrightarrow B_p^1 \longrightarrow G^1$ (resp. $G_r \longrightarrow G^1 = G_r \longrightarrow B_q^1 \longrightarrow G^1$). Hence we have $T = S^1_{ref}$.

Summarizing we have

$$\text{STAR-GLUING}(S^1) = \text{STAR-GLUING}(S^1_{ref}) = \text{STAR-GLUING}(T)$$
$$= \text{STAR-GLUING}(\bar{T}) = G^1$$

This completes the proof for the case n=1. For n>1 this step can be iterated because we have shown the same properties for G^1 and S^1 as we have assumed for G and S respectively where the K_{pq} are unchanged. The graph morphisms $K_{pq} \longrightarrow B_p^{n+1}$ in step n+1 are constructed as $K_{pq} \longrightarrow B_p^n \dashrightarrow B_p^{n+1}$. But we have by induction hypothesis $K_{pq} \longrightarrow B_p^n = K_{pq} \longrightarrow B_p \dashrightarrow B_p^n$ and $B_p \dashrightarrow B_p^n \dashrightarrow B_p^{n+1}$ is the derivation map $MAP(B_p \overset{*}{\Longrightarrow} B_p^{n+1}): B_p \dashrightarrow B_p^{n+1}$ such that $K_{pq} \longrightarrow B_p^{n+1} = K_{pq} \longrightarrow B_p \dashrightarrow B_p^{n+1}$. □

As pointed out in the abstract the main aim of this paper is to find a locally star-gluing formula for the graph sequence $G^0, G^1, G^2, \ldots$ of a simple HPG-grammar. In Lemma 10 we have already a similar property provided that the graphs B_p and B_q are predecessors of G in the graph sequence. All the graph-stars S^n are built up from the "fixstar" $((B_p)_N \longleftarrow K_{pq} \longrightarrow (B_q/_N)$ by composition with the derivation maps. In the following we will give a general definition of a locally star-gluing formula together with a generating process independent of simple HPG-grammars where the derivation maps are replaced by gluing morphisms. These gluing morphisms are constructed recursively starting with fixed gluing morphisms given in the star-gluing formula. For more motivation we refer to the introduction of Section 7. in /Eh 78/.

11. DEFINITION (LOCALLY STAR GLUING FORMULA)

1. A <u>locally star gluing formula</u> is a triple STARFORM=(TUP,FIXSTAR,fixmor) consisting of
   - a k-tuple $TUP=(t_1,\ldots,t_k)$ of positive integers
   - a graph star $FIXSTAR=(K_i \longleftarrow K_{ij} \longrightarrow K_j)_{1 \leq i<j \leq k}$, called <u>fixstar</u>, where all the graphs K_i and K_{ij} are discrete
   - a k-tuple $fixmor=(fixmor_1,\ldots,fixmor_k)$ of graph morphisms $fixmor_i: K_i \longrightarrow K$ for $i=1,\ldots,k$, called <u>fixed gluing morphisms</u>, where K is the star gluing of FIXSTAR.
2. Given a locally star gluing formula STARFORM and an integer $p \geq \max\{t_i / i=1,\ldots,k\}$ a graph sequence $(G_n)_{n \in \mathbb{N}_0}$ together with graph morphisms $g_{in}: K_i \longrightarrow G_n$ for $n \geq p-t_i$ and $i=1,\ldots,k$ is called <u>locally star glued with cut p</u>, if, for all $n \geq p$, the following holds:

3. $G_n = \text{STAR GLUING}(G_{n-t_i} \xleftarrow{g_{i,n-t_i}} K_i \longleftarrow K_{ij} \longrightarrow K_j \xrightarrow{g_{j,n-t_j}} G_{n-t_j})_{1 \leq i < j \leq k}$ and for all $i=1,\ldots,k$ and $n \geq p$

4. $K_i \xrightarrow{g_{in}} G_n = K_i \xrightarrow{fixmor_i} K \xrightarrow{g_n} G_n$ where g_n is the unique graph morphism such that the following diagram commutes:

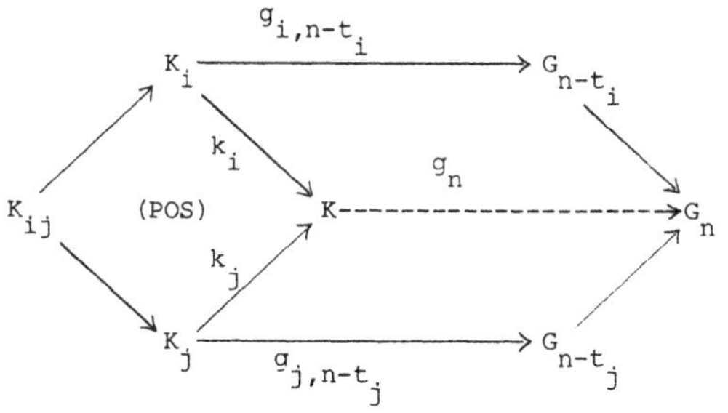

$(1 \leq i < j \leq k)$

The graph morphisms g_{in} will be called <u>gluing morphisms</u> of G_n.

<u>Remark:</u> Note, that in general the graph morphisms $k_i: K_i \longrightarrow K$ in the POS are different from the fixed gluing morphisms $fixmor_i: K_i \longrightarrow K$, and hence $g_{in} \neq g_n \circ k_i$.

A desirable property of such a definition is that we are able to generate graph-sequences for locally star gluing formulas.

12. LEMMA (CONSTRUCTION OF GRAPH SEQUENCES)

Given a locally star gluing formula STARFORM as in 11.1, an integer $p \geq \max\{t_i / i=1,\ldots,k\}$, graphs $G_o,\ldots,G_{p-1}$ and gluing morphisms $g_{in}: K_i \longrightarrow G_n$ for $p-t_i \leq n < p$ and $i=1,\ldots,k$, there exists a unique extension to a graph sequence $(G_n)_{n \in \mathbb{N}_o}$ with gluing morphisms g_{in} for $n \geq p$, $i=1,\ldots,k$ which is locally star glued with cut p.

<u>Proof:</u> The gluing morphisms g_{in} for $n \geq p$ can be iterated by 11.4. □

Now we consider existence and construction of a locally star gluing formula for simple HPG-grammars. First we observe that there exists such a formula iff for some $p > 0$ G_p is the star gluing of graphs G_i' in the graph sequence preceeding G_p.

13. THEOREM (EXISTENCE AND CONSTRUCTION OF LOCALLY STAR GLUING FORMULAS)

Given a simple HPG-grammar with graph sequence $G_o, G_1, G_2, \ldots$ then the following conditions (1) and (2) are equivalent:

(1) There exists a locally star gluing formula STARFORM=(TUP,FIXSTAR,fixmor), an integer $p > 0$ and gluing morphisms $g_{in}: K_i \longrightarrow G_n$

such that the sequence $G_o, G_1, G_2, \ldots$ is locally star glued with cut p.

(2) There exists an integer $p>0$ and a graph star

$$S_p = (G_{p-t_i} \longleftarrow K_{ij} \longrightarrow G_{p-t_j})_{1\leq i<j\leq k}$$

with $1\leq t_i \leq p$ for $i=1,\ldots,k$ and discrete graphs K_{ij} such that G_p=STAR-GLUING(S_p)

<u>Construction:</u> If condition (2) is satisfied the star gluing formula STARFORM and gluing morphisms g_{in} in (1) can be constructed as follows:
Let TUP=$(t_1,\ldots,t_k)$ and K_i be the discrete subgraph of G_{p-t_i} consisting of all nodes such that there is a canonical factorization

$$K_{ij} \longrightarrow G_{p-t_i} = K_{ij} \longrightarrow K_i \longrightarrow G_{p-t_i}$$

Hence we obtain the following fixstar

$$\text{FIXSTAR}=(K_i \longleftarrow K_{ij} \longrightarrow K_j)_{1\leq i<j\leq k}$$

and the gluing morphisms $g_{i,p-t_i}: K_i \longrightarrow G_{p-t_i}$.

For $p-t_i < n \leq p$ we define $g_{in}: K_i \longrightarrow G_n$ to be the derivation map MAP$(G_{p-t_i} \overset{*}{\Longrightarrow} G_n): K_i \longrightarrow (G_n)_N$ followed by the inclusion $(G_n)_N \longrightarrow G_n$. Since K is the gluing of FIXSTAR and $K_i = (G_{p-t_i})_N$ we have $K=(G_p)_N$ and so $g_p: K \longrightarrow G_p$ becomes the inclusion which is bijective on nodes. Hence we can use 11.4 to define fixmor_i by $g_p \circ \text{fixmor}_i = g_{ip}$ for $i=1,\ldots,k$ which completes the construction of STARFORM.

<u>Proof:</u> Clearly (1) implies (2) by Definition 11. Given (2) we define the star gluing formula and gluing morphisms g_{in} for $p-t_i \leq n \leq p$ as given in the construction above. By Lemma 8. we can assume that the star gluing in (2) is locally pullback such that Lemma 10. can be applied.
Hence we have for $n>p$

$$G_n = \text{STAR-GLUING}(G_{n-t_i} \dashleftarrow G_{p-t_i} \longleftarrow K_{ij} \longrightarrow G_{p-t_j} \dashrightarrow G_{n-t_j})_{1\leq i<j\leq k}$$

In order to verify 11.3 and 11.4 it sufficies to show for all $n>p-t_i$ that $g_{in}: K_i \longrightarrow G_n$ is equal to the derivation map $G_{p-t_i} \dashrightarrow G_n$ from $(G_{p-t_i})_N = K_i$ to G_n where for $n>p$ g_{in} is defined by 11.4. For all $p-t_i < n \leq p$ this is true by definition of g_{in} above. Now we will show this property for $n>p$ provided that it is satisfied for all m with $p-t_i < m < n$. In the proof of Lemma 10. the derivation map $G \dashrightarrow G^1$ is uniquely determined by the universal properties of G and the derivation maps $B_p \dashrightarrow B_p^1$. This implies that g_n in 11.4 is the derivation map $G_p \dashrightarrow G_n$ because $g_{i,n-t_i}$ and $g_{j,n-t_j}$ are derivation maps by induction hypothesis (see also /Ld 78/).
Hence we have:

$$K_i \xrightarrow{g_{in}} G_n = K_i \xrightarrow{\text{fixmor}_i} K \xrightarrow{g_n} G_n \qquad \text{(by 11.4)}$$

$$= K_i \xrightarrow{\text{fixmor}_i} K \xrightarrow{g_p} G_p \dashrightarrow G_n \qquad \text{(see above)}$$

$$= K_i \xrightarrow{g_{ip}} G_p \dashrightarrow G_n \qquad \text{(def. of fixmor}_i\text{)}$$

$=G_{p-t_i} \dashrightarrow G_p \dashrightarrow G_n$ (def. of g_{ip})

$=G_{p-t_i} \dashrightarrow G_n$ (def. of composite derivation maps)

which completes the proof. □

Now we are able to attack the main problem: The construction of a locally star gluing formula for a "dependent" simple HPG-grammar. Similar to the string case we define:

14. DEFINITION (DEPENDENT)

Given a simple HPG-grammar as in 6. consider the following dependence graph: The nodes are all the handles and for each handle production $p=(H \longleftarrow K \longrightarrow B)$ and each handle H' of B we have an arc from H to H' in the dependence graph. Now the simple HPG-grammar is called dependent, if each cycle in the dependence graph goes through the axiom H_{ax}.

15. THEOREM (LOCALLY STAR GLUING FORMULAS FOR DEPENDENT SIMPLE HPG-GRAMMARS)

For each dependent simple HPG-grammar with graph sequence $G_o, G_1, G_2, \ldots$ there exists a locally star gluing formula STARFORM=(TUP,FIXSTAR,fixmor) and p>O such that the sequence is locally star glued with cut p, where the gluing morphisms $g_{in}: K_i \longrightarrow G_n$ are given by the derivation maps $MAP(G_{p-t_i} \overset{*}{\Longrightarrow} G_n)$ for $K_i = (G_{p-t_i})_N$, $TUP=(t_1, \ldots, t_k)$, $i=1,\ldots,k$ and $n>p-t_i$.

Construction: The first part of the construction is very similar to the string case. Let p be the maximum of the length of all cycles in the dependence graph. Now we construct the "derivation tree" for the derivation sequence $G_o \Longrightarrow G_1 \Longrightarrow \ldots \Longrightarrow G_p$. The nodes of the derivation tree are colored with handles and for each handle H with production $(H \longleftarrow K \longrightarrow B)$ we have arcs to the handles $H_1, \ldots, H_r$ of B such that in each level n of the derivation tree we have all the handles of G_n (but not the information how to glue them to get G_n). Now for each path from the axiom H_{ax} to a leave in the derivation tree there is - in addition to the root - at least one node colored H_{ax} because of the choice of p. Hence we obtain a collection $n_1, \ldots, n_k$ of nodes in the derivation tree (with distance $t_1, \ldots, t_k$ from the root) such that the subtrees with root $n_1, \ldots, n_k$ are covering the level p of the tree without overlapping. Due to the fact that the handles H_l $(l=1,\ldots,k_i)$ of G_{p-t_i} are also handles of G_p there is a unique graph morphism $G_{p-t_i} \longrightarrow G_p$ such that $H_l \overset{i}{\longrightarrow} G_{p-t_i} \longrightarrow G_p = H_l \rightarrow G_p$ for all $l=1,\ldots,k_i$. Unfortunately the choice of the graph morphisms $H_l \overset{i}{\longrightarrow} G_{p-t_i}$ and $H_l \longrightarrow G_p$ is not uniquely determined if there are handles $H_l = H_{l'}$ for $l \neq l'$.

But there may still be only one graph morphisms $G_{p-t_i} \longrightarrow G_p$, if not the correct choice of this graph morphisms is given by the construction in the proof.
Now let K_{ij} the intersection, or more precisely the pullback in the following diagram

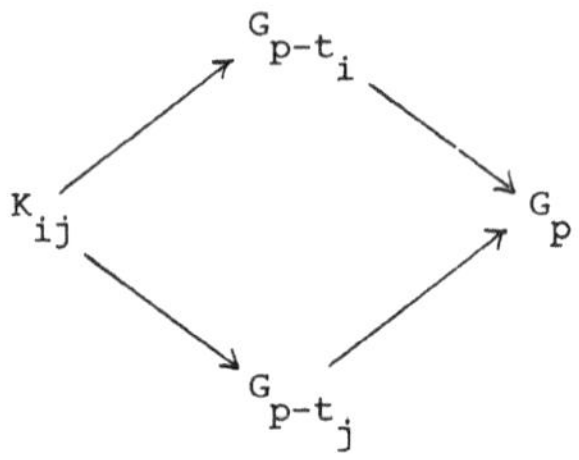

leading to the following GRAPH-star

$$S_p = (G_{p-t_i} \longleftarrow K_{ij} \longrightarrow G_{p-t_j})_{1 \leq i < j \leq k}$$

In fact the star gluing of S_p becomes G_p so that Thm. 13. can be applied to construct the locally star gluing formula for the graph sequence $G_o, G_1, G_2, \ldots$. By construction in Theorem 13. we have $K_i = (G_{p-t_i})_N$ and $g_{in}: K_i \longrightarrow G_n$ is $MAP(G_{p-t_i} \stackrel{*}{\Longrightarrow} G_n)$ followed by the inclusion from $(G_n)_N$ to G_n^1.

<u>Remark:</u> In the construction above it is possible to replace the discrete graphs K_i by those having two nodes only, namely those of the axiom handle, so that g_{in} is given by $MAP(H_{ax} \stackrel{*}{\Longrightarrow} G_n)$.

<u>Proof:</u> It remains to show existence and construction of the graph star S_p above such that the star gluing becomes G_p and the pushout-star is locally pullback.

Let t be the minimum of all the t_i for i=1,...,k and S_t the handle-star of G_t such that $STARGLUING(S_t) = G_t$ by Lemma 4. with pushout-star $(POS)_t$. In the case $t<p$ all handles are axiom handles and we are finished. For $t=p$ due to Lemma 10. we can construct the derived pushout-star $(POS)_t^1$ for G_{t+1}. All graphs derived from the axiom handle in $n \geq 0$ steps will be called stable. (Since there is at least one axiom handle in S_t at least one graph in $(POS)_t^1$ is stable.) For each nonstable gluing graph in the graph-star of $(POS)_t^1$ we construct the handle-star (and for each stable graph the trivial star of degree 1) such that by Lemma 9. we obtain a refined pushout-star $(POS)_{t+1}$ of $(POS)_t^1$ with the same star-gluing G_{t+1}, which can be assumed to be locally pullback after application of Lemma 8.1.
If $t+1<p$ the same construction is repeated: First the derived star is constructed by Lemma 10., then the refined graph star by Lemma 9., where only for nonstable graphs the handle-star is used, and then a locally pullback pushout-star $(POS)_{t+2}$ with star gluing G_{t+2}.

After m=p-t steps all gluing graphs in S_p are stable because the level p of the derivation tree was covered by the subtrees with root $n_1,\ldots,n_k$ respectively. More precisely the gluing graphs in S_p are the derived graphs of the axiom handles in $n_1,\ldots,n_k$ in $p-t_1,\ldots, p-t_k$ steps respectively. That means the gluing graphs in S_p are $G_{p-t_1},\ldots,G_{p-t_k}$ and the stargluing is G_p. □

An example for Theorem 15. is given in 7.7 of /EH 78/ but not for the construction of a graph-star S_p for G_p in the proof of Theorem 15. This will be done in the following example:

16. EXAMPLE

Assume that we have a simple HPG-grammar with the following dependence graph and derivation tree respectively:

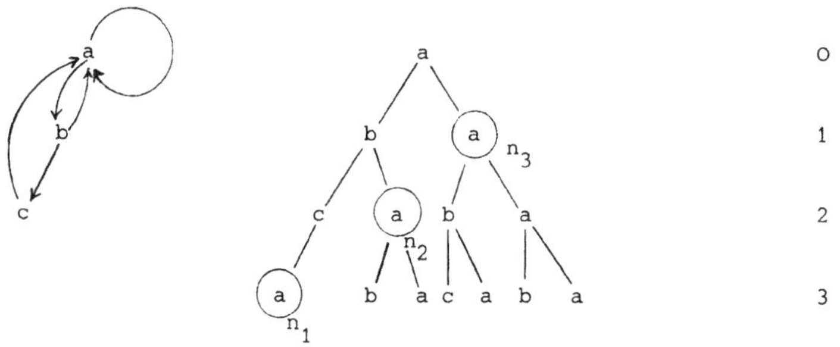

Then p=3 and the level 3 is covered by the subtrees with root n_1, n_2 and n_3 respectively. Then we first construct the handle-star of G_1 in level 1 consisting of the handles H_b and H_a. In the derived graph star with gluing graphs H_b^1 and H_a^1 we construct the handle star of H_b^1 with handles H_c and H_a while H_a^1 is stable to obtain the refined pushout star for G_2 with gluing graphs H_c, H_a and H_a^1. Finally the derived pushout star for G_3 consists of the gluing graphs H_a, H_a^1 and H_a^2 which are the graphs $G_{p-t_1}=G_o$, $G_{p-t_2}=G_1$, and $G_{p-t_3}=G_2$ respectively.

Finally we will show that it is possible to find a slightly more simple star gluing formula as that given in Theorem 15. But there are also examples for simple HPG-grammars satisfying only the more general version (see Example 18.)

17. REMARK (SIMPLIFICATION OF LOCALLY STAR GLUING FORMULAS)

It can be proved that all dependent simple HPG-grammars are locally star glued with a cut p>O with a locally star gluing formula STARFORM=(TUP,FIXSTAR,fixmor) satisfying the following two properties:

1) In the star graph FIXSTAR=$(K_i \longleftarrow K_{ij} \longrightarrow K_j)_{1\leq i<j\leq k}$ we have constant gluing graphs $K_i = (H_{ax})_N$.

2) $fixmor_i = fixmor_j$ for all i,j=1,...,k.

For each graph G_n of a graph sequence $(G_n)_{n\in \mathbb{N}_0}$ generated by a simple HPG-grammar there is the graph morphism $(H_{ax})_N \longrightarrow G_n$ and the morphism i the composition of the derivation map $H_{ax} \dashrightarrow G_n$ and the inclusion $(G_n)_N \longrightarrow G_n$. This might lead to the conclusion that each locally star gluing formula has always the properties 1) and 2) of Remark 17. Unfortunately this is not true. To show that consider the following example.

18. EXAMPLE

Given the simple HPG-grammar $Q=(C,H\text{-}Prod,C_{ax})$ with

$C=(C_A,C_N)$, $C_A = \{a,b,c,d,e\}$ and $C_N = \{\bullet\}$,

$C_{ax} = \bullet \xrightarrow{a} \bullet$ and the handle-productions:

$$p_1 = a \ \uparrow^t_s \Longrightarrow b \ \uparrow^t_s \quad ; \quad p_2 = b \ \uparrow^t_s \Longrightarrow c \ \uparrow^t_s \quad ; \quad p_3 = c \ \uparrow^t_s \Longrightarrow \bullet \xrightarrow{\ d\ }{}_s \bullet \xrightarrow{\ e\ }{}_t$$

$$p_4 = d \ \uparrow^t_s \Longrightarrow {}_a \nearrow \xrightarrow{\ d\ } {}^t \searrow {}_b \quad ; \quad p_5 = e \ \uparrow^t_s \Longrightarrow \bullet \xrightarrow{\ e\ }{}_s \bullet \ {}_t \circlearrowleft c$$

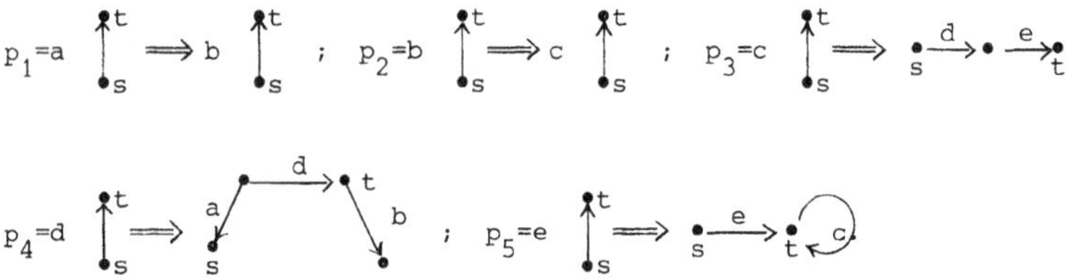

Note that this grammar is not dependent.

We get the following graph sequence:

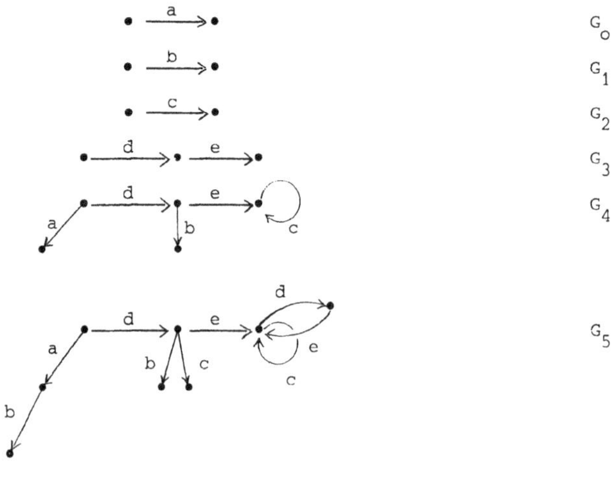

The graph G_4 can be defined as a star gluing of G_0, G_1, G_2 and G_3. Using Theorem 13. we find that the sequence is locally star glued with cut p=4. But in this analysis the graph G_3 is glued in three items. Therefore there must exist a gluing graph K_i in the fixstar of the locally star gluing formula, which has three nodes: $K_i = (G_3)_N$.

REFERENCES

/CuLi 76/ Culik, K. II./Lindenmayer, A.: Parallel Rewriting on Graphs and Multidimensional Development, Int. Journ. of Gen. Systems 3, 53-66 (1976)

/Eh 78/ Ehrig, H.: Introduction to the Algebraic Theory of Grammars, Proc. International Workshop on Graph Grammars and Their Applications to Computer Science and Biology, Bad Honnef 1978

/EhKr 76/ Ehrig, H./Kreowski, H.-J.: Parallel Graph Grammars, in A. Lindenmayer/G. Rozenberg(eds.): Automata, Languages, Development, 425-442, Amsterdam: North Holland 1976

/EhRb 76/ Ehrig, H./Rozenberg, G.: Some Definitional Suggestions for Graph Grammars, in A. Lindenmayer/G. Rozenberg (eds.): Automata, Languages, Development, 443-468, Amsterdam: North Holland 1976

/HeRb 75/ Herman, G.T./Rozenberg, G.: Developmental Systems and Languages, North Holland, Amsterdam, 1975

/Ld 78/ Liedtke, A.: Lokale Sternverklebungen in der Algebraischen Theorie paralleler Graph-Grammatiken, Diplomarbeit, TU Berlin (1978)

TRANSFORMATIONS OF DATA BASE STRUCTURES

A.L. Furtado
Departamento de Informática
Pontifícia Universidade Católica do R.J.
Brasil

ABSTRACT

Many of the existing data base models have an underlying graph structure. Even certain models based on set theory rather than graph theory are translatable into some graph representation, an important example being the relational model.

Graphs are used to represent the data base at the schema or at the instances level. Also, the representation may refer to conceptual elements, such as entities, attributes, relationships, or to implementational elements, such as files, records, items, links.

In any case, one wishes to characterize the valid configurations, and the allowable operations which tranform one configuration into another one. Valid configurations are those that conform to the integrity constraints declared for the particular data base.

In this work we investigate the use of graph grammars for the specification of data base operations, in ways that preserve the imposed integrity constraints.

1. INTRODUCTION

Several data base models have an underlying graph structure, whereas other models have been described through algebraic concepts [1]. The relational model belongs to the second class; according to the relational model, a data base is a collection of relations, where each relation is a set of tuples.

More precisely, given n domains $D_1,D_2,\dots,D_n$ not necessarily distinct, an n-ary relation is any subset $R \subseteq D_1 x\ D_2 x \dots x\ D_n$, where "x" denotes the Cartesian product. The members of the set $D_1 x\ D_2 x\ \dots\ x\ D_n$ are called n-tuples or simply tuples.

This simple organization has been constrasted to the complex graph structures arising in the network model. Conceptually, if an item of information a is related to two other items b and c the situtation would be represented in the network model as three nodes a, b, c, with edges connecting a and b, and a and c. In the relational model one does not utilize edges; there would be two tuples (a,b) and (a,c) noting that the item a would appear twice.

However, one sort of link still remains in the relational model. The values of data items must be compared to decide whether certain updates on tuples shall or shall not be performed (the conditions of the operation) and which other tuples would be affected (the side-effects of the operation). Such testing is also involved, of course, in simply searching for a tuple.

Such "virtual" comparison links may lead to rather complex configurations that become unclear if we insist in staying with a one-dimensional programming notation. High-level relational languages, such as Sequel and Square, performed badly with the features created for this purpose - correlation variables and free variables - in human factors studies [2].

In fact, Square goes part of the way towards a two-dimensional structure. Other relational languages have been proposed going farther in this direction, namely Query by example [3] and especially Cupid [4]. In Cupid the comparison links are drawn as edges, a graphics support system being used.

In the present work we shall use graph-grammars for expressing update operations on tuples. A tuple will be represented as a two-level tree, where the root is labelled after the name of the relation and the leaves after the names to which its components (values of data items) belong. The trees will be disjoint except for the (virtual) edges denoting the comparisons to be performed.

Gathering in one grammar all the update operations admitted on a given data base allows us to verify whether the generated data base configurations will be exactly the valid ones. By a valid configuration we mean one that obeys all the declared integrity constraints [5]; indeed the reason for including conditions and side effects in an update operation is to guarantee that the integrity constraints be preserved.

For clarity, we base the presentation on a simple example, through which the beginnings of a notation are given in section 2, and used to formulate a grammar in section 3. Section 4 contains conclusions and suggestions for further research.

2. NOTATION AND ASSUMPTIONS

The organization of a particular data base is described in its schema. An important section of the schema, when the relational model is adopted, is the enumeration of the relations and domains involved.

Consider a simple data base with domains:

N - names

S - salaries

J - jobtitles

K - skills

T - tasks

and relations:

EMP $\subseteq$ N x S x J - names, salaries and jobtitles of hired employees

CAP $\subseteq$ N x K - skills possessed by employees

REQ $\subseteq$ T x K - requirement of skills to perform tasks

ASN $\subseteq$ N x T - assignment of employees to tasks

We can represent this organization by figure 1, where the edges connect the relations to the participating domains, and where domains shared by two or more relations have more than one edge incident to them.

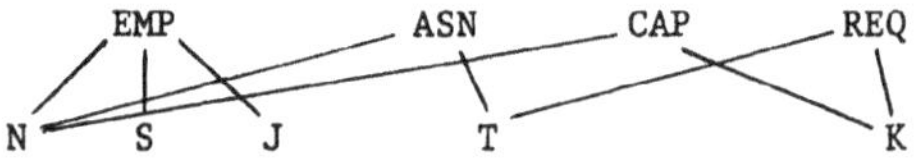

Figure 1

The schema is stored in a special space called data directory, which may be regarded as a meta data-base (since it conveys information about a data base). In the data base itself are stored the individual tuples of each relation; they are called instances of the schema; we shall represent them in a way analogous to figure 1, using however small letters for writing the node labels, and recalling that tuples are seen as disjoint two-level trees (figure 2).

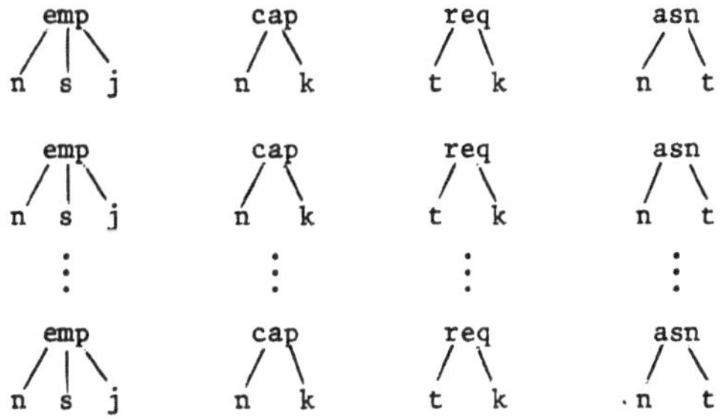

Figure 2

We shall call tuple-nodes the nodes labelled after the relation names, and item-nodes the nodes labelled after the domain names. Tuple-nodes are connected to item-nodes through component-edges. Values stored at the item-nodes are not represented. They are assumed to exist however, and it may happen that different item-nodes have (a copy of) the same value; tuples of the same relation cannot be identical, in the sense of having the same values in all item-nodes corresponding to each domain, because, relations being defined as sets, duplicate tuples are not allowed.

An update operation involves inserting, deleting, or modifying a tuple; modifying a tuple means that the values of certain item-nodes are rewritten, the effect being equivalent to a deletion followed by an insertion.

In a real environment updates make sense only when selected tuples are involved, and, in order to perform the selection, tests on the values in item-nodes must be done. As noted, we did not represent the values in the tuples, but they will be introduced, among other elements, in our notation for patterns, which will be described in the sequel.

Any tuple can be used in a pattern. In addition:

1. special nodes labelled with values (value-nodes) are permitted;
2. the item-nodes of a tuple do not have to be all represented;
3. component-edges (connecting tuple-nodes to item-nodes) may be drawn
   - with interrupted lines,
   - with slashed lines,
   - having a triangular shape;
4. edges between item-nodes, or item-nodes and value-nodes, (comparison-edges) are permitted, labelled with some comparison operator, and having an arrowhead whenever the expressed comparison is not symmetric;
5. node denotations [6], which are numbers associated with item-nodes, are used to distinguish, when necessary, item-nodes having the same label.

Our notation also needs the notion of parameter lists, which are sets of two-level trees each having its root labelled after a domain name, linked to a single square-shaped parameter-node.

A production rule has the form

$\langle\text{parameter list}\rangle\text{: }\langle\ell\text{hs}\rangle \Longrightarrow \langle\text{rhs}\rangle$

where ℓhs (left hand side) and rhs (right hand side) are both patterns, with the restriction that value-nodes and comparison-edges do not appear in rhs patterns.

Production rules are exemplified in section 3 (figures 5 and 6); the reader may find it helpful to look at the examples as he proceeds through the remaining of this section.

The application of a production rule to a data base must be preceded by the assignment of values to all parameter-nodes. One might say that only after this assignment we have real productions rather than production schemes (cf. the Post Production Systems [7]).

The application of a production rule (with all parameter-nodes "filled in") is processed in two phases; matching and replacement. We begin by explaining the first phase.

As happens with graph grammars in general, matching involves a search through the entire graph (here, the data base) looking for a sub-graph that meets the conditions expressed in the ℓhs of the production rule; if this happens, the sub-graph is said to match the ℓhs.

Every tuple in the ℓhs appears with its tuple-node, hence the relation to which a matching tuple in the data base should belong is always indicated. On the other hand, only item-nodes to be tested need be included.

The tests on values possessed by item-nodes of matching tuples are indicated in the ℓhs by:

a. the correspondence between parameters, with assigned values, and ℓhs item-nodes with the same label (and denotation), requiring item-nodes of matching tuples to possess such values;

b. comparisons expressed through comparison-edges connecting item-nodes, requiring the successful corresponding comparison between the values of item-nodes of matching tuples;

c. in a similar way, comparisons expressed through comparison-edges connecting item-nodes to value-nodes.

For simplifying the drawings, we adopt the convention that, whenever two (or more) ℓhs item-nodes have the same label and are linked by a comparison edge expressing equality, we shall represent them as a single item-node (we shall also allow this representation in the rhs). Figure 3(a) shows what we mean by the notation in 3(b).

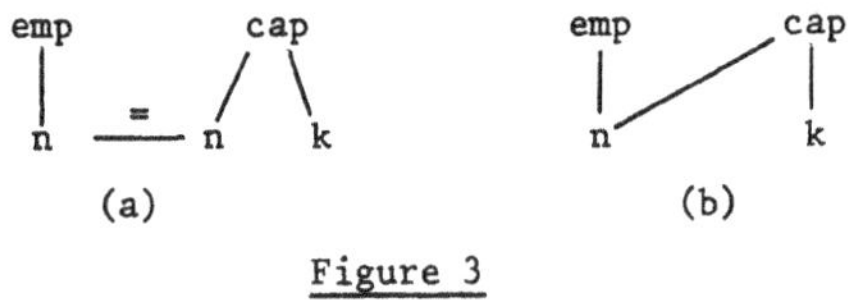

Figure 3

Testing is affected if one of the special notations for component-edges are used:

a. slashed lines indicate that there must be no such tuple (a negative applicability condition [8]);

b. interrupted lines indicate that the tuple may or may not be present; thus this test does not influence the success or failure of the matching phase, but will produce an effect in the replacement phase;

c. triangular lines indicate that sets of tuples are involved, and allow set comparisons on grouped item-nodes.

The third feature deserves further explanation. Suppose that we want to consider all skills required for performing a given task 't'. Such skills would be found as the values in K item-nodes of possibly several tuples from REQ, all having the same value 't' in the T item-nodes. Figure 4(a) shows what we mean by the notation in 4(b).

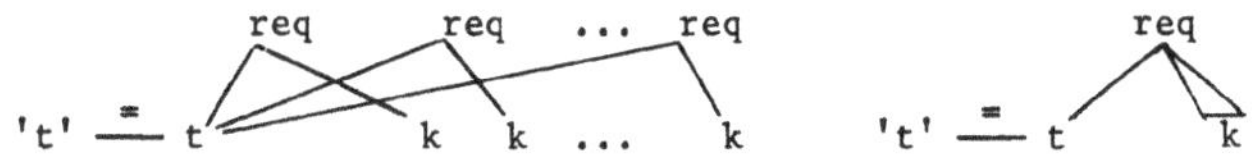

(a) (b)

Figure 4

The process of finding such tuples from REQ consists of partitioning [9] REQ by the domain T, so that tuples corresponding to the same task are placed in the same block, and then selecting the block corresponding to task 't'. Now it becomes possible to consider the set of skills in the selected block and use the set in some test, as we shall do in section 3. Partitioning provides one convenient way to handle situations that in the relational calculus require universal quantifiers [5].

We now turn to the replacement phase. Again, as usual with graph grammars, this phase involves the substitution of a sub-graph created in correspondence with the rhs for the sub-graph located in the matching phase. The determination of the replacing sub-graph depends on information supplied in the parameter list and also on information obtained during the matching phase. Gluing [6] or embedding [8] the replacing sub-graph is trivial, since only disjoint trees are really involved.

The result of the replacement phase can only involve the insertion, deletion, and modification of tuples. Tuple-nodes mentioned in both the ℓhs and the rhs are kept; those appearing only in the ℓhs are deleted, and those appearing only in the rhs are created. Modification occurs with tuples that are kept but appear with different denotations on corresponding item-nodes in the ℓhs and rhs. Tuples with component-edges drawn with interrupted lines do not constitute conditions in the matching phase, as noted, but matching tuples (if any) found in correspondence to them are affected in the same way just described.

3. SPECIFYING DATA BASE OPERATIONS

Suppose the following integrity constraints have been imposed for the data base used as an example:

1. an employee must have exactly one salary and one jobtitle;

2. salaries must be at least equal to the minimum wage 'm';

3. information about skills of an employee is of interest only as long as he stays in the company;

4. only current employees can be assigned to tasks;

5. an employee can only be assigned to a task if, at the moment when he is assigned, he possesses all the skills then required for the task;

6. at least one skill is required for each task;

7. while an employee is attached to at least one task he cannot be fired.

And now consider the following operations as the only updates that can be performed on the data base, being useable as "routines" to be called from an arbitrary number of application programs:

1. hire (n,s,j) - hire employee n with salary s and jobtitle j;

2. learn (n,k) - register the fact that employee n learned (or already possessed when hired) skill k;

3. require (t,k) - require skill k for the execution of task t;

4. assign (n,t) - assign employee n to task t;

5. release (n,t) - release employee n from task t;

6. fire (n) - fire employee n.

Due to the constraints, these operations cannot always be executed, depending on appropriate conditions; also, when executed, certain complementary or compensatory side - effects must take place. Such conditions and side-effects will be incorporated in the production rules to be introduced.

First, let us consider a preliminary operation that "opens" the data base by declaring its schema, which may be thought to be inserted into a data directory. The corresponding production rule appears in figure 5. S_α represents the start symbol of the grammar designed for our example data base α.

0. $S_\alpha \Longrightarrow$

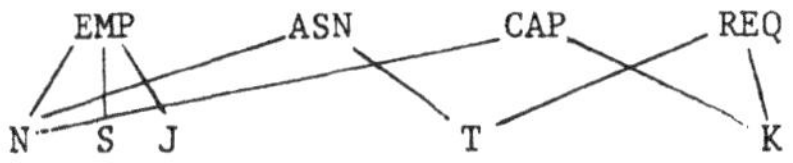

Figure 5

The rhs of production rule 0 is assumed to be part of the ℓhs and rhs of all the other production rules, which are given in figure 6, each one corresponding to one of the described operations. The reader is urged to remark the conditions and side-effects incorporated in the production rules.

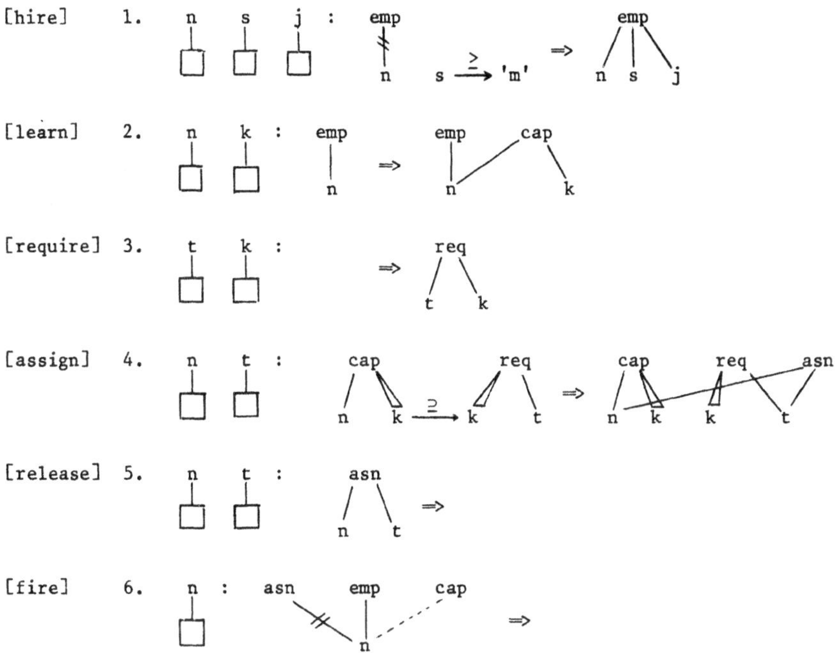

Figure 6

That this grammar generates exactly the intended data base can be verified in two steps:

1. all valid configurations can be generated. Having generated a data base with m tuples it is always possible to insert another tuple belonging to any of the four relations, unless this would violate some of the stated constraints. Production rule 1 will add a new tuple to EMP, except if there already exists a tuple with n (constraint 1) or if s is less than 'm' (constraint 2). Production rule 2 will add a tuple to CAP, except if n is not currently an employee (constraint 3). Production rule 3 will add a tuple to REQ. Production rule 4 will add a tuple to ASN, except if n is not an employee (constraint 4) having all skills required for task t (constraints 5 and 6).

Also, given any valid configuration, it is possible to find a sequence of applications of production rules leading to its generation. For example, a configuration containing a tuple with n and t in ASN, for any n and t, can be generated through suitable applications of production rule 1 (once), followed by production rule 2 (as often as there are tuples with t in REQ), followed by production rule 4 (once).

It is easy to show that any configurations that can be generated by sequences of applications including production rules 5 and 6 can be generated by sequences of applications not including them (see the notion of a constructor set of operators in [10]).

2. only valid configurations can be generated. Assuming that at a stage s of derivation one has a valid configuration, it is easy to show that the application of any of the production rules applicable at such stage will lead to a configuration that is also valid. This is done by checking that configurations violating any of the constraints cannot be generated. Take, for example, constraint 3; a tuple with n and k can only be created by production rule 2, which tests if n is a hired employee; on the other hand, n can only cease to be an employee through production rule 6, which as a side effect deletes all tuples containing skills of n from CAP. In turn this implies that if n appears in CAP then n must also appear in EMP, and we do not need to check constraint 4 in production rule 4; in fact, as the reader may note, constraint 4 is not independent, being a consequence of other constraints. Constraint 7 is enforced by the condition in production rule 6 that an employee n to be fired must not appear in any tuple of ASN; if he does, a stage can still be reached where, by deleting the ASN tuples through applications of production rule 5, constraint 7 would no longer be violated.

One especially difficult issue is to ensure that precisely the verbally stated constraints are enforced, given the ambiguities of natural language. We do not wish to impose weaker or stronger constraints than the intended ones, but misunderstandings may occur.

Note in particular that constraint 5, as phrased, is quite different from

5'. an employee can only be and stay assigned to a task if he possesses all skills required for the task.

The grammar that we present does not enforce this stronger constraint 5', because, after an assignment of n to t, further applications of production rule 3 may require new skills, not possessed by n, for executing t.

While showing one way for enforcing 5', we shall mention a number of useful concepts that we had not introduced yet.

Additional production rules will be used (figure 7).

7.

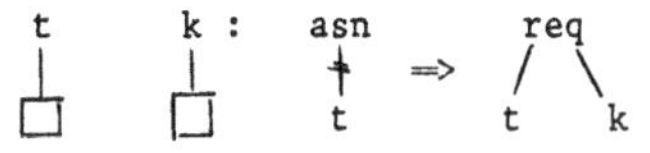

8.

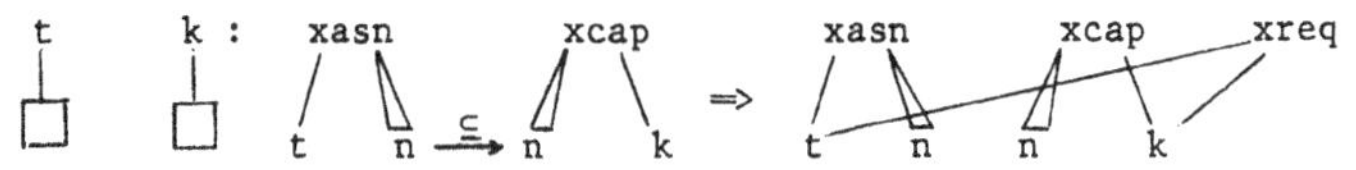

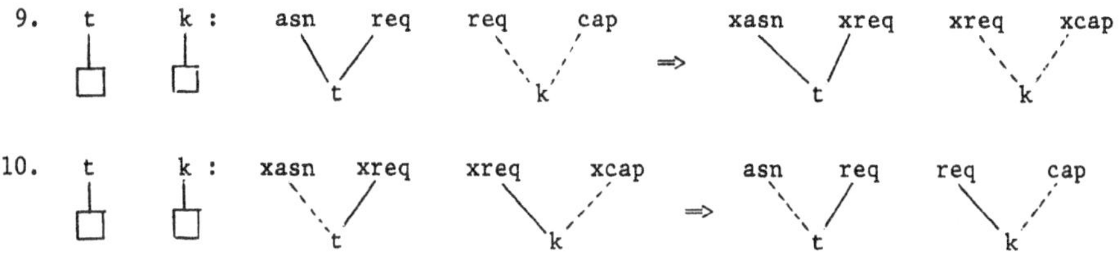

Figure 7

Until now we had not distinguished between terminal and nonterminal node labels. All node labels that we have been using can appear in a valid configuration, and in this sense are terminal; since we can transform a valid configuration into another valid configuration, some node labels must be also regarded as nonterminal in the sense that they can be replaced. We might say that the node labels in the schema are both terminal and nonterminal, and that their presence is the justification for adding tuples of the corresponding types to the data base (the notion of populating the schema in [11]); also terminal and nonterminal are the node labels in tuples that can be deleted. Thus, in these grammars, the sets of terminals and nonterminals need not be disjoint.

The case where a nonterminal is not also a terminal has an interesting interpretation here. Node labels such as xasn, xreq, xcap in production rules 8, 9 and 10 can be added or deleted (i.e. are nonterminal) and characterize a temporarily invalid configuration (i.e. are not terminal). We use them to indicate that all tuples in ASN, REQ and CAP having the given values for t and/or k are locked (unaccessible to other concurrent users).

Locking must be indicated whenever an operation cannot be specified by a single production rule. The strategy that we propose in order to enforce 5' involves replacing production rule 3 by a programmed sequence of production rules [6,12], as follows:

1. apply 7; if the application succeeds, exit, else continue;

2. apply 9;

3. until 8 is applicable
   3.1. apply 2' zero or more times;
   3.2. apply 5' zero or more times;
   [2' and 5' are like 2 and 5 with xcap and xasn substituted for cap and asn]

4. apply 8;

5. apply 10.

In words: if nobody is currently assigned to task t, the requirement of k can be safely made; otherwise a sequence of steps is initiated, which begins by locking the "sensitive" part of the data base, and proceeds by considering each employee assigned to t who does not possess skill k and either declaring that he has learned the skill or releasing him from the task; when all employees that remain assigned possess the task, the requirement of k for t is recorded and the locking is disabled.

The evolution of the data base may dictate other changes to the grammar. For example, the minimum wage appearing as a constant in production rule 1 may be raised. This would require that production rule 1 be rewritten, and also that the new production rule of figure 8 be applied to all current employees (note the need for node denotations, shown as subscripts of node labels).

11.

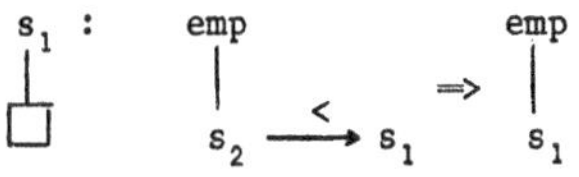

Figure 8

As anticipated in the introduction, we have presented only the beginnings of a notation. Possible additions include the representation of set unions and the superposition of and/or trees.

4. CONCLUDING REMARKS

The proposed notation is still incomplete, but we feel that it is sufficient to demonstrate the feasibility of a formalism for the conceptual characterization of data bases. By allowing one to specify the operations that end users will be authorized to perform, in such a way that integrity constraints are preserved, the formalism also provides part of the mapping from the conceptual to the external schemas, in the terminology of [13].

Another line of investigation might consider the mapping from the conceptual to the internal schema [13], still using graph grammars. Suppose that a grammar G, of the kind we have been discussing here, is used to transform some conceptual configuration C into another equally valid conceptual configuration C'. Both C and C' must have some internal representation, say I and I' respectively, and we might design some graph grammar H able to specify the transformation of I into I'. Also the conversion of C into I and C' into I' would be specified by the (same) grammar T, which would correspond to a transducer [14] (a category theorist might find place for a functor here [15]). Verifying that all these grammars can be composed so that the data base has the intended behavior is equivalent to proving that the diagram in figure 9 commutes [16].

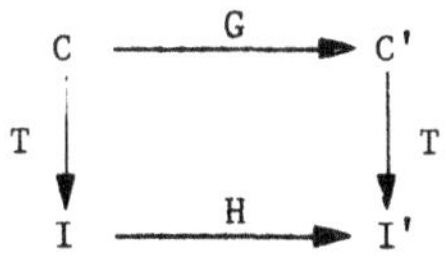

Figure 9

Alternatively, the translation of the operations themselves might be investigated, which would be performed through another grammar $\hat{T}$, also behaving as a transducer, taking, as input, pairs of patterns (ℓhs, rhs) from G and yielding pairs that would constitute H.

The development of the formalism into a language may also be a useful effort. We have shown how update operations can be represented; the simpler case of interrogate operations is analogous to the matching phase of the application of a production rule (with the ℓhs pattern only) with the sole purpose of making available the values of certain of the located nodes.

ACKNOWLEDGMENTS

The author is grateful to P.A. Veloso who made many valuable suggestions, and to D. Bovet for helpful comments. He is indebted to N. Ziviani for several features of the proposed notation, and to K.C. Sevcik who participated in another stage of this research. Financial help from IBM do Brasil is gratefully acknowledged.

REFERENCES

1. Kerschberg, L., Klug, A. and Tsichritzis, D. - "A taxonomy of data models" - Proc. of the Very Large Data Bases Conference (1976).
2. Reisner, P. - "Use of psychological experimentation as an aid to development of a query language" - IEEE Transactions on Software Engineering, SE-3,3 (1977) 218-229.
3. Zloof, M.M. - "Query by example" - Proc. of National Computer Conference (1975).
4. Mc Donald, N. and Stonebraker, M. - "Cupid: the friendly query language" - Proc. of ACM Pacific Conference (1975).
5. Date, C.J. - "An introduction to data-base systems" - Addison-Wesley (1975).
6. Schneider, H.J. - "Conceptual data base description using graph-grammars" - in "Graphen, Algorithmen, Datenstrukturen" - Noltemeier (ed.) - C. Hanser Verlag (1976).

7. Brainerd, W.S. and Landweber, L.H. - "Theory of Computation" - John Wiley (1974).

8. Montanari, U. - "Separable graphs and web grammars" - Information and Control 16 (1970) 243-267.

9. Furtado, A.L. and Kerschberg, L. - "An algebra of quotient relations" - Proc. of the SIGMOD Conference (1977).

10. Guttag, J.V. and Horowitz, E. - "The design of data type specifications" - in "Current trends in programming methodology" v. IV - Yeh (ed.) - Prentice-Hall (1978).

11. CODASYL Systems Committee - "Feature analysis of generalized data base management systems" - report (1971).

12. Rosenkrantz, D.J. - "Programmed grammars and classes of formal languages" - JACM 16 (1969) 107-131.

13. ANSI/X3/SPARC Study Group - interim report - bulletin FDT of ACM SIGMOD 7,2 (1975).

14. Booth, T.L. - "Sequential machines and automata theory" - John Wiley (1967).

15. Goguen, J.A. et al - "An introduction to categories, algebraic theories and algebras" - IBM report RC 5369 (1975).

16. Paolini, P. and Pelagatti, G. - "Formal definition of mappings in a data base" - Proc. of the SIGMOD Conference (1977).

EXPLICIT VERSUS IMPLICIT PARALLEL REWRITING ON GRAPHS

Eberhard Grötsch
Siemens AG
E STE 374, Forschungszentrum,
Günther-Scharowsky-Str. 1
D-8520 Erlangen

Manfred Nagl
Universität Erlangen-Nürnberg
Lehrstuhl f. Programmiersprachen
Martensstr. 3
D-8520 Erlangen

ABSTRACT

For the definition of parallel rewriting systems on graphs there are two different classes of approaches in literature which we call explicit and implicit in the following. In explicit approaches besides replacement rules governing which graph is to be replaced by which one, connection rules are introduced which define the connections between the inserted graphs. In implicit systems, graph replacement rules have a third component, called connection transformation, which provides for connecting the edges. Common to all parallel rewriting systems is that in any direct derivation step the whole host graph is rewritten. In the following several explicit and implicit approaches are compared with respect to their generative power. This leads to a hierarchy of graph languages generated by parallel graph rewriting systems.

1. INTRODUCTION

Parallel rewriting systems on graphs, called graph L-systems, GL-systems or parallel graph grammars, have been introduced with the same motivation as common L-systems, namely to describe the development of regularly growing organisms. While in common L-systems the shape of the organism is coded by a string, in GL-systems this coding is done by a directed graph with labelled nodes and edges. The nodes correspond to the cells of the organism, the different types of which are indicated by different node labels while the labelled directed edges correspond to different relations between the cells. A GL-system describing the development of an organism is a generative device which, starting with an axiom graph, generates an infinite sequence of labelled graphs coding the organism during the steps of development. As strings can only be used to code linear or tree-like structures in a simple way, usual L-systems are restricted to describe the development of filamentous organisms. This restriction does not hold for GL-systems.

The graph substitution in GL-systems is done in parallel, i.e. all one-node subgraphs of a graph g are replaced by other graphs according to a finite set of rules. These rules have to specify which one-node subgraph of g (mother node) is to be substituted by which graph (daughter graph) and which edges between daughter graphs have to be generated in order to get the graph g' which is a direct derivation of g. There are various ways to define these rules for substitution and connection, which nearly all can be found in /LiRb76/. In the following two different approaches to GL-systems are studied in more detail.

In *explicit* GL-systems (in the sequel indicated by the prefix "e-") as defined in /CuLi74/ we have two kinds of rules, replacement rules and connection rules. Each replacement rule $r=(\mathfrak{g}_m, \mathfrak{g}_d)$ consists of a single node $\mathfrak{g}_m$ as left hand side and a graph $\mathfrak{g}_d$ as right hand side. Thus, replacement rules specify the graphs which are substituted for the nodes of g. To generate the connecting edges between daughter graphs connection rules of the form $c=(\mathfrak{g}_e, \mathfrak{g}_{st})$ are used. The left hand side of a connection rule is an edge (mother edge), the right hand side is a graph, called stencil. This stencil $\mathfrak{g}_{st}$ is a bipartite graph divided into a source graph, a target graph and edges which connect nodes of these two subgraphs. These connecting edges link the daughter graphs together which are inserted for the two mother nodes of the mother edge, if the source graph is embedded in the daughter graph substituted for the source node of the mother edge, and if the target graph is embedded in the daughter graph substituted for the target node of the mother edge. Thus, in a direct derivation step $\mathfrak{g} \rightarrow \mathfrak{g}'$ all nodes of $\mathfrak{g}$

have to be substituted by replacement rules and all edges of g by connection rules. The GL-systems as definied in /CuLi74/ contain an environment node and are defined with a maximality condition which, roughly spoken, means that a connection rule c must not be applied if there is another applicable one, c', the stencil of which contains the stencil of c. Systems in the above sense are abbreviated as e-max-env-GL-systems. In /Na76b/ a simplified version of these explicit systems was defined which avoids the "open hands" and "matching hands" mechanism and the environment node of /CuLi74/. These systems are called e-GL-systems and with maximality condition e-max-GL-systems, respectively. In /EhRb76/ the reader can find another simplification of /CuLi74/.

In *implicit* systems (in the following indicated by the prefix "i-") as defined in /Na76a/ there is only one type of rules of the form $p=(g_m, g_d, C)$ with g_m and g_d being the mother node and the daughter graph if the rule is actualized and a third part C called connection transformation. This connection transformation is an algorithmic specification which determines how to connect daughter graphs, depending on the connection between mother nodes. For edges of a certain label going into the daughter graph g_d, C spezifies the target nodes for these edges. Moreover, C has to determine those daughter graphs where these edges are to come from. The latter determination is done in the graph before the derivation step is applied, by specifying the corresponding mother nodes. For that /Na76a/ contains a very powerful method for determination of subsets of the node set of a labelled graph. Analogously outgoing edges of g_d are handled. Thus, the connection transformation can be considered as specifying half-edges of a certain label, and a labelled edge between two daughter graphs is inserted iff two half edges of the same label fit together.

The language of an explicit or implicit GL-system G is defined as the set of all graphs derivable from the axiom graph in 0,1,2,... steps. Both i-GL-systems and e-GL- (or e-max-GL-systems) can be generalized to extended systems (abbr. i-EGL- and e-EGL-systems). This means that the node and the edge label alphabet is splitted into a terminal and a nonterminal one. The language of an EGL-system contains only those graphs derivable in G, all node labels and all edge labels of which are terminal.

If *A* is an abbreviation for the class of languages of systems of type A then the following results for language classes hold true (for further results see /Gr76/):

$$\begin{array}{ccccccc}
i\text{-}depth1\text{-}EGL & \subsetneq & e\text{-}max\text{-}env\text{-}EGL \;=\; e\text{-}EGL & \subsetneq & i\text{-}EGL \;=\; e\text{-}context\text{-}EGL \\
 & & \cup \qquad\qquad \cup & & \cup \\
 & & e\text{-}max\text{-}GL \quad \not\subseteq,\ \not\supseteq & & i\text{-}GL \\
 & & \cup \qquad\qquad \cup & & \\
 & & e\text{-}max\text{-}env\text{-}GL \quad \not\subseteq,\ \not\supseteq \quad e\text{-}GL & &
\end{array}$$

Here depthl in *i-depth1-EGL* means that the connection transformation is restricted to direct neighbourhood. Furthermore, e-context-EGL-systems are e-EGL-systems where connection rules with an additional node and edge as context condition occur. The parallel rewriting systems considered in this paper are a special case in the sense that in a rewriting step only single nodes are replaced instead of arbitrary graphs. Therefore, they are classified as *node substitution* rewriting systems in the introductory paper of this volume. All definitions, however, can easily be extended to the general case.

This paper is a short version of /Gr76/ and therefore contains only a part of the results and examples given there. Especially, most of the proofs are only sketched here.

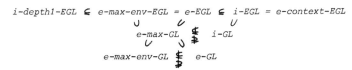

2. BASIC DEFINITIONS FOR EXPLICIT GRAPH L-SYSTEMS

In the following the basic definitions for explicit graph L-systems as defined in /Na76b/ are given. Those systems are only a slight modification and simplification of L-systems for graphs with an environmental node as introduced by CULIK/LINDENMAYER in /CuLi74/. The differences to the notions of /CuLi74/ are only given informal by remarks.

Def. 2.1: A *labelled graph* d (abbr. *l-graph*) over the alphabets Σ_v, Σ_E for node and edge labels is a tuple $d = (K, (\rho_a)_{a\in\Sigma_E}, \beta)$ where+)
1) K is a finite set, the node set,
2) ρ_a is a relation over K for any $a\in\Sigma_E$, i.e. $\rho_a \subseteq K\times K$,
3) $\beta: K \longrightarrow \Sigma_v$ is a function, the labelling function for nodes.

Each pair $(k_1,k_2)\in\rho_a$ can be regarded as directed edge from node k_1 to node k_2 labelled with a symbol $a\in\Sigma_E$. Each node k is labelled with a symbol $\beta(k)\in\Sigma_v$. Usually we take nonnegative integers as node denotations, i.e. $K\subset\mathbb{N}_0$.

Graphs with an environmental node (abbr. env-l-graphs) are special l-graphs: Each env-l-graph d has a distinguished node k_∞ which does not belong to the node set K of d, namely the environmental node. This node is labelled with a special label $e\notin\Sigma_v$ which does not occur anywhere else in d. The environmental node is imagined as infinitely distant and, therefore, it does not appear in a graphical representation of d. Incoming or outgoing edges from or to the envitonmental node simply show to or come from the "environment" of the env-l-graph. Therefore, in /CuLi74/ they have been called "open hands".

Let $d(\Sigma_v, \Sigma_E)$ denote the set of all l-graphs over the alphabets Σ_v, Σ_E, and let d_ε denote the empty graph.

Def. 2.2: Two l-graphs d, $d'\in d(\Sigma_v,\Sigma_E)$ are *equivalent* (abbr. $d\equiv d'$) iff there is a bijective mapping $f: K\rightarrow K'$ with
1) $(k_1, k_2)\in\rho_a \Longleftrightarrow (f(k_1),f(k_2))\in\rho_a'$ for some $a\in\Sigma_E$, $k_1, k_2\in K$, $f(k_1), f(k_2)\in K'$,
2) $\beta = \beta'\circ f$.

Equivalence of env-l-graphs is defined in the same manner. In addition to the above conditions it is required, that $f(k_\infty) = k_\infty$ (the environmental node is mapped onto itself).

Let $B\subseteq d(\Sigma_v,\Sigma_E)$ and $d\in d(\Sigma_v,\Sigma_E)$. The graph d is *contained* in B *up to equivalence* ($d \underline{\in} B$) iff there is a $d'\in B$ with $d\equiv d'$.

The relation $\equiv$ is an equivalence relation over subsets of $d(\Sigma_v,\Sigma_E)$. Let D denote the set of all graphs from $d(\Sigma_v,\Sigma_E)$ equivalent to d, and analogously for other graph denotations, e.g. $d_1\in D_1$, $d'\in D'$ etc. and let $D(\Sigma_v,\Sigma_E) := d(\Sigma_v,\Sigma_E)/_{\equiv}$.

Def. 2.3: A graph d' is a *partial graph* of d ($d'\sqsubseteq d$) iff $K'\subseteq K$, $\rho_a'\subseteq\rho_a$ for any $a\in\Sigma_E$, and $\beta' = \beta|_{K'}$.
A graph d' is a *subgraph* of d ($d'\subseteq d$) iff $d'\sqsubseteq d$ and $\rho_a' = \rho_a\cap(K'\times K')$, i.e. all edges connecting nodes of K' also belong to d'.
Let d',d'' be graphs, where $\beta'(k) = \beta''(k)$ for all $k\in K'\cap K''$. The graph d is called the *union graph* of d' and d'' ($d=d'\cup d''$) iff
$K = K'\cup K''$, $\rho_a = \rho_a'\cup\rho_a''$ for arbitrary $a\in\Sigma_E$,
$\beta(k) = \beta'(k)$ if $k\in K'$ and $\beta(k) = \beta''(k)$ if $k\in K''$.
Let $d'=(K', (\rho_a')_{a\in\Sigma_E}, \beta')$, and $K''\subseteq K'$. Then we call the subgraph with the node set K'' the *subgraph generated by* K'', written as d'(K'').

Def. 2.4: Two l-graphs d_1 and d_2 are called *node disjoint* iff $K_1\cap K_2 = \emptyset$. (As k_∞ is not contained in the node set of any env-l-graph, two node disjoint env-l-graphs both contain the environmental node.)

Def. 2.5: A *replacement rule* is a tuple $r = (d_\ell, d_r)$, where
$d_\ell\in d(\Sigma_v,\Sigma_E)$ is a one node graph,
$d_r\in d(\Sigma_v,\Sigma_E)$ is an arbitrary l-graph which is possibly empty.

+) To avoid confusion with the letter G which is used as abbreviation for grammars we abbreviate l-graphs by d.

By means of replacement rules all nodes of a graph are substituted: The node to be replaced (mother node) must have the structure of the left hand side, the graph which is inserted (daughter graph) that of the right hand side of a replacement rule. So any pair (mother node, daughter graph) represents one actualization of a replacement rule. As one rule may be applied more than once in a parallel rewriting step, there usually is more than one actualization of a replacement rule. Furthermore, the daughter graphs have to be connected by edges. Therefore, we introduce the following definition (cf. /CuLi74/):

Def. 2.6: An *l-stencil* $d_{st} \in d(\Sigma_v, \Sigma_\ell)$ is a bipartite l-graph, i.e. $d_{st} = (K_s \cup K_t, (\rho_a)_{a \in \Sigma_\ell}, \beta)$ with $K_s \cap K_t = \emptyset$. As the order of K_s and K_t is important in the following we write $d_{st}(K_s; K_t)$. The subgraphs $d_s := d_{st}(K_s)$ and $d_t := d_{st}(K_t)$ are called *source graph* and *target graph* of d_{st} respectively.

Def. 2.7: An l-stencil $d_{st}(K_s; K_t)$ is called *applicable* to an ordered pair of l-graphs $(d,d') \in (d(\Sigma_v, \Sigma_\ell))^2$ iff d and d' are node disjoint and $d_s \sqsubseteq d$, $d_t \sqsubseteq d'$. Let $d_{st}(K_s;K_t)$ be applicable to (d,d') then $d \cup d' \cup d_{st}(K_s;K_t)$ is called the *gluing* of (d,d') *along the stencil* d_{st}.

Def. 2.8: Let ST be a finite set of l-stencils over Σ_v, Σ_ℓ. The stencil d_{st} is called *ST-maximal* for a pair (d,d'), iff d_{st} is applicable to (d,d') and there is no $d'_{st} \in$ ST applicable to (d,d') with $d_s \cup d_t \subset d'_s \cup d'_t$ and $d_s \sqsubseteq d'_s$, $d_t \sqsubseteq d'_t$, where d_s, d'_s, d_t, d'_t are the source and target graphs of d_{st} and d'_{st} respectively.

Def. 2.9: A *connection rule* is a pair $c = (d_e, d_{st})$ with d_e being an l-graph of the form 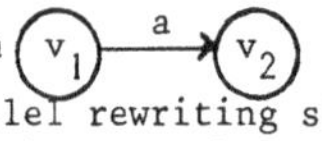 with $v_1, v_2 \in \Sigma_v$, $a \in \Sigma_\ell$ and $d_{st}(K_s; K_t)$ being a stencil.

In a parallel rewriting step all nodes of a host graph are simultaneously replaced by daughter graphs and all mother edges by stencils, which may be elucidated by Fig. 10 of the introductory paper of this volume.

Def. 2.10: Two replacement rules $r=(d_\ell, d_r)$, $r'=(d'_\ell, d'_r)$ are called *equivalent*, iff $d_\ell \equiv d'_\ell$ and $d_r \equiv d'_r$. Two connection rules $c=(d_e, d_{st})$, $c'=(d'_e, d'_{st})$ are called *equivalent* iff $d_e \equiv d'_e$, $d_{st} \equiv d'_{st}$ where additionally $d_s \equiv d'_s$, $d_t \equiv d'_t$. A set of replacement rules is called *node disjoint* iff all left hand sides are pairwise node disjoint and the same holds true for all right hand sides. A set of connection rules is called *edge disjoint* iff all left hand sides are different, i.e. they differ in either the labels or the node denotations.

Def. 2.11: Let $d \in d(\Sigma_v, \Sigma_\ell) - \{d_\varepsilon\}$ and $d' \in d(\Sigma_v, \Sigma_\ell)$. The l-graph d' is *directly explicit parallel derivable* from d ($d \text{ —pe}\rightarrow d'$) iff there is a set $\{r_1, \ldots, r_k\}$ of node disjoint replacement rules and a set $\{c_1, \ldots, c_q\}$ of edge disjoint connection rules such that

$$d_{\ell_i} \subseteq d\,, \quad \bigcup_{i=1}^{k} K_{\ell_i} = K, \quad \text{and } d_{r_i} \subseteq d', \quad \bigcup_{i=1}^{k} K_{r_i} = K',$$
$$d = \bigcup_{i=1}^{k} d_{\ell_i} \cup \bigcup_{j=1}^{q} d_{e_j} \quad \text{and} \quad d' = \bigcup_{i=1}^{k} d_{r_i} \cup \bigcup_{j=1}^{q} d_{st_j}$$

with the following restriction:
Let d_{ℓ_μ} and d_{ℓ_ν} be two mother nodes contained in an edge d_{e_π} (up to eventual loops), i.e. d_{e_π} is an a-edge from d_{ℓ_μ} to d_{ℓ_ν} and let $c_\pi = (d_{e_\pi}, d_{st_\pi})$ be the corresponding connection rule. Then the stencil d_{st_π} is applicable to (d_{r_μ}, d_{r_ν}) and the gluing of (d_{r_μ}, d_{r_ν}) along d_{st_π} is contained in d'. The left hand sides of applied connection rules we call *mother edges*.

Def. 2.12: A *graph L-system with explicit connection transformation (e-GL-system)* is a tuple $G = (\Sigma_v, \Sigma_\ell, d_0, RR, CR, \text{—pe}\rightarrow)$, where Σ_v, Σ_ℓ is the alphabet of node and edge labels, and $d_0 \in d(\Sigma_v, \Sigma_\ell) - \{d_\varepsilon\}$ is the *axiom graph*. RR is a finite set of replacement rules which is *complete* in the sense that for any one-node subgraph of the axiom graph or the right hand sides of replacement rules there is a replacement rule in RR having this one-node graph as left hand side. CR is a finite set of connection rules which is *complete* in the sense that for any triple $(v_1, a, v_2) \in \Sigma_v \times \Sigma_\ell \times \Sigma_v$ there is a connection rule where v_1, v_2 are the labels of the source and target node and a is the label of the edge of the left hand side of the connection rule. Finally, $\text{—pe}\rightarrow$ is the direct derivation mechanism of Def. 2.11. A direct derivation step $d \;\text{—pe}_G\!\rightarrow d'$ within G means that all applied rules are equivalent to some of RR and CR respectively. The *language* of an e-GL-system G is defined as

$$\mathcal{L}(G) := \{D \mid D \in D(\Sigma_v, \Sigma_e) \wedge D_0 \;\text{—pe}^*_G\!\rightarrow D\},$$

where $\text{—pe}^*_G\!\rightarrow$ is the reflexive and transitive closure of $\text{—pe}_G\!\rightarrow$, and where $D \;\text{—pe}_G\!\rightarrow D'$ means that there exists a $d \in D$ and a $d' \in D'$ with $d \;\text{—pe}_G\!\rightarrow d'$.

A set of 1-graphs is called an e-GL-language iff there is an e-GL-system generating it.

The following example of an e-GL-system may improve the understanding of the above notations.

Example 2.13:

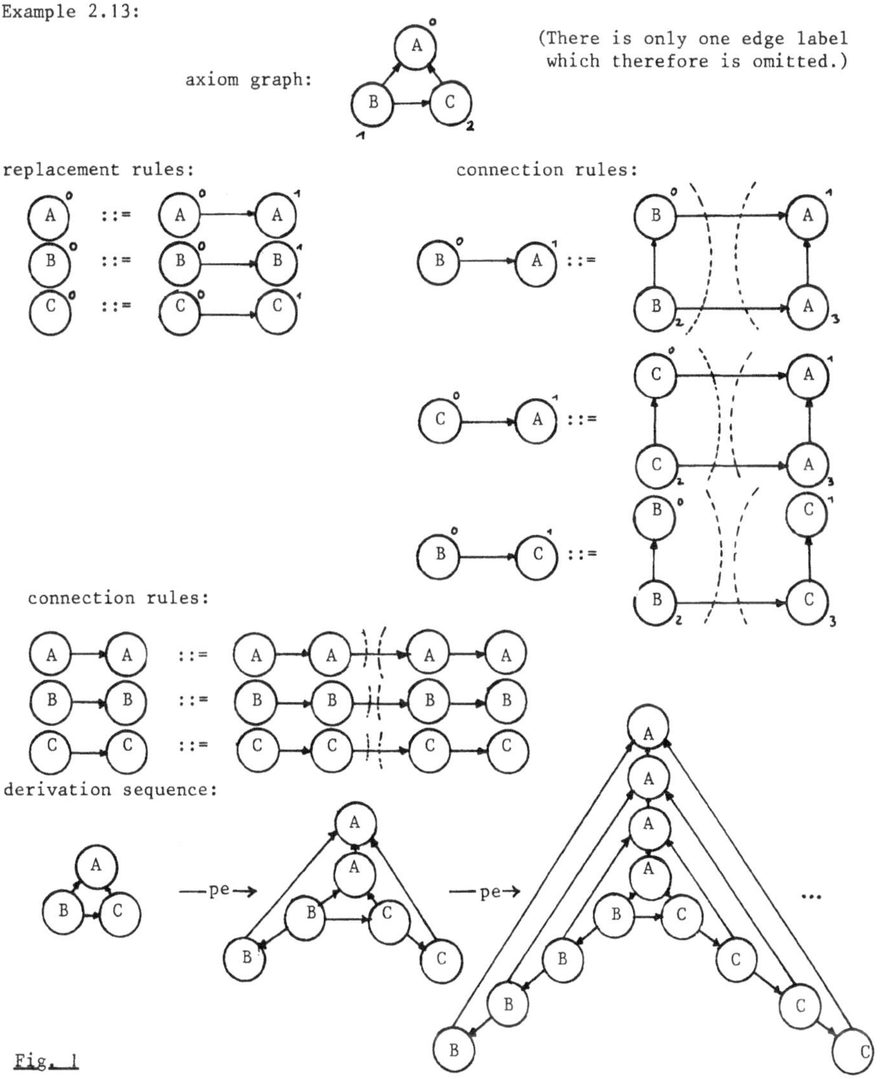

Fig. 1

To avoid a formal introduction of e-max-env-GL-systems as defined in /CuLi74/, we just compare the properties of e-GL-systems and e-max-env-GL-systems:

Remark 2.14:

	e-GL	e-max-env-GL
replacement rules:	Each node is replaced by a daughter graph (without open hands at the daughter graphs).	Each node is replaced by a daughter graph which usually has open hands.
connection of daughter graphs:	by stencils without open hands	by stencils which in general have open hands
left hand side in a connection rule:	edge graph of the form $(v_1) \xrightarrow{a} (v_2)$	edge without nodes $\xrightarrow{a}$
applicability of a stencil:	The source graph and the target graph of the stencil must be contained in the daughter graphs to which the stencil is to apply. The mother nodes of the daughter graphs have the same node labels as the nodes on the left hand side of the connection rule.	The source and the target graph of the stencil must be contained in the daughter graphs to which the stencil is to apply. We cut off the edges between source and target graph within the stencil and regard the resulting half-edges as open hands. Then all these open hands must also appear at the corresponding daughter graph, otherwise the stencil is not applicable. Furthermore, the condition of maximality must be satisfied: There is no "larger" applicable stencil.
programming of connections:	by mother node labels and the structure of source and target graphs in stencils.	by open hands and the structure of source and target graphs in stencils.

In the definition of a derivation in an e-max-env-GL-system there are furthermore special rules for open hands:

If there had been an a-labelled open hand at the mother node (outward), and there is an a-labelled open hand (outward) at the replaced daughter graph, then there is also an a-labelled open hand (outward) in the derived graph at the corresponding place, i.e., in this case the open hand is preserved. Open hands at a daughter graph, which had not been at the mother node, or vice versa, are eliminated. Analogously for incoming open hands.

There is another deviation in the definition of an e-max-env-GL-system to the above definitions: In e-max-env-GL-systems *strong completeness* of connection rules is required for the set CR, i.e. for each mother edge in the host graph there exists at least one connection rule which is applicable to the daughter graphs of the corresponding mother nodes. Above, we only required *weak completeness*: For each mother edge graph exists a connection rule, the applicability of that rule was not required. So, in e-max-env-GL-systems a derivation never abrupts which, however, is possible in e-GL-systems.

Def. 2.15: A GL-system is called *propagating*, if d_ε does not occur as right hand side of any replacement rule. Two GL-systems are called equivalent, if both generate the same language. This definition is assumed to be generalized to all kinds of GL-systems regarded in the following.

Def. 2.16: Two graphs d,d' are called *kernel equivalent* ($d \overset{K}{\equiv} d'$) iff both are equivalent after deleting the environmental node and the open hands. (if $d,d' \in d(\Sigma_V,\Sigma_E)$ then kernel-equivalence is equal to the equivalence of Def. 2.2).

In the following an example of an e-max-env-GL-system is given, the derivation sequence of which is kernel-equivalent to that of Ex. 2.13.

Example 2.17:

axiom graph as in Ex. 2.13
replacement rules:

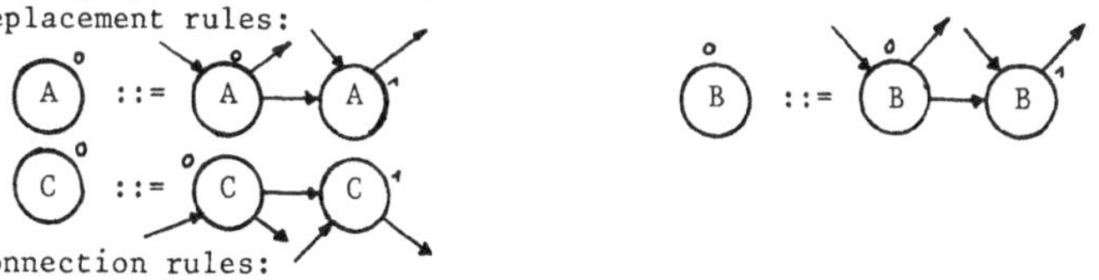

connection rules:

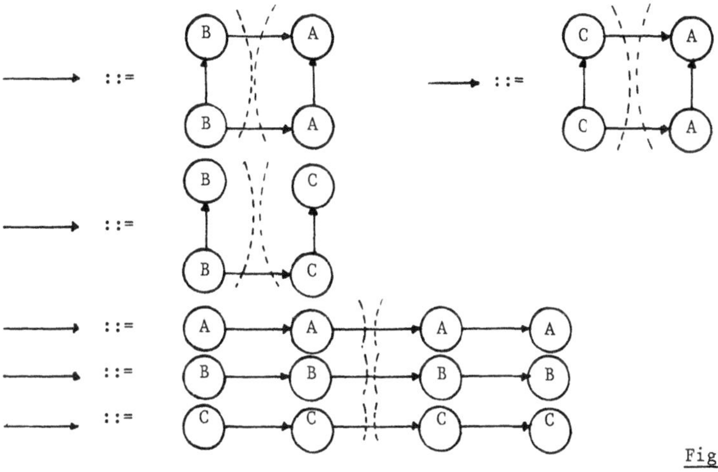

Fig. 2

The open hands at the daughter graphs are required to ensure the applicability of the stencils. A stencil can only create an edge between nodes of two daughter graphs, if each of the two nodes has an open hand in the same direction as the edge to be generated.

Def. 2.18: A stencil d_{st} with source graph d_s and target graph d_t is called a *complete* stencil in an e-GL-system G, iff there are replacement rules in G which have d_s and d_t as right hand sides, respectively.

3. SOME RESULTS FOR EXPLICIT SYSTEMS

Thm. 3.1: For any e-GL-system an equivalent one with complete stencils can be constructed.

Proof: Let $G=(\Sigma_v,\Sigma_\varepsilon,d_0,RR,CR,\text{—pe}\rightarrow)$ be an e-GL-system with $CR = \{c_1,\ldots,c_q\}$. Blow up all connection rules until source and target graphs are right hand sides of replacement rules:
Let $c_i=(d_{e_i},d_{st_i})$ be a connection rule with d_{e_i} = 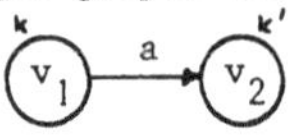

. Let, furthermore $D^{1\text{-node}}(G,v_1)$, $D^{1\text{-node}}(G,v_2)$ be the set of all one-node graphs (equivalence classes) occuring in an arbitrary sentential form of G. As connection rules cannot generate loops, $D^{1\text{-node}}(G,v_1)$ can be found by only looking at the axiom graph and the right hand sides of replacement rules.
Regard all two-node graphs of the following form: ${}^{\lambda}d^{compl}_{e_i}$ = 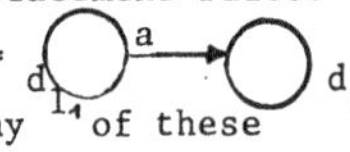

with $d_{l_1}\in D_{l_1}\in D^{1\text{-node}}(G,v_1)$, $d_{l_2}\in D_{l_2}\in D^{1\text{-node}}(G,v_2)$. For any of these graphs regard all graphs ${}^{\lambda_j}D^{compl}_{st_i}$ which are the result of a direct derivation step ${}^{\lambda}D^{compl}_{e_i}\text{—pe}\rightarrow{}^{\lambda_j}D^{compl}_{st_i}$. Let $M^{compl}_{st_i}$ the set of all graphs generated in this way if D_{l_1} and D_{l_2} run through $D^{1\text{-node}}(G,v_1)$ and $D^{1\text{-node}}(G,v_2)$ respectively. For any ${}^{\lambda_j}D^{compl}_{st_i}\in M^{compl}_{st_i}$ we construct a connection rule $(d_{e_i}, {}^{\lambda_j}d^{compl}_{st_i})$ with ${}^{\lambda_j}d^{compl}_{st_i}\in{}^{\lambda_j}D^{compl}_{st_i}$. Let $C^{compl}_{st_i}$ the set of connection rules resulting in this manner and let $CR^{compl} := \bigcup_{i=1}^{q} C^{compl}_{st_i}$. Then G' = $(\Sigma_v,\Sigma_\varepsilon,d_0,RR,CR^{compl},\text{—pe}\rightarrow)$ trivially has the desired property.

Note that in an complete e-GL-system there is no guarantee that applied stencils completely contain the corresponding daughter graphs: There may be replacement rules the right hand sides of which are contained in right hand sides of other replacement rules.

Analogously but more tedious the following result can be proved (cf. /Gr76/):

Cor. 3.2: For any e-max-env-GL-system an equivalent one with complete stencils can be constructed.

Because of Thm. 3.1 and Cor. 3.2 we consider in the following only explicit systems with complete stencils.

In /CuLi74/ and /Na78/ some results are given concerning the relation between string L-systems and explicit GL-systems which are not repeated here. Furthermore, some results of the theory of context free string grammars are generalized there to explicit GL-systems which can be used to reduce these systems.

Def. 3.3: Let $G = (\Sigma_v,\Sigma_\varepsilon,d_0,RR,CR,\text{—pe}\rightarrow)$ be an e-GL-system and ST the set of all stencils occurring in CR. Then G is called an e-GL-system with *maximality condition (e-max-GL-system)* if in any derivation step $d\text{—pe}\rightarrow d'$ all applied stencils are ST-maximal. The *language* of an e-max-GL-system and e-max-GL-languages are defined as usual.

Lemma 3.4: Any e-GL-language is also an e-max-GL-language.

Proof: Let $\mathcal{L}(G)$ be an e-GL-language. Construct the equivalent e-GL-system G' with complete stencils and regard G' as e-max-GL-system. Then trivially $\mathcal{L}(G)$ and $\mathcal{L}(G')$ are equal.

Note, that in a system with complete stencils and with maximality condition replacement rules are superflous as the information by which daughter graph a node is to be substituted is also contained in connection rules. This is, however, only true for graphs without loops and without isolated nodes. The set of connection rules thereby is strongly redundant.

The rest of this section is devoted to interrelate e-GL-systems, e-max-GL-systems and e-max-env-GL-systems.

Thm. 3.5: There is an e-max-env-GL-language which is not kernel equivalent to any e-GL-language.

Sketch of the proof: Let G_{ENV} be the following e-max-env-GL-system:

axiom graph:

d_0:

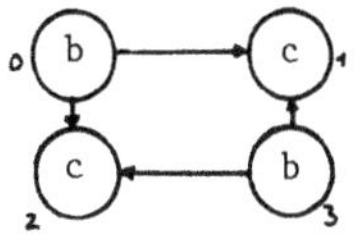

replacement rules:

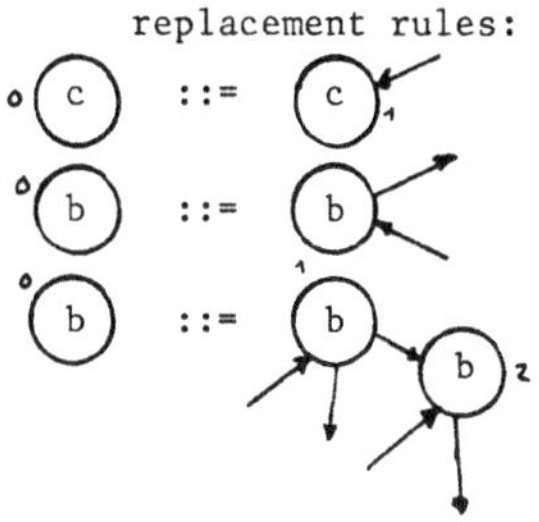

connection rules:

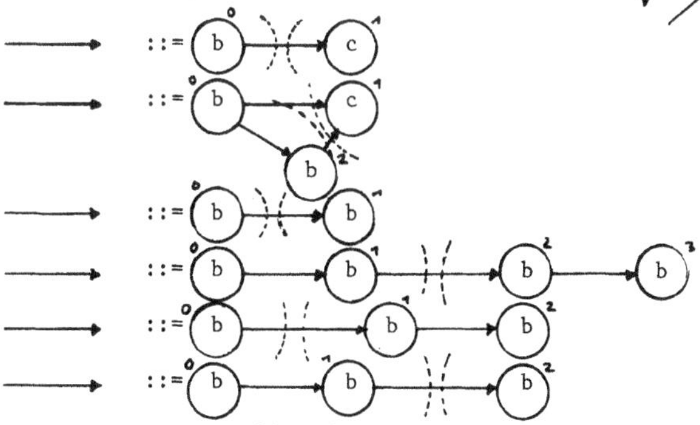

Fig. 3a

The generated language $\mathcal{L}(G_{ENV})$ is the set of graphs occurring in the following derivation sequence:

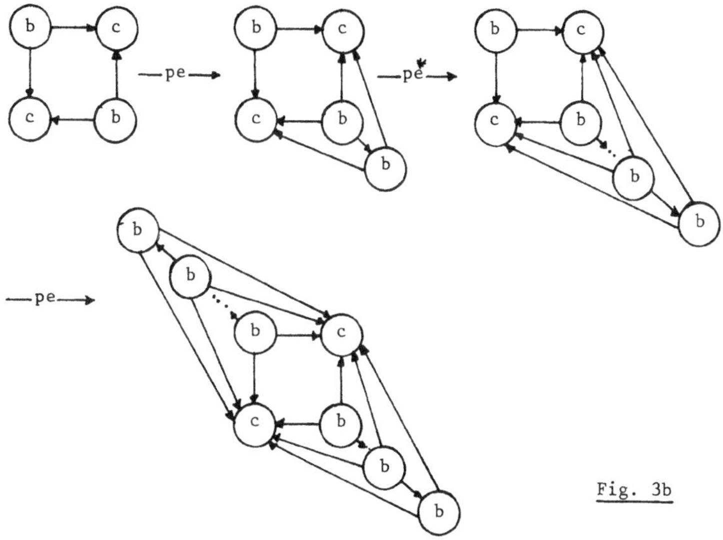

Fig. 3b

Why is that not an e-GL-language? Assume that it were one, generated by the e-GL-system G. It is easy to show that:

1) There are no erasing rules in G.
2) The graph d_0 is also the axiom graph of G.
3) It is impossible to avoid the derivation of the graph of Fig. 3c in G.

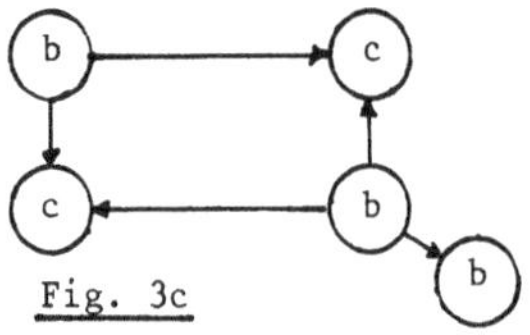

Fig. 3c

Reason: missing condition of maximality.

With a slight modification of the GL-system G_{ENV} by deleting the open hands we can prove the following:

Cor. 3.6: There is an e-max-GL-language which is not an e-GL-language.

Thm. 3.7: For any e-max-env-GL-system G an equivalent[+)] e-max-GL-system G' can be constructed, which generates the same language.

Algorithm 3.8 and sketch of the proof:

1) Add to the mother edge (left hand side of an env-connection rule) those mother nodes as source or target nodes, the daughter graphs of which are the source or target graphs of the env-stencil on the right hand side of the env-connection rule. Remember, that we assume complete stencils. In general, we get an increasing number of connection rules.

Example:

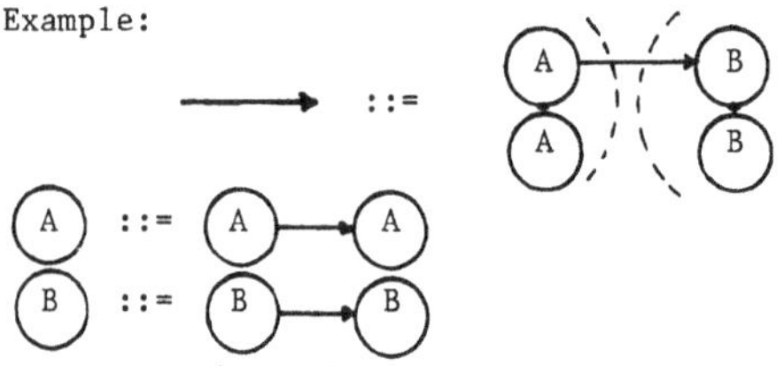

New connection rule:

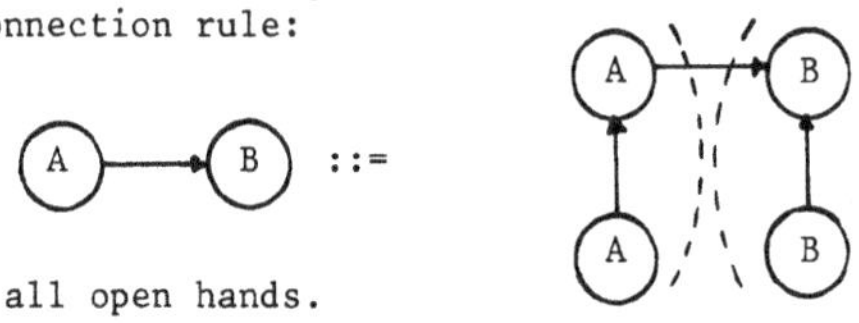

Fig. 4

2) Erase all open hands.

Why is it allowed to erase the open hands?
Open hands program the applicability of a stencil for a pair of daughter graphs. However, the way to program the applicability with mother edge graphs and without open hands is more powerful:

In e-env-max-GL we can only determine (by open hands) whether a stencil is applicable to a daughter graph or not (whether the open hands coincide or they do not). Hereby, we neglect the mother node.
In e-max-GL we determine by the mother edge graph whether a stencil is applicable to the daughter graph of a well-defined mother node (if mother node and daughter graph in the replacement rule coincide with mother node and source or target graph in the connection rule).

Thm. 3.9: There is an e-max-GL-language for which there exists no kernel-equivalent e-max-env-GL-language.

Proof: There exist trivial examples because of the weak completeness[++)] of the set of connection rules in e-max-GL, which allows sequences of derivations to abrupt, e.g. {(a), (a)⟶(a)} is a e-max-GL-language, but not an e-max-env-GL-language.
But there are also examples which fulfill the condition of (strong) completeness as demanded in e-max-env-GL-systems, e.g.

+) up to kernel equivalence

++) The reader must not confuse the completeness of stencils with the completeness or weak completeness of connection rule sets.

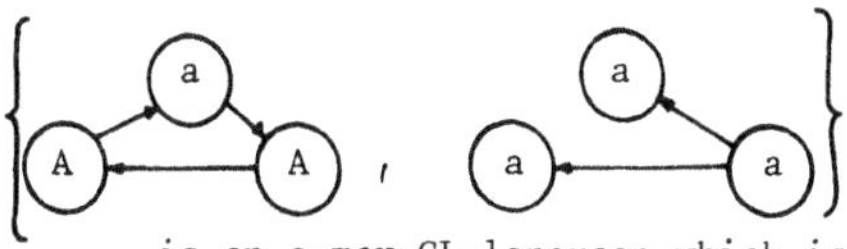

Fig. 5

is an e-max-GL-language which is not an e-max-env-GL-language. Reason: In e-max-env-GL we cannot program the connection between daughter graphs depending on their mother node labels. Here, it is important, whether (A) or (a) is the mother node.

Thm. 3.10: There is an e-max-GL-language which is neither an e-GL-language nor an e-max-env-GL-language.

Proof: An example for such a language is a combination of the examples of Thm. 3.5 and 3.9:

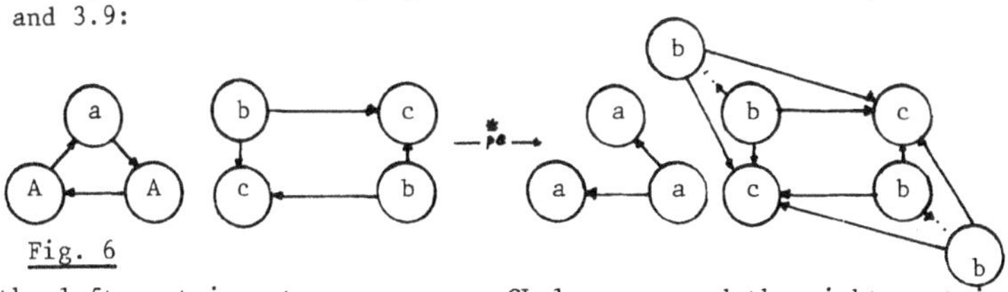

Fig. 6

As the left part is not an e-max-env-GL-language and the right part is not an e-GL-language, the combination is neither the one nor the other.

Cor. 3.11: The following diagram of inclusions holds true:

e-max-GL

$\cup$ $\cup$

e-max-env-GL $\not\subseteq\not\supseteq$ *e-GL*

4. COMPARISON WITH EXTENDED EXPLICIT SYSTEMS

Def. 4.1: An *extended e-GL-system (e-EGL-system)* is a tuple $G=(\Sigma_V,\Sigma_E,\Delta_V,\Delta_E,d_0,$ RR, CR, —pe→) with Σ_V,Σ_E,d_0,RR,CR, —pe→ as above, $\Delta_V\subseteq\Sigma_V$, $\Delta_E\subseteq\Sigma_E$ either called the *terminal* node and edge label alphabet. Derivation in G means derivation in the underlying e-GL-system $G'=(\Sigma_V,\Sigma_E,d_0,$RR,CR, —pe→). The *language* of G is defined as $\mathcal{L}(G) := \mathcal{L}(G') \cap D(\Delta_V,\Delta_E)$, i.e. only those graphs are regarded to belong to the language the node and edge labels of which are terminal. *e-max-EGL-systems* and *e-max-env-EGL-systems* are defined analogously.

Thm. 4.2: For any e-max-GL-system an equivalent e-EGL-system can be constructed.

Proof: Let G be an e-max-GL-system and let G' be the corresponding e-max-GL-system with complete stencils which is constructed analogously to Thm. 3.1. Analogously means here that the graphs derived from d_{l_1} ( ) —a→ ( ) d_{l_2} are derived within an e-max-GL-system, i.e. only maximal stencils are applied. The system G' understood as e-EGL-system is not equivalent to G, as in e-EGL-systems there is no maximality condition. Therefore, we have to prevent that there are replacement rules (d_l,d_{r_1}), (d_l,d_{r_2}) with $d_{r_1}\subseteq d_{r_2}$.
Let t be the label of a node in d_{r_j} of a replacement rule r_j of G'. We introduce a new nonterminal node label t_j. Let r_j' the replacement rule which is the result of r_j by relabelling all nodes with their new node label. Furthermore, we need replacement rules to eliminate the new node labels, e.g. $\overset{\circ}{(t_j)}$ ::= $\overset{\circ}{(t)}$. As the right hand sides of replacement rules are part of the connection rules in the construction of Thm. 3.1 these connection rules must be modified correspondingly. The construction is finished by adding all trivial connection rules of the form $(t_j) \xrightarrow{a} (t_j')$ ::= $(t) \xrightarrow{a} (t')$, $(t_i) \xrightarrow{a} (t_i)$ ::= $(t) \xrightarrow{a} (t)$. Within the resulting

e-EGL-system G" any step of G' is simulated by two steps.

Thm. 4.3: There is an e-EGL-language, which is not an e-max-GL-language.

Sketch of the proof: The following language is an e-EGL-language, as each finite language is an e-EGL-language, but it is not an e-max-GL-language.

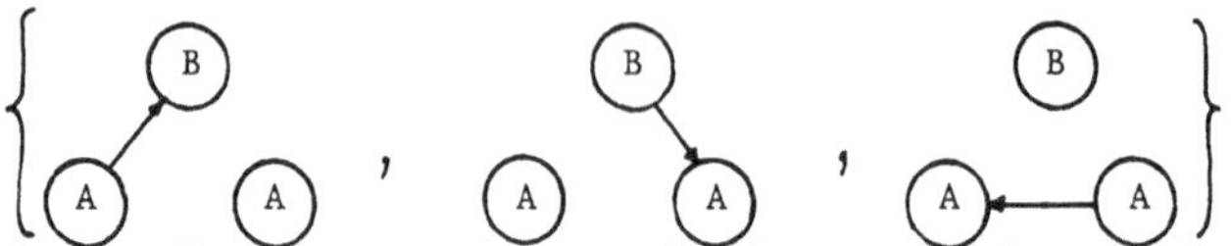

Fig. 7.a

Reason: We cannot generate an edge between daughter graphs, if there is no edge between the corresponding mother nodes, i.e. the edge cannot circulate. Thus, we have to try to circulate the node labels. But then we need the following replacement rules:

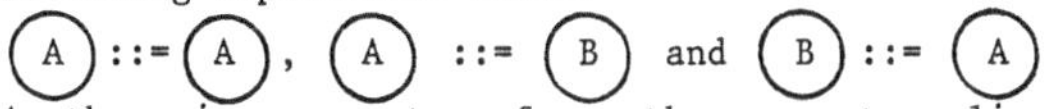

Fig. 7.b

As there is no way to enforce the correct application of the first two rules, such an e-max-GL-system would generate more than the above three graphs.

Cor. 4.4: *e-max-GL* $\subset$ *e-EGL*

Proof: Follows from Thm. 4.2 and 4.3.

Thm. 4.5: For any e-GL-system an equivalent e-max-env-EGL-system G' can be constructed.

The idea of the proof is shown by an example (for the formal proof cf. /Gr76/):

Example 4.6: In the following we give an e-GL-system which is changed into an e-max-env-EGL-system, such that both have the same language.

axiom graph:

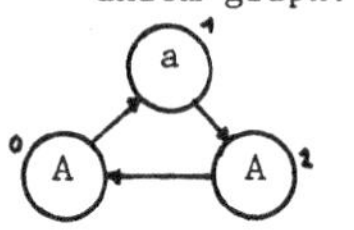

replacement rules:

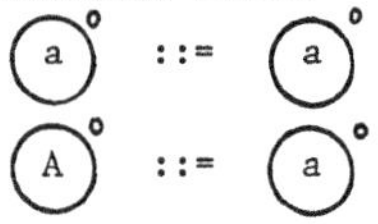

connection rules:

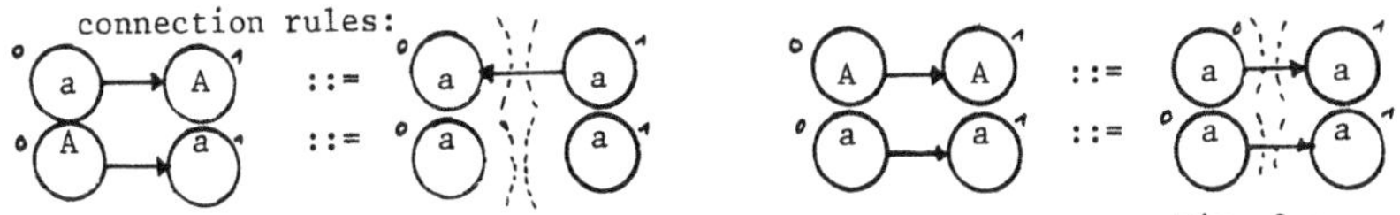

Fig. 8.a

The generated language is:

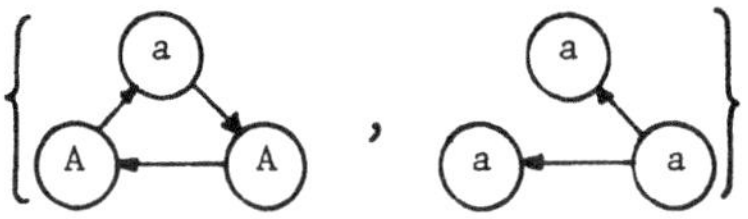

The e-max-env-EGL-system is determined by:

axiom graph as above

step 1): replacement rules:

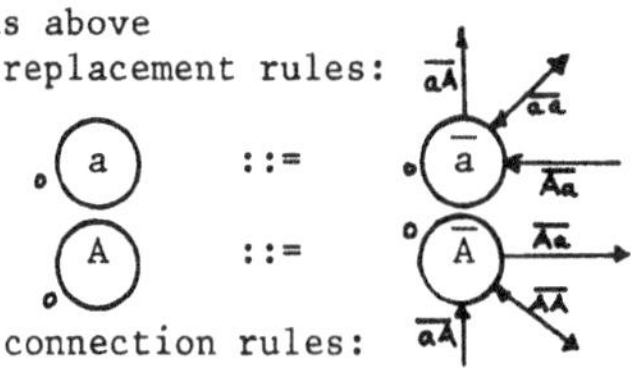

connection rules:

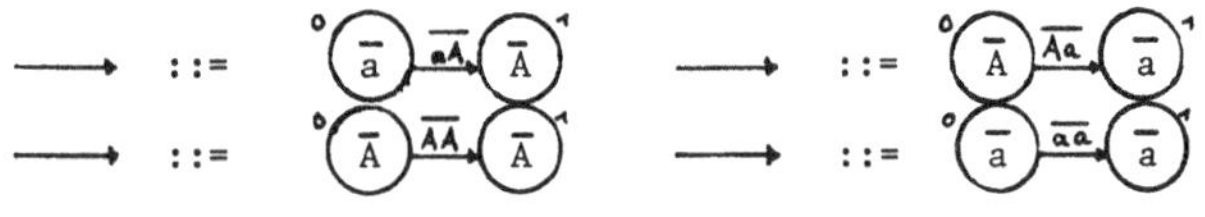

Fig. 8.b

step 2): replacement rules:

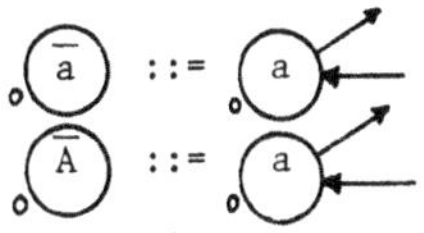

connection rules:

Fig. 8.c

derivation sequence:

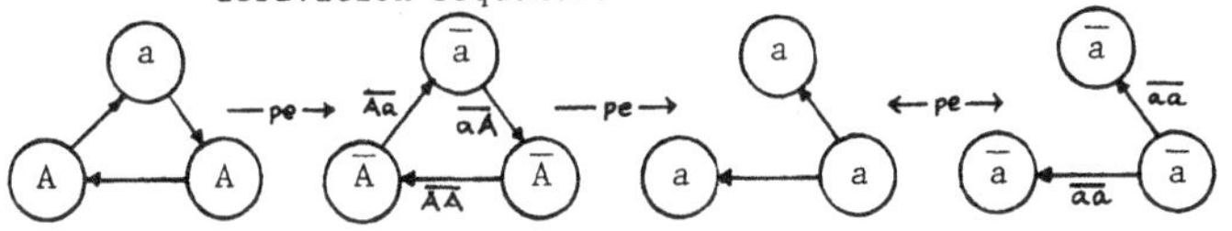

Fig. 8.d

As that language is finite, it can be generated much simpler in *e-max-env-EGL*. The aim of this example was, however, to show the basic idea of the proof of Thm. 4.5.

e-EGL and *e-GL* do not differ in the definition of a derivation but they differ in what graphs belong to the language. So, we can conclude from Thm. 4.5:

Cor. 4.7: *e-EGL* $\subseteq$ *e-max-env-EGL*

Analogously from the construction of Thm. 3.7 and Thm. 4.2:

Cor. 4.8: *e-max-env-EGL* $\subseteq$ *e-EGL*

Now we summarize the results:

Thm. 4.9:

e-max-env-EGL = *e-EGL*
$\cup$ $\cup$
e-max-GL
$\cup$ $\not\subseteq$ $\cup$
e-max-env-GL $\not\supseteq$ *e-GL*

5. IMPLICIT SYSTEMS AND THEIR RELATIONS TO EXPLICIT SYSTEMS

Before we start to compare explicit systems with implicit systems we have to cite the basic notions for i-GL-systems (cf. e.g. /Na76a/).

The most important difference between explicit and implicit systems is that in the latter there is only one type of rules, which we call *productions* in the sequel. The third part of such a production, called connection transformation, is an algorithmic specification determining how daughter graphs have to be connected. As an edge, connecting two daughter graphs, trivially corresponds to two daughter graphs which belong to two productions, the following approach causes a half-edge mechanism rather than an edge mechanism. For an edge, connecting two daughter graphs, two half-edges have to fit together.

The following definition is only an instrument to define subsets of the node set of a graph in a very general way:

Def. 5.1: Words over the alphabet Σ with $\Sigma := \Sigma_v \cup \{L_a \mid a \in \Sigma_\varepsilon\} \cup \{R_a \mid a \in \Sigma_\varepsilon\} \cup \{\complement, \cup, \cap, (,)\}$ are called *operators*, iff they are formed according to the following rules:

1) L_a and R_a are operators for any $a \in \Sigma_\varepsilon$,
2) if A is an operator then $(\complement A)$ and (vA) are operators for any $v \in \Sigma_v^+$, [+)]
3) if A and B are operators then also AB, $(A \cup B)$, and $(A \cap B)$.

+) Do not confuse the special symbol $\complement$ with letter C.

Let op(Σ) denote the set of all words of Σ generated by this recursive scheme. Let $d \in d(\Sigma_v,\Sigma_e)$, d' a subgraph of d, and $k \in K$ be an arbitrary node. An *interpretation* yields for any operator A, any d, d', k as above, a subset of the node set K written as $A^{d',d}(k)$. The definition of an interpretation of an operator is recursive according to the above scheme:

1') $L_a^{d',d}(k) := \{\underline{k} \mid \underline{k} \in K-K' \wedge (\underline{k},k) \in \varrho_a\}$,
1") $R_a^{d',d}(k) := \{\underline{k} \mid \underline{k} \in K-K' \wedge (k,\underline{k}) \in \varrho_a\}$.

$L_a^{d',d}(k)$ specifies the set of source nodes (not contained in K') of a-labelled edges which end in k, and $R_a^{d',d}(k)$ denotes the set of target nodes ($\notin$ K') of a-labelled edges leaving k. Thus "L" is an abbreviation for left and "R" for right.

2') $(\complement A)^{d',d}(k) := \{\underline{k} \mid \underline{k} \in K-K' \wedge \underline{k} \in K-A^{d',d}(k)\}$,

determines the complement of $A^{d',d}(k)$ and

2") $(v_1 v_2 \ldots v_m A)^{d',d}(k) := \{\underline{k} \mid \underline{k} \in A^{d',d}(k) \wedge \beta(\underline{k}) \in \{v_1, v_2, \ldots, v_m\}\}$

yields the subset of $A^{d',d}(k)$ the nodes of which are labelled with one of the symbols of the word $v_1 \ldots v_m$.

3') $AB^{d',d}(k) := \{\underline{k} \mid \exists \underline{\underline{k}} (\underline{\underline{k}} \in B^{d',d}(k) \wedge \underline{k} \in A^{d',d}(\underline{\underline{k}}))\}$
3") $(A \cap B)^{d',d}(k) := A^{d',d}(k) \cap B^{d',d}(k)$
3"') $(A \cup B)^{d',d}(k) := A^{d',d}(k) \cup B^{d',d}(k)$

specifies the subsets of nodes K-K' which are generated by sequencing, parallel connection, or branching of operators.

Remark 5.2: The set $A^{d',d}(k)$ can be empty for any interpretation, e.g. the operator $O:=(v_1(v_2 L_a))$ yields the empty set for any two symbols $v_1, v_2 \in \Sigma_v$, with $v_1 \neq v_2$ because of the uniqueness of node labels. On the other hand there are operators, which always yield all nodes of a given host graph outside of a specified subgraph, i.e. the operator $I:=(\complement O)$.

Def. 5.3: A *graph production* is a triplet $p=(d_\ell,d_r,C)$, where (d_ℓ,d_r) is a replacement rule and C, called *connection transformation*, is a tuple of the form $C=((l_a,r_a)_{a \in \Sigma_E})$. The components of C, called *connection components*, have the form:

$$l_a = \bigcup_{\lambda=1}^{q} A_\lambda(k_\ell) \times \{k_\lambda\}, \qquad r_a = \bigcup_{\lambda=1}^{p} \{k_\lambda\} \times A_\lambda(k_\ell), \qquad a \in \Sigma_E,\ p,q \geq 1,$$

where k_ℓ is the node of d_ℓ, k_λ an arbitrary node of K_r, and A_λ is an operator.

Abbreviations 5.4:

$(A(k);k') := A(k) \times \{k'\}$

$(A(k);k'_1,k'_2,\ldots,k'_m) := \bigcup_{\mu=1}^{m} (A(k);k'_\mu)$

$(A(k_1,k_2,\ldots,k_m);k') := \bigcup_{\mu=1}^{m} (A(k_\mu);k')$

$(k';A(k)) := \{k'\} \times A(k)$

$(k'_1,k'_2,\ldots,k'_m;A(k)) := \bigcup_{\mu=1}^{m} (k'_\mu;\ A(k))$

$(k';A(k_1,k_2,\ldots,k_m)) := \bigcup_{\mu=1}^{m} (k';A(k_\mu))$.

Def. 5.5: Two productions are called *equivalent* ($p \equiv p'$) iff $d_\ell \underset{f}{\equiv} d'_\ell$, $d_r \underset{g}{\equiv} d'_r$ with equivalence functions f,g, and C' is generated from C by the following substitution: k_ℓ is replaced by $f(k_\ell)$, and all node denotations of K_r are replaced by their image in K'_r according to g.
A set of productions is *node disjoint* iff the set of corresponding replacement rules is node disjoint.

Def. 5.6: Let be $d \in d(\Sigma_v,\Sigma_E) - \{d_\varepsilon\}$, $d' \in d(\Sigma_v,\Sigma_E)$. The graph d' is in G *directly implicit parallel derivable* from d ($d \overset{pi}{\longrightarrow} d'$) iff there is a set of node disjoint productions $\{p_1,\ldots,p_q\}$ such that:

1) $K = \bigcup_{i=1}^{q} K_{\ell_i}$, $\quad d_{\ell_i} \subseteq d$,

2) $K' = \bigcup_i K_{r_i}$, $\quad d_{r_i} \subseteq d'$,

3) Two daughter graphs d_{r_m} and d_{r_j} are connected by an edge from $k_1 \in K_{r_m}$ to $k_2 \in K_{r_j}$ with label a iff
   - The connection component l_a of production p_j contains an embedding part $(A(k_{\ell_j});k_2)$, where $k_{\ell_m} \in A^{d_{\ell_j} \cdot d}(k_{\ell_j})$.
   - The connection component r_a of production p_m contains an embedding part $(k_1;B(k_{\ell_m}))$, where $k_{\ell_j} \in B^{d_{\ell_m} \cdot d}(k_{\ell_m})$.

The above conditions guarantee:
- For each node there is a corresponding production in $\{p_1,\ldots,p_q\}$. The production has that node as mother node.
- All daughter graphs of the applied productions are subgraphs of d', and their node sets are a partition of the node set K'.
- Each of the last two conditions generates a half edge: The first of them assures that an a-labelled edge beginning somewhere in d_{r_m} ends in k_2 of d_{r_j}. So, the right half edge in Fig. 9 is generated. Analogously the second condition generates the left half edge. An edge is generated iff two half-edges fit together.

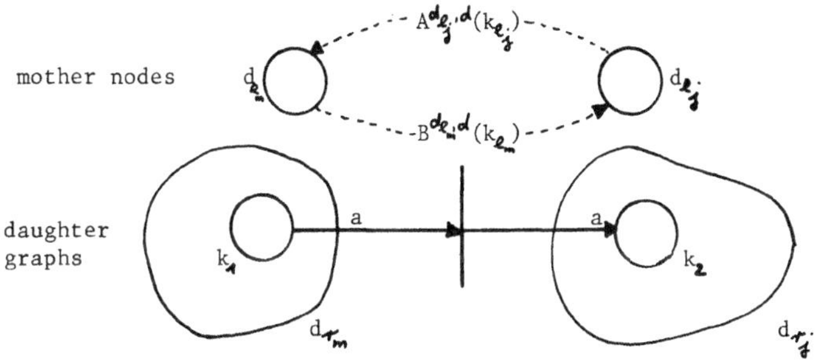

Fig. 9

Def. 5.7: A *graph l-system with implicit connection transformation (i-GL-system)* is a tuple $G=(\Sigma_V,\Sigma_E,P,d_o,\xrightarrow{\text{pi}})$ with Σ_V, Σ_E, d_o as above, and P is a finite set of productions which is complete in the above sense for replacement rules, $\xrightarrow{\text{pi}}$ is the derivation mechanism of Def. 5.6 in the sense that all applied productions are equivalent to some of P.

An example elucidating the half-edge mechanism can be found in the introductory paper of this volume. For results corresponding to implicit systems the reader is referred to /Na78/. The notions derivable, language, extended etc. are used in i-GL-systems analogously to the corresponding notions for e-GL-systems. In the remaining part of this section we investigate the relations between explicit and implicit systems.

Thm. 5.8: There is an i-GL-language which is not an e-max-GL-language.

Proof: Example:

productions:

$A ::= A$
$B ::= B$

$C_1: 1=(RCL(0);0), \quad r=(0;CL(0))$
$C_2 = C_1$

derivation sequence and generated language:

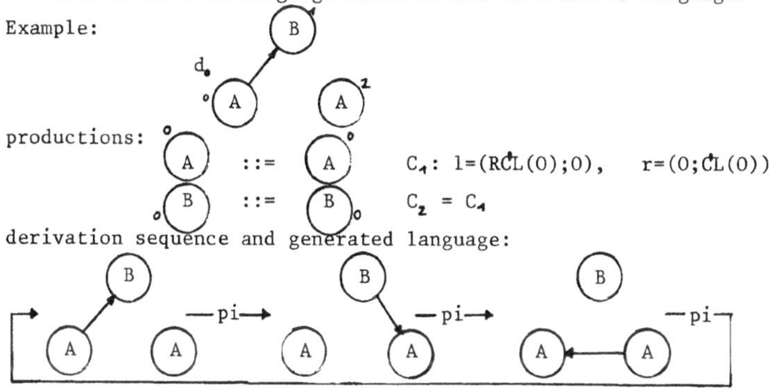

Fig. 10

From Thm. 4.3 we know that this is not an e-max-GL-language.

Thm. 5.9: There is an e-max-GL-language which is not an i-GL-language.

Proof: It is trivial to find an example. By implicit connection transformation we cannot connect two daughter graphs in the following way:

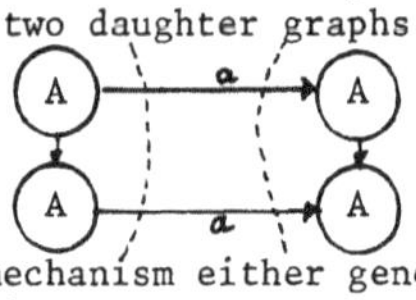

The half-edge mechanism either generates less or more connections as

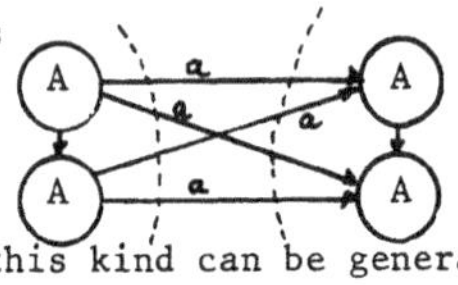

Fig. 11

It is trivial to remark that connections of this kind can be generated within i-EGL-systems.

Thm. 5.10: For any e-max-GL-system an i-EGL-system can be constructed which generates the same language.

Proof: (cf. /Gr76/, pp. 73-87):
The basic idea is that the stencils of e-max-GL are simulated by connection transformations. To prevent the derivation of "wrong" graphs, the node and edge labels (nonterminal) have to be indexed very carefully.
The main problem is that the connection transformations of a pair of daughter graphs have to simulate exactly one stencil between them (as replacement of one mother edge graph).
The derivation is such that in the case of an error we run into a blind alley, i.e. we generate a graph from which no terminal graph can be derived.
Scheme of derivation:

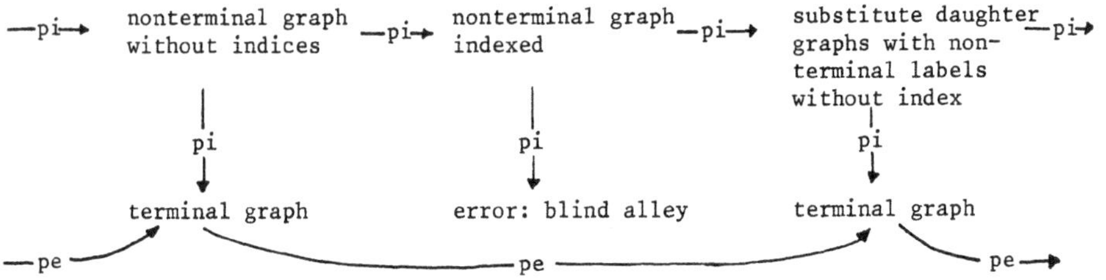

Cor. 5.11: *e-EGL* $\subseteq$ *i-EGL*

Now we get the main result of this paper:

Thm. 5.12:

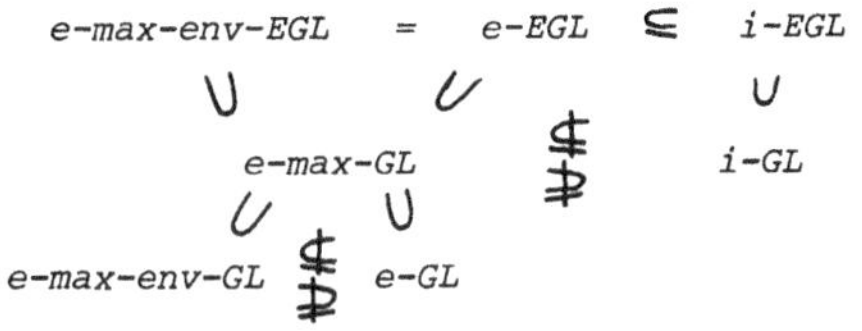
e-max-env-EGL = e-EGL ⊆ i-EGL
e-max-GL
i-GL
e-max-env-GL
e-GL

6. SOME REMARKS ON FURTHER RESULTS

To prove the relation *e-EGL* $\subseteq$ *i-EGL* in /Gr76/ we introduced a standard form of graphs which may be useful for further investigations. This standard form is some kind of coding. Let us explain it by an example.

$\Sigma_E = \{a,b,c\}$

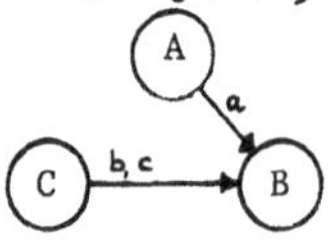

standard form:

$\Sigma'_E = \{(a,\bar{b},\bar{c}),\ (\bar{a},b,c),\ (\bar{a},\bar{b},\bar{c})\}$

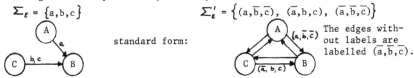

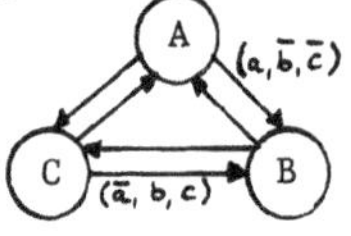

The edges without labels are labelled $(\bar{a},\bar{b},\bar{c})$.

An $\bar{a}$ stands for: in the original graph there is no edge labelled with a which is going in this direction.

A graph in standard form has the following properties:
- Each pair of nodes is connected by exactly one edge in each direction.
- The edge label of the standard form says exactly which edges are contained in the original graph and which edges are not (the latter case is very important for the simulation of the $\complement$-operator in e-EGL). It is easy to expand the standard form so that also the information of the counter-edge is coded in one label only.

Using that standard form we can simulate in e-EGL a subset of i-EGL which we call i-depth1-EGL.+) Such systems only manipulate direct neighbourhood, i.e. a connection between daughter graphs can only be generated if there was a connection between the corresponding mother nodes.

Another approach was to modify e-EGL: We introduced a context node with an edge at the left hand side of any connection rule:

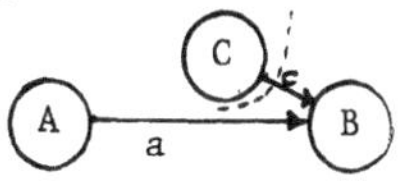

as generalization of 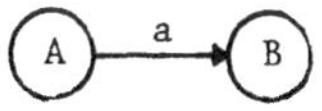

, where

C is the label of the context node and c the label of the context edge. A connection rule may only be applied to the daughter graphs of 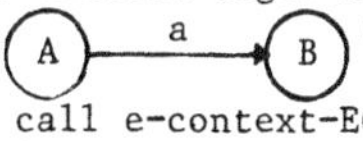

if the context condition (context node plus context edge) is a partial graph of the host graph. These systems, which we call e-context-EGL (context stands for context node and edge) turn out to be equivalent to i-EGL-systems. So we have:

e-EGL $\subseteq$ *i-EGL* = *e-context-EGL*
$\cup\!\mathrm{I}$ $\quad$ $\cup\!\mathrm{I}$
i-depth1-EGL

+) Operators in i-depth1-systems are built up by the following restricted rules: 1) L_a, R_a are admissable, 2) If A, B are admissable then also $(A \cup B)$, $(A \cap B)$, and $(v_1 \ldots\ldots v_m A)$ with $v_i \in \Sigma_v$.

REFERENCES

/CuLi74/ CULIK, K. II/LINDENMAYER, A.:
Parallel Rewriting on Graphs and Multidimensional Development, Techn. Report CS-74-22, University of Waterloo, Canada (1974).

/CuLi76/ CULIK, K. II/LINDENMAYER, A.:
Parallel Graph Generating and Graph Recurrence Systems for Multidimensional Development, Int. J. General Systems 3, 53-66 (1976).

/EhKr76/ EHRIG, H./KREOWSKI, H.J.:
Parallel Graph Grammars, in /LiRb76/, 425-442 (1976).

/EhRb76/ EHRIG, H./ROZENBERG, G.:
Some Definitional Suggestions for Parallel Graph Grammars, in /LiRb76/, 443-468 (1976).

/Gr76/ GRÖTSCH, E.:
Vergleichende Studie über parallele Ersetzung markierter Graphen, Arbeitsber. d. Inst. f. Math. Masch. u. Datenverarb. 9, 6, 1 - 152, University of Erlangen (1976).

/GrNa77/ GRÖTSCH, E./NAGL, M.:
Comparison between Explicit and Implicit Graph L-Systems, Arbeitsber. d. Inst. f. Math. Masch. u. Datenverarb. 10, 8, 5 - 23, University of Erlangen (1977).

/LiRb76/ LINDENMAYER, A./ROZENBERG, G. (Eds.):
Automata, Languages, Development, Amsterdam: North Holland (1976).

/Ma74/ MAYOH, B.H.:
Multidimensional Lindenmayer Organisms, Lect. Notes Comp. Sci. 15, 302-326, Berlin: Springer Verlag (1974).

/Ma76/ MAYOH, B.H.:
Another Model for the Development of Multidimensional Organisms, in /LiRb76/, 469-486 (1976).

/Na76a/ NAGL, M.:
On a Generalization of Lindenmayer-Systems to Labelled Graphs, in /LiRb76/, 487-508 (1976).

/Na76b/ NAGL, M.:
Graph Rewriting Systems and their Application in Biology, Lecture Notes in Biomathematics 11, 135-156 (1976).

/Na77/ NAGL, M.:
On the Relation between Graph Grammars and Graph L-Systems, Lect. Notes Comp. Sci. 56, 142-151, Berlin: Springer-Verlag (1977).

/Na78/ NAGL, M.:
Graph-Ersetzungssysteme: Theorie, Anwendungen, Implementierung, Habilitationsschrift, University of Erlangen (1978).

TWO-LEVEL GRAPH GRAMMARS

Wolfgang Hesse

Institut für Informatik der Technischen Universität München, Postfach 20 24 20, D-8 München 2

Abstract: Two-level graph grammars (2GG) combine the concepts of (one-level) graph grammars - as defined by PRATT - and of two-level (string) grammars - as introduced by v. WIJNGAARDEN for the formal definition of ALGOL 68. 2GG's settle both the inadequacies of one-level graph grammars and of two-level string grammars, the former resulting from the lack of parameters, the latter from the general lack of structure of string manipulation systems. As a field of application of 2GG's, the formal description of programming languages is focussed.

1 Introduction

Graph grammars have been introduced and successfully been used at various places in computer science and biology, wherever sets of more-dimensional objects are involved. Even for the formal description of (one-dimensional) programming languages graph grammars have proved useful, whether for the definition of the "abstract syntax" using a graph structure, or for the specification of control and data structures or for the formulation of semantical models. The application of graph models for the formal description of programming languages has been investigated by several authors (CULIK, PRATT, the VIENNA group etc.). PRATT used some sort of context-free graph grammars for the syntax and hierarchical graphs (H-graphs) for the formal definition of the semantics (/PRA 69/, /PRA 71/). PRATT's method provides for an adequate description of many control and data structures, his language descriptions, however, suffer from two drawbacks: The first is the context-free character of his grammars, which does not admit the formalisation of so-called "context conditions". The other is the lack of parameters in the H-graph model, which e.g. prohibits from directly modelling recursive functions with parameters by H-graphs.

W-grammars ("van WIJNGAARDEN grammars", "two-level string grammars") do away with both these difficulties. Parametrisation was the basic idea for the introduction of metanotions in W-grammars. The adequacy of W-grammars for the description of arbitrary context conditions has been confirmed theoretically and practically (/SIN 67/, /A68R/, /A68RR/). Even for the description of the semantics, W-grammars may be used very well, as is shown in /C-U 75/, /HES 76/ and /HES 77b/. Objections to W-grammars usually aim at the weak point, that they exclusively deal with strings, which forces one to represent all objects by strings, without regard to their natural structure.

Two-level graph grammars (2GG's) are the consequent answer to the objections to both one-level graph grammars and two-level string grammars. They provide metanotions acting as parameters and allowing the formalisation of the context conditions and of the semantics, as W-grammars do. On the other hand, they offer the facilities of graph grammars on both their two levels.

The definitions of one-level graph grammars in section 2 and of W-grammars in section 3 essentially follow PRATT and v. WIJNGAAARDEN et al. (/PRA 71/, /A68R/). Two-level graph grammars are defined in section 4 and some of their properties are considered in section 5. The W-grammar concept of "predicates" is extended to 2GG's in section 6. The use of 2GG's for complete formal language descriptions is outlined in section 7. Section 8 contains some remarks about the implementation of 2GG's.

2 One-level graph grammars

2.1 Basic sets

Let be given the following nonempty, finite, pairwise disjoint sets:

$\hat{N}$: a set of nodes,

S: a set of nonterminal atoms,

T: a set of terminal atoms,

L: a set of edge labels containing the label "o".

$V = S \cup T$ is called the set of atoms.

2.2 F-graphs

By means of an inductive definition, sets $\hat{F}_n(S,T,L)$ of F-graphs of degree n ($n \geq 1$) over S, T and L are introduced.

Let $\hat{F}_0(S,T,L)$ be $S \cup T$. An F-graph of degree n is a 4-tuple $F = (Q_F, c_F, E_F, N_F)$, where

- $Q_F \subset \hat{N}$,
- $c_F : Q_F \dashrightarrow \bigcup_{j=1}^{n-1} \hat{F}_j(S,T,L)$ (the node value function of F) ,
- $E_F \subset Q_F \times L \times Q_F$ (the set of edges of F) ,
- $N_F \in Q_F$ is a distinct node, the frame node of F, with the following properties:
  - there is exactly one edge $e_i \in E_F$ with $e_i = (N_F, o, K)$, $K \in Q_F$, called the entry edge of F (K is the entry node of F),
  - there is at most one edge $e_o \in E_F$ with $e_o = (K, o, N_F)$, $K \in Q_F$, called the exit edge of F (K is the exit node of F), if any.

Let $\hat{F}(S,T,L)$ denote the union $\bigcup_{j=1,2,..} \hat{F}_j(S,T,L)$ and $\hat{F}^+(S,T,L) = \hat{F}(S,T,L) \cup \hat{F}_0(S,T,L)$.

In the following, graph indices ("F" in Q_F, c_F etc.) are omitted, if no confusion may arise.

2.3 Notational conventions

The following notational conventions will be used without further explanation:

- n,x,y,z denote nonterminal values,
- q,s,t denote terminal values,
- l,r,o denote edge labels,
- K,N,X,Y,Z denote nodes, particularly N denotes a frame node,
- F,G,H,J denote F-graphs,
- W denotes an element of $\hat{F}^{+}(S,T,L)$.

All above letters are possibly indexed by natural numbers.

2.4 Graphical representation

In diagrams, nodes with nonterminal values are represented by rectangular boxes, nodes with terminal values by ovals, and frame nodes by large rectangles surrounding the rest of the graph. Node identifiers usually are not written. Edge labels are ascribed to the line representing the corresponding edge, "o" is usually omitted.

Example 1: Let $T = \{s,t\}$, $S = \{n,x\}$, $L = \{o,l_1,l_2,l_3\}$ and $F = (Q,c,E,N)$ with
$Q = \{N,X,Y,Z\}$,
$c(N) = n$, $c(X) = x$, $c(Y) = s$, $c(Z) = t$,
$E = \{(N,o,Y)$, (Y,l_1,X) , (X,l_2,X) , (X,l_3,Z) , $(Z,o,N)\}$.

F is represented by the diagram in the margin:

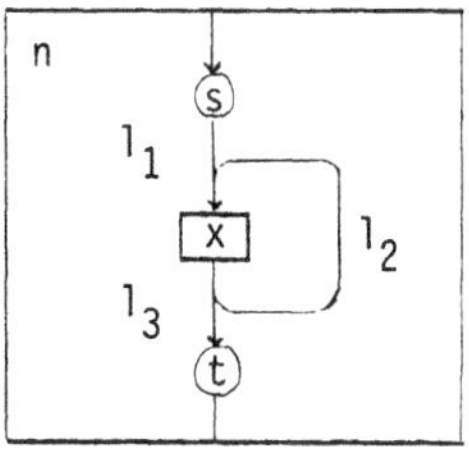

2.5 F-graphs and H-graphs

F-graphs differ from H-graphs (cf. /PRA 69/) by the inclusion of frame nodes. These allow to represent graph names by (nonterminal) atoms rather than to treat them on a metalinguistic level as PRATT does. The extension of H-graphs to F-graphs will facilitate the formal treatment of graph substitution, graph grammars and two-level graph grammars in the following sections.

If the value of a frame node has no further significance (particularly, if it is not used within graphs), this is indicated by the "dummy" nonterminal atom ж. If an F-graph with frame node value ж has no exit edge, its frame may be omitted and "ж" may be ascribed to the entry node.

Example:

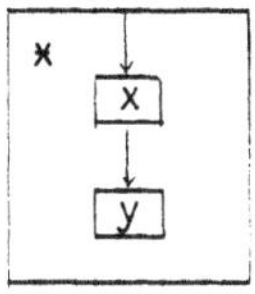

may be shortened to

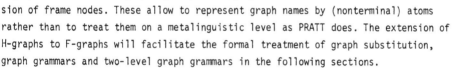

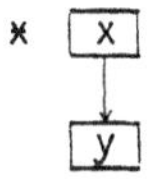

The right hand side graph may be viewed as an analogon to an H-graph with an entry node marked by ж . By $\hat{H}(V,L)$, we denote the subset of F-graphs of $\hat{F}(\{ж\},V,L)$, which have no exit edge. Note that the inclusion of nonterminal atoms in the F-graph formalism makes recursive hierarchical graphs - as used by PRATT - superfluous.

2.6 Isomorphic F-graphs

$G,H \in \hat{F}_i(S,T,L)$ are called isomorphic (denoted by $G \sim H$), iff there is a bijection $f\colon Q_G \dashrightarrow Q_H$, such that

- $\begin{cases} c_G(K) = c_H(f(K)), & \text{if } c_G(K) \in V \\ c_G(K) \sim c_H(f(K)) & \text{otherwise} \end{cases}$ (shortly denoted by $c_G(K) \simeq c_H(f(K))$),
- $(K_1,l,K_2) \in E_G \iff (f(K_1),l,f(K_2)) \in E_H$,
- $f(N_G) = N_H$.

2.7 Replacement of node values

Let $G,H,J \in \hat{F}(S,T,L)$, $W \in \hat{F}^+(S,T,L)$, $X \in Q_G \setminus \{N_G\}$, $c_G(X) \simeq W$ and $c_J(N_J) \sim W$. H is obtained from G by replacement of W by J in X (denoted by $G[\![X_W^J]\!] \sim H$), iff there is a bijection $f\colon Q_G \dashrightarrow Q_H$, such that

- $c_G(K) \simeq c_H(f(K))$ for all $K \in Q_G$ with $K \neq X$,
- $c_H(f(X)) \sim J$.

Remark: For the definition of one-level graph grammars, W is always a single non-terminal of S; proper F-graphs W are only used for two-level graph grammars.

2.8 Elimination of frame nodes

Let G,H,J be F-graphs and $X \in Q_G$ with $c(X) \sim J$. Let I be the entry node of J, and O, if present, be the exit node of J. H is obtained from G by elimination of X, iff

- $Q_H = (Q_G \setminus \{X\}) \cup (Q_J \setminus \{N_J\})$,
- $c_H(K) = \begin{cases} c_G(K), & \text{if } K \in Q_G \\ c_J(K), & \text{if } K \in Q_J \end{cases}$,
- $E_H = E_G \cup E_J$ with the exception that one has to replace
  $(K,a,X) \in E_G$ by (K,a,I) and, if O is present,
  $(X,a,K) \in E_G$ by (O,a,K) and
  $(X,a,X) \in E_G$ by (O,a,I), otherwise, these edges are dropped.

2.9 Substitution of F-graphs

Let $G,H,J \in \hat{F}(S,T,L)$, $W \in \hat{F}^+(S,T,L)$, $X \in Q_G \setminus \{N_G\}$. H is obtained from G by substitution of W by J in X (denoted by $G[X_W^J] \sim H$), iff there is a $H' \in \hat{F}(S,T,L)$, such that

- $G[\![X_W^J]\!] \sim H'$,
- H is obtained from H' by elimination of X.

Example 2: Let J be the F-graph used in example 1 and G, H' and H be the graphs shown below. Then H' and H are obtained from G by resp. replacement and substitution of n by J:

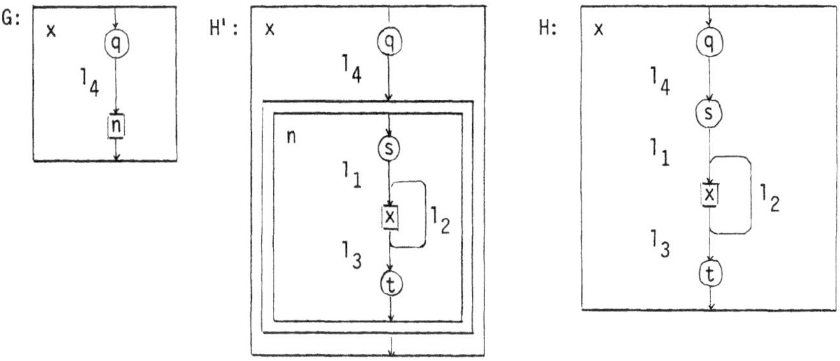

2.10 One-level F-graph grammars and their languages

A (one-level) F-graph grammar is a 5-tuple (S,T,L,R,z), where S,T and L are defined as in 2.1, $R \subset F(S,T,L)$ is a finite set of F-graphs (the rule graphs), and $z \in S$ is a distinct start atom.

Let $FG = (S,T,L,R,z)$ be a F-graph grammar and $G,H \in \hat{F}(S,T,L)$. H is directly derivable from G in FG (short: $G \xrightarrow[FG]{} H$ or simply $G \dashrightarrow H$), iff there are $J \in R$, $n \in S$, and $X \in Q_G$ with $X \neq N_G$, such that $G\left[X\ {J \atop n}\right] \sim H$. H is derivable from G in FG (short: $G \overset{*}{\underset{FG}{\dashrightarrow}} H$ or simply $G \overset{*}{\dashrightarrow} H$), iff there are $G_1, \ldots, G_n$ $(n \geq 0)$ in $\hat{F}(S,T,L)$, such that $G \dashrightarrow G_1 \dashrightarrow \ldots \dashrightarrow G_n \dashrightarrow H$.

For every $y \in S$, the graph $(\{X,Y\}, \{(X,*),(Y,y)\}, \{(X,o,Y)\}, Y)$ is called the singular graph sg(y).

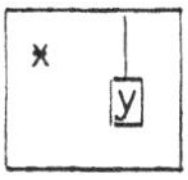

Let $y \in S$ and Y be the singular graph sg(y). $L_{FG}(y) = \{G \in \hat{H}(T,L) \ / \ Y \overset{*}{\underset{FG}{\dashrightarrow}} G\}$ is called the set of graphs generated by y. Particularly, $L_{FG} = L_{FG}(z)$ is called the graph language generated by FG.

Example 3: Let FG = (S,T,L,R,expr), where S = {expr,atom,op} , T = {t,f,⌢,⌣} , L = {l,r,o} , and R consists of the following F-graphs:

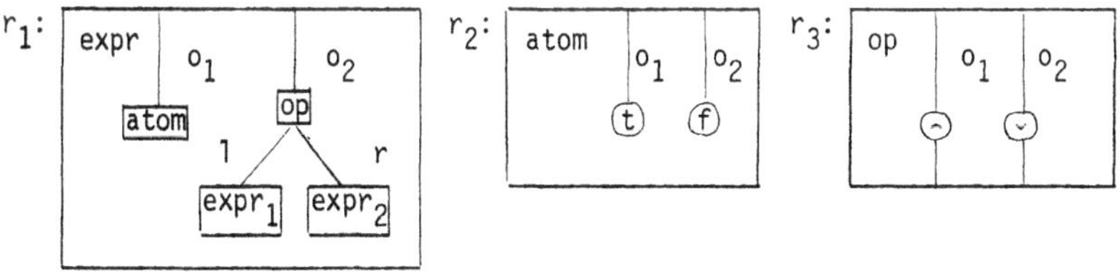

(Alternative rule graphs are contracted in a straightforward manner, arrow directions are not drawn for trees. The indices in "o_1", "o_2", "$expr_1$", "$expr_2$" are of significance only for section 5.2.)

The language L_{FG} consists of all binary trees with leaves marked by "t" or "f" and other nodes marked by "⌢" or "⌣".

3 W-grammars

Let M be an additional finite set, disjoint from S,T and L. M is called the set of meta-atoms. A W-grammar over M,S and T is a 6-tuple WG = (M,S,T,WM,WH,z), where

- $WM \subset M \times (M \cup S)^*$ is a set of metarules,
- $H \subset (M \cup S)^+$ is a set of hypernotions,
- $WH \subset H \times (H \cup T)^*$ is a set of hyperrules, and
- $z \in S^+$ is the start symbol.

(For brevity, we omit extra separation symbols within meta- and hyperrules and suppose, that all members of the right hand sides can always uniquely be separated, as is done e.g. in /A68R/.)

For $x \in M$, $L(x) = \{m \in S^* \ / \ x \overset{*}{\underset{WM}{\dashrightarrow}} m\}$ (where $\overset{*}{\dashrightarrow}$ denotes the usual context-free production relation) is called the metalanguage of x. From the hyperrule set WH, a (possibly infinite) set $WP \subset S^+ \times (S^+ \cup T)^*$ of production rules is obtained by consistent substitution. Consistent substitution (meta-substitution) is a homomorphism

$$j: \ WH \dashrightarrow WP \ \text{ with } \begin{cases} j(x) = x & \text{for } x \in S \cup T \text{ , and} \\ j(x) \in L(x) & \text{for } x \in M \text{ .} \end{cases}$$

The set S^+ may be divided into the two subsets $SN = \{n \in S^+ \ / \ \exists p \in WP \text{ with } p = (n,y)\}$, and $SB = S^+ \setminus SN$. SN is called the set of notions, SB is called the set of blind alleys, because its elements are "unproductive nonterminals" in the sense of CFG's.

M, S and WM constitute the "meta-level" of a W-grammar, S, T and WP constitute its "basic level".

For $x,y \in (N \cup T)^*$, we call y derivable from x (shortly: $x \overset{*}{\dashrightarrow} y$), iff $x \overset{*}{\underset{WP}{\dashrightarrow}} y$.

The language generated by a W-grammar WG is $L_{WG} = \{t \in T^* \ / \ z \overset{*}{\underset{WP}{\dashrightarrow}} t\}$.

4 Two-level graph grammars

4.1 Definitions

The above defined (one-level) graph grammars are extended to two-level graph grammars in a similar way as W-grammars are constructed from context-free grammars.

Let M be defined as in section 3. $\hat{H}(M \cup S,L)$ is called the set of meta-graphs, $K \in \hat{N}$ is called a metanode, if $c(K) \in M$, and a hypernode, if $c(K) \in \hat{H}(M \cup S,L)$. $F(H(M \cup S,L),T,L)$ is called the set of hyper-F-graphs over M,S,T and L.

A two-level F-graph grammar (short 2GG) is a 7-tuple GG = (M,S,T,L,RM,RH,z), where

- M,S,T and L are defined as above,
- $RM \subset \hat{F}(M,S,L)$ is a finite set of metarule graphs,
- $RH \subset \hat{F}(\hat{H}(M \cup S,L),T,L)$ is a finite set of hyperrule graphs, and
- $z \in S$ is the start atom.

Derivation in 2GG's will be explained in three steps: meta-derivation (4.2), construction of production rule graphs from hyperrule graphs by consistent substitution (4.3), and derivation using production rule graphs (4.4).

4.2 Meta-derivation

Let $G,H \in \hat{F}(M,S,L)$. H is called direct metaproduction of G, iff $G \xrightarrow[RM]{} H$, metaproduction of G, iff $G \xrightarrow[RM]{*} H$. G is called a terminal metagraph, iff $G \in H(S,L)$. Let $x \in M$ and $X = sg(x)$ (cf. 2.10), then $L(x) = \{Y \in H(S,L) \;/\; X \xrightarrow[RM]{*} Y\}$ is called the metalanguage of x.

4.3 Consistent substitution

Consistent substitution is a graph homomorphism $j\colon RH \dashrightarrow RP \subset \hat{F}(\hat{H}(S,L),T,L)$ with the following properties:

If $F = (Q,c,E,N) \in RH$, then $j(F) = (Q,c_j,E,N) \in RP$ with

- $c_j(K) = c(K)$, if $c(K) \in \hat{H}(S,L) \cup T$, i.e. if c(K) does not contain any metanode,
- $c_j(K) \sim X \in L(m)$, if $c(K) = m \in M$.

Note that for the homomorphism j and a node K containing the metanodes $K_1,\ldots,K_n$
$c_j(K) = (\ldots((c(K)\begin{bmatrix}K_1 & X_1\\ & m_1\end{bmatrix})\begin{bmatrix}K_2 & X_2\\ & m_2\end{bmatrix})\ldots)\begin{bmatrix}K_n & X_n\\ & m_n\end{bmatrix}$ and $X_i = X_k$ for $m_i = m_k$ (consistent substitution of meta-atoms).

By the mechanism of consistent substitution, the set RP of production rule graphs (which in general is infinite) is obtained from the hyperrule set RH. The set H(S,L) of protographs (corresponding to the set of nonterminals in a one-level grammar) may be split into the two subsets $HN(S,L) = \{G \in \hat{H}(S,L) \;/\; \exists F \in RP$ with $c(N_F) = G\}$, and $HB(S,L) = \hat{H}(S,L) \setminus HN(S,L)$. HN(S,L) is called the set of productive graphs, HB(S,L) is called the set of unproductive graphs or blind alleys.

4.4 Derivation

Let $G \in \hat{F}(HN(S,L),T,L)$, $H \in \hat{F}(\hat{H}(S,L),T,L)$. H is (direct) production of G or (directly) derivable from G, iff $G \xrightarrow[RP]{*} H$ ($G \xrightarrow[RP]{} H$). Let $y \in S$ and $Y = sg(y)$. Then,

$L(y) = \{H \in \hat{H}(T,L) \;/\; Y \xrightarrow[RP]{*} H\}$ is called the set of graphs generated by y. Particularly, $L(z) = L_{GG}$ is called the graph language generated by GG.

4.5 Graphical representation

On the basic level, the conventions of 2.4 for the graphical representation of F-graphs apply. On the meta-level, meta-nodes are represented by rectangular boxes with meta-atoms written in capital letters; nodes with S-values (acting as meta-terminals) are represented by ovals. For meta-graphs in tree form, we omit the entry node marker ⋆ and the labels "l" and "r".

4.6 Example

Let GG = (M,S,T,L,RM,RH,prog) with M = {TYPE}, S = {expr, atom, op, num, bool, nat}, T = {t, f, e, i, +, -, $\frown$, $\smile$} , L = {o, 1, r} , and RM and RH are given by the following graphs:

rm:
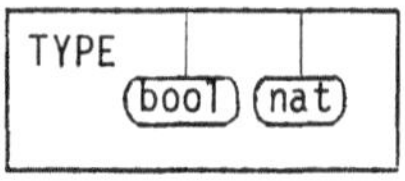

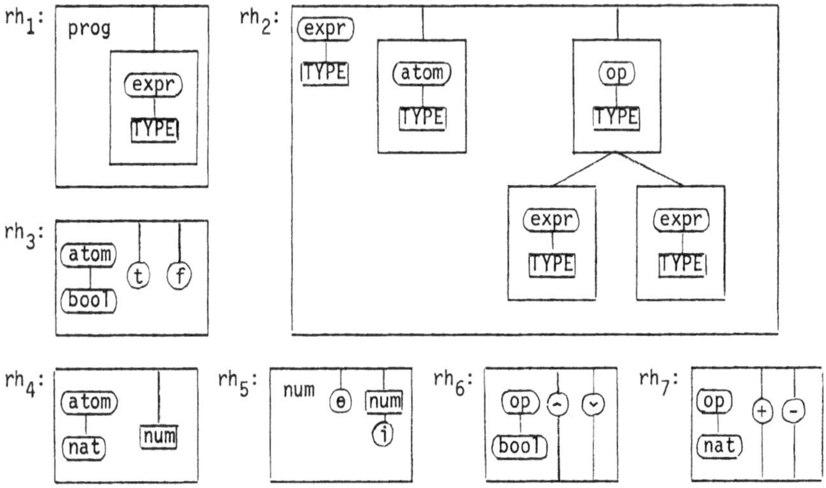

The grammar GG is an extension of the grammar FG (cf. 2.10) adding "natural numbers" and the "operators" "+" and "-". The meta-atom TYPE is used as a parameter for the formulation of "context conditions" concerning types: The consistent substitution guarantees, that e.g. in (rh_2) TYPE has always to be replaced by the same meta-terminal ("bool" or "nat"). Thus, the tree 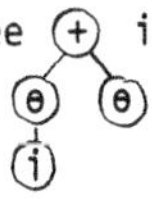 is derivable, 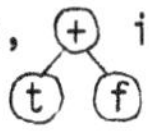 is not.

5 Some properties of two-level graph grammars

5.1 Two-level graph grammars and W-grammars

In order to compare graphs and strings, we associate with every string $s = s_1 s_2 \dots s_n$ ($n \geq 0$) over T the graph f(s) = $*$(s_1)-(s_2)- ... -(s_n) of $\hat{H}(T,\{o\})$. For a set L of strings over T, we define $f(L) = \{f(s) \mid s \in L\} \subset \hat{H}(T,\{o\})$. Now the following theorem holds:

For every W-grammar WG = (M,S,T,WM,WH,z) there is a two-level graph grammar FG = (M,S,T,{o},FM,FH,z) with $L_{FG} = f(L_{WG})$.

The proof and a table showing the corresponding terminologies of W-grammars and 2GG's may be found in the technical report /HES 78/.

Thus two-level graph grammars are analogous extensions of W-grammars as one-level graph grammars are of context-free grammars (cf. /PRA 71/). The following diagram depicts the relationship of the four grammar types (---> means generalisation) :

W-grammars	--->	two-level graph grammars
↑		↑
context-free grammars	--->	(one-level) graph grammars

From the undecidability of W-grammars, we get as a corollary:

> For an arbitrary 2GG GG and an arbitrary graph G, it is in general undecidable, whether $G \in L_{GG}$ or not.

5.2 Two-level graph grammars and pair grammars

In /PRA 71/, PRATT introduced pair grammars in order to describe translations of context-free (string- or graph-) languages. A pair grammar is a pair (LG,RG) of context-free graph grammars, the nonterminals and rules of which are paired, i.e. may be mapped to each other in a bijective manner. As an example, we pair the grammar FG of example 3 (cf. 2.10) with the following grammar FG':

FG' = (S,T',L,R',expr), where $T' = T \cup \{(,)\}$ and R' consists of the following rules:

r_1':

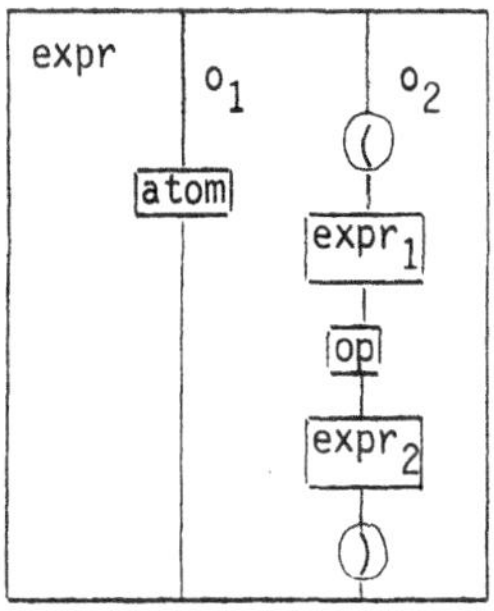

r_2':

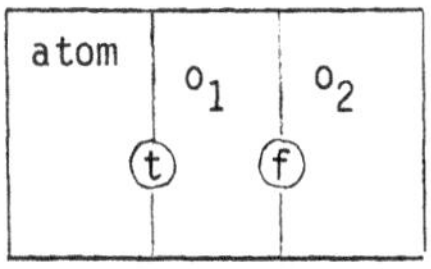

r_3':

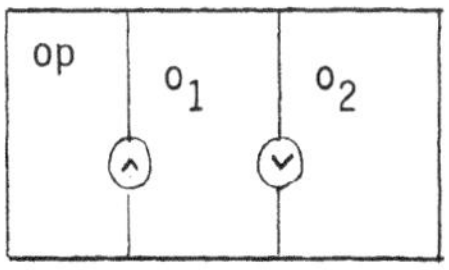

The entry edge labels "o_1" and "o_2" are used in order to pair alternatives of R' with alternatives of R. In a similar manner, nonterminals are supplied with indices, whenever this is necessary for an unambiguous pairing.

Pair grammars may be simulated by (single) 2GG's, as follows from the next theorem:

> For every pair grammar PG = (LG,RG) (with z_L = start symbol of LG and z_R = start symbol of RG) there is a 2GG GG with start symbol z, such that
>
> $(z_L,z_R) \overset{*}{\underset{PG}{\Longrightarrow}} (G,H) \iff z \underset{GG}{\Longrightarrow} (z_L) - \bar{G} \overset{*}{\underset{GG}{\Longrightarrow}} H$ with $\bar{G} \in \hat{H}(S_{GG},L)$ isomorphic image of $G \in \hat{H}(T_{LG},L)$

Instead of giving the rather lengthy proof, we show the construction of GG for our example pair grammar (FG,FG'): Let GG = (M,S,T,L,RM,RH,z), where M = {EXPR,ATOM,OP} , S = {z,expr,atom,op,tt,ff,and,or} , T = {t,f,∧,∨,(,)} , L = {o,l,r} and $RM = \{rm_1,..,rm_3\}$, $RH = \{rh_1,..,rh_6\}$ as follows:

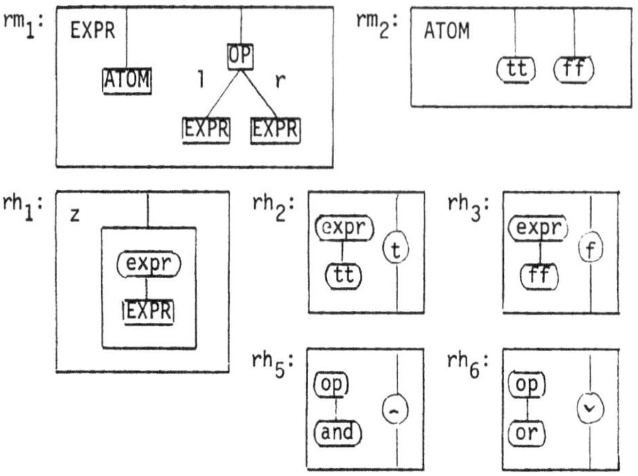

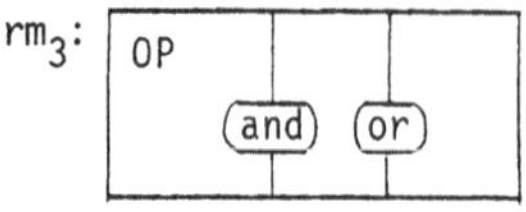

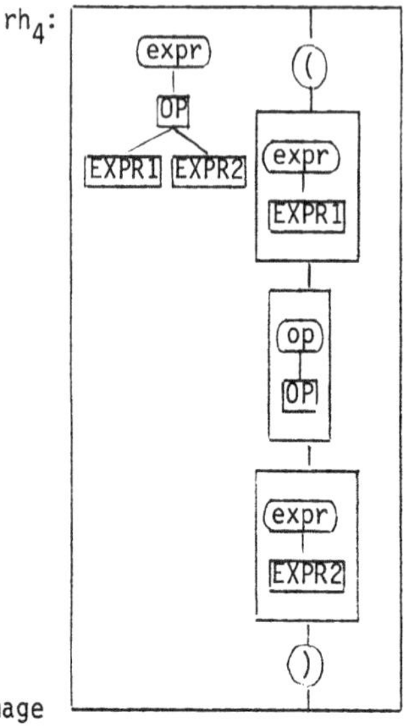

Remark: Analogously to the W-grammar conventions, meta-rules

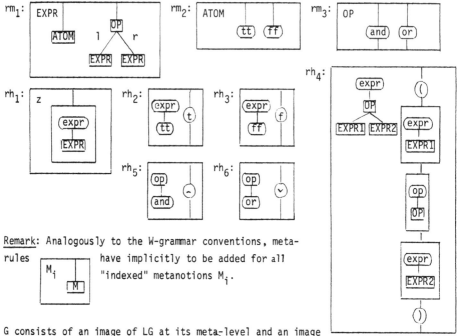

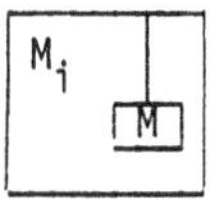

have implicitly to be added for all "indexed" metanotions M_i.

G consists of an image of LG at its meta-level and an image of RG at its basic level. The "pairing" is simulated by the parametrisation of hyperrules by LG-images. Of course, there is an analogous 2GG GG' with LG and RG interchanged, such that $(z_L, z_R) \xrightarrow[PG]{*} (G,H) \Longleftrightarrow z \xrightarrow[GG']{} \underset{H}{(z_R)} \xrightarrow[GG']{*} G$.

The images of graphs of L_{LG} occur at the meta-level of GG, correspondingly the images of graphs of L_{RG} occur at the meta-level of GG'. We call those images <u>nonterminal representations</u> of the resp. graphs of L_{LG} and L_{RG}. By a simple extension of the grammar, nonterminal representations can always be mapped into terminal ones (/HES 76/, /HES 77a/). With this mapping we get the corollary

> For every pair grammar PG (as above), there is a 2GG G" with $p \in T_{GG''}$, such that
> $(z_L, z_R) \xrightarrow[PG]{*} (G,H) \Longleftrightarrow z \xrightarrow[GG'']{*} \underset{G \quad H}{(p)}$.

5.3 Structured two-level graph grammars

Experiences with the practical use of W-grammars have shown that their readability highly depends on the structure of the hypernotions. Since both, human and automatic parsers, normally try (and should try!) to anlyse two-level hyperrules like parametrised context-free rules, it is rather natural to restrict the form of hypernotions in a "procedure"-like manner, i.e. every hypernotion consists of a "head" $h \in S$ (the procedure name) and a number n(h) (which is fixed for every "call" of h) of "parameters" (strings over $M \cup S$). It is easily shown, that the power of W-grammars is not decreased by this restriction (cf. /HES 76/). An analogous restriction on two-level graph grammars leads to the following definition:

A structured two-level graph grammar (S2GG) is a 2GG with the following restriction on the values v of hypernodes: v = 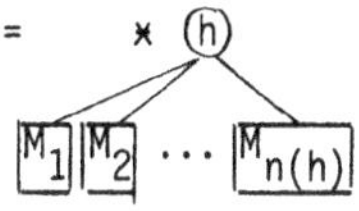 with $h \in S$, $M_i \in \hat{H}(M \cup S, L)$ $(i=1,\dots,n(h),\ n(h) \geq 0)$

For example, the 2GG GG of 5.2 is structured, because all values of hypernodes are trees with the heads "z", "expr", or "op" and n(z) = 0, n(expr) = n(op) = 1. GG is no longer structured, if we add to M a new meta-atom X with the meta-rule

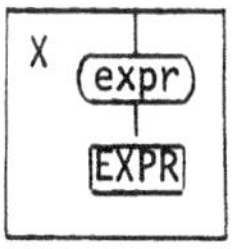

and replace rh_1 by rh_1': 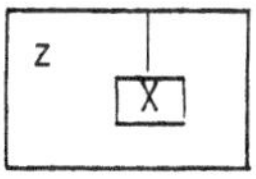

because in rh_1', X has not the required form.

The following theorem shows, that the power of 2GG's is not restricted by "structuring":

For every 2GG G there is a structured 2GG G' with $L_{G'} = L_G$.

The proof is analogous to that given in /HES 76/ for W-grammars.

Remarks: Note that for a structured two-level (graph) grammar the "referencing problem", i.e. the problem to determine all rules applicable to a given hypernotion (hypernode) is trivially solved by looking for the given "head".

The undecidability of two-level grammars, which is implied by the emptyness problem of the intersection of CF- (meta-) languages, is not touched by the above restriction.

6 Predicates

6.1 Predicates in W-grammars

From section 5.1, it follows immediately, that 2GG's may be used for syntax descriptions as well as W-grammars. But W-grammars have proved not only a successful tool for syntax description but also for the description of the semantics of programming languages (cf. /C-U 73/, /HES 76/, /HES 77b/). Semantics description by W-grammars is based on the use of predicates, i.e. hypernotions which either produce the empty string or produce no string at all ("blind alleys"). By simply transferring the idea of predicates to 2GG's, rather delicate problems as the description of complicated context conditions, graph transformations and "dynamic" semantics become manageable.

6.2 The empty graph

The empty graph ε is defined by $\varepsilon = (\{N\}, (N,*), (N,o,N), N)$

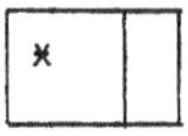

6.3 Predicate nodes

Let GG be a 2GG and F be a hyperrule graph of GG. A predicate node is a hypernode P of F, for which $L_{GG}(c_F(P)) \subset \{\varepsilon\}$, i.e. a hypernode, which produces either the empty graph or no graph at all. If P is a "protonode", i.e. $c_F(P)$ contains no metanode, and $c_F(P) \overset{*}{\dashrightarrow} \varepsilon$, we call P a true predicate, otherwise, if $c_F(P)$ does not produce any graph, we call P a false predicate and denote this by $c_F(P) \dashrightarrow \omega$.

6.4 Example (the "is"-predicate)

Suppose the sets M and RM of grammar GG of 5.2. Let (rh) (cf. diagram) be the only hyperrule having "is" in its frame node.

rh:

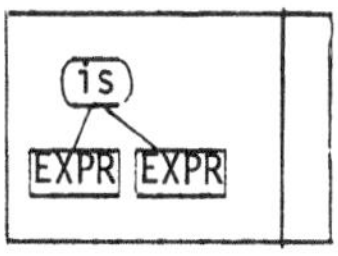

Then, every hypernode P (with metagraphs M1 and M2, cf. diagram) occuring anywhere in a hyperrule is a predicate. For, if $M1 \overset{*}{\underset{RM}{\dashrightarrow}} m_1$ and $M2 \overset{*}{\underset{RM}{\dashrightarrow}} m_2$ and $m_1 \sim m_2$, then $P \dashrightarrow \varepsilon$ by rule rh. Otherwise, if $m_1 \not\sim m_2$, the rule of consistent substitution prevents from any application of rule rh and as by our assumption there is no other node with an "is" at its frame, $p \dashrightarrow \omega$.

P:

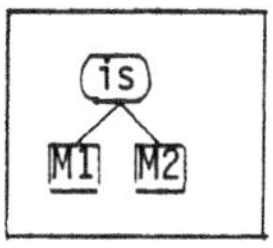

Of course, "is" is a predicate which models the comparison of two EXPR's for equality. Note that the definition of an analogous "isnot"-predicate (cf. /HES 78/) is not as simple, because the mechanism of consistent substitution is not symmetric with respect to "equality" and "inequality".

6.5 Description of recursive functions by predicates

In a structured 2GG, the values of predicate nodes are trees with a root $p \in S$ and a fixed number $n = n(p)$ of descendents. We shortly express this fact by "p is a n-ary predicate". E.g. the above defined "is" is a binary predicate.

The next theorem is fundamental for the use of predicates in formal language descriptions by 2GG's:

> For every n-ary partial recursive function f there is a (n+1)-ary predicate p_f of a 2GG GG, such that $f(a_1, \ldots, a_n) = a_0 \iff$
>
> 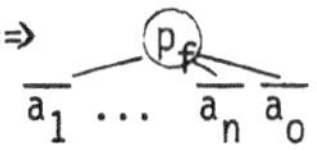
>
>
> $\dashrightarrow \varepsilon$ with $\overline{a_i}$ = non-terminal representation of a_i $(i=0,..,n)$.

The proof follows readily that for W-grammars given in /HES 76/. As an example we give a 2GG-description of the (unary) factorial function by a (binary) predicate "fac". Let M contain a meta-atom NUM and $\{e, i, fac, mult\} \subset S$. The metarules for NUM and the hyperrules for "fac" are given by the following F-graphs:

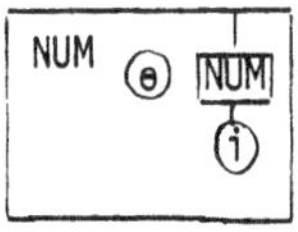

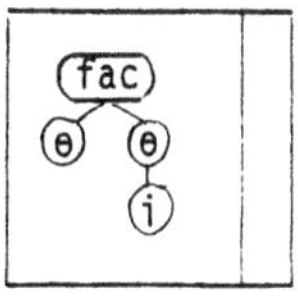

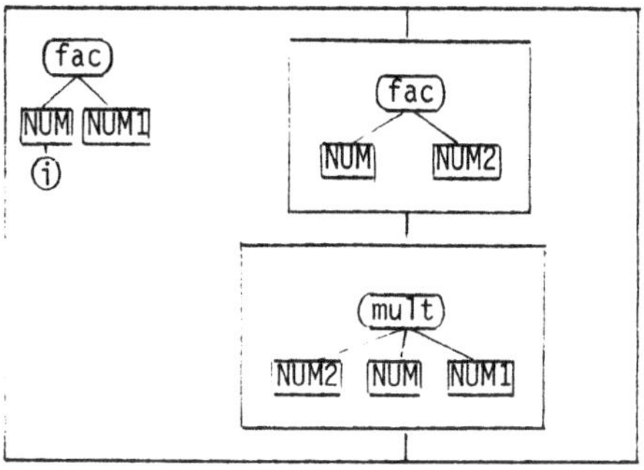

The correspondence between the factorial function "fact" and the predicate "fac" (with two metapositions for the argument (NUM) and the result (NUM1)) is given by

fact(a) = b ⟺ (fac) with sons $\bar{a}$, $\bar{b}$ $\xrightarrow[GG]{*} \varepsilon$. (The multiplication function "mult" with arguments NUM2 and NUM and result NUM1 has to be described in an analogous way.)

Note the essential differences to PRATT's semantics description (/PRA 69/, /PRA 73/). The lack of parameters in PRATT's H-graph formalism causes the necessity of additional "data H-graphs" (acting like global variables in a programming language) and even of a stack for the arguments and results of function calls.

For more examples of the use of predicates for the description of context conditions, graph transformations and semantics we refer to /HES 76/ and /HES 78/.

7 The use of 2GG's for formal language descriptions

7.1 Two-level string- and graph- grammar types

Graph grammars are a proper extension of string grammars, as shown in /PRA 71/. Two-level string grammars may be extended to graph grammars by the inclusion of graphs in their meta-level and/or their basic level. Thus we obtain four possible types of two-level string-/graph- grammars:

grammar type	meta-level	basic level	comment
$\begin{bmatrix}S\\S\end{bmatrix}$	string	string	W-grammars
$\begin{bmatrix}S\\G\end{bmatrix}$	string	graph	graph grammars parametrised by strings
$\begin{bmatrix}G\\S\end{bmatrix}$	graph	string	two-level grammars with graph meta-languages
$\begin{bmatrix}G\\G\end{bmatrix}$	graph	graph	(full) two-level graph grammars

The type $\begin{bmatrix}S\\G\end{bmatrix}$ may be viewed as an extension of PRATT's graph grammars by string parameters. An example of this type is the grammar GG of 4.6.

Our main interest was drawn to the type $\begin{bmatrix}G\\S\end{bmatrix}$ for the formal description of programming languages. Of course, we do with the "S" on the basic level for this purpose. Some reasons for our preference of the "G" for the meta-level are:

- Pure (string-) W-grammars tend to be hard to read (or even to be unreadable) for both human and automatic parsers - one of the most frequent objections to that grammar type. The lack of structure of such a pure string manipulation system is one of the main reasons for this drawback.
- A complete language description including the semantics requires an "abstract syntax", i.e. an image of the concrete syntax (represented by the terminals of T) on the (nonterminal) S-layer. Graph - and in particular tree-structures have widely been accepted to be most appropriate for this purpose.
- Implementation descriptions may considerably profit from the direct representation of the appropriate data structures (which normally are graphs) in the formal description.

7.2 A model for complete formal language descriptions by $\begin{bmatrix}G\\S\end{bmatrix}$-grammars

"Complete" formal language description means a description which includes syntax, context conditions and semantics. In /HES 76/ and /HES 77a/, we proposed a model for such descriptions by W-grammars. Following that model, a complete language description consists of a (rather trivial) syntactical part G_0, which manages the translation between terminal representations ("concrete syntax") and nonterminal representations ("abstract syntax"), of a semantical part G_1, and, possibly, of a number of subgrammars $G_2,\dots,G_n$ $(n \geq 2)$, which describe intricate context conditions. $G_1,\dots,G_n$ are purely "predicative", i.e. their hypernodes are all predicates.

If a $\begin{bmatrix}G\\S\end{bmatrix}$- grammar is used for a complete language description, the syntactical part models the string-to-graph translation between concrete and abstract syntax as sketched in section 5.2. Possible context conditions and the semantics are described by predicates which operate on the graphs representing the abstract syntax.

Complete language descriptions by 2GG's have been given in /HES 76/ for an ALGOL-like language and in /HES 78/ for LISP.

8 Implementation

For the reasons mentioned above, structured $\begin{bmatrix}G\\S\end{bmatrix}$-grammars are the most appropriate variant of two-level graph grammars for the formal definition of programming languages. For this grammar type, an implementation has been designed at the Technische Universität München (/LAU 77/). As implementation language, structured $\begin{bmatrix}G\\S\end{bmatrix}$-grammars themselves have been used (and shown their usefulness). In order to make the system available, a simple bootstrap (preferably using CDL2, cf./CDL2/) is necessary.

For the implementation, some further restrictions, but also some extensions of 2GG's have been made. These are listed in /HES 78/; for details cf. /LAU 77/.

Acknowledgement:

The author is grateful to A. FURTADO, who stimulated the work on this paper by valuable discussions, and to A. LAUT, who worked out the implementation and carefully read the paper.

References:

/A68R/ van WIJNGAARDEN, A. (Ed.), MAILLOUX, B.J., PECK, J.E.L., KOSTER, C.H.A.: Report on the algorithmic language ALGOL 68, Num. Math. 14, 79-218 (1969)

/A68RR/ van WIJNGAARDEN, A. (Ed.) et al.: Revised report on the algorithmic language ALGOL 68, Acta Informatica 5 (1-3), 1-236 (1975)

/CDL2/ DEHOTTAY, J.P., KOSTER, C.H.A., STAHL, H.M.: Syntaktische Beschreibung von CDL2, Arbeitspapier, TU Berlin (1975)

/C-U 75/ CLEAVELAND, J.C., UZGALIS, R.C.: Grammars for programming languages: What every programmer should know about grammar, Lecture notes UCLA (1975)

/HES 76/ HESSE, W.: Vollständige formale Beschreibung von Programmiersprachen mit zweischichtigen Grammatiken, Dissertation, Inst. für Informatik, Technische Universität München, Bericht Nr. 7623 (1976)

/HES 77a/ HESSE, W.: A correspondence between W-grammars and formal systems of logic and its application to complete formal language descriptions, TUM-INFO-7727, Technische Universität München (1977)

/HES 77b/ HESSE, W.: Formal semantics of programming languages described by predicative W-grammars, TUM-INFO-7728, Technische Universität München (1977)

/HES 78/ HESSE, W.: Two-level graph grammars, TUM-INFO-7833, Technische Universität München (1978)

/LAU 77/ LAUT, A.: Zur Implementierung zweischichtiger Graphen-Grammatiken, Diplomarbeit, Inst. für Informatik, Technische Universität München (1977)

/PRA 69/ PRATT, T.W.: A hierarchical graph model of the semantics of programs, Proc. AFIPS Spring Joint Comp. Conf. 34, 813-825 (1969)

/PRA 71/ PRATT, T.W.: Pair grammars, graph languages and string-to-graph translations, J. of Comp. Sys. Sci. 5, 560-595 (1971)

/PRA 73/ PRATT, T.W.: A formal definition of ALGOL 60 using hierarchical graphs and pair grammars, Report TSN-33, Univ. of Texas Comp. Center, Austin (1973)

/SIN 67/ SINTZOFF, M.: Existence of a van Wijngaarden syntax for every recursively enumerable set, Ann. Soc. Scientifique de Bruxelles 81, 115-118 (1967)

A PUMPING LEMMA FOR CONTEXT-FREE GRAPH LANGUAGES

Hans-Jörg Kreowski
Technische Universität Berlin

ABSTRACT

Each sufficiently large graph belonging to a context-free graph language (generated by an edge-replacement system) can be decomposed in three subgraphs FIRST, LINK and LAST, such that a suitable chain gluing of FIRST, LAST and N examples of LINK for each natural number N is also member of the language. This generalization of the well-known pumping lemma (also called Bar-Hillel's lemma, uvwxy lemma etc.) for context-free Chomsky languages is formulated and proved, where the iteration of LINK in the chain gluing leads to the pumping effect. The proof is based in canonical derivations and the embedding theorems studied in the algebraic theory of graph grammars.

INTRODUCTION

Graph grammars generalize the notion of Chomsky grammars by changing the underlying data structure from strings to graphs. How the generative machanisms are carried over, one can learn - instead of having to list many of the references in /Na 78b/ - from H. Ehrig's /Eh 78/ and M. Nagl's /Na 78b/ surveys on graph grammars. However, little is known up to now which results of formal language theory remain true in the more general setting of graph rewriting. How must the formulations be modified, how the proof techniques adapted, to generalize theorems? Some exemplifying answers are given by K. Culik and D. Wood in /CuWo 78/, P. Della Vigna and C. Ghezzi in /DeGh 78/, H. Ehrig and A. Liedtke in /EhLi 78/, R. Franck in /Fr 78/, by M. Nagl in /Na 78a/ and surely also by a few other authors.

To extend those experiences and considerations this paper presents a graph grammar version of the well-known pumping lemma for context-free languages (cf. e.g. /HoUl 69/, Theorem 4.7.).

In Chomsky case the pumping lemma states that (up to a finite number) each string z in a context-free language L is compound by five substrings uvwxy of which v and x can be interated simultaneously, i.e. uv^iwx^iy is in the given language L for each natural number i. The decomposition of the strings as well as the pumping make use of the linear order of strings, which is no longer available for graphs in general. Actually, the crucial part in generalizing the pumping lemma to graph languages is to find an alternative to uvwxy and uv^iwx^iy.

Sequences of graphs, of which every two succesive members are glued together in two nodes, solve this problem. If a graph G is composed by such a sequence of three graphs FIRST, LINK and LAST, LINK is provided with two gluing points to attach it to FIRST as well as with two other ones to couple it to LAST. Therefore pumping can be defined by sequences FIRST, LINK, LINK,...,LINK and LAST, where every two successive LINKs are glued together by identifying the two LAST-nodes of the predecessing LINK with the two FIRST-nodes of the successing one (cf. section 3.).

In addition to this pumping property a pumping lemma in the graph case requires a notion of context-free graph grammars and languages. For this purpose edge replacement is introduced in section 1. (Node replacement provides a possible alternative notion for context-freeness preferred by some authors. But which of both is favorite, seems a matter of taste mainly.) In section 2. an example of a context-free graph grammar is designed and special derivation is studied to demonstrate cause and effect of graph pumping. In section 3. the main result in this paper, the pumping lemma for context-free graph languages, is formulated and proved. Finally, some additional aspects are discussed in section 4. concerning specialization to the string case, an analogon for a sort of regular graph languages and non-context-freeness of some graph classes.

With respect to the main results this paper is based on parts of the author's Ph.D. thesis /Kr 77b/ and on a technical report /Kr 77a/. The pumping lemma for context-free graph languages is also reviewed in /Eh 78/, 8.3, but proofs are omitted. Independently quite a similar pumping lemma - indeed for graph languages generated by a special type of node replacement as introduced by T. Pratt /Pr 71/ - is given by P. Della Vigna and C. Ghezzi in /DeGh 78/. There is also a result closely related to a pumping lemma in H.W. Heibey's diploma thesis /He 75/. However, he does not describe the pumping of his graph-like "V,B-diagrams" (generated by a kind of node replacement) explicitly, but he quantifies only the growth.

It should be mentioned that the presented paper is not completely self-contained. But the reader is supposed to be familiar with the notions of labeled directed graphs and graph morphisms as defined in /Eh 78/, 2.3. + 5. Moreover some concepts and results studied in the algebraic approach to graph grammars are used to prove the pumping lemma. Those are the operations CLIP and JOIN, the canonical derivation and some of their properties (cf. /Kr 77b/). Most of them are also summarized in /Eh 78/, a part of this volume. (Apart from the different notion for context-freeness Della Vigna and Ghezzi /DeGh 78/ do not introduce any analogon to CLIP and JOIN. Hence the so important connection between constructed derivations and derived graphs remains a little vague in the proof of their pumping lemma.) Furthermore, for an explicit algebraic construction of the gluing of graphs in two nodes the reader should consult the more general case in /Eh 78/, 2.6. + 8.

1. CONTEXT-FREE GRAPH LANGUAGES

Edge replacement is proposed to specify the notion of context-free graph grammars and languages. It is defined by context-free productions and their applications to graphs.

The left-hand side of a context-free production p is a nonterminal A. Its right-hand side consists of an arbitrary graph B and two distinguished nodes s and t of B.

This situation is equivalently represented by two mappings (in fact graph morphisms)

$$A^{\S} \longleftarrow 2 \longrightarrow B,$$

- where $A^{\S}$ is a handle, i.e. an edge labeled with A together with its source and target nodes,
- 2 is a two-nodes graph without any edge
- and the mappings do not identify the both nodes of 2 (injectivity).

Note that for simplicity all nodes of all considered graphs are assumed to be unlabeled or, more exactly speaking, labeled with the same color.

In analogy to Chomsky grammars such a context-free production $p=(A^{\S}\longleftarrow 2 \longrightarrow B)$ can be applied to a graph G to obtain a direct derivation $G \Longrightarrow H$ via p if and only if the nonterminal A (of the left-hand side of the production) occurs in G. If occurring, the actual location within the graph G is fixed by a graph morphism $A^{\S} \longrightarrow G$ relating the both edges labeled with A. In this case the derived graph H can be constructed in two steps. First the nonterminal edge indicated by $A^{\S} \longrightarrow G$ is removed from G, the remaining graph is called R. Secondly, the right-hand side B of the production is attached to R defining H by identifying the original source of the removed edge with the distinguished node s of B and the original target with t.
This construction is well-defined because all nodes of G belong to R, too, such that the mapping $2 \longrightarrow A^{\S} \longrightarrow G$ can be restricted to $2 \longrightarrow R$. Note that by definition R is subgraph of G and that R and B can be embedded into H. Hence there are graph morphisms $G \longleftarrow R \longrightarrow H$ and $B \longrightarrow H$.

All graph morphisms constituting a direct derivation can be grouped into two squares

$$\begin{array}{ccccc} A^{\S} & \longleftarrow & 2 & \longrightarrow & B \\ \downarrow & & \downarrow & & \downarrow \\ G & \longleftarrow & R & \longrightarrow & H \end{array}$$

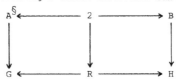

which are actually gluing diagrams in the sense of /Eh 78/, 2.6. This means that direct derivation via context-free production is a special case of graph grammar derivation defined in /Eh 78/, 3.1. The explicit construction of the derived graph given above corresponds to gluing analysis and construction in /Eh 78/, 2.8. + 3.1.

Now context-free graph grammars and languages can be defined.

DEFINITION

A context-free graph grammar $\mathcal{G}$=(N,T,P,S) consists of an initial nonterminal $S \in N$ and a set P of context-free productions, which left-hand sides are nonterminals in set N and which right-hand sides are labeled with nonterminals in N and/or terminals in set T.

Given such a grammar $\mathcal{G}$, all terminal graphs which are derivable from the initial nonterminal form the context-free graph language L($\mathcal{G}$) generated by $\mathcal{G}$:

$$L(\mathcal{G})=\{ G/S^{\S} \overset{*}{\Longrightarrow} G \text{ and } G \text{ terminal}\} .$$

Accordingly, a graph language L is context-free if a generating context-free graph grammar $\mathcal{G}$ exists: L($\mathcal{G}$)=L.

The fixed node color is viewed as terminal. Hence a graph is terminal, if all its edges are terminal labeled. Derivability is used as usual, this is the reflexive, transitive closure of direct derivation denoted by $\overset{*}{\Longrightarrow}$. Moreover, to avoid unnecessary trouble (proving the pumping lemma) context-free graph grammars are assumed to be cycle-free, this means no nonterminal is derivable from itself. The assumption does not really matter because each context-free graph grammar can be transformed into a cycle-free one analogously to the Chomsky case.

2. EXAMPLE

The following seven productions are context-free

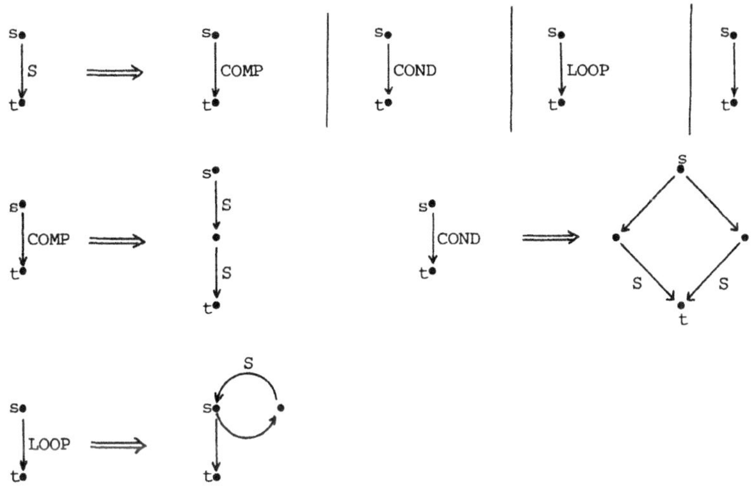

The mappings from 2 to the left- and right-hand sides are not given explicitly, but the images of the both nodes are indicated by s and t in each case (in particular s and t are not labels).

S, COMP, COND and LOOP are nonterminals. And there is meant to be only one terminal label. Hence terminal edges are sufficiently represented by unlabeled ones. Distinguishing S as initial, one obtains a context-free graph grammar in this way.

The graphs generated by this grammar are flow diagrams of a simple type. (But this does not matter with respect to pumping.) For instance, the following derivation can be constructed applying the given productions

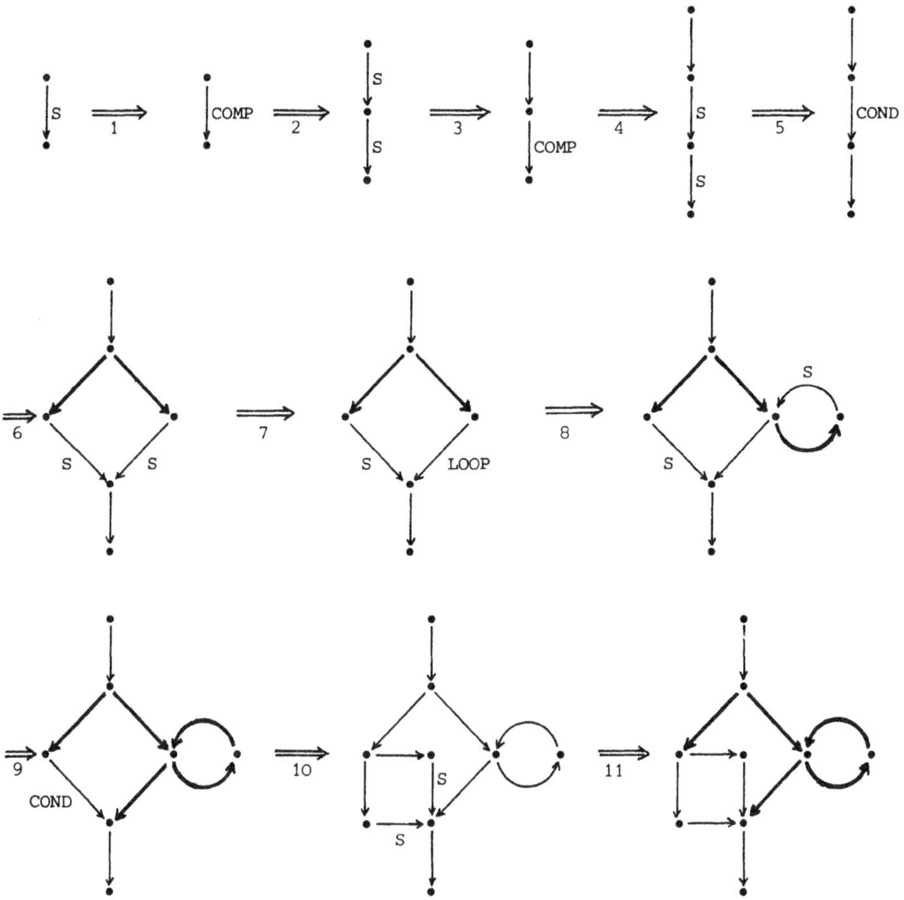

The direct derivation step 10, for example, is explicitly described by the following gluing diagrams

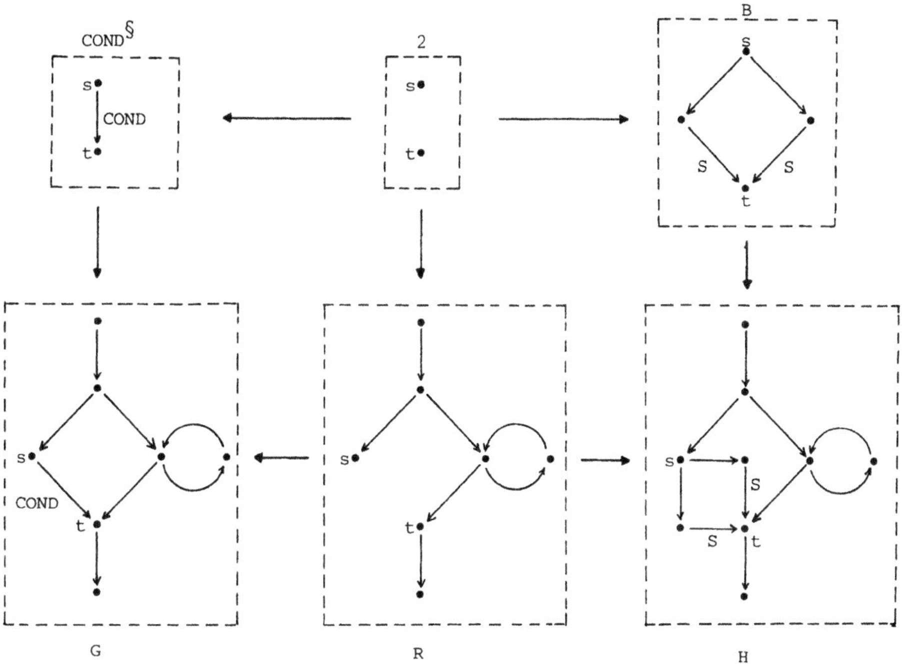

All mappings are uniquely induced by shape of graphs or by the images of s and t indicated in each graph.

REMARK: In some derivation steps above some productions are applied in parallel. Context-free productions can be applied simultaneously to a graph G if (and only if) they replace different edges of G. The explicit definition of parallel productions and parallel derivations is given in /Kr 77b/, 1.1., and in /Eh 78/, 4.6. It is important that parallel replacement of nonterminal edges allows common sources and targets. So it is possible to derive all occurring nonterminals of each graph in one parallel step. This defines the canonical derivation (cf. /Kr 77b/,5.1. and /Eh 78/, 5.5.) in the special case of context-freeness if the derived graph is terminal, in addition. These observations will be used in the proof of the pumping lemma.

The sample derivation is appropriate for demonstration of the pumping effect, as generally described in the following pumping lemma. The first five steps derive a graph with COND as only nonterminal. After another four steps a graph is derived again with COND as only nonterminal. Obviously the self-embedding property (COND derived from COND) allows arbitrary iteration of those four derivation steps. Doing this, the terminal part of the derived graph which is generated between the both occurrences of COND (recognizable by bold face) is copied - one copy for each iteration. For instance, the derivations, in which the part between COND and COND occurs two and three times resp., derive the following graphs

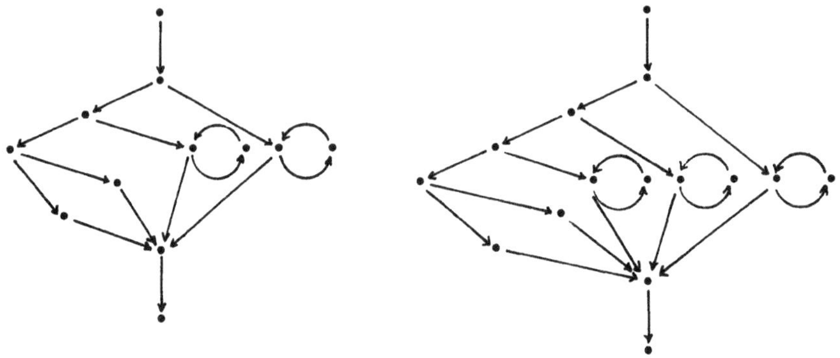

3. PUMPING LEMMA

Now we are able to formulate and prove the main result of this paper: a pumping lemma for context-free graph languages.

To describe the pumping effect, a gluing of graph sequences or chains, where successive members are glued together in two nodes, is used in the theorem. The necessary gluing points in each graph G of the sequence are indicated by mappings 2⟶ G (as known from context-free productions) so that such a graph sequence can be denoted by

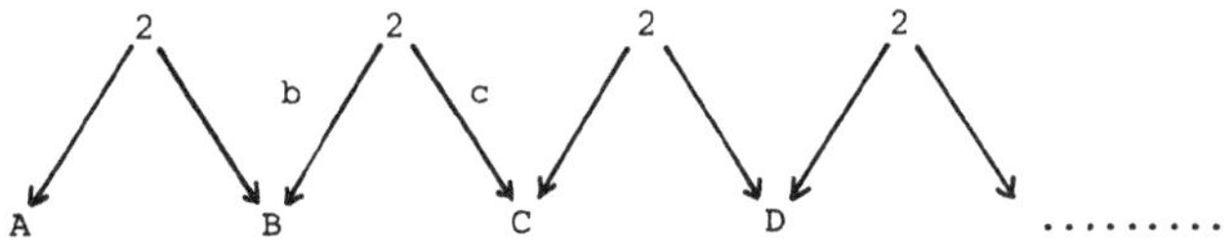

If s and t are the both nodes of the graph 2, the graphs B and C of the sequence, for example, are glued together by identifying corresponding nodes b(s) and c(s) as well as b(t) and c(t), the images of s and t in B and C resp.. After that the given graph sequence is shorter. So the gluing of the whole sequence is defined inductively. In fact, the induction step is the gluing of two graphs in two nodes as used already to define direct derivations. For a more general case a simple explicit construction is given in /Eh 78/, 2.8. It is important that the result, the gluing of a graph sequence, is independent of the order in which successive members are glued together. This associativity follows from the fact, that chain gluing in the sense above is a special case of star gluing defined in /Eh 78/, 2.9. (cf. also ditto, 8.3.).

THEOREM (Pumping Lemma)

Let L be a context-free graph language.
Then there exist constants p and q such that each graph G in L with number-of-edges(G) > p is gluing of a sequence of three subgraphs FIRST, LINK and LAST

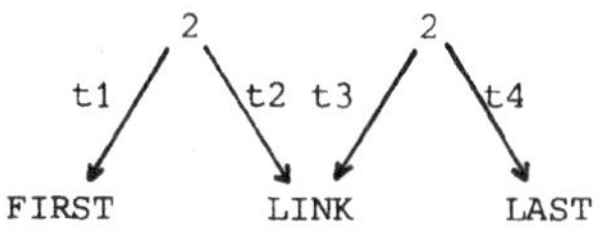

where number-of-edges(LINK)+number-of-edges(LAST) $\leq$ q and LINK$\neq$2, such that pumping is possible, i.e. for each natural number $i \in \mathbb{N}$ the gluing of the graph sequence

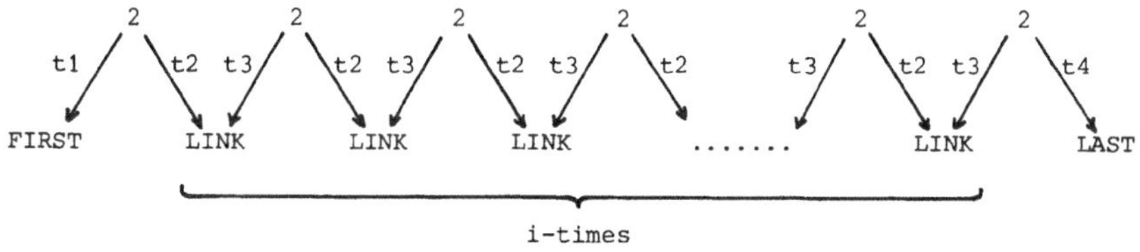

belongs to the language L.

REMARK: The requirement LINK$\neq$2 guarantees that the pumped graphs are different from the given one and from each other. (Hence in analogy to context-free languages of Chomsky type the pumping lemma provides a finiteness test for languages generated by context-free graph grammars.)

PROOF

Let $\mathcal{G}$=(N,T,P,S) be a context-free graph grammar generating L.
For $G \in L$ let $s: S \overset{*}{\Longrightarrow} G$ via parallel productions $q_1 \ldots q_m$ be a canonical derivation in $\mathcal{G}$ corresponding to a derivation tree in the string case (for definition and construction of canonical derivations see /Kr 77b/, chap. 5 and /Eh 78/, 5.5.+6.; cf. also remark in 2.).

By definition one finds a sequence of productions $p_1 \ldots p_m$ (p_i used in the parallel productions q_i) such that for each i=1,...,m-1 p_i and p_{i+1} are dependent in s. In the context-free case dependence means that the nonterminal to be replaced by p_{i+1} is just generated by p_i in the previous direct derivation of s.

The left-hand sides of those productions form a sequence of nonterminals $A_1 \ldots A_m$.

If the length m of s is greater than the number /N/ of nonterminals in N (cf. the end of the proof), at least two items in this sequence must be equal. Then choose $A_\mu = A_\nu = A$ with $1 \leq \mu < \nu \leq m$ and $m-\mu \leq$ /N/.

This means one nonterminal $A=A_\nu$ occurs in a graph derived from this very nonterminal $A=A_\mu$. Such a situation provides a self-embedding property (cf. /HoUl 69/,4.5.). Using the operations ANALYSIS and SHIFT in a suitable way (cf. /Kr 77b/,3.3.+ 8.3. and /Eh 78/,4.7.+5.5.), the given canonical derivation s can be transformed into an equivalent derivation of the form

$$S \overset{*}{\underset{s1}{\Longrightarrow}} G_\mu \overset{*}{\underset{s2}{\Longrightarrow}} G_\nu \overset{*}{\underset{s3}{\Longrightarrow}} G$$

where G_μ and G_ν are terminal up to one nonterminal edge labeled A.

Intuitively, it is clear that the middle part of the derivation can be iterated. But it does not seem obvious, how the derived graphs can be described explicitly - or whether the description in the pumping lemma in correct. More detailed consideration is necessary.

By construction G_μ is gluing of its terminal part FIRST and an edge labeled A glued together in source and target of the edge

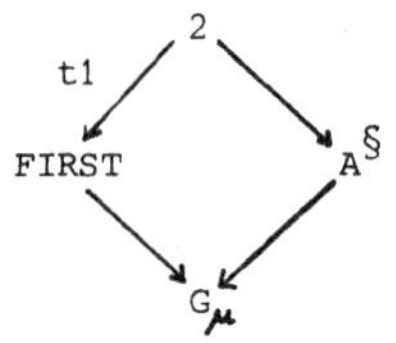

Because context-free derivations are not influenced by terminal parts, the derivation s2 above can be restricted to $A^§$ leading to $s4: A^§ \overset{*}{\Longrightarrow} F_\nu$. An explicit construction of $s4 = CLIP(s2, A^§ \longrightarrow G_\mu)$ uses the operation CLIP defined in /Kr 77b/,7.3. and /Eh 78/,5.3.

Moreover deriving G_ν from G_μ the terminal part FIRST remains unchanged. Therefore G_ν is gluing of FIRST and F_ν

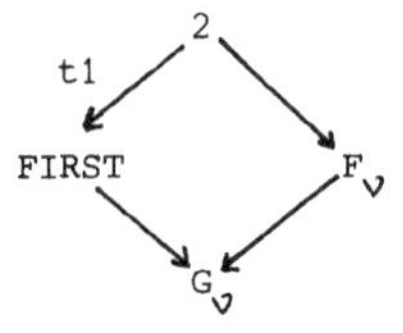

Repeating the arguments, F_ν turns out to be gluing of its terminal part, called LINK, and of the handle $A^§$ such that G_ν is the gluing of FIRST, LINK and $A^§$

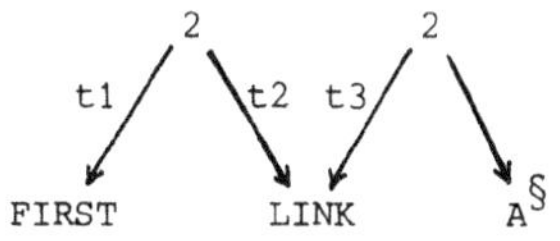

And respectively the derivation s3 can be restricted to $A^{\S}$ defining the derivation s5:$A^{\S} \overset{*}{\Longrightarrow}$ LAST. Because s3 and s5 differ only in terminal context, G is the gluing of FIRST, LINK and LAST

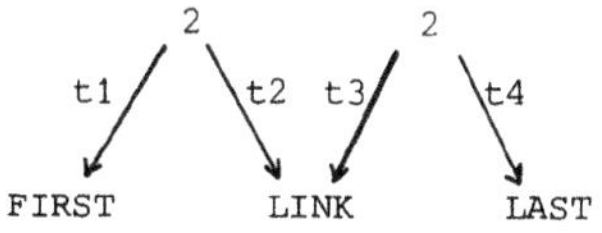

This is the desired decomposition of G.

More explicitly, the derivations s4 and s5 can be embedded in the graphs G_{μ} and G_{ν} along $A^{\S} \longrightarrow G_{\mu}$ and $A^{\S} \longrightarrow G_{\nu}$ respectively using the operation JOIN (see /Kr 77b/, 7.4. and /Eh 78/, 5.3.). Since CLIP and JOIN are inverse to each other (see /Kr 77b/,7.6. and /Eh 78/, 5.3.) one obtains:

JOIN(s4)=JOIN(CLIP(s2))=s2 and

JOIN(s5)=JOIN(CLIP(s3))=s3.

Hence the decompositions of G_{ν} and G stated above follow from JOIN-construction.

Assume now by induction that the gluing $G_{\nu}^{(i)}$ of

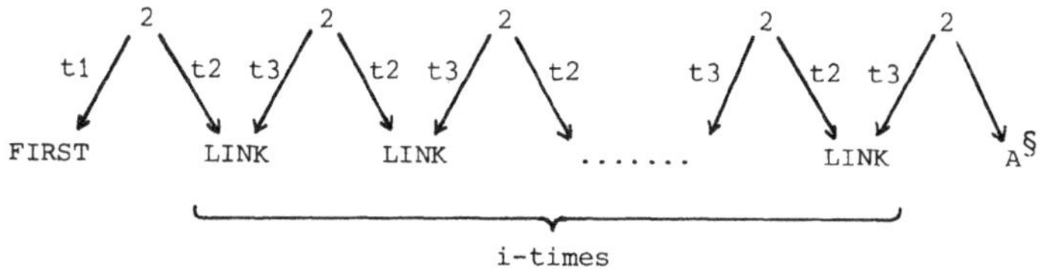

is derivable from the initial nonterminal S (by composition of the derivation s1 and i iterations of s4 embedded in suitable context). Then this derivation can be lengthened by another composition with s4 embedded now in $G_{\nu}^{(i)}$. Hence the derived graph grows out of $G_{\nu}^{(i)}$ by replacing $A^{\S}$ by F_{ν}. This leads to $G_{\nu}^{(i+1)}$ because F_{ν} is gluing of LINK and $A^{\S}$.

The beginning of the induction is given by the derivation s1 deriving $G_{\mu}=G_{\nu}^{(0)}$, the gluing of FIRST and $A^{\S}$ (and no LINK at all).

These inductively defined derivations can be terminated by s5 embedded in $G_\nu^{(i)}$ for all $i \in \mathbb{N}$. That implies, that the derived graphs $G^{(i)}$ grow out of $G_\nu^{(i)}$ if LAST replaces $A^\S$.

Altogether for each natural number i the terminal graph $G^{(i)}$ is the gluing of

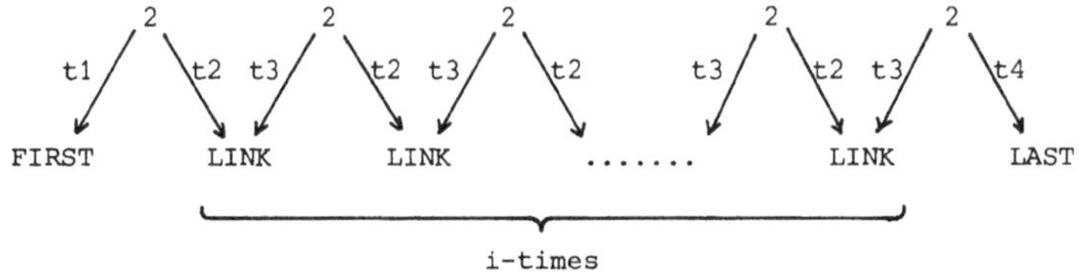

it is derivable from the initial and therefore it belongs to the given context-free language L.

Again the embedding theorem constructing the JOIN operation has been applied to obtain the explicit descriptions of $G_\nu^{(i+1)}$ and $G^{(i)}$.

To complete the proof, we have to show that the length m of the canonical derivation s is greater than the number /N/ of nonterminals.

Say $G_{m-1} \Longrightarrow G$ is the last derivation step. At most all edges of G_{m-1} are replaced simultaneously by at most the maximal number max of edges of right-hand sides of productions. This implies number-of-edges(G) $\leqslant$ max$\cdot$number-of-edges(G_{m-1}). Inductively one obtains: number-of-edges(G) $\leqslant \max^m$. Choose now $p=\max^{/N/}$. Then number-of-edges(G) $>$ p, as assumed in the theorem, implies m $>$ /N/.

It remains to verify the additional requirements. There is a part of the canonical derivation s deriving from $A=A_\mu$ the gluing of LINK and LAST. By choice of μ the length of this derivation (explicitly constructed in /Kr 77b/,8.3.) is $m-\mu \leqslant$ /N/. Using the relation above, one obtains

number-of-edges(LINK)+number-of-edges(LAST) $\leqslant \max^{m-\mu} \leqslant \max^{/N/}$.

Hence choosing $q=\max^{/N/}$ the respective requirement in the pumping lemma is satisfied. Finally we obtain LINK$\neq$2, because cycle-freeness implies that F_ν in s4:$A^\S \overset{*}{\Longrightarrow} F_\nu$ is not $A^\S$, such that the terminal part LINK of F_ν is not the terminal part 2 of $A^\S$.

4. SOME FINAL REMARKS

A. The composition of the graph G in the pumping lemma can be depicted by

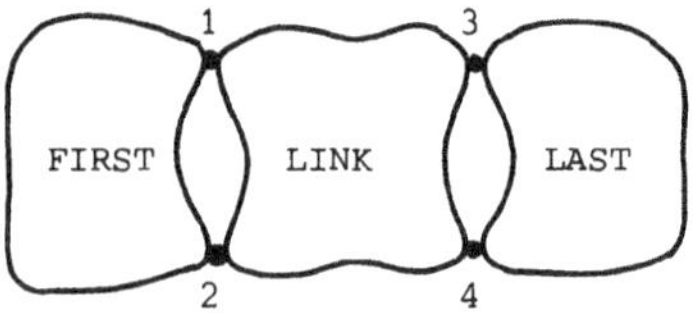

So the pumped graphs have the shape

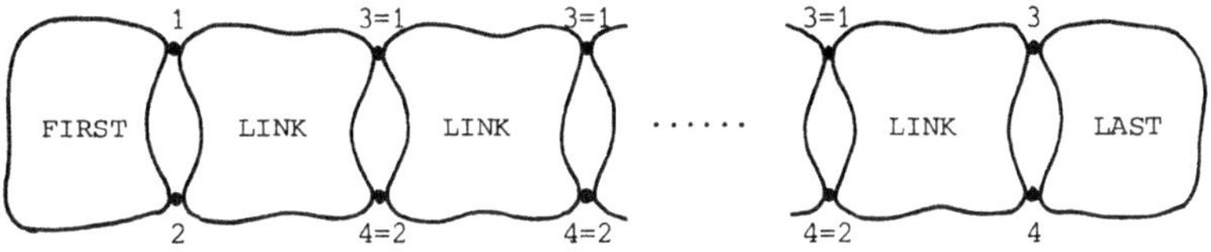

However, in some sense this picture is too intuitive, because it suggests that FIRST, LINK and LAST are connected graphs - but they are not in general.
For example, FIRST and LINK may consist of two components each, so that the graph G can have the form

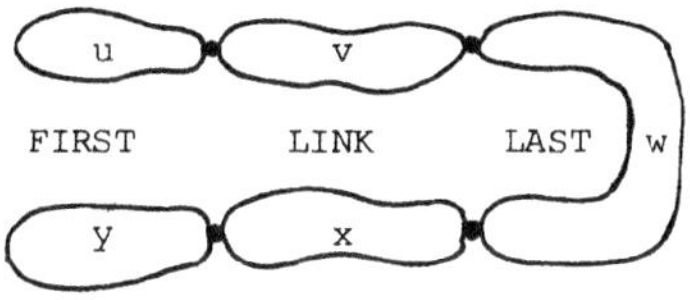

Pumping leads in this case to

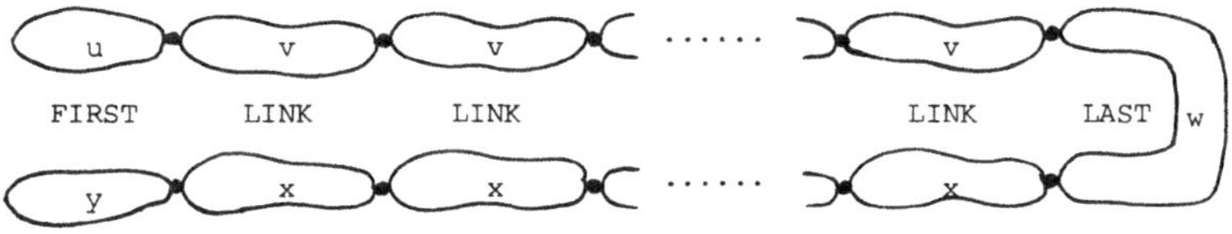

If now all components become thinner and thinner, so that finally all of them are strings, the pumping lemma for context-free Chomsky languages turns out to be a special case of the result for graph languages.

The author is indebted to B.K. Rosen for this pictorial relationship between string and graph case. More formal arguments are given in /Kr 77b/,6.5.

B. Besides context-freeness also an analogon to regularity can be defined for graph grammars and languages.
A regular production is given by two mappings

$$A^{\S} \longleftarrow 1 \longrightarrow B$$

where A is a nonterminal, 1 is a one-node graph without edges, B has at most one nonterminal edge and the node in 1 is mapped to the sources of the nonterminals. This provides a notion of regular graph grammars and languages, which can be viewed

also as a special case of the context-free situation.
As pointed out by H. Ehrig, for these regular graph languages one can prove a pumping lemma, too. Remarkably the formulation of this result arises from the context-free version by assuming a regular language and replacing all occurrences of 2 by 1.

In analogy to the special graphs 1 and 2 each graph defines a pumping property. But it is still an open problem to find appropriate classes of graph languages allowing such pumping.

C. In analogy to the string case the pumping lemma can be applied to prove that some graph languages are not context-free. But in addition some graph theoretical observations can be used to show non-context-freeness.

If a language L satisfies the pumping property, the number of edges of pumped graphs and of all FIRST components can not be limited. So there are nodes in FIRST and LINK in general additional to the both common nodes, if the number of parallel edges is limited for each graph. Hence in most cases a graph G∈L divides in at least two components after having removed the common nodes of FIRST and LINK (as well as adjecent edges). Using Menger's theorem (see e.g. /Wa 70/,9.2.), this means G∈L is at most two-fold connected in general, if L satisfies the pumping property.

Conversely, if infinite many graphs of a language are three-fold connected, the language is not context-free.

Typical examples of three-fold connected graphs are cubes

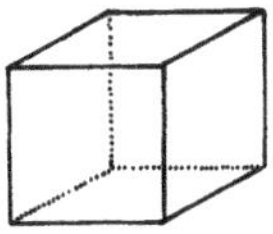

and cube buildings like

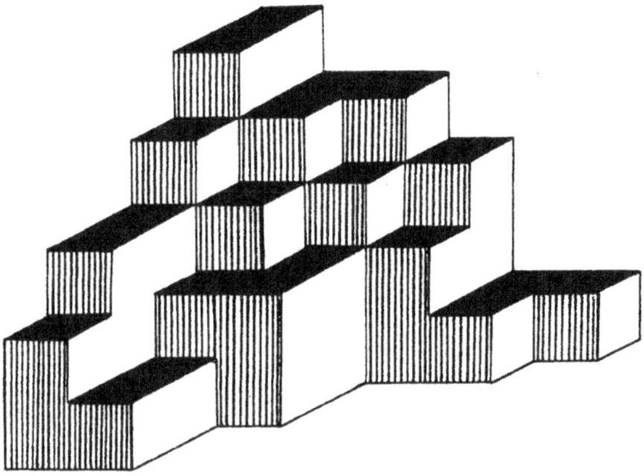

Hence languages of an infinite number of cube buildings are not context-free. A special example of such a language generated by a graph grammar is given in /Kr 77b/, 6.7.

As the one above the cube buildings in that language have the additional property that - suitably drawn - all their top, front and right surfaces are completely visible. This means that the language does not fulfill much stronger pumping properties than the one presented, because the only parts of the cube buildings, where pumping is possible at all, are the topmost, frontmost and rightmost cubes. The author is indebted to M.A. Arbib for this observation.

REFERENCES

/CuWo 78/ Culik, K. II/ Wood, D.: A Mathematical Investigation of Parallel Graph OL-Systems, this volume

/DeGh 78/ Della Vigna, P./ Ghezzi, C.: Context-free Graph Grammars, Inf. Contr. 37, 207-233 (1978)

/Eh 78/ Ehrig, H.: Introduction to the Algebraic Theory of Graph Grammars, this volume

/EhLi 78/ Ehrig, H./ Liedtke, A.: Locally Star Gluing Formulas for a Class of Parallel Graph Grammars, this volume

/Fr 78/ Franck, R.: A Class of Linearly Parsable Graph-Grammars, Acta Informatica 10, 175-201 (1978)

/He 75/ Heibey, H.W.: Ein Modell zur Behandlung Mehrdimensionaler Strukturen unter Berücksichtigung der in ihnen definierten Lagerelationen, Report No. 15, University of Hamburg, (1975)

/HoUl 69/ Hopcroft, J.E./ Ullman, J.D.: Formal Languages and their Relation to Automata, Addison-Wesley 1969

/Kr 77a/ Kreowski, H.-J.: Ein Pumping Lemma für kanten-kontextfreie Graph-Sprachen, Techn. Rep. 77-15, FB 20, TU Berlin (1977)

/Kr 77b/ --: Manipulationen von Graphenmanipulationen, Dissertation, FB Informatik, TU Berlin (1977)

/Na 78a/ Nagl, M.: Graph-Ersetzungssysteme: Theorie, Anwendungen, Implementierung, Habilitationsschrift, University of Erlangen (1978)

/Na 78b/ --: A Tutorial and Bibliographical Survey on Graph Grammars, this volume

/Pr 71/ Pratt, T.: Pair Grammars, Graph Languages and String-to-Graph Translations, Journ. Comp. Syst. Sci. 5, 560-595, (1971)

/Wa 70/ Wagner, K.: Graphentheorie, Bibliographisches Institut, Mannheim 1970

TWO-DIMENSIONAL, DIFFERENTIAL, INTERCALARY PLANT TISSUE GROWTH AND PARALLEL GRAPH GENERATING AND GRAPH RECURRENCE SYSTEMS

Jacqueline Lück and Hermann B. Lück

Laboratoire de Botanique Analytique et Structuralisme Végétal
Faculté des Sciences et Techniques de St-Jérôme - C.N.R.S. / E.R. - 161
Rue Henri Poincaré, 13397 Marseille cedex 4, France

1. INTRODUCTION

Biological morphogenetics operate in the framework of cellular tissue organization. Cellular assemblage and rules for positional order during cell multiplication and cell growth, take their whole importance against the background of individual cellular behavior. In contrast to animal tissues, in which cells can migrate, in plant tissues cell assemblage excludes major gliding arrangement phenomena between cells. The cell-wall network is persistent. The cell assemblage is ordered in regard to polarity axes. There may be apical growth, so that only at the top of an organ meristematic cells divide, or there may be intercalary growth. In either way growth includes cell multiplication and cell enlargement. Overall measurements furnish a first approach to morphogenetic growth. The growth functions are mostly sigmoidal; an exponential growing youthful period is followed by a period of senescence. Statistical methods give a deeper insight. A classical example deals with the length and width variations of squares marked in ink on young tobacco leaves. Conclusions from comparative regression analyses emphasized 'differential growth rates' in different parts of the leaf |1|. Elemental characteristics of overall behavior were later on analysed by microcinematographic methods and the still statistical approach touched elemental behavior in organ growth |2|. In recent years, we analysed in long time-scale experiments the growth behavior of all cells, and of their derivatives, individually recognized, of filaments of the alga *Chaetomorpha*. These investigations allowed us to state that the differentiation of cell length cycles are related to positional order in regard to polarity axes and to the position a cell holds in its own genealogical lineage |3,4,5|.

Both aspects of morphogenesis will be treated in this paper.

In order to describe the morphological features of tissue growth, we use L systems |6,7|. Actually, the discrete structure of these constructions allows the recognition of morphisms in cell arrangements. The recurrent properties of these L systems fit the recurrence in morphological unit patterns: differentiated cells (e.g.stomata) have been demonstrated to be markers of filiation controlled development |8,9|. PDOL systems grow exponentially |10| and thus correspond to the first period of tissue growth. Solutions for the second, senescent period of growth have already been given |11,12|. Surface growth needs an extension of the model structure to parallel rewriting graph grammars. We propose an extension based on the linear *Chaetomorpha*-scheme |3,4,5|, to refer to the theoretical work on graph generating systems |13-17|. Our first attempt to simulate surface growth and cell organization in cellplates led to a quantification of cell surfaces and linear cell dimensions |12|. Here, we propose a generalization of this concept.

2. GROWTH OF CELLULAR FILAMENTS

2.1 Positional control

Cell multiplication - The division of a single plant cell c^0 gives rise to two daughter cells c^1 and c^2, which are in constant positional relationship in regard to the polarity axis $\alpha\beta$ (apical-basal), $c^0 \to \langle c^1, c^2 \rangle$. If the two sister cells c^1 and c^2 divide once again in the same plane, so that the newly formed walls are again perpendicular to the axis $\alpha\beta$, the growth of a cellular filament is incepted.

There are some notable observations that the lifespans of sister cells are not equal. The number m of time steps i between birth, and disappearance by division, depends obviously on the relative position of the cells. In the thoroughly analyzed filamentous alga *Chaetomorpha* the apical sister cell c^1 has a longer lifespan m^1 than the basal cell c^2 with its lifespan m^2. Therefore, we admit the ordered set $\langle m^1, m^2 \rangle$.
A simple PDOL system may account for this situation. Its grammar is $G = \langle \Sigma, P, \omega_0 \rangle$ with the finite alphabet of state symbols $\Sigma = \{c_q^p\}$, the state transition rules $P = \{c_1^p \to c_2^p,\ c_2^p \to c_3^p, \ldots, c_{m^p-1}^p \to c_{m^p}^p,\ c_{m^p}^p \to c_1^1\ c_1^2\}$, the starting set $\omega_0 \varepsilon \Sigma$, and the indices $p \varepsilon \{0,1,$

2}, and $q \varepsilon \{1,2,\ldots,m^p\}$. The upper index p refers to the relative position of sister cells, the lower index q to the state of a cell in its specific life path, $c_1^p \rightarrow c_2^p \rightarrow \ldots \rightarrow c_{m^p}^p$.

The grammar G generates a sequence E(G) of locally catenated strings, $S_i = S_{i-m^1} * S_{i-m^2}$. The corresponding growth function f(i) of the number of elements in a string is exponential, $f(i) = f(i-m^1) + f(i-m^2)$ if $i > m^0 + \max\{m^1, m^2\}$. The case of $\langle m^1, m^2 \rangle = \langle 2,1 \rangle$, the famous standard Fibonacci series, is well known to plant morphologists e.g. phyllotaxis; cf. also a general discussion in |18|.

Cell elongation - To attribute a quantified length to each cell state c at i, we suppose that the symbol l stays for a number of linearily arranged length units. Under G and after j timesteps a state symbol c generates a word ω: $c_q^p \xrightarrow[G]{j} \omega$. The number of symbols in ω, i.e. $|\omega|$, can stay for l_q^p, which is the length of a cell c_q^p, $l_q^p = |\omega|$. If a word ω_i is composed of more than one cell symbol, the length of a cell can be evaluated by the partitioning of ω_{i+j} in regard to the descendants of the elements in ω_i.

2.2 Positional and lineage control

So far, these constructions which relay the multiplication of length units to cell lengths and to growth behavior, are strong enough to simulate statistically described real growth phenomena, but they cannot respond to differential growth rates, between parts of a growing entity. As there are pertinent biological observations that a 'memory' over successive generations is working during cell multiplication and growth, bootstrap recurrent systems |4,5| are adapted to these kinds of biological problems. Recently, an intensive theoretical discussion on memory mechanisms in cell differentiation during cell lineage development was given in |19,20|.

In a bootstrap system, the alphabet is stretched out over one (or more) generations: $\Sigma = \{c_q^p\}$ with $p \varepsilon \{0, 1, 2, 1.1, 1.2, 2.1, 2.2\}$ and $q \varepsilon \{1,2,\ldots,m^p\}$. The binary index p now takes into account the successive relative positions of mother and daughter cells in the path of cell filiation, i.e. $c^0 \rightarrow c^1 c^2 \rightarrow c^{1.1} c^{1.2} c^{2.1} c^{2.2}$ and $c^{1.1} \rightarrow c^{1.1} c^{1.2}, c^{1.2} \rightarrow c^{2.1} c^{2.2}$,

$c^{2,1} \to c^{1,1}c^{1,2}$, $c^{2,2} \to c^{2,1}c^{2,2}$. The growth function becomes $f(i) = f^1(i) + f^2(i)$ with $f^1(i) = f^1(i-m^{1,1}) + f^2(i-m^{1,2}-d)$ and $f^2(i) = f^1(i-m^{2,1}+d) + f^2(i-m^{2,2})$, $d = m^1-m^2$. As these formulations are based on two different complementary series, the f^1 and the f^2 series, differential cell division and growth rates can be simulated in developing cell descendances.

Applications - This expansion of grammar construction over time (generation sequences) allows an approach to cell configuration typology |4,5|:the character of the four cells of, for example the second generation, is in a positional order, such that each of the two apical cells $c^{1,1}$ and $c^{2,1}$ alternate with the two basal cells $c^{1,2}$ and $c^{2,2}$. At a given timestep, such a cell 'family' is frequently observable, as the underlying lifespan parameter set is not sufficiently asymmetrical to conceal the incidence of the binary division structure of cell multiplication.

In this context, four cases of invariant order of length relations between the four cells could be related to cell cycle length variations:(1) The apical cells, $c^{1,1}$ and $c^{2,1}$, are smaller than the complementary basal ones, $c^{1,2}$ and $c^{2,2}$: *Chaetomorpha* under optimal culture conditions. The lifespan parameter set $M = \langle m^{1,1},\dots,m^{2,2}\rangle = \langle 7,5,8,3\rangle$ produces such a configuration.(2) The two inner cells, $c^{1,2}$ and $c^{2,1}$, are smaller than the two marginal ones, $c^{1,1}$ and $c^{2,2}$: *Chaetomorpha* under limited culture conditions. The configuration is obtainable by $M = \langle 7,10,8,7\rangle$. (3) The two marginal cells, $c^{1,1}$ and $c^{2,2}$, are smaller than the two inner cells, $c^{1,2}$ and $c^{2,1}$: *Anabeana* |21|. $M = \langle 5,4,4,5\rangle$ satisfies this configuration.(4) The cell $c^{1,1}$ is longer than $c^{1,2}$ and its lifespan longer than that of the latter |22|. For this case holds $M = \langle 5,4,9,6\rangle$ if $c^{2,1}$ and $c^{2,2}$ are of equal length (*Ulothrix aequalis!*).

These results, and moreover the simulability of real cell length development in a filament emphasize that the coupling of two grammars, one for cell multiplication and the other for multiplication of hypothetical cell length units, is justified.

3. SURFACE GROWTH OF CELLPLATES

Here is the most primitive case: we assume each cell division to be alternatively directed 'horizontally' (h) and 'vertically' (v); if its directional index u is h, u' will be v, and vice versa, if u=v, u'=h. Two polarity axis are thus operative, $\alpha\beta$ and $\gamma\delta$. Each cell state is labelled ${}^{u}c_{q}^{p}$. As the cell population is supposed to grow in the context of a continuous surface, all different cells of the meristematic tissue have to be recognized in regard to their relative positional relationship, and this recognition has to be examined in a developmental aspect. We propose an extension of the *Chaetomorpha*-scheme.

Parallel graph generating system - The framework will be a di-graph D = {N,A} with the set of node labels $N = \{{}^{u}c_{q}^{p}\}$, $p\varepsilon\{0,1,2\}$, $q\varepsilon\{1,2,\ldots,{}^{u}m^{p}\}$, $u\varepsilon\{h,v\}$, and the set of binary labelled arcs $A = \{u^{z}\}$, with the attribute for division hierarchy z written as a universal address system in the ordered genealogical tree, $z\varepsilon\{1, 1.1, 1.2, 1.1.1, 1.1.2, 1.2.1,\ldots\}$. The parallel graph generating system $G_D = \{N,A,P,C,\gamma_0\}$ procures the deterministic algorithm for the growth of D: The set of substitution rules for node states is $P = \{{}^{u}c_{1}^{p} \rightarrow {}^{u}c_{2}^{p},\ldots,{}^{u}c_{{}^{u}m^{p}}^{p} \rightarrow {}^{u'}c_{1}^{1} \xrightarrow{u'^{z}} {}^{u'}c_{1}^{2}\}$ (fig.1a-d).

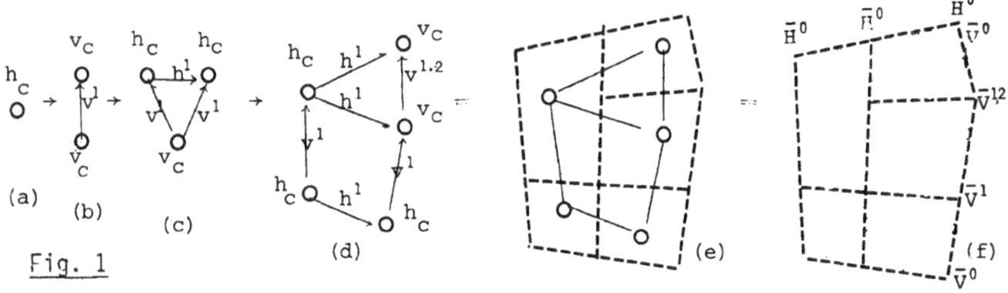

Fig. 1

The substitution rule for ${}^{u}c_{{}^{u}m^{p}}^{p}$ institutes a node division (cell division) and the addition of a new u'^{z} labelled arc (a new cell wall). For the index z of the label of the newly formed arc u'^{z} between daughter nodes, z = z'.2 if an arc $\underrightarrow{u'^{z'}}$ ends in ${}^{u'}c_{1}^{1}$, or z = z".1 if an arc $\underrightarrow{u'^{z''}}$ begins in ${}^{u'}c_{1}^{2}$, so that z = max{z' ,z"} determines the application of one of these transition rules; the absence of such an arc is equivalent to $\underrightarrow{u'^{0}}$; in this way, without ending and beginning of the u' arcs, z = 1.

Example: if u = h, i : $\underrightarrow{h^{z'}} \cdot \underrightarrow{h^{z''}}$

i+1 : $\underrightarrow{h^{z'}} \cdot \underrightarrow{h^{z}} \cdot \underrightarrow{h^{z''}}$, if z'> z", z=z'.2 , if z'< z", z=z".1 .

All h^{z} labelled arcs and all v^{z} arcs in D constitute, respectively, sets of chains H and V, such that each chain H cuts a chain V only once. This device does not exclude bifurcations of chains (fig.1d). In a chain, two immediately following arcs are always differently labelled. As arc labels indicate the relative age of the cell walls at the moment of their formation, the labels are conserved during the further development of the system.

A node division introduces new relationships between two newly formed nodes and their adjacent nodes. These connection rules are given by the set C and may be described as follows: a node of a chain U, such as $U \varepsilon \{H,V\}$ is connected by a u'^{z} arc to one node or nodes of a chain segment of an immediately adjacent chain U, if the node(s) source and the node(s) target, both lie between the arcs $u^{z'}$ and $u^{z''}$ $(z' \neq z'')$, and if $u^{z''}$ follows $u^{z'}$ in U (fig.2).
The starting graph is $\gamma_0 \varepsilon N$.

Fig. 2

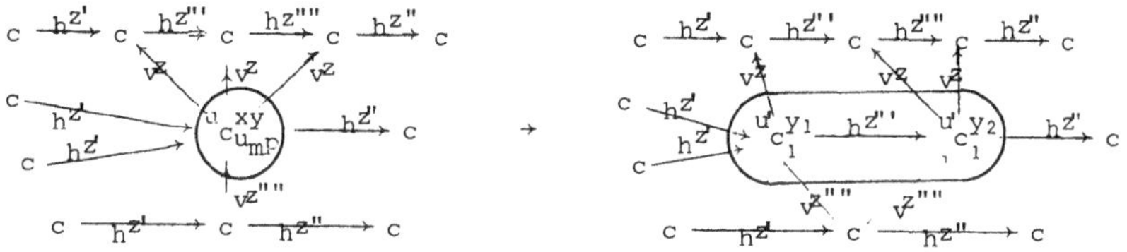

For a morphogeneticist it is interesting to see that in a planar map representation, the dual $\bar{D}$ (fig.1e,f) of the di-graph D is the image of the relative, generation dependent, cell wall age pattern of a cell population. Actually, each of the $\bar{H}$ chains, if $\bar{D} = \{\bar{H},\bar{V}\}$, intersects arcs with the same label h^{z} in D, and each of the $\bar{V}$ chains intersects arcs with the same label v^{z} in D.

The growth function of the number of nodes in the sequence of generated graphs becomes: $s(i) = s(i-({}^{h}m^{1}+{}^{v}m^{1})) + s(i-({}^{h}m^{1}+{}^{v}m^{2})) + s(i-({}^{h}m^{2}+{}^{v}m^{1})) + s(i-({}^{h}m^{2}+{}^{v}m^{2}))$, which is simply a Fibonacci-scheme formulated over two following generations.

Recurrence graph systems - Both the attributes of node labels in D and chain labels in $\bar{D}$, establish the basis for the formulation of a recurrence graph system, in which γ_i is a graph in the sequence of generated graphs $E(G_D)$. The growth function s(i) of the node numbers furnishes the recurrence indices of each of the 4 subgraphs of the recurrent graph. If the first cell division leads to two sister cells with v indices and for $i > {}^{u}m^{0} + \max\{{}^{u'}m^{p}\} + \max\{{}^{u}m^{p}\}$, then the recurrence graph γ_i can be constructed in the following manner:

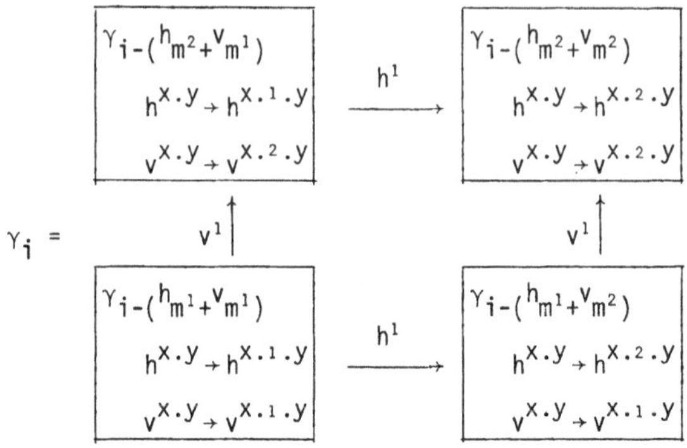

The configuration and
their node state symbols
of the 4 copied graphs
figuring in γ_i as subgraphs remain unaltered.
To the contrary, the arc
labels have to be adjust-
ed in regard to the two

$$\gamma_i = \begin{array}{ccc}
\boxed{\begin{array}{c} \gamma_{i-(h_{m^2}+v_{m^1})} \\ h^{x\cdot y} \to h^{x\cdot 1\cdot y} \\ v^{x\cdot y} \to v^{x\cdot 2\cdot y} \end{array}} & \xrightarrow{h^1} & \boxed{\begin{array}{c} \gamma_{i-(h_{m^2}+v_{m^2})} \\ h^{x\cdot y} \to h^{x\cdot 2\cdot y} \\ v^{x\cdot y} \to v^{x\cdot 2\cdot y} \end{array}} \\
v^1 \uparrow & & v^1 \uparrow \\
\boxed{\begin{array}{c} \gamma_{i-(h_{m^1}+v_{m^1})} \\ h^{x\cdot y} \to h^{x\cdot 1\cdot y} \\ v^{x\cdot y} \to v^{x\cdot 1\cdot y} \end{array}} & \xrightarrow{h^1} & \boxed{\begin{array}{c} \gamma_{i-(h_{m^1}+v_{m^2})} \\ h^{x\cdot y} \to h^{x\cdot 2\cdot y} \\ v^{x\cdot y} \to v^{x\cdot 1\cdot y} \end{array}}
\end{array}$$

intervening cell generations between the occurence of the copied graph and its occur-
rence as a subgraph in γ_i. For example the arc label rule $h^{x\cdot y} \to h^{x\cdot 1\cdot y}$ of the subgraph $\gamma_{i-(h_{m^2}+v_{m^1})}$, means that x.y = z and y is the last integer in z. This procedure
contrasts with that of the parallel graph generating systems, in which the node states
change by rewriting the graph while the arc labels are persistent.

For the subgraph gluing, all node(s) of a source chain U in a subgraph and the node(s)
of an immediately adjacent target chain U belonging to another subgraph, with identical in- and outcoming labelled arcs, have to be connected as mentioned for C in the
case of the generating grammar. All connecting arcs between the 4 subgraphs are labelled so that z=1.

The biological incidence of these recurrence graph grammars is evident: the two-dimensional meristematic cell pattern at i may be considered as a mosaic of subplates
of cells in the same state as the tissue at defined number of previous timesteps.
Nevertheless, the rules for the labels u^z of the chains in the dual $\bar{D}$ emphasize the
progression in relative cell wall age.

Cell surface enlargement and corresponding length and width growth - The growth function s(i) of nodes in D can, in regard to surface growth, be attributed to cell surface increase, just as f(i) was at the base of the quantification of cell length
growth. The trivial graph labelled $^u c^p_q$ generates under G_D after j applications the

the graph γ, ${}^{u}c_q^p \xrightarrow[G_D]{i} \gamma$. Thus the number of nodes in γ, $|\gamma|$, quantifies the surface state symbol ${}^{u}s_{c_i}^p$ of a cell, ${}^{u}s_q^p = |\gamma|$.

Each graph γ_i or subgraph of the recurrence graph, under the constraint of the grid of chains which are defined by U, is bordered by the four chains *A*, *B*, *C* and *D*, each

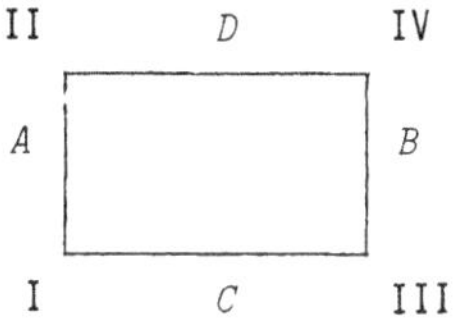

of them beginning and ending with a node I, II, III, IV. These nodes are characterized by the fact that they have only one incoming or outcoming arc in each chain to which they belong. Since the border-chains are subgraphs under the grammars G_A, G_B, G_C and G_D of the graph γ_i under G_D, their development depends upon the development of γ_i. The alphabet of the chain grammars remains obviously N of G_D. The sets of the arc labels A_A, A_B, A_C and A_D are inclusions in A of the overall grammar. The arc labels of the chains *A* and *B* are only constituted by v^z labels, those of the chains *C* and *D* by h^z labels. The sets of production rules P_A, P_B, P_C and P_D of the chain grammars are subsets of P in G_D. For example in P_A the state transition rule ${}^{v}c^p_{v_{mp}} \to {}^{h}c^1_1 \longrightarrow {}^{h}c^2_1$ inducing in P a node division, is reduced in P_A to the transition ${}^{v}c^p_{v_{mp}} \to {}^{h}c^1_1$, linking by that a sequence of two cellcycles without intervening division, and in consequence without forming a new arc.

In *B* , ${}^{v}c^p_{v_{mp}} \to {}^{h}c^1_1 \longrightarrow {}^{h}c^2_1$ is reduced to ${}^{v}c^p_{v_{mp}} \to {}^{h}c^2_1$,

in *C* , ${}^{h}c^p_{h_{mp}} \to {}^{v}c^1_1 \longrightarrow {}^{v}c^2_1$ is reduced to ${}^{h}c^p_{h_{mp}} \to {}^{v}c^1_1$, and

in *D* , ${}^{h}c^p_{h_{mp}} \to {}^{v}c^1_1 \longrightarrow {}^{v}c^2_1$ is reduced to ${}^{h}c^p_{h_{mp}} \to {}^{v}c^2_1$. The connection rules of the chain grammars are given by the general rule specified for C in the graph grammar G_D. And the starting set in the chain grammars is obviously identical with γ_0 in G_D.

According to the suppression respectively of the horizontal or the vertical node divisions in a chain, a cycle length, example ${}^{A}m^1$ or ${}^{A}m^2$ in *A*, between two successive divisions of a node in a chain, is composed of the sum of a v cellcycle and a h cellcycle. They are $\langle {}^{A}m^1, {}^{A}m^2 \rangle = \langle {}^{v}m^1 + {}^{h}m^1, {}^{v}m^2 + {}^{h}m^1 \rangle$, $\langle {}^{B}m^1, {}^{B}m^2 \rangle = \langle {}^{v}m^1 + {}^{h}m^2, {}^{v}m^2 + {}^{h}m^2 \rangle$,

$\langle {}^{C}m^1, {}^{C}m^2 \rangle = \langle {}^{h}m^1 + {}^{v}m^1, {}^{h}m^2 + {}^{v}m^1 \rangle$ and $\langle {}^{D}m^1, {}^{D}m^2 \rangle = \langle {}^{h}m^1 + {}^{v}m^2, {}^{h}m^2 + {}^{v}m^2 \rangle$.

The growth function of the border-chains, $l_A(i)$, $l_B(i)$, $l_C(i)$ and $l_D(i)$ can be formulated as simple Fibonacci series (as in § 2.1), for example $l_A(i) = l_A(i - {}^{A}m^1) + l_A(i - {}^{A}m^2)$. Nevertheless, the recurrence index must be corrected according to the axiom γ_0.

Biologically, this property is of importance, as it holds for differential meristematic length and width growth. Together with $\bar{V}$ and $\bar{H}$, the relative cell wall generation age, s(i) and $l_A(i),\ldots,l_D(i)$ are terms which permit the quantified simulation of form variations in cellular surface growth within the context of tissue growth. Curled or planar surface growth are programable |12|.

4. TOWARDS A GENERALIZATION

Filamentous (§ 2) and surface growth (§3) of plant tissue may be described by means of positional control devices (§ 2.1 and 3) and positional and filiation control devices, bootstrap systems (§2.2). Now, we demonstrate a way to unify the different approaches - those of memory free constructions and constructions with memory, and those of filamentous and surface growth - by help of a generalized expression of the recurrent growth function.

Each cell c of the hierarchically ordered binary genealogical tree T with its root R generates after n generations a 2^n-tuple X of cells, $X = \langle c^{1\cdots},\ldots,c^p,\ldots,c^{\cdots 2}\rangle$, to which are attributed different lifespans, the set $M = \langle m^{1\cdots},\ldots,m^p,\ldots,m^{\cdots 2}\rangle$, with n terms in the binary index p. From this n^{th} generation on, the label p of the derivatives c are those of X and M, according to the position and origin of each cell c, i.e. without an extension of the binary n termed p values, but also, without repeating lower-levelled labels. The cells of X are isochronous in the generation timed

Fig. 3

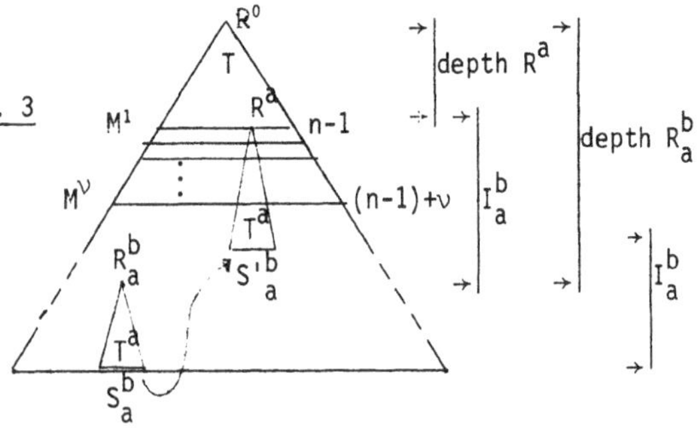

tree, but are not necessarily isochronous in the real timed one. There are 2^{n-1} different partial trees T^a in T. Each partial tree T^a is rooted R^a at the generation level n-1, and $a\epsilon\{1,\ldots,2^{n-1}\}$, the positional rank index from left to right in T, stands for the type of partial tree. Starting with the root R^a, then only, and only after n generations the whole parameter set M is again effectively operative in each T^a.

The development of T may be governed by the application of ν different, sequential and recycling, parameter sets M, specified as M^h, M^v, etc. Such 'zebration' may be, for example the image of a switch between succeeding horizontal and vertical cell division planes, bi-dimensional cell multiplication, or only the structure of periodicity in filamentous growth which can be called 'accordion' growth. If $\nu = 3$ volume growth may be induced.

It appears that the ordered representation of elements in one, two or even three dimensions at timestep i can always be given by the monodimensional representation of a string S_i. This string S_i can be partitioned into 2^{n-1} substrings, each of these belongs to a partial tree T^a which is rooted at the generation level n-1. The partition of S_i in this case is said to be of degree $l = n-1$. The description of S_i by means of recurrence formulas needs at least one further degree of partitioning, (n-1) +1, i.e. the substrings ensuing belong to subtrees which are rooted by the cells of the nth generation of T.

One cycle over the ν different M in T leads to a minimum partitioning degree l of S_i, so that $l = (n-1) + \nu$. The catenation of the different outcoming substrings S_a^b make up in order the string S_i. Each S_a^b is a section of a partial tree, and this tree is one of 2^{n-1} T^a-types that have been defined at the generation level n-1. In this way a is the type index of the partial tree to which belongs S_a^b and which is rooted by R_a^b. The rank of substrings from left to right is $b \in \{1,2,\ldots,2^{(n-1)+\nu}\}$. The string S_i is

$$S_i = \overset{(2^{(n-1)+\nu},2^{n-1})}{\underset{(b,a)=(1,1)}{*}} S_a^b .$$

Substrings of higher partitioning degree than $l = (n-1)+\nu$ are still ascribed to partial trees of type T^a for $l = (n-1)+\mu$, if μ is a multiple of ν. As each S_a^b of a partial tree rooted R_a^b has its image $S_a'^b$ in the corresponding initial partial tree T^a

rooted R^a, the recurrence indices I_a^b are equal to the difference between the depths of these partial trees (fig.3), $I_a^b = \langle R^0, R_a^b\rangle - \langle R^0, R^a\rangle$. Intuitively, the index a stands for a general index of growth differentiation. This differentiation appears also in the formulation of the growth function f(i). Obviously this growth function is composed of $2^{(n-1)+\mu}$ terms which are distributed over the 2^{n-1} partial growth functions

$$f(i) = \sum_{a=1}^{2^{n-1}} f^a(i) \; .$$

The composition of each of these partial functions $f^a(i)$ is

$$f^a(i) = \sum_{(r,s,b)=(r_j,1,b_j)}^{(r_k,\, 2^\mu,\, b_k)} f_s^r(i-I_r^b) \; ,$$

with r_j to r_k as the a-indices of the $f_s^r(i-I_r^b)$ terms in $f^a(i)$,

$$r \in \langle 1,\ldots,\overset{j}{\downarrow}\ldots,2^{n-1},\ldots,\ldots,\overset{k}{\downarrow}\ldots,1,\ldots,2^{n-1}\rangle \; ,$$

and the addresses $j = (a-1)2^\mu+1$ and $k = a2^\mu$, which depend on the a-index in $f^a(i)$. The number of terms in each $f^a(i)$ is $s = 2^{(n-1)+\mu}/2^{n-1} = 2^\mu$.

The index r in $f_s^r(i-I_r^b)$ defines also the a-index of the corresponding recurrence index I_a^b, i.e. I_r^b. The rank b of this index is determined by the addresses from j to k, which depend on a in $f^a(i)$,

$$b \in \langle 1,\overset{j}{\downarrow}\ldots\overset{k}{\downarrow},2^{(n-1)+\mu}\rangle \; .$$

5. A BIOLOGICAL APPLICATION

The procedure of generating a quantified cellplate by means of the proposed bootstrap constructions will be shown in the following botanical example. The small lycopod *Selaginella kraussiana* has special organs, which have intermediate morphological characteristics between roots and shoots. Fig.4 shows a part of the epidermis (80 cells) of such a rhizophore. The differing thicknesses of the cell walls indicate the division hierarchy of the constituting epidermal cells and show that transverse and longitudinal di-

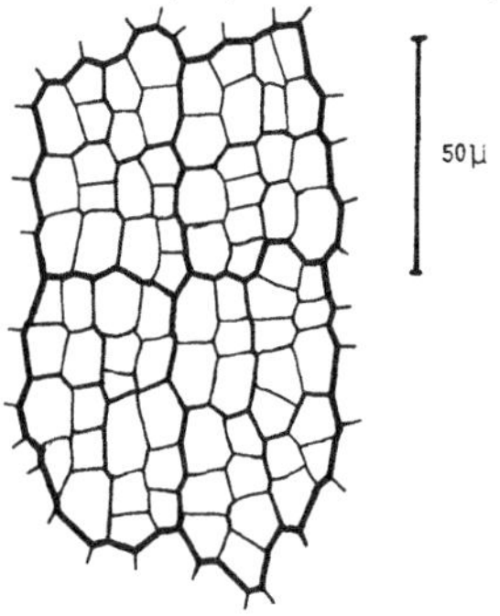

(after B. Fouletier Ann.Sc.Nat.Bot.,1969)

vision planes have alternated.

The di-graph and its growth function - In order to generate a similar cellplate by means of a graph grammar, we adopt a 'two-stripped bootstrap' system, i.e. $\nu = 2$. Each of the two lifespan parameter sets, M^h and M^v, is assumed to be composed of 2^3 parameters, n = 3, M^h = <7,5,8,6,6,9,8,7> and M^v = <4,3,3,2,4,5,4,4>, respectively governing the horizontally (transverse) or vertically (longitudinal) orientated division planes of nodes (the cells). The hierarchy of the initial parameters for $p\varepsilon\{0,1,\ldots,22\}$ in n=0, 1 and 2, and the following parameters with three digit indices of M^v in n = 3 and M^h in n = 4 is

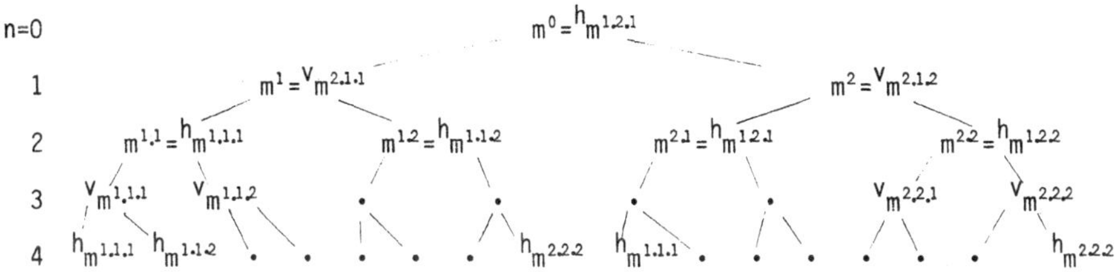

etc.

The corresponding values are

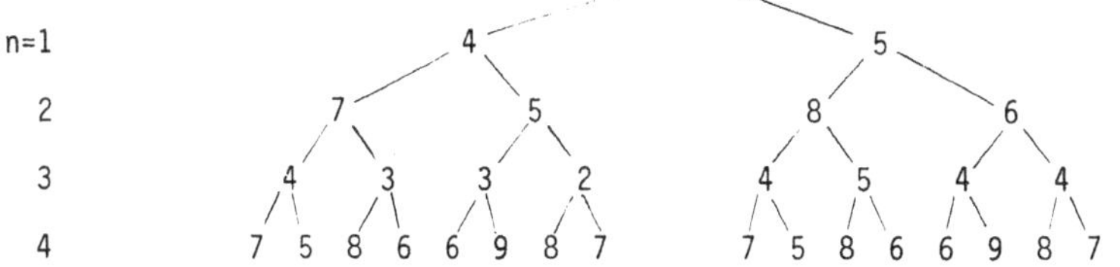

The alphabet is $N = \{{}^uc^p\}$ with $p\varepsilon\{0,1,\ldots,222\}$ and $u\varepsilon\{h,v\}$. The state transition rules can be deduced from the preceeding division hierarchy. The starting node is ${}^hc_1^{1.2.1}$. These devices generate at the 38th timestep the graph of the fig.5, composed of 84 nodes.

The corresponding growth function of node numbers or cells is f(i),(§4). As there are 2^{n-1}= 4 different partial growth functions with $a\varepsilon\{1,\ldots,4\}$, each of them is composed of $s = 2^{\mu}$= 4 terms, here $\mu=\nu$. For the different a-types, j, k, r_j, r_k, b_j and b_k are

a	j	k	r_j	r_k	b_j	b_k
1	1	4	1	1	1	4
2	5	8	2	2	5	8
3	9	12	3	3	9	12
4	13	16	4	4	13	16

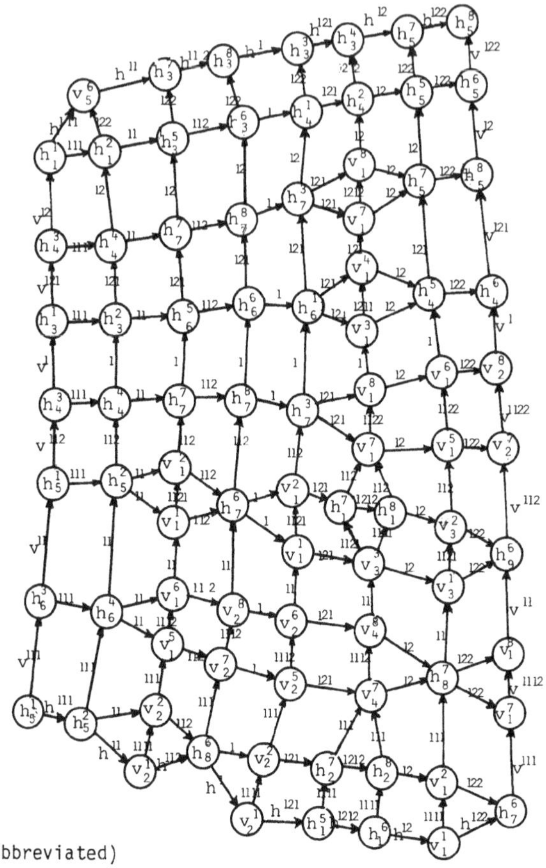

Fig. 5
(labels abbreviated)

The ordered set of recurrence indices I_a^b is, from b = 1 to $b = 2^{(n-1)+\mu} - 16$,

$$\langle 11, 11, 9, 9, 7, 12, 6, 7, 13, 13, 13, 13, 10, 15, 10, 11 \rangle.$$

The growth function f(i) can now be established,

$$f(i) = f^1(i) + f^2(i) + f^3(i) + f^4(i), \text{ with}$$

$$f^1(i) = f^1(i-11) + f^2(i-11) + f^3(i-9) + f^4(i-9)$$

$$f^2(i) = f^1(i-7) + f^2(i-12) + f^3(i-6) + f^4(i-7)$$

$$f^3(i) = f^1(i-13) + f^2(i-13) + f^3(i-13) + f^4(i-13)$$

$$f^4(i) = f^1(i-10) + f^2(i-15) + f^3(i-10) + f^4(i-11).$$

Cell surface growth - In order to calculate the surface of the constituting cells, we take arbitrarily j = 20 in ${}^u s_q^p \xrightarrow[G_D]{j} |\gamma|$ (§ 3). The number of states ${}^u c_q^p$ in D is

$$\max_{y=1.1}^{2.2}\{{}^{u}m^{1.y}, {}^{u}m^{2.y}\} = 45$$

with $u\varepsilon\{h,v\}$, and 1.y or 2.y = p, where y holds for the two last terms in p. Consequently, there are 45 surface states ${}^{u}s_{q}^{p}$ which describe the cells in the developing cellplate.

The general growth function f(i) is here composed of 4 different partial growth functions. As there are h and v cells, for each of them there exists 4 different growth functions, i.e. a differentiation between cells into 8 different modes of behavior. This can also intuitively be deduced from the state transition flow graph,

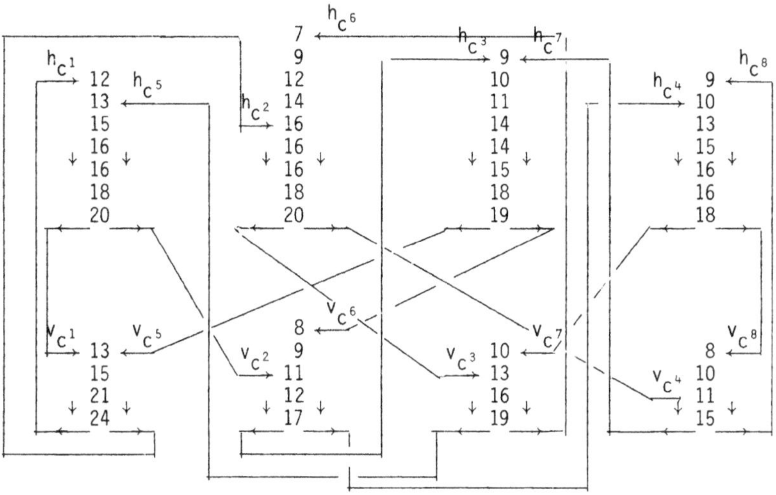

The system provides 16 different initial and 8 different final cell surfaces.

<u>Cell length and width growth</u> - As the overall grammar G_D refers to n=3 and ν=2, the subgraphs which describe the development of the border-chains *A*, *B*, *C* and *D*, are based on systems with n=2 and ν=1, i.e. on bootstrap systems with 4 lifespan parameters (§ 2.2). For example for the chain *A* the parameter set is $<{}^{A}m^{1.1}, {}^{A}m^{1.2}, {}^{A}m^{2.1}, {}^{A}m^{2.2}>$. Each of these 4 parameters is composed of the sum of 2 lifespan parameters belonging to

G_D , $<{}^{A}m^{1.1},\ldots,{}^{A}m^{2.2}> = <{}^{v}m^{1.1.1}+{}^{h}m^{1.1.1},\ {}^{v}m^{1.1.2}+{}^{h}m^{1.2.1},\ {}^{v}m^{2.1.1}+{}^{h}m^{1.1.1},\ {}^{v}m^{2.1.2}+{}^{h}m^{1.2.1}>$,

$<{}^{B}m^{1.1},\ldots,{}^{B}m^{2.2}> = <{}^{v}m^{1.2.1}+{}^{h}m^{2.1.2},\ {}^{v}m^{1.2.2}+{}^{h}m^{2.2.2},\ {}^{v}m^{2.2.1}+{}^{h}m^{2.1.2},\ {}^{v}m^{2.2.2}+{}^{h}m^{2.2.2}>$,

$<{}^{C}m^{1.1},\ldots,{}^{C}m^{2.2}> = <{}^{h}m^{1.1.1}+{}^{v}m^{1.1.1},\ {}^{h}m^{1.1.2}+{}^{v}m^{1.2.1},\ {}^{h}m^{2.1.1}+{}^{v}m^{1.1.1},\ {}^{h}m^{2.1.2}+{}^{v}m^{1.2.1}>$,

$\langle {}^{D}m^{1.1}, \ldots, {}^{D}m^{2.2} \rangle = \langle {}^{h}m^{1.2.1} + {}^{v}m^{2.1.2},\ {}^{h}m^{1.2.2} + {}^{v}m^{2.2.2},\ {}^{h}m^{2.2.1} + {}^{v}m^{2.1.2},\ {}^{h}m^{2.2.2} + {}^{v}m^{2.2.2} \rangle.$

Each cell surface state ${}^{u}s^{p}_{q}$ may now be described by the set of 5 attributes, a surface value and the length of the 4 border-chains, ${}^{u}s^{p}_{q} = \langle {}^{u}s^{p}_{q}, l_A, l_B, l_C, l_D \rangle$. According to these values, the dual of the graph γ_i (fig.5) can be quantified. This is done for i = 38 in fig.6.

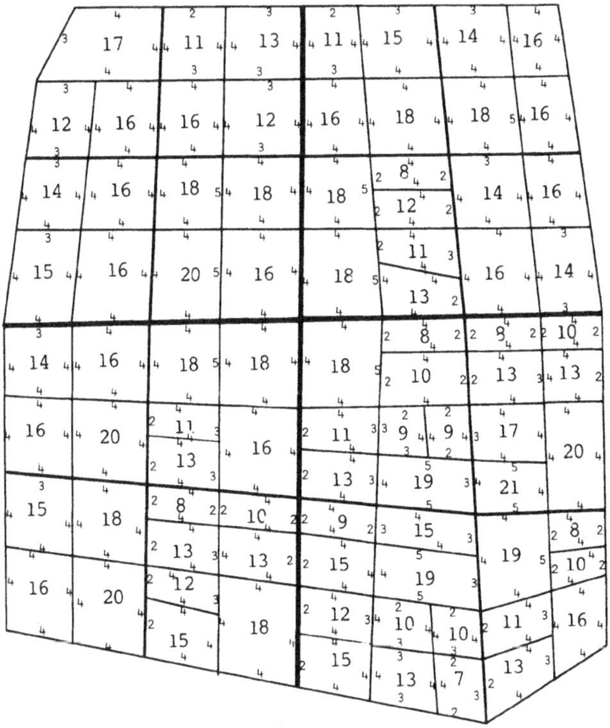

Fig. 6

Bootstrap reccurence systems and their gluing - The recurrence of the growth function f(i) of γ_i allows the construction of the cellplate of fig. 6 directly by means of a recurrence graph bootstrap system. The bootstrap characteristic prescribes that only parts of the formerly existing graphs of the developmental sequence enter as subgraphs into the recurrence graph.

Each graph γ_i can be partitioned into 2^{n-1} subgraphs γ_i^a which depict at timestep i the cell configuration in the 2^{n-1} initial partial T^a trees. In the proposed example $2^{n-1} = 4$, and as the first division in the development is a v division, the configuration of this partition graph (P-graph or γ_i^P) becomes

$$\gamma_i \quad \text{as} \quad \gamma_i^P \quad = \quad \begin{array}{ccc} \gamma_i^3 & \xrightarrow{h^1} & \gamma_i^4 \\ v^1 \uparrow & & \uparrow v^1 \\ \gamma_i^1 & \xrightarrow{h^1} & \gamma_i^2 \end{array}$$

(h^1 and v^1 arcs are not copied)

The partition degree of the recurrence graph (R-graph or γ_i^R) is $(n-1)+\mu$, that means for this example a partition into $2^4 = 16$ subgraphs $\gamma^b_{r(i-I^b_r)}$ with b, r and I^b_r as in the generalized growth function. The index r indicates which part has to be copied in the graph $\gamma_{i-I^b_r}$ and b indicates the site where this part has to figure like a subgraph in γ_i^R. The gluing of these 16 subgraphs is dominated by the sequence of the directions of the first $(n-1)+\mu$ division planes in the developmental graph, here 4 ones. The R-graph is

$$\gamma_i \text{ as } \gamma_i^R = \begin{array}{ccccccc} \gamma^{11}_{3(i-13)} & \rightarrow & \gamma^{12}_{4(i-13)} & \rightarrow & \gamma^{15}_{3(i-10)} & \rightarrow & \gamma^{16}_{4(i-11)} \\ \uparrow & & \uparrow & & \uparrow & & \uparrow \\ \gamma^{9}_{1(i-13)} & \rightarrow & \gamma^{10}_{2(i-13)} & \rightarrow & \gamma^{13}_{1(i-10)} & \rightarrow & \gamma^{14}_{2(i-15)} \\ \uparrow & & \uparrow & & \uparrow & & \uparrow \\ \gamma^{3}_{3(i-9)} & \rightarrow & \gamma^{4}_{4(i-9)} & \rightarrow & \gamma^{7}_{3(i-6)} & \rightarrow & \gamma^{8}_{4(i-7)} \\ \uparrow & & \uparrow & & \uparrow & & \uparrow \\ \gamma^{1}_{1(i-11)} & \rightarrow & \gamma^{2}_{2(i-11)} & \rightarrow & \gamma^{5}_{1(i-7)} & \rightarrow & \gamma^{6}_{2(i-12)} \end{array}$$

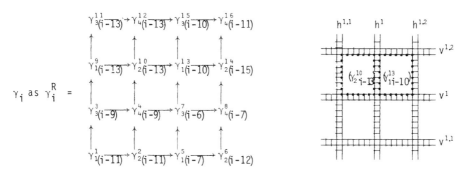

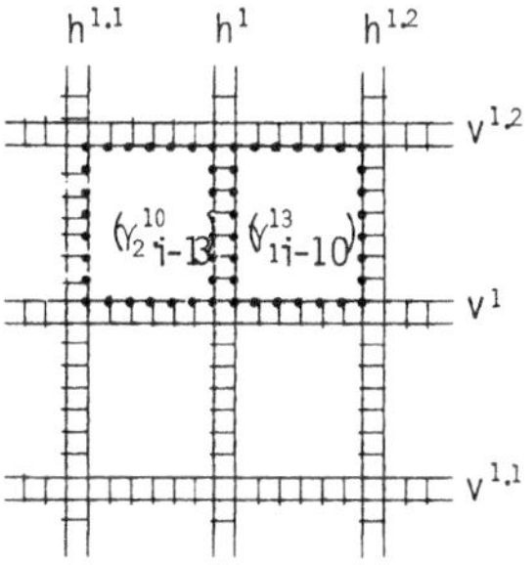

It should be mentioned that the node labels in the subgraphs remain invariant, but the arc labels have to be readjusted.

The gluing of the subgraphs $\gamma^b_{r(i-I^b_r)}$ works by the connection of the nodes of border-chains of adjacent subgraphs. Analogously to the star gluing device |23| we propose 'ratlin' gluing. Instead of nodes, the border-chains taken off from the subgraphs, constitute a grid of connected double chains like rope-ladders (sketched above, at the right). This grid which is itself a subgraph of G_D, procures at each timestep the frame into which fit the subgraphs of γ_i^R: (1) the growth functions of border-chains define the 'shrouds' length, (2) the node connections between chains (ratlin fixations on shrouds) follow the rule of C (§ 3), and (3) all connections (ratlins) of a ladder are equally labelled according to the initial division hierarchy of D.

This recurrence system works after the maximal path through the first 4 cell generations, i.e. $i > m^0 + \max\{m^1, m^2\} + \max\{m^{1.1}, \ldots, m^{2.2}\} + \max\{{}^{v}m^{1.1.1}, \ldots, {}^{v}m^{2.2.2}\} + \max\{{}^{h}m^{1.1.1}, \ldots, {}^{h}m^{2.2.2}\}$. It is obvious that a cellplate as in fig. 6 can be constructed immediately as a map representation of the dual of the graph D, with the aid of the P- and R-graphs.

In biology, the above construction of a growing quantified network answers many classical questions of morphology. For example, proportionality between cell size and cell lifespan |24| is not necessarily required . From the P-graph may be deduced a limited number of growth modalities appearing at defined places in the quantified network. The resulting form variations, based on elemental behavior, can replace classical allometric growth relationships |25|. The description of these variations by means of the gluing grid is close to cartesian transformation grids |26,27|.

We thank Prof. G. Rozenberg for his suggestion of the word 'bootstrap' and Dr D.R. McQueen for reviewing the english text.

7. REFERENCES

|1| G.S. Avery, Jr, *Am.J.Bot.* 20: 565-592; 1933. |2| R.O. Erickson, in |7|: 39-56; 1976. |3| H.B.Lück, *J.theor.Biol.* 54: 23-34; 1975. |4| H.B. and J. Lück, in |7|: 109 -124; 1976. |5| J. Lück, *Cah.Biol.theor.* 1: 1-362; 1977. |6| G.T. Herman and G. Rozenberg, Developmental systems and languages, *North-Holland Publ.Co., Amsterdam*; 1975. |7| A. Lindenmayer and G. Rozenberg (eds), Automata, Languages, Development, *North-Holland Publ.Co., Amsterdam*; 1976. |8| H.B. Lück, *Ann.Sci.nat.(Bot.), 12e sér.* 3: 1-23; 1962. |9| H.B. Lück, Coll.'Recherches interdisciplinaires', P. Delattre (ed.), *Maloine, Paris*; 1979. |10| G.T. Herman and P.M.B. Vitányi, *Amer.Math.Monthly* 83: 1-15; 1976. |11| P.M.B. Vitányi, Lindenmayer systems, *Math.Centrum, Amsterdam*; 1978. |12| H.B. and J. Lück, *Proc.Intern.Symp.on Mathem.Topics in Biol., Kyoto*: 174-185; 1978. |13| K. Čulik II and A. Lindenmayer, *Int.J.Gen.Systems* 3: 53-66; 1976. |14| A. Lindenmayer and K. Čulik II, *preprint*, 1978. |15| H. Ehrig and G. Rozenberg, in |7|: 443-468; 1976. |16| M. Nagl, in |7|: 487-515; 1976. |17| B.H. Mayoh, in |7|:469-485; 1976. |18| J.M. Legay, *Bull.Math.Biophys.* 30: 33 -46 ; 1968. |19| H. Nishio, *Information and Control* 37: 280-301; 1978. |20| H. Nishio, *Proc.Intern.Symp.on Mathem.Topics in Biol., Kyoto*: 164-173; 1978. |21| G.J. Mitchison and M. Wilcox, *Nature* 239: 110-111; 1972. |22| P. Marvan and F. Hindák, *Arch.Hydrobiol.Suppl.* 39: 178-205; 1971. |23| H. Ehrig, Introduction to the algebraic theory of graph grammars (surv.), *T.U. Berlin*; 1978. |24| R.W.Korn, *manuscript*; 1978. |25| J.S. Huxley, Problems of relative growth, *Methuen, London*; 1932. |26| D'A.W. Thompson, On growth and form, *Cambridge, Cambridge Univ.Press*; 1917. |27| O. Schüepp, Meristeme, *Birkhäuser Vlg., Basel*; 1966.

PARALLEL GENERATION OF MAPS:

DEVELOPMENTAL SYSTEMS FOR CELL LAYERS

Aristid Lindenmayer

Vakgroep Theoretische Biologie, Rijksuniversiteit Utrecht

and

Grzegorz Rozenberg

Instituut voor Toegepaste Wiskunde en Informatica,
Rijksuniversiteit Leiden

ABSTRACT

In this paper we extend parallel string generating systems (string L-systems) to parallel map generating systems(BPMOL-systems). The main distinguishing feature of of these constructs is that they generate map patterns by rewriting the graph of the map directly, and not its dual graph. These systems and their languages and sequences are illustrated in particular by applying them to the development of epidermal cell layers in which hexagonal arrays of cells are generated from previous hexagonal arrays.

INTRODUCTION

In recent years efforts have been made to extend one-dimensional developmental systems to those generating multidimensional structures. In making such an extension to the two-dimensional case, one has a choice of either transforming maps or of transforming the dual graphs of maps in a parallel way. Both of these approaches were initiated by Mayoh [1,2]. Sequential map grammars were already defined in [3]. Parallel map generating systems have been further investigated in [4,5,6]. The approach using dual graphs have been continued, among others, in [7,8,9,10,11], while most of the other work on parallel and sequential graph grammars is reviewed in this volume [12,13,14]. Many other approaches to the algorithmic generation of two-dimensional structures (tesselation, web, array, matrix grammars) have contributed to our understanding of the underlying problems (see reviews in [15,16]).

The intuitive idea in all these constructs is to replace each subunit in a connected structure by some "daughter" structures, and then connect these daughter structures in a neighborhood-preserving way, in each of the derivation steps. The parallel replacement of all subunits in a derivation step has the advantage that it is not necessary to select arbitrarily one or more of the subunits which should be replaced. The interpretation of such a parallel procedure is also much easier since in any physical or biological object every part of the object changes simultaneously in time (whether we think of a planetary system or a developing organism).

In two-dimensional parallel generating systems the advantage of transforming maps directly is that this allows one to provide rather precise information about the "geometry" of the structure. This is in contrast to processing graphs as duals of maps where only topological representations of the structures can be given. From the point of view of applications (the visual similarity of the generated pattern to the multicellular organism) maps systems are certainly more desirable. Graph representations, on the other hand, are not restricted to two-dimensional objects and can usually be formulated in a more concise way. An important distinguishing feature between map and graph generating systems is that in a map system when from structure M_1 structure M_2 is directly derived, a large part of structure M_1 remains invariant in the sense that one can actually find it in M_2. In a graph generating system in general no part of the previous structure is preserved in successor structures. For instance, in a map generating system once corners are introduced they remain present in "fixed" relationships to each other in all subsequent structures. In our systems the walls of the map do not remain invariant in the same sense as corners do. But the stable structure of corners implies that while walls evolve into sequences of walls, these sequences still connect the same corners that the original wall did.

In the map generating systems we propose here, a direct derivation step consists of two stages. In the first stage each wall of the map is subject to rewriting, and in the second stage new walls are spanned on the structure of walls and corners obtained in the first stage (inducing in this way cell divisions). Thus in these systems one processes maps by directly processing their own "graphs", not their dual graphs. This independent processing of the graph of a map is the main distinguishing feature between our model and that of [4,6]. Other differences between the models are that our model is essentially context-independent, and that our model does not require an a-priori-fixed bound on the number of walls of a cell.

With respect to our map generating systems and their various restrictions and extensions we follow the terminology established for the string generating L-systems (for reviews see [17,18,19,20]). Their biological usefulness is discussed in the section on generating hexagonal cellular arrays.

THE BASIC MODEL

We introduce in this paper a biologically motivated terminology for a "map". The terms are therefore somewhat different from the usual geographically oriented ones (countries, boundaries, etc.). The notion of a map is introduced here informally, it is not significantly different from the formal definitions in the literature (e.g. in [3]), except for the use of wall and cell labels and wall directions.

A map consists of a finite set of cells. Each cell is surrounded entirely by a finite sequence of walls (called the boundary of the cell). Walls meet in corners. Each wall has a direction, an associated arrow pointing from one to the other of its corners. Each cell has a label and each wall has a label, chosen from symbols in two finite, disjoint alphabets. The rest of the plane outside of the map is the environment, which we label with ∞, a symbol not in either of the two alphabets. Two neighboring cells touch each other along one or more shared walls. At a corner one, two, or more walls may meet. A corner at which at most two walls meet we call a virtual corner. Thus, for example, in the following map there are three corners, one of which (in the center) is a virtual corner (figure on the left). In the map shown in the figure on the right there are two cells, labelled a and b, which touch each other along two walls that do not have a common corner.

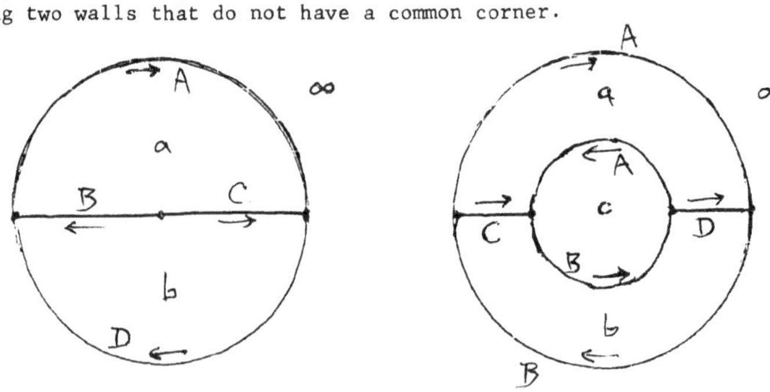

We shall give a definition of parallel map generating systems with the following characteristics:

(1) only binary cell divisions are allowed, i.e., in a single derivation step each cell gives rise to one or two successor cells,

(2) walls cannot be erased, hence cells cannot fuse or "disappear",

(3) the productions for rewriting of wall symbols or of cell symbols do not take into account their positions in the map.

Using terminology analogous to that of string L-systems, we thus refer to these systems as binary, propagating, map OL-systems, abbreviated as BPMOL-systems.

Such a system G consists of

(1) a finite cell alphabet Σ,

(2) a finite wall alphabet Δ,

(3) a finite set of wall productions P,

(4) a finite set of cell productions R, and

(5) the axiom (or starting map) ω.

Alphabets Σ and Δ are disjoint. Moreover we use three special symbols: ∞ (the label of the environment, usually not shown on the maps), and +,- (orientation signs associated with wall labels in productions).

Let the oriented wall alphabet Δ_o be the Cartesian product of Δ and $\{+,-\}$. For any $D = (A,x)$ in Δ_o, we refer to A as the label of D (denoted by $\ell(D)$), and to x as the sign of D (denoted by $s(D)$). For convenience we will usually write D in the form A^x.

Wall productions are of the form $A \longrightarrow \alpha$, where $A \in \Delta$ and $\alpha \in \Delta_o^+$. We require that for every wall label there is at least one production.

Cell productions are of two kinds:

(1) the first kind are of the form $a \longrightarrow b$, with $a,b \in \Sigma$ (we refer to these as chain productions), and

(2) the second kind are of the form $a \longrightarrow (K_1, b, K_2, c, D)$, where $a,b,c \in \Sigma$, $D \in \Delta_o$, and $K_1, K_2 \subseteq \Delta_o^*$ (we refer to these as division productions). We assume that K_1 and K_2 are finitely specified languages over Δ_o. Different ways of specifying K_1 and K_2 lead to a possible classification of these systems. In this paper we consider only systems with finite K_1 and K_2.

A single (direct) derivation step in a BPMOL-system is performed as follows:

(1) First of all, every wall is rewritten as a sequence of walls. This rewriting is governed by a wall production $A \longrightarrow \alpha = D_1 \cdot \ldots \cdot D_t$, where A is the label of the wall to be rewritten. Since every wall in the map is directed (has an associated arrow), the spanning of the initial and terminal corners of the wall labelled A is unambiguous. After rewriting, these two corners are connected by the sequence of walls corresponding to $D_1, \ldots, D_t$ in the proper order (i.e., D_1 leaves the initial corner and D_t arrives at the terminal corner). The arrow associated with the newly introduced wall D_i points in the direction of the original wall (labelled A) if $s(D_i) = +$, and is opposite to the direction of the original wall if $s(D_i) = -$. Thus, for example, if the wall production is $A \longrightarrow B^-C^+D^-$, then the following diagram shows a single derivation step.

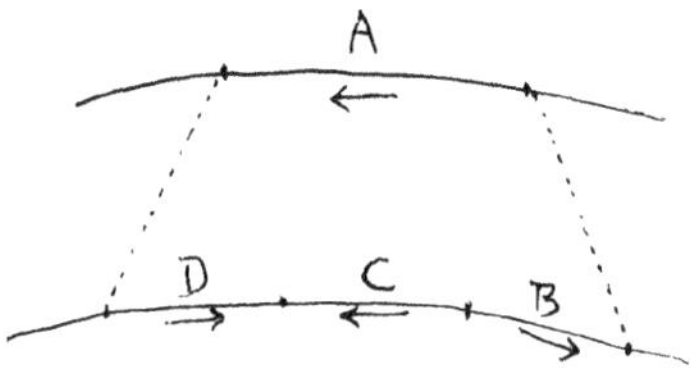

(2) After each wall of the map has been rewritten, we apply the cell productions.

(2.1) If the set of cell productions P contains a chain production $a \longrightarrow b$ then a cell labelled a can change its label to b.

(2.2) If P contains a division production $a \longrightarrow (K_1, b, K_2, c, D)$ then a cell labelled a can acquire a division wall between its two corners u_1 and u_2 only if the sequence β of directed walls leading from u_1 to u_2 in the clockwise direction is an element of K_1, and the sequence γ of directed walls leading clockwise from u_2 to u_1 is an element of K_2. The sequences β and γ are constructed in such a way that each of their elements is of the form B^x where B is the label of the wall considered and **x** is + if the direction of this wall is clockwise and x is - otherwise. The division wall will be labelled by $\ell(D)$ and its associated arrow points from u_1 to u_2 if s(D) is +, or its direction is from u_2 to u_1 if s(D) is -. The labels of the two new cells are assigned according to the rule: the cell to whose boundary the sequence of walls leading from u_1 to u_2 belongs gets the label b, and the other cell gets the label c. Thus, for example, let R contain the production

$$a \longrightarrow (\{A^-A^-\},\ b,\ \{B^+A^-B^+A^-,\ A^-B^+A^-B^+,\ A^+B^+A^-B^+\},\ c,\ B^-).$$

(i) If a cell labelled a after wall rewriting looks like this

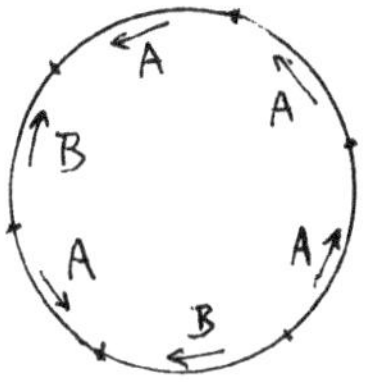

then it becomes in the second stage of the derivation step

either 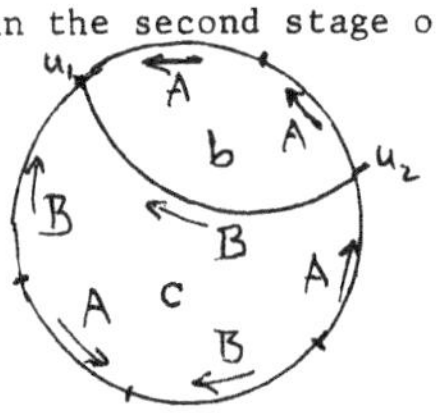

or 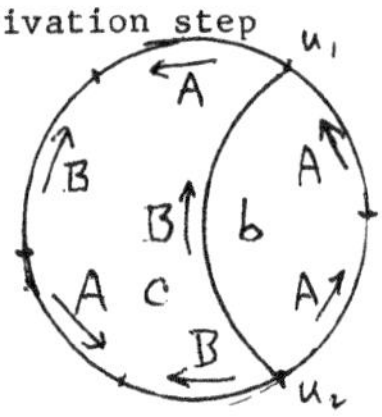

(ii) If a cell labelled a looks like the left-hand map after wall rewriting, then according to the above production the only possible derivation yields the following right-hand map.

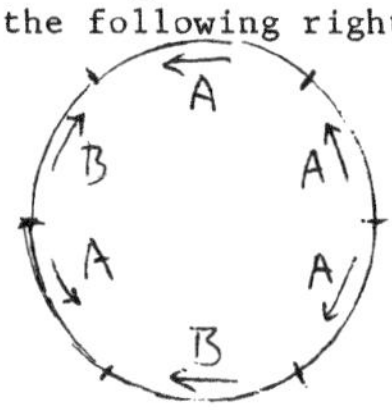

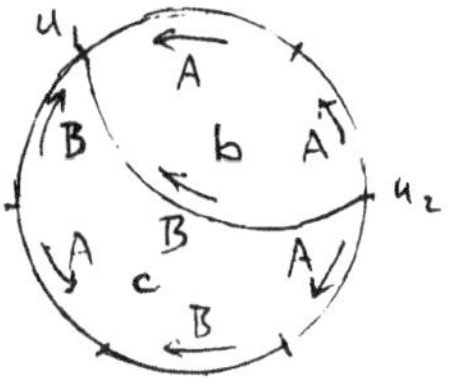

(iii) If a cell labelled a after wall rewriting is of the form

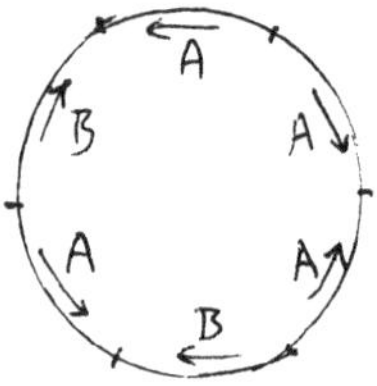

then on the basis of the above production no cell division is possible (what happens to this cell depends on some other cell production or on the clause that follows).

(2.3) If P contains neither a chain production nor a division production for a given cell then the label of the cell remains unchanged in this derivation step. (Note that the new boundary of this cell may be different from its previous one because wall rewriting was already performed as the first stage of this derivation step.) This clause insures that BPMOL-systems are complete in the usual sense of L-system theory.

As usual in formal language theory, a derivation is a finite iteration of single derivation steps. Note that by our definition such an iteration can always be carried out. If a derivation leads from a map M_1 to a map M_2 in a system G then we say that M_1 derives M_2 in G, and write

$$M_1 \overset{+}{\underset{G}{\Longrightarrow}} M_2.$$

Moreover we write

$$M_1 \overset{*}{\underset{G}{\Longrightarrow}} M_2$$

if $M_1 = M_2$ or if M_1 derives M_2 in G.

A trace in G is a finite sequence of maps $\tau = M_o, M_1, \ldots, M_n$ with $n \geq 2$ such that for $0 \leq i \leq n-1$, M_i directly derives M_{i+1} in G. We say that τ is reachable if

$$\omega \overset{*}{\underset{G}{\Longrightarrow}} M_o.$$

A developmental sequence in G is an infinite sequence ρ of maps starting with ω such that every finite segment of ρ is a trace in G.

The set of sequences of G, denoted by E(G), consists of all developmental sequences of G. The language of G, denoted by L(G), is defined as follows

$$L(G) = \{M \mid \omega \overset{*}{\underset{G}{\Longrightarrow}} M\}.$$

If E(G) consists of one developmental sequence only then we say that G is deterministic. A complete set of wall and cell productions, i.e., a BPMOL-system without an axiom, is called a BPMOL-scheme.

EXAMPLES

(1) Perhaps the simplest BPMOL-system is the following one:

wall alphabet: $\{1\}$
wall production: $1 \longleftrightarrow 1^+$
cell alphabet: $\{a\}$
cell production: $a \longrightarrow (\{1^+\}, a, \{1^-\}, a, 1^+)$.

Beginning with the axiom shown below it produces a series of pumpkin-like patterns

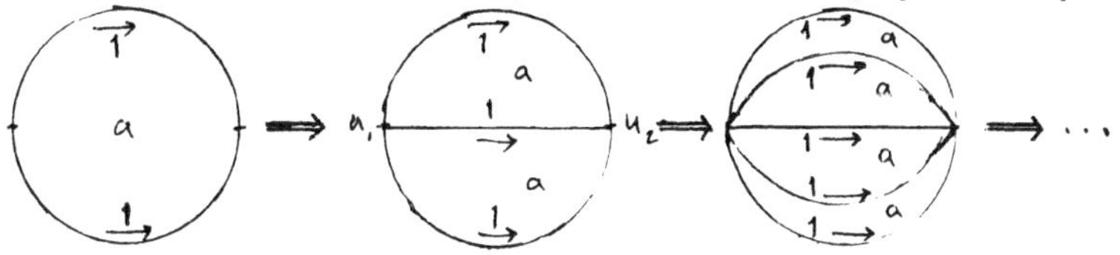

(2) Square grids (maps consisting of four-sided cells) are generated by the system:

wall alphabet: $\{1,2\}$
wall productions: $1 \longrightarrow 2^-2^-$
$2 \longrightarrow 1^+$
cell alphabet: $\{a\}$
cell production: $a \longrightarrow (\{2^-1^+2^+\}, a, \{2^+1^-2^-\}, a, 1^+)$.

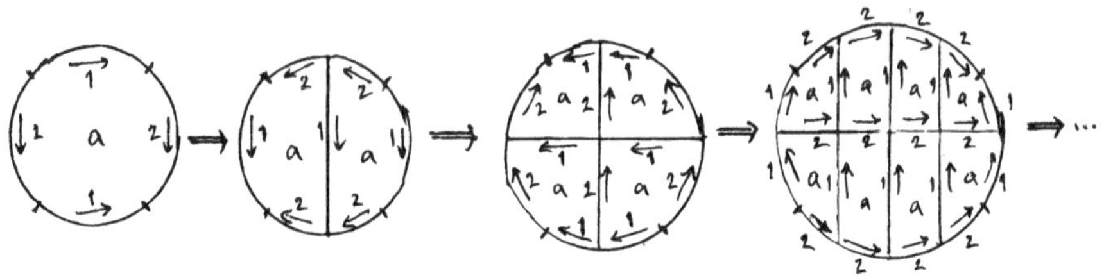

(3) The following system, with the same wall and cell alphabets, gives rise to polar filaments of four-sided cells. The structures have apical and basal ends, dorsal and ventral sides, and each cell is individually polar both ways.

Wall productions: $1 \longrightarrow 1^{+}1^{+}$
$2 \longrightarrow 2^{+}$
Cell production: $a \longrightarrow (\{1^{+}2^{+}1^{-}\}, a, \{1^{-}2^{-}1^{+}\}, a, 2^{+})$

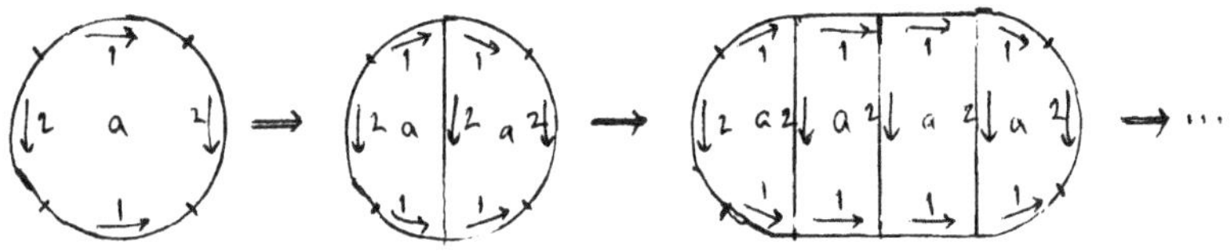

(4) Wheel-like and radiating patterns are produced by the same wall productions and the following cell production:

$$a \longrightarrow (\{1^{+}2^{+}\}, a, \{2^{-}1^{+}\}, a, 2^{+})$$

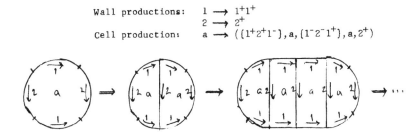

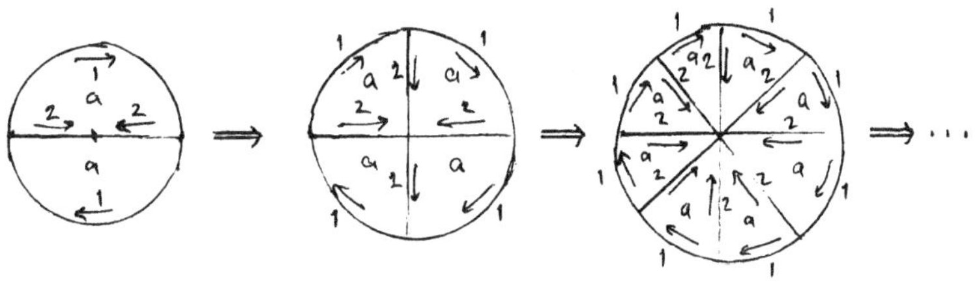

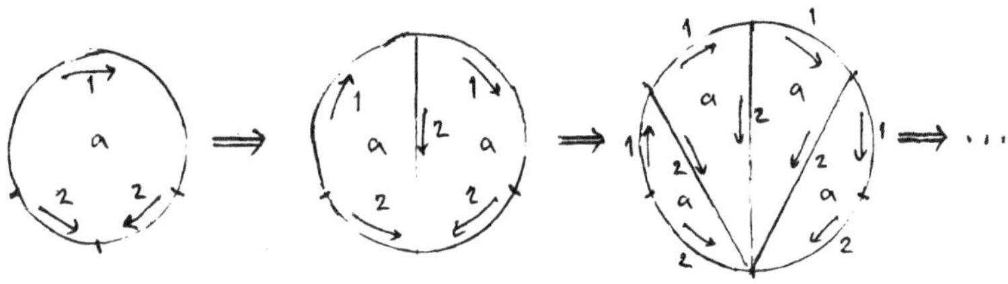

Comments: The map system of Example 3 can be used to construct BPMOL-systems which correspond to binary, propagating, string OL-systems. One needs only to include cell productions of the form $a \longrightarrow (\{1^{+}2^{+}1^{-}\}, c, \{1^{-}2^{-}1^{+}\}, b, 2^{+})$ in the map system for each division production $a \longrightarrow bc$ in the string system, as well as taking over all chain productions of the string system. The disadvantage of this construction is that virtual corners accumulate when cells do not divide. To avoid this, one would have to introduce as many wall symbols as cell symbols.

In some of the above examples the same map patterns could be generated without wall directions. For this reason we use the convention of omitting signs from wall labels where the directions of walls are not essential. To conform to the definition, all combinations of missing signs should be provided (or a suitable subset of these combinations).

(5) We use this convention in this example which demonstrates how alternating left and right apical divisions can be programmed. This corresponds to the developmental pattern found in moss leaves and fern gametophytes and to the graph system to produce ladder-like structures in [11].

Wall alphabet: $\{0,1,2\}$
wall productions: $0 \rightarrow 0$
$1 \rightarrow 1^{-}0$
$2 \rightarrow 00$
cell alphabet: $\{a,b\}$
cell productions: $a \rightarrow (\{01^{-},1^{+}0\},a,\{000\},b,2)$
$b \rightarrow b$

Due to the second wall production the direction of walls labelled 1 alternates in consecutive derivation steps, and this forces us to use alternately different elements of K_1 in applying the division production.

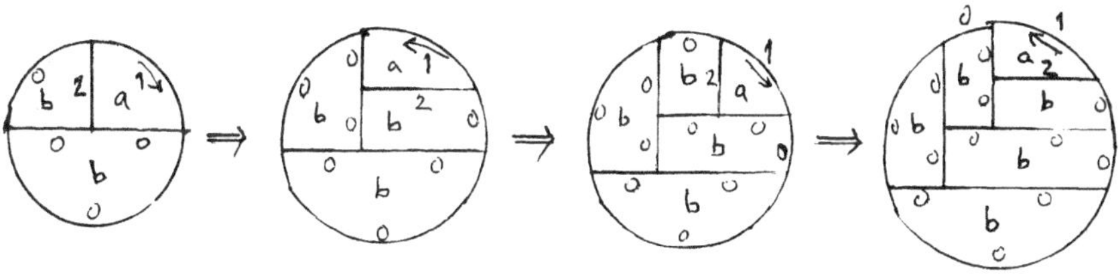

GENERATION OF HEXAGONAL CELL LAYERS

In most epidermal and epithelial cell layers in plants and animals the average number of neighbors each cell has is six. The question arises how does one get such cell arrays which grow by binary cell divisions and have this property at every cell generation. The first time this question was clearly stated in the biological literature was by Lewis [21]. Since that time several kinds of division patterns have been formulated which would result in the transformation of an arbitrarily large hexagonal cell array (each cell having exactly six neighbors) into a new hexagonal array by binary divisions (see [22] for a survey of these patterns). These patterns are usually presented by showing division walls in a regular hexagonal array, resulting in six-sided cells which are not regular hexagons any more. The disadvantage of this presentation is that one cannot carry out the same transformation iteratively without redrawing the array each time. The map generating systems proposed here, on the other hand, enable us to carry out as many derivation steps as we wish while maintaining the structural framework. At the same time we do not need to rely on our geometric intuition to be sure that in each step the same set of division rules is being applied. We illustrate this on the following map generating system.

(1) The following hexagonal cell generating pattern was shown by Korn and Spalding in [23]. Abbott [22] gives the name "compact" to the four-cell pattern which arises from any two of the original cells which are next to each other in a row (see figure on right).

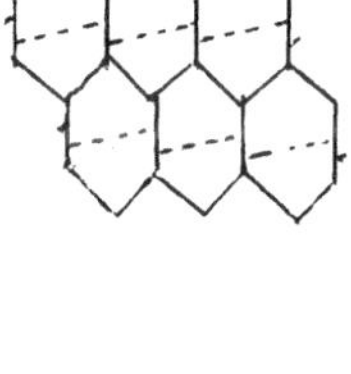

As we see, by adding division walls as indicated by the broken lines we obtain two new hexagonal cells from each previous cell (at the edges one must also consider the division walls which would be present in the neighboring cells). Repeating this operation is, however, quite cumbersome and it is ambiguous (there are several ways in which the next step can be carried out). By constructing the following map generating system we avoid these difficulties. Since wall directions are not needed to generate this pattern we omit them according to the convention mentioned before Example 5.

Wall alphabet: {1,2,3}
wall productions: 1 $\rightarrow$ 323
2 $\rightarrow$ 1
3 $\rightarrow$ 2
cell alphabet: {a}
cell production: a $\rightarrow$ ({23123},a,{23123},a,1)
axiom: a hexagonal cell with walls labelled 123123 in the clockwise direction

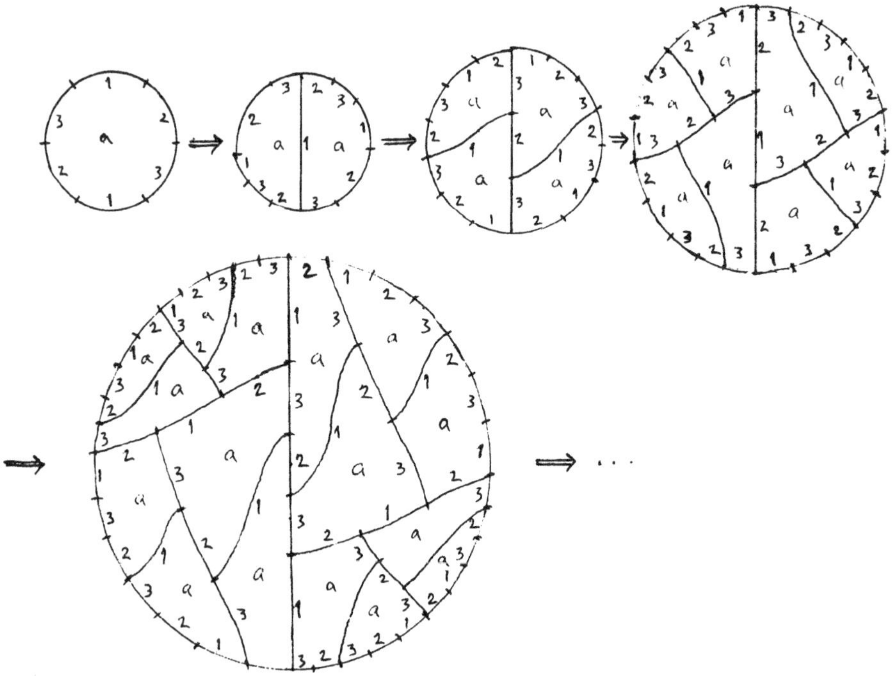

This map generating system is one of the simplest ones, requiring only a single cell symbol and three wall symbols, with which hexagonal arrays can be generated from previous hexagonal arrays with binary divisions. We call this a "clockwise" system because in every cell the order of wall labels runs in the clockwise direction. It has a twin system in which the opposite is true, as shown next.

(2) The counterclockwise pattern which is mirror-symmetric to the previous one is generated by the following map system.

Wall alphabet and wall productions are the same.
Cell alphabet: {a}
cell production: a $\rightarrow$ ({32132},a,{32132},a,1)
axiom: a hexagonal cell with walls labelled 123123 in the counterclockwise direction.

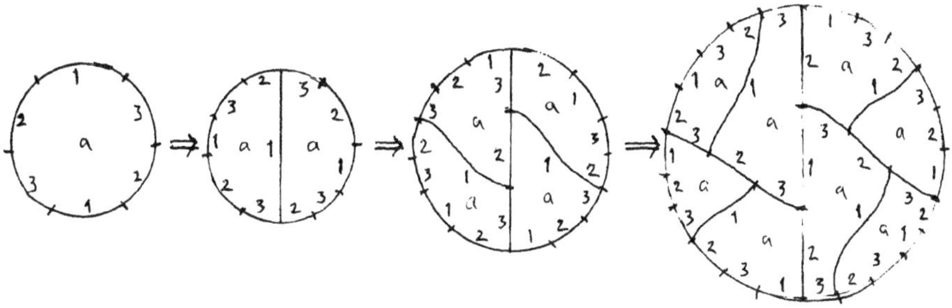

Both clockwise and counterclockwise cell division patterns of this type can be seen in plant epidermal cell layers, as shown in the following figure.

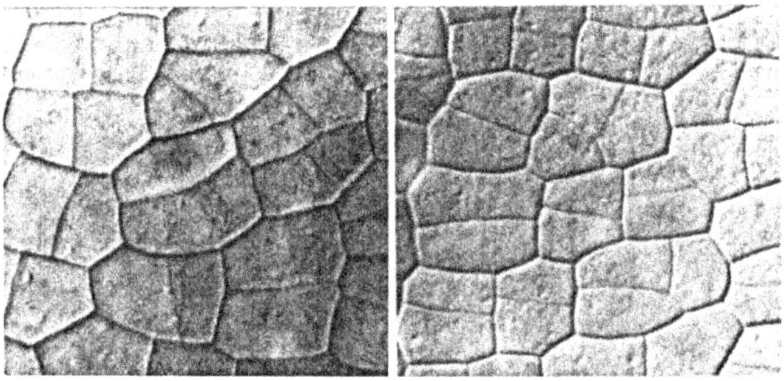

This figure shows the epidermis of young leaves of the aquatic plant Aponogeton elongatus MÜLLER(from [24]). One can find groups of cells which are descendants from a common ancestor cell since the cell walls become thicker and the corresponding grooves deeper with age. It is interesting to see that in the photograph on the left side there are two groups of four cells exhibiting the clockwise division pattern, while in the one on the right-hand side there are two tetrads showing the counterclockwise pattern (in the lower left corner and at the right edge) and there is one group (at the upper edge) which is showing the clockwise pattern. As far as we know there has not been any investigation of this characteristics of cell division patterns which is clearly the result of a cellular mechanism regulating spindle orientation in consecutive cell divisions. Map generating systems can also be used to formulate division mechanisms for groups of cells larger than tetrads.

(3) The following hexagonal generating system has also three wall labels and a single cell label. There are actually two mirror-image systems of this kind, we present only the clockwise one here.

Wall alphabet: {1,2,3}

wall productions: 1 ⟶ 313

2 ⟶ 1

3 ⟶ 2

cell alphabet: {a}

cell production: a ⟶ ({31231},a,{31231},a,2)

axiom: a hexagonal cell with wall labels 123123 in the clockwise direction

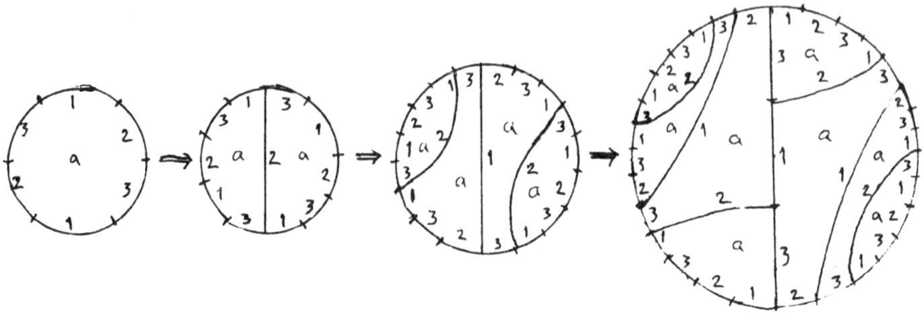

In the four-cell stage this pattern is called the "constellation" by Abbott [22]. Drawn on a hexagonal grid the cell tetrad looks like this if generated by a clockwise system of this sort:

(4) Still another hexagonal system with three wall symbols and a single cell symbol is the following (again only the clockwise version is presented).

Wall alphabet: {1,2,3}
wall productions: 1 → 131
2 → 2
3 → 3
cell alphabet: {a}
cell production: a → ({31231},a,{31231},a,2)
axiom: a hexagonal cell with wall labels 123123 clockwise

While all the cells in the arrays which are generated are six-sided, they form a filament, i.e., each has not more than two neighbors in the array.

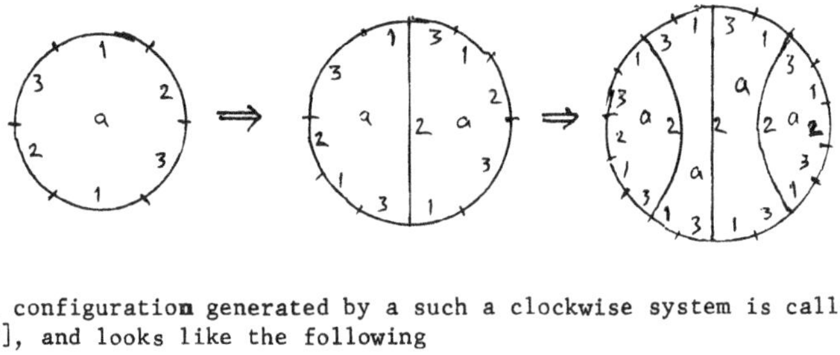

The four-cell configuration generated by a such a clockwise system is called a "line" in [22], and looks like the following

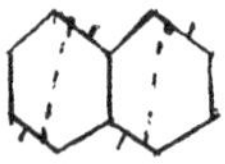

Note that the tetrad patterns which have been mentioned, namely the "compact," the "constellation" and the "line", can all be found in the hexagonal division pattern given by Korn and Spalding [23], shown under (1). The compact and the line patterns are present there in the clockwise orientation, while the constellation is in the counterclockwise one.

(5) There is also an alternating clockwise and counterclockwise pattern corresponding to those given under (1) and (2).

Wall alphabet: {1,2,3}
wall productions: 1 → 323
2 → 2
3 → 1
cell alphabet: {a}
cell production: a → ({32132,23123},a,{32132,23123},a,1)
axiom: a hexagonal cell with wall labels 123123 clockwise

This system gives an interesting alternating division pattern which may well be found in nature. It has the feature that walls labelled 2 do not produce corners for division walls.

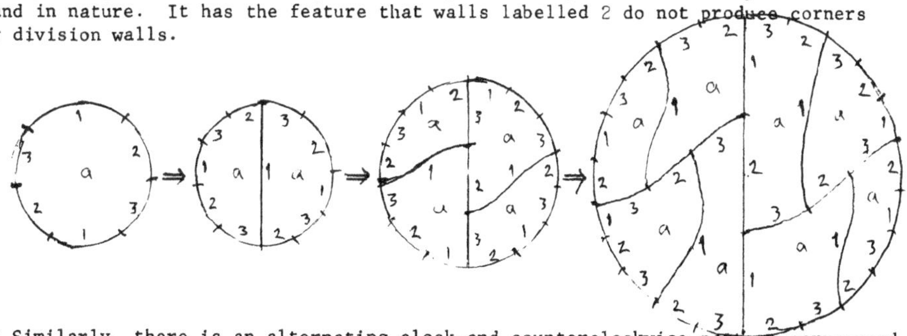

(6) Similarly, there is an alternating clock-and counterclockwise pattern corresponding to that shown under (3).

Wall alphabet: {1,2,3}
wall productions: 1 → 313
2 → 2
3 → 1
cell alphabet: {a}
cell production: a → ({13213,31231},a,{13213,31231},a,2)
axiom: a hexagonal cell with wall labels 123123 clockwise

This system produces a "line" pattern, again walls labelled 2 do not produce corners.

(7) Finally, there is an alternating clock- and counterclockwise pattern corresponding to that shown under (4).

Wall alphabet: {1,2,3}
wall productions: 1 → 131
2 → 3
3 → 2
cell alphabet: {a}
cell production: a → ({13213,31231},a,{13213,31231},a,2)
axiom: a hexagonal cell with wall labels 123123 clockwise

This system produces an interesting "wobbly line" pattern. Here neither walls labelled 2 nor those labelled 3 produce corners.

(8) There are also three systems, without clockwise and counterclockwise alternatives, which produce all hexagonal cells in "line" configuration with two wall labels and single cell label. These are the following:

Wall alphabet: {1,2} , cell alphabet: {a} in each system,

wall productions:	1 → 1	1 → 212	1 → 121
	2 → 22	2 → 2	2 → 2
cell productions:	a → ({22122},a,{22122},a,1)		a → ({12212},a,{12212},a,2)
	for first two systems		for the third system

axiom in all three systems: a hexagonal cell with 122122 wall label sequence.

Comments: We have given here a long list of hexagonal map generating systems with single cell label in order to demonstrate that the class of map systems we propose in this paper can cope efficiently with classes of pattens that are mathematically interesting and biologically feasible. Moreover, the sequence of systems presented above covers exhaustively an important geometrically defined class of division patterns as explained below.

We call a map regularly hexagonal if every cell in it has six walls, no two cells share more than one wall, and at every corner, except those on walls bordering on the environment, exactly three walls meet. Further, we call two dividing cells in such a regularly hexagonal map simply isomorphic if their division walls and all their corners have respectively the same geometric positions in the two cells when they are drawn on a regular hexagonal grid. That is, the two original cells with added division walls and new corners can be brought into exact overlap by translation in the grid, without rotation or mirror transformation. Cell and wall labels, and wall directions are not to be taken into account when establishing this relationship. Examples of pairs of neighboring dividing cells which are simply isomorphic are shown under (1),(3) and (4) where they are called "tetrads". We can now state:

Proposition. The only BPMOL-schemes which generate in one derivation step a regularly hexagonal map from another regularly hexagonal map in such a way that in the preceeding map all cells divide and every pair of dividing cells is simply isomorphic, are the six sets of wall and cell productions given under (1),(3),(4),(5),(6),(7), their counterclockwise counterparts, and the three sets given under (8).

Proof (sketch). First of all we can show that it may be assumed that in a map, which is regularly hexagonal and which generates a regularly hexagonal map by admitting simply isomorphic dividing cells only, the following are satisfied:
(a) all the cells have the same label,
(b) there are no more than three wall labels, and
(c) opposite walls of a cell have the same label and opposite orientation along the cell boundary.
As far as (b) is concerned, one easily sees that the case of a single wall label is impossible. If two wall labels are assumed, then we can immediately conclude that the only three possible systems are the ones listed under (8). Hence we proceed to consider the case of systems with three distinct wall labels. Since wall orientation is fixed by requirement (c), wall direction cannot be used as control factor in these systems. One also notices that (c) implies that reading labels around the boundary of a cell always gives a word of the form ww where w is a sequence of length three consisting of wall labels without signs. This results in the fact that in a dividing cell a sequence of three walls must produce a sequence of five walls. Moreover, all wall productions must have palindromes at their right-hand sides. But certain palindromic configurations are impossible by the ww consideration, such as strings consisting of the same symbol twice. This leaves us with only the following six sets of wall productions (with division wall label 1 in all cases):

$1 \longrightarrow 232$	$1 \longrightarrow 232$	$1 \longrightarrow 1$	$1 \longrightarrow 3$	$1 \longrightarrow 1$	$1 \longrightarrow 3$
$2 \longrightarrow 1$	$2 \longrightarrow 3$	$2 \longrightarrow 232$	$2 \longrightarrow 232$	$2 \longrightarrow 3$	$2 \longrightarrow 1$
$3 \longrightarrow 3$	$3 \longrightarrow 1$	$3 \longrightarrow 3$	$3 \longrightarrow 1$	$3 \longrightarrow 232$	$3 \longrightarrow 232$

Note that they are the sets given under (1),(3),(4),(5),(6),(7) under simple recoding of the labels. Thus the theorem holds. □

It is instructive to note at this point that if one does not require a hexagonal map to be regularly hexagonal then such maps can be generated by systems having three or more wall labels and with non-palindromic right-hand sides in the wall productions, single cell label, and making essential use of wall directions. An example is the following system:

(9) Wall alphabet: $\{1,2,3\}$, wall productions: $1 \longrightarrow 3^-2^-$
$2 \longrightarrow 1^-$
$3 \longrightarrow 1^+2^+$

cell alphabet: $\{a\}$,
cell production: $a \longrightarrow (\{2^-1^-1^+2^+3^+\}, a, \{3^-2^-1^-1^+2^+\}, a, 3^+)$,
axiom: a hexagonal cell with wall labels and directions described by the sequence $1^+2^+3^+3^-2^-1^-$.

(10) The last hexagonal division pattern we wish to present is based on the one proposed in his first paper in 1926 by Lewis [21]. There are two different division orientations in the array as shown below, thus we need at least two cell labels.

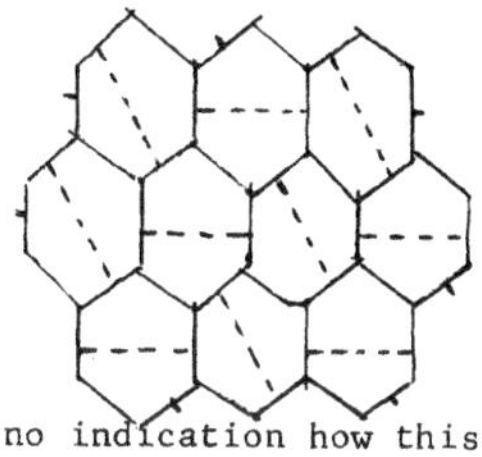

In Lewis's paper there was no indication how this array should divide in a second step, and for a while we thought that the cells must be relabelled after each step by an interactive algorithm. At the end it turned out to be possible to construct a BPMOL-system with two cell labels, six wall labels, and directed walls by which the same pattern can be continued for arbitrary number of generations. In the patterns produced by this system the rows of cells which divide in the same direction turn in each derivation step by 120°. Again there is a mirror-image counterpart of this pattern which we do not give here.

Wall alphabet: $\{1,2,3,4,5,6\}$

wall productions:

$1 \longrightarrow 2^{+}$

$2 \longrightarrow 3^{+}1^{-}$

$3 \longrightarrow 5^{-}6^{-}$

$4 \longrightarrow 1^{-}5^{-}$

$5 \longrightarrow 6^{-}3^{+}$

$6 \longrightarrow 4^{+}$

cell alphabet: $\{a,b\}$

cell productions:

$a \longrightarrow (\{1^{+}2^{+}3^{+}1^{-}5^{-}\}, a, \{6^{-}2^{-}3^{-}6^{+}5^{+}\}, b, 4^{+})$

$b \longrightarrow (\{3^{+}1^{-}5^{-}4^{-}1^{+}\}, a, \{3^{-}6^{+}5^{+}4^{+}6^{-}\}, b, 2^{-})$

axiom: as below

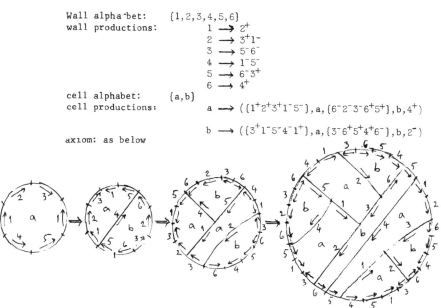

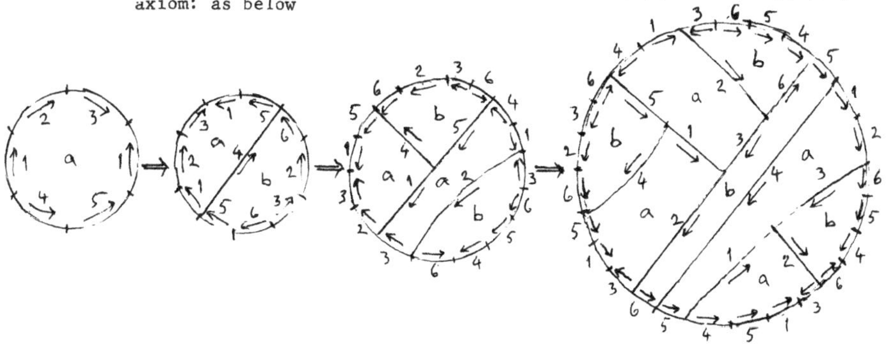

Abbott [22] calls the tetrads which occur in the Lewis pattern "acute type-1" and "acute type-2". They are shown below. Tetrads which were called "lines" can also be found in this division pattern.

All of the tetrad types mentioned in this section, as well as some others, were found in cell layers on Drosophila wings [22]. The analysis of cell tetrads and larger groups of cells with common ancestors can be facilitated by using map generating systems. Large numbers of growing hexagonal cell patterns are known, but their systematic study is only now beginning.

DISCUSSION

Our aim in this paper has been to introduce the basic notion of a BPMOL-system and to illustrate it by examples mainly chosen from hexagonal cell generating systems. In a forthcoming paper we deal more extensively with the theory of map generating systems. We are rather convinced that these systems and their natural extensions represent a useful tool both for describing concrete developmental patterns and for constructing a systematic theory of (parallel) map grammars. We would like to conclude this paper with a discussion of possible directions for restricting or extending the BPMOL model. First the restrictions.

(1) In our cell productions of the form $a \rightarrow (K_1, b, K_2, c, D)$ we could put various restrictions on the complexity of the division-controlling pair of languages (K_1,K_2). In the systems we have treated so far K_1 and K_2 were singletons or pairs only. We could build up a hierarchy of systems on the basis of considering singletons, finite, regular, linear, and context-free languages. Note that if we restrict K_1 and K_2 to finite languages, then cells with lengths of boundary exceeding certain constants (depending on the specification of the system only) will not be subject to cell division.

(2) If all wall productions have palindromes on their right-hand sides then wall directions are not needed in the wall rewriting stage of a derivation step. One can then allow or forbid the use of wall directions in the second stage (cell rewriting) of the derivation step.

(3) It is easy to motivate biologically the restriction of these systems to deterministic ones on the basis that physiological and cellular control mechanisms can be very precise and predictable. There are various ways of insuring that a given BPMOL-system G would be such that E(G) is a singleton set.

We now come to the possible extensions.

(1) A BPMOL-system admits only binary cell divisions. It would be feasible to extend them to allow divisions of a cell into more than two daughter cells.

(2) Erasing is not allowed in these systems. There are several ways in which erasing could be introduced. First of all, one could admit wall erasing by including wall productions of the form $A \rightarrow \Lambda$. These could be employed to let cells fuse with each other or with the environment (in which case the cell disappears). Secondly, one can admit erasing cell productions $(a \rightarrow \Lambda)$. This would mean that a cell would contract to a point and all its walls disappear. Thirdly, one can admit cell productions of the form $a \rightarrow \infty$. In a certain sense these productions would be analogous to fragmenting productions in L-systems with fragmentation [25].

(3) In our cell productions we have required that neither K_1 nor K_2 contain the empty word. If we should allow this then systems could be specified which would produce islands in the maps. Also, we could allow for a dividing cell a sequence of walls between the two daughter cells, rather than a single division wall.

(4) There are various unexplored ways to define the languages or the sequences of BPMOL-systems. For instance one could disregard wall directions and/or wall labels and/or cell labels when defining the language or the set of sequences of a system. This leads us to consider the trade-offs between various control elements of a system in generating map patterns of various complexity.

(5) A way to extend the pattern-generating power of BPMOL-systems is by admitting various features making the resulting systems "context-dependent". Thus, for example, the application of a wall production $A \to \alpha$ would only be allowed if a wall labelled A is present between cells labelled a and b, and not otherwise (in this case productions will be of the form $(a,A,b) \to \alpha$). In the same way cell productions can also be made dependent on the labels of the neighbor cells.

(6) Obviously one could also use corners to control the rewriting process. For instance corners could give rise to walls (or wall sequences), or they could disappear. Labelled corners could be included in the division-controlling languages K_1 and K_2.

(7) In BPMOL-systems cells are units of considerable autonomy. But a wall between two cells belongs to the boundary of both cells which results in a certain degree of rigidity of the generating process. In many cases it would be desirable to have a wall programmed independently with respect to the two cells which share it. The idea of introducing double walls between cells (two labels and directions on either side of a wall) of Nyrup and Mayoh and of J. and H.B.Lück in their papers in this volume appears therefore attractive to us.

In further publications we plan to discuss in more detail the above outlined topics as well as the relationship of the model presented here to other map and graph generating systems encountered in the literature.

ACKNOWLEDGEMENT

We thank Prof. J.I. Malitz and Dr. Lois A.B. Abbott for many interesting discussions on hexagonal cell generating systems, and Dr. Valerie B. Morris and Dr. R.W. Korn for drawing our attention to regular division patterns in cell layers. The support provided for this work by the Netherland Organisation for the Advancement of Pure Research (Z.W.O.) is gratefully acknowledged.

REFERENCES

1. B.H. Mayoh, Mathematical models for cellular organisms. Datalogisk Afdeling, Aarhus Univ., Report No. DAIMI PB-12, 38 pp., 1973.

2. B.H. Mayoh, Multidimensional Lindenmayer organisms. In: "L-systems", edited by G. Rozenberg and A. Salomaa, Lecture Notes in Computer Science 15, Springer-Verlag, Berlin-Heidelberg, pp. 302 -326, 1974.

3. A. Rosenfeld and J.P. Strong, A grammar for maps. In: "Software Engineering", edited by J.Tou, Academic Press, New York, Vol.2, pp. 227 - 239, 1971.

4. J.W. Carlyle, S.A. Greibach, and A. Paz, A two-dimensional generating system modeling growth by binary cell division. In: 15th Annual Symp. on Switching and Automata Theory, Proceedings, New Orleans, IEEE Computer Soc., Long Beach, Calif., pp. 1 - 12, 1974.

5. B.H. Mayoh, Another model for the development of multidimensional organisms. In: "Automata, Languages, Development", edited by A. Lindenmayer and G. Rozenberg, North-Holland Publ. Co., Amsterdam, pp. 469 - 485, 1976.

6. A. Paz and Y. Raz, Complexity of pattern generation by map-L-systems. In this volume.

7. K. Culik II and A. Lindenmayer, Parallel rewriting on graphs and multidimensional development. Faculty of Mathematics, Univ. of Waterloo, Report No. CS-74-22, 41 pp., 1974.

8. M. Nagl, Graph Lindenmayer-systems and languages. Inst. für math. Maschinen und Datenverarbeitung, Univ. Erlangen-Nürnberg, Arbeitsberichte, Vol.8, No. 1, pp. 16 -63, 1975.

9. K. Culik II and A. Lindenmayer, Parallel graph generating and graph recurrence systems for multicellular development. Int. J. General Systems, 3: 53 - 66, 1976.

10. H.B. Lück and J. Lück, Automata theoretical explanation of tissue growth. In: Proc. of the Int. Symp. on Mathematical Topics in Biology, Kyoto, pp.174-185, 1978. See also paper by J. Lück and H.B. Lück in this volume.

11. A. Lindenmayer and K. Culik II, Growing cellular systems: Generation of graphs by parallel rewriting. Int. J. General Systems, to appear; and paper by K.Culik II and D. Wood in this volume.

12. H. Ehrig, Introduction to the algebraic theory of graph grammars. In this volume.

13. M. Nagl, A tutorial and bibliographical survey of graph grammars. In this volume.

14. E. Grötsch and M. Nagl, Explicit versus implicit parallel rewriting on graphs. In this volume.

15. A.R. Smith III, Introduction to and survey of polyautomata theory. In: "Automata, Languages, Development", edited by A. Lindenmayer and G. Rozenberg, North-Holland Publ. Co., Amsterdam, pp. 405 - 422, 1976.

16. A. Rosenfeld, Array and web grammars: An overview. Ibid., pp. 517 - 529, 1976.

17. G.T. Herman and G. Rozenberg, "Developmental Systems and Languages" (with a contribution by A. Lindenmayer). North-Holland Publ. Co., Amsterdam, 363 pp., 1975.

18. G. Rozenberg and A. Salomaa, "The Mathematical Theory of L Systems". Academic Press, New York, to appear.

19. A. Lindenmayer, Developmental algorithms for multicellular organisms: A survey of L-systems. J. Theor. Biol., 54: 3 - 22, 1975.

20. A. Lindenmayer, Algorithms for plant morphogenesis. In: "Theoretical Plant Morphology", edited by R. Sattler, Leiden Univ. Press, The Hague, pp. 37 - 81, (Supplement to Acta Biotheoretica, Vol. 27), 1978.

21. F.T. Lewis, The effect of cell division on the shape and size of hexagonal cells. Anatomical Record, 33: 331 - 355, 1926.

22. Lois A.B. Abbott, A biological and mathematical analysis of wing morphogenesis in Drosophila. Ph. D. Thesis, Dept. of Environmental, Population and Organismic Biology, Univ. of Colorado, Boulder, 127 pp., 1977.

23. R.W. Korn and R.M. Spalding, The geometry of plant epidermal cells. New Phytologist, 72: 1357 - 1365, 1973.

24. R.W. Korn, Quantitative aspects of "cell net" analysis. Manuscript, 1976.

25. G. Rozenberg, K. Ruohonen and A. Salomaa, Developmental systems with fragmentation. Int. J. Computer Math., 5: 177 - 191, 1976.

PROCESSES IN STRUCTURES

Andrea Maggiolo-Schettini
Ist. Scienze Informazione, Università di Salerno
84100-Salerno, Italy

Józef Winkowski
Instytut Podstaw Informatyki PAN
00901-Warszawa, PKiN, Skr.p.22, Poland

Introduction

In [EKMRW 78] a general definition of structures has been considered and a method to derive structures from structures has been introduced. Now we are going to show that compound derivations can be considered as compound processes in the sense of [Wi 77] and [Wi 78] and that both the formalisms are equivalent with respect to what can be derived. We are able to define directly compound processes and see whether the processes defined apply to certain structures. This is an obvious advantage with respect to using complex derivations and their applications. Besides, as the processes can be combined both sequentially and in parallel, we may consider concurrent transformations on a given structure.
In section 1 we shall recall the concept of partial sequences and explain how the partial sequences represent processes.
In section 2 the concept of partial sequences will be applied to represent processes of transforming structures, and we shall show the main result connecting derivations and processes of transforming structures.
A part of the material has been the subject of [MW 78].

1. Partial sequences

We shall exploit the idea to represent processes by partial sequences which are defined as classes of isomorphic labelled partially ordered sets satisfying certain special conditions.

1.1. Labelled partially ordered sets

Definition 1.1.1 By a labelled partially ordered set (l.p.o. set) we mean a triple $H=(X, \leqslant, l)$ such that:

(H1) $(X, \leqslant)$ is a partially ordered set,

(H2) every element of X has a lower bound which is minimal and an upper bound which is maximal,

(H3) $l: X \rightarrow L$ is a mapping (a labelling) assigning elements of a certain set L (labels) to the elements of X,

(H4) $l(x)=l(y)$ implies $x \leqslant y$ or $y \leqslant x$,

(H5) given a maximal antichain Y with

$$h(X, \leqslant, Y) := \{x \in X: x \leqslant y \text{ for some } y \in Y\}$$
$$t(X, \leqslant, Y) := \{x \in X: y \leqslant x \text{ for some } y \in Y\}$$

and a maximal chain Z, the intersection $Z \cap Y$ is non-empty (Fig.1) or for every $x \in Z \cap h(X, \leqslant, Y)$ and $y \in Z \cap t(X, \leqslant, Y)$ there are $p \in Z \cap h(X, \leqslant, Y)$ and $q \in Z \cap t(X, \leqslant, Y)$ such that $x \leqslant p \leqslant q \leqslant y$ and $l(p)=l(q)$ (Fig.2).

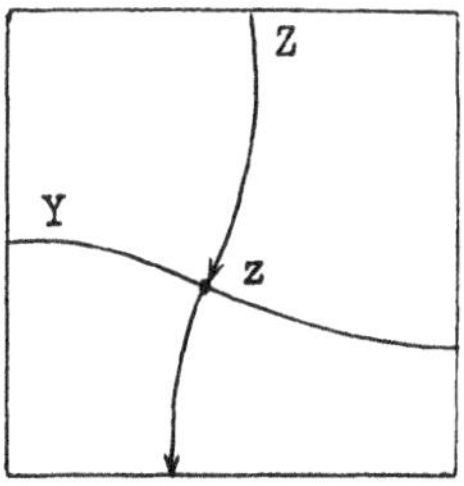

Fig.1

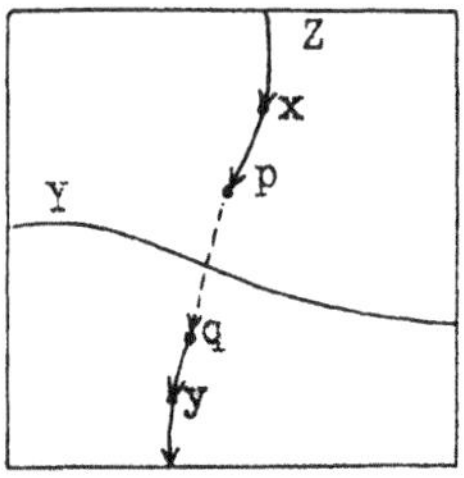

Fig.2

One may interprete such an l.p.o. set H as a history of a process of activating certain resources. The resources, whose nature is irrelevant, are represented by the elements of L. Particular activations of resources are represented by the elements of X. The activations of a particular resource $r \in L$ are represented by the elements with the label r. No assumption is made on the presence of a time scale. The ordering $\leqslant$ reflects only a causal relation between particular activations. Namely, an activation y of $r=l(y)$ is understood to be a consequence of all activations x such that $x \leqslant y$. Maximal antichains represent global configurations of activations that could possibly arise in the history. Maximal chains represent what we may call signal lines through the history. A completeness of the causal relation $\leqslant$ is assumed such that all the activations of a particular resource are causally connected (condition (H4)), and all the signal lines are represented in all the global configurations either by a presence of an activation of a resource or by a presence of a passivation of a resource (condition (H5)).

1.2. Internal structures of l.p.o. sets

Definition 1.2.1 Given any maximal antichain Y of an l.p.o. set $H=(X,\leqslant,l)$, the l.p.o. set $(Y,\leqslant|Y,l|Y)$, where $\leqslant|Y$ and $l|Y$ are the restrictions of $\leqslant$ and l, respectively, to Y, is called a cut of H. Every such a cut $c=(Y,\leqslant|Y,l|Y)$ determines two l.p.o. sets, namely

$$\underline{head}(H,c):=(h(X,\leqslant,Y),\leqslant|h(X,\leqslant,Y),l|h(X,\leqslant,Y))$$
$$\underline{tail}(H,c):=(t(X,\leqslant,Y),\leqslant|t(X,\leqslant,Y),l|t(X,\leqslant,Y))$$

where

$$h(X,\leqslant,Y):=\{x\in X\colon\ x\leqslant y \text{ for some } y\in Y\}$$
$$t(X,\leqslant,Y):=\{x\in X\colon\ y\leqslant x \text{ for some } y\in Y\}$$

Definition 1.2.2 The cuts of H can be ordered as follows:

$$c\sqsubseteq d \quad \text{iff} \quad c \text{ is a cut of } \underline{head}(H,d)$$

The set of cuts of H with this ordering is called the cut structure of H and denoted by cuts(H).

One can prove that such a structure is a lattice. The bottom element of this structure corresponds to the set of minimal elements. The top element corresponds to the set of maximal elements.

Definition 1.2.3 The bottom element of cuts(H) will be called the origin of H and denoted by origin(H). The top element of cuts(H) will be called the end of H and denoted by end(H).

Another structure of an l.p.o. set $H=(X,\leqslant,l)$ can be derived by considering suitable partitions of X.

Definition 1.2.4 Given an l.p.o. set $H=(X,\leqslant,l)$, we consider ordered pairs (X_1,X_2) of disjoint subsets of X such that $X_1\cup X_2=X$ and x is incomparable with y for every $x\in X_1$ and $y\in X_2$. Every such a pair has the property $l(X_1)\cap l(X_2)=\emptyset$ and it determines two l.p.o. sets, namely: $s_1=(X_1,\leqslant|X_1,l|X_1)$ and $s_2=(X_2,\leqslant|X_2,l|X_2)$. The pair $s=(s_1,s_2)$ is called a splitting of H and we denote s_1,s_2 by left(H,s), right(H,s).

Definition 1.2.5 Let H be an l.p.o. set. Given a splitting s of H determined by a pair (X_1,X_2) and a splitting t determined by a pair (U_1,U_2), we define an ordering:

$$s \sqsubseteq t \quad \text{iff} \quad X_1 \subseteq U_1 \quad (\text{and } U_2 \subseteq X_2)$$

The set of splittings of H with this ordering is called the splitting structure of H and is denoted by splittings(H).

It is easy to see that such a structure is a lattice with the bottom element corresponding to $(\emptyset,X)$ and the top element corresponding to $(X,\emptyset)$.

1.3. Partial sequences

Definition 1.3.1 Two l.p.o. sets $H=(X,\leqslant,l)$ and $H=(X',\leqslant',l')$ are said to be isomorphic iff there is a bijection $f:X \to X'$ such that:

(I1) $x \leqslant y$ iff $f(x) \leqslant' f(y)$,
(I2) $l(x)=l'(f(x))$ for every $x \in X$.

Definition 1.3.2 The class of l.p.o. sets which are isomorphic with an l.p.o. set H is called a partial sequence and denoted by $[H]$.

A partial sequence P can be interpreted as a process of activating resources. Such a process is understood as a pattern that shows which resources and according to which causal ordering should be activated. When realized it gives isomorphic histories $H \in P$. To every realization a particular history $H \in P$ with particular activations of resources corresponds. For instance, the process in which resources a,b,c are activated and the activation of c is a consequence of the activations of a,b can be represented by the "l.p.o. set with unnamed elements" shown in Fig.3. A particular history corresponding to the realization of this process with activations x,y,z of a,b,c, respectively, can be represented by the l.p.o. set shown in Fig.4.

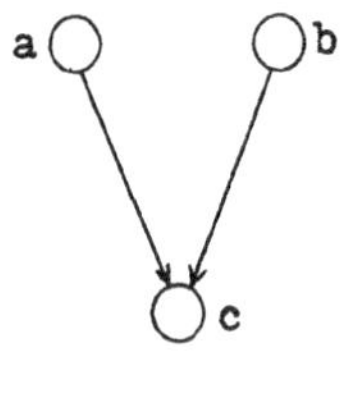

Fig.3

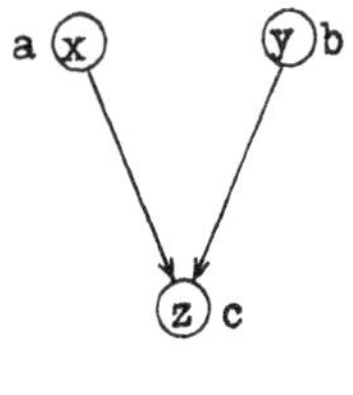

Fig.4

1.4. Operations on partial sequences

Definition 1.4.1 To every cut c of an l.p.o. set H the partial sequence [c] corresponds which can be identified with the set of labels of the elements of c. The set [origin(H)] depends on the partial sequence [H] only. It will be called the source of [H] and denoted by $\partial_0([H])$. Similarly, the set [end(H)], depending on [H] only, will be called the target of [H] and denoted by $\partial_1([H])$.

If a partial sequence P=[H] is interpreted as a process the sets [c] corresponding to the cuts of H will be interpreted as states or cases of this process. In particular, $\partial_0(P)$ denotes the initial state and $\partial_1(P)$ the final state.

Definition 1.4.2 Given two partial sequences P=[H] and Q=[I], we have at most one partial sequence R=[J] such that there is a cut c of J with head(J,c)$\in$P and tail(J,c)$\in$Q. Such a partial sequence R will be called the sequential composition of P and Q and denoted by P·Q.

One can prove the following theorem.

Theorem 1.4.1 The sequential composition P·Q of two partial sequences P and Q exists iff $\partial_1(P)=\partial_0(Q)$.

The sequential composition P·Q can be constructed taking l.p.o. sets H$\in$P, I$\in$Q, identifying every maximal element of H with the minimal element of I that has the same label, and extending the orderings of H and I to the weakest ordering with the property (H4). An example is shown in Fig.5 (the arrows resulting from the transitivity of the ordering are omitted).

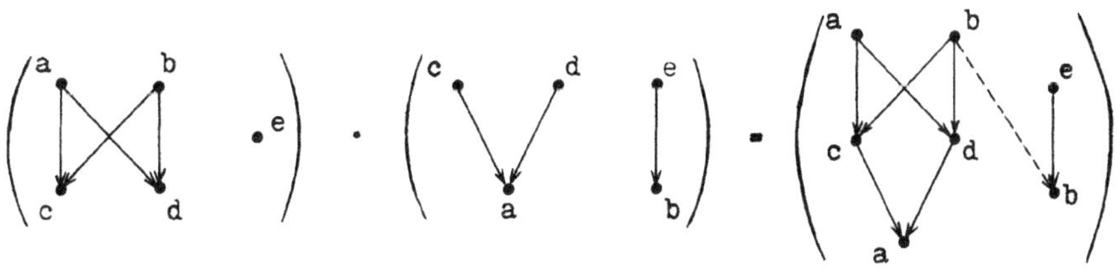

Fig.5

The sequential composition P·Q represents the process of executing the processes represented by P and Q one after another. The final state

$\partial_1(P)$ of the first process must be exactly the initial state $\partial_0(Q)$ of the second.
The class of partial sequences, when endowed with the operations of taking sources, targets, and sequential compositions, is a category. Sets of labels play the role of objects. Partial sequences play the role of morphisms.

Definition 1.4.3 Given two partial sequences $P=[H]$ and $Q=[I]$, there is at most one partial sequence $R=[J]$ such that there is a splitting s of J with left(J,s) $\in$ P and right(J,s) $\in$ Q. Such a partial sequence R will be called the parallel composition of P and Q and denoted by P+Q.

One can prove the following theorem.

Theorem 1.4.2 The parallel composition P+Q of two partial sequences P and Q exists iff the sets of labels occurring in P and Q are disjoint.

The parallel composition P+Q can be constructed taking an l.p.o. set which consists of two independent parts $H \in P$, $I \in Q$. An example is shown in Fig.6.

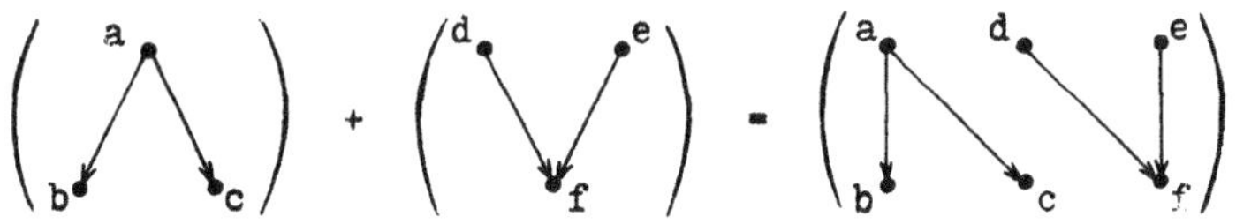

Fig.6

The parallel composition P+Q represents the process of executing independently (concurrently) the processes represented by P and Q. Such a process exists if the components are really independent, i.e., do not use common resources.
The parallel composition is associative $(P+(Q+R)=(P+Q)+R$ whenever either side is defined), commutative ($P+Q=Q+P$ whenever either side is defined), and has the neutral element $0=[(\emptyset,\emptyset,\emptyset)]$ (such that $0+P=P+0=P$ for every partial sequence P). If P+Q exists then $\partial_0(P)+\partial_0(Q)$ and $\partial_1(P)+\partial_1(Q)$ also exist and $\partial_0(P+Q)=\partial_0(P)+\partial_0(Q)$, $\partial_1(P+Q)=\partial_1(P)+\partial_1(Q)$.
The connection between the sequential composition and the parallel one

is given by the following theorem.

Theorem 1.4.3 If $(P\cdot Q)+(R\cdot S)$ exists then also $(P+R)\cdot(Q+S)$ exists and $(P\cdot Q)+(R\cdot S)=(P+R)\cdot(Q+S)$.

One can also prove that every finite partial sequence (corresponding to a finite l.p.o. set) can be decomposed into partial sequences which either are one-element partial sequences or correspond to l.p.o. sets with minimal and maximal elements only such that every minimal element is comparable with every maximal element.

2. Processes of transforming structures and derivations

In the rest of the paper we shall apply partial sequences to represent processes of transforming structures. Following [EKMRW 78] we shall deal with structures which are sets of atomic formulas and with transformations of structures called derivations. Our main aim is to show the connections between the formalism of partial sequences and that of derivations.

2.1. Processes of transforming structures

Processes of transforming structures will be represented by partial sequences whose labels are (atomic) formulas.

Definition 2.1.1 By a formula (or more precisely an atomic formula) we mean any ordered $(a(w)+1)$-tuple

$$F=(w,b_1,\ldots,b_{a(w)})$$

where w is a predicate symbol of the arity $a(w)$ and $b_1,\ldots,b_{a(w)}$ are arbitrary (not necessarily different) objects. Such a formula will be written as

$$w(b_1,\ldots,b_{a(w)})$$

The objects $b_1,\ldots,b_{a(w)}$ will be called atoms of F. The set of atoms of a formula F will be denoted by $|F|$.

Definition 2.1.2 By a structure (or more precisely a relational structure) we mean any set of (atomic) formulas. By $|S|$ we shall denote the set of atoms of the formulas belonging to a structure S.

Definition 2.1.3 By a process (of transforming structures) we mean any partial sequence P whose labels are (atomic) formulas and which has the following property (see Fig.7):

(P1) if $H=(X, \leq, l) \in P$ and c,d are any cuts of H with a common element x and u is an atom of the formula $l(x)$ then for every element y in c such that u occurs in the formula $l(y)$ there is an element z in d such that u occurs in the formula $l(z)$ and $y \leq z$ or $z \leq y$.

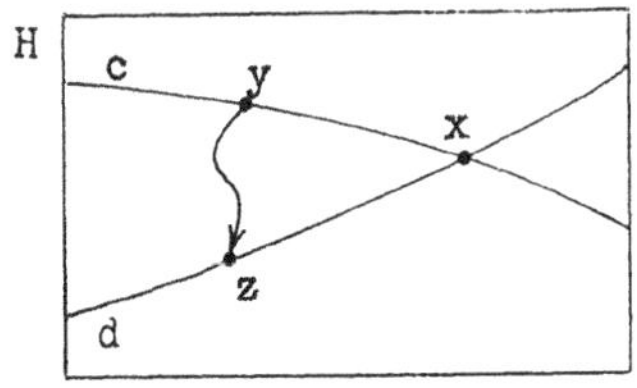

Fig.7

We interprete P as a process that transforms structures by removing some of the existing formulas and introducing new ones. Together with formulas also atoms are considered to be removed (if they do not occur in the formulas which remain) or introduced (if the process introduces a formula with atoms which do not occur in the existing formulas). The meaning of the property (P1) is that no process which is a part of P and removes or introduces an atom can be concurrent in P with a separate formula containing this atom.

A difficulty arises with composing processes. There may be processes which can be composed (sequentially or in parallel) as partial sequences but such that the result of the composition does not enjoy the property (P1).

A theorem can be proved that gives a sufficient condition under which the sequential composition of two given processes is a process.

<u>Theorem 2.1.1</u> Let P and Q be processes such that $\partial_1(P) = \partial_0(Q)$. If the formulas of Q do not contain any atom which occurs in the formulas of P but does not occur in the formulas of $\partial_0(Q)$ then the partial sequence $P \cdot Q$ is a process.

A sufficient condition ensuring that the parallel composition of two given processes is a process is formulated in the following theorem.

<u>Theorem 2.1.2</u> Let P and Q be processes such that there exists the partial sequence P+Q. If every atom occurring in a formula of P (of Q) either occurs in a formula of every cut of Q (of P) or does not occur in any formula of any cut of Q (of P) then P+Q is a process.

What we have observed shows that, in the case of processes, the concepts of parallel and sequential compositions have to be modified.

Definition 2.1.4 By the sequential (parallel) composition of processes we mean the restriction of the sequential (parallel) composition of partial sequences to such processes P and Q for which the result P·Q (resp.: P+Q) is a process.

In the following, when speaking on a sequential (parallel) composition of processes we shall always have in mind such a restricted operation. We shall use the same symbol "." ("+") for the restricted sequential (parallel) composition.
The processes can be applied to structures and transform them in the following sense.

Definition 2.1.5 We shall say that a process P applies to a structure A iff there are two structures A_1 and A_2 such that $A=A_1+A_2$, $\partial_0(P)=A_1$, and there exists the parallel composition $P+A_2$. In such a case there exists the parallel composition $\partial_1(P)+A_2$ and this composition, which is a structure B, will be called the result of the application of P to A. In particular, any process P applies to the structure $\partial_0(P)$ and $\partial_1(P)$ is the result of the application.

Example 2.1.1 Consider the process P in Fig.8. This process applies to the structure $A=\{c(1,2),b(2,3)\}$. It is sufficient to take $A=A_1+A_2$ with $A_1=\{b(2,3)\}$, $A_2=\{c(1,2)\}$. Then we have the parallel composition $Q=P+A_2$ which is shown in Fig.9. Thus P applies to A and the result of the application is $B=\{c(1,2),c(2,4),a(4,3)\}$.

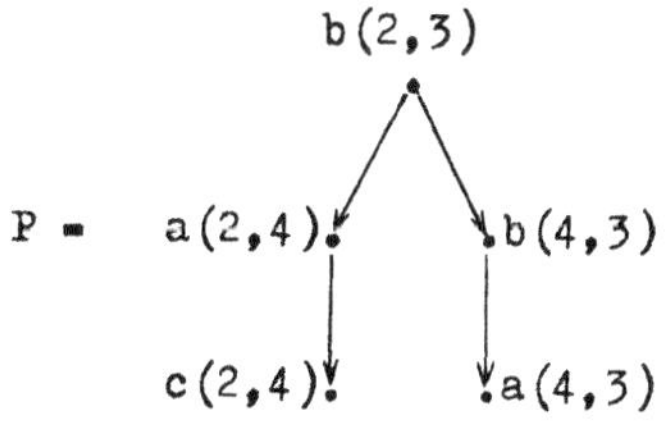

Fig.8

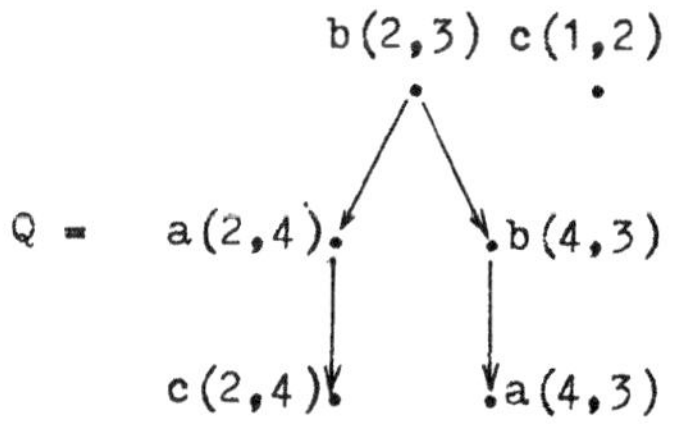

Fig.9

The idea to apply processes to structures will be the subject of the rest of the paper. We shall show some connections of this idea with deriving structures via productions.

2.2. Structure derivations

To show the relations between the processes of transforming structures and the derivations of structures in the sense of [EKMRW 78] we shall recall the concept of derivation. For simplicity the original definitions of [EKMRW 78] will be slightly restricted and modified.

Definition 2.2.1 For any formula $F=w(b_1,\dots,b_{a(w)})$ and any mapping h assigning some objects to the atoms of F the symbol hF will denote the formula $w(h(b_1),\dots,h(b_{a(w)}))$. The formula hF will be called the image of F under h. For any structure S and any mapping h assigning some objects to the atoms of the formulas of S the symbol hS will denote the structure consisting of all the images of the formulas of S under h. Given two structures S and T, by a morphism $h:S\longrightarrow T$ we mean any mapping $h:|S|\longrightarrow|T|$ such that $hS\subseteq T$.

Definition 2.2.2 A production is a pair $p=(L,R)$ of structures. The structure L will be called the left side of p and denoted by L(p). The structure R will be called the right side of p and denoted by R(p). The elements of $|L|\cap|R|$ will be called the glueing atoms of p.

Definition 2.2.3 An instance of a production $p=(L,R)$ is a pair $I=(p,i)$ consisting of p and of a one-to-one correspondence i between the atoms of L and R and some objects.

Definition 2.2.4 We say that an instance $I=(p,i)$ of a production $p=(L(p),R(p))$ (and the production p itself) applies to a structure G iff:

(D1) the formulas of iL(p) are in G,

(D2) no formula of iR(p)-iL(p) is in G,

(D3) the atoms of iL(p) which are not in $|iR(p)|$ do not belong to $|G-iL(p)|$,

(D4) the atoms of iR(p) which are not in $|iL(p)|$ do not belong to $|G-iL(p)|$.

A structure H is called the result of the application of I to G iff:

(D5) $H=(G-iL(p))\cup iR(p)$

Definition 2.2.5 A direct derivation is a triple

$$G\overset{I}{\Longrightarrow}H$$

where G and H are structures, I is an instance of a production,

I applies to G, and H is the result of applying I to G. Any sequence

$$G_0 \xRightarrow{I_1} G_1 \xRightarrow{I_2} \cdots \xRightarrow{I_n} G_n$$

(with $n>0$) is said to be a <u>derivation</u>

$$G_0 \Longrightarrow G_n \text{ applying } (I_1,\dots,I_n)$$

We say that a structure H is <u>derivable</u> from another one G using productions $p \in \Pi$ iff H is isomorphic with G or there is a derivation $G \Longrightarrow S$ applying some instances of productions $p \in \Pi$ and such that H is isomorphic with S.

<u>Example 2.2.1</u> Words over a certain alphabet can be represented as structures consisting of formulas showing particular letter occurrences. One may think that such occurrences in a word separate some objects called positions, and make use of the formulas of the type:

$$a(x,y),\ b(x,y),\ c(x,y),\dots$$

where $a(x,y)$ (resp.: $b(x,y)$, $c(x,y),\dots$) stands for "an occurrence of the letter a (resp.: b,c,...) separates the position x from the position y". For instance, the word cb can be represented as the structure $\{c(1,2),b(2,3)\}$.

The context-free rewriting rules $b \rightarrow ab$, $a \rightarrow c$, $b \rightarrow a$ can be considered as the following productions:

$$p_1 = (\{b(x,y)\},\{a(x,z),b(z,y)\})$$
$$p_2 = (\{a(x,y)\},\{c(x,y)\})$$
$$p_3 = (\{b(x,y)\},\{a(x,y)\})$$

We have the following derivation:

$$cb \xRightarrow{(p_1,i_1)} cab \xRightarrow{(p_2,i_2)} ccb \xRightarrow{(p_3,i_3)} cca$$

with

$$i_1(x)=2,\ i_1(y)=3,\ i_1(z)=4,$$
$$i_2(x)=2,\ i_2(y)=4,$$
$$i_3(x)=4,\ i_3(y)=3.$$

<u>Remark</u>: To see how our concept of derivation is related to that of [EKMRW 78] we have to define a structure as a pair $G=(G_A,G_F)$ consisting of a set G_A of atoms and a set G_F of formulas such that $|G_F| \subseteq G_A$. Also a morphism $h:G \longrightarrow H$ has to be defined as a mapping $h:G_A \longrightarrow H_A$ such that $hG_F \subseteq H_F$. Then a production p in our sense can be considered as the following (fast) production in the sense of [EKMRW 78]:

$$(|L(p)|, L(p)) \xleftarrow{\supseteq} (|L(p)| \cap |R(p)|, \emptyset) \xrightarrow{\subseteq} (|R(p)|, R(p))$$

A set H of formulas is the result of applying an instance (p,i) of p to a set G of formulas iff we have the following pair of pushouts in the category of structures:

$$\begin{array}{ccccc}
(|L(p)|, L(p)) & \xleftarrow{\supseteq} & (|L(p)| \cap |R(p)|, \emptyset) & \xrightarrow{\subseteq} & (|R(p)|, R(p)) \\
\downarrow g & \text{p.o.} & \downarrow d & \text{p.o.} & \downarrow h \\
(|G|, G) & \xleftarrow{\supseteq} & D & \xrightarrow{\subseteq} & (|H|, H)
\end{array}$$

where $D=(|G-iL(p)| \cup (|iL(p)| \cap |iR(p)|), G-iL(p))$, $g=i\,\big|\,|L(p)|$, $h=i\,\big|\,|R(p)|$, $d=i\,\big|\,(|L(p)| \cap |R(p)|)$. This means that our direct derivations are direct (injective, natural) derivations in the sense of [EKMRW 78].

2.3. Derivations and processes

Now we are able to establish the connection between the derivability and the processes of transforming structures.

Definition 2.3.1 By the process corresponding to an instance $I=(p,i)$ of a production p we mean the following process $\underline{Pr}(I):=[(X, \leqslant, l)]$:

$X=\{1\} \times iL(p) \cup \{2\} \times iR(p)$,

$x \leqslant y$ iff $x=y$ or $x=(1,u)$ and $y=(2,v)$ for some $u \in iL(p)$, $v \in iR(p)$,

$l(x)=u$ for every $x=(k,u) \in X$ with $k=1$ or 2 and $u \in iL(p) \cup iR(p)$.

It is easy to see that $\underline{Pr}(I)$ is really a process of transforming structures. It can be interpreted as a process of replacing (in one step) the structure $iL(p)$ by the structure $iR(p)$.

Example 2.3.1 For the instances $I_1=(p_1,i_1)$, $I_2=(p_2,i_2)$, $I_3=(p_3,i_3)$ in Example 2.2.1 we have the following processes $P_1=\underline{Pr}(I_1)$, $P_2=\underline{Pr}(I_2)$, $P_3=\underline{Pr}(I_3)$:

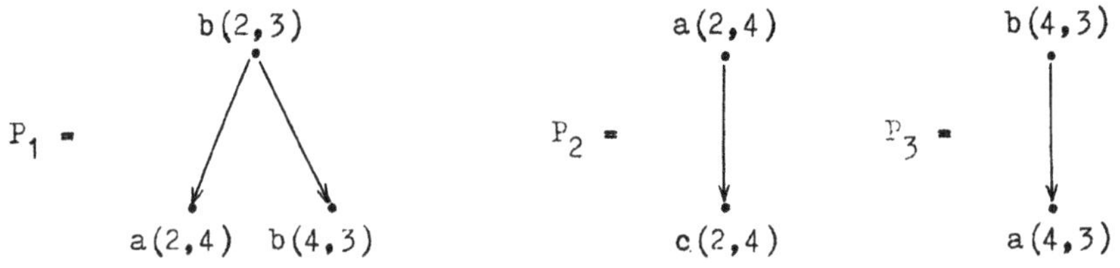

The applicability of instances of productions to structures is equivalent to the applicability of the corresponding processes:

Theorem 2.3.1 An instance I of a production applies to a structure G iff the corresponding process Pr(I) applies to G. The results of the applications are identical.

To formulate our main result we need some further notions.

Definition 2.3.2 Let Str be the class of structures. Given a production p, by Pro(p) we denote the class of processes Pr(I) corresponding to instances I of p. Given a set Π of productions, we define:

$$\underline{Pro}(\Pi) = \bigcup_{p\in\Pi} \underline{Pro}(p) \cup \underline{Str}$$

and denote by Proc(Π) the closure of Pro(Π) with respect to the sequential and parallel composition of processes.

The connection between the derivability and the processes of transforming structures is the following:

Theorem 2.3.2 Given two structures G and H, the structure H can be derived from G applying instances of productions $p\in\Pi$ iff there is a process $P\in$ Proc(Π) which applies to G with the result isomorphic with H.

The idea of the proof is that the elements of Proc(Π) are exactly those processes whose histories can be decomposed by means of cuts into "slices" corresponding to direct derivations.

Example 2.3.2 The process Q in Example 2.1.1 can be decomposed as follows:

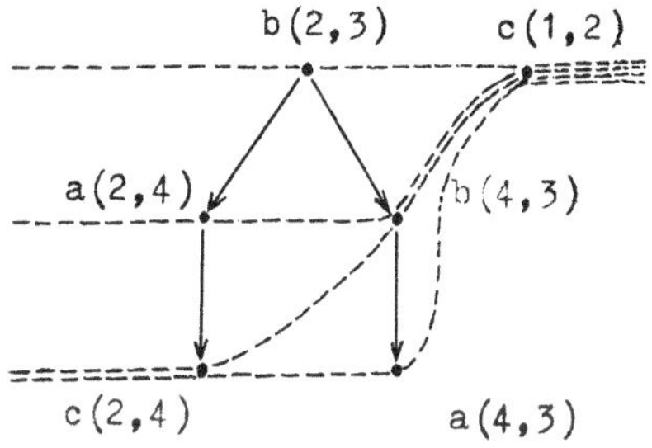

Fig.10

The "slices" corresponding to this decomposition (which is not unique) are $P_1+\{c(1,2)\}$, $P_2+\{b(4,3),c(1,2)\}$, $P_3+\{c(2,4),c(1,2)\}$, where P_1, P_2, P_3 are as in Example 2.3.1. They correspond to the direct derivations in Example 2.2.1. We have

$$Q=(P_1+\{c(1,2)\})\cdot(P_2+\{b(4,3),c(1,2)\})\cdot(P_3+\{c(2,4),c(1,2)\})$$
$$=(P_1\cdot(P_2+P_3))+\{c(1,2)\}$$

The internal structure of Q describes the way of deriving the structure representing the word cca from the one representing the word cb. The process applied is $P_1\cdot(P_2+P_3)$. The first step is represented by the process P_1. The next two are represented by P_2 and P_3, and they are independent. So $P_1\cdot(P_2+P_3)$ is an information similar to a derivation tree and it plays a similar role.

References

[EKMRW 78] Ehrig,H., Kreowski,H.J., Maggiolo-Schettini,A., Rosen, B.K., Winkowski,J.: Deriving Structures from Structures, Springer-Verlag Lecture Notes in Computer Science, Vol 64, 1978

[MW 78] Maggiolo-Schettini,A., Winkowski,J.: An Algebraic Characterization of Derivability Relations, ICS PAS Report 307, 1978

[Wi 77] Winkowski,J.: An Algebraic Characterization of the Behaviour of Non-Sequential Systems, Inf. Proc. Letters, Vol 6, No 4, August 1977 (and ERRATUM in Vol 7, No 1)

[Wi 78] Winkowski,J.: An Algebraic Approach to Non-Sequential Computations, ICS PAS Report 312, 1978

MAP GRAMMARS: CYCLES AND THE ALGEBRAIC APPROACH

Kristian Nyrup and Brian Mayoh
Department of Computer Science
Aarhus University
8000 Aarhus C, Denmark

Abstract

Some real world phenomena are essentially two dimensional; they are more naturally modelled by map grammars than graph grammars. The planarity of maps can be captured by cycles and converted into a form suitable for abstract manipulation. This insight suggests (section 1) a new definition of map grammars, (section 2) some theorems, (section 3) and a generalization of the algebraic approach to graph grammars.

1. Grammars for planar organisms

Because Lindenmayer systems [2] have been useful in the description of filamentous organisms, it is natural to suppose that suitable generalizations may also help in the description of the development of biological organisms that are essentially two or three dimensional. Unfortunately the basic concept of dimensionality evaporates in the generalization to parallel graph grammars [GL-CaGrPa74, Culi76, Na76]. The generalization to map grammars does not have this weakness, but the presentation in [GL-Ma74, Ma76] is imprecise and unnecessarily complicated. Here we give a more precise and simple definition of a map grammar suggested by Maclane's characterization of planar graphs [3, 4].

Definition 1

A graph is a binary relation on a finite set of vertices. A graph G is proper, if it is undirected, loopless, connected and satisfies: there are at least two vertices and G cannot be disconnected by removing a vertex. A proper graph G has an associated directed graph $\vec{G}$ defined by:

1) $\vec{G}$ has the same vertices as G;
2) if there is an edge between vertices s and t in G, then the relation $\vec{G}$ holds for both (s,t) and (t,s), otherwise the relation $\vec{G}$ holds for neither (s,t) nor (t,s);

A cycle of the proper graph G is a set of vertex pairs, (s_i, t_i) for i = 1, 2, ..., k, such that

3) $k > 1$ and $s_1, s_2 \ldots s_k$ are distinct,
4) $s_1 = t_k,\ s_2 = t_1,\ s_3 = t_2 \ldots s_k = t_{k-1}$
5) the relation $\vec{G}$ holds for each (s_i, t_i).

A cycle basis for a proper graph G is a partition of $\vec{G}$ into a set of disjoint cycles one of which is designated the skin.

Example

Figure 1 shows how we depict graphs and cycle bases. The counter clockwise cycle is the skin of the cycle basis.

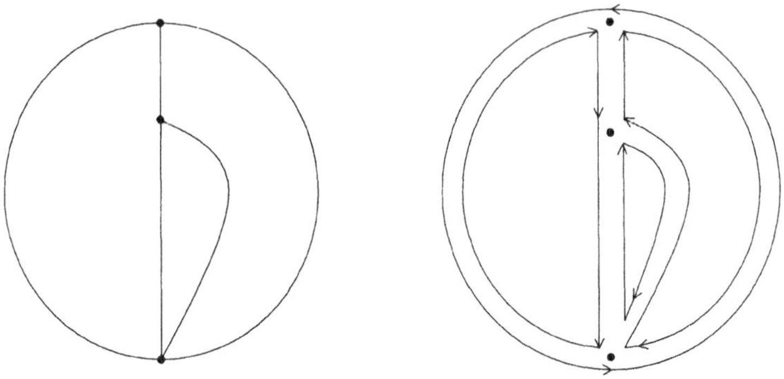

Figure 1. Spinning Spider's Spiral

Definition 2

Suppose we have a finite set Δ called the edge alphabet, and a finite set Σ with distinguished element called the state alphabet. A (Σ,Δ)-map consists of a proper graph G, a cycle basis $\mathcal{C}$ for G, and a function L such that

1) L assigns an element of Σ to each cycle in $\mathcal{C}$;
2) L assigns the distinguished element of Σ to the skin of $\mathcal{C}$;
3) L assigns an element of Δ to each edge in G.

Example

Figure 2 shows how we depict a map as a pair, a labelled graph and a labelled cycle basis.

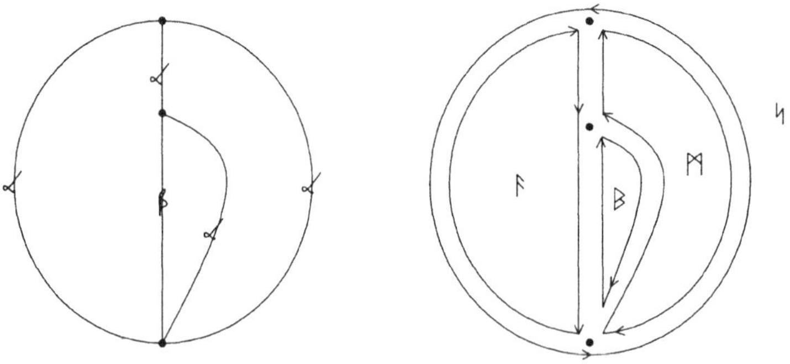

Figure 2. Spinning Spider's Spiral (as Runic Map)

As representations of life stages of a biological organism we like maps better than graphs drawn in the plane because they are more amenable to grammar and computer manipulation. Each cell of a life stage is represented by a non-skin cycle, and each such cycle represents an individual cell. A cell C_1 is the neighbour of a cell C_2 if and only if there is a vertex pair (s, t) in the cycle for C_1 such that (t, s) is in the cycle for C_2. It is easy for the computer to find all neighbours of a given cell. It is also easy for it to simulate the development of one life stage from another in four stages (see figure 3):

1) each mother cell in the life stage changes into a latent organism, more formally: each non-skin cycle is replaced by a map M (the non-skin cycles of M are the daughter cells);

2) the latent organisms are aligned with the mother cell edges, more formally: the edges in the skin of each latent organism are assigned to the edges in the cycle of its mother cell;

3) each mother cell edge is matched with a "stencil";

4) these stencils direct the joining of all the latent organism maps into the map for the new life stage.

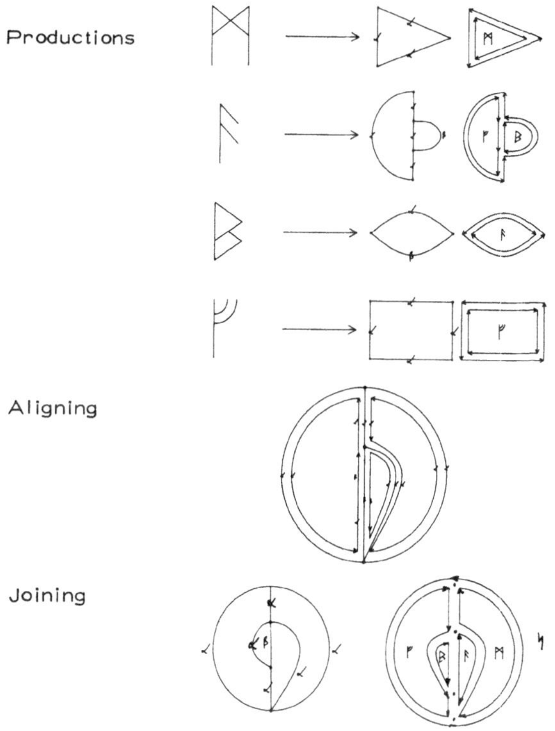

Figure 3. The next stage of the Spinning Spider's Spiral

Definition 3 (can be skipped with no great loss)

The set of non-empty sequences on a set Δ is denoted by Δ^+. A Δ-partition is a non-empty sequence on the set Δ^+. Two Δ-partitions are compatible if the result of concatenating the two partition sequences gives the same element of Δ^+. A Δ-skin stencil is a triple (a,b,c) where $a \in \Delta$, $b \in \Delta^+$, and c is a Δ-partition with the same length as b. A Δ-boundary stencil is a five tuple (a, b_1, c_1, b_2, c_2) where $a \in \Delta$, $b_1 \in \Delta^+$, c_1 is a Δ-partition with the same length as b_1, $b_2 \in \Delta^+$, c_2 is a Δ-partition with the same length as b_2, and the two Δ-partitions are compatible.

Example

In Figure 3 we used the skin stencil

$$(\alpha,\ (\alpha),\ ((\alpha)))$$

and the boundary stencils

$$(\alpha,\ (\alpha),\ ((\alpha)),\ (\alpha),\ ((\alpha)))$$
$$(\beta,\ (\beta),\ ((\beta\alpha)),\ (\beta\alpha),\ ((\beta),\ (\alpha)))$$

It is easy to invent more readable representations of stencils.

Definition 4

Let Σ and Δ be as in definition 2. A (Σ,Δ)-production is a pair consisting of an element of Σ (the left side) and a (Σ,Δ)-map (the right side). A (Σ,Δ)-map grammar consists of: a (Σ,Δ)-map called the seed, a finite set of (Σ,Δ)-productions, and a finite set of Δ-stencils.

Example

We get the Spinning Spider Spiral map grammar by taking the map in figure 2 as the seed, the productions in figure 3, and the three stencils given above.

Our earlier informal description of a derivation step in a map grammar is precise except for "the edges in the skin of each latent organism are assigned to the edges of the cycle of its mother cell". We interpret this as "split zero, one or more skin edges, then choose an order preserving map of the skin to the cycle". We do not have the space here to give either the formal definition or the proof of the next theorem which shows that our map grammars are a natural generalization of one dimensional Lindenmayer systems.

Theorem 1

Map grammars can simulate Turing machines, tag systems, and propagating Lindenmayer systems with interaction.

Comment

For the most natural way of simulating one dimensional Lindenmayer systems map grammars are equivalent to a slight extension of the "propagating, regular global context L-systems" [1].

2. Do map grammars always produce planar maps?

Clearly any labelled proper graph drawn in the plane gives a map. The converse is false, the map in figure 4 cannot be drawn in the plane because

number of vertices - number of edges + number of regions = $12 - 18 + 6 \neq 2$.

Figure 5 shows that this map can be drawn on a surface with a "handle".

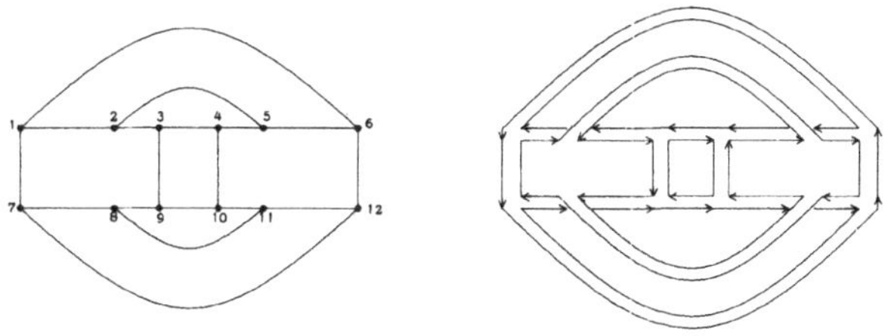

Figure 4. A non-planar map

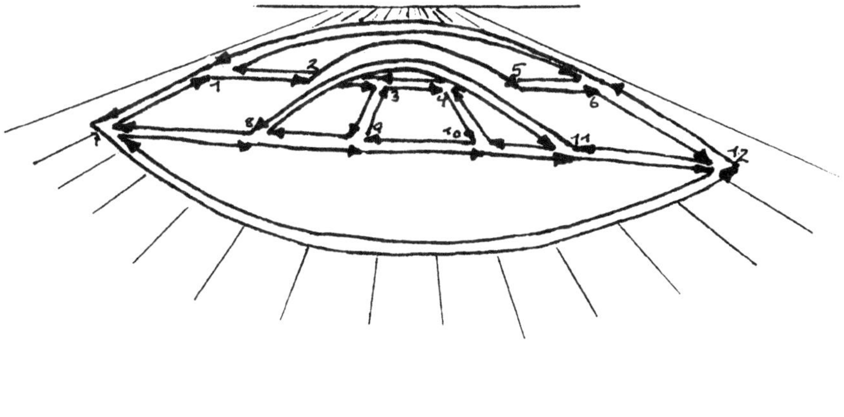

Figure 5. Realising a non-planar map

Definition 5

A map is planar if it can be drawn in the plane so that the resulting regions correspond to the cycle basis of the map. A map grammar is planar if its seed and the right side of each production are planar.

Theorem 2

If all the maps generated by a map grammar are planar, then there is a planar map grammar that generates the same maps and no others.

Proof: The seed is generated so it must be planar. If a production has a non-planar right side, it cannot be used for the derivation of a new map because the new map would be non-planar. Dropping all such productions gives a planar map grammar.

Corollary

Planar map grammars suffice for the description of two dimensional biological organisms.

Theorem 3

(1) The problem "Is a given map generated by a given map grammar" is decidable.

(2) There is a (Σ,Δ)-map grammar that generates all planar (Σ,Δ)-maps.

(3) The problem "Is a given map grammar planar" is decidable.

(4) The problem "Does a given map grammar generate only planar maps" is undecidable.

Proof: (1) There are only finitely many (Σ,Δ)-maps with a given number of edges, and a derivation step in a (Σ,Δ)-map grammar does not decrease the number of edges.

(2) Suppose there is a planar (Σ,Δ)-map that cannot be derived in the grammar of Figure 6. Let M be such a map with the least number of edges and cycles. Because M is connected and has no cut vertices, dropping a vertex lying on just two edges and joining the edges would give a map with fewer edges. Since M is minimal each of its vertices lies on at least three edges, neighbouring cycles are connected by single edges, and there are neighbouring cycles. As one of the grammar productions gives two neighbouring cells connected by a single edge, there is no minimal M. (We do not give more detail because the argument is so like that in [GL-CaGrPa74].

(3) One can use the algorithm of (1) to check if the seed of a given grammar and the right side of each production can be derived in the grammar of figure 6.

(4) By theorem 1 each Turing machine T can be simulated by a map grammar Γ_T. Let Γ_T' be Γ_T with an extra production for each final state of T whose right side is the map in figure 4. A non-planar map can be derived in Γ_T' if and only if T stops.

Seed:  for some $\delta \in \Delta$, $\sigma \in \Sigma$

Productions: for all σ_1, σ_2, σ_3 in Σ

$\sigma_1 \longrightarrow$ 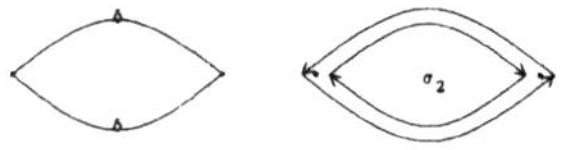

$\sigma_1 \longrightarrow$ 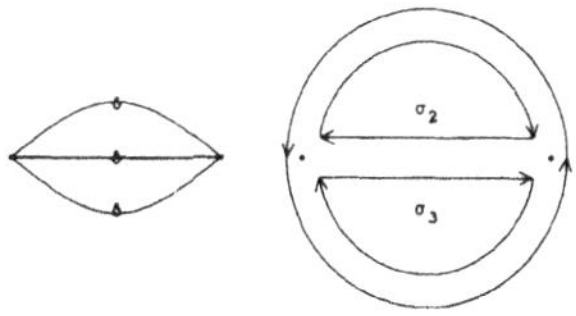

Stencils: for all δ_1, δ_2 in Δ

$(\delta_1, (\delta), ((\delta_2)))$

$(\delta_1, (\delta), ((\delta_2)), (\delta), ((\delta_2)))$

Figure 6. Universal (Σ, Δ)-map grammar

3. The algebraic approach

The algebraic approach to graph grammars is described in [OV-Eh78]. The key idea is that a grammar derivation step from 'G to G' corredponds to a diagram:

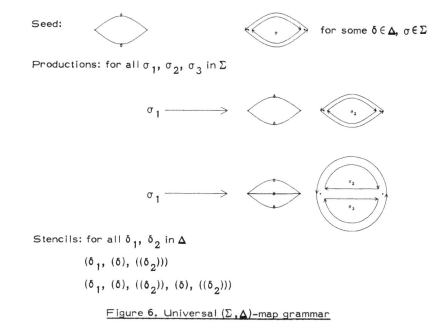

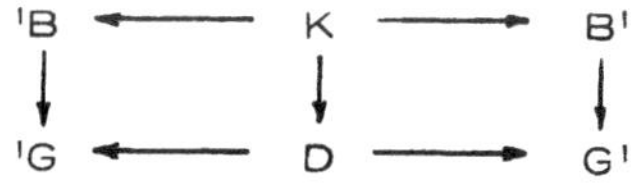

Figure 7

where D is a covering and K is an interface between the left side 'B and the right side B' of a production. Other papers in this proceedings show that powerful general theorems can be proved if the arrows in our diagram can be interpreted as morphisms in a category and the two squares are pushouts. Do we have this interpretation for our map grammars?

First we must decide what an interface should be. The most appropriate choice depends on the precise definition of how "the edges in the skin of each latent organism are assigned to its mother cell cycle". Figure 8 shows the effect of defining an interface K to be an undirected graph with labelled edges.

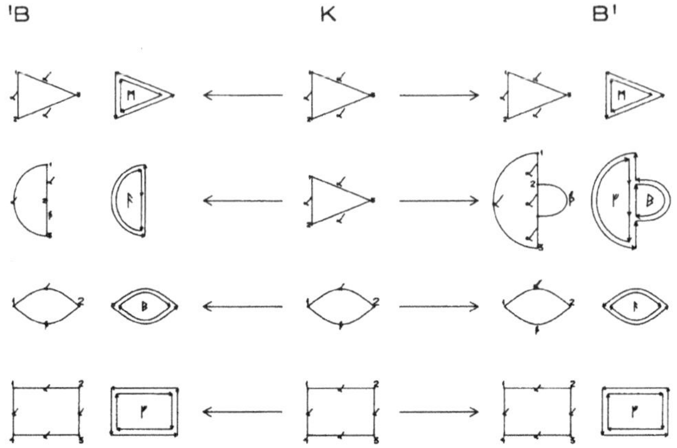

Figure 8. Productions using interfaces

Next we must decide on the most appropriate definition of a covering. Because our map grammars are parallel, not sequential, this is easy - a covering is also an undirected graph with labelled edges. As we see in figure 9 a map 'G uniquely determines the covering D.

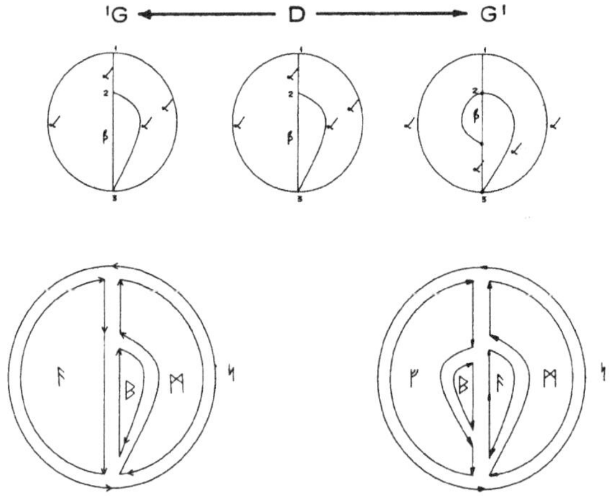

Figure 9. Derivations using coverings

Figures 8 and 9 show that interpreting the horizontal arrows of figure 7 as morphisms in a category requires care. This is also true of the vertical arrows. Figure 10 and the star constructions in [OV-Eh78] show that vertical arrows from interfaces to coverings are very like sums and integrals. The vertical arrow from 'B to 'G is represented in figure 11, and the more complicated vertical arrow from B' to G' is represented in figure 12. Note the natural role of stencils in the construction of the undirected labelled graph part of G'.

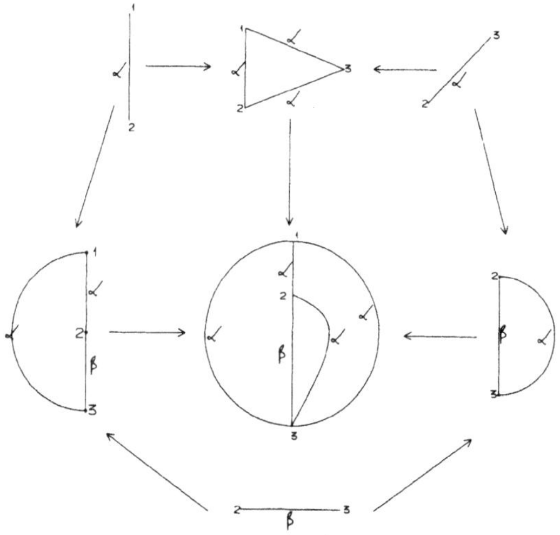

Figure 10. Coverings as integrals of interfaces

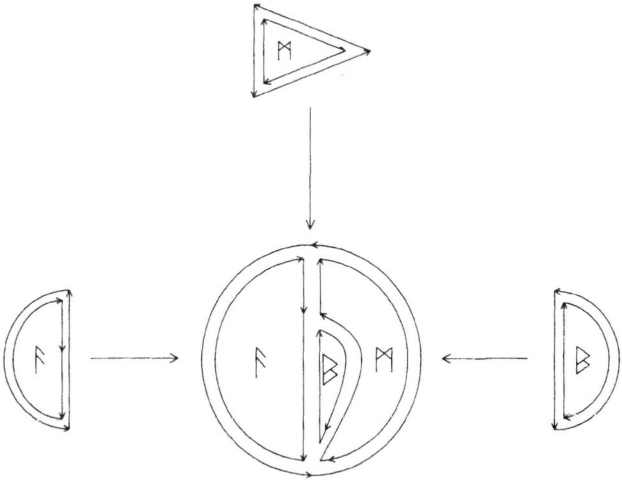

Figure 11. Old map as integral of left sides

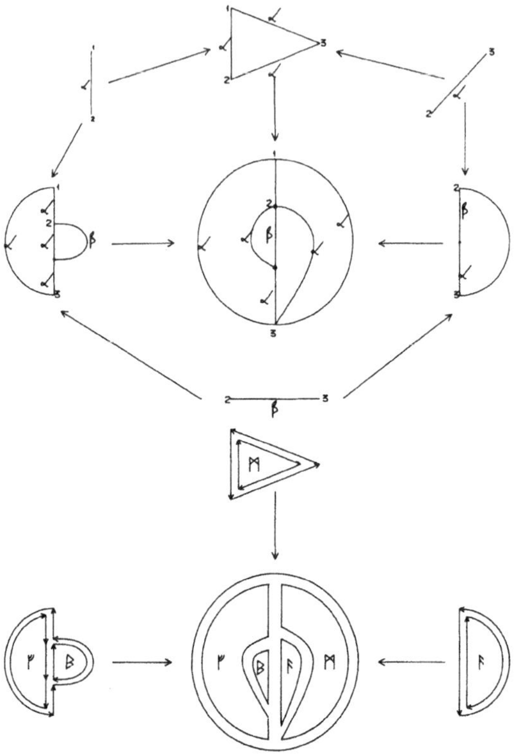

Figure 12. New map as integral of right sides

The algebraic approach to map grammars may be very rewarding, certainly our analysis of a derivation step in a map grammar reminds one of a pushout construction in a category.

Numbered References (unnumbered references are to the bibliography in this proceedings)

[1] K. Culik & J. Opatrny: Context in Parallel Rewriting, Springer Lecture Notes 15(1974) 230-243.

[2] A. Lindenmayer: Mathematical models for cellular interaction in development, J. Theor. Biology 18(1968) 280-315.

[3] S. Maclane: A combinatorial condition for planar graphs, Fund. Math. 28 (1937) 22-32.

[4] W.T. Tutte: Convex representation of graphs, Proc. London Math. Soc. 10 (1960) 304-320.

ON MULTILEVEL - GRAPH GRAMMARS

Alexander Ollongren
Dept. of Mathematics, Leiden University, the Netherlands

0. *INTRODUCTION*

The so-called operational definition of the semantics of programming languages is often based upon the idea that the meaning of a program is determined by its interpretation by an abstract machine. During interpretation the machine carries out state transitions, the states being vectors in some appropriate set. In this spirit the Vienna definition method and the Vienna definition language for the formal semantics of procedural programming languages have been developed, and to a certain extent also the Vienna development method for programming concepts. The present author has worked on the Vienna method a number of years; at first the Vienna interpreting machine was used, later it was modified [1, chapter 8], but still using the selector-labelled trees as the basic data objects. In more recent work our group has generalised both the abstract machine [2], and the basic data objects [3,4,5]. The latter have been replaced by abstract objects defined over a set of selectors and a set of elementary objects, and representable as multi-level selector-labelled rooted digraphs. In the present note I give the general definition of the abstract machine, a definition of the abstract objects and abstract grammars over them, and, finally, an example (the interpretation of binary expressions) to show possible uses of the multi-level graphs.

1. *ABSTRACT MACHINES*

An abstract machine is considered to be a set of states and a binary relation over that set. Since we wish to distinguish initial and terminal states, we define formally

Definition 1.1 An abstract machine M is a 4-triple (S, S_I, S_T, δ) where S is a non-empty set of *states*, $S_I \subseteq S$ is the set of *initial states*, $S_T \subseteq S$ is the set of *terminal states* and $\delta \subseteq S \times S$ is the *state transition relation*. ▪

If $s_i \, \delta \, s_{i+1}$ $i = 0,1,\ldots,n-1$ with $s_i \in S$, then M is said to *compute* s_n from s_0. We write $s_0 \, \delta^* \, s_n$ or $s_0 \overset{*}{\rightarrow} s_n$ where δ^* is the reflexive, transitive closure of δ. The *domain* of M is

$$\mathcal{D}(M) = \{s \mid s \in S_I \wedge \exists_{t \in S_T} (s \delta^* t)\}$$

and the *range* of M is

$$\mathcal{R}(M) = \{t \mid t \in S_T \wedge \exists_{s \in S_I} (s\delta^* t)]$$

M computes a binary relation ϕ over S, defined as follows

$$s \phi t \leftrightarrow s \in \mathcal{D}(M) \wedge t \in \mathcal{R}(M)$$

M is in general non-deterministic as (s,r) as well as (s,r') can be in δ, with $r \neq r'$. Certain operations, depending upon the application considered, must be assumed to be primitive for M, i.e. they may be used in the definition of δ.

Example 1 (non-prime testing machine).

Denote the set $\{2,3,4,5,6,\ldots\}$ by N and suppose that multiplication of natural numbers and the testing of equality of natural numbers is primitive for the abstract machine M, defined by $S_I = N$ $\quad S_T = \{\text{true}\}$ $\quad S = S_I \cup S_T \cup N^3$ and δ given by

$$\begin{array}{ll} a \ \delta \ (x,y,a) & \\ (x,y,a) \ \delta \ \text{true} & \text{provided } x \cdot y = a \\ (x,y,a) \ \delta \ (u,v,a) & \text{provided } x \cdot y \neq a \end{array}$$

For this case $\mathcal{D}(M) = N$ and $\mathcal{R}(M) = \{\text{true}\}$. Any non-prime number a can be found in at least two steps to be non-prime. For a prime number a the computation does not terminate. ⊠

Elsewhere [2] we have shown that by specification of the above definition of abstract machines, finite automata, pushdown automata etc. are obtained, but also grammars, for instance in the Chomsky hierarchy. By choosing for S the set of Vienna trees and appropriate rules for δ, also the Vienna interpreting machine for PL/I (say) can be seen as a special case.

Example 2 (finite automaton)

Suppose that Q is a finite non-empty alphabet, $q_0 \in Q$, $Q_t \subseteq Q$, and that Σ is a finite non-empty set of imput symbols. Consider now the following abstract machine M:

$$S = Q \circ \Sigma^* \qquad S_I = \{q_0\} \circ \Sigma^* \qquad S_T = Q_t$$

and δ given by a finite number of rewriting rules of the form $pa \rightarrow q$, where

$$pa \rightarrow q \leftrightarrow \exists_{\alpha \in \Sigma^*}[pa\alpha \delta q\alpha]$$

M is then a finite automaton and the language accepted by it is $\{\alpha \in \Sigma^* \mid \exists_t \ q_0 \circ \alpha \phi t\}$. The right-linear grammar associated with M has $p \rightarrow aq$ as production rule iff pa $\rightarrow$ q is a rewriting rule in δ . See also [6]. ∎

2. *MULTI-LEVEL DATA OBJECTS*

Let S be an at most countable, but non-empty set of *selectors* and let E be a countable non-empty set of *elementary data* and let Ω be a constant, the *empty object*. n - tuples of empty objects $(\Omega,\ldots,\Omega)$ are identified with Ω . We define the set of *data objects* $\mathcal{O}$ as follows:

<u>Definition 2.1</u> $\mathcal{O} = \bigcup_{i\geq 0} \mathcal{O}_i$ with $\mathcal{O}_0 = E \cup \{\Omega\}$

and for sufficiently large n

$$\mathcal{O}_{i+1} = \{f:S\rightarrow(\bigcup_{k=0}^{i} \mathcal{O}_k)^n \mid \exists_1{}^m(\alpha)\ f(\alpha)\neq\Omega\}$$

where $\exists_1{}^m(\alpha)\ f(\alpha) \neq \Omega$ means that there exists at least one selector α and at most finitely many selectors α such that $f(\alpha) \neq \Omega$. ∎

In above definition we can distinguish special cases:

(i) n = 1 and i = 0 . This gives the zero-level data objects studied by H.D. Ehrich [7], but then restricted to the finite case.

(ii) n = 1 and i not fixed. This gives the multilevel objects studied by us in [3,4]. These are multilevel objects because $f(\alpha_1)(\alpha_2)\ldots(\alpha_p)$ are in general defined and not empty.

(iii) n fixed and i not fixed. This gives also multilevel objects since $f(\alpha)$ is a vector the components of which are also in $\mathcal{O}$.

For a data object $A \in \mathcal{O}$ but $A \neq \Omega$ and $A \notin E$, $A(\alpha)$ is defined for $\alpha \in S$. We can write

$$A(\alpha) = \langle A_1,A_2,\ldots,A_n\rangle$$

and considering this as a stack we can define

$$top(A(\alpha)) = A_1 \qquad rest(A(\alpha)) = \langle A_2,\ldots,A_{n-1},\Omega\rangle$$
$$push\ (A(\alpha),B) = \langle B,A_1,A_2,\ldots A_{n-1}\rangle$$

For the case $A \in E \cup\{\Omega\}$ we define $A(\alpha) = \Omega$ for all $\alpha \in S$, and $top(A(\alpha)) = rest(A(\alpha)) = \Omega$. Further $push(A(\alpha),B) = \langle B\rangle$.
We are now able to define two operators: ν(stack) of type $\mathcal{O} \times S \times \mathcal{O} \rightarrow \mathcal{O}$ and ν' (unstack) of type $\mathcal{O} \times S \rightarrow \mathcal{O}$ as follows:

Definition 2.2 $\nu(A,\alpha,B) = \underline{\text{if}}\ A \in \mathcal{O}_0 \wedge B = \Omega\ \underline{\text{then}}\ A$

$\underline{\text{else}}\ \underline{\text{if}}\ A \in \mathcal{O}_0\ \underline{\text{then}}\ \lambda\beta\ .\ [\underline{\text{if}}\ \beta = \alpha\ \underline{\text{then}}\ \text{push}(\Omega,B)\ \underline{\text{else}}\ \Omega]$

$\underline{\text{else}}\ \lambda\beta\ .\ [\underline{\text{if}}\ \beta = \alpha\ \underline{\text{then}}\ \text{push}(A(\alpha),B)\ \underline{\text{else}}\ A]$

$\nu'(A,\alpha) = \lambda\beta\ .\ [\underline{\text{if}}\ \beta = \alpha\ \underline{\text{then}}\ \text{rest}(A(B))\ \underline{\text{else}}\ A]$ ⊠

From above definitions we can immediately derive the following lemma's.

Lemma 2.3 (extensionality)

For $A,B \notin E$: $\forall_\alpha [A(\alpha) = B(\alpha)] \Rightarrow A = B$

Lemma 2.4

$A \in \mathcal{O}_0 \wedge A = \nu(B,\alpha,C) \Rightarrow A = B \wedge C = \Omega$

$\nu(A,\alpha,B) = \nu(A,\alpha,C) \Rightarrow B = C$

$\alpha \neq \beta \Rightarrow \nu(\nu(A,\alpha,B),\beta,C) = \nu(\nu(A,\beta,C),\alpha,B)$

Lemma 2.5

$\nu'(\nu(A,\alpha,B),\alpha) = A$; $\nu'(\nu(A,\alpha,B),\beta) = \text{rest}(A(B)),\ \alpha \neq \beta$

$\text{top}(\nu(A,\alpha,B)(\alpha)) = B$

$\text{rest}(\nu(A,\alpha,B)(\alpha)) = A(\alpha)$ ⊠

In definition 2.1 we have the condition $\exists_1^m(\alpha)\ f(\alpha) \neq \Omega$. This means that any $A \in \mathcal{O}$ can be constructed by a finite sequence of ν operations, starting from Ω . Also $B = \nu'(A,\alpha)$ for any $A \in \mathcal{O}$ and $\alpha \in S$ can be constructed by a finite number of ν operations, starting from Ω . In view of this the following lemma, also provable from the definitions, is evident.

Lemma 2.6 (ν - induction)

If Φ is a property of objects such that $\Phi(A)$ is true for all $A \in \mathcal{O}_0$ and if $\Phi(A) \wedge \Phi(B) \Rightarrow \Phi\ (\nu(A,\alpha,B))$ for all α , then $\Phi(A)$ is true for all $A \in \mathcal{O}$. ⊠

This lemma is useful in those cases where objects are built, say by an abstract machine, using only ν and ν' operations. We shall meet such a situation in section 4.

Definition 2.1 introduces sequences of objects which are accessible via selectors in a given object. The sequences have a fixed length n . If A is an object, $n = 1$ and α a selector, then in general $A(\alpha) \neq A$; i.e. circularities in the multilevel structure are not admitted. Also for larger n no circularities can occur in the levels, although circularities at a given level are possible [8]. Further we remark that in definition 2.2 a special interpretation is given to the sequences:

they are considered to be pushdown stacks of finite depth. This has been chosen in view of the usefulness of such objects, but it is by no means the only possible choice. See also [5].

3. *REPRESENTATION*

By special choices of the underlying set of selectors we obtain special cases of multi-level data objects. In this and the next section we shall consider data objects representable as multi-level selector-labelled graphs. In order to do this we choose a subset of the free monoid $(\Sigma^*, \circ, \varepsilon)$ over some alphabet Σ, as the underlying set. In particular we specify S to be the language accepted by a deterministic finite automaton. We allow the following property: if Q is the set of states and Q_t is the set of final states, then $Q_t = Q$. So S is in general infinite and it may contain ε.

Definition 3.1

A (zero-level) selector-labelled graph G_0 is a collection of nodes N and a binary relation B over N together with an arc labelling function $c_a : B \to \Sigma$. Exactly one node is the root. Further $q \neq q' \Rightarrow c_a(p,q) \neq c_a(p,q')$.

Definition 3.2

A multi-level selector-labelled graph G (or ml-sl graph) is a selector-labelled graph G_0 together with a node labelling function $c_n : N \to E \cup \{G' | G'$ is a ml-sl graph$\}$; here E is a set of elementary objects. We request the number of distinct levels to be finite. ⊠

For sake of simplicity we have restricted definition 3.2 to the case that the nodes are labelled by just one elementary object or ml-sl graph, instead of a vector of those.

Given a finite automaton, we can represent its state-transition function as a (zero-level) selector-labelled graph as follows (see also example 2):

$ps \to q$ is a rewriting rule iff
$p,q \in N \wedge c_a(b,q) = s$

Theorem 3.3 (representation theorem)

A multi-level data object can be represented by a ml-sl graph and a ml-sl graph is the representation of a multi-level data object.

Proof: If A is a multi-level data object we can define its domain $\mathcal{D}(A)$ as the set of selectors for which $f(\alpha) \neq \Omega$. Since this is a finite set, it is regular and there exists a deterministic finite automaton which accepts this set. The state-transition function can be represented by a ml-sl graph, which then is a representation of the zero-level part of A . Using the node-labelling function c_n and using ν - induction we conclude the proposition of the theorem.

If G is a ml-sl graph we consider the zero-level part G_0 of it. Let the nodes be $n_0(\text{root}), n_1, \ldots, n_p$. Consider the sets

$$V_m = \{(n_0, c_a(n_0, n_{i_1}) \circ c_a(n_{i_1}, n_{i_2}) \circ \ldots \circ c_a(n_{i_{m-1}}, m_{i_m}), n_{i_m} \mid n_{i_1}, n_{i_2}, \ldots, n_{i_m} \in \{n_0, \ldots, n_p\}\}$$

for $m = 0,1,2,\ldots$.

For sufficiently large q the sets $V_0, V_1, \ldots, V_q$ determine G_0 completely, i.e. the function c_a . Select from $V_0, V_1, \ldots, V_q$ the subset of Σ^* by considering the second elements of the triples. This subset is finite. Identify this set with the domain of the data object which G_0 represents.

Finally, if α is selected from some V and n' is last element of the triple, put $f(\alpha) = c_n(n')$.

Repeat the procedure for higher levels of G . ⊠

Example 3

A ml-sl graph G is given by $N = \{0,1,2\}$, root 0, $\Sigma = \{s,t\}$ and

$c_a(0,1) = s$ $c_a(1,0) = t$ $c_a(2,0) = s$

$c_a(0,2) = t$ $c_a(1,2) = s$ Further $c_n(i) = e_i$ $i = 0,1,2$

We construct first

$V_1 = \{(0,s,1),(0,t,2)\}$ $V_2 = \{(0,s\circ t,0),(0,s\circ s,2),(0,t\circ s,0)\}$

so that the domain of the data object G represents is $\{\varepsilon, s, t, s\circ t, s\circ s, t\circ s\}$

The data object is then given by

$f(\varepsilon) \;= e_0$

$f(s) \;= c_n(1) = e_1 \qquad f(t) = c_n(2) = e_2$

$f(s \circ t) = c_n(0) = e_1$

$f(s \circ s) = c_n(2) = e_2$

$f(t \circ s) = c_n(0) = e_0$ ⊠

4. *AN APPLICATION*

In this section we consider the evaluation of binary arithmetic expressions by an abstract machine. For the set of states we use the set of multilevel data objects, and as primitive operations we admit $a * b$, where a and b are numerical values and $*$ is some binary operator; further ν, ν', selection, concatenation and the deletion of postfixes of composite selectors is assumed to be primitive. An arithmetic binary expression is considered to be a multilevel data object representable as a ml-sl tree over an alphabet $\{\ell, r\}$; ℓ denotes "left" and r denotes "right". The class of expressions $is\hat{-}exp$, is given by the abstract grammar

exp: (bin-op;ℓ,r) $\vee$ const
ℓ : exp
r : exp.

This is interpreted as follows: if is-exp(E) then top(E(ε)) is either a constant or top(E(ε)) is a binary operator and $\ell \circ E$ is the left-hand operand and $r \circ E$ is the right-hand operand which both satisfy the same abstract grammar. $\alpha \circ E$ or $\alpha(E)$ is the standard Vienna selection operation. For $\alpha \circ (\beta \circ E)$ we write $\alpha \circ \beta \circ E$.

The abstract machine M will have at its disposal two stacks ST_i $i = 1,2$, for which $ST_i(\varepsilon)$ is a sequence of composite selectors in $\{\ell, r\}^*$, and $ST_i(\alpha) = \Omega$ $i = 1,2$ for all $\alpha \neq \varepsilon$. Let $is\hat{-}stack$ denote the class of this type of stacks. Finally denote by $is\hat{-}val$ a set of numerical values.

Consider then the following abstract machine

$$S_I = is\hat{-}exp \qquad S_T = is\hat{-}val$$
$$S = S_I \cup S_T \cup is\hat{-}stack \times is\hat{-}stack \times is\hat{-}exp$$

and δ to be defined presently. For sake of convenience we display in the definition of δ only the top of the push-down stacks $top(ST_i(\varepsilon)) = x$ $i = 1,2$. Further the pushdown operation $\nu(ST_i,\varepsilon,x)$ is written $\downarrow x$ and the pop-up operation $\nu'(ST_i,\varepsilon)$ is written $\uparrow x$ where $x = top(ST_i(\varepsilon))$ again. With these conventions we define the state transition relation by the following table

Definition 4.1

		conditions	
		is-const	is-const
1.	E δ E	top(E(ε))	
2.	E δ ($\downarrow\ell$,$\downarrow$r,E)		
3.	(ℓ,r,E) δ eval	top(E(ℓ))	top(E(r))
4.	(x,y,E) δ ($\uparrow$x,$\uparrow$y,ν[E,x-ℓ,eval])	top(E(x))	top(E(y))
5.	(x,y,E) δ ($\downarrow$y$\circ\ell$,$\downarrow$y$\circ$r,E)	top(E(x))	
6.	(x,y,E) δ ($\downarrow$x$\circ\ell$,$\downarrow$x$\circ$r,E)		top(E(y))
7.	(x,y,E) δ ($\downarrow$x$\circ\ell$,$\downarrow$x$\circ$r,E)		
8.	(x,y,E) δ ($\downarrow$y$\circ\ell$,$\downarrow$y$\circ$r,E)		

In this definition we have written $\alpha - \beta$ for the deletion of the postfix β of α . Further we have written (on line 3) eval for the primitive operation $top(E(\ell)) * top(E(r))$ where $* = top(E(\varepsilon))$ is a binary operator; on line 4 we have eval for the primitive operation $top(E(x)) * top(E(y))$ where $* = top(E(y-r))$ is the binary operator to be used.

Note that the evaluation of E proceeds in the following way: two terminal nodes in the tree representing E are located in a non-deterministic way (lines 7 and 8) and then, using the binary operator in the father node, a "local" evaluation is carried out and pushed down in the mentioned father node; at the same time the selectors x and y pointing at the terminal nodes are deleted from the stacks and the process starts anew. Termination is guaranteed by line 3. Lines 1 and 2 start the process. The process of evaluation is correct because:

1) $top(ST_1(\varepsilon)) - \ell = top(ST_2(\varepsilon)) - r$
and 2) $\text{is-exp}(x\circ E) \wedge \text{is-exp}(y\circ E)$

are invariant under δ . So we can use lemma 2.6 (ν - induction) for the formal proof of $E \,\phi\, value(E)$ (see section 1), which will not be given here.

REFERENCES

[1] A. Ollongren 1974, "Definition of programming languages by interpreting automata", Acad. Press, APIC Studies in Dataprocessing No. 11, London.

[2] A. Ollongren, Th.P. van der Weide 1978, "Abstracte automaten en grammatica's", Syllabus, Dept. of Mathematics, Leiden University (in Dutch).

[3] J.A. Bergstra, H.J.M. Goeman, A. Ollongren, G.A. Terpstra, Th.P. van der Weide 1978, "Axioms for multilevel objects", submitted for publication in Fundamenta Informaticae.

[4] H.J.M. Goeman, A. Ollongren, Th.P. van der Weide 1978, "Axiomatiek van datastructuren", MC Syllabus 37, Colloquium Data structuren, Math. Centr, Amsterdam (in Dutch), p. 85-98.

[5] Th.P. van der Weide 1979, thesis, to appear.

[6] A. Salomaa 1973, "Formal languages", Academic Press, New York.

[7] H.D. Ehrich 1976, "Outline of an algebraic theory of structured objects", Automata, Languages and Programming, Third International Colloquium, Edinburgh University Press, p. 508-530.

[8] J.A. Bergstra, A. Ollongren, Th.P. van der Weide 1977, "An axiomatization of the rational data objects", in: Fundamentals of Computation Theory, Springer Lecture Notes in Computer Science 56, p. 33-38.

GRAPH GRAMMARS AND OPERATIONAL SEMANTICS

Peter Padawitz
Technische Universität Berlin
Fachbereich Informatik (20)

Oktober 1978

ABSTRACT

Transformations of graphlike expressions are called correct if they preserve a given functional semantics of the expressions. Combining the algebraic theory of graph grammars (cf./Eh 78/) and the ADJ approach to semantics of programming languages it will be proved that the correctness of transformation rules carries over to the correctness of derivations via such rules. Applying this result to LISP we show that a LISP interpreter represented by a graph grammar is correct with respect to the functional semantics of graphlike LISP expressions.

1. INTRODUCTION

Starting from the theory of context-free languages, Cadiou, Nivat, Rosen, Vuillemin and others describe symbolic expressions and their evaluation in principle by the following approach (cf. /CM 72/, /Niv 74/, /Ros 73/, /Vui 74/):

A set of symbols for constants and basic functions is separated from a set of symbols for recursively defined functions. Expressions composed of these symbols always have tree representations. They are evaluated by "simplification" of (basic function, argument)-pairs and by "substitution" of defining terms for recursive function symbols.

Derivations of expressions via such evaluation rules are "parallel independent" so that the rules yield a Church-Rosser system. Therefore normal forms of expressions are unique and define an OPERATIONAL SEMANTICS. Substitution rules constitute a system of equations that is solvable in the lattice of partial functions. Evaluating an expression after replacing its recursive function symbols by those solutions yields its FUNCTIONAL SEMANTICS.

An important result of /Niv 74/ and /Ros 73/ is that each normal form of an expression coincides with its functional semantics:

Operational and functional semantics are equivalent.

We drop the restrictions concerning the structure of symbolic expressions and their evaluation rules by introducing Σ-graphs and Σ-grammars. The Σ-graph representation of expressions allows the collapsing of variables on the right side of substitution rules so that copying of subexpressions during the derivation process is avoided. Furthermore, LABEL-operators as in LISP can be evaluated by generating cycles.

Σ-grammars cover more applications than the simplification / substitution systems mentioned above. Especially, lazy evaluation rules (cf. /HM 76/) can be formulated. They allow the reduction of certain subexpressions before their arguments have been completely evaluated. Therefore, such rules mostly have trees of height >1 on their left side.

Recent approaches to functional programming (cf. /Backus 78/) and the consideration of direct implementations for algebraically specified data types (cf. /GHM 76/) let us suppose that "applicative" programming and execution by replacement will achieve great importance in practical computer science.

Using the initial algebra approach of /GTW^2 77/, we define the functional semantics of Σ-graphs as an extension of Dana Scott's fixed point semantics of flow diagrams. (cf. /GTW^2 77/, section 5.2) We prove that derivations via a Σ-grammar $\mathcal{G}$ preserve the functional semantics of Σ-graphs if the productions of $\mathcal{G}$ are "correct relative to a given semantical algebra" (cf. Thm. 3.9).

Derivations via Σ-grammars do not yield unique normal forms in general. But there are sufficient conditions for a weak Church-Rosser property of Σ-grammars which hold true for special classes of Σ-grammars. This subject will be treated only informally in this paper. Concerning details the interested reader is referred to /Pad 78/.

An extended version of this paper containing all proofs is available as a technical report (/Pad 78 a/).

NOTATIONS:

ω is the set of natural numbers. The composition of two functions $f:A \longrightarrow B$ and $g:B \longrightarrow C$ is denoted by $g \circ f$ or gf.

If A is a set, then /A/ is its cardinal. A word w has length lg(w). λ is the empty word. w_i is the i-th symbol of w. Let $f:A \longrightarrow B$ a function and $A' \subset A$. Then the domain restriction of f to A' is denoted by f/A'. The value f(a) where $a \in A$ is often abbreviated by fa. If $b \in B$, then $f^{-1}b = \{a \in A / fa = b\}$. For $n \in \omega$, $[n] = \{1,\dots,n\}$.

2. Σ-GRAPHS AND THEIR FUNCTIONAL SEMANTICS

2.1 DEFINITION (cf. /GTW^2 77/, chapter 2)

Let S be a set. The elements of S are called sorts. An S-sorted operator domain Σ is a family of sets $\Sigma_{w,s}$ for all $w \in S^*$ and $s \in S$ where S^* denotes the free monoid over S.

$\sigma\in\Sigma_{w,s}$ is called operation symbol with arity w, sort s, and rank lg(w). We also write $\sigma: w \longrightarrow s$ for $\sigma\in\Sigma_{w,s}$. $\sigma\in\Sigma_{\lambda,s}$ is called a constant. □

For chapters 2 and 3, we fix a set S of sorts and an S-sorted operator domain Σ.

2.2 DEFINITION

Let C be a set. The elements of C are called colors. A C-colored directed graph $G=(G_N,G_E,s_G,t_G,m_G)$ is given by a set G_N of nodes, a set G_E of edges, source and target maps s_G and t_G, resp., from G_E to G_N, and a color map $m_G: G_N \cup G_E \longrightarrow C$. Sometimes $G_N \cup G_E$ is denoted by G.

A pair $g=(g_N,g_E)$ of functions from the node resp. edge sets of a graph G to a graph H is called graph morphism if $s_H g_E = g_N s_G$ and $t_H g_E = g_N t_G$. If $x\in G_N$, then $g_N(x)$ is abbreviated by $g(x)$. Analogously for $e\in G_E$. □

2.3 DEFINITION

Let G be a C-colored directed graph with nodes colored by elements of Σ or $S\times\omega$ and edges colored by natural numbers. We call $C_{fix}=\Sigma\cup\omega$ fixed colors and $C_{var}=S\times\omega$ variable colors. G is a Σ-graph if G_N is the union of disjoint sets $G_{N,s}$, one for each $s\in S$, such that for all $s\in S$ and $x\in G_{N,s}$ we have either

1) $m_G x=(s,i)$ for some $i\in\omega$ and $/s_G^{-1}x/=\emptyset$, or
2) there is $w\in S^+$ with $m_G x\in\Sigma_{w,s}$, $/s_G^{-1}x/=lg(w)$, $m_G s_G^{-1}x=\left[lg(w)\right]$, and $t_G e\in G_{N,w_i}$ for $e\in s_G^{-1}x$ with $m_G e=i$.

$G_I=\{x\in G_N/m_G x\in\Sigma\}$ is the set of internal nodes of G while the nodes of $G_P=G_N-G_I$ are called parameters of G. If $x\in G_{N,s}$ then s is the type of x. □

Since we shall define the substitution of fixed colors for variable colors by a function from colors to colors called recoloring we must distinguish the colors of variable colored nodes which have the same type. Therefore parameters are not only colored by their type but also by an additional natural number.

Example:

Given the sort set S={val,exp,env} and the operator domain

Σ = {EVAL:exp env — val,
LAMBDA-X:exp — exp,
ATTR-Y:val env — env},

the following graph G is a Σ-graph:

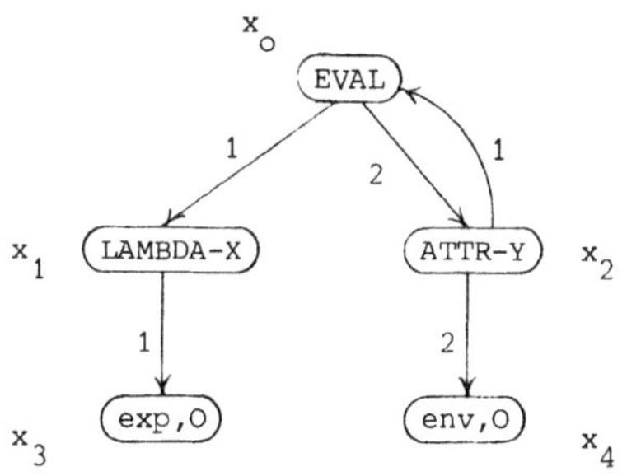

We observe that $G_I=\{x_o,x_1,x_2\}$, $G_P=\{x_3,x_4\}$, $G_{N,val}=\{x_o\}$, $G_{N,exp}=\{x_1,x_3\}$ and $G_{N,env}=\{x_2,x_4\}$. □

Let G and H be Σ-graphs. A graph morphism $g:G \longrightarrow H$ that preserves types and fixed colors is called Σ-graph morphism. The restriction of g to G_I is denoted by g_I. g_P is defined analogously. Note that g fixed color preserving implies $g(G_I) \subset H_I$ but $g(G_P) \subset H_P$ does not hold in general.

Before we turn to "semantic algebras" let us first represent each Σ-graph G by a system $\tilde{G}$ of equations such that the semantics of G can be considered as the "least solution" of $\tilde{G}$ in an appropriate algebra.

2.4 DEFINITION (cf. /GTW[2] 77/)

Let X be the union of a family $\{X_s\}_{s\in S}$ of disjoint sets. The set $T_\Sigma(X)$ of Σ-terms over X is inductively defined by

1. For all $s\in S$ $X_s \cup \Sigma_{\lambda,s} \subset T_\Sigma(X)_s$
2. $\sigma:s_1,\dots,s_n \longrightarrow s$, $t_i \in T_\Sigma(X)_{s_i}$ for all $1\leq i\leq n$
   $\Longrightarrow \sigma(t_1,\dots,t_n)\in T_\Sigma(X)_s$
3. $T_\Sigma(X)=\bigcup_{s\in S} T_\Sigma(X)_s$ □

2.5 DEFINITION

Let G be a Σ-graph. Then the funtion

$$\tilde{G}:G_I \longrightarrow T_\Sigma(G_N)$$

defined by

$$\tilde{G}x=\sigma(x_1,\dots,x_n)$$

for all $x\in G_I$ where $\sigma=m_G x$, $n=\text{rank}(\sigma)$, and $t_G e=x_i$ for $e\in s_G^{-1}x$ with $m_G e=i$ is called equational representation of G. □

2.6 DEFINITION (cf. /GTW[2] 77/)

A Σ-algebra A consists of a carrier set A_s for each $s\in S$ and a function $\sigma_A:A_{s_1}\times\dots\times A_{s_n} \longrightarrow A_s$ for each $\sigma:s_1\dots s_n \longrightarrow s$ in Σ. σ_A is called operation. $\sigma:\lambda \xrightarrow{1} s$ yields a constant $\sigma_A\in A_s$.

If A and B are Σ-algebras, a family $f=\{f_s\}_{s\in S}$ of functions $f_s:A_s \longrightarrow B_s$ is a <u>Σ-homomorphism</u> if

$$\begin{array}{ccc} A_{s_1}\times\ldots\times A_{s_n} & \xrightarrow{\ \sigma_A\ } & A_s \\ {\scriptstyle f_{s_1}\times\ldots\times f_{s_n}}\downarrow & & \downarrow{\scriptstyle f_s} \\ B_{s_1}\times\ldots\times B_{s_n} & \xrightarrow{\ \sigma_B\ } & B_s \end{array}$$

commutes for all $\sigma:s_1\ldots s_n \longrightarrow s$ in Σ.

A Σ-Algebra A is <u>ω-continuous</u> if for each $s\in S$ there is a partial order $\leqslant_s$ on A_s such that a least element $\perp_s$ exists, all ω-chains $\{a_i\}_{i\in\omega} \subset A_s$ have suprema $\bigsqcup_{i\in\omega} a_i$ in A_s, and all operations preserve these suprema (are ω-continuous). □

2.7 <u>DEFINITION</u>

Let X be the union of a family $\{X_s\}_{s\in S}$ of disjoint sets and A a Σ-algebra. A function $\alpha:X \longrightarrow A$ is an <u>assignment</u> if for all $s\in S$, $x\in X_s$ implies $\alpha x\in A_s$. The set of assignments from X to A is denoted by $X[A]$.

Since $T_\Sigma(X)$ can be extended to the free Σ-algebra over X, each $\alpha\in X[A]$ has a unique Σ-homomorphic extension $\alpha^*:T_\Sigma(X)\longrightarrow A$.

Let G be a Σ-graph. If $\iota\in G_I[A]$ and $\pi\in G_P[A]$, then $[\iota,\pi]\in G_N[A]$ is the coproduct extension of ι and π.

Moreover, if A is ω-continuous, then $\tilde{G}$ yields for all $\pi\in G_P[A]$ an ω-continuous function+)

$$G_{A,\pi}:\{\alpha\in G_N[A] \mid \alpha/G_N=\pi\} \longrightarrow G_N[A]$$

defined by $G_{A,\pi}(\alpha)=[\alpha^*\circ\tilde{G},\pi]$. The least fixed point $/G_{A,\pi}/$ of $G_{A,\pi}$ is called <u>(functional) semantics of G</u> relative to A and π. Note that $/G_{A,\pi}/=\bigsqcup_{i\in\omega} G^i_{A,\pi}([\perp,\pi])$ where $x\in G_{N,s}$ implies $\perp x=\perp_s$.

$/G_{A,\pi}/(x)$ is the <u>(functional) semantics of x</u>. □

The following proposition says that $/G_{A,\pi}/$ is the least solution in A of the system of equations given by G. It also shows that the semantics of a node is derivable from the semantics of its successors.

2.8 <u>PROPOSITION</u>

Let G,A and π as in 2.7. Then $Gx=\sigma(x_1,\ldots,x_n)$ implies $/G_{A,\pi}/(x)=\sigma_A(/G_{A,\pi}/(x_1),\ldots,/G_{A,\pi}/(x_n))$.

+) The ω-continuity of $G_{A,\pi}$ is proved analogously to the Δ-continuity of E_A in /GTW[2] 77/, section 5.1.

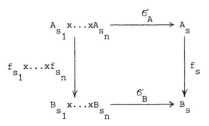

Proof:

$$/G_{A,\pi}/(x)=G_{A,\pi}(/G_{A,\pi}/)(x)=[/G_{A,\pi}/^{*}\circ \tilde{G},\pi](x)=$$
$$=/G_{A,\pi}/^{*}(\tilde{G}x)=/G_{A,\pi}/^{*}(\sigma(x_1,\ldots,x_n))=\sigma_A(/G_{A,\pi}/(x_1),\ldots,/G_{A,\pi}/(x_n)).$$ □

Example:

Given the operations for LISP-graphs in 4.1 and the "semantical" algebra A in 4.2, the semantics of node x_o of the Σ-graph example in 2.3 is evaluated as follows:

$$/G_{A,\pi}/(x_o)=EVAL_A(/G_{A,\pi}/(x_1),/G_{A,\pi}/(x_2))=$$
$$=/G_{A,\pi}/(x_o)(/G_{A,\pi}/(x_2))=$$
$$=LAMBDA\text{-}X_A(/G_{A,\pi}/(x_3))(ATTR\text{-}Y_A(/G_{A,\pi}/(x_o),/G_{A,\pi}/(x_4)))$$
$$=LAMBDA\text{-}X_A(\pi x_3)(ATTR\text{-}Y_A(/G_{A,\pi}/(x_o),\pi x_4))$$
$$=abstract((\pi x_3)\circ ATTR\text{-}X_A)(ATTR\text{-}Y_A(/G_{A,\pi}/(x_o),\pi x_4))$$

so that

$f=/G_{A,\pi}/(x_o):A_{val}\longrightarrow A_{val}$ is given by

$$f(v)=(\pi x_3)\circ ATTR\text{-}X_A(v,ATTR\text{-}Y_A(f,\pi x_4)),$$

i.e. evaluating the expression πx_3 after assigning v to X and f to Y and executing the assignments of πx_4 yields f(v). The reader may convince himself that this is really the intended semantics of G. □

Later we shall see (cf. proposition 3.7) that the fixpoint property of $G_{A,\pi}$ and therefore ω-continuity of A is only needed for cyclic graphs. In the acyclic case, there is a finite Σ-term t_x for each node x such that $\pi^{*}t_x$ yields the semantics of x.

2.9 LEMMA

Let A be a Σ-algebra and $\alpha\in H_N[A]$. Each Σ-graph morphism $g:G\longrightarrow H$ induces a unique Σ-homomorphism $g^{+}:T_{\Sigma}(G_N)\longrightarrow T_{\Sigma}(H_N)$ such that

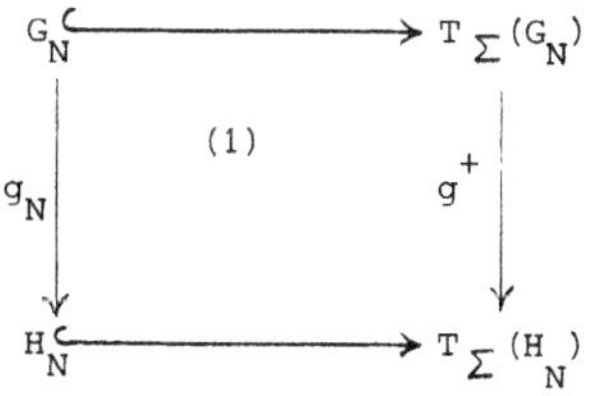

commutes. Moreover, the following diagrams (2) and (3) commute

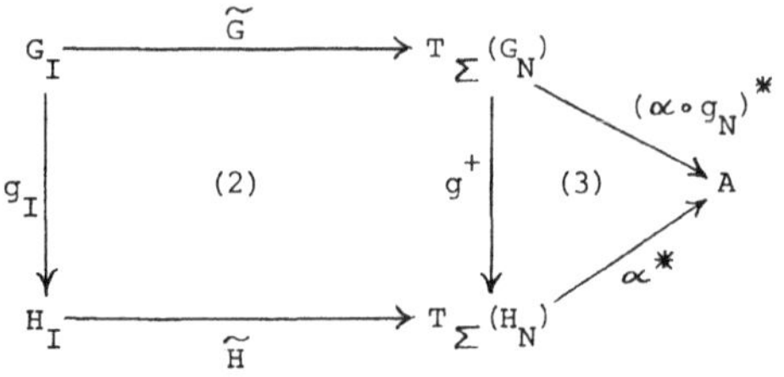

□

2.10 THEOREM (Σ-graph morphisms preserve the semantics of Σ-graphs)

Let $g:G \longrightarrow H$ be a Σ-graph morphism, A an ω-continuous Σ-algebra and $\pi \in H_P$ A .

Then $\rho = /H_{A,\pi}/ \circ g_P$ implies $/G_{A,\rho}/ = /H_{A,\pi}/ \circ g_N$, and $\rho_n = H^n_{A,\pi}([\bot,\pi]) \circ g_P$ implies $G^n_{A,\rho_n}([\bot,\rho_n]) \geqslant H^n_{A,\pi}([\bot,\pi]) \circ g_N$ for all $n \in \omega$. □

3. TRANSFORMATIONS OF Σ-GRAPHS

3.1 DEFINITION (cf. /Eh 78/,3.1)

Let C be a set of colors. A graph production $p=(B_1 \xleftarrow{b_1} K \xrightarrow{b_2} B_2)$ consists of two C-colored directed graphs B_1 and B_2, a non-colored directed graph K called gluing graph, and two graph morphisms b_1 and b_2.

We write s_i, t_i, m_i for the source, target, resp. color maps of B_i (i=1,2).

3.2 DEFINITION

A graph production $p=(B_1 \xleftarrow{b_1} K \xrightarrow{b_2} B_2)$ is called Σ-production if B_1 and B_2 are Σ-graphs, b_1 and b_2 are graph inclusions, $B_{1,N,s} \subset B_{2,N,s}$ for all $s \in S$, $B_{1,P} = B_{2,P}$, $m_1 x = m_2 x$ for all $x \in B_{1,P} \cup K_E$, and K is defined as follows:

Let alter $(p) = \{x \in B_{1,N} / m_1 x \neq m_2 x\}$. Then

$K = (B_{1,N}, K_E, s_1/K_E, t_1/K_E)$ where $K_E = \{e \in B_{1,E} / s_1 e \notin \text{alter}(p)\}$.

Moreover, each two nodes x,y in B_1 such that $m_1 x = m_1 y$ is a constant must be the same. (Clearly, for each Σ-graph G there is a Σ-graph G' that has the same functional semantics as G but has no two equally colored leaves.)

p is "fast" which means that the applicability of p to a Σ-graph G does not depend on the context of the embedding of B_1 in G (cf. /ER 77/, chapter 2).

A Σ-grammar is a set of Σ-productions. An example of a Σ-grammar is the interpreter for graphlike LISP expressions given in section 4.3. For all productions p of this grammar, alter (p) consists of the single node x_o.

3.3 DEFINITION (cf. /Eh 78/,3.1)

Let C be a set of colors, $p=(B_1 \xleftarrow{b_1} K \xrightarrow{b_2} B_2)$ a graph production, and G,H two colored directed graphs. Then two pushouts

$$\begin{array}{ccccc} B_1 & \xleftarrow{b_1} & K & \xrightarrow{b_2} & B_2 \\ \downarrow g & & \downarrow d & & \downarrow h \\ G & \xleftarrow[c_1]{} & D & \xrightarrow[c_2]{} & H \end{array} \qquad (1)$$

in the category of graphs and graph morphisms define a direct derivation $G \overset{p}{\Longrightarrow} H$ if g and h are color preserving and $m_G c_1 x = m_H c_2 x$ holds for all $x \in D - dK$. □
The details of a direct derivation will always be denoted as in Fig. (1). Concerning the interpretation of this notion of a direct derivation we refer to /Eh 78/,3.1.

3.4 <u>DEFINITION</u>

Let $C = C_{fix} \cup C_{var}$ (cf. 2.3). A fixed color preserving function $r: C \longrightarrow C$ with

$$r(s,i) \in \left(\bigcup_{w \in S^*} \Sigma_{w,s}\right) \cup (\{s\} \times \omega)$$

for all $(s,i) \in C_{var}$ is called <u>Σ-recoloring</u>.
If G is a Σ-graph, then define the graph $rG = (G_N, G_E, s_G, t_G, rm_G)$ which, in general, is not a Σ-graph because leaves may be colored by Σ. Moreover, for each Σ-production $p = (B_1 \xleftarrow{b_1} K \xrightarrow{b_2} B_2)$ define $rp = (rB_1 \xleftarrow{b_1} K \xrightarrow{b_2} rB_2)$. □
A direct derivation via rp is called <u>direct Σ-derivation</u>.

3.5 <u>THEOREM</u>

Given a direct Σ-derivation $G \overset{rp}{\Longrightarrow} H$, H is a Σ-graph, and the color preserving graph morphisms $g: rB_1 \longrightarrow G$ and $h: rB_2 \longrightarrow H$ are Σ-graph morphisms from B_1 to G and from B_2 to H, resp. □

3.6 <u>DEFINITION</u>

Let $p = (B_1 \xleftarrow{b_1} K \xrightarrow{b_2} B_2)$ be a Σ-production and A an ω-continuous Σ-algebra. p is <u>correct relative to A</u> if

$$/B_{1,A,\tau}/(x) = /B_{2,A,\tau}/(x)$$

holds true for all $\tau \in B_{1,P}[A]$ and $x \in alter(p)$. □

The following proposition supplies a simple method for proving the correctness of p in the case that B_1 and B_2 are acyclic graphs.

3.7 <u>PROPOSITION</u>

Let A be a Σ-algebra and G an acyclic Σ-graph. Then for each $x \in G_N$ a term $t_x \in T_\Sigma(G_P)$ is inductively defined by

1. $x \in G_P \Longrightarrow t_x = x$,

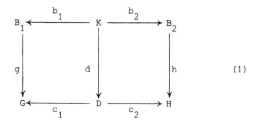

2. $x \in G_I$, $\tilde{G}x = \sigma(x_1,\dots,x_n) \Longrightarrow t_x = \sigma(t_{x_1},\dots,t_{x_n})$

Moreover, if A is ω-continuous, then

$$/G_{A,\pi}/(x) = \pi^* t_x$$

for all $\pi \in G_p \lceil A \rceil$ and $x \in G_N$. □

An example of a Σ-production p where B_1 or B_2 are not acyclic, is the evaluation rule for LABEL-operators in LISP which is given in section 4.3 as production p_4. The correctness proof for p_4 is worked out in section 4.5.

3.8 DEFINITION

Let $G \xRightarrow{rp} H$ be a direct Σ-derivation. Since c_1 is bijective on nodes, we have a well-defined residue map $f_N = c_{1,N}^{-1}\ c_{2,N}$ (cf. 3.3 fig.(1)).
Pushout properties imply $f_N(G_P) = H_P$ so that π can be applied to $f_P = f_N/G_P$.
$G \xRightarrow{rp} H$ is correct relative to A if

$$/G_{A,\pi} \circ f_P/ = /H_{A,\pi}/ \circ f_N$$

holds true for all $\pi \in H_P[A]$. □

3.9 MAIN THEOREM

Let $G \xRightarrow{rp} H$ be a direct Σ-derivation and A an ω-continuous Σ-algebra. The correctness of p relative to A implies the correctness of $G \xRightarrow{rp} H$ relative to A. □

The statement of theorem 3.9 holds also true for sequences of direct Σ-derivations:

3.10 COROLLARY

Let A be an ω-continuous Σ-algebra, $\mathcal{G}$ a Σ-grammar whose productions are correct relative to A, and $G_o \xRightarrow{p_1} G_1 \xRightarrow{p_2} \dots \xRightarrow{p_n} G_n$ a sequence of direct Σ-derivations such that $p_i \in \mathcal{G}$ and f_i is the residue map of $G_{i-1} \xRightarrow{p_i} G_i$ for all $1 \leq i \leq n$. Then $f_N = f_n \circ \dots \circ f_1$ and $f_P = f_N/G_{O,P}$ satisfy

$$/G_{O,A,\pi} \circ f_P/ = /G_{n,A,\pi}/ \circ f_N$$

for all $\pi \in G_P[A]$. □

3.11 REMARKS CONCERNING GARBAGE COLLECTION AND CHURCH-ROSSER PROPERTIES OF Σ-GRAMMARS

We assume that initially each Σ-graph G has an "entry node" x such that all nodes of G are reachable from x. During the evaluation of G by Σ-derivations a subgraph G' of the derivative of G may become unreachable from x. But we are only interested in the semantics of x (cf. 2.7) so that G' can be deleted without affecting the semantics of x. If G is acyclic, this "garbage collection" can be performed by successive deletions of "bunches" in G whose roots have no ingoing arcs. A theorem of Ehrig and Rosen (cf. /ER 77/, Thm. 6.4) implies that a Church-Rosser system of "treelike" Σ-productions remains Church-Rosser if it is extended by the bunch deletions described above. Therefore, the evaluation and the garbage collection processes can run concurrently without influencing each other. But if we admit cyclic graphs, cycles which are not reachable from the entry node must be considered, too. One way for recognizing those cycles is to define rules for searching and marking all reachable nodes. We have shown elsewhere that the "weak Church-Rosser property" of a "weakly independent" set $\mathcal{G}$ of "treelike" Σ-productions is preserved if $\mathcal{G}$ is extended by such search rules. But garbage collection will be simpler if there is only a finite set of cycles that possibly occur during the evaluation process of an initially acyclic graph. In such cases we can extend the Σ-grammar by deletion rules not only for "unreferenced" bunches but also for "unreferenced" cycles. The LISP interpreter presented in /Pad 78/ as an example of a Σ-grammar even generates at most one cycle up to isomorphism.

A grammar $\mathcal{G}$ is called weak Church-Rosser if for all $p,p' \in \mathcal{G}$ and two direct derivations $G \overset{p}{\Longrightarrow} H$ and $G \overset{p'}{\Longrightarrow} H'$ there is a graph X such that X is derivable via $\mathcal{G}$ both from H and H'.

Roughly spoken, a Σ-grammar $\mathcal{G}$ is called weakly independent if for all $p,p' \in \mathcal{G}$ there is at most one gluing graph V(p,p') of the left sides of p and p' where nongluing points of p or p' are identified with arbitrary points.

The embedding theorem for derivation sequences (cf. /EK 76/,Thm. 4) yields a "local" criterion for the weak Church-Rosser property of a weakly independent Σ-grammar (cf. /Pad 78/, IV.10). Using this criterion we have shown that the LISP interpreter mentioned above is weak Church-Rosser (cf. /Pad 78/,V.14-17).

A weak Church-Rosser grammar $\mathcal{G}$ is already Church-Rosser if there is a "weight" on graphs that properly decreases with every direct derivation via $\mathcal{G}$. But the existence of such a weight in the case that $\mathcal{G}$ is our LISP interpreter would imply that the evaluation of each LISP expression terminates. Hence, the halting problem of Turing machines would be solved because every partial-recursive function F is representable by a LISP expression that has the functional semantics of f.

In the last chapter, we present parts of the LISP interpreter and prove their correctness using the theory of chapters 1-3.

4. A Σ-GRAMMAR FOR EVALUATING GRAPHLIKE LISP EXPRESSIONS

4.1 Let S be a sort set that consists of the four elements atom, val (values), exp (expressions) and env (environments). The S-sorted operator domain Σ=LISP is given by

$a_i : \lambda \longrightarrow$ atom for all $i \in \omega$

true, false: $\lambda \longrightarrow$ atom

quote: atom $\longrightarrow$ val

car, cdr, is-atom: val $\longrightarrow$ val

cons, eq, apply: val val $\longrightarrow$ val

ite: val val val $\longrightarrow$ val

$X_i : \lambda \longrightarrow$ exp for all $i \in \omega$

QUOTE: atom $\longrightarrow$ exp

CAR, CDR, IS-ATOM: exp $\longrightarrow$ exp

LAMBDA-X_i, LABEL-X_i: exp $\longrightarrow$ exp for all $i \in \omega$

CONS, EQ, APPLY: exp exp $\longrightarrow$ exp

ITE: exp exp exp $\longrightarrow$ exp

EVAL: exp env $\longrightarrow$ val

NIL: $\lambda \longrightarrow$ env

ATTR-X_i: val env $\longrightarrow$ env for all $i \in \omega$

Example:

The application of the factorial function to 6 is represented by the following LISP'-graph where

LISP'=LISP $\cup$ {MULT, SUB: exp exp —— exp,
mult, sub: val val —— val},

$\mathbb{N} \subset \{a_i\}_{i \in \omega}$ and N, FAC $\subset \{X_i\}_{i \in \omega}$.

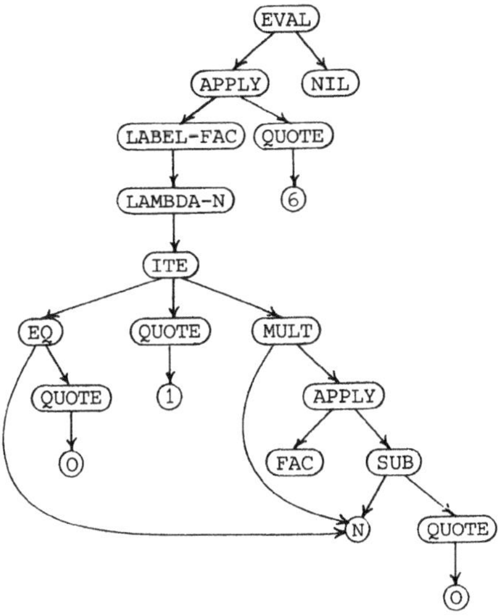

(The edge labels are omitted.)

4.2 Let $\{a_i\}_{i\in\omega}$ be an arbitrary countable set and $\underline{A_{atom}} = \{a_i\} \dot{\cup} \{true, false\} \dot{\cup} \{\perp\}$. A partial order $\leq$ on A_{atom} is defined by

$$a \leq b \implies a=b \text{ or } a=\perp .$$

The category CPO^{ω} has all posets with least elements and ω-chain suprema as objects and all pairs (f,g) of ω-continuous functions with gf=id and fg$\leq$id as morphisms. Let $+, x, \longrightarrow$ be the coproduct, product, resp. power functors in CPO^{ω}. Then the functor $F: CPO^{\omega} \longrightarrow CPO^{\omega}$ defined by $FC = A_{atom} + CxC + [C \longrightarrow C]$ has an "initial" fixed point called $\underline{A_{val}}$ (cf. /LS 77/, chapt.2/3).
Let Var= $\{X_i\}_{i\in\omega}$ be a countable set. Then $\leq$ induces a partial order on $\underline{A_{env}} = A_{val}^{Var}$, the set of all functions from Var to A_{val}. $\underline{A_{exp}} = [A_{env} \longrightarrow A_{val}]$ is partially ordered, too.
Moreover, for all s$\in$S, A_s has ω-chain suprema and a least element. Thus, we have defined the carrier sets of an ω-continuous Σ-algebra A. Operations σ_A are not given for all $\sigma\in\Sigma$ but for the most interesting ones (domain and range sets are determined by the presentation of Σ at the beginning of this chapter and the carrier set definitions given above):

$a_{i,A} = a_i$ for all $i\in\omega$

$true_A = true$

$false_A = false$

$$car_A(v) = \begin{cases} v_1 & \text{if } v=(v_1,v_2) \\ \perp & \text{if } v \notin A_{val}^2 \end{cases}$$

$cons_A(v_1,v_2) = (v_1,v_2)$

$X_{i,A}(f) = f(X_i)$ for all $i\in\omega$

$CAR_A(e) = car_A \circ e$

$CONS_A(e_1,e_2)(X) = cons_A(e_1(X), e_2(X))$

$NIL_A = \perp_{env}$

$$ATTR\text{-}X_{i,A}(v,f)(X_j) = \begin{cases} v & \text{if } i=j \\ f(X_j) & \text{otherwise} \end{cases}$$

$LAMBDA\text{-}X_{i,A}(e) = abstract(e \circ ATTR\text{-}X_{i,A})$

$LABEL\text{-}X_{i,A}(e) = lfp \circ (LAMBDA\text{-}X_{i,A}(e))$

$EVAL_A(e,f) = e(f)$

where $abstract(g): A_{env} \longrightarrow [A_{val} \longrightarrow A_{val}]$ is defined for all $g: A_{val} x A_{env} \longrightarrow A_{val}$ by

$$abstract(g)(f)(v) = g(v,f),$$

and $lfp: [A_{val} \longrightarrow A_{val}] \longrightarrow A_{val}$ supplies the least fixed point of ω-continuous functions from A_{val} to A_{val}.
All these operations are ω-continuous (cf. /Scott 72/, chapt.3, /Scott 74/, chapt.4).

4.3 The following Σ-productions for evaluating graphlike LISP expressions (Σ-graphs) are derived from the "lazy evaluator" of Henderson and Morris (cf. /HM 76/). The whole Σ-grammar is given in /Pad 78/.

1)

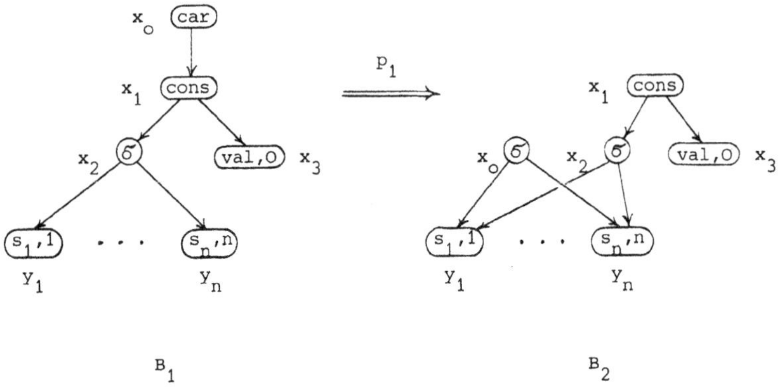

where $\sigma: s_1 \dots s_n \longrightarrow$ val

2)

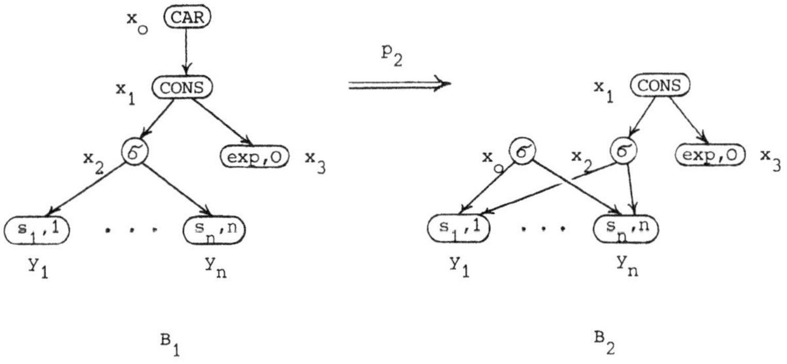

where $\sigma: s_1 \dots s_n \longrightarrow$ exp

3)

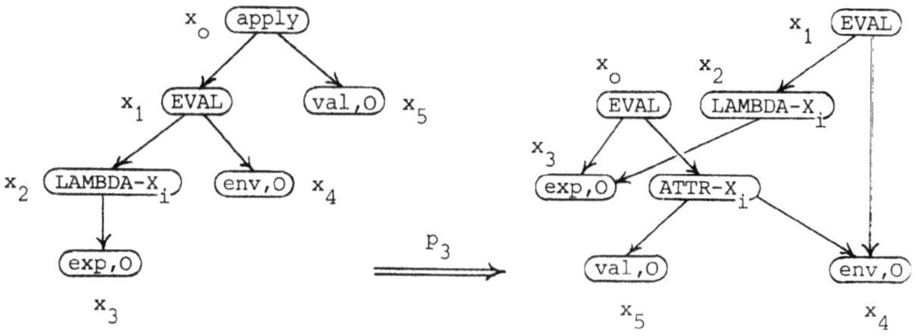

B_1 B_2

where $i \in \omega$

4)

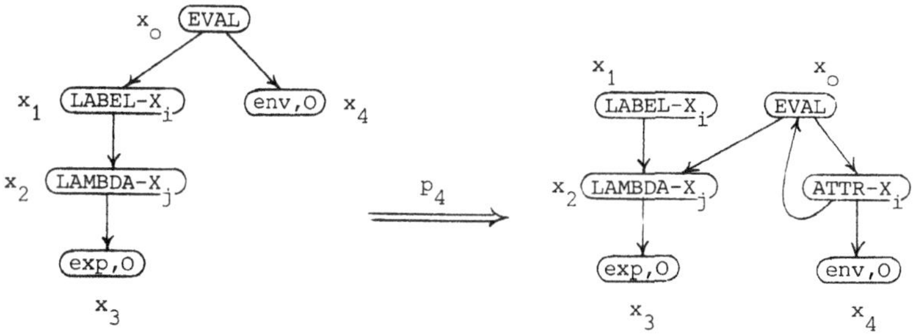

B_1 B_2

where $i,j \in \omega$

5)

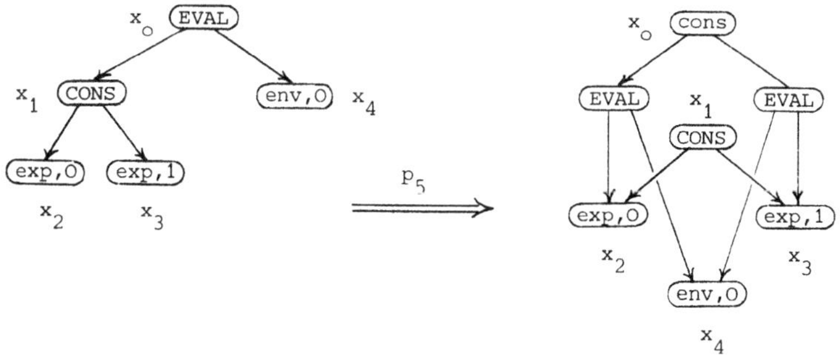

B_1 B_2

6)

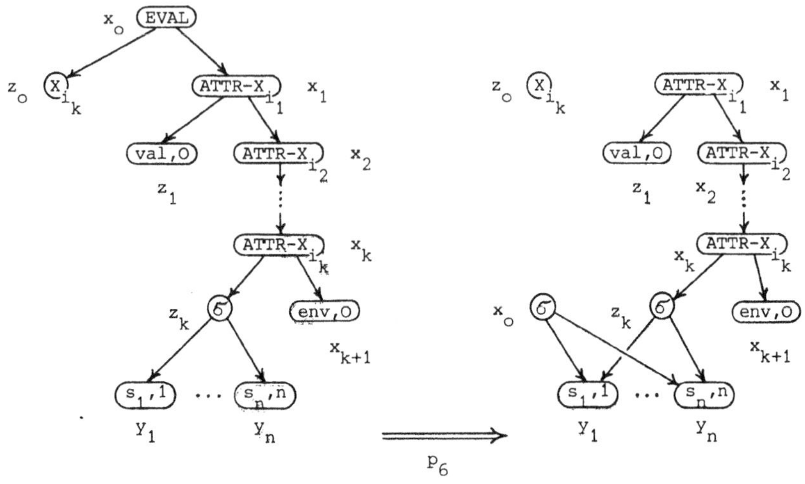

B_1 B_2

where $\sigma: s_1 \dots s_n \longrightarrow$ val.

Now we will show that the Σ-grammar above is correct relative to the "semantical algebra" A given in section 4.2.

4.4 Let $\mathcal{G}=\{p_1,\dots,p_6\}$ and A an ω-continuous Σ-algebra. If $p=(B_1 \xleftarrow{b_1} K \xrightarrow{b_2} B_2)\in \mathcal{G}-\{p_4\}$, then B_1 and B_2 are acyclic so that there are terms $t_{1,x_o}, t_{2,x_o} \in T_\Sigma(B_{1,P})$ with $/B_{i,A,\tau}/(x_o)=\tau^* t_{i,x_o}$ (i=1,2) for all $\tau \in B_{1,P}[A]$ (cf. prop. 3.7). Hence, by theorem 3.9, derivations via $\mathcal{G}-\{p_4\}$ preserve the semantics of Σ-graphs if

$$\tau^* t_{1,x_o} = \tau^* t_{2,x_o} \qquad (1)$$

holds true for all $p\in\mathcal{G}-\{p_4\}$ and $\tau\in B_{1,P}[A]$.

The proof of (1) is straightforward, e.g. let $p=p_6$ and $k>1$. Then

$\tau^* t_{1,x_o} = \mathrm{EVAL}_A(X_{i_k,A}, \tau^* t_{1,x_1}) = X_{i_k,A}(\tau^* t_{1,x_1}) =$

$= \tau^* t_{1,x_1}(X_{i_k}) = \mathrm{ATTR\text{-}X}_{i_1,A}(\tau^* t_{1,z_1}, \tau^* t_{1,x_2})(X_{i_k}) = \tau^* t_{1,x_2}(X_{i_k}) =$

$= \dots = \tau^* t_{1,x_k}(X_{i_k}) = \mathrm{ATTR\text{-}X}_{i_k,A}(\sigma_A(\tau y_1,\dots,\tau y_n), \tau x_{k+1})(X_{i_k}) =$

$= \sigma_A(\tau y_1,\dots,\tau y_n) = \tau^* t_{2,x_o}$.

4.5 For $p=p_4$, $/B_{1,A,\tau}/(x_o)=/B_{2,A,\tau}/(x_o)$ must be proved directly. Let $L=/B_{1,A,\tau}/$, $R=/B_{2,A,\tau}/$ and

$$f=\text{LAMBDA-X}_{i,A}(Lx_2)(\tau x_4).$$

By definition of $B_1, B_2, \text{EVAL}_A, \text{LABEL-X}_{i,A}$ and $\text{ATTR-X}_{i,A}$, we get

$$Lx_o=\text{lfp}(f) \qquad \text{(cf. 4.2)}$$

and

$$Rx_o=f(Rx_o)$$

which implies $Lx_o \leq Rx_o$. $Rx_o \leq Lx_o$ follows from

$$B^n_{2,A,\tau}([\bot,\tau])(x_o) \leq Lx_o \qquad (2)$$

for all even $n \in \omega$. We show (2) by induction on n.

Clearly, (2) holds true for n=0. Let (2) be satisfied for n. Then

$B^{n+2}_{2,A,\tau}([\bot,\tau])(x_o)=$

$=\text{EVAL}_A(\text{LAMBDA-X}_{j,A}(\tau x_3),\text{ATTR-X}_{i,A}(B^n_{2,A,\tau}([\bot,\tau])(x_o),\ \tau x_4))$ by definition of $\tilde{B}_2$

$=\text{EVAL}_A(Lx_2,\text{ATTR-X}_{i,A}(B^n_{2,A,\tau}([\bot,\tau])(x_o),\tau x_4))$ by definition of $\tilde{B}_1(x_2)$

$\leq \text{EVAL}_A(Lx_2,\text{ATTR-X}_{i,A}(Lx_o,\tau x_4))$ by induction hypothesis

$=(Lx_2)(\text{ATTR-X}_{i,A}(Lx_o,\tau x_4))$ by definition of EVAL_A

$=\text{abstract}((Lx_2)\circ \text{ATTR-X}_{i,A}(\tau x_4)(Lx_o)$ by definition of abstract (cf.4.2)

$=f(Lx_o)$ by definition of $\text{LAMBDA-X}_{i,A}$

$=Lx_o$. since $Lx_o=\text{lfp}(f)$

REFERENCES

/Backus 78/ J. Backus: Can Programming be Liberated from the von Neumann Style? A Functional Style and its Algebra of Programs; CACM Vol. 21, No.8, August 1978

/CM 72/ J.M. Cadiou/ Z. Manna: Recursive Definitions of Partial Functions and their Computations; SIGPLAN Notices, Vol.7, No.1, 58-65, 1972

/Eh 78/ H. Ehrig: Introduction to the Algebraic Theory of Graph Grammars; this volume

/ER 77/ H. Ehrig/ B.K. Rosen: The Mathematics of Record Handling; Proc. 4th International Colloquium on Automata, Languages and Programming, Turku 1977, Springer Lect. Notes in Comp. Sci. 52, 206-220

/GHM 76/ J.V. Guttag/ E. Horowitz/ D.R. Musser: Abstract Data Types and Software Validation; University of Southern California Information Sci. Institute RR-76-48, 1976

/GTW^2 77/ J.A. Goguen/ J.W. Thatcher/ E.G. Wagner: Initial Algebra Semantics and Continuous Algebras; J.ACM, Vol.24, No. 1, 68-95, 1977

REFERENCES (cont'd)

/HM 76/ P.Henderson/J.H.Morris: A Lazy Evaluator; Proc.Third ACM Symposium on Principles of Programming Languages (1976), 95-103

/LS 77/ D.J.Lehmann/M.B.Smyth: Data Types; University of Warwick, Dept.of Comp.Sci., Theory of Computation Report No.19,1977

/Niv 74/ M.Nivat: On the Interpretation of Recursive Program Schemes; Universität Saarbrücken, Technical Report A74/09, 1974

/Pad 78/ P.Padawitz: Operationelle und funktionale Semantik von Σ -Graphen; Forschungsbericht der TU Berlin, FB 20, Nr.78-23, 1978

/Pad 78a/ ---: Graph Grammars and Operational Semantics; Forschungsbericht der TU Berlin, FB 20, Nr.78-33,1978

/Ros 73/ B.K.Rosen: Tree-Manipulating Systems and Church-Rosser Theorems; J.ACM,Vol.20,No.1,160-187, 1973

/Scott 72/ D.Scott: Continuous Lattices, in: Toposes, Algebraic Geometry and Logic (ed. by F.W.Lawvere), Springer Lect. Notes in Mathematics 274, 97-136, 1972

/Scott 74/ ---: Data Types as Lattices; Proc.International Summer Institute and Logic Colloquium, Kiel 1974, Springer Lect. Notes in Math. 499, and SIAM Journ. on Computing 5(1976) 522-587

/Vui 74/ J.Vuillemin: Correct and Optimal Implementations of Recursion in a Simple Programming Language, J.Comp. Syst.Sci., Vol.9,No.3, 332-354, 1974

COMPLEXITY OF PATTERN GENERATION BY MAP-L SYSTEMS*

Abridged Version

by

A. Paz and Y. Raz

Computer Science Department
Technion - Israel Institute of Technology
Haifa, Israel

1. INTRODUCTION

A certain type of two-dimensional generative grammars has been introduced in [1] intended as a theoretical model for the development of organisms with two-dimensional characteristics. Such a grammar will generate out of a single cell (egg) a sequence of plannar topological patterns (maps) according to a preassigned finite set of context sensitive rules. At each stage of the generation the rules are applied simultaneously to the existing pattern in order to create the next pattern by a binary (at most) splitting of its "cells" (a process which is similar to the generation process of an actual living organism). In order to account for the environmental context governing the splitting process, the cells are assumed to be in one out of a finite set of "states" (represented by letters or colors belonging to a given alphabet) at each stage of the generation. The pattern is thus assumed to be "colored", and the coloration changes from generation to generation according to the rules of the two-dimensional grammar. The model described intuitively above allows one to define and study the complexity of pattern generation by two-dimensional grammars in several aspects such as: (a) Is it possible to find a number m such that for any given specific uncolored pattern in the plane, there exists a grammar with no more than m colors which will generate the given pattern among all the patterns generated by it? (b) What is the relation between the number

---

* This work is based on the D.Sc. research of the second author under the supervision of the first.

of colors of a given grammar and the speed of generation of the patterns generated by it?

Those and similar questions are investigated in this paper. It is shown e.g. that the answer to the question (a) above is negative and that there actually exists an infinite sequence of patterns $\{M_i\}$ such that the pattern M_i in the sequence cannot be generated by a grammar with less than i colors, but can be generated by a grammar with $i+k$ colors for some k. This result and others enable one to establish hierarchies of complexity classes induced by two-dimensional grammars in the set of all uncolored maps, from the points of view of both speed of generation and number of letters in the alphabet.

It would be clear from the text that all the results achieved for two-dimensional grammars can be generalized to 3-dimensional grammar in an easy way.

2. DEFINITIONS AND NOTATIONS

The systems dealt with in this paper are as defined in [1] with some changes to be described below. The reader is referred to that paper for the basic definitions. Some of the definitions are repeated here for the sake of completeness. The systems described are a generalization of a special case of one-dimensional Lindenmayer systems (string producing systems) defined first in [3] and described in [4], [5], [6].

A <u>map</u> is a "plannar topological graph" as defined in [7]. The faces of the map are called countries or <u>cells</u>. A cell may be adjacent to another one through one boundary (edge) or more. Two cells having at least one common edge are <u>neighbours</u>. Every map has exactly one unbounded cell called the infinite cell or "infinity".

The maps considered in this paper are assumed to be connected and legal (i.e. without islands or island groups). (See [1] for exact definition of these concepts.) A pair of neighboring cells is <u>legal</u> if its merger does not create islands or island-groups.

A <u>colored map</u> is a map such that a label belonging to some alphabet Σ is associated with every cell in it. The symbol M will denote both colored and uncolored maps. (The type of map considered will depend on the context.) The uncolored map associated with a colored map M will be denoted $\bar{M}$. We shall use the notation $M_1 = M_2$ in two cases :

(1) M_1, M_2 are isomorphic uncolored maps.

(2) M_1, M_2 are colored maps, $\bar{M}_1 = \bar{M}_2$ according to (1) above, and the isomorphism between $\bar{M}_1$, $\bar{M}_2$ induces the identity correspondence on the cells' labels. (Corresponding cells have the same label.)

The size of a map M (notation: $|M|$) is the number of finite cells in M.

PDBIML System. A grammar or a PDBIML system G (Propagating Deterministic, with Binary division, Interactive Map Lindenmayer) is a triplet (Σ, P, MI) where:

(1) Σ, the alphabet, is a finite set of labels for the finite cells in the maps produced by G. $\infty \notin \Sigma$ is a special lable for the infinite cell.

(2) MI is the initial map. It is legal and colored by elements of Σ.

(3) P is a set of production rules — the explicit rules of G — where every rule is expressed by one of the following types of formulae:

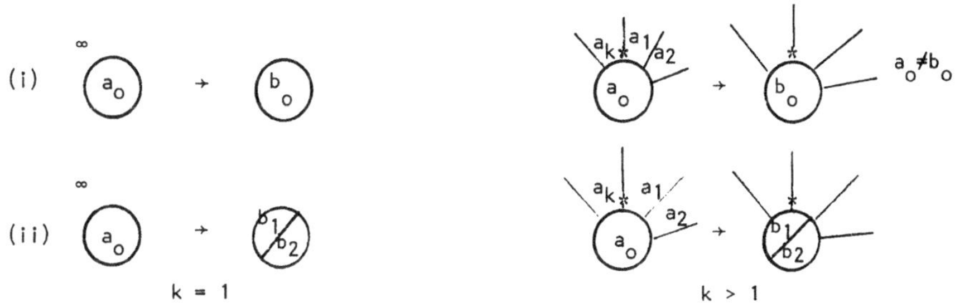

$a_0, b_0, b_1, b_2 \in \Sigma \qquad a_1, \ldots, a_k \in \Sigma \cup \{\infty\}$

Remarks. (1) The rules' graphical representation is topologically invariant.

(2) The patterns in both sides of the formulae are identical, except of an additional edge in the right side of formulae (ii).

(3) The marks '*' in the formulae define a common reference point for both sides of the formulae. The reference point is chosen arbitrarily so that every rule is invariant with regard to simultaneous rotation of both of its sides.

(4) The new edge in the right hand side of formulae (ii) may connect any two

distinct points on the boundary of the cell that splits.

(5) It is assumed in formulae (ii) that $a_1a_2 \dots a_k \neq \pi(a_1 \dots a_k)$ for any cyclic permutation π which differs from identity. (The grammar is assumed to be deterministic.)

(6) There are no two rules in P with the same left hand side.

(7) The set of words: $a_1a_2 \dots a_k$ and all its cyclic permutations is called the context of the rule. k is the rule's context height.
The explicit context's height of a grammar G (notation: $|G|$) is the highest context height of some explicit rule of G. (It is always a finite natural number.)

The production of maps induced by grammars. $M_G(1)$, the first map generated, is MI. $M_G(n+1)$ is produced from $M_G(n)$ (the n-th map) the same way as in [1].
A submap is a connected (by neighbourhood relationship) set of finite cells in a map. (Notation: A(n) is a submap of $M_G(n)$.)

We are now able to define complexity measures on legal uncolored maps. These measures are the basis for the main investigation of this paper and are described below. The complexity classes introduced are defined by PDBIML systems with a single cell initial map ("egg").

(1) C_m^n - The set of uncolored maps produced by some grammar with m letters at the n-th step.

(2) $C_m^{(n)}$- As in (1), but the maps are not produced by any m letter grammar at a step $n' < n$.

(3) C_m - The set of uncolored maps produced by some grammar with m letters.

(4) C^n - The set of uncolored maps produced by some grammar at the n-th step.

3. THE PRODUCTION POWER OF PDBIML SYSTEMS

It is shown in [1] that every map can be produced by a grammar. We shall give here a different proof which will imply some additional results.

Theorem 3.1. For every uncolored map M with size ℓ $M \in C_\ell^\ell$.

Proof. To prove that M with $|M| = \ell$ is in C_ℓ^ℓ we construct a grammar G which produces M as follows:

A cell A in M is chosen arbitrarily together with a neighbour B such that (A,B) is a legal pair. (The existance of such a B for every A is proved in [1].) The cells A and B are labelled with the labels a_ℓ and b respectively. All other cells are labelled c. This colored map will be $M_G(\ell)$. Merging A, B into a cell A' we get a new map M' with $|M'| = \ell-1$. The labels $a_{\ell-1}, b, c$ are now set on A', B' — a legal neighbour of A' — and all the other cells respectively. The resulting map is the colored map $M_G(\ell-1)$. In the same way $M_G(n-1)$ is constructed from $M_G(n)$, $3 < n < \ell$, and the relation $|M_G(n-1)| = |M_G(n)| - 1$ holds. Thus $|M_G(n)| = n$ and we can define:

$M_G(2) =$ 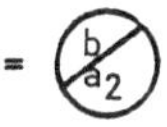

 ; $M_G(1) =$ 

 .

This process defines the grammar G as follows:

$\Sigma = \{a_1, a_2, \ldots, a_\ell, b, c\}$

$MI =$ 

and the production rules are:

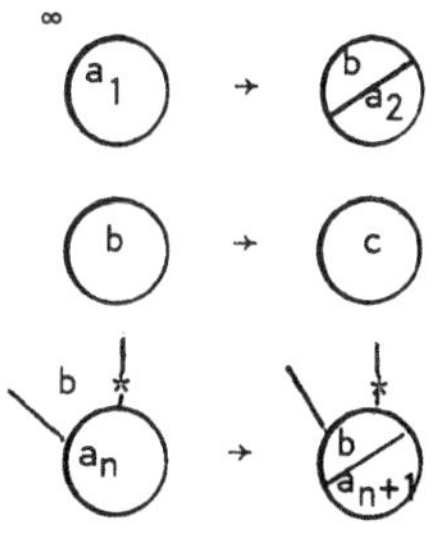

{ in any possible context of b in the sequence $M_G(n)$ $n = 2, \ldots \ell-1$.

{ according to the structure of $M_G(n)$, $M_G(n+1)$ $n = 2, \ldots \ell-1$.

Rewriting the labels a_1, a_ℓ by b and c respectively will save two letters.

Q.E.D.

4. COMPLEXITY OF STRINGS

Strings are considered here as a special case of two-dimensional maps, i.e. a cell in a string (except the first and the last one) has in fact three neighbours and not two.

Definition: A string is either a single cell or a sequence of cells having the following shape:

The notation $a_1 a_2 \ldots a_k$ denotes the colored string

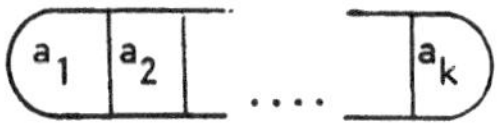

Remark. A simpler notation for the production rules for strings can be used:

(1) $a \to b|bc$ for

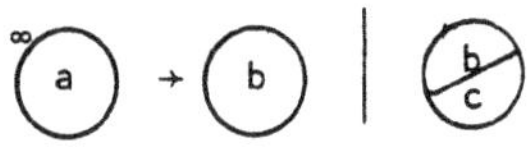

(2) $(\infty,a,b) \to c|cd$ or $(b,a,\infty) \to c|dc$ for

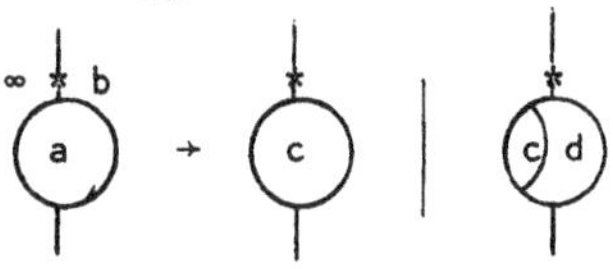

(3) $(b,a,c) \to d|de$ or $(c,a,b) \to d|ed$ for

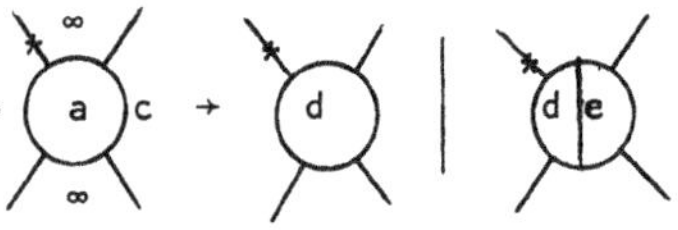

Theorem 4.1. For every string M, $|M| = \ell$ we have that $M \in C_2^{\ell}$.

Proof. The following grammar $G = (\Sigma,P,I)$ produces all the (uncolored) strings.

$$\Sigma = \{a,b\} \ ; \qquad IM = b$$

$$P = \{b \to ab,\ (a,b,\infty) \to ab\}$$

Q.E.D.

Theorem 4.2. For every string M of length ℓ we have that $M \in C_{n-2}^{(n)}$ where $n = \lceil \log_2 \ell \rceil + 1$.

Proof. Let $(b_1 b_2 \ldots b_k)$ be the binary representation of $\ell-1$ thus $\ell-1 = b_1 \cdot 2^{k-1} + b_2 \cdot 2^{k-2} + \ldots + b_k\ 2^0$, where

$$b_1 = 1 \ ; \quad b_i = \{^0_1 \quad k \geqslant i > 1 \ ; \quad k = \lceil \log_2 \ell \rceil \ .$$

Let G be the following grammar :

$G = (\Sigma, P, \bar{b}_1)$ where

$\Sigma = \{a, \bar{b}_1, \bar{b}_2 \dots \bar{b}_k\}$ (k+1 letters)

P consists of the following rules :

$$\bar{b}_1 \to \bar{b}_2 a$$

$$\begin{matrix} (\infty, b_i a) \\ 1 < i < k \end{matrix} \to \begin{cases} \bar{b}_{i+1} a & \text{if } b_i = 1 \\ \bar{b}_{i+1} & \text{if } b_i = 0 \end{cases}$$

$$\left.\begin{matrix} (x,a,\infty) \to aa \\ (x,a,a) \to aa \end{matrix}\right\} \text{ for every } x \in \Sigma$$

It is easy to verify that

$$M_G(i) = \bar{b}_i aa \dots a \qquad i \geq 2$$

where the number of cells labelled "a" is

$$|M_G(i)| -1 = b_{i-1} + 2(|M_G(i-1)| -1) .$$

Hence $|M_G(k+1)| = \ell$.

The letters $\bar{b}_1$, $\bar{b}_k$ can be saved replacing them by "a" in the rules in which they appear.

As $|M_G(i)| \leq 2^{i-1}$ (binary division), ℓ cannot be constructed in less than k+1 steps. Q.E.D.

The last theorem gives us the maximal speed at which a string can be constructed. The next theorem will give a lower bound for the number of letters needed (the worst case) for producing a string at maximal speed.

Lemma 4.3. Let G be a grammar of m letters, and let $M_G(n_o)$ be a string of length ≥ 3. Suppose that starting at step n_o for $(m+1)^5$ consecutive steps every cell splits in a way such that the resulting maps are strings. Then only the rules that were active during these steps can be active in the consequent generation.

Corollary. All the consequent maps will be stringlike doubling their length at every step.

Proof. Let $A(n+1) = x_1x_2x_3x_4x_5$ be any submap of $M_G(n+1)$ of size 5. This submap is derived in one of the following two types of derivation :

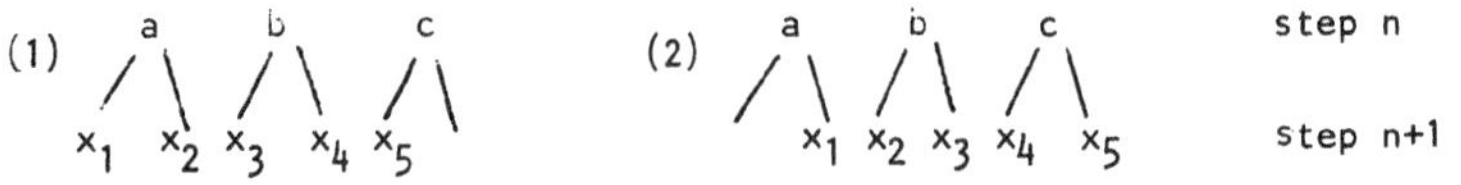

$$a,b,c,\ x_i \in \Sigma \quad i = 1 \ldots 5 .$$

The above observation shows that the substring of $M_G(n)$ which determines the generation of a substring in $M_G(n+1)$ of length 5 is of length $\leqslant 5$ (three generating cells and two celss to fix the context, including the case where one of those two is ∞).

Denote by $F(n)$ the number of all different substrings of length 5 of all the strings $M_G(n_o)$, $M_G(n_o+1)$ ... $M_G(n)$, where n_o is the smallest integer such that $|M_G(n_o)| \geqslant 3$ and $n \geqslant n_o$. By definition $F(n+1) \geqslant F(n)$ and it follows from the remark above that if for some k, $F(n_o+k) = F(n_o+k+1)$ then $F(n_o+k) = F(n_o+j)$, $j > k$. Thus we have that for some k

$$F(n_o) < F(n_o+1) < \ldots < F(n_o+k-1) = F(n_o+k) = \ldots$$

As there are at most $(m+1)^5$ different substrings of length 5 ($m+1$ is the number of letters in $\Sigma \cup \{\infty\}$) it is clear that $k < (m+1)^5$. Hence only production rules which were active during the steps $n_o, n_o+1 \ldots n_o+k-1$ can be active later on.

Q.E.D.

Theorem 4.4. Every string M of size $2^{n-1}-1$, $n > 1$, has the property that if $M \in C_m^{(n)}$ then $(m+1)^5 > n-4$.

Proof. Let $|M| = 2^{n-1}-1$. Hence $M \in C_m^{(n)}$ for some m (Theorem 4.2) and $M = \overline{M_G(n)}$ for G with m letters. If in $M_G(n_o)$, $n_o < n-1$, there is a cell which does not split when $M_G(n_o+1)$ is formed then $|M_G(n)| \leqslant 2^{n-1}-2^{n-n_o-1}$ (binary division), and hence $|M_G(n)| < 2^{n-1}-1$ — a contradiction.

Thus $M_G(n-1)$ is the first configuration in which some cell does not split, and at the first $n-2$ steps all the rules used are splitting rules. Hence $|M_G(3)| = 4$ and $(m+1)^5 > n-4$. (It follows from Lemma 4.3 that the condition $2+(m+1)^5 \leqslant n-2$ ensures that all the cells in $M_G(n-1)$ split.) Q.E.D.

5. THE CHANGES INDUCED BY THE VARIATION OF m ON THE CLASS C_m^n

One can easily show that:

$$C_m^n \subset C_{m+1}^n \quad . \tag{1}$$

The number of grammars with m letters and explicit height not greater then r is finite. A subset of those grammars generate finite languages only. Let $k(m,r)$ be the maximal size of a map generated by any grammar in the above (finite) subset of grammars. Let $M_G(n_o)$ be a map generated by some grammar with m letters and explicit heights not greater than r at time n_o. It follows from the above considerations that

$$\text{if} \qquad |M_G(n_o)| > k(m,r) \quad \text{then} \quad \lim_{n\to\infty}|M_G(n)| = \infty \ . \tag{2}$$

(Notice also that $k(m,r) \leqslant k(m+1,r)$.)

Given a grammar G it is clear that if $|M_G(n)|$ does not grow for too many consecutive steps then it will not grow any more. Therefore, there exists a function $f_m(n)$ such that

$$\lim_{n\to\infty}|M_G(n)| = \infty \Rightarrow |M_G(n)| \geqslant f_m(n) \ . \tag{3}$$

It can be shown that the function $f_m(n) = \log_m[(m-1)n+m]-1$ has the above property (3). In addition this function satisfies the following relations :

$$f_{m'}(n) > f_m(n) \qquad \text{for} \quad m > m' \geqslant 2 \tag{4}$$

$$\lim_{n\to\infty} \frac{f_m(n)}{\log_m n} = 1 \ . \tag{5}$$

<u>Lemma 5.1.</u> No string M such that $k(m,4) < |M| < f_m(n)$ can be generated by a grammar G with m letters or less at time n.

<u>Proof.</u> Follows from (2), (3), (4).

<u>Lemma 5.2.</u> There is a string M and a number n such that $k(m,4) < |M| < f_n(n)$ and M is generated by a grammar G with $m+3$ letters at time n.

The proof is based on the construction of a grammar as specified in the lemma with growth asymptotic to $\log_{m+1}n$ (see (5) above).

Theorem 5.3. For every m there is n_o such that :

$$C_m^n \subsetneq C_{m+3}^n \qquad \text{for } n \geq n_o .$$

Proof. Follows from (1) and Lemmas 5.1 and 5.2.

Conjecture: $C_m^n \subsetneq C_{m+1}^n$.

6. THE SEQUENCE C_m IS AN INFINITE HIERARCHY

It is clear that :

$$C_m \subset C_{m+1} \quad . \tag{*}$$

In order to prove the main result of this section we shall need the following facts:

(a) The number of different grammars single-cell initial map, m letters in the alphabet and explicit context height not greater than r is finite and depends on r and m. Denote this number by $NG(m,r)$.

Definition. A three-arm is a map having the following shape:

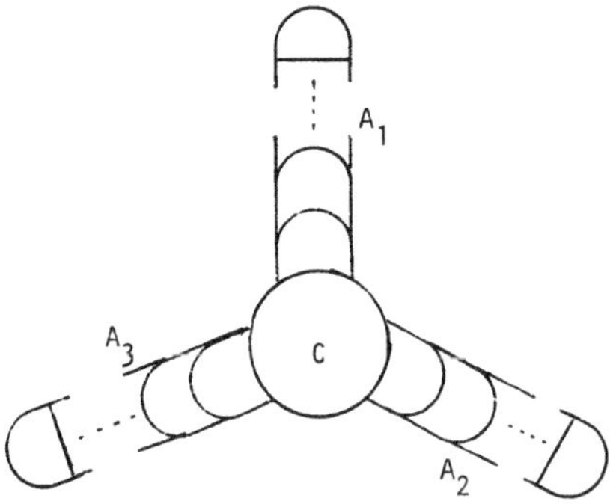

The submaps A_1, A_2, A_3 are the "Arms" and C is the "Center".

(b) Let $M_G(n_o)$ be a three-arm generated by a grammar G with alphabet Σ, then there exists a grammar G' over the same alphabet with an explicit context height not greater than 6, such that $M_G(n) = M_{G'}(n)$, $1 \leq n \leq n_o$.
G' can be constructed using the fact that every mother map of a three arm is itself either a three arm or a string, so that every rule in G with context height bigger than 6 can be omitted.

(c) Let $(a_1a_2a_3)$ be a vector of numbers associated with a three arm such that a_i

is the length of the arm A_i. It is clear that the number of different such vectors with the property that $a_1+a_2+a_3 = \ell$ is $\geqslant k\ell^2$ where k is a constant.

(d) Let G be a given grammar and let ℓ be an integer. The number of different uncolored 3-arms generated by G with associated vector (a_1,a_2,a_3) and $a_1+a_2+a_3 = \ell$ is zero or one. This follows from the fact that the only way to generated a new uncolored 3-arm from an existing one is by increasing some of its arms.

We are able now to prove the main result of this section.

Lemma 6.1. For every m there is a three-arm M which cannot be constructed by a grammar with m letters or less ($M \notin C_{m'}$ for $m' \leqslant m$).

Proof. The number of different 3-arms with associated length vector $(a_1 a_2 a_3)$ and $a_1+a_2+a_3 = \ell$ which can be generated by some grammar with m-letters or less is at most $NG(m,6)$ by (a), (b) and (d) above. On the other hand the number of different such 3-arms $\geqslant k\ell^2$ by (c) and for large enough ℓ $k\ell^2 > NG(m,6)$.

Theorem 6.2: For every m there is $k > 0$ such that

$$C_m \subsetneqq C_{m+k} \quad .$$

Proof. It follows from (*) that $C_m \subset C_{m+k}$, $k > 0$.
By Lemma 6.1 there is a map $M \notin C_m$. If $|M| = \ell$ then $M \in C_\ell$ (Theorem 3.1). It is clear that $\ell > m$ hence for $k = \ell-m$ $M \in C_{m+k}$.

Q.E.D.

Conjecture:
$C_m \subsetneqq C_{m+1}$

7. SUMMARY

There are additional results which can be proved such as the following:

Theorem 7.1: (1) $C_m^n \subsetneqq C_{m+1}^{n+1}$ (2) $C^n \subsetneqq C^{n+1}$.

Theorem 7.2: For every m there is n_o such that for any $n \geqslant n_o$ there is $k_o(m,n)$ such that C_m^n, C_m^{n+k} are incomparable but not disjoint for $k \geqslant k_o(m,n)$.

Conjecture: $k_o(m,n) \equiv 1$.

One can summarize the results exhibited in this paper in the following two-dimensional infinite diagram:

$$
\begin{array}{ccccccccccc}
 & \vdots & & \vdots & & \vdots & & & & \vdots \\
\cdots & C^{n}_{m} & \rightarrow & C^{n}_{m+1} & \rightarrow & C^{n}_{m+2} & \rightarrow & \cdots & \rightarrow & C^{n} \\
 & & \searrow & & \searrow & & \searrow & & & \downarrow \\
\cdots & C^{n+1}_{m} & \rightarrow & C^{n+1}_{m+1} & \rightarrow & C^{n+1}_{m+2} & \rightarrow & \cdots & \rightarrow & C^{n+1} \\
 & & \searrow & & \searrow & & \searrow & & & \downarrow \\
\cdots & C^{n+2}_{m} & \rightarrow & C^{n+2}_{m+1} & \rightarrow & C^{n+2}_{m+2} & \rightarrow & \cdots & \rightarrow & C^{n+2} \\
 & & \searrow & & \searrow & & & & & \downarrow \\
 & \vdots & & \vdots & & \vdots & \searrow & & & \vdots \\
 & \downarrow & & \downarrow & & \downarrow & & & & \\
\cdots & C_{m} & \rightarrow & C_{m+1} & \rightarrow & C_{m+2} & \rightarrow & \cdots & &
\end{array}
$$

The symbol ' $\rightarrow$ ' stands for inclusion relation and strict inclusion or equality appear according to the theorems in this paper.

BIBLIOGRAPHY

[1] Carlyle, J.W., Greibach, S.A., Paz, A., "A Two-Dimensional Generating System Modelling Growth by Binary Cell Division", IEEE 15th Annual Symposium on Switching and Automata Theory, October 1974, 1-12.

[2] Mayoh, B.H., "Mathematical Models for Cellular Organisms", T.R. DAIMI PB-12, Datalogiok Afdeling, Aarhus Universitet, April 1973.

[3] Lindenmayer, A., "Mathematical Models for Cellular Interactions in Development", Part I, J. of Theoretical Biology, 1968, Vol.18, 280-299.

Lindenmayer, A., "Mathematical Models for Cellular Interactions in Development", Part II, J. Of Theoretical Biology, 1968, Vol. 18, 300-315.

[4] G.T. Herman & G. Rozenberg, Developmental Systems and Languages. North - Holland Publishing Co., 1975.

[5] Rozenberg, G. and A. Salomaa (ed.) L Systems, Springer lecture notes in Computer Science, Vol. 15, 1974.

[6] A. Lindenmayer and G. Rozenberg (ed.) Automata, Languages, Development. North-Holland Publishing Co., 1976.

[7] Berge, C. The Theory of Graphs and its Applications. Methuen & Co., Ltd., London, 1962.

A GRAPH GRAMMAR THAT DESCRIBES THE SET OF
TWO-DIMENSIONAL SURFACE NETWORKS

John L. Pfaltz
University of Virginia
Charlottesville, Virginia

By a grammar one means a set of rewrite rules (or productions) which are applied in some systematic way to generate (or parse) objects in some set comprising the language of the grammar. We call it a graph (or web) grammar if elements (or symbols) within an object of the language may have more than two immediate neighbors. This is in contrast to a traditional string grammar in which any element may have at most one left-hand and one right-hand neighbor. Such a general notion of a "graph grammar" proviede a wide latitude for application; from the piecewise definition of a single state-space graph used in problem solving [5], to relatively trivial "context-free" phrase structure type grammars which define a set of rooted trees [3]. The application of the rewrite rules may be sequential, in a standard Chomsky fashion [7], or may be parallel as in a Lindenmayer system [4]. Object in the language may be irregularly shaped graphs, or they may be regular arrangements of cells, such as images [10].

Our formulation of the rewriting process will be as follows. Let ϕ be any rewrite rule that is to be applied to some (intermediate) graph G. Typically ϕ will take some subgraph H in G (in all our cases H will be only a single point) and replace it with (rewrite it as) some new subgraph, H'. Thus the basic rewrite rule may be expressed in the form

$$\phi: H \Longrightarrow H'$$

where it is customary to specify H and H' as pictures, for example,

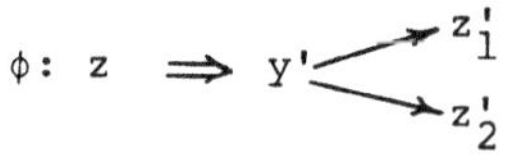

ϕ is assumed to be the identity map on all other points in $G \sim H$, and on all edges (p,q) where $p,q \in G \sim H$. Now "surrounding" H in G is some kind of context, call it C_H, consisting of all points that are adjacent to H and possibly some more that are "near", but not adjacent to H. $C_H \subseteq G \sim H$. ϕ can not be simply defined to be the identiy map on these edges. Instead the rewrite rule must explicitly specify some set of edges, E_ϕ, between $\phi(H) = H'$ and $\phi(C_H)$ which "embeds" H' in the "hole" left in $\phi(G \sim H)$. We call the specification of such edges the embedding of ϕ, [6]. Since the context C_H of H in G can normally be quite varied, embeddings can seldom be specified by a "pictorial graph" as above, but rather require an algorithmic specification. To all our rewrite rules we will append this embedding algorithm.

A surface is a smooth differentiable function, $f(x_1,...,x_n)$ of several variables. In this paper we will always let n = 2. One can visualize the surface by means of a standard contour map, as in figure L. Points on the surface where f is "locally flat", that is

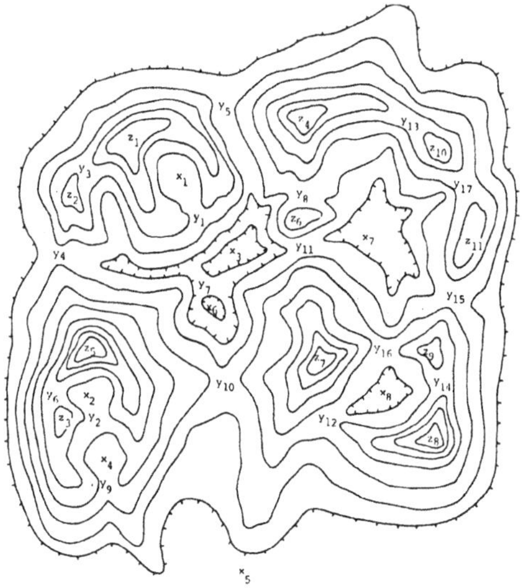

Figure 1
A Hypothetical
Surface

$\nabla f = 0$, are called points of equilibrium, or critical points of the surface. The critical points of a surface of two variables may be classified as pits (relative minima), passes (saddles), or peaks (relative maxima) and denoted by the sets $\{x_i\}$, $\{y_j\}$, $\{z_k\}$. These are shown on figure 1.

The critical points may be joined together to form a surface network by connecting each pit to its associated passes by directed edges which follow the course (stream) lines, and by connecting each pass to its associated peaks by directed edges which follow the ridge lines. Figure 2 illustrates the surface network associated with the functional surface of figure 1. Here we have represented a relation (x_i,y_j) between a pit and a pass by a dashed edge; a relation (y_j,z_k) between a pass and a peak by a solid edge. Note that: 1) edges in a surface network are abstract relationships

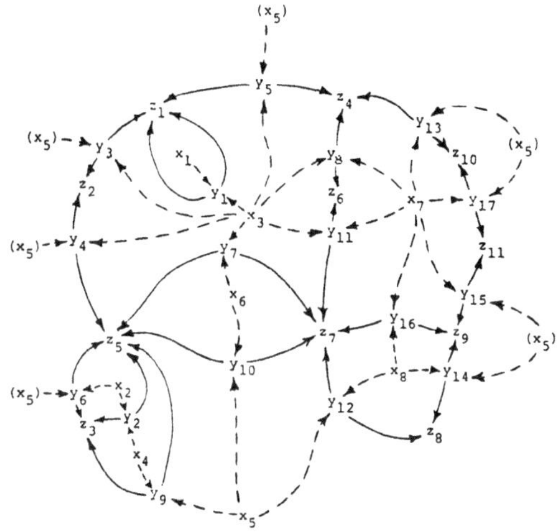

Figure 2

The Surface Network Associated with the Surface of Figure 1

without shape, however we draw them in this paper so as to follow the courses and ridges of figure 1 for a kind of intuitive clarity; 2) the pit x_5 corresponds to the "ocean" surrounding this "topological island" and is connected to many passes, for example y_3 and y_5; 3) the presence of a circuit of "dashed" course edges surrounding each peak and a circuit of "solid" ridge edges surrounding each pit. Much of the terminology in surface networks has been coined by geographers who use them as a tool for studying topographic terrain and spatial functions; for example, Warntz [11] calls the regions enclosed by the circuits above, "hills" and "dales".

Surface networks therefore constitute an "interesting" class of graphs. They can be arbitrarily large, and of varying complexity. Moreover, since they are derived from real physical phenomena (actual functional surfaces), the class as a whole has definite structure. An arbitrarily generated graph is unlikely to be a surface network. But how can we characterize the class of surface networks? I tried in [8] to define a surface network as:

a tri-partite graph $G = (X,Y,Z,E)$, where $X = \{x_i\}$, $Y = \{y_j\}$, and $Z = \{z_k\}$ are the three disjoint sets of points and E is a set of edges of the form (x_i,y_j) or (y_j,z_k), such that

1. G is connected,
2. $|X| - |Y| + |Z| = 2$,
3. for all $y \in Y$, $id(y) = od(y) = 2$,
4. $val(x,y_j) = val(y_j,z) = 1$ implies there exists $y^* \in Y$

such that (x,y^*) and $(y^*,z) \varepsilon E$,

5a. (x,y) is an edge of a circuit in the bipartite subgraph $[X,Y]$ if and only if $val(y,z) \neq 2$ for any $z \varepsilon Z$,

5b. (y,z) is an edge of a circuit in the bipartite subgraph $[Y,Z]$ if and only if $val(x,y) \neq 2$ for any $x \varepsilon X$.

In this definition, $val(y,z)$ denotes the "valency" of an edge. Normally an edge is a simple edge with valency = 1, but we may have edges that actually correspond to two ridge or course lines, for example see the edge(s) (y_1,z_1) in figure 2. Such an edge (pass-peak relationship) is said to have valency 2.

It can be shown that properties 1 thru 5b are necessary conditions for a graph to be a surface network. It was stated in [8] that it was unknown if they were sufficient conditions, which is just as well since they are indeed not sufficient, as was pointed out by Dave Mark in [1]. An effective sufficient characterization is still undemonstrated. Instead in this paper we will characterize the class of surface networks by means of a grammar, G, in which the rewrite rules (or productions) correspond to physical processes. Visualize an existing surface (possibly represented by a flexible rubber sheet or a clay model) in which a peak z is in a "hill" bounded by a circuit of alternating passes and pits with their joining course lines. We wish to split the existing peak by "punching up", or otherwise adding, a second peak within this region. Call this operation α. Figure 3 shows some possible resulting configurations in the case of a peak with 4 incident ridges. We can represent the the physical operation α as the following rewrite rule.

$$\alpha_{m,n}: z \Longrightarrow y' \begin{array}{l} \nearrow z'_1 \\ \searrow z'_2 \end{array}$$

embedding procedure

1. Let $\langle x_1\ y_{1,2}\ x_2 \ldots x_n\ y_{n,1}\rangle$ be the bounding circuit of z, $n \geq 2$.
2. Choose m, $1 \leq m \leq n$.
3. If $2 \leq m \leq n$

$$E_\alpha = \{(x_1,y')(y_{1,2},z'_1) \ldots (y_{m-1},z'_1)$$
$$(x_m,y')(y_{m,m+1},z'_2) \ldots (y_{n,1},z'_2)\}$$

if $m = 1$

$$E_\alpha = \{val(x_1,y')=2\ (y_{1,2},z'_1) \ldots (y_{n,1},z'_1)\}$$

4. If for some y, $val(y,z)=2$ then $val(y,z'_1)=2$.

The reader should convince himself that this rewrite rule, with

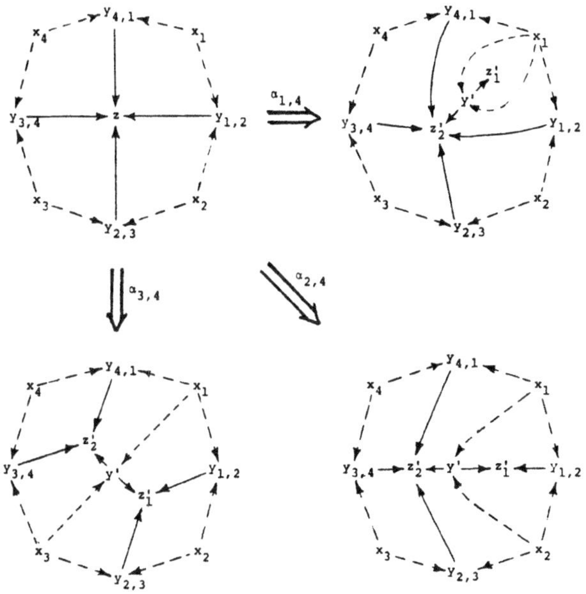

Figure 3

Operation α
(peak splitting)

embedding steps 1, 2, and 3, does in fact capture the physical splitting process shown in figure 3. (Step 4 merely asserts, if there is an additional double ridge connected to z, preserve it.) Note that the choice of the pit in the circuit to be x_1 is arbitrary. Cyclic rotation yields different (and all possible) configurations.

However, process $\alpha_{m,n}$ is insuficient by itself. Figure 4 shows a peak creation process which affects a small dale created by a double ridge. A second peak splitting rewrite rule describes

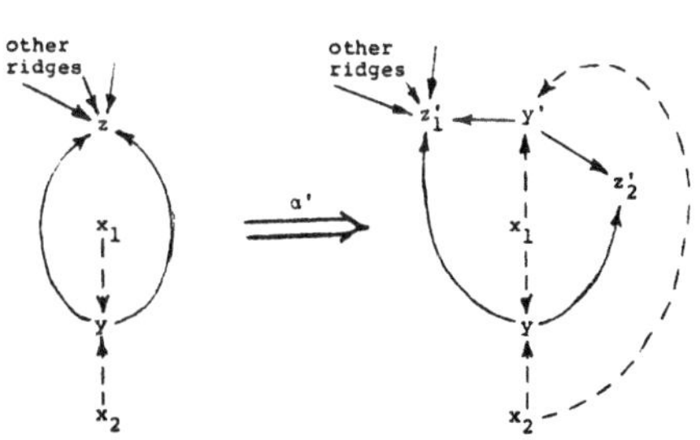

Figure 4

Operation α'
(peak splitting)

this process.

$$\alpha': z \Longrightarrow y' \begin{array}{l} \nearrow z'_1 \\ \searrow z'_2 \end{array}$$

embedding procedure

1'. val(y,z)=2, so there exists x_1, x_2 such that (x_1, y) and $(x_2, y) \in E$. (See lemma 1 [8])

$E_{\alpha'} = \{(x_1, y')(x_2, y')(y, z_1')(y, z_2')\}$

2'. If $<x_1\ y_{1,2}\ x_2\ \ldots\ x_n\ y_{n,1}>$ is a bounding circuit then $(y_{i,i+1}, z_1')$ for all i.

Note that step 2' (as step 4 above) simply preserves the surrounding circuit if one exists. Further both α and α' can be regarded as a single rewrite process with two alternative embedding procedures, one, or either, of which may be used depending on the configuration of ridges incident to the peak z, provided there are at least two.

In a completely analogous fashion one can visualize the splitting of an existing pit, x, by "punching down" a second pit within the "dale" bounded by a circuit of alternating passes and peaks with their joining ridge lines. To same space we will present the evuivalent rewriting process, β, as a single rule with two alternative embedding procedures.

$$\beta_{m,n}: x \Longrightarrow \begin{matrix} x_1' \dashrightarrow \\ \\ x_2' \dashrightarrow \end{matrix} y'$$

embedding procedure(s)

1. Let $<z_1\ y_{1,2}\ z_2\ \ldots\ z_n\ y_{n,1}>$ be a bounding circuit of x, n > 2.
2. Choose m, $1 \leqslant m \leqslant n$
3. If $2 \leqslant m \leqslant n$

   $E_\beta = \{(y', z_1)(x_1', y_{1,2})\ \ldots\ (x_1', y_{m-1,m})$
   $(y', z_m)(x_2', y_{m,m+1})\ \ldots\ (x_2', y_{n,1})\}$

   if m = 1

   $E_\beta = \{val(y', z_1)=2\ (x_1', y_{1,2})\ \ldots\ (x_1', y_{n,1})\}$
4. If for some y, val(x,y)=2 then $val(y, z_1')=2$.

1'. val(x,y)=2 for some y, so there exist z_1, z_2 such that (y, z_1) and $(y, z_2) \in E$.

$E_{\beta'} = \{(y', z_1)(y', z_2)(x_1', y)(x_2', y)\}$

2'. If $<z_1\ y_{1,2}\ z_2\ \ldots\ z_n\ z_{n,1}>$is a bounding circuit then $(y_{i,i+1}, z_1')$ for all i.

The graph grammar, G, of the title consists of the rewrite rules $\alpha_{m,n}$, α', $\beta_{m,n}$, and β'; together with the two initial networks of figure 5. (We require that a surface network have at least one pass so that it will be tri-partite. These are the simplest such

Figure 5

Initial Graphs
for the Grammar *G*

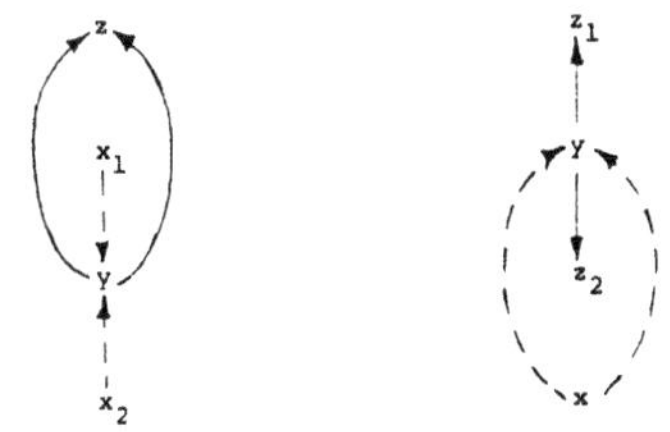

surface networks.) Since every intermediate graph is a well-formed surface network, the generation process can be terminated whenever desired; there is not need to specify either a terminal or non-terminal vocabulary.

The best feeling for this grammar can be obtained by following a few steps in the generation process. Suppose that the graph G_1 of figure 6 has been generated by a sequence of applications of the rewrite rules. It is sufficiently complex that it will provide an interesting context for the application of further rules. For each

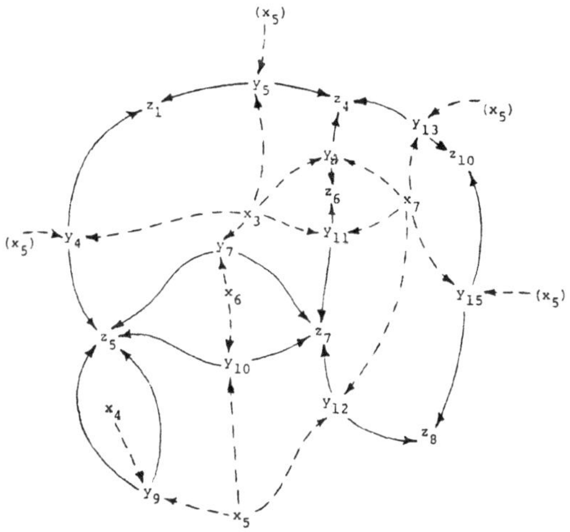

Figure 6

An Intermediate
Surface Network, G_1

rule applied we will specify the point being rewritten, the new rewritten subgraph, the surrounding context of the rewritten point, and the edges of the derived embedding. We may apply the following three rewrite rules (either sequentially or in parallel).

$$\alpha_{2,2}\colon z_1 \Longrightarrow y_3' \begin{matrix} \nearrow z_1' \\ \searrow z_2' \end{matrix}$$

$$C_{z_1} = \langle x_5\ y_5\ x_3\ y_4 \rangle$$
$$E_\alpha(z_1) = \{(x_5,y_3')(y_5,z_1')(x_3,y_3')(y_4,z_2')\}$$

$$\beta_{4,5}\colon x_7 \Longrightarrow \begin{matrix} x'_7 \dashrightarrow \\ x'_8 \dashrightarrow \end{matrix} y'_{16}$$

$C_{x_7} = \langle z_6\ y_8\ z_4\ y_{13}\ z_{10}\ y_{15}\ z_8\ y_{12}\ z_7\ y_{11}\rangle$

$E_\beta(x_7) = \{(y'_{16},z_6)\,(x'_7,y_8)\,(x'_7,y_{13})\,(x'_7,y_{15})$
$(y'_{16},z_8)\,(x'_8,y_{12})\,(x'_8,y_{11})\}$

- -

$$\alpha'\colon z_5 \Longrightarrow y'_6 \begin{matrix} \nearrow z'_5 \\ \searrow z'_3 \end{matrix}$$

$$C_{z_5} = \begin{cases} \langle x_5\ y_4\ x_3\ y_7\ x_6\ y_{10}\rangle \\ \mathrm{val}(y_9,z_5)=2 \end{cases}$$

$E_{\alpha'}(z_5) = \{(x_4,y'_6)\,(x_5,y'_6)\,(y_9,z'_5)\,(y_9,z'_3)$
$(y_4,z'_5)\,(y_7,z'_5)\,(y_{10},z'_5)\}$

Application of the rewriting processes $\alpha_{2,2}(z_1)$, $\beta_{4,5}(x_7)$, and $\alpha'(z_5)$ to G_1 produces the surface network G_2 of figure 7, below.

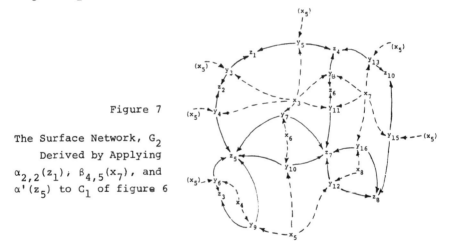

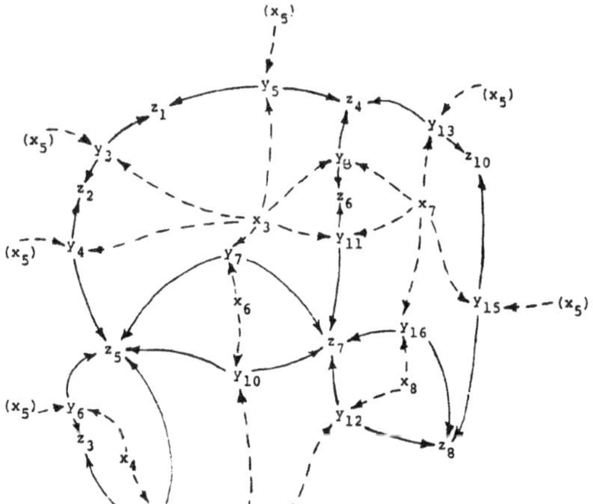

Figure 7

The Surface Network, G_2 Derived by Applying $\alpha_{2,2}(z_1)$, $\beta_{4,5}(x_7)$, and $\alpha'(z_5)$ to G_1 of figure 6

To this intermediate graph we may apply the following four rewrite rules.

$$\beta_{1,6}\colon x_3 \Longrightarrow \begin{matrix} x'_1 \dashrightarrow \\ x'_3 \dashrightarrow \end{matrix} y'_1$$

$C_{x_3} = \langle z_1\ y_5\ z_4\ y_8\ y_{11}\ z_7\ y_7\ z_5\ y_4\ z_2\ y_3\rangle$

$E_\beta(x_3) = \{\mathrm{val}(y'_1,z_1)=2\ \ (x'_3,y_5)\ \ldots\ (x'_3,y_3)\}$

$\alpha_{2,2}: z_{10} \Longrightarrow y'_{17}$ (branching to z'_{10} and z'_{11})

$C_{z_{10}} = \langle x_7\ y_{13}\ x_5\ y_{15} \rangle$

$E_\alpha(z_{10}) = \{(x_7,y'_{17})(y_{13},z'_{10})(x_5,y'_{17})(y_{15},z'_{11})\}$

- -

$\alpha_{3,3}: z_8 \Longrightarrow y'_{14}$ (branching to z'_9 and z'_{10})

$C_{z_8} = \langle x_8\ y_{16}\ x_7\ y_{15}\ x_5\ y_{12} \rangle$

$E_\alpha(z_8) = \{(x_8,y'_{14})(y_{16},z'_9)(y_{15},z'_9)(x_5,y'_{14})(y_{12},z'_8)\}$

- -

$\beta_{2,2}: x_4 \Longrightarrow$ x'_2 and x'_4 (both joined to y'_2)

$C_{x_4} = \langle z_3\ y_6\ z_5\ y_9 \rangle$

$E_\beta(x_4) = \{(y'_2,z_3)(x'_2,y_6)(y'_2,z_5)(x'_4,y_9)\}$

The rewriting processes $\beta_{1,6}(x_3)$, $\alpha_{2,2}(z_{10})$, $\alpha_{3,3}(z_8)$, and $\beta_{2,2}(x_4)$ applied to surface network G_2 of figure 7 generate the original surface network of figure 2.

This grammar *G* thus provides a tool: (1) for characterizing the class of surface networks associated with functions of two variables, (2) for generating arbitrary examples of surface networks (a computer process can implement and apply the rewrite rules in a non-deterministic manner), and (3) for abstracting important features from an existing surface network by employing the same rewrite rules in a parsing mode. This latter provides a solution to one of the unrealized goals stated in [8].

The discovery and location of the critical points of an analytic function is important in the description of the "global" behavior of the function; it is one of the major purposes of the differential calculus! Relationships between the numbers of different types of critical points in real analytic functions of n variables over arbitrary manifolds have been extensively studied by Marston Morse, c.f. [2],[3], using methods of differential topology. Indeed, this field is called variously, "critical point theory" or "Morse theory". For example, in a smooth differentiable function, $f(x_1,x_2)$ defined on the 2-sphere, S^2, (the implicit domain that has been used in the definition and examples of surface networks in this paper) it can be shown that $|X| - |Y| + |Z| = 2$, as stated in property 2. of the surface network "definition". A different equation would hold if the function, $f(x_1,x_2)$, is defined over a subset of the plane, over a torus, etc. But while much is known regarding the possible cardinalities of the sets of different types of critical points, no results have been established regarding possible configurations of critical points, that is, permissible relationships (or interactions) between individual critical points in a well-formed surface network. The grammar *G* provides such a result for the case of two variables.

The surface network associated with a function, $f(x_1,x_2,x_3)$, of three variables is more complex. There are relative maxima (peaks), relative minima (pits) as before, together with two different types of saddles, thus yielding a 4-partite graph. These surface networks offer a useful tool for the global description, analysis, and display of such functions of three variables found in computer-aided tomography, in radion astronomy mapping, and especially in the interpretation of electron density maps used in the analysis of molecular structure, [9]. But again, what constitutes a well-formed configuration is unknown. The author is trying to characterize such 3-dimensional configurations by means of a similar grammar.

References

[1] Mark, D., "Topological Properties of Geographic Surfaces", Proc. Advanced Study Symposium on Topological Data Structures, Harvard Univ., Oct. 1977.

[2] Morse, M. and Van Schaack, "The critical point theory under general boundary conditions", Ann. of Math., v.35,3 (July 1934) 545-571

[3] Morse, M. and S.S. Cairns, Critical Point Theory in Global Analysis and Differential Topology, Academic Press, 1970

[4] Nagl, M., "Graph Lindenmayer-systems and Languages", Arbeitsber. d. Inst. f. Math. Masch. u. Datenvar., v.8,1 Erlangen, 1975

[5] Nilsson, N., Problem Solving Methods in Artifical Intelligence, McGraw-Hill, 1971

[6] Pfaltz, J. and A. Rosenfeld, "Web Grammars", Proc. Int. Joint Conf. Art. Intel., Washington 1969, 609-619

[7] Pfaltz, J., "Web Grammars and Picture Description", Comput. Graphics and Image Process., v.1,2 (Aug 1972) 193-219

[8] Pfaltz, J., "Surface Networks", Geograph. Analysis, v.8,2 (April 1976) 77-93

[9] Pfaltz, J. "Surface Networks: An Analytic Tool for the Study of Functional Surfaces", Final NSF report under grant DCR-74-13353, (July 1978)

[10] Rosenfeld, A., "Isotonic Grammars, Parallel Grammars, and Picture Grammars", Machine Intell., v.6 (1971) 281-294

[11] Warntz, W., "The Topology of a Socio-Economic Terrain and Spatial Flows", Papers of the Regional Sci. Assoc., v.17, (1966) 47-61

DEFINITION OF PROGRAMMING LANGUAGE SEMANTICS USING GRAMMARS FOR HIERARCHICAL GRAPHS*

by

Terrence W. Pratt

Directed graphs are a useful formal structure in the modeling and definition of programming language semantics. Graph grammars are a valuable tool for defining sets of directed graphs in this setting. The goal of this paper is to describe this application of graph grammars and to provide the underlying formal definitions for the particular graph structures and graph grammars used. Translation of programming languages into graph structures may also be defined using graph grammars paired with ordinary BNF (context-free) grammars. This closely related application is also described.

The graph grammar form used here and the theory underlying its application were developed about 1970 (see [1]). Graph grammars have been used regularly since then in the definition of a number of programming languages, including ALGOL 60, PASCAL, LISP, and HAL/S.

1. The Problem Setting: Definition of Programming Language Semantics

A number of techniques have been developed for the formal definition of the meaning (semantics) of programming languages, including the axiomatic approach of Hoare [2], the "denotational" approach of Scott and Strachey [3], and the "Vienna Definition Language" of the IBM Vienna Laboratory [4]. Marcotty, Ledgard, and Bochmann [5] provide a survey of various approaches and issues.

The approach to semantic definition taken in this work, which is termed the "H-graph" approach, defines semantics in terms of a model of program execution. This model takes the form of an abstract machine (equivalently, "virtual computer", "virtual machine", or executing automaton") that is capable of executing any program in the language, together with a "translation" mapping that maps program text into initial states of the abstract machine. To determine the meaning of a given program, one first maps the program into the corresponding

---

*This research is supported in part by NSF Grant MCS78-00763 and NASA Grant NSG 1458.
Author's address: Dept. of Applied Math and Computer Science
University of Virginia
Charlottesville, VA 22901
USA

initial state of the abstract machine and then observes the actions of the abstract machine as the translated program is executed. The results that are output during this execution determine the meaning of the original program for the input data set used, i.e., determine the function represented by the program. This general approach to semantic definition is common to a number of definitional techniques, e.g., the same approach is used in the Vienna Definition Language [4].

The most important difference between the H-graph approach and other methods based on abstract machines lies in the use of modeling techniques that provide realistic models of actual language implementations and yet which preserve formal simplicity. This approach results in programming language definitions that provide a guide for the language implementor and that can be analyzed mathematically to discover important properties of the language and its possible implementations. These aspects of the definitional method are described more fully in [6].

2. Abstract Machines

At the center of the definition of a programming language is the abstract machine that models program execution. In the H-graph approach the basic definition is:

Definition 1. An abstract machine (or virtual computer), V, is a quadruple $V = (H,O,T,H_o)$, where

H, the state set, is a non-empty set of H-graphs,

O, the operation set, is a finite non-empty set of transformations on H-graphs,

T, the transition rule, is a transition rule over H and O,

and H_o, the initial state set, is a non-empty subset of H.

A few additional definitions for transition rule, instructions, and execution sequences are needed to complete the definition. Since it is not the intent here to develop fully the H-graph approach, these definitions are omitted. Instead we now narrow our focus to the particulars of H-graphs and the application of graph grammars in their definition.

3. Hierarchical graphs (H-graphs)

Directed graphs have long been widely used in modeling programs and data structures, both formally and informally, e.g., in the form of program flowcharts and data structure diagrams. In such uses the arcs and nodes of the graphs are ordinarily labeled. In simple cases it suffices to restrict these labels to "atomic" elements such as elementary data items or instructions.

As one moves to modeling the larger structures found in complete programming languages, such as the sets of highly interconnected programs and data structures that appear in realistic programs, some extension to ordinary directed graph concepts is needed. First, it becomes increasingly desirable to allow the labels on nodes to be complex structures themselves, rather than just simple atomic elements. Second, the hierarchical nature of many of the objects in programs and data structures also influences the extensions desired: subprogram hierarchies, data structure hierarchies, and similar structures seem to abound in most practical programming languages. Unfortunately these hierarchies often contain anomalies: structures overlap or are recursive, pointers exist between structures that are at different levels in the hierarchy, etc.

Hierarchical graphs (H-graphs) are an extension to ordinary directed graphs that provide a tool for direct modeling of most program and data structures with the desired degree of intuitiveness and formal simplicity. H-graphs are also implementable on conventional computers using straightforward representations. An H-graph is a finite set of directed graphs over a common set of nodes, organized into a hierarchy:

Definition 2. (H-graph) Assume two base sets: a set N of nodes and a set A of atoms.

2.1. An extended directed graph, G, over N and A is a triple, G = (M,E,S), where

M, the node set, is a finite non-empty subset of N,

$S \in M$, the initial node of G, and

E, the arc set, is a finite set of triples of the form (n,a,m) where $n,m \in M$ and $a \in A$.

If $(n,a,m) \in E$ there is said to be an arc labeled a from node n to node m of G.

Extended directed graphs are ordinary finite directed graphs with labeled arcs and with an initial node singled out.* Note that multiple arcs with different labels between the same pair of nodes are allowed.

---

*Initial nodes of graphs are primarily important to the definition of graph transformations; they will be ignored in the remainder of this paper.

2.2. An H-graph, H, over N and A is a pair, H = (M,V), where
M, the node set, is a finite non-empty subset of N, and
V, the value or contents function, is a function mapping M into $A \cup \{X \mid X$ is an extended directed graph over M and A$\}$.

If n is a node in M, then V(n) is called the value or contents of n.

An H-graph is built up from a pool of nodes, N, that intuitively represents a pool of abstract storage locations. Some of these nodes are assigned atoms from A as values and thus model elementary data items of various sorts in an abstract machine state. More complex structures are constructed by defining directed graphs containing these elementary nodes (graphs with labeled arcs). Each new graph is the value of another "higher level" node, which then becomes, intuitively, a model for a larger program or data structure. Continuing in a similar fashion, graphs containing these higher level nodes may be constructed and assigned as the values of yet other nodes, until hierarchical structures of the desired degree of complexity have been fashioned.

Figure 1 shows a LISP list structure represented as an H-graph in which each level of sublist appears at a different H-graph level. For simplicity, atoms are represented by nodes containing the atom itself rather than by property lists. In the figure node values are written within the rectangle representing the node.

Within an H-graph, a particular directed graph may only exist as the value of some node, and the arcs and initial node designation are "local" to that graph. The nodes, however, are not local to the graph; a node is inherently "global" in that it may appear in many different graphs within an H-graph, and its value is independent of the particular graph within which it is found.

Global nodes combined with local graphs in H-graphs are important for natural modeling of many programming language structures. For example, two nodes containing graphs may represent different data structures, with the nodes in the graphs representing the elements of the structures and the arcs the access paths to the elements. In many programming languages the two data structures may share some storage, as in PASCAL variant records, FORTRAN equivalenced arrays, LISP lists with common atoms, or COBOL redefined records. Using H-graphs, these structures may be directly modeled by separate graphs for each data structure using common nodes representing the shared storage. Global nodes combined with local graphs also allow straightforward modeling

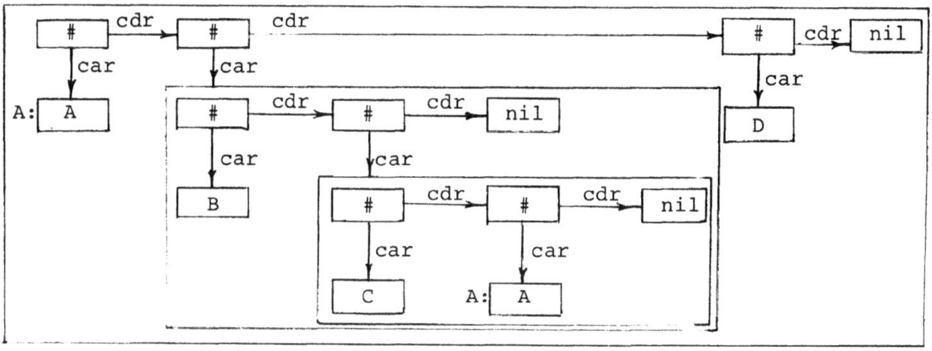

An H-graph of four levels corresponding to the LISP list
(A (B (C A)) D).
Fig. 1

of recursive structures: the contents of a node may be a graph that contains that same node in its node set.

Figure 1 illustrates a node common to two graphs. The atom "A" appears in both the main list and a sublist. In a LISP implementation the same storage location would represent the atom in both occurrences (the location representing the head of the property list for atom A). The two occurrences of the node labeled "A:" in Fig. 1 (which contain the atom A) represent occurrences of the same node in two different graphs.

Abstract machine states and state transitions.

An H-graph that represents the state of an abstract machine during execution of a program in a high-level programming language may contain thousands of nodes and hundreds of graphs. For example, HAL/S is a complex high-level language similar to PL/I with extensions for real-time programming. The HAL/S abstract machine contains 19 top-level nodes representing the various system data structures required for control of program execution, such as queues of active and waiting processes, stacks of activation records, lists of input-output channels, etc. Thus most of these top-level nodes contain graphs whose nodes themselves represent complex structures, such as processes, each modeled by many further levels of graph structure. All of the modeling power of H-graphs must be used to provide an intelligible, analyzable model of such a complex machine state.

The situation is made more difficult by the fact that each step in program execution results in a transformation of the state H-graph, and program execution may involve thousands of execution steps. Most of the analysis that one wishes to do of the abstract machine involves predicting the structural properties of the H-graphs that result during program execution from the structure of the initial state H-graph that exists at the start of program execution (which itself is derived directly from the program text). For example one might wish to prove that if the initial state had certain properties, such as no recursive subprogram hierarchies, that then the storage used during program execution, as measured by the number of new nodes created during program execution, was bounded in a predictable way. Similarly one might wish to prove that no execution path could lead to a state with certain undesirable properties, such as an unchecked operand type error.

Both the definition of the H-graphs representing abstract machine states and the analysis of the resulting abstract machines requires a convenient means of representing and studying sets of H-graphs with particular properties. Graph grammars for H-graphs provide such a means.

4. H-graph Grammars

The H-graph grammars that have been used in this work are of a relatively simple form. The concepts of terminal and non-terminal symbol, derivation, and language follow closely those used in ordinary BNF (context-free) grammars.

Definition 3. An H-graph grammar, F, is a quadruple, F = (B,A,S,R),
where B, the set of non-terminal symbols, is a finite alphabet,
A, the set of terminal symbols, is an alphabet,
$S \in B$ is the start symbol, and
R, the production set, is a finite set, each member of which is a quintuple (C,K,G,I,O), where
$C \in B$, the left-hand nonterminal,
K = (M,V) is an H-graph with atoms in $B \cup A$, and arc labels restricted to elements of A,
G is an extended directed graph over M and A, and
I and O, the input and output connections, are nodes in the node set of G.

Definition 4. (Derivation)

4.1. Let F be an H-graph grammar and H be an H-graph containing a node n whose value is a nonterminal C of F. Let P = (C,K,G,I,O) be a production of F. Then H-graph H' is directly derived from H by application of production P to node n if and only if H' is identical with H except that:

a. Node n has been replaced by a copy of graph G (including the H-graph K defined over the nodes of G),

b. The arcs entering node n in H have been replaced by arcs entering node I in the replacement graph, and

c. The arcs leaving node n in H have been replaced by arcs leaving node O in the replacement graph.

4.2. An H-graph H" is said to be <u>derived</u> from H-graph H if there exists a sequence $H_1H_2...H_k$, with $H=H_1$ and $H"=H_k$, for $k \geq 1$ where each H_i is directly derived from the preceding H_{i-1} by application of some production of the grammar.

<u>Definition 5.</u> The <u>H-graph language</u> (alternatively, the <u>set of H-graphs</u>) defined by an H-graph grammar F = (B,A,S,R) is the set of all H-graphs containing no nonterminal symbols in B that may be derived by productions of F from the graph of the single node whose value is a node n with contents S.

Because the concepts of derivation and language for H-graph grammars closely parallel the corresponding concepts for context-free grammars, the definitions above have been left somewhat informal. Note that H-graph grammar productions are "context-free" in that the applicability of a production is not dependent on the surrounding context of a node whose value is the left-hand nonterminal of the production. Also note that when a production is applied to replace a nonterminal node (node whose value is a nonterminal symbol) with the graph specified in the production, the "embedding" rule is particularly simple: all arcs incoming to the original nonterminal node are connected to the same node, I, in the replacement graph, and likewise all arcs outgoing from the original nonterminal node are connected to the node O after the replacement.

<u>Node labels</u>.

One final notational question remains: how to specify nodes that are common to more than one graph when writing the productions of an H-graph grammar. The use of node labels allows this specification. There are two cases to consider:

<u>Case 1</u>. <u>Within the right-hand side H-graph in a single production the same node appears in two or more graphs</u>. In this case, each time the production is applied, a single new node must be introduced and used in all of the relevant graphs. For this case each occurrence of the common node is labeled with a single lower-case letter in the production.

Case 2. Within the right-hand side H-graph in a production a node appears that may also appear in the right-hand side H-graph of some other production. In this case, each time the production is applied, if the node already exists in the H-graph being derived then that node must be used again in the introduced graphs, and otherwise a new node must be introduced. For this case, an upper-case label is used to label the node. In the final H-graph derived from the start symbol, all nodes with the same label are coalesced.

In either case, two restrictions apply: only terminal nodes (nodes containing graphs or terminal symbols) may be labeled, and each production that contains a labeled node must assign the same value to the node.

Note that node labels are only a notational convention used during derivation of an H-graph (or in drawing H-graphs). The node labels are not part of the H-graph itself. Reference [1] develops the complete set of definitions for H-graph grammars.

Figure 2 shows an H-graph grammar for LISP lists in which the node labeling convention is used for nodes representing atoms. The notation is an extended BNF. Nonterminals are written inside hexagonal nodes; rectangles are used for terminal nodes. The tags I and O on nodes in the right-hand side graphs indicate the input and output connection nodes respectively. Figure 3 illustrates a derivation of a list H-graph using the grammar.

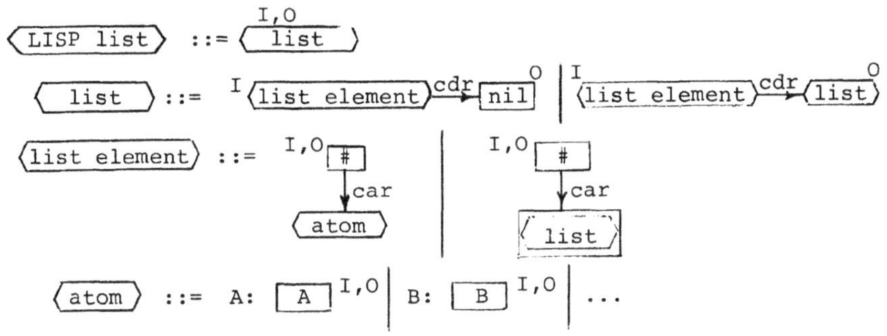

An H-graph grammar for LISP lists.

Fig. 2

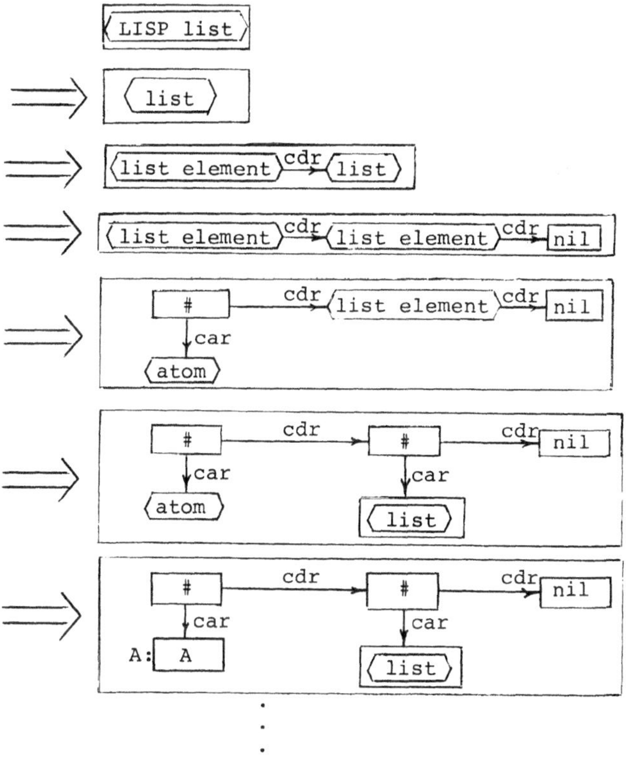

Initial steps in the derivation of the list (A (B A))

Fig. 3

5. Defining Translations: Pair Grammars

The original motivation for the development of H-graph grammars arose from the need to specify the correspondence between syntactic elements in a programming language and structures in the abstract machine initial state. Where the syntax of the language is defined by a BNF grammar it is natural to define the correspondence using the syntactic classes already present in the BNF grammar. A graph grammar production may be paired with each BNF production to define the graph structure in the abstract machine state that corresponds to the syntactic structure defined by the BNF production. Such a grammar form, called a "pair grammar", is defined as follows:

Definition 6. A pair grammar, G, is a quadruple, G = (K,T,S,P),where
K, the set of nonterminal symbols, is a finite alphabet,
T, the set of terminal symbols, is an alphabet,
$S \in K$, the start symbol, and
P is a set of productions, each composed of a pair (R,R')
where R is an ordinary BNF production, and
R' is an H-graph grammar production, with R and R' having the same left-hand nonterminal, and with the right-hand parts of R and R' containing the same nonterminals in 1-1 correspondence.

The complete set of definitions for pair grammars is given in [1]. Figure 4 illustrates a pair grammar defining the translation (i.e., the correspondence) between the usual LISP list syntax and the H-graph representation used in the preceding examples.

6. Application of H-graph Grammars and Pair Grammars in Programming Language Definition

H-graph grammars have played an increasingly valuable role in each programming language definition undertaken in this research. In a current definition of the complex language HAL/S, which has been used for a number of years by the United States space agency, NASA, for large real-time programs (in particular spacecraft software), two graph grammars are used.

One grammar is used to define the general form of each construct that may appear in a state H-graph of the abstract machine for executing HAL/S programs. At the top level the grammar defines the structure of the system data structures needed to support program execution: queues of processes awaiting various events such as clock interrupts, run-time stacks of process activation records, error indicators, etc. These structures exist for every program and are not created in response to any particular declarations or statements in the user program. As one moves from the top level down the hierarchy to the lower levels the graph structures correspond to programs, procedures, functions, and individual data and code structures.

The second grammar is used to define the structure of the initial state H-graphs for the abstract machine, which are special cases of the forms defined by the first grammar. For each H-graph construct that corresponds to a particular syntactic element in the original program text, such as a declaration or statement, a BNF production is paired with the H-graph grammar production to define the translation

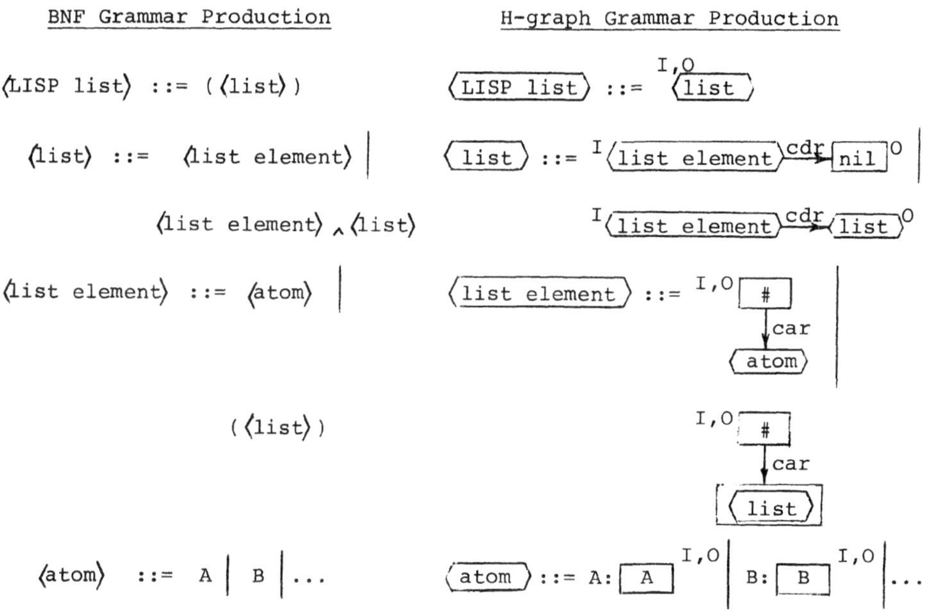

Pair grammar defining the correspondence between
LISP syntax and H-graph representation.
Fig. 4

from program text into initial abstract machine state. Thus the result is a partial pair grammar.

Programming languages contain many constructs in both syntax and semantics that cannot be directly represented using the tools described here. The many context-sensitive aspects of programming language syntax, which are well-known in the literature, are matched by an equally numerous set of "context related" restrictions on program execution. These appear in a language definition either as restrictions on the initial state structure of the machine or as restrictions on the states that may be produced during program execution. In this research such restrictions are usually stated informally in whatever form seems most appropriate, much as context-sensitive restrictions on syntax are usually introduced informally as an addendum to a BNF grammar.

In this application it is the graph grammars that define the central framework of the language definition: the state structure of the abstract machine. It is a credit to the power and elegance of the graph grammar concept that the additional restrictions needed may be filled in informally without sacrificing the overall integrity and precision of the definition. Further description of this work in programming language definition may be found in [6-9].

7. References

1. Pratt, T. "Pair grammars, graph languages, and string-to-graph translations", J. Comp.Sys.Sci., 5,6,1971,560-595.
2. Hoare, C.A.R. and N. Wirth, "An axiomatic definition of PASCAL", Acta Infor., 2, 1973, 335-355.
3. Tennent, R., "The denotational semantics of programming languages", Comm. ACM, 19,8, 1976, 437-453.
4. Lucas, P. and K. Walk, "On the formal description of PL/I", Annual Rev.Auto. Prog., 6,3, 1969,105-182.
5. Marcotty, M, H. Ledgard and G. Bochmann, "A sampler of formal definitions", Comp. Surveys, 8,2, 1976, 191-276.
6. Pratt, T. "A theory of programming languages, Part I", Univ. of Texas Comp. Center Report UTEX-CCSN-41, July 1975, 200pp.
7. ----, "Application of formal grammars and automata to programming language definition" in Applied Computation Theory, R.T. Yeh (ed.), Prentice-Hall, 1976.
8. ----, "Semantic definition of programming languages: Prospects for the 1980's", Proc. 17th ACM/NBS Annual Tech. Symp., June 1978, Washington, D.C., 71-77.
9. ---- and G. Maydwell, "A semantic definition of HAL/S" (in preparation).

DETERMINISM IN RELATIONAL SYSTEMS

Václav Rajlich
Research Institute for Mathematical Machines
Loretánské nám. 3, 118 55 Praha 1, Czechoslovakia

Relational systems are defined as a triple consisting of : set of (relational) structures, substitutions into structures (each substitution transforms a structure into another one), and successor function which gives to each formula its successor in the next structure.

A system is deterministic iff during any admissible sequence of substitutions, each formula has the same sequence of successors. It is proved that noninterferring persistent systems are deterministic. Counterexample to opposite implication is given.

1. Introduction

Relational systems were investigated for example in [2,3,4]. Their philosophy could be summarized in the following way :

The basic mathematical formalism used is that of relational structures, which intuitively represent a static arrangement of interrelated objects in the real world. The arrangement is static except for short moments of change, which are formalized as substitutions into relational structure. In [2], biologically motivated pattern reproduction was investigated and in [3], semantics for data structure was defined within this framework.

In this paper, the discrete systems were modified in the following sense : The formalism is based on substitutions (Definition 2.2) rather than productions of [2,4]. The relationship of productions and substitutions is illustrated by Example 2.6. We have chosen this formalism because all notions concerning determinism are more readily expressed within the framework of substitutions than within the framework of productions. Also the apparatus of substitutions seems to be more general than that of productions as seen in [3].

In the discrete systems, we may execute one substitution at a time. However refering back to the real world, changes occuring simultaneously may be formally described by commutative substitutions, i.e. substitutions which may occur in any order. This intuition has led to definition 2.9, where a system was defined to be deterministic, iff each of its formulas has a unique history of changes, affecting it.

Section 3 contains a sufficient condition for a system to be deterministic and counterexample to the opposite implication.

2. Definitions and notation

In this chapter, we shall give notation for discrete systems and determinism. We start with the next definition :

Definition 2.1

Let L be a set of predicates and X a set of atoms, then (atomic) formula is a sequence $A\langle a_1,\ldots,a_n\rangle$ where $A \in L$ and $a_1,\ldots,a_n \in X$. We shall distinguish unary, binary, ..., n-ary predicates in the usual sense. Structure is a set of formulas. Let S be a structure, then $\mathrm{At}\ S = \{x \mid \text{there exists } A\langle a_1,\ldots,a_n\rangle \in S \text{ such that } x \in \{a_1,\ldots,a_n\}\}$.

Next definition defines substitution into a structure :

Definition 2.2

Substitution is a couple of structures $s = \langle {}^\bullet s, s^\bullet \rangle$, sometimes also denoted ${}^\bullet s \Rightarrow s^\bullet$. We shall call ${}^\bullet s$ and $s^\bullet$ left and right side of substitution s, respectively. Substitution s into structure S gives T (written $S.s = T$ or $S \Rightarrow_s T$) iff ${}^\bullet s \subset S$, $s^\bullet - {}^\bullet s \cap S = \emptyset$, and $T = (S - {}^\bullet s) \cup s^\bullet$.

Note that each substitution s consists of three parts : part which disappears i.e. ${}^\bullet s - s^\bullet$, part which is created i.e. $s^\bullet - {}^\bullet s$, and context which remains intact ${}^\bullet s \cap s^\bullet$.

Next, we shall give definition of systems. Intuitive discussion and examples follow.

Definition 2.3

Let T be a set of substitutions and let φ be a set of structures closed under T, i.e. whenever $S \in \varphi$ and $t \in T$, then also $S.t \in \varphi$.

Denote $p(\varphi) = \bigcup_{S \in \varphi} S \cup \{\emptyset\}$.

Then define successor function $h : T \times p(\varphi) \to p(\varphi)$ which satisfies the following properties (a denotes a formula) :

i) If $a \notin {}^{\bullet}t - t^{\bullet}$, then $h(t,a) = a$,

ii) If $a \in {}^{\bullet}t - t^{\bullet}$, then $h(t,a) \in (t^{\bullet} - {}^{\bullet}t) \cup \{\emptyset\}$.

System is a triple $\langle \varphi, T, h \rangle$.

Elementary system hence consists of structures, substitutions, and successor functions. Successor function retains the same formula in case the substitution does not affect it (condition i). In the opposite situation (case ii), successor function gives either a new formula, or it gives empty set. The empty set in this setting means the ultimate disappearance of the formula, i.e. the formula does not have a successor.

We shall give the following examples :

Example 2.4

Let $T = \{s,t\}$ be the following substitutions :

$s : \{A\langle 1\rangle, A\langle 2\rangle\} \Rightarrow \{B\langle 1\rangle, B\langle 2\rangle\}$,
$t : \{A\langle 2\rangle, A\langle 3\rangle\} \Rightarrow \{B\langle 2\rangle, B\langle 3\rangle\}$.

Let $S = \{A\langle 1\rangle, A\langle 2\rangle, A\langle 3\rangle\}$ be a structure. Then $S.s = (S - {}^{\bullet}s) \cup s^{\bullet} = \{B\langle 1\rangle, B\langle 2\rangle, A\langle 3\rangle\}$, $S.t = (S - {}^{\bullet}t) \cup t^{\bullet} = \{A\langle 1\rangle, B\langle 2\rangle, B\langle 3\rangle\}$. Let $\varphi = \{S, S.s, S.t\}$, then $p(\varphi) = \{A\langle 1\rangle, B\langle 1\rangle, A\langle 2\rangle, B\langle 2\rangle, A\langle 3\rangle, B\langle 3\rangle\}$.

Define successor function in the following way :

$h(s, A\langle 1\rangle) = B\langle 1\rangle$,	$h(t, A\langle 1\rangle) = A\langle 1\rangle$,
$h(s, A\langle 2\rangle) = B\langle 2\rangle$,	$h(t, A\langle 2\rangle) = B\langle 2\rangle$,
$h(s, A\langle 3\rangle) = A\langle 3\rangle$,	$h(t, A\langle 3\rangle) = B\langle 3\rangle$,
$h(s, B\langle 1\rangle) = B\langle 1\rangle$,	$h(t, B\langle 1\rangle) = B\langle 1\rangle$,
$h(s, B\langle 2\rangle) = B\langle 2\rangle$,	$h(t, B\langle 2\rangle) = B\langle 2\rangle$,
$h(s, B\langle 3\rangle) = B\langle 3\rangle$,	$h(t, B\langle 3\rangle) = B\langle 3\rangle$.

Then conditions i) and ii) of previous definition are satisfied and $\langle \varphi, T, h \rangle$ is a system.

Example 2.5

Let $\mathcal{Y}$,T be the same as in Example 2.4. Define a successor function h' so that h'(s,A⟨1⟩) = ∅. For all formulas a ≠ A⟨1⟩, h'(s,a) = h(s,a) and for all formulas b, h'(t,b) = h(t,b). Then again h' satisfies conditions of definition 2.3 and ⟨$\mathcal{Y}$,T,h'⟩ is a system. ∎

For readers familiar with [2,4] , substitutions could be considered to be "instances of productions", as illustrated by the following example :

Example 2.6

Isomorphism of structures S and T is an isomorphism of atoms e : At S → At T such that $A\langle a_1,\dots,a_n\rangle \in S$ iff $A\langle e(a_1),\dots, e(a_n)\rangle \in T$. Production p is a couple of structures p = ⟨•p,p•⟩ , also denoted •p ⇒ p•. Each production defines a set of substitutions

$$\{{}^\bullet s \Rightarrow s^\bullet \mid \text{there exists isomorphism } e: {}^\bullet p \cup p^\bullet \to {}^\bullet s \cup s^\bullet \text{ such that } e({}^\bullet p) = {}^\bullet s, e(p^\bullet) = s^\bullet\}.$$

Let us have a production p: {A⟨11⟩, A⟨12⟩} ⇒ {B⟨11⟩, B⟨12⟩} and structure S = {A⟨1⟩, A⟨2⟩, A⟨3⟩} of example 2.4. Then production p defines three substitutions into S, i.e. substitutions s,t of example 2.4 and additional substitution u: {A⟨1⟩, A⟨3⟩ ⇒ ⇒ {B⟨1⟩, B⟨3⟩} . ∎

In certain situations, it is convenient (or necessary) to define substitutions (or rather sets of substitutions) in other ways then by productions, as in the following example :

Example 2.7

Define T as a set of all substitutions A⟨1⟩ ∪ G ⇒ A⟨1⟩ where G consists of any set of binary formulas of the type B ⟨j,1⟩ , where j is any atom.

Examples of such substitutions are

{A⟨1⟩, B⟨2,1⟩} ⇒ A⟨1⟩,
{A⟨1⟩, B⟨2,1⟩, B⟨3,1⟩} ⇒ A⟨1⟩, ...

There are infinitely many substitutions of this type and they cannot be expressed by a finite number of productions. Let $\mathcal{Y}$ consist of any structure containing many formula A⟨1⟩ and any set of binary formulas B $\langle i,j \rangle$.

Define successor function in the following way :

Let $t \in T$, $i \in At\,\varphi$, then $h(t,B\langle i,1\rangle) = \emptyset$ and for all remaining formulas $a \in p(\varphi)$, $h(a) = a$. Then $\langle \varphi,T,h\rangle$ is a system. ∎

We shall give the following definitions :

Definition 2.8

Let $w = a_1 \ldots a_n$ be a word where $a_1,\ldots,a_n$ are substitutions. Then $S.w = (\ldots((S.a_1) . a_2)\ldots). a_n$. Empty word is denoted by λ and $S . \lambda = S$. Length of w is denoted $|w| = n$. Infinite word $v = b_1 b_2 \ldots$ is of length $|v| = \infty$. If $i \in \{0,\ldots,n\}$ then ${}_iw = a_1.a_2\ldots a_i$, ${}_iv = b_1,b_2\ldots b_i$. If $i \in \{n+1, n+2,\ldots\}$ then ${}_iw = w$.

Complete sequence of substitutions for structure S is finite or infinite word w such that for every $i = 1,2,\ldots$, $S . {}_iw$ is defined. If w is finite, then for every $t \in T$, s.w.t is undefined and S.w is called terminal structure.

Let w be a word consisting of substitutions, $a \in S$ be a formula. Then history of a (in S and w) is defined inductively in the following way :

History of a in S and λ is $\langle a\rangle$. If $\langle a_1,\ldots,a_n\rangle$ is history of a in S and w, S.w.t is defined, and $a_n \notin {}^\bullet t\text{-}t^\bullet$, then $\langle a_1,\ldots, a_n\rangle$ is history of a in S and w.t. If $a_n \in {}^\bullet t\text{-}t^\bullet$ and $h(t,a_n) = a_{n+1}$, then $\langle a_1,\ldots,a_n,a_{n+1}\rangle$ is history of a in w.t.

Hence history reflects all substitutions which change the formula while ommitting substitutions which did not interferre with it.

We shall classify systems according to certain properties which are given in the next definitions :

Definition 2.9

Let $\langle \varphi,T, h\rangle$ be a system. Two substitutions s,t are parallel iff there exists $S \in \varphi$ such that S.s, S.t are defined.

Substitution s is persistent iff for every $S \in \varphi$ for which S.s is defined, and for every complete sequence of substitutions w for S, $w = w_1.s.w_2$.

A system is persistent iff all its substitutions are persistent.

System is <u>deterministic</u> iff for each formula $a \in S$, there is a unique history of a in S.

Substitutions s,t are <u>noninterferring</u> iff $^\bullet s \cap (^\bullet t - t^\bullet) = {}^\bullet t \cap (^\bullet s - s^\bullet) = \emptyset$. A system is noninterferring iff its parallel productions are noninterferring.

3. Results

In this section, we shall prove that noninterferring persistent systems are deterministic. Also we shall give a counterexample to the opposite implication.

Theorem 3.1

If a system is noninterferring persistent then it is deterministic.

Proof follows idea of [1].

Let $\langle \varphi, T, h \rangle$ be a noninterferring persistent system. First we shall prove the following statement :

(1) Let $t \in T$, $S \in \varphi$ and S.t be defined. Let w be a complete sequence of substitutions for S. Then $w = w_1.t.w_2$ where w_1 consists of substitutions which are parallel and noninterferring with t.

For proof of (1) by induction, let $w_1 = w_1'.w_1''$ and (1) can be proved by the help of the following inductive statement :

(2) If assumptions of (1) are satisfied, then w_1' consists of substitutions parallel and noninterferring with t.

Proof of (2) is by induction on the length of w_1'. Statement (1) then follows when we take $w_1' = w_1$.

The theorem will be proved with the help of the following statement :

(3) Let $S \in \varphi$, $a \in S$ and let x,y be complete sequences of substitutions for S. Denote H(a,x) history of a in x. Then for every $i \in \{0,1,\dots\}$ there exists a complete sequence of substitutions z^i such that ${}_iz^i = {}_ix$ and for every $a \in S$, $H(a,z^i) = H(a,y)$.

Proof of (3) is by induction on i. For i = 0, take $z^0 = y$ and

(3) holds.

For induction step, suppose $x = {}_i x.s.w$, $z^i = {}_i x . w'$. Then by (1), $w' = w_1.s.w_2$ where w_1 consists of substitutions parallel and noninterferring with s. Take $z^{i+1} = {}_i x.s.w_1.w_2$ and then for every $a \in S$, $H(a,z^{i+1}) = H(a,z^i)$ which proves (3).

For proof of the theorem, take i equal to the length of x, and this completes the proof. ∎

The opposite implication does not hold as seen from the following counterexample, where we present a system which is deterministic persistent, but is not noninterferring.

Example 3.2

Take system $\langle \varphi, T, h \rangle$ of example 2.4 and define $T' = T \cup \{u,v\}$, where

$u : \{B\langle 1\rangle, B\langle 2\rangle, A\langle 3\rangle\} \Rightarrow \{B\langle 1\rangle, A\langle 2\rangle, A\langle 3\rangle\}$,
$v : \{A\langle 1\rangle, B\langle 2\rangle, B\langle 3\rangle\} \Rightarrow \{A\langle 1\rangle, A\langle 2\rangle, B\langle 3\rangle\}$.

$\varphi' = \{S, S.s, S.t, S.s.u, S.t.v, T\}$ where $T = S.s.u.t = S.t.v.s$.

Define successor function h' in the following way : For every $a \in p(\varphi)$, $h'(s,a) = h(s,a)$, $h'(t,a) = h(t,a)$. Moreover define h' for remaining substitutions u,v in the following way :

$h(u,B\langle 2\rangle) = h(v,B\langle 2\rangle) = A\langle 2\rangle$ and for every $a \neq B\langle 2\rangle$, $h(u,a) = h(v,a) = a$.

Then for structure S, there exist two complete sequences of substitutions s.u.t and t.v.s, but for every $a \in S$, there exists unique history;

history of $A\langle 1\rangle$ is $\langle A\langle 1\rangle, B\langle 1\rangle\rangle$,
history of $A\langle 2\rangle$ is $\langle A\langle 2\rangle, B\langle 2\rangle, A\langle 2\rangle, B\langle 2\rangle\rangle$,
history of $A\langle 3\rangle$ is $\langle A\langle 3\rangle, B\langle 3\rangle\rangle$.

All substitutions are persistent, but they are not noninterferring, because $^\bullet s \cap (^\bullet t - t^\bullet) = \{A\langle 1\rangle, A\langle 2\rangle\} \cap \{A\langle 2\rangle, A\langle 3\rangle\} = \{A\langle 2\rangle\} \neq \emptyset$. ∎

LITERATURE

[1] Karp,R.M., Miller,R.E., Parallel program schemata, J. of Computer and System Sci. 3, 1969, pp. 147-195.

[2] Rajlich,V., Dynamics of discrete systems and pattern reproduction, J. of Computer and System Sci., 11, 1975, pp.186-202.

[3] Rajlich, V., Partial universal algebras : semantics for data structures and assignment, submitted to Information and Control.
Preliminary version : Theory of data structures by relational and graph grammars, in Salommaa, Steinby ed., Automata, Languages and Programming, Lecture Notes in Computer Science, Vol. 52, Springer-Verlag, Berlin, 1977, pp. 391-411.

[4] Ehrig,H., Kreowski,H.J., Magiolo-Schettini,A., Rosen,B.K., Winkowski,J., Deriving structures from structures, in : Winkowski,J., ed. : Mathematical Foundations of Computer Science, Lecture Notes in Computer Science 64, Springer-Verlag, Berlin, 1978, pp. 177-190.

ANALYSIS OF PROGRAMS BY REDUCTION OF THEIR STRUCTURE*)

Manfred Rosendahl
Seminar für Informatik
Erz. Wiss. Hochschule Rheinl.-Pfalz
Rheinau 3-4
5400 Koblenz
Germany

Karl Peter Mankwald
Bergbau Forschung
Friedrichstr. 1
4300 Essen
Germany

Abstract - The program and data flow of a program given in a line oriented programming language is analised according to the rules of structured programming. This allows a structured representation of arbitrary programs as far as possible

*) The work started, when both authors were at the Computing Centre of the Ruhr University Bochum.

1. Introduction

The structure of a program, given in a line oriented programming language like FORTRAN, BASIC, Assembler is analysed. The aim is to find in programs, written in such a non-structured programming language, the structures well known from the ideas of structured programming. In chapter 2 a definition of these structures used here is given.
The analysis is done by an algorithm, which uses graph manipulations given by a graph grammar in chapter 3.
For certain programs, which are called well structured the algorithm reduces the program graph to one edge. Because the programming languages, we deal with, allow all type of programs, we also want to find the structured parts in not totally well structured programs. Therefore we add a new rule which isolates self contained part-programs (chapter 4). These are the smallest surroundings of unstructured parts of a program.
So far only the program flow is investigated. In chapter 5 we modify our representations of the program to a graph, which deals with the data flow, too.

The results of the paper help to develop software products which consider the program structure e.g. flowcharts, Nassi-Shneiderman diagrams, structured cross reference lists or HIPO structures.

2. Program representation and program structures

The programs, we consider, are given in a line oriented language. They are represented by a graph $G = (B, E)$ were B is a set of nodes and E the set of directed edges. The set B corresponds to the program lines and $(b_1, b_2) \in E$ with $b_1, b_2 \in B$ if it is possible in the program flow that line b_2 will be executed directly after line b_1. For instance if there is a (conditional)-jump in b_1 to b_2 or b_2 is directly under b_1 with b_1 not containing an unconditional jump.

We choose this representation, the actions as nodes, because this can easily be obtained from the source text of the program. If we take the program lines as edges, we start with a set of edges and have to construct the nodes corresponding to the program flow.

In the literature there are a lot of definitions for structured programming, but we only consider the program flow and therein the following structures:

(1) compound statement
<u>begin</u> <statement>; ...; <statement> <u>end</u>

(2) conditional statement
<u>if</u> <condition> <u>then</u> <statement> [<u>else</u> <statement>] <u>fi</u>

(3) <u>while</u> - loop
<u>while</u> <condition> <u>do</u> <statement> <u>od</u>

(4) <u>until</u> - loop
<u>do</u> <statement> <u>until</u> <condition> [<u>else</u> <statement>] <u>od</u>

If <statement> is a node with one incoming and one outgoing edge the 4 structures would be represented by the following 4 production rules:

(1) compound statement

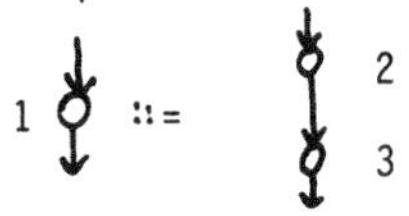

$\pi_+ = (1, 3)$ $\pi_- = (1,2)$

(2) conditional statement

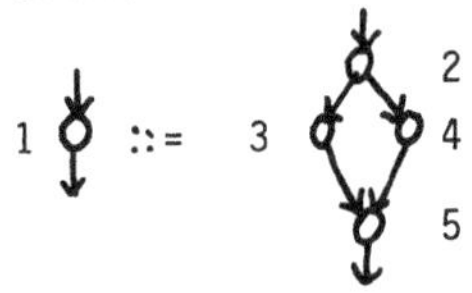

$\pi_+ = (1, 5)$ $\pi_- = (1, 2)$

(3) <u>while</u>-loop

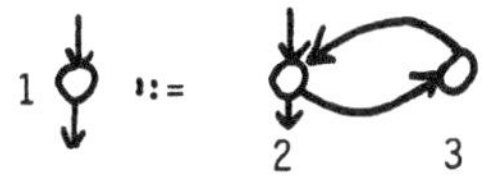

$\pi_+ = (1, 2)$ $\pi_- = (1, 2)$

(4) <u>until</u>-loop

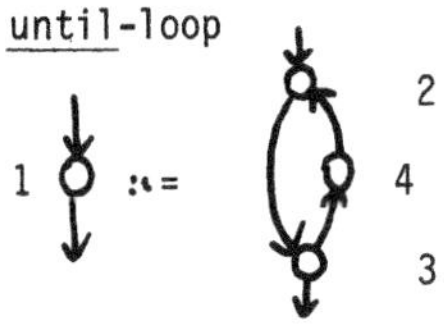

$\pi_+ = (1, 3)$ $\pi_- = (1, 2)$

The relation π_+ and π_- define the embeddings: $\pi_+ \ni (i, j)$ ::= outgoing edges from node i on the left side, are outgoing from node j on the right side.

$\pi_- \ni (i, j)$ ::= incoming edges to node i on the left side, are incoming to node j on the right side. This notation see [3].

<u>Definition 1:</u> A <u>classical structured program</u> is a program, which corresponding graph can be derived by rules (1), (2), (3), (4).

But in our application we do not have only to deal with fully structured programs, but we want to find a structure as far as possible in every program for instance the following diagram, could not be derived by these productions:

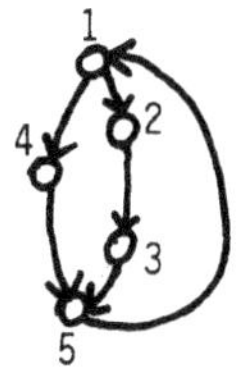

But the program:

```
(1)  10 IF   (A.GT.0)  GOTO  20
(2)       A = A + 1
(3)       GOTO  30
(4)  20  A = A - 1
(5)  30 IF   (A.NE.0)  GOTO 10
```

is represented by this graph and contains an until-loop with a conditional statement.
Therefore we have to choose reduction rules, which would reduce for instance this program, too.

3. Graph-grammar for the program analysis

In the following chapter we will give a grammar, which productions reduce the graph given by a structured program to a graph with one edge. To receive this we have to demand the following conditions to the start-graph.

Definition 2: A program is called allowed if the induced graph fulfils the following conditions:
(1) exact one entrance node (outgoing edges only)
(2) exact one exit node (incoming edges only)
(3) any node can be reached from the entrance node
(4) from any node the exit node con be reached.

---

(5) exact one edge outgoing from the entrance node
(6) exact one edge going into the exit node.

The conditions (5) and (6) can always be fulfiled, by just adding two nodes to the graph. In this way every classical structured program is allowed, too.
The reduction is now by the following 4 rules:

(S)

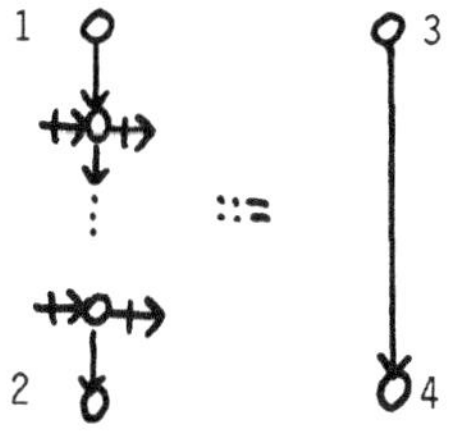

$\pi_- = \{(1, 3), (2, 4)\}$

$\pi_+ = \{(1, 3), (2, 4)\}$

(A) 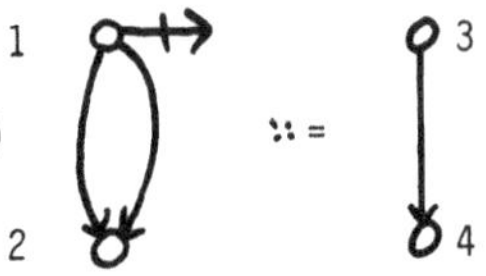

$\pi_- = \{(1,3), (2, 4)\}$

$\pi_+ = \{(1, 3), (2, 4)\}$

(L1) 

$\pi_- = (1, 2)$

$\pi_+ = (1, 2)$

(L2) 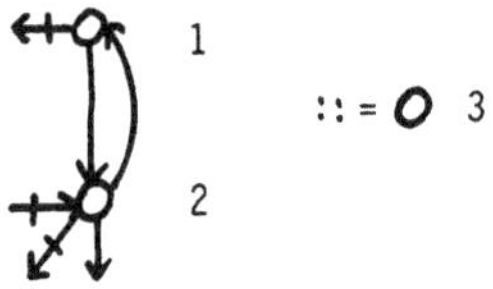

$\pi_- = (1, 3)$

$\pi_+ = (2, 3)$

The notations  resp.  on the left side mean, that the application of the rule is only allowed, if there are no additional incoming resp. outgoing edges.

Rule (S) reduces maximum ways without junctions to one edge. These infinite number of rules can be simulated by the following rule:

(S') 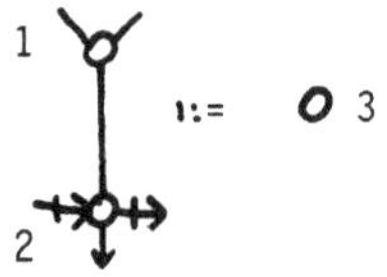

$\pi_- = (1, 3)$

$\pi_+ = \{(1, 3), (2, 3)\}$

applied repeatedly. The rule can only be applied if node 1 has 3 or more edges.

The rules are applied according to the following control diagram C:

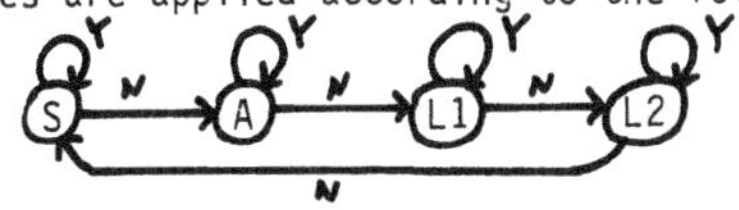

with (N, N, N, N) as excit.

Lemma: Each graph, derived from a well structured and allowed program can be reduced by Rule (S), (A),(L1) and (L2) to one edge.

Proof: We have to show, that all structures derived by the rules (1), (2), (3), (4) of Definition 1 are reduced by the Rules (S), (A), (L1) and (L2):

(1) compound statement

 by (S) to 

(2) conditional statement

 by (S) to  by (A) to 

by (S) to 

(3) while-loop

(4) until-loop

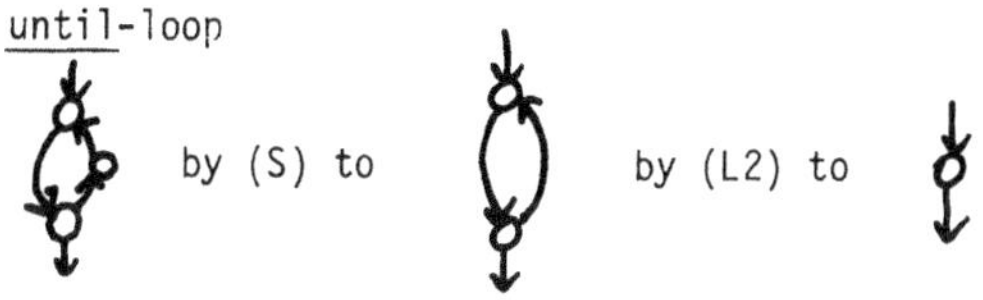

At any step the applied rule is the only possible. So the control-diagram includes just this reduction.

But as shown in the example above the rules (S), (A), (L1), (L2) can reduce programs wich are not classical structured programs following definition 1. So we define:

Definition 3: A program is fully well structured if it is allowed and its corresponding graph can be reduced by rules (S), (A), (L1), (L2) with control diagram C to one edge.

4. Closed part-programs

Because we have to deal with unstructured programs, too and we want to find as many structure as possible, we have to isolate the unstructured parts. Therefore we define:

Definition 4: A program given by a graph $G = (B, E)$ has a closed part-program $B' \subset B$ if the subgraph $G' = (B', E')$ fulfils the following conditions:

(1) G' has exact one entrance (b_E) and exact one exit (b_A)

(2) Every node of B' can be reached from b_E

(3) From every node of B' the node b_A can be reached

(4) There is no edge from $B - B'$ to $B' - \{b_E\}$

(5) There is no edge from $B - \{b_A\}$ to $B - B'$.

A closed part program is a subgraph connected to the rest only over one entrance and one exit. Without interference to the rest of the program, it can be reduced to one edge. Our problem is to find a minimal non trivial closed part-program. Non trivial means that B' has more than two nodes.

Lemma 2: Given a program, it can be decided whether a non trivial closed part-program exist and when it exists it can be constructed.

Proof: We give an overview of the algorithm:

```
        Given the graph G = (B,E).
   var B̄, B', B_E, B_A: set of nodes;
        b_E, b_A : nodes; γ: integer;
   begin
        B̄:= B; γ:= 0; B_E:= B;
        while  B_E ≠ ∅ do
   begin b_e ∈ B_E  (choosen); B_A:= B̄;
```

<u>while</u> $B_A \neq \emptyset$ <u>do</u>
$b_A \in B_A$ (choosen);
$B' := R(b_E) \cap Q(b_A$

$R(b_E)$ is the set of nodes, which can be reached in G from b_E.
$Q(b_A)$ is the set of nodes, from which b_A can be reached in G.
<u>if</u> $|B'| \geq 3$ <u>and</u> no edges from $B' - \{b_A\}$ to $B - B'$ or from $B - B'$ to $B' - \{b_E\}$.
<u>then</u> <u>begin</u> $\gamma := 1$; $\bar{B} := B_E := B_A := B'$;
$b_E \in B_E$ (chosen);
<u>end</u> <u>else</u> $B_A := B_A - \{b_A\}$
<u>end</u>;
$B_E := B_E - \{b_E\}$
<u>end</u>;
<u>if</u> $\gamma = 0$ <u>then</u> no closed part-program
<u>else</u> B' is minimal closed part-program
<u>end</u>.

So we add the new reduction rule

(PP) minimal closed part-program ::=

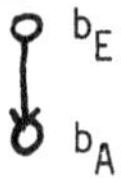

<u>Definition 5:</u> A program, which graph can be reduced by (S), (A), (L1), (L2) and (PP) to one edge is called <u>partly well structured</u>.

The reduction algorithm will be demonstrated by the following example:

Program:

```
(1)     START
(2)  40 READ CA)
(3)     IF (A.EQ.0) GOTO 10
(4)     GOTO 20
(5)  10 B = 2
(6)  20 C = A + 2
(7)     IF (C.EQ.0) GOTO 30
(8)     STop
(9)  30 IF (C.LT.0) GOTO 40
(10)    B = A - 1
(11)    GOTO 30
```

The graph has the form:

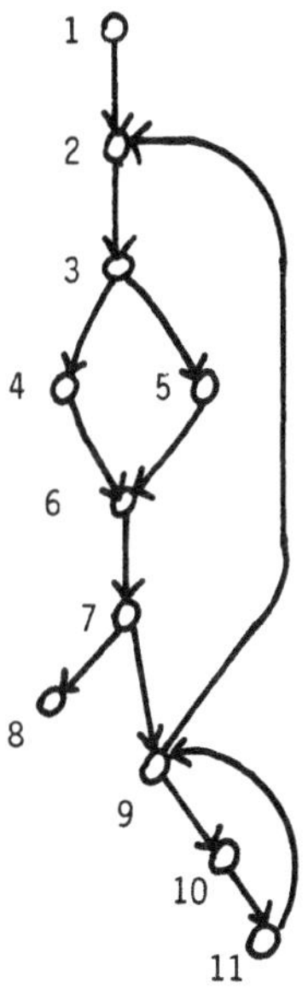

In the reducing process the reduced information is put into the node labelling, only application of (S) is put into the edge labelling.
The steps are:

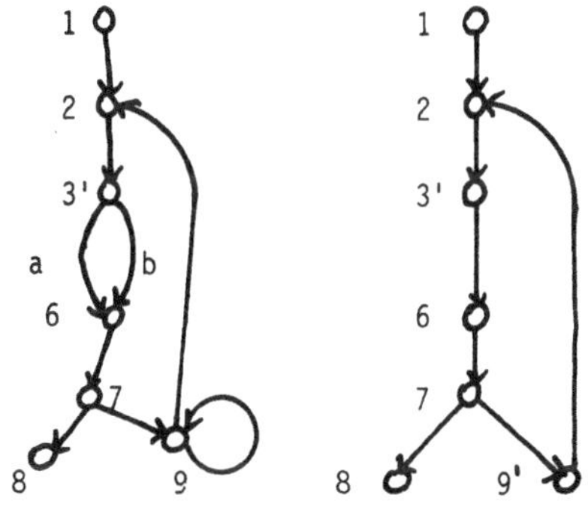

a= (4)

b= (5)

c= (10; 11)

3'= if 3 then a else b fi

9'= while 9 do c od

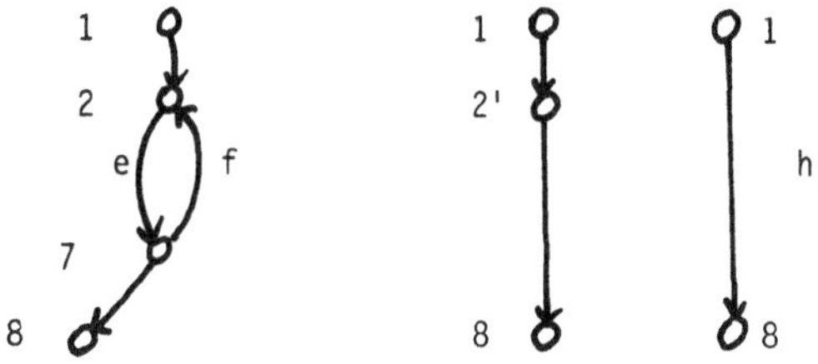

e= (3; b)

f= (9)

2' = do 2; e until 7 else f od

h= (2')

By inserting we get the following structured program:

```
begin
1;
do 2;
   if 3 then 4 else 5 fi;
   6
until 7
else while 9 do 10; 11 od
od;
8
end
```

We can also use the reduction to construct a structured flow chart or Nassi/ Shneiderman diagram [1].

5. Analysis of the data flow

So far we have only looked for the control flow of the program. To investigate the data flow, we modify the corresponding graph to a 3-diagram.

Definition 6: Given a line oriented program, the corresponding graph with regard of the data is defined as the 3-diagram $G = (B, E, D, L, S)$.
B the set of nodes corresponding to the program lines
$E \subseteq B \times B$ the program flow
D the set of nodes corresponding to the data variables.
L and $S \subseteq D \times B$
$(d, b) \in L$ if data d can be used in line b
$(d, b) \in S$ if data d can be modified in line b.

Example:

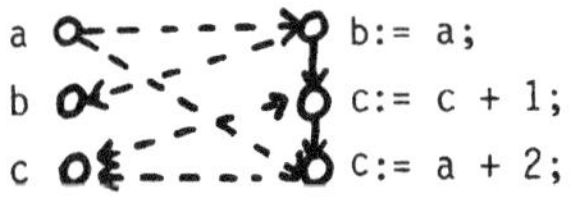

For further representation of data flow see [2].

The reduction rules have then to be modified:

($\bar{S}$)

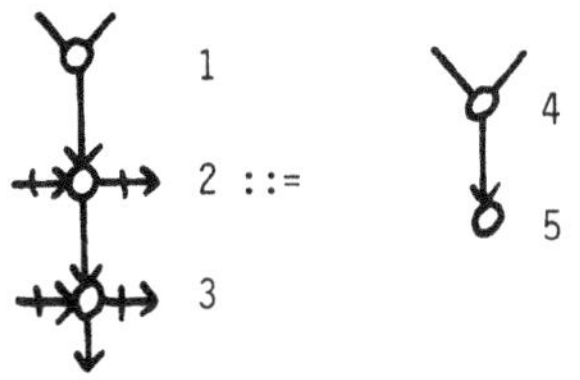

$\pi_- = \pi_+ = (1, 4)$

$\pi_L = \pi_S = \{(1, 4), (2, 5), (3,5)\}$

Data references to node (2) and (3) are collected to node (5).

($\bar{A}$)

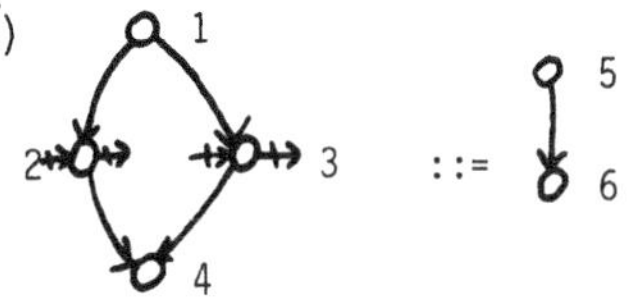

$\pi_- = \pi_+ = \{(1, 5), (4, 6)\}$

$\pi_L = \pi_S = \{(1, 5), (2, 5), (3, 5), (4,6)\}$

($\overline{A}$a) as ($\overline{A}$) without node (3)
($\overline{A}$b) as ($\overline{A}$) without node (2) and (3)

($\overline{L1}$)

::= O 3 $\pi_- = \pi_+ = (1, 3)$
$\pi_L = \pi_S = \{(1, 3), (2, 3)\}$

($\overline{L2}$)

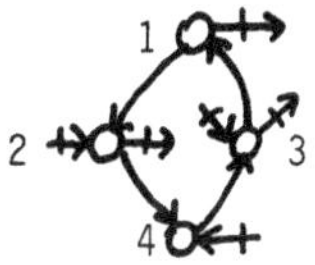

::= O 5 $\pi_- = \pi_+ = \{(1, 5), (4, 5)\}$
$\pi_L = \pi_S = \{(1, 5), (2, 5), (3, 5), (4, 5)\}$

($\overline{L2}$a) as ($\overline{L2}$) without node (3)
($\overline{L2}$b) as ($\overline{L2}$) without node (2) and (3)

The last rule (PP) will also be modified.

Definition 7: A closed part-program with regard of data flow as defined as
$\overline{EP} = (B', b_E, b_A, D', D_E, D_A)$
with (B', b_E, b_A) a closed part-program concerning program flow and:
$\overline{B} = B - B'$, $D' \subset D$, $D_E \subset D - D'$, $D_A \subset D - D'$

$\left.\begin{array}{l} L \cap D' \times \overline{B} = \emptyset \\ S \cap D' \times \overline{B} = \emptyset \end{array}\right\} D'$ (only used locally in B')

$\widehat{d \in D_E} \quad \widecheck{b \in B'} \quad (d, b) \in L$ (used as input in B')

$\widehat{d \in D_A} \quad \widecheck{b \in B'} \quad (d, b) \in S$ (used as output in B')

The new rule is then:

($\overline{PP}$) minimal closed part-program ::=

b_E $\pi_L = \{D_E \times b_E\}$
b_A $\pi_S = \{D_A \times b_A\}$

with these rules
which regard the data, we can construct structured cross reference lists or HIPO, that are diagrams, which show Hierachically the Input, the Processing and the Output .

Literatur:

[3] Schneider, H.J.: Chomsky Systeme für partielle Ordnungen, Arbeitsberichte des Inst. f. Mathe. u. Datenv. 3, 3, Erlangen (1970)

[1] Nassi, I. Shneiderman, B.: Flowcharting Techniques for Structured Programming, Sigplan Notices Vol. 8, 8 (1973), 12-26

[2] Rosen, B.K.: High Level Data Flow Analysis, Comm. ACM, Vol. 20 (1977), 712-724

GRAPHS OF PROCESSORS

Walter J. Savitch

Computer Science Program
Department of Applied Physics and Information Science
University of California at San Diego
La Jolla, California 92093

1. INTRODUCTION

With the recent rapid advances in hardware technology, it is clear that multiprocessing computer systems are growing in importance and availability. Some highly parallel machines are already available, such as the ILLIAC IV and CDC STAR computers. Eventually, systems with a large number of processors will become common. When this occurs, parallel processors may come to be thought of as a computational resource in much the same way that storage is now.

The computational power of such highly parallel machines depends on the number of parallel processors available. The computational power also depends on a number of other factors. One factor that can greatly affect the computing power of a highly parallel machine is the pattern of interconnections by which processors communicate with one another. In this paper, we survey some of the work that has been done on models for parallel machines and analyze the effect that different interconnection patterns have on the computing power of a machine configuration.

The models for multiprocessing machines considered here do not have a common memory. Instead, each processor has its own memory that can only be accessed directly by that processor. Also, it is customary, and reasonable, to choose all processors in the multiprocessing machine to be identical. Under these assumptions, a multiprocessing machine is characterized by two objects: the type of processor used and a directed graph. Each node of the graph is a processor. A directed edge from node n_1 to node n_2 means that the processor at node n_1 can pass information to the processor at node n_2. As might well be expected, the power of a multiprocessing system can be affected by the power of the individual processors. However, we will see that the choice of the directed graph can affect the computing power of the system at lease as much as the choice of processors.

In this paper we will adopt the conventions which are standard for the field of machine-based complexity theory: All resources are allowed to be potentially infinite. So, in particular, the above mentioned directed graphs will usually be infinite. The only tasks considered will be testing for membership in a set. Run times and other computational costs will be measured as a function of the size of the input. The input will always be a string over some alphabet and its size is just its length.

We assume that the reader is familiar with the basic results of complexity theory as found in, for example, chapter one of Aho, Hopcroft and Ullman (1974). Since the main results discussed here are not new, proofs will usually be omitted or limited to a brief sketch.

2. TREES

The most widely studied pattern of processor interconnections consists of a tree of processors in which each processor may communicate directly only with the processors directly above and below it in the tree. Models by Chandra and Stockmeyer (1976), by Kozen (1976) and by Savitch and Stimson (1976,1978) use such tree-structured interconnections. In order to have a concrete model to work with, we will describe the PRAM model of Savitch and Stimson in some detail. The reader who desires a more complete description of the model should consult their 1978 paper. For simplicity, we are considering only binary trees but the binary branching is of no significance to the results discussed here.

A *parallel random access machine* or *PRAM* consists of an infinite binary tree of processors. Each processor is a random access machine with its own infinite memory. The random access machines are of the Cook-Reckhow (1973) type. In particular, the only arithmetic operations allowed are addition and substraction. The uniform cost criterior is used. That is, any memory access or operation can be performed in one time unit.

Each processor can communicate directly only with the processors directly above and below it in the tree. The communication is, in essence, restricted to a question and answer protocol. At the start of a computation, only the processor at the root of the tree is active. This root processor may activate the processors directly below it in the tree by passing each of them a finite list of parameters. These processors may, in turn, activate the processors directly below them in a like manner and so forth. These pasted parameters may be thought of as questions, or at least as parameters for some general class of questions. A processor may communicate with the processor directly above it in only one way. It can give a single answer to its "question." That is, it can pass back a finite list of parameters to the processor that activated it. When a processor gives such an "answer," it and all processors below it in the tree stop computing and return to their initial state. A processor may be called again at a later time to answer another "question." Notice that, with this communication pattern, the root node processor can activate exponential in t processors in t time units.

A PRAM also has a program associated with it. In the formal definition of a PRAM, this program is recursive and all processors use the same program (although they each have a separate instruction counter so that they can each be executing different parts of the same program). A processor activates another processor by making a recursive call. The processor activated begins computing on the passed parameters by starting at the first instruction of the PRAM program. Both the calling and the called processor compute in parallel. However, the details of how the program structure is defined are not critical to the results. Any reasonable notion of programming which conforms to the above outlined question and anwer protocol will yield the same results.

The input to a PRAM is a number placed in the first register of the root node processor. Initially, all other registers for the processor and all registers for the other processors are set to zero. The input is said to be *accepted* if the root node processor executes an accept instruction. The PRAM is said to *accept the set* A of integers, provided that it accepts exactly those integers which are in A.

When measuring run times, we identify integers with their binary numerals. So the length of an integer is just the length of the binary numeral for that integer. A PRAM is said to be T(n) *time bounded* provided that: for any input x of length n, if x is accepted, then x can be accepted in T(n) or fewer steps.

A PRAM program may be deterministic or nondeterministic. However, as our first theorem indicates, this distinction does not appear to be as significant for parallel machines as it is for serial machines. The proof may be found in Savitch and Stimson (1978). Similar proofs of very similar results can be found in Chandra and Stockmeyer (1976) and in Kozen (1976).

THEOREM 1. For any set A of integers, the following are equivalent:

(1) A is accepted by a nondeterministic PRAM in polynomial time.

(2) A is accepted by a deterministic PRAM in polynomial time.

(3) A is accepted by an ordinary, serial computer using polynomial storage.

There are a number of things to note about the above theorem. First, we did not specify the model used for a serial computer. That is because it is well known that, to within a polynomial, all standard models yield the same storage complexity classes. In fact, it does not matter whether the serial model is deterministic or nondeterministic. Since the integers can easily be identified with strings over a finite alphabet, it also does not matter whether the serial computer model has symbolic or numeric input. The second major point to note is that the result generalizes to arbitrary time bounds and does not apply only to polynomials. Finally, we should discuss in some detail the extent to which this result depends on the tree-structured interconnections.

Theorem 1 says that parallel machines appear to be much more powerful than serial machines and gives a characterization of this power in terms of the well-known notion of storage complexity. Chandra and Stockmeyer (1976) showed that it is primarily the tree-structured interconnections and not so much the particular type of processors used that gives this parallel processing machine its power. They show that

Theorem 1 remains true when the type of processor used at each node is changed from a random access machine to a Turing machine, a finite state machine or any of a number of other machine models.

It is hard to imagine a reasonable processor model that is simpler than the finite state model and, as noted above, Theorem 1 remains true even if the individual processors are changed from random access machines to finite state machines. So it is fair to say that the power of parallel processing expressed in Theorem 1 is due primarily to the interconnection pattern and not to the power of the individual processors. This power can, however, be increased by using a very powerful processor model. Savitch (1978) presents a version of the PRAM model which has powerful string manipulation operations available to the random access machines that serve as the individual processors. This version of the PRAM model is, at least in the nondeterministic case, much more powerful than the model used for Theorem 1. It is also interesting to note that there are versions of the random access machine which have no overt parallelism at all, and yet have exactly the same computing power as that proven for PRAMs in Theorem 1. Such models have been given by Pratt and Stockmeyer (1976) and by Hartmanis and Simon (1974).

3. FEASIBLE GRAPHS

Recall that we characterized a multiprocessing machine by two things: The type of processor used and a directed graph which specifies the communication paths between processors. In order to compare the computing power of various directed graphs for multiprocessing systems, we will fix the type of processor and vary the directed graph. The simplest choice for a processor model is the finite state machine. Also, since a finite state machine is of fairly limited power, this will help insure that we focus on the power of the directed graph. We have already noted that Theorem 1 remains true when we replace the random access machines of the PRAM model by finite state machines. So, choosing finite state machines as our model for the individual processors will certainly not produce a trivial model of multiprocessing systems. For these reasons, we will from now on assume that the individual processors of a multiprocessing machine are identical finite state machines. Our approach in this section and the next section follows that of Goldschlager (1977 and 1978).

Goldschlager defines a *conglomerate* as an infinite directed graph, with nodes labeled by the set of integers, together with a deterministic finite state machine, a copy of which serves as the processor for each node. The edges of the graph are labeled and give the directed transmission lines by which the finite state machines communicate. Since the finite state machines at the nodes are all identical, the directed graph must have bounded fan in. For simplicity, it is assumed that each finite state machine has exactly one output line which may feed into any number of other machines. Hence there is no bound on the fan out of the graph. Input is implemented by identifying an input alphabet Σ with a subset of the states of the finite state machine model. In this way, a string $a_1a_2...a_n$ of n symbols from Σ can be thought of as a sequence of n states. At the start of a computation, the conglomerate is given this input by placing the machines at nodes number one through n in states $a_1,a_2,...,a_n$ respectively. All other machines are placed in a designated start state. All transmission lines are set to a designated start signal and the computation proceeds from this initial configuration. In any one step, each finite state machine reads its input signals and, on the basis of these inputs and its own internal state, it changes state and issues a signal on its output line. The input is *accepted* provided that the processor at node number zero enters a designated accepting state. Definitions of accepting a set of input strings and of running within a time bound T(n) are defined analogously to how they were defined for PRAMs.

The directed graph of a conglomerate has bounded fan in. If it is bounded by r, then the arcs entering a node can be labeled by 1,2,...r or some initial segment of this list. The directed graph can be characterized by a function f from $\{1,2,...,r\}^*$ to Z∪{NIL}, where Z is the set of integers and hence node labels and NIL is a marker to indicate the absence of a node. The function f is called the *connection function* and basically tells which finite state machines can have outputs which effect the machine at node zero within some bounded time period. Since node zero is where acceptance takes place, this is a useful way of viewing the graph. To be specific, $f(i_1i_2...i_n)$ is the integer labeling the node reached by tracing backwards, from node zero along input lines labeled $i_1,i_2,...,i_n$ in that order. If there is no such node (because some node has fewer than r input arcs), then $f(i_1i_2...i_n)$ = NIL. So, for example, f(3) labels the node with an output line feeding directly into the third input line of node zero; f(32) is the node with an output line feeding directly into the second input line of f(3).

It is generally accepted that any feasibly realizable connection function must be moderately easy to compute and certainly must be computable in polynomial storage. Goldschlager has shown that the tree type connection function is at least as powerful as any other directed graph whose connection function can be computed in polynomial storage on a serial machine. Hence, it appears that, at least up to a polynomial, the tree type connection function is as powerful as any other feasible realizable connection function. A precise statement of Goldschlager's result follows. The proof can be found in Goldschlager (1977).

THEOREM 2. For any set A of strings over a finite alphabet, the following are equivalent.

(1) A is accepted in polynomial time by a conglomerate whose directed graph is a binary tree with directed arcs in both directions between adjacent nodes of the tree.

(2) A is accepted in polynomial time by a conglomerate whose connection function can be computed in polynomial storage on a serial computer.

(3) A is accepted in polynomial storage on a serial computer.

4. ARBITRARY GRAPHS

Theorem 2 places a limit on the computing power of conglomerates which have feasibly realizable connection functions. It is of some theoretical interest to ask how much more computing power a conglomerate can realize by using connection functions that are extremely complex and possibly not even practically realizable. The answer is that there really is no limit to the power one can add to a conglomerate by making its connection function more complicated. Goldschlager (1977) showed that with non-recursive connection functions, conglomerates can accept non-recursively-enumerable sets. Using Goldschlager's techniques it is easy to build a connection function to store the membership table for any given set. If this is done with a little care we get

THEOREM 3. If A is any set (possibly even non-recursively-enumerable) of strings over a finite alphabet, then there is some conglomerate that accepts A in polynomial time.

The use of a non-effectively-computable connection function in the conglomerate of Theorem 3 places that conglomerate outside the class of things that we commonly think of as computers. Hence, it is worth noting that the effective version of Theorem 3 also holds.

THEOREM 4. If A is a recursive set, then there is some conglomerate M with a total recursive connection function such that M accepts A in polynomial time.

Since Theorems 3 and 4 do not already appear in the literature, we will present a very brief sketch of the proof.

Proof sketch for Theorems 3 and 4: The directed graph for the conglomerate consists of a countably infinite collection of infinite binary trees. The trees are thought of as being lined up in a row so that there is a first, second, etc. tree. Corresponding tree nodes are connected. So, for example, the root node of the first tree is connected to the root node of the second tree, the root node of the second tree is connected to the root node of the third tree and so forth. Hence, the conglomerate can also be thought of as a single binary tree each node of which is a semi-infinite linear array. Each element of A is associated with one such linear array. The input is placed in the root linear array and is passed down the tree to each linear array. It is easy to arrange things so that the linear array for a string of length n can be reached in a polynomial in n steps.

Node zero, which is the node that performs any acceptance, is an additional node not in this tree. We will also add other nodes as we explain the construction of the conglomerate.

The output lines from each linear array branch in three. Two sets of output lines pass the input string down the tree. The other set of output lines are fed into a subconglomerate which checks to see if the input is the particular string in A associated with that linear array. The subconglomerate outputs a signal if and only if the input was this particular string. The output line from each of these subconglomerates are fed into the zero node. So node zero will receive a signal if and only if the input is in A. The zero node accepts if it receives such a signal.

If the above description is taken literally, the zero node has infinite fan in. However, this can be replaced by a binary tree which combines lines two at a time. In fact, the first binary tree in the array of trees can be used for this purpose.

The above described tree type construction allows signals to travel fast enough to achieve the desired run time. □

5. NONDETERMINISTIC MACHINES

A *nondeterministic conglomerate* is a conglomerate in which the finite state machine is allowed to be nondeterministic. As we already noted, if we only measure time up to a polynomial, then nondeterminism adds no power to the class of conglomerates with tree type interconnections. However, some other types of interconnections can be made extremely powerful by the use of nondeterminism.

THEOREM 5. There is a connection function f such that:

(1) f can be computed by a deterministic polynomial time bounded serial computer and,

(2) for any set A and any time bound T(n), if A is accepted by a nondeterministic T(n) time bounded single tape Turing machine, than A is accepted in time O(log T(n)) by a nondeterministic conglomerate with connection function f.

Proof Sketch. Let Z be a T(n) time bounded single tape Turing machine and let w be an input to Z of length n. A computation of Z or input w can be viewed as a T(n)-by-T(n) array of squares. The first row is the first ID, the second row the second ID and so forth. Hence each individual square in this array can assume a value equal to a tape symbol of Z plus possibly a state of Z. To test if an arbitrary such array represents a possible action of Z, we need only check that each square satisfies certain simple relationships with its immediate neighbors and check that exactly one square per row contains a state.

A T(n)-by-T(n) array of nondeterministic finite state machines can tell if Z accepts w as follows. Each finite state machine quesses the contents of one square of the array discussed in the previous paragraph. The finite state machines then communicate with their neighbors to see if their guesses are consistent with those of their neighbors. If all guesses are consistent and there is exactly one state per row of the array, then an action of Z has been correctly guessed. The checking for consistency takes only a constant amount of time. To test if Z accepts w, five additional things are needed: the input w must be delivered to the appropriate squares; the information that all squares made consistent guesses must be transmitted to node zero of whatever conglomerate this is inbedded in; the conglomerate must somehow check that the guessed array contains exactly one state per row; it also must check that an accepting state occurs in the array; also, it is necessary that whatever conglomerate this is imbedded in can activate a T(n)-by-T(n) array in time O(log T(n)).

It is not too difficult to design a nondeterministic conglomerate to simulate A in the manner outlined above. The nodes of Z are arranged in successively larger square arrays with the single node numbered zero being the first such array. The interconnections within an array are such that each node is connected to its four neighbors. The interconnections between arrays are such that each array can activate the next and such that signals can also return on these activation lines.

To test whether Z accepts w, the conglomerate does the following. It activates a T(n)-by-T(n), or larger, square array. It then performs the type of simulation outlined above. Finally, the result of the simulation is passed back up to the zero node. If the rate of growth of the successive arrays is exponential, then the conglomerate will simulate Z in time O(log T(n)).

Some care must be taken with the input. The idea that we wish to simulate is that the input is placed in the first row of the array activated. Since the input can only go one place but any array might be activated, we do the following: We put as much as possible of the input into the first row of the first array. In one move this much of the input shifts to the second array. More of the input is placed in those squares of the first row of the second array which are not needed to receive input from the first array. In two steps all this gets to the first row of the third array and so forth.

To check for one state per row and to check for an accepting state, each array has an additional tree-like configuration attached. This tree-like configuration performs the tests and delivers the final result to some node in the array. This node can then pass the desired information up the configuration so it eventually reaches node zero.

The above connection pattern between processors is independent of Z and can be computed in determinate polynomial time on a serial computer. □

Definitional Mechanisms for Conceptual Graphs

John F. Sowa
IBM Systems Research Institute
205 East 42nd Street
New York, N. Y. 10017

ABSTRACT: Conceptual graphs formalize the semantic networks used to represent meaning in artificial intelligence and computational linguistics. This paper presents mechanisms for defining new types of concepts, conceptual relations, and composite entities that have other entities as parts. It gives a formal calculus for operating upon the graphs; applications and philosophical interpretations are treated in other papers.

1. Conceptual Graphs

Graph notations called semantic networks, conceptual dependency graphs, or cognitive nets are used in artificial intelligence for processing natural language. Although various authors use different terminology and notations, some themes are common to most of them:

- Nodes of the graphs, which are usually called *concepts,* represent such things as entities, attributes, and events.
- Different nodes of the same concept type represent distinct individuals or instances of that type, unless they are marked with a *name* or *index* to indicate the same individual.
- Arcs of the graphs, called *relations, conceptual relations,* or *case roles,* represent relationships that hold between the concepts linked by the arcs.
- Types of concepts are ordered according to levels of generality, such as COLLIE, DOG, ANIMAL, LIVING-THING, ENTITY. This ordering is variously called *subtype, subset, subsort,* or simply *IS-A*.
- Commonly occurring patterns of concepts and conceptual relations are grouped in stereotyped units called *conceptual schemata, frames, templates, scenarios,* or *scripts.*
- Schemata that determine properties for one type of concept may be applied to any of its subtypes.

Articles on various forms of these graphs have been collected by Schank and Colby (1973), Bobrow and Collins (1975), Charniak and Wilks (1976), and Findler (1979). The notation in this article follows Sowa (1976). That paper discussed a variety of issues—quantifiers, functions, and applications to data base systems. This one, however, concentrates on definitional mechanisms, which the previous article merely hinted at. Readers should see the earlier article for examples and applications, but some of the terminology has been changed: "sort label" is now called "type label", "well-formed" is now "canonical", and some of the arrows on conceptual relations have been reversed, following a suggestion by Pedersen (1978).

Definition 1: A *conceptual graph* is a finite, connected, bipartite graph with nodes of the first kind called *concepts* and nodes of the second kind called *conceptual relations*.

The conceptual graph (1) shows concepts and relationships in the sentence "Seymour cut the salami with a knife." The boxes are *concepts* and the circles are *conceptual relations*. Inside each box or circle is a *type label* that designates the type of concept or relation. After the type label on a concept, there may be a name of some individual (such as Seymour) or a marker that designates a particular, but unnamed, individual (such as the salami i23017). A concept that has only a type label is generic: the concepts KNIFE and CUT do not specify any particular knife or act of cutting. The conceptual relations labeled AGNT, INST, and PTNT represent the relations agent, instrument, and patient in case grammar (Fillmore, 1968).

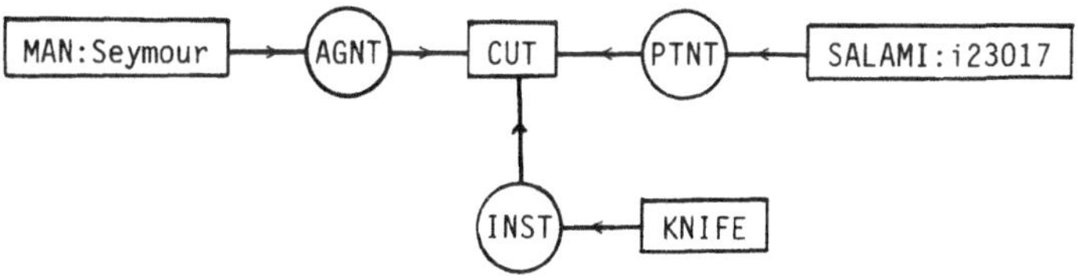

(1)

Definition 2: Every conceptual relation has one or more *arcs*, each of which must be attached to a concept. If the relation has n arcs, it is said to be *n-adic*, and its arcs are labeled 1, 2, ..., n.

The most common conceptual relations are dyadic (2-adic), but the rules for defining new relations can create ones with any number of arcs. Although the formal definition says that arcs are numbered, for dyadic relations, arc 1 is drawn as an arrow pointing towards the circle, and arc 2 as an arrow pointing away from the circle.

Axiom 1: There is a set L of *type labels* and a function *type*, which maps concepts and conceptual relations into L.

- If $type(a)=type(b)$, then a and b are said to be of the *same type*.
- Type labels are partially ordered: if $type(a) \leq type(b)$, then a is said to be a *subtype* of b.
- Type labels of concepts and conceptual relations are disjoint, noncomparable subsets of L: if a is a concept and r is a conceptual relation, then a and r may never be of the same type nor may one be a subtype of the other.

Type labels are the character strings that are written inside the boxes and circles of a conceptual graph. The partial ordering of type labels represents the generalization hierarchies in semantic networks. Although some notations draw explicit arcs for subtypes, such notations tend to be cluttered. Since the partial ordering of types is so pervasive, it is not drawn explicitly, but it underlies the formation rules defined below.

Not all combinations of concepts and conceptual relations are meaningful. Yet to say that some graphs are meaningful and others are not is begging the question, because the purpose of conceptual graphs is to form the basis of a theory of meaning. Therefore, to avoid prejudging the issue, the more neutral term *canonical* is adopted. Canonical graphs model real world situations and can be mapped to sentences in natural language.

Axiom 2: There is a finite set of conceptual graphs called the *canon*. There are four rules for deriving conceptual graphs called the *canonical formation rules*. A conceptual graph is said to be a *canonical graph* if either it is in the canon or it is derived from canonical graphs by a canonical formation rule.

Canonical formation rules serve the same purpose as selectional constraints in linguistics (Chomsky, 1965). Canonical graphs are like frames or scripts in artificial intelligence, and the formation rules generate bigger frames. The rules defined by Sowa (1976) were copy, detach, restrict, and join on a concept. The rules defined in this paper include copy, restrict, and join on a concept, but detach has been replaced by join on a star. This change imposes tighter constraints on a derivation: every graph that is derivable by the new rules was derivable by the old rules, but the old rules permitted some undesirable combinations. Before stating the formation rules, the definitions of *star graph* and *joinable* are necessary.

Definition 3: A *star graph* is a conceptual graph consisting of a single conceptual relation and the concepts attached to each of its arcs. (Two or more arcs of the conceptual relation may be attached to the same concept.)

Definition 4: Two concepts a and b are said to be *joinable* if $type(a)=type(b)$. Two star graphs with conceptual relations r and s are said to be *joinable* if r and s have the same number of arcs, $type(r)=type(s)$, and for each i, the concept attached to arc i of r is joinable to the concept attached to arc i of s.

Axiom 3: Let u and v be canonical graphs (u and v may be the same graph). Any graph derived by one of the following *canonical formation rules* is also canonical:

- Copy: An exact copy of u is canonical.
- Restrict: Let a be a concept in u, and let t be a type label where $t \leq type(a)$. Then the graph obtained by replacing a with a concept of type t is canonical.
- Join on a concept: Let a be a concept in u, and b a concept in v. If a and b are joinable, then the graph derived by the following steps is canonical: First delete b from v; then attach to a all arcs of conceptual relations that had been attached to b.
- Join on a star: Let r be a conceptual relation in u, and s a conceptual relation in v. If the star graphs of r and s are joinable, then the graph derived by the following steps is canonical: First delete s and its arcs from v; then for each i, join the concept attached to arc i of r to the concept that had been attached to arc i of s.

Restriction replaces a type label in a graph by the label of a subtype; this rule lets subtypes inherit the structures that apply to more general types. Join on a concept combines graphs that have concepts of the same type: one graph is overlaid on the other so that two concepts of the same type merge into a single concept; as a result, all the arcs that had been connected to either concept are connected to the single merged concept. Join on a star is the counterpart for conceptual relations: two conceptual relations are overlaid so that their star graphs are merged.

The number of possible canonical graphs may be infinite, but the canon contains a finite number from which all the others can be derived. With an appropriate canon, many undesirable graphs are ruled out as noncanonical. Anything that can be said in English must be representable in a canonical graph; but to distinguish true graphs from merely possible graphs, Sowa (1976) gives rules of inference that preserve the truth of a derivation.

Definition 5: Let v be a conceptual graph, let v' be a subgraph of v in which every conceptual relation has exactly the same arcs as in v, and let u be a copy of v' in which zero or more concepts may be restricted to subtypes. Then u is called a *projection* of v, and v' is called a *projective origin* of u in v.

According to the 1976 rules, a projection of a canonical graph was also canonical. But according to the new rules, a projection is not necessarily canonical. The main purpose of projections, however, is to define the rule of join on a common projection, which is a generalization of the rules for joining on a concept or a star.

Definition 6: If v and w are canonical graphs, u is a projection of v, and u is a projection of w, then u is said to be a *common projection* of v and w.

Theorem 1: If u is a common projection of v and w, then v and w may be *joined on the common projection* u to form a canonical graph by the following steps:

- Let v' be a projective origin of u in v, and let w' be a projective origin of u in w.
- Restrict each concept of v' and w' to the type label of the corresponding concept in u.
- Join each concept of v' to the corresponding concept of w'.
- Join each star graph of v' to the corresponding star of w'.

The concepts and conceptual relations in the resulting graph consist of those in $v-v'$, $w-w'$, and a copy of u.

Proof: The resulting conceptual graph is canonical because all of the operations performed on v and w were canonical: restrictions, joins on concepts, and joins on stars. The operations of restricting all concepts in v' and w' to the corresponding types in u had the effect of making the graphs v' and w' copies of u, since they were originally identical to u except for having possibly different type labels. The operations of joining corresponding concepts and star graphs in v' and w' had the effect of merging both graphs into a single graph that is identical to u. The final graph therefore consists of a copy of u together with all concepts and conceptual relations that were outside of the subgraphs v' and w', i.e. $v-v'$ together with $w-w'$.

2. Individuals and Names

Section 1 presented a theory of generic concepts: the type CAT, for example, could apply to any cat in the world or to any fictional cat in a possible world. This section extends the theory with markers on concepts to designate particular individuals.

Axiom 4: There is a countably infinite set I={i1, i2, i3, ...} whose elements are called *individual markers.* The function *referent* applies to concepts:

- If *a* is a concept, then *referent(a)* is either an individual marker in I or the special marker *undef.*
- When *referent(a)* is in I, then *a* is said to be a concept of an *individual.*
- When *referent(a)=undef,* then the *referent* of *a* is said to be *undefined,* and *a* is said to be a *generic* concept.

Diagram (2) shows a generic concept of type CAT and an individual concept of type CAT. A generic concept has only a type label in the box; an individual concept has a colon following the type label and an individual marker after the colon. A concept of any type may have an individual marker: for a concept of type CAT, the marker would specify a particular cat; for a concept of type JUMP, a particular instance of jumping; for a concept of type HAPPY, a particular instance of the state of happiness.

(2)

In data base systems, individual markers correspond to the unique identifiers that distinguish between persons or things that happen to have the same name. In linguistics, Chomsky (1965) introduced unique indices as a notation for specifying which noun phrases referred to the same individuals. Since then, some linguists have suggested that the indices reflect underlying mental structures; McCawley (1971) said, "Indices exist in the mind of the speaker rather than in the real world: they are conceptual entities which the individual creates in interpreting his experience." (pp. 223-224)

Once the theory can specify individuals, it has a basis for naming them. Axiom 5 introduces the conceptual relation NAME, which links a name to a concept of an individual. This axiom provides a way of naming individual entities.

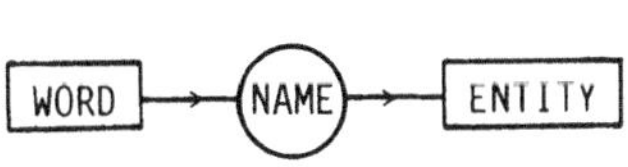

(3)

Axiom 5: Graph (3) is in the canon.

- If a relation of type NAME occurs in a canonical graph, then its star graph must be derivable from (3) by restriction.
- When the concept attached to arc 2 of NAME is a concept of an individual, then the concept attached to arc 1 (which must be a subtype of WORD) is called a *name* of that individual.

If the type ENTITY is restricted to PERSON and WORD to "John", graph (3) becomes a graph for a person named John. Graph (4) shows the generic concept "John", which is a subtype of MASCULINE-NAME, which is a subtype of WORD. That graph indicates that a use of "John" is a name of the person i3074.

(4)

If there is only one person named John, then the name itself is sufficient to identify the individual, and the marker i3074 is not necessary. The notation PERSON: John is an abbreviation for graph (4) when the name is unique; this form deletes the quotation marks and substitutes the name for the marker i3074. Formally, however, all definitions and axioms are stated in terms of (4). Furthermore, the abbreviation may only be used when the name is unique (within some context) and when the individual does not have multiple names or aliases. This notation applies equally well to names of entities in the real world, other possible worlds, or fictional worlds.

Definition 4 for *joinable* does not apply to concepts of individuals; definition 4a extends 4 to include concepts of individuals. If both concepts are individual, then their markers must be identical.

Definition 4a: If *a* and *b* are concepts of the same type, then they are *joinable* if either *referent(a)=undef, referent(b)=undef,* or *referent(a)=referent(b).* Otherwise, they are not joinable.

To accommodate individual markers, the canonical formation rules must specify a referent for each concept in the derived graphs. As before, the copy rule is the simplest: it copies everything including the individual markers. An additional test is necessary for the rule of restriction: the concept ANIMAL: i98077 cannot be restricted to CAT: i98077 if the particular individual i98077 happens to be a dog. Before restricting the type label ANIMAL to the type label CAT, a test must determine whether the label CAT is applicable to i98077; the predicate *applicable* makes that test.

Axiom 6: Let *t* be a type label of a concept and let *i* be an individual marker. The predicate *applicable* tests whether the marker *i* may be the referent of a concept of type *t*: if *applicable(t,i)* is true, then *t* is said to be *applicable* to *i*. For all *t*, *applicable(t,undef)* is defined to be true.

Axiom 3a extends the formation rules to concepts of individuals. If the referents of all concepts in a graph are undefined (generic concepts), then Axiom 3a is equivalent to Axiom 3. If some or all of the concepts have individual markers, then the formation rules carry the markers along to the derived graphs.

Axiom 3a: Let *u* and *v* be canonical graphs (*u* and *v* may be the same graph). The following rules generalize the canonical formation rules of Axiom 3 to accommodate individual markers:

- Copy: An exact copy of *u* is canonical.

- Restrict: Let *a* be any concept in *u* and *t* be a type label, where *t≤type(a)* and *applicable(t,referent(a))*. Then the graph obtained by changing *type(a)* to *t* and leaving *referent(a)* unchanged is canonical.

- Join on a concept: The operations are the same as in Axiom 3, but with Definition 4a for joinable concepts. Let the concept *c* be derived by joining *a* and *b*. If *referent(a)=undef,* then *referent(c)=referent(b),* else *referent(c)=referent(a).*

- Join on a star: The operations are the same as in Axiom 3, but with Definition 4a for joinable concepts. Referents are determined as in join on a concept.

3. Defining Concept Types

For many applications, a fixed set of concept types is adequate. In conceptual dependency theory, Schank (1975) claims that a limited set of primitive types is sufficient for understanding a wide range of natural language. For complex types such as BUY and SELL, he requires the language processor to analyze the input into primitive types such as transfers of money and goods; he has no formalism for defining new types of concepts and relations. Other systems, such as Heidorn's NLP (1974), are not dogmatic about which concepts are primitive and let the language designer choose a suitable set, but most of these systems have no convenient way of defining new types in terms of more primitive ones. A system that implements definitional methods is OWL (Szolovits, Hawkinson, & Martin, 1977), which takes an Aristotelian approach in defining new types by means of genus and differentiae. This paper adopts an Aristotelian approach with mechanisms similar to the lambda calculus (Church, 1941), but extended to graphs.

Definition 7: Let *u* be a canonical graph and let *a* be a generic concept in *u*. Then the pair *(a,u)* is called a *type definition*, where *a* is called the *genus* and *u* is called the *differentia*.

Axiom 7: The function *label* maps type definitions into the set L. If *(a,u)* is a type definition, *label(a,u)* is a type label in L.

Graph (5) is the differentia for a new type that could be labeled CIRCUS-ELEPHANT. The genus, which is flagged with an asterisk, has type label ELEPHANT. This graph defines a subtype of ELEPHANT that performs in circuses. By designating one of the other concepts as genus, the same graph could be used as the differentia for either a type of circus that has performing elephants or a type of performing done by elephants in circuses.

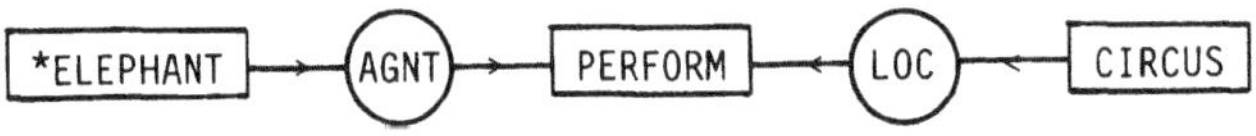

(5)

Once a mechanism is available for defining new types, the definitions can be used to simplify the conceptual graphs. Type contraction replaces an entire subgraph with a single concept that incorporates equivalent information in its type label.

Definition 8: Let *v* be a canonical graph, let *b* be a concept in *v*, and let *u* be a canonical subgraph of *v* that contains *b* and which is connected to the rest of *v* only by arcs attached to *b*. Then the operation of *type contraction* has the following steps:

- Detach all of the graph *u* from *v* except for the concept *b*,
- Replace *b* in *u* with the concept *a*, whose type label is *type(b)* but whose referent is *undef*,
- Replace the concept *b* in what's left of *v* with a concept whose type is *label(a,u)* and whose referent is *referent(b)*.

Axiom 8: If type contraction is performed on a canonical graph, the resulting graph is canonical.

Axiom 1 introduced the partial ordering of type labels as an *a priori* assumption. If the type labels correspond to type definitions, Axiom 9 relates the partial ordering to the structure of the definitions. This axiom states the usual Aristotelian principle that adding more differentiae to a concept restricts it to a lower subtype. Commutativity of type contractions is another common principle: if the type label CIRCUS-ELEPHANT is defined by ELEPHANT which performs in a circus and GRAY-ELEPHANT by ELEPHANT which is gray, then the type label GRAY-CIRCUS-ELEPHANT defined by ELEPHANT which is gray and performs in a circus should be equivalent to CIRCUS-ELEPHANT which is gray and to GRAY-ELEPHANT which performs in a circus.

Definition 9: Let the notation $((a,u),v)$ represent a type definition (b,v) where $type(b)=label(a,u)$.

Axiom 9: If (a,u) is a type definition, the position of $label(a,u)$ in the partial ordering over the set L of type labels is determined by the following conditions:

- If the graph u consists of the single concept a,
  then $label(a,u)=type(a)$,
  else $label(a,u)<type(a)$.
- Type contraction is commutative: if the graph u is derivable by joining canonical graphs v and w on the concept a, then $label(a,u) = label((a,v),w) = label((a,w),v)$.

Because of Axiom 9, if the label of a type definition is a subtype of some concept, then there must be some graph that states the differentia between the new definition and the more general concept. This graph may, in fact, be the join of a large number of graphs if there are many intervening levels in the partial ordering. The existence of this graph can be proved as Theorem 2.

Theorem 2: If (a,u) is a type definition and c is a generic concept where $label(a,u)<type(c)$, then there exists a canonical graph w such that $label(a,u)=label(c,w)$. The graph w is called the *differentia* between (a,u) and c.

Proof: If $label(a,u)<type(c)$, then either $type(a)=type(c)$, or else there exists a sequence of type definitions $(a_1,u_1),\ldots,(a_n,u_n)$ where

- $label(a,u) = label(a_1,u_1)$,
- $type(a_n) = type(c)$,
- $label(a_i,u_i) < label(a_{i+1},u_{i+1})$ by Axiom 9; hence $type(a_i) = label(a_{i+1},u_{i+1})$.

If $type(a)=type(c)$, the differentia is u. Otherwise, $label(a_i,u_i)=label((a_{i+1},u_{i+1}),u_i)$ for each i from 1 to $n-1$. Therefore, $label(a,u)=label((\ldots(c,u_n)\ldots),u_1)$, and the differentia w is the join of the graphs u_n through u_1 on the concept that corresponds to c.

If new type labels are introduced by definitions, there must be at least one primitive label. Axiom 10 states that the set of all type labels has a subset M of primitive labels that are not subtypes of anything else. For Aristotle, the primitive type labels are the categories: SUBSTANCE, QUANTITY, QUALITY, RELATION, TIME, POSITION, STATE, ACTIVI-

TY, and PASSIVITY. For OWL, the only primitive label is SUMMUM-GENUS. Axiom 10 permits any number of primitive labels.

Axiom 10: The set L of type labels contains a subset M of *maximal type labels*. If p is in M, then there is no q in L for which $p<q$. Further, if t is a type label not in M, then there exists a type definition *(a,u)* where *t=label(a,u)* and *type(a)* is in M.

Since Axiom 8 makes type contraction a canonical operation, the formation rule of restriction is redundant: if all subtypes are introduced by type definition, then restriction is equivalent to join on a concept followed by type contraction.

Theorem 3: Let v be a graph derived from a canonical graph w by restricting a concept a in w to type t. Then v could also be derived from w by a join on a concept and a type contraction.

Proof: Since $t \leq type(a)$, by Axiom 10 and Theorem 2 there must be a type definition (a,u) where *t=label(a,u)*. Join u and w on the concept a. Then perform a type contraction by removing the graph u that had just been joined to w and replace the type label of a with *t=label(a,u)*.

Type expansion replaces a concept type with its definition: the type label of the genus replaces the defined type label and the graph for the differentia is joined to the concept. Although type contraction always produces a canonical graph from a canonical graph, the result of type expansion is not necessarily canonical.

Definition 10: Let v be a conceptual graph, and let b be a concept in v where *type(b)=label(a,u)*. Then *type expansion* is the operation of replacing the type label of b with *type(a)*, leaving *referent(b)* unchanged, and joining the graphs u and v on the concept a in u and the newly modified b in v.

No axiom makes type expansion a canonical rule. The reason why it is not canonical is that it overrides the constraints imposed by the canonical formation rules. In a system that had a single maximal type label, say SUMMUM-GENUS, any two graphs could be joined simply by performing repeated type expansions to obtain two concepts of type SUMMUM-GENUS and then joining them.

4. Defining Conceptual Relations

New conceptual relations may be defined by a mechanism similar to type definition for concepts. For an inventory system, Graph (6) may represent the sentence "A catalog number characterizes an item and a number is the quantity of such items located in a stock room."

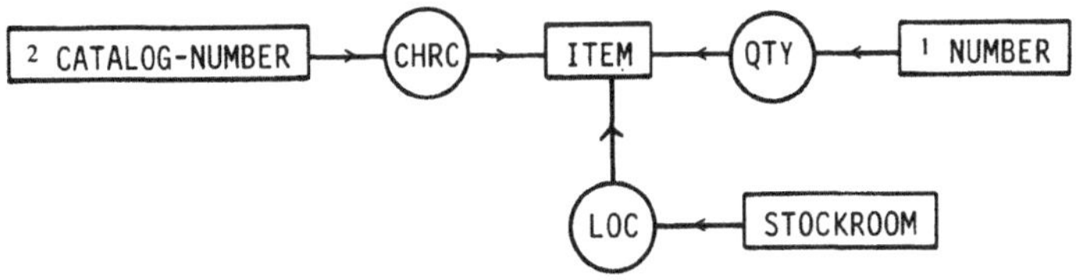

(6)

If (6) is a useful configuration, the entire graph may be defined as a conceptual relation of type QOH that represents quantity of items on hand. The superscripts [1] and [2] on the concepts of type NUMBER and CATALOG-NUMBER indicate that they are associated with arcs 1 and 2 of the new relation QOH. Then (7) is a relational contraction of (6).

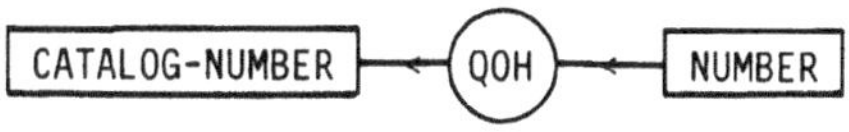

$$\boxed{\text{CATALOG-NUMBER}} \ \longleftarrow \bigcirc\!\!\text{QOH}\!\!\bigcirc \longleftarrow \ \boxed{\text{NUMBER}} \tag{7}$$

Definition 11: An *n-adic relational definition* is a sequence $(u,a_1,...,a_n)$, where u is a conceptual graph called the *relator*, n is a positive integer, and $a_1,...,a_n$ are n distinct generic concepts in u called the *formal parameters*.

Axiom 11: The function *label* maps relational definitions into the set L of type labels:

- If r is a relational definition, then there is no type label t where $label(r)<t$ or $t<label(r)$.

- If r and s are two relational definitions, then $label(r)=label(s)$ implies that r and s are either the same or exact copies of each other.

Axiom 12: Let r be an n-adic relational definition $(u,a_1,...,a_n)$ and c be a conceptual relation where $type(c)=label(r)$:

- c must have n arcs,

- In a canonical graph containing c, the concept attached to arc i of c must be a subtype of a_i.

Just as all type definitions for concepts could be reduced to a single primitive type such as SUMMUM-GENUS, all relational definitions could be reduced to the single dyadic relation type, LINK. Even the linguistic relation AGNT could be introduced first as the concept type AGENT, and then Graph (8) could be used as the relator to define the conceptual relation. The concept type labels ANIMATE, AGENT, and ACT could themselves be defined in terms of more primitive concept types.

$$\boxed{\text{\small 2 }\text{ANIMATE}} \longrightarrow \bigcirc\!\!\text{LINK}\!\!\bigcirc \longrightarrow \boxed{\text{AGENT}} \longleftarrow \bigcirc\!\!\text{LINK}\!\!\bigcirc \longleftarrow \boxed{\text{\small 1 }\text{ACT}} \tag{8}$$

Axiom 13: There is a type label LINK in L where $LINK=type(c)$ for some dyadic conceptual relation c. If d is a conceptual relation where $type(d)\neq LINK$, then there exists a relational definition r where $type(d)=label(r)$.

Relational contraction and expansion are the counterparts of type contraction and expansion. Graph (7) is a relational contraction of (6), and (6) is a relational expansion of (7).

Definition 12: The operation of *relational contraction* replaces a subgraph v of a conceptual graph w with a star graph of some conceptual relation c. Let $b_1,...,b_n$ be n distinct concepts of v, let v have no arcs attached to concepts in $w-v$, and let u be a copy of v with the concepts $b_1,...,b_n$ replaced by generic concepts $a_1,...,a_n$ where each b_i is a subtype of a_i. Then relational contraction consists of the following steps:

- Delete all of v from w except for $b_1,\ldots,b_n$,
- Let $type(c)=label(u,a_1,\ldots,a_n)$,
- For each i, attach arc i of c to concept b_i.

Axiom 14: If relational contraction is performed on a canonical graph, the resulting graph is canonical.

Definition 13: The operation of ***relational expansion*** replaces a star graph of a conceptual relation c where $type(c)=label(u,a_1,\ldots,a_n)$ with the relator u of the relational definition. Let w be a conceptual graph containing c; then relational expansion consists of the following steps:

- Detach c and its arcs from w,
- For each i, if b_i is the concept that was attached to arc i of c, then restrict a_i to $type(b_i)$,
- For each i, join the restricted form of a_i to b_i.

As before, contraction is a canonical operation, but expansion is not. Note that Definition 11 merely required the relator to be a conceptual graph, not necessarily a canonical graph. If the relator was required to be canonical, one could prove that all canonical graphs containing relations of types other than the primitive LINK could be built up by joining star graphs and then possibly doing some type contractions. This property is too strong: it rules out the possibility of declaring complex graphs canonical that could not be built up from canonical star graphs. Further issues about the choice of canonical graphs are discussed in Section 6.

5. Defining Composite Individuals

Goodman (1951) populates the world with individuals that have other individuals as parts. Mathematicians define sets that have other things, possibly other sets, as elements. Programming languages define structures that have data elements and other structures as parts. The human body has parts like head, hands, and feet. Books have chapters, chapters have sections, sections have paragraphs, paragraphs have sentences, sentences have words, words have letters, and letters have strokes. Clubs have members, gaggles have geese, and even situations, events, and states may have subevents and aspects.

Definition 14: Let $t=(a,u)$ be a type definition where u is larger than the single concept a and where every concept of u is generic. Then t is called a *pattern* for a *composite individual.*

Axiom 15: There is a function *part* defined over pairs of concepts. Let c be a concept where $type(c)=label(a,u)$, (a,u) is a pattern for a composite individual, and $i=referent(c)$ is an individual marker.

- For the genus concept a, $part(c,a)=i$. The marker i is called a *composite individual marker*.
- For any other concept b in u, $j=part(c,b)$ where j is either *undef* or an individual marker where $applicable(type(b),j)$. If $j \neq undef$, then j is called a *part* of i.
- For any other concepts x and y not meeting the above conditions, $part(x,y)=undef$.

Axiom 15 means that some individual markers correspond to composite individuals. The pattern for a composite individual induces a mapping from a composite individual marker i to the individual markers for the parts of i. Graph (5) for defining CIRCUS-ELEPHANT is a pattern for a composite individual since all concepts in it are generic. Suppose c is a concept of type CIRCUS-ELEPHANT for the individual named Jumbo. Then the three concepts of (5) each determine a specific part of Jumbo in his role as circus elephant: the ELEPHANT part is Jumbo himself, the CIRCUS part is the Barnum & Bailey Circus, and the PERFORM part is a performance of Jumbo in the Barnum & Bailey Circus. The circus is not part of Jumbo in his role as elephant, but it is a necessary part of Jumbo in his role as circus elephant.

There are a number of important topics which are beyond the scope of this paper: Definition 14 and Axiom 15 allow patterns for composite individuals with a fixed number of parts, but in patterns for sets, the number of elements should be arbitrary. Some patterns of individuals might require quantifiers or concepts of individuals in the type definition. And for the example of Jumbo, the PERFORM part of Jumbo in his role as circus elephant should probably be the set of all his performances rather than some single performance. These extensions, however, will be left for a forthcoming book.

6. Constructing Possible Worlds

Concepts and conceptual relations are the building blocks for constructing possible worlds. Any such world may contain at most a countable number of discrete entities with discrete relationships between them. They cannot simulate continuous processes in the real world to an arbitrary degree of precision, but they are probably adequate for representing the kinds of things that people think about conceptually and express in the discrete words of a natural language. If there are continuous processes in human thought, then they cannot be represented accurately with conceptual graphs—neither could they be represented on a digital computer in any form.

Besides building blocks, a theory must supply blueprints for specifying how the blocks are assembled. That is the purpose of the graphs in the canon. For any particular application, someone must decide which relationships are so important that they must be canonized in the privileged set. In data base systems, the data base designer or administrator would be responsible for defining the canon. In an artificial intelligence system, one might experiment with methods for letting the computer discover its own optimal set of canonical graphs. Once the canon is specified, it determines permissible structures for an entire family of possible worlds. This philosophy is consonant with current research in the semantics of modal logic (e.g. Rescher, 1975).

All of the operations and formation rules defined in this paper fall within the scope of context-free graph grammars. The canon imposes some of the restrictions that might otherwise require context-sensitive rules. Unfortunately, there are fundamental features of logic that cannot be handled with a purely context-free system. Implication and negation both require context-sensitive operations that imply some sort of pattern matching. The canonical graphs should be viewed as a system for filtering out many undesirable combinations, but further context-sensitive rules are needed to guarantee that a true state of the world always evolves out of another true state.

One point that was not fully explained in Sections 3 and 4 was why type and relational contractions are canonical operations, but expansions are not canonical. The reason is that everything can be built up from a primitive base: one type for concepts, one type for conceptual relations, a countable set of distinguishable labels, such as character strings, and a countable set of individual markers. Type and relational contraction make the graphs smaller by using more complex types: a great deal of information can be packed into each node. And the formation rules, although basically context-free, can take account of a complex structure by testing only a single type label. When all graphs are fully expanded, however, every concept is labeled SUMMUM-GENUS, and every relation is labeled LINK. In the fully expanded form, type labels are meaningless, and complex pattern matching would be needed to determine what was being represented. Therefore, to take maximum advantage of the constraints imposed by the canon, the graphs should not be expanded unless absolutely necessary. One reason for doing expansions is to perform certain kinds of inferences that do require pattern matching—but that is a topic for another paper.

Many other topics have not been mentioned here: quantifiers, computations, and applications. Furthermore, the operations defined in this paper provide only a formal calculus that says nothing about the "meaning" of the graphs. The meaning would be determined by syntactic rules for mapping sentences from English or other languages to and from the graphs, by rules of perception and action that would relate the graphs to the real world, and by a detailed philosophical analysis that would justify the term *concept* for the boxes in these graphs. Some of these topics were mentioned by Sowa (1976), and others are left for the forthcoming book.

Acknowledgment

I would like to thank George Heidorn for making many detailed comments on this paper and forcing me to clarify a number of points. Since he did not have a chance to review the final draft, he is not responsible for any obscurities that remain.

References

Bobrow, Daniel G., & Allan Collins, eds. (1975) *Representation and Understanding*, Academic Press, New York.

Charniak, Eugene, & Yorick Wilks, eds. (1976) *Computational Semantics*, North-Holland Publishing Co., Amsterdam.

Chomsky, Noam (1965) *Aspects of the Theory of Syntax*, MIT Press, Cambridge, Mass.

Church, Alonzo (1941) *The Calculi of Lambda Conversion*, Princeton University Press, Princeton, N. J.

Fillmore, Charles J. (1968) "The Case for Case" in E. Bach & R. T. Harms, eds., *Universals in Linguistic Theory,* Holt, Rinehart and Winston, New York, pp. 1-88.

Findler, N. V., ed. (1979) *Associative Networks, The Representation and Use of Knowledge in Computers,* Academic Press, New York.

Goodman, Nelson (1951) *The Structure of Appearance,* Harvard University Press, Cambridge, Mass.

Heidorn, George E. (1974) "English as a Very High Level Language for Simulation Programming," Proc. Symp. Very High Level Languages, *SIGPLAN Notices,* vol. 9, April 1974, pp. 91-100.

Hendrix, Gary G. (1975) "Expanding the Utility of Semantic Networks through Partitioning," in *Proc. of the Fourth IJCAI,* Tbilisi, Georgia, USSR, pp. 115-121.

McCawley, James D. (1971) "Where do Noun Phrases Come from?" in D. D. Steinberg & L. A. Jakobovits, eds., *Semantics,* Cambridge University Press, pp. 217-231.

Pedersen, Gert Schmeltz (1978) *Conceptual Graphs I,* Technical Report 78/9, DIKU, Copenhagen University.

Rescher, Nicholas (1975) *A Theory of Possibility,* University of Pittsburgh Press, Pittsburgh.

Schank, Roger C., ed. (1975) *Conceptual Information Processing,* North-Holland Publishing Co., Amsterdam.

Schank, Roger C., & Kenneth M. Colby, eds. (1973) *Computer Models of Thought and Language,* W. H. Freeman & Co., San Francisco.

Sowa, John F. (1976) "Conceptual Graphs for a Data Base Interface," *IBM Journal of Research & Development,* vol. 20, pp. 336-357.

Sowa, John F. (forthcoming) *Conceptual Structures: Information Processing in Mind and Machine,* Addison-Wesley.

Szolovits, Peter, Lowell B. Hawkinson, & William A. Martin (1977) *An Overview of OWL, A Language for Knowledge Representation,* Report TM-86, MIT Laboratory for Computer Science.

A GRAPH-LIKE LAMBDA CALCULUS FOR WHICH LEFTMOST-OUTERMOST REDUCTION IS OPTIMAL

John Staples

Department of Mathematics and Computer Science,
Queensland Institute of Technology,
Brisbane, Australia.

1. Introduction

The problem of giving an optimal reduction algorithm for a suitable representation of the lambda calculus has been open at least since Wadsworth's thesis (10). Although Lévy (4) has developed a theory of optimal reduction for the lambda calculus, his theory has not so far led to an algorithm. Indeed Lévy (4, page 217) described the finding of an algorithm as the most important of the problems left unresolved by his thesis.

This paper gives a weak solution to the problem, though the algorithm of the present paper has not been developed from Lévy's theory. The representation of the lambda calculus which we give faithfully models reduction to normal form of terms of the classical lambda calculus which have normal forms; we prove for this representation that leftmost-outermost reduction is optimal.

The solution that we give is a weak one because optimal reductions in the calculus considered here are not always faster than optimal reductions in the classical lambda calculus; see section 8.

The lambda calculus which we consider is a calculus of graph-like expressions in the sense of (8), and the proof of optimality applies the abstract optimality theory of (7). Although it is essential for the optimality of leftmost-outermost reduction that graph-like expressions (in some sense) be used, the basic rules of the calculus can be simply explained, to those having a little familiarity with the classical lambda calculus, by describing a corresponding calculus of linear expressions, as follows.

The terms of this corresponding calculus of linear expressions are either variables x_0, x_1, x_2, ..., or are built up from these variables by recursive use of the following construction rules.

(i) <u>Application</u>; if T_1 and T_2 are terms then so is (T_1T_2).

(ii) <u>Abstraction</u>; if T is a term then so is $\lambda x_i.T$, for each variable x_i.

(iii) <u>Suspension</u>; if T_1, T_2 are terms and x_i is a variable, then $\sigma(x_i,T_1,T_2)$ is a term.

We assume the usual conventions for the omission of parentheses.

The rules of this corresponding linear calculus, apart from change of bound variable, are as follows.

(i) β-rule: $\lambda x_i AB \rightarrow \sigma(x_i, A, B)$

(ii) $\sigma\omega 0$-rule: $\sigma(x_i, x_i, B) \rightarrow B$

(iii) $\sigma\omega 1$-rule: $\sigma(x_i, x_j, B) \rightarrow x_j$, provided $j \neq i$

(iv) $\sigma\lambda 0$-rule: $\sigma(x_i, \lambda x_i A, B) \rightarrow \lambda x_i A$

(v) $\sigma\lambda 1$-rule: $\sigma(x_i, \lambda x_j A, B) \rightarrow \lambda x_k \sigma(x_i, \sigma(x_j, A, x_k), B)$, provided $j \neq i$, and where x_k is the first variable which does not occur in $\lambda x_j A$ or B.

(vi) σa-rule: $\sigma(x_i, x_j A_1 \ldots A_{n+1}, B) \rightarrow (\sigma(x_i, x_j A_1 \ldots A_n, B)\sigma(x_i, A_{n+1}, B))$.

Again we emphasise that it is not the calculus just described, but an analogous graph-like calculus, for which leftmost-outermost reduction is optimal.

The classical lambda calculus can be formulated in a similar way, except that the σa-rule is replaced by the stronger rule

$$\sigma(x_i, (AB), C) \rightarrow (\sigma(x_i, A, C)\sigma(x_i, B, C)).$$

It is the weakening of this stronger rule to the σa-rule, together with the use of graph-like expressions, which allows the optimality of leftmost-outermost reduction to be proved very simply. This weakening limits the operation of substitution so that it cannot proceed past any β-redex; neither can it commute with any other partially completed substitution. It is therefore intuitively clear why this calculus can represent reductions to normal form of the classical lambda calculus, but not reductions in general. For, in a reduction to normal form all β-redexes are eventually removed, so that all partially completed substitutions can be completed. In an arbitrary reduction however, β-redexes may remain throughout the reduction, preventing the completion of certain substitutions.

An optimal reduction procedure is by definition one which reduces terms which have a normal form , to a normal form in a minimal number of contractions. Thus a calculus such as the above, which correctly models reductions to normal form, is sufficient for solution of the optimal reduction algorithm problem.

The use of the suspension construction,

$$\sigma(x_i, A, B),$$

is not essential to our calculus. Each of its occurrences could be replaced by an occurrence of $\lambda x_i AB$, in which case the β-rule is of course omitted. The suspension construction has been introduced merely to allow a simple motivation and explanation of the rules of the calculus; it will have a technical value later in the paper. Suspension is well-known in the theory of the classical lambda calculus (5, 6); and in the interpretation of LISP greater attention has been given recently to the similar 'funarg' concept (1).

2. Definition of the terms of the graph-like lambda calculus G

2.1. The work of this paper is not much dependent on which notion of graph-like expression is used; the basic ideas are simple and robust. For definiteness however the work is expressed using the rather simple notion of graph-like expression (or, term) given in (8). First we summarise this formalism.

2.2. Terms are constructed from the following components:

(i) an infinite set of addresses;

(ii) a finite or infinite set of function letters, each of which has associated with it a unique nonnegative integer called its arity. Function letters with arity n may be called n-ary; 0-ary function letters may be called constants. The uniqueness of the arity of a function letter is not essential, but removing this restriction gives no real increase in generality.

2.3. A graph-like expression, or term, in the sense of (8) is by definition an ordered pair (r,P) which satisfies the following conditions.

(i) P is a finite set of ordered pairs (s,v), usually denoted s := v, and called assignments.

(ii) For each assignment s := v of P, s is a set of addresses which is called the address set of the assignment, and v is a symbol string which is either the empty string e or is of the form

$$f(a_1, \ldots, a_n),$$

where f is an n-ary function letter and $a_1, \ldots, a_n$ are occurrences of addresses. The string v may be called a value, or the value of an element of s, or the value of s.

(iii) The address sets of distinct assignments of P are disjoint. The union of the address sets of the assignments of P may be called the set of addresses of P. The address sets of P thus partition the set of addresses of P into equivalence classes; the equivalence relation so defined we call simply equivalence of addresses.

(iv) Every address which occurs in a value of an assignment of P also occurs in some address set of P.

(v) The address r is an address of P.

(vi) Every address of P is the end of some path in P which starts at r; where paths are defined in the following natural way.

A path in P is defined to be a sequence

$$a_1, n_1, a_2, n_2, \ldots, a_k, n_k, a_{k+1} \quad , \quad k \geq 0,$$

where for all i = 1, ..., k, a_i is an address of P with nonempty value of the form

$$f(b_1, \ldots, b_m), \quad m \geq 1,$$

where $b_{n_i} = a_{i+1}$.

The length of such a path is k, a_1 is its start, and a_{k+1} is its end.

2.4 Within the context of the above notion of term the terms of the graph-like lambda calculus G to be considered in this paper can be defined as follows. The terms of G are acyclic (no path with positive length has its start and end equivalent), all addresses of a term of G have nonempty value, and the following condition are also satisfied.

(i) There are just two 2-ary function letters which may occur in terms of G; λ ("abstraction") and α ("application").

(ii) There is just one 3-ary function letter which may occur in terms of G; σ ("suspension").

(iii) There are infinitely many constants which may occur in terms of G; $x_0, x_1, x_2, \ldots$ ("variables").

(iv) In every value $\lambda(p_1,p_2)$ or $\sigma(p_1,p_2,p_3)$ of a term T of G, p_1 has as value in T some variable x_i. Note that the value of an address in a term is local to that term; the same address may play differing roles in different terms of G. Such an occurrence of an address p_1 is called a binding occurrence. Intuitively, the occurrences of addresses which are bound by such a binding occurrence are those which are below p_2 (that is, at the end of some path which starts at p_2), are equivalent to p_1 and are not bound by any binding occurrence which is below p_2.

3. Definitions of the contractions of G

3.1. A single computational step performed on a term of G, which transforms it into another term of G, will be called a contraction. First we summarise the approach of (8), then we indicate the slight extension of that definition which is required for the present calculus.

3.2. The idea of a rule is basic to our notion of contraction. For our purpose here it is sufficient to use the following definition of rule, which is slightly less general than the definition of (8).

A rule ρ is by definition an ordered pair $((r_\rho, R_\rho),(c_\rho, C_\rho))$ of terms, generally not terms of G, which satisfies the following conditions. Note that (r_ρ, R_ρ) is called the redex of the rule, (c_ρ, C_ρ) is its contractum, and the addresses of C_ρ which are also addresses of R_ρ are called the committed addresses of C_ρ.

(i) All committed addresses of C_ρ are empty-valued addresses of C_ρ.

(ii) All addresses of C_ρ which are equivalent to committed addresses are also committed.

(iii) Committed addresses of C_ρ which are equivalent in C_ρ are also equivalent in R_ρ.

(iv) R_ρ is not a trivial term. That is, its root r_ρ is not empty-valued.

3.3. In order to define contractions of terms by the application of rules, we now define an instance $h:\rho \rightarrow T$ of a rule ρ applied to a term T to be a function from addresses of R_ρ to addresses of T which satisfies the following conditions; we write T = (r,P).

(i) h preserves equivalence. That is, for all $(s := v) \in R_\rho$ there is $(s' := v') \in P$ such that $h(s) \subseteq s'$.

(ii) h preserves nonempty values. That is, whenever $(s := f(p_1, \ldots, p_m)) \in R_\rho$, $m \geq 0$, and $(s' := v') \in P$ is such that $h(s) \subseteq s'$, then v' has the form $f(q_1, \ldots, q_m)$, where $h(p_i)$ and q_i are equivalent, i = 1, ..., m.

3.4. The process of contraction, which is discussed in detail in (8), can now be informally described as follows.

The contraction defined by an instance $h:\rho \rightarrow T$, where T = (r,P), consists of the following three steps, performed in order.

(i) Add to P those assignments s := v of C_ρ such that the addresses of s are uncommitted, to give say P'.

(ii) Replace the assignment s := v of P' such that $h(r_\rho) \in s$ by

$$s \cup s' := v',$$

where s' := v' is the assignment of C_ρ such that $c_\rho \in s'$ (if c_ρ is uncommitted in C_ρ) or $h(c_\rho) \in s'$ (if c_ρ is committed in C_ρ), to give a set P" say.

(iii) Discard each address of P" which is not the end of some path in P' which starts at r, and discard assignments all of whose addresses are then discarded; iterate this garbage collection process to give a set $P^{(3)}$. The pair $(r,P^{(3)})$ is a term which is the result of the contraction.

Remark. Actually it is necessary to carry out the above steps using a suitable copy $i(C_\rho)$ of C_ρ rather than C_ρ itself. In particular, the committed addresses of $i(C_\rho)$ are to be the same as the corresponding addresses of C_ρ, but the uncommitted addresses of $i(C_\rho)$ are to be distinct from all addresses of P. This necessity introduces an arbitrariness into the definition of contraction, with the result that it is actually isomorphism classes of terms, rather than the terms themselves, which are significant in the theory. This minor complication is inessential and will be ignored in the remainder of this paper. It is treated in detail in (8).

3.5. The notion of contraction of (8), as outlined above, needs to be refined slightly in order to define the contractions of G. Instead of accepting as contractions in G, arbitrary contractions of terms of G according to the rules of G, we accept as contractions of G only a subset of them. This restriction raises the question of whether, and if so how, membership of the subset can be decided. In practice the subsets we choose will be described by very simple predicates, the

testing of which is easy. From the theoretical point of view, restriction of the contractions of a system to only a subset of those defined by the rules of the system causes no difficulty, indeed makes no significant difference at all to the theory of (8, 9), provided that the following condition is satisfied.

3.6. <u>Whenever a term</u> T <u>in such a system</u> S <u>has two contractions,</u> T → T' <u>and</u> T → V, <u>which are both contractions of</u> S, <u>and when the contraction</u> T → V <u>induces a contraction</u> T' → V' <u>of</u> T', <u>then</u> T' → V' <u>is also a contraction of</u> S.

<u>Remarks</u> (i) In order that this condition should have a precise meaning it is necessary to define "induce"; for systems such as G that is done in (8).

(ii) It will soon be clear that G satisfies 3.6.

3.7. We now define the contractions of the system G. The rules which define the contractions are indicated diagrammatically in Figures 1 to 6. In each case the conditions under which a contraction defined by the rule is a contraction of G are given in the legend to the Figure. For the sake of completeness, and so as to give examples of our notation for graph-like expressions, we also give complete descriptions of the rules in the notation outlined above.

The rules of G will be named **β**, **σω0**, **σω1**, **σλ0**, **σλ1** and **σa**. Strictly, **σa** is a scheme of rules. The terms occurring in these rules are not themselves terms of G, since they include empty-valued addresses (which play the role of parameters). In the description of the address sets of the assignments of these terms we may denote a singleton set by its unique element.

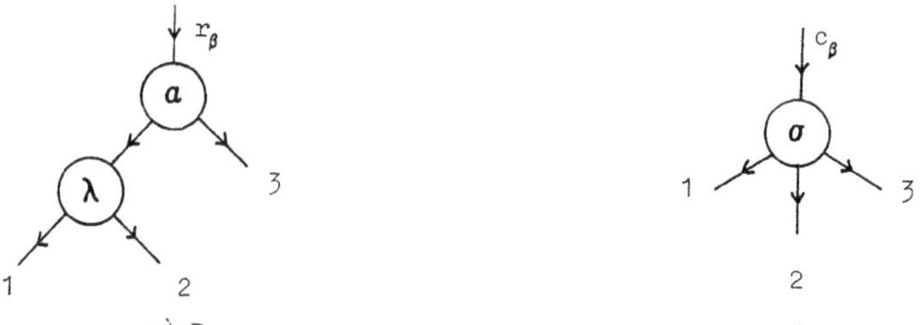

a) R_β b) C_β

Figure 1. **β**-rule. No restriction on the application of the rule.

a) $R_{\sigma\omega 0}$ b) $C_{\sigma\omega 0}$

Figure 2. **σω0**-rule. No restriction on the application of the rule.

a) $R_{\sigma\omega1}$ b) $C_{\sigma\omega1}$

Figure 3. $\sigma\omega1$-rule. An instance $h:\sigma\omega1 \to T$ of this rule defines a contraction of G only when the images in T of 1 and 2 are inequivalent, and both have variables as values.

a) $R_{\sigma\lambda0}$ b) $C_{\sigma\lambda0}$

Figure 4. $\sigma\lambda0$-rule. No restriction on the application of this rule.

a) $R_{\sigma\lambda1}$ b) $C_{\sigma\lambda1}$

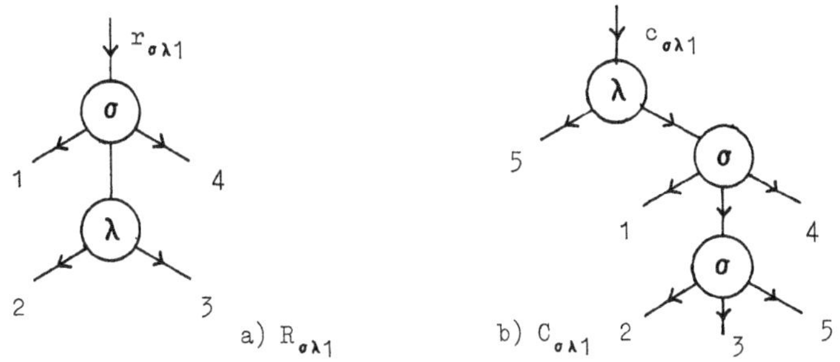

Figure 5. $\sigma\lambda1$-rule. An instance $h:\sigma\lambda1 \to T$ of this rule defines a contraction of G only when the images in T of 1 and 2 are inequivalent.

a) $R_{\sigma a}$ b) $C_{\sigma a}$

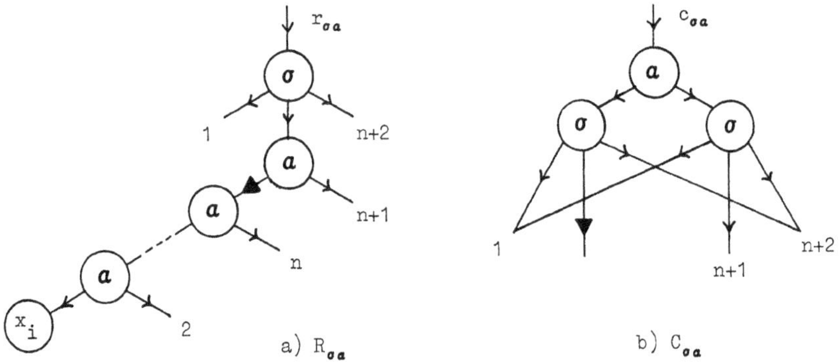

Figure 6. σa-rule. No restriction on the application of this rule.

(i) The β-rule $((r_\beta, R_\beta), (c_\beta, C_\beta))$, indicated in Figure 1, is defined by:

$$R_\beta = \{r_\beta := \alpha(q_0, p_3),\ q_0 := \lambda(p_1, p_2),\ p_1 := e,\ p_2 := e,\ p_3 := e\},$$
$$C_\beta = \{c_\beta := \sigma(p_1, p_2, p_3),\ p_1 := e,\ p_2 := e,\ p_3 := e\}.$$

(ii) $\sigma\omega 0$, indicated in Figure 2, is defined by:

$$R_{\sigma\omega 0} = \{r_{\sigma\omega 0} := \sigma(q_1, q_2, c_{\sigma\omega 0}),\ \{q_1, q_2\} := e,\ c_{\sigma\omega 0} := e\},$$
$$C_{\sigma\omega 0} = \{c_{\sigma\omega 0} := e\}.$$

(iii) $\sigma\omega 1$, indicated in Figure 3, is defined by:

$$R_{\sigma\omega 1} = \{r_{\sigma\omega 1} := \sigma(p_1, c_{\sigma\omega 1}, p_3),\ p_1 := e,\ c_{\sigma\omega 1} := e,\ p_3 := e\},$$
$$C_{\sigma\omega 1} = \{c_{\sigma\omega 1} := e\}.$$

(iv) $\sigma\lambda 0$, indicated in Figure 4, is defined by:

$$R_{\sigma\lambda 0} = \{r_{\sigma\lambda 0} := \sigma(p_0, c_{\sigma\lambda 0}, p_3),\ c_{\sigma\lambda 0} := \lambda(p_1, p_2),\ \{p_0, p_1\} := e,\ p_2 := e,\ p_3 := e\},$$
$$C_{\ \lambda 0} = \{c_{\sigma\lambda 0} := e\}.$$

(v) $\sigma\lambda 1$, indicated in Figure 5, is defined by:

$$R_{\sigma\lambda 1} = \{r_{\sigma\lambda 1} := \sigma(p_1, q_1, p_4),\ q_1 := \lambda(p_2, p_3),\ p_2 := e,\ p_3 := e,\ p_4 := e\},$$
$$C_{\sigma\lambda 1} = \{c_{\sigma\lambda 1} := \lambda(p_5, q_2),\ q_2 := \sigma(p_1, q_3, p_4),\ q_3 := \sigma(p_2, p_3, p_6),\ p_1 := e,$$
$$p_2 := e,\ p_3 := e,\ p_4 := e,\ \{p_5, p_6\} := e\}.$$

(vi) $\sigma\alpha$, indicated in Figure 6, is defined by:

$$R_{\sigma\alpha} = \{r_{\sigma\alpha} := \sigma(p_1, q_1, p_{n+2}),\ q_1 := \alpha(q_2, p_{n+1}),\ \ldots,\ q_n := \alpha(q_{n+1}, p_2),$$
$$q_{n+1} := x_i,\ p_1 := e,\ \ldots,\ p_{n+2} := e\},$$
$$C_{\sigma\alpha} = \{c_{\sigma\alpha} := \alpha(q_1, q_2),\ q_1 := \sigma(p_1, q_2, p_{n+2}),\ q_2 := \sigma(p_1, p_{n+1}, p_{n+2}),$$
$$p_1 := e,\ q_2 := e,\ p_{n+1} := e,\ p_{n+2} := e\}.$$

3.8. The following lemma allows condition 3.6 to be verified for G, so that the theory of (8, 9) can be applied.

Whenever p, q are addresses of a term T of G such that p has a binding occurrence in T, and whenever T → U is a contraction in G of T such that p, q have descendants in U, then p and q are equivalent in T if and only if they are equivalent in U.

Proof. No instance of any rule makes equivalent addresses of T inequivalent in U. If p, q are inequivalent in T and equivalent in U then from the definition of contraction, writing ρ for the rule of which T → U is an instance, c_ρ occurs in T and p, q are equivalent in T to r_ρ, c_ρ. Therefore neither p nor q has a binding occurrence in T, in view of the particular definitions of the rules ρ of G.

4. Subcommutativity of the calculus G

It is evident from the definitions just given that distinct instances of contractions of G are *disjoint*, in the sense that if $h:\rho \to T$ and $k:\sigma \to T$ are instances of rules of G which define contractions of G, then $k(r_\sigma)$ is not equivalent to any address h(p) such that p has nonempty value in R_ρ. Thus the theory of (8, 9) applies to G. In particular G is a *subcommutative* system, in the sense that if $T \to U$, $T \to V$ are contractions of G, then either U = V, $U \to V$, $V \to U$ or there is W in G such that $U \to W$ and $V \to W$.

This observation allows the application of the relatively simple optimality theory of (7, 9), as indicated in the following section.

5. Optimality of leftmost-outermost reduction in G

5.1. Although the theory of (9) can be applied straightforwardly to prove the optimality of leftmost-outermost reduction in G, the situation is so simple that we shall instead prove optimality directly from the abstract optimality theorem for subcommutative systems of (7, section 5.2). In particular it is enough to prove the following result, in which all the contractions mentioned are contractions of G.

5.2. (i) *Every term of G which is not in normal form has a leftmost-outermost contraction (briefly, a left contraction).*

(ii) *If* $T \to U$ *is left contraction and* $T \to V$ *is another contraction, then either* U = V, *or* $V \to U$ *is left contraction, or there is* W *such that* $U \to W$ *and such that* $V \to W$ *is left contraction (see Figure* 7).

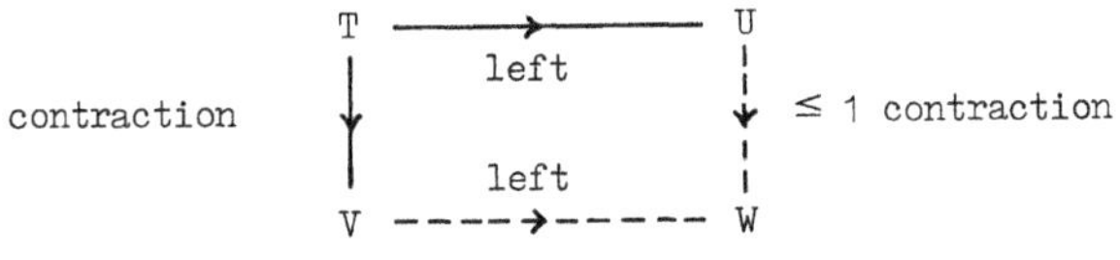

Figure 7. (Case $U \neq V$)

Proof. (i) is evident. In view of the theory of (8), to prove (ii) we have only to show, in the case $U \neq V$, that the instance $h:\rho \to T$ which defines $T \to U$ induces an instance $\bar{h}:\rho \to V$ which defines the left contraction in G of V. We see that as follows.

The leftmost path π in T from the root of T to a root of the contraction $T \to U$ (a root of the contraction is an address of T which is equivalent to the image under h of the root of the rule redex) includes no address which is equivalent to the root of $T \to V$; otherwise the contraction $T \to V$ would be to the left of $T \to U$, contradiction. Therefore π has a descendant in V, which we call π also, so $T \to U$ induces

a contraction of V as required. We also need to know that this contraction is a contraction in G; but that follows immediately from the facts that $T \rightarrow U$ is a contraction in G, and G is disjoint.

To see that the contraction of V so defined is the left contraction of V, suppose to the contrary that some initial path π' in V is to the left of π and ends in a root of a contraction of V. Consider the maximal initial subpath π'' of π' which is a descendant of a path π'' of T under the contraction $T \rightarrow V$. If π'' is a proper subpath of π', then in T, π'' ends in a root of a contraction of T which is to the left of $T \rightarrow U$, contradiction. Thus π' is a descendant of a path of T, and is to the left of π in V and therefore in T. Therefore the end of π' is not a root of a contraction of T in G. As it is a root of a contraction of V in G, then a root of $T \rightarrow V$ is the end of some path $\pi^{(3)}$ which is an extension of π' and which is therefore either equal to, or to the left of, π. It cannot be equal to π, since $U \neq V$, so it is to the left of π, contradicting the definition of π.

6. The related system G^{β}_{n}

6.1. Starting from G we can define as follows a related system G^{β}_{n} which is closer in spirit to the classical lambda calculus in the sense that all possible σ-contractions are carried out immediately after each β-contraction. In this section we define G^{β}_{n} and observe that it is subcommutative.

6.2. First we define the calculus G^{σ} to be the system obtained from G by omitting the rule β. A term of G^{σ} which is in normal form in G^{σ} will be said to be in σ-normal form. Evidently G^{σ} is disjoint, so that it is subcommutative and has the normal form property. Further, G^{σ} is evidently noetherian (there are no reductions of infinite length; so every term has a σ-normal form). We may also write G^{β} for the system obtained from G by omitting all rules except the β-rule.

6.3. The system G^{β}_{n} defined below is not a system of graph-like expressions with contractions defined by rules in the sense outlined in earlier sections. Rather, each contraction of G^{β}_{n} is a certain reduction of G.

In particular, the terms of G^{β}_{n} are those terms of G which are in σ-normal form, and a contraction $T \rightarrow U$ of G^{β}_{n} is a reduction $T \rightarrow V \rightarrow^{*} U$ of G, where $T \rightarrow V$ is a contraction of G^{β} and $V \rightarrow^{*} U$ is a reduction in G^{σ} of V to σ-normal form.

6.4. G^{β}_{n} __is subcommutative__.

Proof. This assertion requires for its proof only a very simple application of the "requests" Church-Rosser theorem of Rosen (6). The argument is indicated in Figure 8, wherein $\leq$ denotes at most one contraction of G^{β}, and σn denotes a reduction in G^{σ} to σ-normal form. Parts a) and b) of Figure 8 are the lemmas which allow c). In reading c) one should observe that $Z_1 = Z_2$, and one should realise that if for example $V_1 = X_1$ then $V_1 = Z_1$.

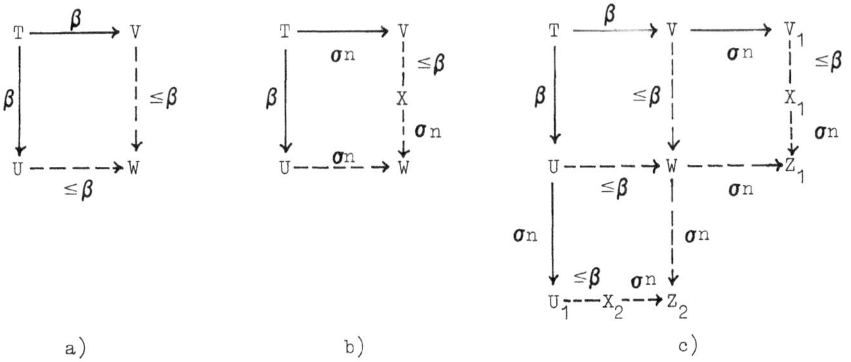

Figure 8.

7. Correctness of G and G_n^β as normal representations of the lambda calculus

7.1. We show in this section that G_n^β, and therefore G, correctly models reductions to normal form in the classical lambda calculus. This result is our justification for calling G and G_n^β graph-like lambda calculi. Before doing so however we observe that G and G_n^β cannot model arbitrary reductions of the classical lambda calculus. Figure 9 a) shows an example of a term of G which cannot be reduced in G to the term of Figure 9 b), though the former term models a term of the classical lambda calculus which can be reduced (by one contraction) to the classical term which is modelled by the term of Figure 9 b).

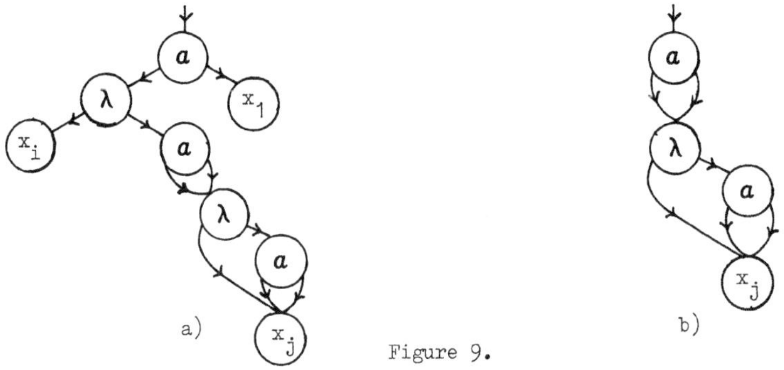

Figure 9.

We shall denote the classical lambda calculus by G^c.

7.2. First we define, for each term T of G, s(T) to be the result of replacing, in the set of assignments of T, each assignment of the form $s := \sigma(p_1,p_2,p_3)$ by two assignments, of the forms $s := a(q_1,p_3)$ and $q_1 := \lambda(p_1,p_2)$, where q_1 does not occur in T, and where a different such q_1 is used for each such replacement.

7.3. For each T in G, s(T) defines in an evident way a term (more precisely an equivalence class of terms with respect to the change-of-bound-variable equivalence relation) of G^c; we denote this term by t(T).

7.4. For each T $\in$ G and each β-redex of s(T) there are one or more corresponding β-redexes in t(T), which we may call the descendants of that β-redex of s(T). We write u(T) for that term of the classical lambda calculus G^c which is obtained from t(T) by a complete development of all descendants in t(T) of redexes of s(T) which replace occurrences of in T. It will be useful to recall that all complete developments are finite, from (2), and all reduce to the same term of the classical lambda calculus, from (3).

Our correctness result is that if T is a term of G^β_n and u(T) has a left reduction in the classical lambda calculus to normal form V, of length n, then T has a left reduction in G^β_n to normal form W of length at most n, where u(W) = V. Thus G^β_n, and hence G, are normal representations (in the sense of (7)) of the classical lambda calculus.

The following lemmas lead up to the result.

7.5. <u>For every term T of G^β_n and every occurrence in T of an address with value $\sigma(p_1,p_2,p_3)$ there is an instance of the β-rule whose image is in the cofinal subterm of T whose root is p_2.</u>

Proof. Straightforward, by noetherian induction. That is, if no left path starts at p_2 and ends at an address with value $\sigma(q_1,q_2,q_3)$, then as T is in σ-normal form, some left path starting at p_2 ends at a β-redex. If however some left path which starts at p_2 does end at an address with value $\sigma(q_1,q_2,q_3)$ then the inductive hypothesis applies to this address to give the required result.

In this proof, a left path means a path

$$p_1,\ n_1,\ \ldots,\ p_k,\ n_k,\ p_{k+1}$$

such that if the value of p_i has the form $a(a_1,a_2)$ (respectively $\lambda(a_1,a_2)$, $\sigma(a_1,a_2,a_3)$) then $n_1 = 1$ (respectively $n_i = 2$, $n_i = 2$).

7.6. <u>For all terms T of G^β_n which are not in normal form, the leftmost-outermost G^c-redex r_u of u(T) is a descendant of the leftmost-outermost redex r of T.</u>

In this assertion the G^c-redex r_u means the leftmost-outermost subterm of u(T) which matches the β-rule of the classical lambda calculus, and similarly r denotes the leftmost-outermost subterm of T which is the image under an instance h of the β-rule of G, of R_β.

Proof. In view of 7.5, the only occurrences in T of addresses with value of the form $\sigma(p_1,p_2,p_3)$ which are earlier than r in the leftmost-outermost ordering are equivalent to intermediate addresses of the leftmost path in T from the root to r. Thus the only β-redexes in s(T) which are earlier than r in the ordering have roots which are equivalent to intermediate addresses on the leftmost path from the root of s(T) to r. Hence the same is true of the leftmost descendant r_t of r in t(T).

Since those β-redexes are contracted to produce u(T), and since any new redexes which those contractions create are later than r_t in the ordering, then the descendant r_u in u(T) of r_t is the leftmost-outermost redex of u(T).

7.7. For all T in G_n^β which are not in normal form; if T $\rightarrow$ V is leftmost-outermost contraction of T then there is a G^c-reduction u(T) $\rightarrow$ W $\rightarrow$ * u(V) such that u(T) $\rightarrow$ W is left G^c-contraction and W $\rightarrow$ * u(V) is a development of residuals of redexes of u(T), which is a special reduction of W.

Proof. Consider the redexes of t(T) which are either

(i) descendants in t(T) of occurrences of σ in T, or

(ii) descendants in t(T) of the β-redex of T $\rightarrow$ V.

We have already remarked that all complete developments of sets of redexes are finite and reduce to the same G^c-term. One such development is first to G^c-contract all redexes of u(T) descending from the redex of T $\rightarrow$ V, to give a term which is reached by the development of some of the σ-descended redexes of t(V), then to contract the remaining redexes to give u(V). Another complete development is first to contract all those redexes which descend from occurrences of σ in T, to give u(T), then to contract the remaining redexes, which are those descending from the redex of T $\rightarrow$ V, choosing to begin with the leftmost-outermost, and from then on always contracting innermost redexes, so as to give a special reduction W $\rightarrow$ * u(V). Since, from 7.6, the leftmost-outermost of these latter redexes is the leftmost-outermost redex of u(T), we have the desired result.

7.8. To complete the argument we also need some elementary results about the classical lambda calculus, as follows. We write |T| for the length of the left reduction to normal form of a term T which has a normal form. This notation will be applied both to G^c and to G_n^β, as required. The interpretation will be clear from the context.

7.9. If T $\rightarrow$ U is left G^c-contraction of T, and if T $\rightarrow$* V is a special G^c-reduction, then either U $\rightarrow$ * V is a special G^c-reduction or there is W in G^c such that V $\rightarrow$ W is left G^c-contraction and there is a special G^c-reduction U $\rightarrow$ * W.

Proof. This is a special case of the basic lemma in the theory of the classical lambda calculus which says that special reductions commute.

7.10. (Corollary of 7.9) If T is in G^c, if T $\rightarrow$ * V is a special reduction and if |T| = n, then |V| $\leq$ n.

Proof. By induction on n. The case n = 0 is trivially true, so suppose that n > 0. In the notation of 7.9, |U| = n-1 (in the case U $\rightarrow$ * V) or |W| $\leq$ n-1 (in the case U $\rightarrow$ * W). In the latter case |V| $\leq$ n as required since V $\rightarrow$ W is left contraction.

We can now prove:

7.11. _If_ $T \in G_n^{\beta}$ _and_ $|u(T)| = n$ _then_ $|T| \leq n$ _and, writing_ X _for the_ G_n^{β}_-normal form of_ T, u(X) _is the_ G^c_-normal form of_ u(T).

Proof. By induction on n. The case n = 0 is trivially true, since from 7.5 u(T) is in normal form. Hence we suppose that n > 0.

In the notation of 7.7, $|W| = n-1$, and from 7.10 $|u(V)| \leq n-1$. Hence by inductive hypothesis $|V| \leq n-1$, so $|T| \leq n$ as required.

8. Discussion

In the previous section we saw that leftmost-outermost reduction in our graph-like system speeds up leftmost-outermost reduction in the classical lambda calculus. However the following example, due to J.-J. Lévy and G. Huet, shows that the classical calculus can sometimes give shorter reductions than the system given here. The shortest reduction to normal form in G_n^{β} of (in classical notation)

$$\lambda x.(\lambda y.(yy)(xa))(\lambda z.z)$$

has length four; but there is a reduction in the classical calculus of length three. Further work is needed to refine G_n^{β} so as to match the performance of the classical calculus in all cases.

It is also natural to ask whether the method of this paper can be extended to cope with additional reduction rules. The work of (9) together with the appropriate extension of the σa-rule copes with many rules which are graph-like versions of rules of the type known as δ-rules in the classical theory of the lambda calculus. However graph-like versions of the classical η-rule,

$$\lambda x(Mx) \rightarrow M, \quad \text{provided x does not occur free in M,}$$

raise questions which there is not space to discuss here.

The author thanks J.-J. Lévy and M. Bunder for helpful criticism of a draft of this paper.

References

1. Peter Henderson and James H. Morris Jr., A lazy evaluator, Proceedings of the Third A.C.M. Symposium on the Principles of Programming Languages, 1976, 95-103.
2. Roger Hindley, Standard and normal reductions, duplicated notes, Swansea, 1975.
3. Roger Hindley, The equivalence of complete reductions, Trans Amer. Math. Soc. 229 (1977) 227-248.
4. J.-J. Lévy, Réductions correctes et optimales dans le λ-calcul, Thesis, Paris, 1977.
5. G. Mitschke, Eine algebraische Behandlung von λ-K-Kalkül und Kombinatorischer Logik, Ph.D. thesis, Bonn, 1970.
6. Barry K. Rosen, Tree-manipulating systems and Church-Rosser Theorems, J.A.C.M. 20 (1973) 160-187.
7. John Staples, A class of replacement systems with simple optimality theory, Bull. Austral. Math. Soc. 17 (1977) 335-350.
8. John Staples, Computation on graph-like expressions, Report No. 2/77, Dept Maths and Comp. Sci., Queensland Institute of Technology, Brisbane, 1977.
9. John Staples, Optimal evaluations of graph-like expressions, Report No. 2/78, Dept Maths and Comp. Sci., Queensland Institute of Technology, Brisbane, 1977.
10. C.P. Wadsworth, Semantics and Pragmatics of the lambda-calculus, Ph.D. thesis, Oxford, 1971.

A Bibliography of General Replacement Systems
(grouped by author, in rough chronological order)

M.H.A.Newman, On theories with a combinatorial definition of equivalence, Ann. of Math. (2) 43 (1942) 223-243

R. Hindley, An abstract form of the Church-Rosser theorem I, J.Symbolic Logic 34 (1969) 545-560

— An abstract form of the Church-Rosser theorem II: Applications, J. Symbolic Logic 39(1974) 1-21

B.K.Rosen, Tree-manipulating systems and Church-Rosser theorems; J.A.C.M. 20 (1973), 160-187

R.Sethi, Testing for the Church-Rosser property, JACM 21 (1974) 671-679; erratum 22 (1975), 424.

J.Staples, Church-Rosser theorems for replacement systems, "Algebra and Logic", 291-306 (L.N. Math. 450, Springer 1975)

— Optimal reduction in replacement systems, Bulletin Austral. Math. Soc. 16 (1977) 341-349.

— A class of replacement systems with simple optimality theory, Bulletin Austral. Math. Soc. 17 (1977) 335-350.

G.Huet, Confluent reductions: abstract properties and applications to term rewriting systems, Proceedings 18th Annual Symposium on Foundation of Computer Science, Providence, R.I., Oct. 1977, pp. 30-46

Relationships Between Graph Grammars and the Design and Analysis of Concurrent Software

Jack C. Wileden

Department of Computer and Information Science
University of Massachusetts, Amherst, Massachusetts 01003

Abstract - Formal models of parallel computation provide a basis for several techniques employed in the design and analysis of concurrent software systems. We consider the relationships between these models and graph grammars, with particular emphasis upon the Dynamic Process Modelling Scheme (DPMS). This scheme, developed to study concurrent software systems in which both processes and interprocess communication channels may be created or destroyed during system operation, is shown to have an especially strong connection to graph grammars.

1. Introduction

There are two fundamental aspects to the problem of designing a large-scale, concurrent software system. The first of these is to produce a suitable description of the proposed system. Such a description should be sufficiently abstract to permit a succinct statement of the design, yet must be both comprehensible and unambiguous if it is to serve as a useful guide to the system's eventual implementation. Ideally, the description should also be malleable, permitting easy elaboration or revision as the design evolves. Much of our recent work has been directed toward the development of a software design description language (called the DREAM Design Notation, or DDN) which possesses these and other desirable properties [11].

The second aspect of the design problem arises from the need to analyze a design. Since the majority of errors discovered in large-scale, concurrent software systems can be traced to mistaken designs, it is extremely desirable to begin analyzing (i.e., assessing the appropriateness of) a system's design at the earliest possible point in its development. In order for such analysis to be possible at all stages of the design process, techniques supporting the analysis of partial, incomplete designs are required. Our goal in developing the DREAM design aid system (of which DDN is a part) has been to provide software designers with analysis tools having these capabilities [12].

Formal models of parallel computation play an important role in our efforts at attacking both aspects of the concurrent software design problem. Such models offer a substantial basis for abstract and unambiguous representations of software system designs and also furnish the foundation for developing analysis techniques applicable to those designs. Thus, we and other researchers in this area are continually seeking suitable formalisms which might prove useful in our attempts at constructing tools to aid designers of concurrent software.

This paper represents a preliminary exploration of the potential utility of graph grammars as a formalism on which to base techniques for concurrent software design and analysis. We begin by briefly discussing standard formal models of parallel computation and sketching their possible relationships to graph grammars. We then proceed to focus upon a new formalism developed for studying a special class of software design problems. This formalism, the Dynamic Process Modelling Scheme (DPMS), is considered in some detail, and its particularly natural relationship to graph grammars is outlined and explored. Finally we offer some tentative observations on the prospects for using graph grammars in software design and analysis, suggesting in this regard some questions which might merit further attention.

2. Standard Parallel Computation Models

Numerous formal models of parallel computation have been defined and studied (see [3], [7], [8] and [9] for surveys). Generally these models resemble the original computation model developed by Petri [10]. Moreover, Peterson has shown that nearly all of these models are essentially equivalent to Petri's formalism [9]. For these reasons, and because it captures the fundamental properties of concurrency, we will restrict our attention here to Petri's model.

A Petri net (fig. 1) consists of a bipartite directed graph whose vertices are known as places (e.g., p1, p2, in fig. 1) and transitions (e.g., t1 in fig. 1), and a set of rules governing the movement of tokens (represented by dots in the places in fig. 1) from place to place within the graph. Under specified enabling conditions, a transition may "fire", removing tokens from all places adjacent to the transition and placing tokens in all places adjacent from the transition. Thus, for instance, a firing of transition t1 in fig. 1(a) would result in the new configuration (called a "marking") shown in fig. 1(b).

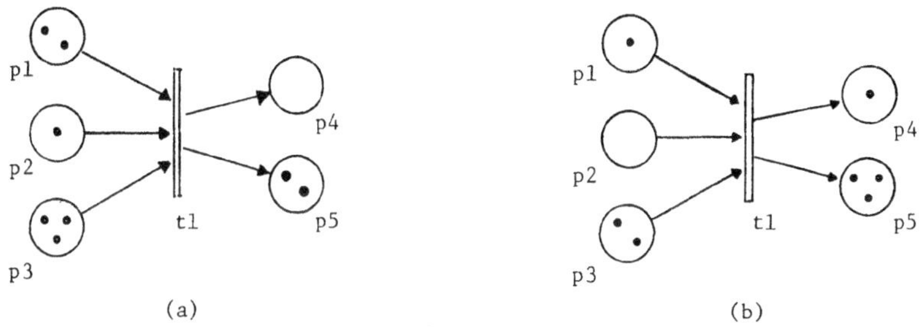

figure 1

It is possible to formulate the Petri net model in graph grammar terms. A straightforward approach is to use productions to simulate the firing rules (e.g., the production of fig. 2 simulates the firing shown in fig. 1), with the net and its initial marking given as an axiom. For general Petri nets this approach has the unpleasant characteristic of requiring an infinite number of productions, one corresponding to each of the infinite number of possible markings which could serve to enable any given transition.

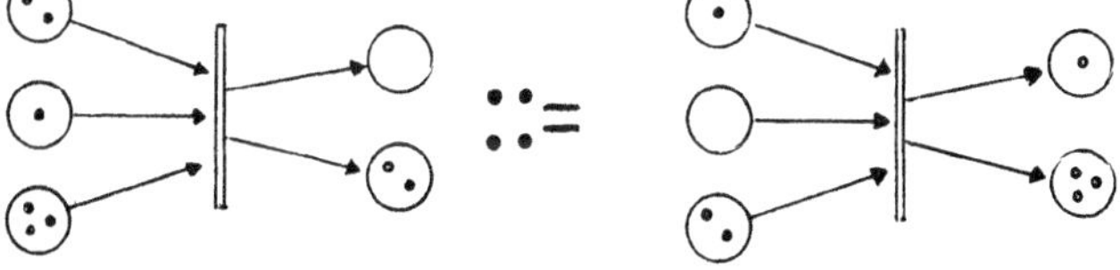

figure 2

A finite number of productions can be obtained, however, if there is a known bound on the number of tokens which can reside in any individual place at one time. Thus, if the bound is one (a situation known as a 1-safe net), and if the maximum transition indegree is m and the maximum transition outdegree is n, then at most (m+1)(n+1) productions are needed. Similarly, if at most k tokens may reside in any single place at one time, and assuming the same maximum transition indegree and outdegree, at most $k^{m+n}(m+1)(n+1)$ productions are required. Alternatively, the infinite number of productions needed in the general case could be represented by a finite number of <u>production schemata</u> such as the schema shown in fig. 3. It has further been suggested [2] that, based upon

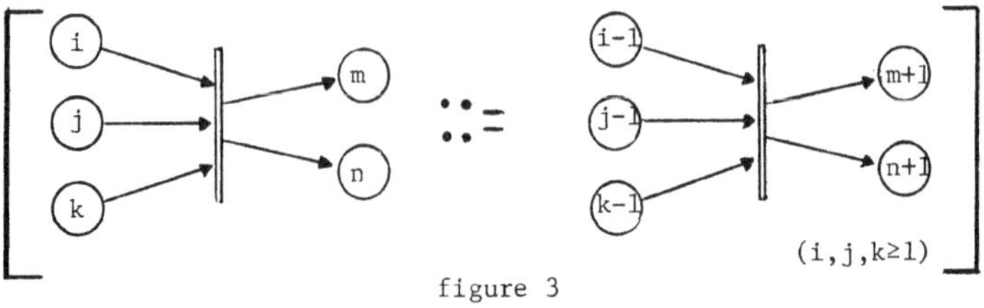

figure 3

this latter formulation, a somewhat less obvious graph grammar representation for general Petri nets can be given which has only a finite number of productions.

So it is clear that graph grammars may be used to construct models of parallel computation. It is also apparent that graph grammar results on independence, Church-Rosser properties and so forth are related to properties such as safeness, conflict-freeness and determinism in models like Petri's. However, from the viewpoint of research on concurrent software design and analysis, a graph grammar model of parallel computation would be useful only if it could provide modelling capabilities or techniques for analysis which surpass those available from the standard models. While such developments are certainly possible with further research in this area, our subjective feeling is that the graph grammar formalism is most likely more powerful than is required for situations captured by the standard models. None of these standard models actually deals with changing graphical structures, to which graph grammars seem most naturally applicable, but only with changing markings in fixed graphical structures. (An exception is Adams' model [1] which does admit a limited amount of graph restructuring and might fruitfully be represented by graph grammars.) Thus, while graph grammars are definitely related to standard parallel computation models, substantial additional effort will be required to demonstrate their potential utility in the area of concurrent software design and analysis.

3. The Dynamic Process Modelling Scheme

In the course of our work on problems in concurrent software design, we have encountered a class of software systems which cannot be naturally described using any of the standard parallel computation models. Systems in this class may be characterized as collections of interacting parallel processes, in which processes may be created or destroyed and patterns of process interaction may be altered during system execution. We call a system having these properties a parallel system with dynamic structure (PSDS). Among the software systems which come under the PSDS heading are the HEARSAY speech understanding system [6] and the RC 4000 operating system [4]. Since we hope to extend our design aid system to handle software systems such as these, we sought to develop a formal model of parallel computation capable of describing a PSDS.

The Dynamic Process Modelling Scheme (DPMS) is the result of our efforts at finding a formalism for representing parallel systems with dynamic structure. In the remainder of this section we outline the features of DPMS (details may be found in [14]) and illustrate its use in describing and analyzing a dynamically-structured, concurrent software system. Then in the next section we sketch the relationship between DPMS and graph grammars.

We distinguish three kinds of representational capabilities required in a formal modelling scheme for parallel systems with dynamic structure. First, such a scheme must offer a means for describing the components which might exist in the system at some time, that is, the processes which might be instantiated in the system at some point during its operation. The modelling scheme must also include a technique for representing interaction among the components in the modelled system. Finally, the modelling scheme must provide for the description of the system's configuration at a given point in time and for describing changes in that configuration.

The first of these requirements is fulfilled in DPMS by <u>process templates</u>, such as those shown in fig. 4 and fig. 5, which are used to describe the behavior and interaction possibilities for potential processes in a DPMS model. Each process template represents a class of potential processes; at any given time the modelled system may include zero or more instantiations of any particular process class. A process template is specified in a simple abstract

```
SUBTASK:
  st1:  DO FOREVER
          BEGIN
  st2:      RECEIVE in;
  st3:      SEND out
        END.
```

```
SYNCH:
  sy1:  DO FOREVER
          BEGIN
  sy2:      RECEIVE v;
  sy3:      SEND p
        END.
```

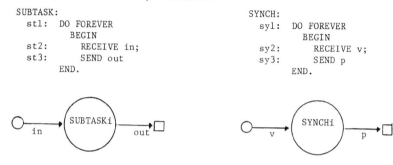

figure 4

```
SCHED:

  sc1:  WHILE INTERNAL TEST DO
          BEGIN
  sc2:      WHILE INTERNAL TEST DO
              BEGIN
  sc3:          CREATE subtask tvar;
  sc4:          ESTABLISH tvar.out synch1.v;
  sc5:          ESTABLISH synch1.p tvar.in;
  sc6:          /subs/ := tvar
              END;
  sc7:      WHILE INTERNAL TEST DO
              BEGIN
  sc8:          FOR SOME tvar :- /subs/ DO
                  BEGIN
  sc9:              DESTROY tvar
                  END
              END
          END.
```

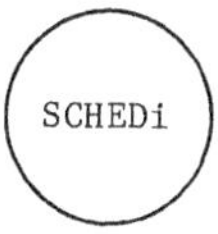

figure 5

programming language called the Dynamic Modelling Language or DYMOL. (Graphical representations, like those shown in fig. 4 and fig. 5, are normally associated with the formal DYMOL specifications.) For our present purposes, the most significant of the DYMOL instructions are those used for process creation and destruction (CREATE and DESTROY) and for alteration of interprocess connectivity (ESTABLISH and CLOSE), since these serve to alter the (graphically-represented) structure of the modelled system. Complete details on DYMOL may be found in [14].

Component interaction is represented in DPMS by message transmission. Processes may send and receive messages by issuing the DYMOL commands SEND and RECEIVE. Message routing possibilities are determined by intercomponent connectivity as controlled by the ESTABLISH and CLOSE commands; any process may or may not be capable of communicating with some other process at a given point in time, depending upon the current interprocess connectivity. Since no process is allowed to progress past a RECEIVE instruction until a message has been made available for it to receive (through the execution of a SEND by some process connected to the receiver), the communication mechanism also provides for coordination of component activity (as detailed in [14]).

The final requirement for a modelling scheme for parallel systems with dynamic structure is fulfilled in DPMS by the instantaneous configuration concept. An instantaneous configuration represents the complete state of a modelled system at some point in time, largely in terms of the current configuration matrix, a dynamically-structured matrix whose indices represent the currently active (instantiated) processes in the system and whose entries indicate the current pattern of interprocess connectivity. The instantaneous configuration also includes information regarding the current state of each active process and any interprocess communication currently in progress in the system. The formal semantics of DYMOL (as defined in [14]) specify the permissible sequences of instantaneous configurations, or computations, which may occur for a given collection of process templates and a given initial instantaneous configuration.

A graphical representation may be given which captures most of the information in an instantaneous configuration. Therefore, a computation in a DPMS model may be represented by a sequence of graphs, one corresponding to each instantaneous configuration in the computation. For example, a model whose initial instantaneous configuration included one instance of each of the processes defined by the SYNCH and SCHED templates of fig. 4 and fig. 5 could eventually produce an instantaneous configuration represented by the graph of fig. 6. In [14] we illustrate how consideration of the possible subsequent instantaneous configurations reachable from the fig. 6 graph can be employed to reveal an anomolous behavior which could occur in the software system modelled by the SCHED,SYNCH and SUBTASK templates and the above-described initial instantaneous configuration. In the present context it suffices to observe that a DPMS model, which essentially represents a collection of graphs, can serve to represent a design for a dynamically-structured, concurrent software system and hence analysis techniques applicable to DPMS models can serve as a basis for analysis tools applicable to software designs. DPMS has also been used to study decidability properties for dynamically-structured parallel systems and to define PSDS subclass and alternative analysis techniques applicable to those subclasses [14].

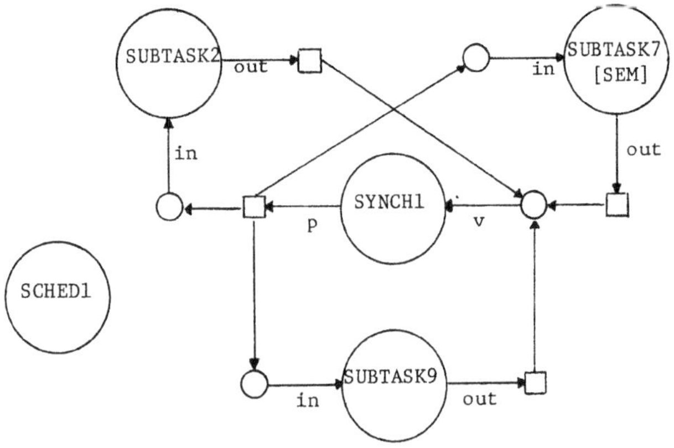

figure 6

4. DPMS and Graph Grammars

It should be clear from the preceding discussion that a very natural relationship exists between graph grammars and the Dynamic Process Modelling Scheme. Indeed, a DPMS model implicitly defines a graph rewriting system, as demonstrated by the example of the previous section. We now focus in on this relationship by considering how a DPMS model might be represented in the graph grammar formalism.

There are two aspects to the graph rewriting which is defined by a DPMS model. One involves the actual structural changes arising from process creation and deletion and from the alteration of interprocess connectivity. The second comes from the model's message transmission activity and corresponds closely to the marking changes brought about by transition firings in Petri nets.

To illustrate a graph grammer representation of the first aspect of DPMS-defined graph rewriting, in fig. 7 we give productions corresponding to three of the DYMOL statements found in the SCHED process template of fig. 5. The first of these shows how new nodes could be added to an instantaneous configuration graph through process creation. The marked arc from SCHEDi to TASKj, not found in the graph of fig. 6, serves as the "memory" implemented by the DYMOL result parameter tvar. In the second production, this memory information is used as context in assuring that the appropriate nodes are connected by the newly-added arc (SUBTASKj.out, synchl.v). Then the marked arc is replaced by a doubly-marked arc, which will enable application of the production corresponding to statement sc5 (not shown here). Finally, the third production in fig. 7 deletes nodes and arcs from an instantaneous configuration graph, and corresponds to a DESTROY operation. The triply-marked arc again provides enabling context; the small square node and its outbound arc are not deleted by this production due to a technicality of DYMOL semantics which is explained in [14].

The message transmission aspect of a DPMS model's graph rewriting activity can be cast into the graph grammar formalism using very much the same approach applied to Petri net firing rules in section 2. To complete the graph grammar formulation of a DPMS model, we also need a means of sequencing the application of productions, corresponding to the sequential execution of DYMOL statements by an instantiated process. This can be done through adding labels to the graph's nodes, thereby encoding state information which will serve as context in controlling the order of production application. Alternatively, a programmed graph grammar like that described in [5] could be employed.

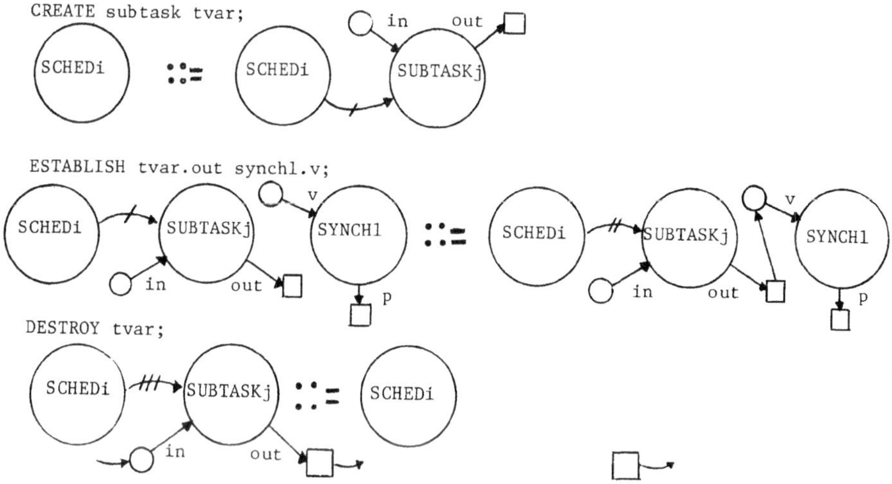

figure 7

The preceding, while by no means a complete treatment, does serve to demonstrate the feasibility of modelling parallel systems with dynamic structure using the formalism of graph grammars. As we observed in the case of standard parallel computation models, the use of a modelling scheme based on graph grammars is worthwhile in our view only if it can augment the description or analysis capabilities already offered by existing models. However, given the very natural relationship between dynamically-structured parallel systems and graph grammars, we are more inclined to anticipate such results in this case than we were for standard parallel computation models. We conclude this section by considering several ways in which a graph grammar approach to PSDS modelling could prove beneficial to designers of dynamically-structured, concurrent software systems.

In terms of descriptive capability, we would not expect the graph grammar approach to be an improvement upon DPMS. Rather, we would expect designers to be more comfortable with a programming language-based notation than with a set of graph rewriting rules. However, a graph grammar description could well prove a useful alternative means of representing a design stated in DYMOL, and a design aid system might do well to include a facility for automatically translating a DYMOL description into the equivalent graph grammar. We have argued elsewhere [13] that comparison of two such redundant descriptions is a potentially valuable analysis technique for software designers.

Through analogy to standard formal language theory, we can envision other possible applications of a graph grammar modelling scheme to the problems of software design and analysis. Such a scheme could, for instance, permit the definition of PSDS subclasses based upon the form of the productions used in their defining graph grammars. Properties of entire subclasses might then be established, as they have been for regular, context-free and context-sensitive languages, and a designer could be assured that some property held for a given design based simply upon the form of its graph grammar productions. Furthermore, graph grammar analogs to parsing might be used to determine if, and how, a given configuration could arise during the execution of a dynamically-structured concurrent software system, by discovering a sequence of graph grammar productions yielding that configuration when applied to the axiom graph. Such a capability would offer a powerful analysis technique to the software designer, who could use it to check a design for the possibility of attaining either desirable or undesirable configurations. With the well-developed theory of formal languages as a source of inspiration, it seems likely that many other fruitful techniques for graph grammar analysis could be found and applied to software design and analysis problems.

Thus we have seen that graph grammars are closely related to parallel systems with dynamic structure and have definite potential as a useful PSDS modelling tool. Further research is called for to establish the actual extent of this potential and to seek additional graph grammar results which could enhance the formalism's usefulness in the realm of concurrent software design and analysis.

5. Summary

In this paper we have described the significance of formal models of parallel computation to our work on methods for concurrent software design and analysis, and considered the prospects for using graph grammars as a basis for such models. We have illustrated the relationships between models currently in use and graph grammars, and pointed out the particularly strong connection between graph grammars and the Dynamic Process Modelling Scheme. We have also tried to suggest how graph grammars might provide a basis for analysis techniques applicable to designs of dynamically-structured, concurrent software systems. Based upon our observations here, it seems probable that continued developments in graph grammar theory may have an important impact on the search for concurrent software design and analysis tools.

6. References

1. Adams, D. A.
   A computation model with data-flow sequencing, Ph.D Thesis and Technical Report CS-117, Computer Science Department, Stanford University, Stanford, California, December 1968.

2. Arbib, M. A.
   Private communication, November 1978.

3. Bredt, T. H.
   A survey of models for parallel computing. Digital Systems Lab Technical Report 8, Stanford University, Stanford, California, August 1970.

4. Brinch Hansen, P.
   The nucleus of a multiprogramming system. Comm. ACM, 13, 4 (April 1970), 238-241, 250.

5. Bunke, H.
   Programmed graph grammars, (this volume).

6. Fennel, R. D. and Lesser, V. R. Parallelism in AI problem solving: A case study of HEARSAY-II. IEEE Trans. Comp., C-26, 2 (February 1977), 98-111.

7. Miller, R. E.
   A comparison of some theoretical models of parallel computation. IEEE Trans. Comp., C-22, 8 (August 1973), 710-717.

8. Peterson, J. L.
   Modelling of parallel systems. Ph.D. Thesis, Department of Electrical Engineering, Stanford University, Stanford, California, 1974.

9. Peterson, J. L. and Bredt, T. H.
   A comparison of models of parallel computation. Proc. IFIP Cong. 74, North-Holland Publishing Company, Amsterdam, 1974, pp. 446-470.

10. Petri, C. A.
    Kommunikation mit automatin, U. Bonn, Bonn, Germany, 1962.

11. Riddle, W. E. et al.
    Behavior modelling during software design. IEEE Trans. Soft. Eng., SE-4, 4 (July 1978), 283-292.

12. Riddle, W. E. et al.
    DREAM--A software design aid system. Information Technology, (JCIT3), North Holland Publishing Company, Amsterdam, 1978. pp. 373-380.

13. Riddle, W. E. and Wileden, J. C.
    Languages for representing software specifications and designs. Software Engineering Notes, 3, 4 (October 1978), 7-11.

14. Wileden, J. C.
    Modelling parallel systems with dynamic structure. Ph.D. Thesis, Dept. of Computer and Comm. Science, University of Michigan, Ann Arbor, Michigan, January 1978.

Cellular Graph Automata

Angela Wu
Azriel Rosenfeld

Computer Science Center
University of Maryland
College Park, MD 20742

ABSTRACT

Labelled graphs of bounded degree, with numbers assigned to the arcs at each node, are called d-graphs. A class of generalized automata, called cellular d-graph automata, in which the intercell connections define a d-graph, is introduced. It can be shown that a cellular d-graph automaton can measure various properties of its underlying graph; can detect graph or subgraph isomorphism; and can recognize various basic types of graphs. Most of these tasks can be performed in time proportional to the diameter of the given graph. Closure properties of d-graph languages are also briefly discussed.

1. Introduction

The generalization of sequential automata to graph-structured tapes has been studied by Shank [1], Rosenfeld and Milgram [2,3], and Mylopoulos [4]. In these models, a sequential graph automaton is placed on a node (or an arc) of a graph, moves from a node (arc) to neighboring nodes (arcs), changes states and rewrites symbols as directed by the transition function.

Cellular array automata can also be generalized such that the intercell connections define a graph. Rosenstiehl, Fiksel and Holliger [5], Shah, Milgram and Rosenfeld [6], and Rosenfeld [7] have studied such networks of automata.

Rosenstiehl's "intelligent graph" is a multigraph of bounded

The support of the U.S. Air Force Office of Scientific Research under Grant AFOSR-77-3271 is gratefully acknowledged, as is the help of Ms. Kathryn Riley in preparing this paper.

degree d, whose arcs at each node are uniquely identifiable by arc labels, and having a finite automaton at each node. All the automata are identical and they can sense the states of the automata at adjacent nodes. The state transition is thus a function of the states of the given node and its adjacent nodes. The authors exhibit algorithms to solve labyrinths; to find Eulerian paths, spanning trees, and Hamiltonian cycles; to construct node orderings and block decompositions; and to solve the network firing squad problem. They also define a type of symmetry in a network that would prevent the detection of certain adjacency relations. This situation of symmetry can be avoided if the graph has a distinguished node whose automaton is initially in a state distinct from those of the other automata.

The "parallel web automata" (PWA) of Shah et al. do not require bounded degree at each node, and do not allow unique identification of the edges at each node. However, there is an a priori ordering of the states and node symbols. The input tape to a node is the lexicographic reordering of the states of its neighbors. The PWA is said to make a parallel transition when each automaton has scanned its input tape, changing state as necessary, until the end is reached. In [7], Rosenfeld defined a PWA as a graph in which there is an automaton M_N at each node and an automaton M_A at each arc. Each M_N can sense the states of the M_A's on its arcs and each M_A can sense the states of the M_N's at its two ends; they then all change their own states in accordance with their transition functions. In both definitions of PWA, the neighbors of a node are all indistinguishable from one another. For this reason, PWA's are not good recognizers of their own graph structure. For example, a PWA whose graph structure is a cycle cannot tell the size of that cycle. This problem with cycles can be eliminated if the graph has a distinguished node. However, if the graph is a clique, a PWA still cannot tell its size even if there is a distinguished node. Rosenfeld showed that even though PWA's are poor acceptors, they can perform parallel pattern matching and constraint checking.

In this paper, we will study cellular graph automata with distinguished nodes on d-graphs. d-graphs are labelled graphs of bounded degree d,where each node has d arcs emanating from it and each arc end at a node is distinctly labelled. (Such graphs have also been studied by Mylopoulos [21]. Unlike the graphs treated by Rosenstiehl et al., they are not multigraphs, and they have a distinguished node.) It is not unreasonable to assume bounded degree, since the automaton at each node only has a fixed amount of memory. Note also that n-dimensional array automata operate on graphs of degree 2n and implicitly have distinguished nodes (for example, the top cell of the leftmost column in a two-dimensional array) which can always be identified.

The present paper presents the basic definitions and summarizes the main results. The details can be found in Wu [8].

2. Cellular d-graph acceptors

Let L be a finite nonempty set of labels with a distinguished element #. A d-graph on L is a 4-tuple $\Gamma = (N, A, f, g)$ where

N is a finite nonempty set of nodes

$A \subseteq N \times N$ is a symmetric relation on N, called the set of arcs

f is a function from N into L, called the labelling function, such that if $(m,n) \in A$, $f(m)=\#$ implies $f(n) \neq \#$.

g is a function from A into D, where $D = \{1,2,\ldots,d\}$, such that, for any $n \in N$, if we let $A_n = \{(n,m) \in A\}$ be the set of arcs having n as first term, then:

a) If $f(n) \neq \#$, then the cardinality of A_n is d, and $g|_{A_n}$ (g restricted to A_n) is a bijection of A_n onto D.

b) If $f(n) = \#$, then the cardinality of A_n is 1.

Informally, Γ is a graph whose nodes are labelled with symbols from L, and whose arcs at each node have numbers in $\{1,\ldots,d\}$. If a node has label other than #, it has exactly d arcs emanating from it, while if it has label #, it has exactly one arc. Note that we have said nothing about consistency of the arc numbering; if arc (n,m) is the ith arc at node n, we have no information about the arc number of arc (m,n) at node m.

The underlying graph G of a d-graph Γ is the graph resulting from discarding all the nodes labelled #; hence the node set of G is $N - \{n|n \in N \text{ and } f(n) = \#\}$, and its arc set is $A - \{(n,m)|(n,m) \in A \text{ and } f(n) = \# \text{ or } f(m) = \#\}$. We will always assume that the underlying graph is connected.

A cellular d-graph automaton $\mathcal{M}$ is a triple (Γ,M,H), where

Γ is a d-graph (N,A,f,g) on the label set L

M is a finite-state automaton (Q,δ), where

Q is a finite nonempty set of states such that $L \subseteq Q$.

δ is a transition function from QxD^dxQ^d into Q (or into finite subsets of Q, in the nondeterministic case), which maps any triple whose first term is # into #.

H is a mapping from N into D^d; the image $H(n) = (t_1,\ldots,t_d) \in D^d$ is called the neighbor vector of n.

Informally, there is an automaton M at each node n of Γ, and the input state of the automaton at node n is just $f(n) \in Q_I$. (We then say that Γ is the input d-graph of M.) At each time step, each M senses the states of its neighbors, reads its neighbor vector, and changes its own state according to the transition function δ. The neighbor vector tells each node which neighbor of each of its neighbors it is. Thus if $f(n) \neq \#$ and $H(n) = (t_1,\ldots,t_d)$, then m is the ith neighbor of n iff. n is the t_ith neighbor of m, i.e., $g(n,m) = i$ iff. $g(m,n) = t_i$. This allows the automaton at n to decide whether or not to use information from a given neighbor m, depending on which neighbor of m n is. If f(n)=#, n has only one neighbor m; in this case

$H(n)=(t,t,\ldots,t)$ where $t=g(n,m)$.

A configuration of M is just a mapping from N to Q, which is an assignment of states to the nodes. The application of the transition function δ takes a configuration c into a configuration c', denoted by c $\vdash$ c', as follows: For each non-# $n \in N$, if n is in state $q=c(n)$, and the neighbors $m_1,\ldots,m_d$ of n are in states $q_1=c(m_1),\ldots,q_d=c(m_d)$, then $c'(n)$, the new state of n, is $\delta(q,H(n),q_1,\ldots,q_d)$. If δ does not depend on $H(n)$ -- i.e., it maps $Q^{d+1} \to Q$ at each node -- we call M a weak cellular d-graph automaton.

A cellular d-graph automaton with a distinguished node is a cellular d-graph automaton such that exactly one of the automata M carries a special mark (as part of its state). The mark need not remain at the same node of the graph, but we assume that it always remains at a non-# node.

A cellular d-graph acceptor is a cellular d-graph automaton $M=(\Gamma,M,H)$ with a distinguished node such that M is a finite state acceptor (Q_I,Q,δ,F) where (Q,δ) is a finite state automaton as before, $Q_I=L$ is a set of input states, and $F \subseteq Q$ is a set of final states. An initial configuration of M is a mapping from N into L. A terminal configuration is a mapping c from N into Q such that if n is the distinguished node, then $c(n) \in F$, i.e., the acceptor M of M that has the special mark is in a final state. $M=(\Gamma,M,H)$ accepts the d-graph $\Gamma = (N,A,f,g)$ if there is a finite sequence of configurations $c_0,c_1,\ldots,c_m$ such that $c_0=f$ is an initial configuration, c_m is a terminal configuration, and $c_i \vdash c_{i+1}$ for $0 \le i \le m$ as defined above.

Cellular d-graph automata can be shown to be equivalent to sequential automata on d-graphs (see [8] for the definition and details of the proof). They are also equivalent to the web-bounded automata of Rosenfeld and Milgram [2,3], if we appropriately define acceptance of the underlying graph of a d-graph by a d-graph automaton.

3. Graph property measurement

It is not difficult to define an O(diameter) time cellular-d-graph automaton algorithm for constructing a breadth-first spanning tree of the given d-graph. This algorithm can be applied to the measurement of the radius (from the given distinguished node) and area (=number of nodes) of the graph, as well as to the detection and counting of occurrences of specific node labels, in O(diameter) time. In these counting algorithms, the distinguished node successively outputs the digits of the desired number, least significant first, in base d.

Depth-first spanning tree construction and node ordering requires O(area) time, because of the inherently sequential nature of depth-first search. Using this algorithm, we can identify a central point, measure the radius from that point, or identify all cut nodes, blocks, or bridges of the given graph, in time O(diameter·area).

4. Graph and subgraph isomorphism

Given a graph α, there is a deterministic cellular d-graph acceptor that can decide whether a d-graph Γ is isomorphic to α in diameter(Γ) time. The detection of a subgraph isomorphic to α takes area(Γ) time in general. However, subgraph isomorphism detection can be done in diameter time for certain special types of d-graphs such as trees, k-level colored d-graphs, k-locally homogeneous d-graphs, and homogeneous d-graphs, where special assumptions are made about the "homogeneity" of the d-graphs. These assumptions hold for many important classes of graphs including trees, cliques, and (semi-)regular tessellations.

A d-graph is called <u>k-level colored</u> if any two nodes within distance k of one another have different colors. It is called <u>k-locally homogeneous</u> if at each node, all cycles of lengths up to k (i.e., all paths of length $\le k$ that return to the given node) are known. It is called k-homogeneous if these cycles are the same for all nodes, and homogeneous if it is k-homogeneous for all k. This is true, e.g., for trees, where there are no cycles at all, and for arrays (or, more generally, for all regular or semiregular tessellations).

5. Graph structure recognition

O(diameter) time cellular d-graph recognizers exist for types of graphs such as cycles, strings, trees, binary trees, cliques, rectangular and square arrays, stars, and wheels. Slower recognizers can be exhibited for biconnected graphs (area · diameter time) and line graphs (2^d·area time). Only a very slow recognizer has been found for planar graphs. It can also be shown that d-graphs*) in a deterministic bounded cellular automaton (DBCA) language can be accepted in time proportional to the maximum of the acceptance time of the DBCA language and the time needed to obtain the number representing the measurement. In particular, d-graphs having radius in a linear time DBCA language (e.g., primes) are accepted in diameter time; those having area in a linear time DBCA language are accepted in area time; but those having area in a finite state language, or equal to a power of 2, can be accepted in diameter time.

6. Closure properties

Cellular d-graph languages are closed under set-theoretic operations, including finite union and intersection; and under "geometric" operations, including permutation of arc end numbering, concatenation, closure, and formation of line graphs. Determinism is preserved under the set-theoretic operations; but under the geometric operations, determinism has been shown to be preserved only when the languages are also predicates.

Closure under other common operations on graphs, such as join,

*) having the values of a given property (area, radius, etc.)

product, and composition, will not be considered here, since there is no bound on the degrees of the resulting graphs; their degrees depend on the numbers of nodes in the given graphs.

7. Concluding remarks

The following are some areas that deserve further investigation:

a) Some of the cellular d-graph automaton algorithms discussed above take O(area) time or longer. It would be desirable to find faster algorithms for these tasks, or to show that faster algorithms do not exist. Tasks that should be investigated include the detection of subgraph isomorphism (for arbitrary d-graphs), the identification of cut nodes, and the recognition of planar graphs.

b) The definition of a cellular d-graph acceptor can be easily extended to directed d-graphs. It would be of interest to see how cellular directed d-graph automata can solve various problems concerning directed d-graphs, such as the recognition of acyclic graphs or two-terminal series-parallel networks, or the discovery of strong connectedness or unilateral connectedness.

c) In a cellular d-graph automaton, the configuration of the intercell connections is never altered. Sometimes it would be advantageous to be able to vary the underlying structure. For example, consider the situation in which two nodes m,n at distance k apart in a d-graph communicate with each other frequently. Each message from one node takes k time steps to reach the other node and another k steps for the answer to return. A great deal of time could be saved if an arc could be added to join the two nodes. The deletion of nodes or arcs can be done implicitly by giving the nodes a special inactive state, or giving the states of the end nodes of the arc a mark to signify that no messages are allowed to pass through them. However, the difficulty is that deletion of several arcs simultaneously may disconnect the graph even though the deletion of each individual arc would not.

Growth of a graph, where arcs and nodes are to be added, is even more difficult. Since attaching new nodes requires the creation of arcs, we will consider only the growing of arcs here. An arc can be added between two nodes only if they are not already neighbors and each has at least one # neighbor. The trouble is that too many nodes may all want to be joined with the same node. Hence creation of arcs in parallel may destroy the bounded degree d. More work needs to be done to modify our model or create a new model in order to allow growth of d-graphs, which is important and interesting.

d) Another feature of cellular d-graph automata is that the basic finite state automata at the nodes have a fixed amount of memory regardless of the size of the input graph. However, in practical situations, the memory of the processors is in general large in comparison with the size of the input graphs. This suggests that it is reasonable to allow the automata to have an augmented memory whose size is a moderate function of the size of the input. This idea of giving cellular automata extra memory has been studied by Dyer and Rosenfeld in 1-dimensional and 2-dimensional arrays.

For example, let us consider cellular d-graph automata with augmented memory whose size is log(area of the given graph). This memory can hold numbers as large as the area of the graph. We will show that this automaton M can give each node a unique identifier, hence an address, in diameter time. M first constructs a breadth-first spanning tree T of the d-graph. The identifier given to each node n will be the position of n in a preordering of T, where the position counting starts with zero and the subtrees at each node are ordered by increasing arc end number. In diameter time, the number of nodes in each node's subtree can be obtained and stored in the augmented memory. The identifier assignment starts with the root having identifier zero and proceeds level by level. A node n takes note of the number of nodes in each son's subtree, one digit at a time and least significant digit first. The first son is assigned 1 plus the number representing the identifier of n and the i+1st son is assigned the identifier of the ith son plus the number of nodes in the ith son's subtree ($0<i<$the number of sons of n). It is easy to see that the nodes will have distinct identifiers and the augmented memory is large enough to store them. All this can be done in time proportional to the height of T, which is the diameter of the graph.

From the above example we see that this class of extended cellular graph automata can perform certain tasks efficiently. It deserves further study; in particular, its power and speed in solving graph recognition problems should be assessed.

References

1. H. S. Shank, Graph property recognition machines, Math. Systems Theory 5, 1971, 45-49.

2. D. L. Milgram, Web automata, Information and Control 29, 1975, 162-184.

3. A. Rosenfeld and D. L. Milgram, Web automata and web grammars. In B. Meltzer and D. Michie, eds., Machine Intelligence 7, Edinburgh U. Press, 1972, 307-324.

4. J. Mylopoulos and T. Pavlidis, On the topological properties of quantized spaces, JACM 18, 1971, 239-254.

6. SUMMARY

We characterized multiprocessing computers by two objects: the type of processor used and a directed graph specifying the communication lines between processors. A tree type of directed graph was seen to be as powerful as any feasibly buildable interconnection graph, provided we define feasibly buildable graphs as those whose connection function can be computed in polynomial storage. Finally, we saw that, by either greatly increasing the complexity of the interconnection graph or by introducing nondeterminism, we can create dramatically fast multiprocessing systems.

References

A. Aho, J.E. Hopcroft and J.D. Ullman (1974), The Design and Analysis of Computer Algorithms, Addison-Wesley, Reading, MA.

A.K. Chandra and L.J. Stockmeyer (1976), "Alternation," Proc. 17th IEEE Symposium on Foundations of Computer Science, Houston, Texas, 98-108.

S.A. Cook and R.A. Reckhow (1973), "Time Bounded Random Access Machines," JCSS 7, 354-375.

L.M. Goldschlager (1977), "Synchronous Parallel Computation," Ph.D. Thesis, Computer Science, University of Toronto.

L.M. Goldschlager (1978), "A Unified Approach to Models of Synchronous Parallel Machines," Proc. 10th ACM Symposium on Theory of Computing, San Diego, CA 89-94.

J. Hartmanis and J. Simon (1974), "On the Power of Multiplication in Random Access Machines," Proc. 15th IEEE Symposium Switching and Automation Theory, New Orleans, 13-23.

D. Kozen (1976), "On Parallelism in Turing Machines," Proc. 17th IEEE Symposium on Foundations of Computer Science, Houston, Texas, 89-97.

V.R. Pratt and L.J. Stockmeyer (1976), "A Characterization of the Power of Vector Machines," JCSS 12, 198-221.

W.J. Savitch (1978), "Parallel and Nondeterministic Time Complexity Classes," in G. Ausiello and C. Böhm (Eds.), Automata, Languages and Programming, Fifth Colloquium, Udine, Italy, Springer-Verlag, 411-424.

W.J. Savitch and M.J. Stimson (1976), "The Complexity of Time Bounded Recursive Computations," Proc. Conf. on Information Sciences and Systems, The Johns Hopkins University.

W.J. Savitch and M.J. Stimson (1978), "Time Bounded Random Access Machines with Parallel Processing," JACM (in press).

ACKNOWLEDGEMENT

This research was supported in part by NSF Grant MCS-74-02338A02.

5. P. Rosenstiehl, J. R. Fiksel, and A. Holliger, Intelligent Graphs: Networks of Finite Automata Capable of Solving Graph Problems. In R. C. Read, ed., Graph Theory and Computing, Academic Press, New York, 1972, 219-265.

6. A. N. Shah, D. L. Milgram and A. Rosenfeld, Parallel web automata, University of Maryland Computer Science Center Technical Report 231, 1973.

7. A. Rosenfeld, Networks of Automata -- some applications, IEEE Trans. SMC-5, 1975, 380-383.

8. A. Wu, Cellular graph automata, Ph.D dissertation, University of Maryland, 1978.

List of participants:

Arbib, Michael A., Coins/GRC, Univ. of Mass., Amherst, MA 01003, USA.

D'Atri, Allesandro, Diparto Sistemi Conenza.

Batini, Carlo, Istituto di Automatica Roma, Via Endossiana 18, Roma.

Bunke, Horst, IMMD, Lehrstuhl für Informatik 5, Universität Erlangen-Nürnberg, Martensstr. 3, 852 Erlangen

Claus, Volker, Abt. Informatik, Universität Dortmund, Postfach 500 500, 46 Dortmund 50

Culik, Karel, Department of Computer Science, University of Waterloo, Waterloo, Ontario, Canada N2L 3GI

Ehrich, Hans-Dieter, Abt. Informatik, Universität Dortmund, Postfach 500 500 46 Dortmund 50

Ehrig, H., FB 20 Technische Universität Berlin, Otto-Suhr-Allee 18/20 D-1000 Berlin

Franck, Fa. Softlab, Sederanger 4-6, 8000 München 22

Furtado, Antonio Luz, Departamento de Informatica, Potoficia Universidada Catôlica do Rio de Janeiro Rua Marques des Sao Vincente, 209-4 andar-Gãvea 22453 Rio de Janeiro - Brasil.

Gernert, Dieter, Schluderstr. 2, 8000 München 19

Grötsch, Eberhard, Am Tannenbach 28, 8521 Spardorf

Hesse, Wolfgang, Pienzenauerstr. 5, 8000 München 80.

Le Hoi, Inst. of Mathematics, 208^{D} Doi Can, Hanoi, Vietnam.

Kaul, Manfred, Höschenstr. 31, 4100 Duisburg 14

Kreowski, Hans-Jörg, Techn. Universität Berlin, FB Informatik, Otto-Suhr-Allee 18/20, D-1000 Berlin 10

Kreplin, Klaus-Dieter, Bergstr. 3, D-1000 Berlin 41

Liedtke, Axel, Winterfeldstr. 9, D-1000 Berlin 30

Lindenmayer, Aristid, Vakgruep Theoretische Biologie, Rijksuniversiteit Utrecht, Padualaan 8, Utrecht, Netherlands.

Lück, J. und H.B. Lück, Laboratoire de Botanique et Structuralisme Vêgetâl, Facultê des Sciences et Techniques de Saint-Jérome, Rue Henri-Poincarê, 1397 Marseille Cedex 4, France

Maggiolo-Schettini Andream Instituto die Scienze dell'Informazione, University di Salerno, Via Vernieri 42, 84100 Salerno, Italy

Mayoh, Bryan, Inst. of Math. Univ. of Aarhus, Dept, of Comp. Sc. Ny Munkegade, 8000 Aarhus C, Denmark

Milgram, David, Univ. of Maryland, College Park, MD, USA

Montanari, Ugo, Computer Science Department, University of Pisa, 56100 Pisa, Italy

Nagl, Manfred, Lehrstuhl f. Programmiersprachen der Universität Erlangen-Nürnberg, Martensstr. 3, 852 Erlangen

Ollongren, A., Dept. of Mathematics, University of Leiden, Wassenaarseweg 80, 2300 RA Leiden, Holland.

Padawitz, Peter, Technische Universität Berlin FB 20, Otto-Suhr-Allee 18/20, D-1000 Berlin 10.

Paz, A., Technion IIT - Dept. of Computer Science, Haifa, Israel

Pfaltz, J.L. Dept. Applied Math. & Comp. Science, University of Virginia, Charlottesville, Va. 22903, Bollingwood Rd., 134

Pflüger, J., TH Darmstadt, FB 20, Magdalenenstr. 11, 6100 Darmstadt

Poigné, Axel, Abt. Informatik, Universität Dortmund, Postfach 500 500, 46 Dortmund 50.

Pratt, Terrence W., Dept. of Applied Math. and Computer Science, Thornton Hall, University of Virginia, Charlottesville, VA 22901, USA.

Rajlich, Vaclav, Research Institute for Mathematical Machines, Loretanske n.3, 11855 Praha 1, Szechoslovakia

Raoult, J.C., IRIA University of Paris XI, L.R.I, Bat 490, 91405 Orsay cedex

Raz, Y., Technion, IIT-Dept. of C.S. Haifa, Israel

Rosen, Barry K., Comp. Sci. Dept. IBM, T.J.W. Research Center, Yorktown Heights, N.Y. 10598 USA.

Rosendahl, Manfred, Hünninghauserweg 57, 43 Essen 14.

Rosenfeld, Azriel, Computer Science Center, University of Maryland, College Park,Md 20742 USA.

Rozenberg, Grzegorz, Dept. of Math., Univ. of Antwerp. U.I.A. Universiteitsplein 1, Wilrijk, Belgium

Savitch, Walter, J.Dept, APIS, Univ. of Calif. San Diego, CA 92043, USA

Schmidt, G., Inst. f. Informatik, Techn, Universität München, Postfach 202420, 8000 München 2.

Sowa, John, F., IBM Research Institute, 219 East 42nd Street, New York, N.Y. 10017 USA

Staples, John, Dept, Mathematics and Computer Science, Queensland Institute of Technology, G.P.P. Box 2434, Brisbane 4001, Australia.

Uccella, Giovanni, University di Salterno, Via Vernieri, 42 - 84100 Salerno.

Wileden, J.C. Department of Comander and Information Science, University of Mass., Amherst, Mass., 01003.

Winkowski, Institute of Computer Science of the Polish Ac. od Sciences, 00-901 Warsaw, PkiN, P.O. Box 22.

Vol. 49: Interactive Systems. Proceedings 1976. Edited by A. Blaser and C. Hackl. VI, 380 pages. 1976.

Vol. 50: A. C. Hartmann, A Concurrent Pascal Compiler for Minicomputers. VI, 119 pages. 1977.

Vol. 51: B. S. Garbow, Matrix Eigensystem Routines – Eispack Guide Extension. VIII, 343 pages. 1977.

Vol. 52: Automata, Languages and Programming. Fourth Colloquium, University of Turku, July 1977. Edited by A. Salomaa and M. Steinby. X, 569 pages. 1977.

Vol. 53: Mathematical Foundations of Computer Science. Proceedings 1977. Edited by J. Gruska. XII, 608 pages. 1977.

Vol. 54: Design and Implementation of Programming Languages. Proceedings 1976. Edited by J. H. Williams and D. A. Fisher. X, 496 pages. 1977.

Vol. 55: A. Gerbier, Mes premières constructions de programmes. XII, 256 pages. 1977.

Vol. 56: Fundamentals of Computation Theory. Proceedings 1977. Edited by M. Karpiński. XII, 542 pages. 1977.

Vol. 57: Portability of Numerical Software. Proceedings 1976. Edited by W. Cowell. VIII, 539 pages. 1977.

Vol. 58: M. J. O'Donnell, Computing in Systems Described by Equations. XIV, 111 pages. 1977.

Vol. 59: E. Hill, Jr., A Comparative Study of Very Large Data Bases. X, 140 pages. 1978.

Vol. 60: Operating Systems, An Advanced Course. Edited by R. Bayer, R. M. Graham, and G. Seegmüller. X, 593 pages. 1978.

Vol. 61: The Vienna Development Method: The Meta-Language. Edited by D. Bjørner and C. B. Jones. XVIII, 382 pages. 1978.

Vol. 62: Automata, Languages and Programming. Proceedings 1978. Edited by G. Ausiello and C. Böhm. VIII, 508 pages. 1978.

Vol. 63: Natural Language Communication with Computers. Edited by Leonard Bolc. VI, 292 pages. 1978.

Vol. 64: Mathematical Foundations of Computer Science. Proceedings 1978. Edited by J. Winkowski. X, 551 pages. 1978.

Vol. 65: Information Systems Methodology, Proceedings, 1978. Edited by G. Bracchi and P. C. Lockemann. XII, 696 pages. 1978.

Vol. 66: N. D. Jones and S. S. Muchnick, TEMPO: A Unified Treatment of Binding Time and Parameter Passing Concepts in Programming Languages. IX, 118 pages. 1978.

Vol. 67: Theoretical Computer Science, 4th GI Conference, Aachen, March 1979. Edited by K. Weihrauch. VII, 324 pages. 1979.

Vol. 68: D. Harel, First-Order Dynamic Logic. X, 133 pages. 1979.

Vol. 69: Program Construction. International Summer School. Edited by F. L. Bauer and M. Broy. VII, 651 pages. 1979.

Vol. 70: Semantics of Concurrent Computation. Proceedings 1979. Edited by G. Kahn. VI, 368 pages. 1979.

Vol. 71: Automata, Languages and Programming. Proceedings 1979. Edited by H. A. Maurer. IX, 684 pages. 1979.

Vol. 72: Symbolic and Algebraic Computation. Proceedings 1979. Edited by E. W. Ng. XV, 557 pages. 1979.

Vol. 73: Graph-Grammars and Their Application to Computer Science and Biology. Proceedings 1978. Edited by V. Claus, H. Ehrig and G. Rozenberg. VII, 477 pages. 1979.

This series reports new developments in computer science research and teaching – quickly, informally and at a high level. The type of material considered for publication includes:

1. Preliminary drafts of original papers and monographs
2. Lectures on a new field or presentations of a new angle in a classical field
3. Seminar work-outs
4. Reports of meetings, provided they are
   a) of exceptional interest and
   b) devoted to a single topic.

Texts which are out of print but still in demand may also be considered if they fall within these categories.

The timeliness of a manuscript is more important than its form, which may be unfinished or tentative. Thus, in some instances, proofs may be merely outlined and results presented which have been or will later be published elsewhere. If possible, a subject index should be included. Publication of Lecture Notes is intended as a service to the international computer science community, in that a commercial publisher, Springer-Verlag, can offer a wide distribution of documents which would otherwise have a restricted readership. Once published and copyrighted, they can be documented in the scientific literature.

Manuscripts

Manuscripts should be no less than 100 and preferably no more than 500 pages in length.
They are reproduced by a photographic process and therefore must be typed with extreme care. Symbols not on the typewriter should be inserted by hand in indelible black ink. Corrections to the typescript should be made by pasting in the new text or painting out errors with white correction fluid. Authors receive 75 free copies and are free to use the material in other publications. The typescript is reduced slightly in size during reproduction; best results will not be obtained unless the text on any one page is kept within the overall limit of 18 x 26.5 cm (7 x 10½ inches). On request, the publisher will supply special paper with the typing area outlined.
Manuscripts should be sent to Prof. G. Goos, Institut für Informatik, Universität Karlsruhe, Zirkel 2, 7500 Karlsruhe/Germany, Prof. J. Hartmanis, Cornell University, Dept. of Computer-Science, Ithaca, NY/USA 14850, or directly to Springer-Verlag Heidelberg.

Springer-Verlag, Heidelberger Platz 3, D-1000 Berlin 33
Springer-Verlag, Neuenheimer Landstraße 28–30, D-6900 Heidelberg 1
Springer-Verlag, 175 Fifth Avenue, New York, NY 10010/USA

ISBN 3-540-**09525**-X
ISBN 0-387-**09525**-X